OpenVMS System Management Guide

2nd Edition

IF THIS BOOK SHOULD DARE TO ROAM
BOX ITS EARS AND SEND IT HOME
TO
IAN SURRIDGE

OpenVMS System Management Guide

2nd Edition

Lawrence L. Baldwin, Jr.

Steve Hoffman

David Donald Miller

ELSEVIER
DIGITAL
PRESS

Amsterdam • Boston • Heidelberg • London • New York • Oxford
Paris • San Diego • San Francisco • Singapore • Sydney • Tokyo

Digital Press is an imprint of Elsevier.

∞ Recognizing the importance of preserving what has been written, Elsevier prints its books on acid-free paper whenever possible.

Library of Congress Cataloging-in-Publication Data
Baldwin, Lawrence L., 1965–
OPEN VMS system management guide/Lawrence L. Baldwin Jr., Steve Hoffman, David Miller.–2nd ed.
p. cm.
ISBN: 1-55558-243-5
1. OpenVMS. 2. Operating systems (Computers). I. Hoffman, Steve (Stephen) II. Miller, David, 1959–III. Title.

QA76.76.063B3525 2003
005.4'3–dc22

2003055656

British Library Cataloguing-in-Publication Data
A catalogue record for this book is available from the British Library.

The publisher offers special discounts on bulk orders of this book.
For information, please contact:

Manager of Special Sales
Elsevier
200 Wheeler Road
Burlington, MA 01803
Tel: 781-313-4700
Fax: 781-313-4882

For information on all Digital Press publications available, contact our World Wide Web home page at: http://www.digitalpress.com or http://www.bh.com/digitalpress

10 9 8 7 6 5 4 3 2 1

Printed in the United States of America

Contents

Preface

Steve Hoffman started working on this second edition, but his responsibilities in OpenVMS 8.2 eventually consumed his free time. Pam Chester, an acquisition editor at Digital Press, asked me to finish this edition. My first task was to expand on Hoff's suggestions—such as "put an OVMS 7.3-1 example here," "update this display," and "include ATW comments." And believe me, there were plenty of those to deal with. When I finished with his comments, I made changes and additions I felt were necessary as well.

Chapter 20 and Appendix A are new, and they are entirely my idea. I thought the novice and the hobbyist needed more guidance for buying hardware, installing software, and especially installing freeware. Even though PRODUCT and VMSINSTAL are well documented, I thought it would be handy to have examples in one location.

A major deletion in this edition is all references to OpenVMS versions prior to 6.0. My feeling is that anyone still running 5.5-2 and earlier would already have Lawrence Baldwin's first edition. And those running OpenVMS 6.0 or later would be confused by references to the older versions. The emphasis in this edition is OpenVMS/VAX 7.3 and OpenVMS/Alpha 7.3-1 because these are what I'm using as I am writing. I have tried hard to show commands that are valid over all post-6.0 versions, even though OpenVMS is constantly evolving.

Even so, I still find my gray VMS 5.2 manual is handy and easy to use. For you newbees, the 5.2 System Manager's Manual is about the size of a Clancy paperback, whereas the current two-volume System Manager's Manual is about the size of the Tucson phone book. Sure, the latter has lots more examples and detail, but the 5.2 manual is convenient and concise. Yes, I have a point: many of the OpenVMS essential commands have not changed all that much in 15 years, and I do not expect them to change much over the next 15 years, either. I am keeping my 5.2 manual. However, older versions of OpenVMS will produce more or less information on the displays. Thus, the reader is cautioned against relying on the examples, verbatim.

Examples are from OpenVMS/Alpha 7.3-1 on an AlphaStation 200 and OpenVMS/VAX 7.3 on a VAXstation 3100 M48. A fact of life is that the two versions of OpenVMS differ slightly.

I think I should expand on the last paragraph a bit. Although there is only one OpenVMS, unlike UNIX, which varies from company to company, there are two OpenVMS variations. These are dictated by company policy and computer architecture. For instance, 100-MB Ethernet Network Interface Cards (NICs) have been added to Alpha, but those NICs have never been developed and supported on the VAX. This is not a technical decision, but a policy decision. On the other hand, the Alpha's 64-bit address space results in an entirely new version of the OpenVMS kernel. In particular, VAX paging is based on a two-level translation scheme, whereas the Alpha has a three-level implementation. A few of these differences are summarized in Table P-1. It could be noted that a table of similarities would be much bigger.

Table P.1 *OpenVMS/VAX and OpenVMS/Alpha Differences*

Characteristic	VAX	Alpha
Architecture	32-bit CISC	64-bit RISK
Page size	512 bytes	Variable, currently set to 8,192 (8K) bytes
User-written device drivers	Macro (assembly)	Macro and C
Floating-point format	Digital	Digital and IEEE
Network hardware	10-MB Ethernet	All Ethernet, ATM, fiber channel, memory channel
Mozilla and Java support	No	Yes
HTTPD support	OSU's HTTPD, WASD, others	VAX servers plus APACHE (PHP, TOMCAT)
Multimedia support	No	Yes

I suppose, in mid-2004, there will be a third variation, defined by the Itanium implementation, for OpenVMS/IA-64.

P.1 Conventions

I have retained Baldwin's conventions for the most part. Within a paragraph, both acronyms and Digital Command Language (DCL) commands are capitalized. The reader should be able to distinguish between the two. A sample command is listed together with the resulting output separated from the prose, and monospaced. Examples will look as much like a screen display as possible; for instance:

```
$ INITIALIZE/QUEUE/BATCH –
 _$ /AUTOSTART_ON=(NODE1::, NODE2::)  SYS$BATCH

$ REPLY/DISABLE

%%%%%%%%%%%  OPCOM  23-MAY-2003 17:13:35.45  %%%%%%%%%%%
Operator _MILLER$FTA13: has been disabled, username SYSTEM
```

In the first example, the dash at the right end of the first line is typed by the user and indicates the command is continued on the next line. The second line's prompt is "_$" not "$" to indicate the continuation. To distinguish user input from OpenVMS output, the user's input is presented in bold font.

P.2 Organization

I maintained Baldwin's organization as much as practical. Additional sections are inevitable of course. Chapter 20 and appendix A are new. Baldwin's sample scripts (see appendix E) are available online and are not included with the text.

P.3 References

Although I have included an extensive bibliography, the following are such important starting points, they bear repeating:

The primary news group for OpenVMS is very active. It is called comp.os.vms. This news group is mirrored on a mailing list called INFO-VAX@MVB.SAIC.COM.

The official OpenVMS home page is at http://h71000.www7.hp.com/dec. You can navigate through sales and technical information from this page.

The unofficial OpenVMS FAQ (frequently asked questions) home page is at http://h71000.www7.hp.com/wizard/openvms_faq.html.

The OpenVMS user community is quite active. I have found one good jumping-off point at www.levitte.org/~ava.

Acknowledgments

Writing any book is a labor of love. I love VMS. This is my second publication for Digital Press this year (2003) and my third DP book in print. That is some sort of a personal record. However there is no way in the world I would have been able to do this without the permission and support of Kari, my wife. The number of lost weekends and the length of the honey-do list will also attest to her patience with this project. Thanks, hon!

My Digital Press editor, Pam Chester got me started on this project. Thanks for asking me to work on this, Pam. And thanks for the constant support throughout the project. There were so many issues to address along the way and you always acted promptly on my concerns.

Thanks to my reviewers, Professor Sue Rosselet from Bemidji State University, and Helen Johnson who once again provided me with lots and lots of suggestions. We worked so well together on *Getting Started with OpenVMS System Management* and I was pleased to have them straighten things out on this project as well.

Several others made writing this book a lot easier. David Drier of Building Block Computers gave (and I mean for free!) me a Vaxstation 3100. Without it I would not have been able to create my cluster and would not have had any reliable, up-to-date OpenVMS/VAX examples in the book. Carl Couric gave me several (really old) disk drives that worked perfectly in the VS 3100.

When putting my cluster together I made a plea on comp.os.vms (c.o.v) for OpenVMS/Alpha software because the latest version, 7.3-1, was no longer available on the hobbyist site. Several folks came to my rescue and shipped me CDs. My thanks to William Webb, Mike Rechtman, Randy Doering and Sue Rosselet for the CDs. Others made offers to either ship CDs or allow me to download the files. Thanks to Marty Kuhrt, Hans Vlems, Peter Langstoeger, and Andras Holistska. I was able to buy an

OpenVMS/VAX CD from the hobbyist site; that is a wonderful service and many thanks for all who support that effort.

David Miller

Green Valley, Arizona

August, 2003.

1

Professional System Management

1.1 Chapter Objectives

- Apply classic business-management strategies to system management
- Define service-level objectives and their importance
- Focus on an overall approach to effective system management

1.2 Introduction

The term *system manager* (or *system administrator*) is ambiguous. What exactly does a system manager do? What or whom does a system manager manage? Is the position technical or managerial? Frequently, job descriptions for this position lack or avoid these details, and the default expectation of the position is to do "whatever is necessary" to keep systems running.

To accomplish this, system managers generally perform tasks such as configuring new hardware, upgrading software, managing system-startup procedures, tracking software licenses, configuring print and batch queues, managing user accounts, monitoring disk space, ensuring regular system backups, monitoring system security, and maintaining system performance. Although these tasks require technical skills, applying them to the objectives of an organization is more of a managerial task. Thus, the optimal system manager is a composite technician and manager (that is, a *technomanager.*) Achieving this standing requires the following nontechnical skills:

- Objective-based management
- Good communication
- Logical troubleshooting

1.3 Objective-Based Management

Users complain that systems run slowly or are down frequently, and management insists that you are spending too much money. This leaves you caught in the middle—you have to placate frustrated users with contracting resources.

Peter Drucker, the classic management scientist, frequently wrote about *management by objective*. This strategy is based on the idea that you can only operate effectively when you understand business objectives and direct your efforts toward meeting them. This concept applies well to the process of system management. The enormity of the task leaves many system managers unsuccessfully scrambling to meet ill-defined and unattainable user and management expectations. Clear objectives developed in collaboration with users and management will help you better focus your system-management efforts, moderate user expectations, and justify costs.

The first step is to define exactly what the objectives are. Almost everyone agrees that system managers are supposed to keep systems running. But what does this mean? Exactly when should systems be up? How fast should they perform and based on what metric? At what price? You may find it helpful to start by defining an overall *mission statement* that sums up what everyone agrees should be accomplished. For example, this book focuses on the following mission: keeping applications available at a level of performance that meets user expectations.

After you have developed a mission statement, develop more detailed *service-level objectives* that support the mission; for example:

- System uptime
  - Target scheduled downtime (in hours per year) for upgrades and preventive maintenance
  - Target unscheduled downtime (in hours per year)
- Time to service user requests
  - File restore from backups
  - Add user accounts
  - Answer general technical questions
- Time to service application requests
  - Mount tapes
  - Change printer forms

- Maintain data integrity
  - Determine maximum data loss due to system failure (in minutes, hours, or days)
- Software upgrades
  - Determine frequency with which products should be upgraded (OpenVMS, layered products, etc.)
- Performance
  - Specify the target response time for each key application
- Security
  - Agree on level of protection against
    - User error
    - Internal attacks
    - External attacks

You must be able to measure your ability to achieve each service objective. Whenever possible, quantify exactly what the goal is. For example, you can calculate system uptime by using the following formula:

Uptime (percentage) = [(hours per year – downtime)/hours per year] × 100

If a system were down for 50 hours (about one hour per week) during a year, uptime would be calculated as follows:

Uptime (in percent) = [(365 × 24 – 50)/365 × 24] × 100% = 99.43%

On a regular basis you should post both service objectives and statistics indicating the level of service you actually provided.

1.4 Communication Skills

Although system management is technically oriented, excellent personal skills and a positive attitude are essential. An OpenVMS guru with poor communication skills will never be a good system manager. On the other hand, a novice OpenVMS technician with excellent communication skills, patience, and an ability and desire to learn can become a great system manager with time.

System management requires frequent, sometimes stressful communication with many groups within an organization. To be effective, you must be even tempered, well organized, and extremely patient. Your tone must not be condescending—you need to be able to educate people without making them feel dumb.

Communication is a two-party event. To communicate effectively you need to know your audience and communicate at a level appropriate to its expertise. Do not try to impress people with your knowledge, yet do not insult the more experienced user. For instance, do not try to explain what is wrong to someone who only cares when it will be fixed. Understand your user's objectives and provide only relevant information.

Sometimes you tend to feel users exist only to make your life miserable. Actually, users are your reason for existence. If it were not for users, you would not have a job. If you do not like dealing with users, you are in the wrong profession.

Your door should always be open (if you are lucky enough to have a door). Sometimes it is very hard to concentrate when people are constantly calling and asking questions. However, you will spend far less time helping them now than you will spend cleaning up the results of unanswered questions. Nigel Sharp illustrated this point:

> It should be clear that you *can* be bothered, and that in many cases you would *prefer* to be bothered. A nervous student once ruined one of our printers because he did not want to disturb anyone. (He simply added toner, since that is what it said it needed.) Unfortunately, he poured liquid toner into a dry toner container. ["The Philosophy of System Management," *DECUS Transactions* (Fall 1992), 1–4.]

Users sometimes understand that it will take time for you to solve their problem. However, they should never have to wait to tell you about a problem. Whether you have a secretary, voice mail, answering machine, or e-mail, there should always be a mechanism that allows users to log problems immediately. Imagine how you would feel if you had to call a service department 10 times before someone even answered.

If you already think you are good, you will never get better. If there were people who knew everything there was to know about Hewlett-Packard

(HP) OpenVMS software and systems, then the HP Customer Support Center would be staffed by a few dozen people. There are no such experts, and it takes hundreds of people to provide a pool of knowledge sufficient to support OpenVMS. The true experts are modest about what they do know. Most importantly, they know how to learn what they do not know.

1.5 Logical Troubleshooting Skills

You must be a logical thinker and an expert troubleshooter. You have to be able to transcend a typical user's response (e.g., "it doesn't work") by iteratively dividing up the potential problem areas to determine the actual "it." Avoid asking users questions that are too easily answered without much thought. For example, do not ask, "Has this always worked?" Users will invariably answer yes. Rather, ask, "When was the last time this worked (or didn't work)?" Also remember that what may be obvious to you may not be so obvious to the user (e.g., whether a device is plugged in).

In an emergency, you may have to fix a problem temporarily. However, you should always go back later and permanently solve the problem. Solving a problem means understanding why the problem occurred and taking the necessary steps to prevent it from occurring again. Fixing a problem temporarily is like smothering a fire by throwing a huge pile of leaves on it—the flames temporarily disappear, but soon burst into an inferno twice as large as before. Solve problems—do not go searching for even larger piles of leaves.

Some problems cannot be immediately solved. For example, if disk drives run out of space on a weekly basis, the solution might be to purchase more disk space, but that could take several weeks. In the meantime, you must prevent denial of service to users. At a minimum, you should deploy a disk-space monitoring utility that proactively notifies you when disk space is low so you can purge files before users are affected.

1.6 Conclusion

If you are to have a clear focus, you must demand objectives or develop them yourself. Operating without objectives is attempting to achieve the impossible—infinite service-level expectations. Once you have set objectives, system management is nothing more than classic customer service. As with any job that involves direct customer (user) contact, excellent personal and communication skills are essential. If you can work within these guidelines, you will be well on your way to becoming an effective system manager—a professional system manager.

1.7 Additional Reference

1. Aeleen Frisch. *Essential System Administration*. O'Reilly & Associates, Inc. 1995.

2

Site Configuration

2.1 Chapter Objectives

- Determine site configuration required to meet service-level objectives
- Explore physical, electrical, environmental, and other factors that characterize site configuration
- Suggest management policies and operational procedures necessary to maintain a functioning site
- Briefly discuss disaster planning issues

2.2 Introduction

Within the context of this chapter, *site configuration* refers to the physical, environmental, electrical, safety, and operational characteristics of the space immediately surrounding your computer systems.

- *Physical* characterizes the size, shape, and location of the room or rooms that contain your systems (e.g., the computer room)
- *Environmental* describes computer-room attributes, such as temperature, humidity, airflow, and the existence of airborne contaminants
- *Electrical* addresses the quality and availability of electrical power from the local utility company, as well as in-house equipment used to enhance power
- *Safety* focuses on the equipment necessary to ensure safety of personnel, equipment, and building structures
- *Operational* refers to the procedures and policies used to manage, maintain, and operate site components

These site-configuration features represent the foundation that supports the systems and the applications built upon that foundation. Computer equipment is generally more reliable than mechanical equipment, but only when precise temperature, humidity, airflow, air-quality, and power-level tolerances are maintained. When site support systems fail, any system contained within the site is vulnerable to failure or, at best, will operate less reliably.

Not many system managers have the opportunity to be involved in the initial design and construction of the data centers they manage. As a system manager, you more than likely inherited a site that was configured and constructed by your predecessors. For this reason, you might take for granted the configuration of your site and assume it is acceptable. Or, you might be tempted to ignore the issue altogether and consider it someone else's responsibility.

Site configuration represents a foundation pivotal to achieving service-level objectives. You cannot afford to make any assumptions about it and certainly cannot ignore it. You must ensure that current site characteristics match the needs of the systems they support. You also need to consider whether your site-configuration needs match changing system-configuration or service objectives. For example, as you add computer hardware, you may need to add cooling and power conditioning. Similarly, a change in business objectives might require redundant air conditioners or higher-capacity power backup.

2.3 Site Attributes

The following sections discuss the five aspects of site configuration in more detail.

2.3.1 Physical

2.3.1.1 Location

Elevator capacity, hallway and doorway widths, and any impediments to physical access are central considerations whenever adding or removing computer equipment.

Computer rooms are best located in the center of a building, away from exterior windows. This provides additional security and protects the equipment from the effects of exterior temperature changes. Systems should be located away from vibration (e.g., heavy industry, airports), sources of electrical interference (e.g., welders, large motors), and overhead flood sources (e.g., toilets, water-chilled air conditioners, sprinkler systems).

2.3.1.2 Structural Capacity

Building floors must have the structural capacity to support the weight of equipment, supplies, and personnel.

2.3.1.3 Flooring

A raised floor is essential for many installations. Many HP computer systems and disk subsystems require specific airflow rates for cooling purposes. Raised floors meet these requirements by routing air below the floor and up through vents beneath or immediately behind equipment. If you have more than a few systems or peripherals, a raised floor allows you to isolate and route data and power cables more easily.

The height of the raised floor must be adequate to house the cables that run beneath it and still have additional space for good airflow. Floor tiles themselves should be antistatic and provide a firm footing to prevent slips and falls. Falling on a disk drive is painful to humans and disk heads alike.

A common alternative to a raised-floor computer room involves overhead wiring trays and overhead bus bars for power. Overhead services are easier to retrofit into an existing structure and easy to reconfigure as necessary, but they will not be as photogenic as a raised-floor environment.

2.3.1.4 Equipment Layout

The layout of equipment should facilitate access by service personnel, minimize cable lengths and routing difficulties, maximize airflow, and allow for future reconfiguration. Printers should be located in a separate room to minimize dust generation. The layout should also provide for easy egress of personnel in an emergency.

2.3.2 Electrical

2.3.2.1 Power Basics

More than likely, your electric power is delivered to your site from your local utility company. Power from generating stations flows into a series of grids that satisfy the needs of buildings attached to the grid. As demand changes on these grids, the utility company shifts power to meet those needs. Some locations (usually business areas) are fed by multiple grids. If one grid fails (e.g., a car runs into a utility pole), the remaining grids can pick up the load. These load-switching events can result in surges or drops in power, which some equipment cannot tolerate.

There are two basic concerns with electrical power: *availability* and *quality.* Availability is the percentage of time power is available to equipment. Sometimes events such as fire, flood, wind, or lightning induce failure of all possible power paths to a location, causing an outage. Other times, load switching causes a momentary loss of power. Either of these events may cause unprotected computer systems to crash and require a complete reboot.

Some HP systems and storage controllers can be optionally outfitted with an integrated battery backup. The battery backup preserves the contents of the main memory or the controller cache for a short period of time so that if power is restored quickly, the system can sometimes recover fully. Unfortunately, battery backup provides power only to the main system memory or to controller cache—peripherals such as disks and terminals lose power, rendering the system inoperable during the outage. In addition, devices such as disks do not react well to sudden power loss and may be damaged by the outage. Therefore, even if the main central processing unit (CPU) recovers from the outage because of the memory battery backup, other equipment may be damaged, causing downtime anyway. Also, if data transactions are interrupted by a power failure, data may become corrupted—again requiring system downtime.

Power availability can be improved through the use of an uninterruptible power supply (UPS) or a motor generator. A UPS consists of a series of high-capacity batteries that provide backup power if the local utility fails. As long as all system peripherals (and this can include console displays and critical lighting) are attached through the UPS or motor generator, the system can continue to operate for as long as battery capacity or fuel allows. If you do not protect all remote terminals with a UPS, some users may not be able to access the system during an outage. However, having a UPS or motor generator gives you the time to ensure that key transactions are completed and to perform an orderly system shutdown. This minimizes the risk of outage-induced hardware failures and data corruption.

If your site requires protection against extended power failures, some type of backup generator or motor-generator system will be required. With a backup generator or motor generator, power can be maintained for as long as available fuel allows. If your site uses a backup generator, some form of UPS may be required during the interval when the generator starts and stabilizes. With a motor generator, ride-over is expected.

Power quality measures the consistency of electrical power in terms of voltage fluctuations and power-line noise. Most HP systems can tolerate voltage fluctuations of ±10 percent, but can tolerate only a minimal amount of noise. Power-line noise is commonly caused by electronic arcing within relays, motors, lights, and welders. Computer equipment can be protected from such noise with an *isolation transformer* between computer loads and possible noise-generating loads. Voltage fluctuations can also be caused by utility load switching, as well as by localized load switching caused by heavy equipment. You can isolate equipment from voltage fluctuations by installing a power-conditioning system, which also contains an isolation transformer.

For the most part, local utility companies do an excellent job and have sufficient backup systems to ensure reliable service for most situations. Some critical applications, however, may require a UPS, power-conditioning equipment, or both to meet service objectives. In some areas where power anomalies are frequent because of local weather patterns, additional power protection may be prudent. If you are unfamiliar with the power characteristics in your area, contact your local utility company and ask for a history of voltage fluctuations and outages.

2.3.2.2 Electromagnetic Interference

Another area of concern is electromagnetic interference (EMI). When current flows through a wire, electromagnetic fields develop around the wire. The stronger the current, the larger and stronger these fields are. When equipment or data cables are subjected to magnetic fields, electronic signals can be disrupted. Other sources of electrical disturbances, such as static or lightning, can cause equipment damage.

Current-induced EMI problems can be minimized by using cabling with sufficient shielding and grounding. In addition, data cables should be routed separately from EMI-generating power cables. Where power cables cross data cables, they should be oriented at right angles to minimize the effects of EMI.

2.3.2.3 Electrostatic Discharge

Protection from static discharge can be enhanced by minimizing the use of carpets and by maintaining proper humidity levels. If static is a problem, static discharge mats can be installed at the entrances to the computer room. Lightning is simply a severe form of electrostatic discharge. Although you cannot completely eliminate the risk of equipment damage from lightning, you can greatly enhance protection with proper building grounding and lightning arrestors. In geographic areas where lightning is common, you should carefully assess your protection against such disturbances.

2.3.3 Environmental

2.3.3.1 Temperature

The published operating temperature range for most HP equipment is 70°F ± 5°F. Absolute temperature is important, but the rate of temperature change must also be minimized to 5.4°F/hr. Most importantly, these temperature ranges must be maintained at the inlet to equipment cabinets, not on the wall away from equipment. Air vents must be configured to provide sufficient airflow through or in the immediate vicinity of equipment cabinets.

2.3.3.2 Humidity

Most HP equipment is designed to operate at 50 percent relative humidity ±10 percent with a maximum change rate of 6 percent per hour.

2.3.3.3 Corrosion and Contamination

In some process manufacturing environments, air can become contaminated with chlorine, sulfur, oxides, acids, or dust, all of which can cause premature failure of electronic equipment. Make sure that computer-room air is sufficiently filtered.

2.3.4 Safety Equipment

2.3.4.1 Power

The main safety devices for electric power are remote emergency power off (REPO) switches, which should be located at the main exits of the computer room. These provide a mechanism to quickly de-energize the entire computer room in the event of a serious fire, flood, or electrical problem.

2.3.4.2 Fire

When considering fire, fire detection, and fire suppression, the most important aspect is *life safety.* If the functions performed by the computer(s) are life critical, multiple isolated data centers are a central requirement. No computer itself is worth the life of a person.

The second level of fire protection is *fire prevention.* Fires need fuel to burn, so everything you can do to minimize the amount of combustible material around computer equipment minimizes the possibility of a fire. Walls, floors, ceilings, doors, ceiling tiles, and furniture should be noncombustible or fire resistant. Use of paper should be kept to a minimum, and paper should be disposed of in noncombustible trash containers. Any highly combustible materials (such as tape head cleaner) should be stored away from the computer room.

The second level of fire protection is *fire detection.* Smoke detectors should be deployed not only in the computer room, but also in surrounding rooms. Within the computer room, detectors should be placed in all major air spaces, including under the raised floor, above the false ceiling, and in the computer room itself. Alarms should sound in the computer room, in a security office, and at the local fire department.

The third level of fire protection is *fire suppression.* At a minimum, appropriately rated fire extinguishers should be located at all exits and strategically throughout the computer room. Fire extinguishers located near computers should typically be rated Class AB or Class ABC, suitable for use on conventional (Class A) and electrical fires (Class B).

You must be familiar with legal requirements and standards of practice, necessary personnel-safety training and equipment, potential equipment damage, and environmental factors associated with fire and fire-suppression equipment.

Many of the gasses produced by combustion are toxic, even in small quantities. Evacuate.

2.3.4.3 Water

Water detectors should be placed at the lowest point of the subfloors, where water is most likely to collect. Additional detectors near cooling systems may be required. Alarms should be located in the computer room and in security offices.

2.3.4.4 Security

Once someone has physical access to your computer room, he or she can disrupt power, destroy equipment, and remove confidential information. In other words, this person can bypass any software security you might have in place. If your information is valuable or confidential, you need to consider restricting physical access.

Access to the computer room can be restricted by fitting doors with keyed locks, cipher locks, or card readers. Keyed locks are the least expensive, but it is difficult to track who has keys. Cipher locks are activated by entering a combination on a series of buttons. This eliminates the need for keys, but requires that combinations be changed whenever key personnel leave your organization. Card readers accept cards with a magnetic strip indicating who is attempting access. Readers can be placed at each entrance to the computer room. A central computer database tracks who is allowed access to which rooms and at what times. This system can be especially helpful in determining who entered the computer room and when; however, magnetic cards can be borrowed, duplicated, or stolen.

2.3.5 Operational

2.3.5.1 Procedures

Safety and protection equipment is only as useful as the procedures that describe when and how to operate it. Comprehensive training should be given to all personnel who will be required to interpret equipment alarms, use fire-suppression equipment, or activate REPO switches. Specific procedures explaining how to respond to each type of situation should be in place. For example, you probably do not want the REPO switch pressed in response to a fire drill. In some cases, protection equipment causes more system downtime than it saves, because of inadequate operating procedures.

2.3.5.2 Cleaning Procedures

Dust can reduce the airflow to computer systems, and it can build up on system components. Both result in increased component temperature and failure rates. In addition, excessive dust can trigger certain types of smoke alarms. Computer room floors and subfloors should be cleaned with special vacuums that reduce dust exhaust. Air conditioner and computer air filters should be checked and replaced on a regular basis. Floors can be damp mopped with water only, and antistatic waxes can be applied if necessary. Conventional waxes can lead to static buildup, and other chemicals can cause air contamination.

2.4 Disaster Planning

No matter how redundant your site support systems are, events such as earthquakes, fires, floods, hurricanes, or terrorist acts can occur that in turn cause site failure. Any event that causes extended site failure can be considered a disaster.

As discussed in chapter 1, the service objectives at your site should specify the nature of the service that you need to provide in the event of a disaster and how quickly you need to restore service. In general, you should have an alternative site and equipment that are geographically isolated from any possible localized disaster. Depending on these requirements, you may need to implement one of the following site-backup strategies.

2.4.1 Backup Site

A backup site generally consists of duplicate computer equipment at a second geographic location. In the event of a primary site failure, you can retrieve your backups from off-site storage and restore them at the backup site. Depending on the quantity of data to be restored, you can normally restore service within a day. However, you would only be able to provide a system that was as current as your latest backups.

2.4.2 Hot Site

A hot site is similar to a backup site, except that backups are continually restored to the backup site so that contingent service can be made available much more quickly. With a hot site, some level of service can usually be restored in a matter of hours.

2.4.3 Distributed Site

The highest level of disaster tolerance can be achieved by establishing a distributed site, which consists of multiple physically distant redundant data centers linked by a network. All system transactions are automatically mirrored at both sites instantaneously. In the event that one site fails, the other site is immediately available to provide disaster backup. This strategy allows service to be restored in a matter of seconds or minutes, with all data available and current. This type of configuration is possible using the multiple-data-center capabilities of an OpenVMS cluster environment.

2.5 Conclusion

The first site I ever managed consisted of six VAX systems, an IBM system, and a Prime system all crammed into a narrow room that lacked a raised floor. The equipment was little more than three feet away from the walls, with almost a foot of cabling matted behind the systems. The field service engineers could hardly open the cabinet doors, never mind get behind the machines. Power, networking, and serial data cables were "routed" together in mats. The equipment was cooled by three water-chilled air conditioners, and the humidified water supply ate the stainless steel pans in the humidifier every few months. Because the capacity of each of the air-conditioning units was insufficient to cool the entire room, any failure would send temperatures soaring until someone noticed how hot the equipment room had become. Because there was no UPS, power failures would frequently cause system crashes.

As you can imagine, system reliability was less than optimal. Reliability improved as individual components were improved—replacing the wiring mats with modular wiring, upgrading and simplifying the network, relocating printers out of the computer room, and consolidating storage and expansion racks into fewer cabinets.

2.6 Additional References

1. "Maintaining a Dependable Environment," in *Building Dependable Systems.* Digital Equipment Corporation, March 1994.

2. *Site Environmental Preparation Guide*. Digital Equipment Corporation, November 1990.

3

System Configuration

3.1 Chapter Objectives

- Examine the organization of an OpenVMS system disk
- Review standard OpenVMS logical names
- Present basic OpenVMS cluster configuration options

3.2 OpenVMS System-Disk Organization

By default, when you install OpenVMS, a directory structure is created on the target device as follows:

```
[000000]              ! Master File Directory
   [.SYS0]            ! SYS0 system-specific root
     [.SYSEXE]        ! Specific system files
     [.SYSMGR]        ! Specific management files
     ...
     [.SYSUPD]
     [.SYSCOMMON]     ! Link to common root (VMS$COMMON)
   [VMS$COMMON.]      ! Cluster common directory
     [.SYSEXE]        ! Common system files
        [.SYSLIB]     ! Common utility executables
        [.SYSHLP]     ! HELP files and release notes
     [.SYSMGR]        ! Common management files
        [.SYSMSG]     ! Common error message files
     ...
     [.SYSUPD]        ! System update history
```

By default, the first system root is named SYS0. For each system root that shares a system disk, another SYS*x* (where *x* is a hexadecimal number) directory tree is added. System roots are typically added using the CLUSTER_CONFIG or CLUSTER_CONFIG_LAN utility. For instance, the additional system roots would look as follows:

```
[SYS1.]          ! Second system-specific root
   [SYSEXE.]
   [SYSMGR.]
   ...
   [SYSUPD.]
   [SYSCOMMON.]
 [SYS2.]         ! Third system-specific root
   [SYSEXE.]
   [SYSMGR.]
   ...
   [SYSUPD.]
   [SYSCOMMON.]
```

The directories under each system-specific root contain only the files that cannot or should not be shared in a cluster (e.g., system-parameter files, which are hardware specific, and node-specific network configuration). All other OpenVMS files are located under the cluster-common root VMS$COMMON. For example, all OpenVMS executable images (e.g., DIRECTORY.EXE) are located in [VMS$COMMON.SYSEXE]. Because of restrictions in bootstrap code, an OpenVMS system must boot by referring to the system-specific root (e.g., [SYS0]). This presents a problem because the files needed to boot are actually stored in the root directory [VMS$COMMON]. To handle this problem, there is a directory entry in each system-specific root called SYSCOMMON.DIR, which is an alias for the common root ([VMS$COMMON]). This allows OpenVMS to locate boot files in [VMS$COMMON] by referring to [SYS*x*.SYSCOMMON].

Using the DIR/FILE command you can confirm that the file identification numbers, (11,1,0) in the example below, of both of these directory files are identical; hence, they are the same file:

```
$ DIRECTORY/FILE MASON$DUA1:[SYS0]SYSCOMMON.DIR,-
_$ MASON$DUA1:[000000]VMS$COMMON.DIR
Directory MASON$DUA1:[SYS0]
SYSCOMMON.DIR;1   (11,1,0)
```

```
Total of 1 file.
Directory MASON$DUA1:[000000]
VMS$COMMON.DIR;1   (11,1,0)
Total of 1 file.
Grand total of 2 directories, 2 files.
```

3.3 System Logical Names

To facilitate access to system directories (e.g., to [SYS0.SYSEXE]), OpenVMS defines (at boot time) a number of systemwide logical names. At the lowest level, the logical name SYS$SYSDEVICE is defined as the device name of the system disk; for example:

```
$ SHOW LOGICAL SYS$SYSDEVICE
SYS$SYSDEVICE = "MASON$DUA1:"
```

At the next level, the logical names SYS$SPECIFIC, which locates the local-system root directory, and SYS$COMMON, which locates the cluster-common root directory as follows:

```
$ SHOW LOGICAL SYS$SPECIFIC
  "SYS$SPECIFIC" = "MASON$DUA1:[SYS0.]"
$ SHOW LOGICAL SYS$COMMON
  "SYS$COMMON" = "MASON$DUA1:[SYS0.SYSCOMMON.]"
```

Next, the logical name SYS$SYSROOT is defined as a search list (or search path) that points to both the system-specific and cluster-common roots as follows:

```
$ SHOW LOGICAL SYS$SYSROOT
  "SYS$SYSROOT" = "MASON$DUA1:[SYS0.]"
      = "SYS$COMMON:"
1 "SYS$COMMON" = "MASON$DUA1:[SYS0.SYSCOMMON.]"
```

When you access a file using a search list, OpenVMS attempts to locate the file by sequentially checking each directory included in the list. However, when you create a file, OpenVMS creates the file in the first directory listed. Figure 3.1 shows the relationship between the SYS$SYSROOT, SYS$COMMON, SYS$SPECIFIC, and SYS$SYSDEVICE logical names.

Figure 3.1 *OpenVMS System Disk Logical Structure*

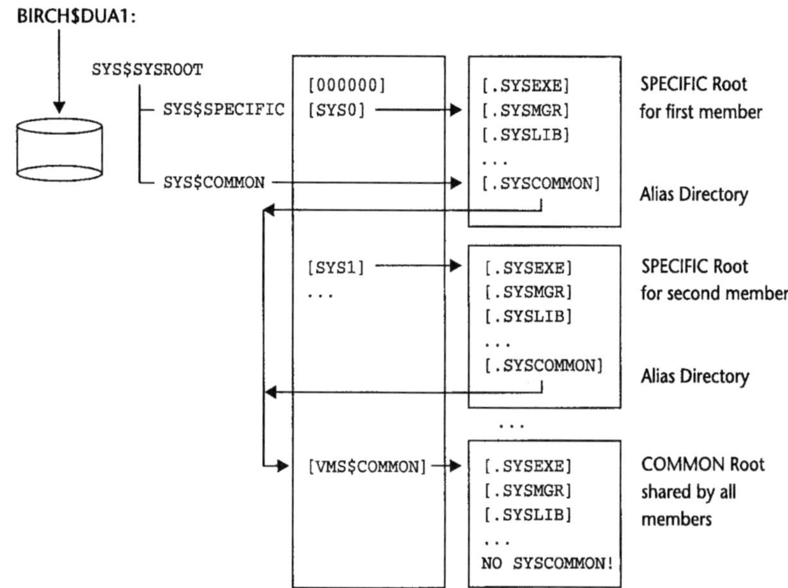

OpenVMS also defines logical names for key system directories in terms of SYS$SYSROOT, as indicated in table 3.1.

Table 3.1 *OpenVMS System Logical Names*

Logical Name	Equivalence	Contents
SYS$ERRORLOG	SYS$SYSROOT:[SYSERR]	System-error log file (ERRLOG.SYS)
SYS$ETC	SYS$SYSROOT:[SYS$ETC]	Miscellaneous useful (and undocumented) tools
SYS$EXAMPLES	SYS$SYSROOT:[SYSHLP.EXAMPLES]	Example command procedures and programs supplied by HP
SYS$HELP	SYS$SYSROOT:[SYSHLP]	Help files and release notes
SYS$I18N_ICONV	SYS$SYSROOT:[SYS$I18N.ICONV.USER], SYS$SYSROOT:[SYS$I18N.ICONV.SYSTEM]	Search list for internationalization (I18N) files
SYS$LIBRARY	SYS$SYSROOT:[SYSLIB]	Object libraries

Table 3.1 *OpenVMS System Logical Names (continued)*

Logical Name	Equivalence	Contents
SYS$LOADABLE_ IMAGES	SYS$SYSROOT:[SYS$LDR]	OpenVMS executable image files and device drivers
SYS$LOCALTIME	Specific file	System time zone rules
SYS$MAINTE-NANCE	SYS$SYSROOT:[SYSMAINT]	Reserved for HP Open-VMS diagnostics
SYS$MANAGER	SYS$SYSROOT:[SYSMGR]	System-management procedures
SYS$MESSAGE	SYS$SYSROOT:[SYSMSG]	System-message text files
SYS$NLSPATH	SYS$SYSROOT:[SYS$I18N.MESSAGES.USER.%L], SYS$SYSROOT:[SYS$I18N.MESSAGES.SYSTEM.%]	I18N files
SYS$SHARE	SYS$SYSROOT:[SYSLIB]	Shareable images
SYS$STARTUP	SYS$SYSROOT:[SYS$STARTUP], SYS$MANAGER	Startup command procedures
SYS$SYSTEM	SYS$SYSROOT:[SYSEXE]	Executable image files for most OpenVMS commands and utilities
SYS$TEST	SYS$SYSROOT:[SYSTEST]	OpenVMS user environment and HP-provided testing tools
SYS$TZDIR	SYS$SYSROOT:[SYS$TIMEZONEINFO.SYSTEM]	Time zone rules
SYS$UPDATE	SYS$SYSROOT:[SYSUPD]	Command procedures to perform system updates and maintain system parameters (e.g., VMSINSTAL, AUTOGEN)

3.4 OpenVMS Cluster Configurations

The reason for the directory structure described above is to support OpenVMS clusters, which consist of hardware and software mechanisms that allow several systems to share resources, primarily disks and printers. A cluster generally consists of two or more members that are physically connected by a common bus (several technologies are supported) or by an Ethernet network. OpenVMS cluster software allows each cluster member to share disks, tapes, queues, files, and other logical structures. Clusters are categorized based on how tightly they are integrated. In a *common-environment* cluster, all members generally boot from a common system disk and present the same applications and devices to users. To a user, a common-environment cluster appears as a single, large system, with all nodes participating. In a *multiple-environment* cluster, members may or may not boot from a common system disk, but system files are not usually shared, and different applications are started on each system. System disks are architecture specific. A cluster comprised of OpenVMS Alpha and OpenVMS VAX systems requires at least two system disks, one containing Alpha system images and the other containing VAX system images. Cluster-configuration data files must be shared across all nodes in the OpenVMS cluster.

The following paragraphs discuss some of the benefits of establishing an OpenVMS cluster.

Common system disk: The most powerful aspect of OpenVMS clusters is the ability to reduce the number of system disks and to configure and share authorization and configuration files. Cluster members can boot from the common system disk(s), allowing members to share key system files. This facilitates system management because you manage only one copy of system-startup files, user-authorization files (UAFs), and queue database files.

Remote File Access: All user file-manipulation commands (e.g., COPY, CREATE, EDIT, DELETE, DIRECTORY, RENAME, TYPE, PRINT) can be used to manipulate files throughout the OpenVMS cluster. Because all storage devices appear to be local, file specifications are the same as for local files. File access is direct and simpler than via DECnet remote file access or DECnet or FTP IP file transfer protocols. Further, existing coordination mechanisms such as file- and record-level locking function transparently across all cluster members. For instance, since the user's file system is served throughout every CPU (or node) in the cluster, the user may issue commands like

```
$ TYPE INSTRUCTIONS.TXT
```

no matter what node he or she has logged into. If the nodes were not clustered, the user would have to know which node was connected to the disk containing his or her data. If he or she were not logged into that node, the above command would become

```
$ TYPE MASON::INSTRUCTIONS.TXT
```

This is the syntax for accessing files via DECnet over the network.

Remote file access is available via DECnet (COPY) and via FTP (COPY/FTP, DIRECTORY/FTP). The point is that the clustered user has transparent access to files.

Clusterwide job submission: Users can directly submit a print or batch job to a queue on any cluster member. The submitted job need only exist somewhere in the cluster. This is much simpler than using SUBMIT/REMOTE, in which the command procedure must already exist on the remote DECnet system.

As in the example above, the user issues a PRINT command no matter what node he or she logged into. No only does PRINT refer to a clusterwide queue manager, but the file to be printed can be transparently accessed by the queue manager. By "transparent" I mean that the user does not have to state specifically which node serves the file.

Increased availability: When an OpenVMS cluster is configured as a common-environment cluster, users can log in to any cluster member and transparently access the same disks, files, queues, and applications. System availability is greatly increased, because users can simply log in to another cluster member if the primary system fails.

3.4.1 OpenVMS Cluster Interconnects

Cluster nodes, that is, CPUs, must be interconnected in order to ascertain the cluster health and to coordinate file access between users. Devices (disks, printers, and tape drives) must be interconnected to facilitate data access from multiple nodes. These two connections may be combined in a single path (e.g., using Ethernet) or may be separated [e.g., using Computer Interconnect (CI) to connect nodes and Small Computer Systems Interface (SCSI) to interconnect disks and tapes.] At least one communications interconnect must be present between all nodes in an OpenVMS cluster, but two interconnects are also permitted to increase reliability. A storage interconnect permits host access to storage, but does not permit direct communications with other hosts. Zero or more storage interconnects can be present.

The following paragraphs briefly present some of the OpenVMS cluster configuration options.

Fibre Channel: OpenVMS permits access to a storage-area network (SAN) via fibre channel communications. Fibre Channel is a storage interconnect and requires one or more additional cluster-communications interconnects.

SCSI: Selected SCSI controllers with support for a SCSI feature known as tagged command queuing (TCQ) can be used for storage access. All SCSI devices configured on a shared SCSI bus must tolerate SCSI bus resets without loosing context. In particular, SCSI tape devices will typically rewind in response to a reset, and thus cannot be configured on a shared SCSI bus. SCSI is a storage interconnect. In certain CPU configurations, SCSI may be used for communications interconnect as well.

Memory Channel: Memory Channel provides a low-latency, high-bandwidth communications connection that is specifically suited to lock management and similar types of cluster traffic. Memory Channel controllers require the assistance of the processor for operation. Configurations of up to 3 km in diameter are permitted. Memory Channel is a communications interconnect.

CI: Clusters that use the CI are connected to a star coupler in a radial configuration, as shown in figure 3.2. Within a CI cluster, disks can be connected to dedicated storage controllers (e.g., HSJ50), which handle disk I/O requests generated by cluster members. The CI supports a maximum bandwidth of 70 Mbps per channel, with two CI channels available. The throughput of a single system depends on its CI adapter. CI is a communications interconnect.

Digital Storage System Interconnect: Clusters that use the Digital Storage System Interconnect (DSSI) are connected to a DSSI bus in a lateral configuration, as shown in figure 3.3. The DSSI bus supports a maximum of eight

Figure 3.2
CI VMS Cluster Configuration

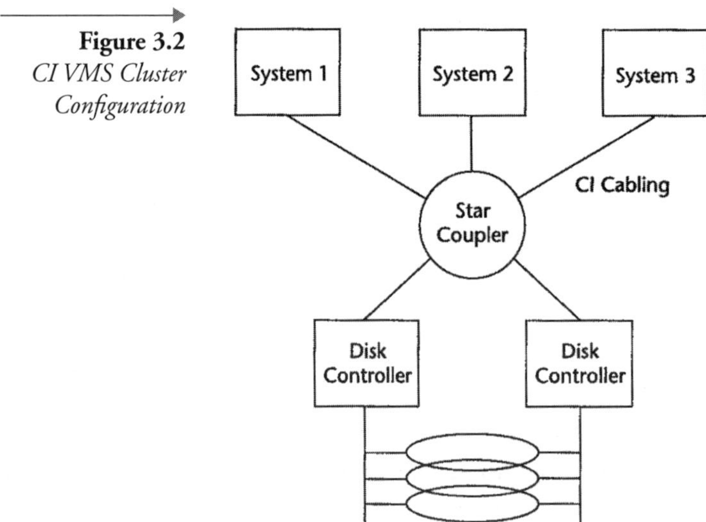

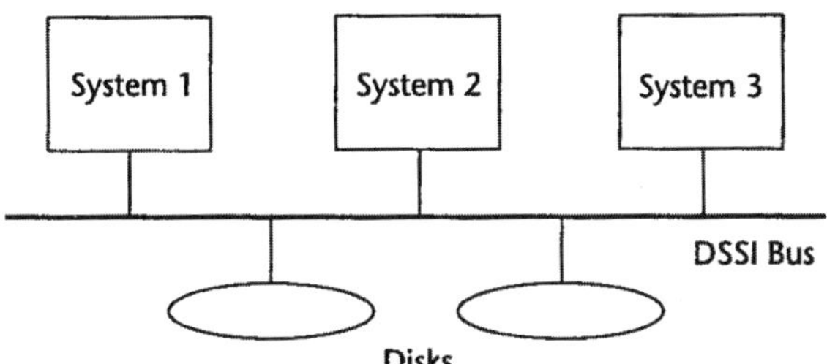

Figure 3.3
DSSI VMS Cluster Configuration

nodes, of which a maximum of four can be OpenVMS systems. The remaining nodes can be integrated storage element (ISE) disks or tapes. The maximum bandwidth of a DSSI bus is 32 Mbps and is generally limited to a total length of about 25m. DSSI is a communications interconnect.

Network Interconnect: You can also establish an OpenVMS cluster simply by connecting several systems to an Ethernet, Fiber Distributed Data Interface (FDDI), or Asynchronous Transfer Mode (ATM) network, as illustrated in figure 3.4. Ethernet clusters are sometimes referred to as local-area clusters. In general, one or more satellite members boot from one or more boot servers that have direct access to an OpenVMS system disk of the appropriate architecture for the satellite host. Network Interconnect is a communications interconnect.

Dual-architecture OpenVMS clusters: A dual-architecture OpenVMS cluster contains both OpenVMS VAX and OpenVMS Alpha members. It is subject to the following configuration restrictions:

- OpenVMS systems must be added or removed only from the OpenVMS cluster using a node of the same architecture. Once a cluster member has been configured, cross-booting systems is supported.
- At least one VAX and one Alpha system disk must be present.
- Additional system disks can be configured.

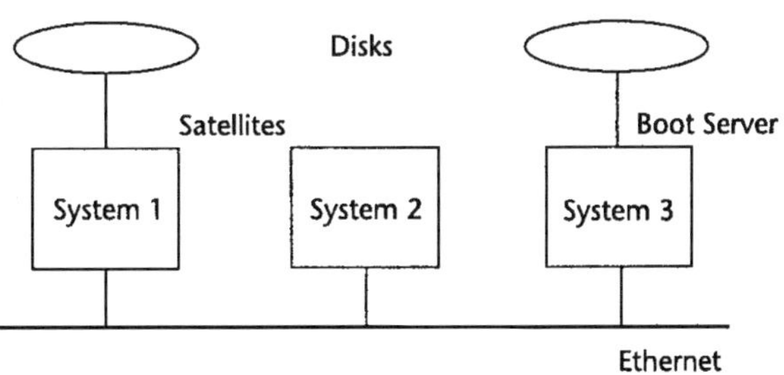

Figure 3.4
Network Interconnect VMS Cluster Configuration

3.5 Conclusion

Although somewhat complicated at first glance, the OpenVMS directory structure is designed for clustering, even if the system is not clustered. With this scheme, it is vital to understand the distinction between the SYS$SPECIFIC and SYS$COMMON directory trees. Likewise, the fact that SYS$SYSROOT is a search path, not a single directory, which points to both trees is a powerful concept that must be understood when configuring a cluster.

The several available cluster technologies are intended for different applications, and the cluster novice would do well to consult with HP engineers before acquiring any hardware.

3.6 Additional References

1. Roy G. Davis. *VAX Cluster Principles*. Digital Press, 1993.
2. Gregory Pfister. *In Search of Clusters*. Prentice Hall, 1998.
3. *Guidelines for OpenVMS Cluster Configurations*, Compaq Computer Corporation, April 2001.
4. *OpenVMS Cluster Systems,* Compaq Computer Corporation, April 2001.

4

Booting OpenVMS

4.1 Chapter Objectives

- Provide a single reference source that details boot procedures for most OpenVMS systems
- Discuss procedures for configuring and initiating various boot methods
- Review procedures for configuring console switches and parameters
- Increase system availability by implementing robust boot procedures

4.2 Introduction

OpenVMS systems normally boot automatically after you power them on or issue the standard BOOT command. As a result, it is easy to take the process of booting for granted. However, things do not always go so smoothly. Sometimes systems hang or will not boot because of misconfigured system parameters, problems with startup procedures, software bugs, or hardware failures. In these situations you may need to use alternative techniques to perform the following procedures:

- Minimal boot
- Conversational boot
- Stand-alone backup boot
- Alternate system-disk boot
- Crash dump
- DECamds and the Availability Manager
- Interrupt Priority C (IPC) utility

Usually you need to employ these techniques when a system is malfunctioning and downtime is accumulating. However, because unscheduled downtime does not happen very often, even more downtime is incurred while you try to remember the necessary procedures. To maximize system uptime, you should carefully review and familiarize yourself with these procedures so that you are ready to use them when needed. You may want to post specific instructions near the system console as a reminder.

This chapter presents the steps necessary to prepare for each booting method, including setting hardware console switches, configuring console subsystem-boot files, setting console parameters, and building stand-alone backup kits. Much of the information presented here is applicable to other processors not mentioned. For example, procedures for booting VAXserver systems are not specifically addressed; however, the procedures are similar to those for the corresponding VAX and MicroVAX systems.

4.3 Console Subsystems

Each VAX and Alpha processor contains a console subsystem that consists of hardware and software mechanisms used to configure and control the booting process. When a system is powered on, the console subsystem loads a console program from a load device. Next, the console program either initiates a system boot or displays a console prompt and waits for manual console commands. Console commands perform limited functions such as loading CPU registers, halting the main system processor, or initiating a boot sequence. Each system model either has a *dedicated* or *nondedicated* console subsystem (figures 4.1 and 4.2).

Processors with dedicated console subsystems typically include a console CPU in addition to the CPU of the main system, and a console load device (usually a floppy drive or small hard disk). On systems with a dedicated console, OpenVMS and application programs can continue to operate while the console is in use, unless OpenVMS is explicitly halted. Boot procedures and console initialization code are usually loaded from the console storage device. You configure boot procedures by modifying boot command files (e.g., DEFBOO.COM or DEFBOO.CMD) located on the console load device.

On processors with nondedicated console subsystems, all console functions are performed by the main CPU of the system. This means that the processing of the OpenVMS operating system and of all applications is halted for the duration of the console operations. The VAX console program is typically read from read-only memory (ROM), although a few VAX

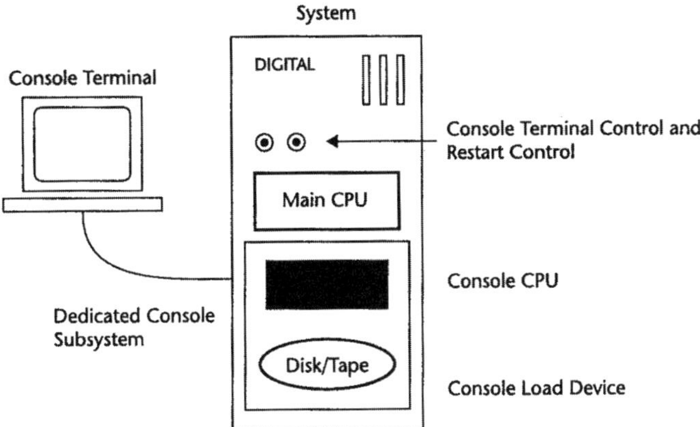

Figure 4.1 *Systems with Dedicated Console Subsystems*

systems use nonvolatile random access memory (NVRAM). The Alpha console program is typically read from SROM. Because these systems may have no console storage device, boot parameters are stored in nonvolatile memory, rather than in boot command files.

4.3.1 Console Terminal

All console functions are performed from the console terminal, which can be a graphics console, a serial connection to a cluster console application running on another system, to a terminal emulator running on another system, or to a traditional video or printing terminal. Certain Alpha systems may have USB console connections.

Most processors support two console modes: *console input/output* (CIO) mode and *program input/output* (PIO) mode. These two modes are henceforth referred to as *console mode* and *program mode*.

In program mode, the console terminal acts like any other user terminal attached to the system. If OpenVMS is already booted, pressing the <RETURN> key initiates an interactive login—the standard Username: prompt is displayed, allowing you to log in and run any OpenVMS program or utility.

In console mode, the console-mode prompt (on most processors, >>>, which is often called the "dead sergeant" prompt) is displayed, allowing console commands to be entered and processed by the console subsystem. You cannot enter OpenVMS commands from console mode.

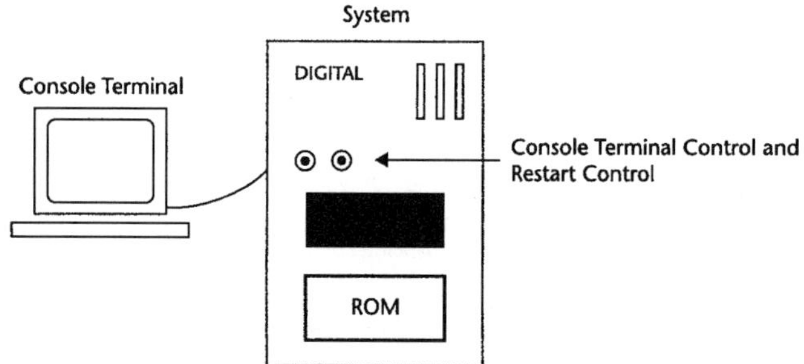

Figure 4.2 *Systems with Nondedicated Console Subsystems*

You switch from program mode to console mode by entering a special key sequence from the console terminal. This switch sequence is either a <CTRL/P> or the <BREAK> key (sometimes labeled F5), depending on the VAX or Alpha system model. On some processors, you switch from program to console mode by pressing the <HALT> switch located on the system chassis. Additionally, specific processors can have a key switch or a console password that is used to control access to the console-program environment.

If the VAX system uses a dedicated console, you can switch from console mode back to program mode on systems with the following commands:

```
>>> SET TERMINAL PROGRAM
>>> BOOT
```

The SET TERMINAL PROGRAM command assumes that OpenVMS VAX was not halted (this is only the case on systems that do not use the VAX CPU as the console CPU) and that you now want to communicate with OpenVMS and not with the console. The latter BOOT command reboots the OpenVMS system.

If the VAX or Alpha system uses a serial or local graphics console, as well as a nondedicated console, the following commands can be used:

```
>>> CONTINUE
>>> BOOT
```

The CONTINUE command restarts OpenVMS where it was when the system was halted and the console program was activated. Depending on the system state when it was halted, OpenVMS may not be restartable. In particular, systems configured in an OpenVMS cluster and systems that do not use graphics or serial consoles are typically not restartable. The BOOT command reboots OpenVMS.

If an OpenVMS system uses a USB console, the OpenVMS system cannot be restarted after it is halted and must be rebooted. This requirement results from the complexity of operating the USB and the inability to restart the OpenVMS host USB device drivers once halted.

4.3.2 Console Terminal Control

Each system has a *console terminal control* mechanism that enables and disables switching the console terminal from program mode to console mode. Normally, terminal control is set with a physical switch located on the system chassis or with a console password.

You should configure the console terminal control mechanism of your system to disable console-mode switching, except when it is absolutely necessary. On systems with nondedicated console subsystems, switching into console mode halts the main processor, forcing suspension of all system activity. Although you can usually resume system activity by issuing the CONTINUE command, you can easily crash the system or cause a reboot by accidentally entering the wrong command (e.g., BOOT). In addition, if the system is a member of an OpenVMS cluster and it is left in console mode for longer than the period specified by the system parameter reconnect interval (RECNXINTERVAL), the cluster connection manager ejects one or more systems from the cluster. This occurs because the halted system cannot respond to periodic polling as required.

On some MicroVAX systems, you have to be especially careful to ensure that terminal control is disabled. If console-mode switching is enabled and you power the console terminal off and back on, a <BREAK> signal is generated that forces the console terminal into console mode, suspending all user activity and resulting in eventual cluster ejection. (Technically, this is caused by a serial line framing error that occurs when certain serial terminals power up. A serial line framing error is identical to a <BREAK>.)

When you enter console mode on a system with a dedicated console, the main processor is not halted. Thus, normal system activity is not affected. Nor is the system susceptible to cluster ejection unless a console HALT command is explicitly executed. As a rule, you should still disable console-mode switching on all system consoles to prevent accidental system halts or reboots.

The terminal control mechanisms for each processor are detailed in appendix C.

4.3.3 System Restart Control

The *restart control* mechanism controls the boot action an Alpha or a VAX system takes when the system is initially powered on. On VAX systems, restart control is either a physical switch or the SET HALT console command, while on Alpha systems the restart control is established by the auto_action console environment variable. Tables 4.1 and 4.2 illustrate each restart control setting and its associated boot action.

Table 4.1 *Alpha Restart Control Settings*

Restart Control Setting	Boot Action
`BOOT`	When the console environment is set to BOOT, the system initiates an automatic boot after power on or system crash. Automatic boot procedures are discussed in section 4.5.1.
`RESTART`	If the console environment variable is set to RESTART and a power-failure recovery occurs, the system attempts to restart the CPU at the point just before the power failure. In many cases, user activity resumes at the point where it was interrupted, and a system boot is not necessary. This functionality exists only for systems that have main-memory battery backup. If the restart attempt fails, an automatic boot is performed. This is often the preferred setting.
`HALT`	When the console environment variable is set to HALT, the system halts and displays the console mode prompt (>>>) after power on or a system crash.

Table 4.2 *VAX Restart Control Settings*

Restart Control Setting	Boot Action
`BOOT`	When restart control is set to BOOT, the system initiates an automatic boot after power on or system crash. Automatic boot procedures are discussed in section 4.5.1.

Table 4.2 *VAX Restart Control Settings (continued)*

Restart Control Setting	Boot Action
`RESTART/BOOT`	If restart control is set to RESTART/BOOT (or RESTART_BOOT) and a power-failure recovery occurs, the system attempts to restart the CPU at the point just before the power failure. In many cases, user activity resumes at the point where it was interrupted, and a system boot is not necessary. This functionality exists only for systems that have main-memory battery backup. If the restart attempt fails, an automatic boot is performed. This is often the preferred setting.
`RESTART/HALT`	If restart control is set to RESTART/HALT, the system initiates a restart attempt after recovery from a power failure. However, if the restart fails, the system halts and displays the CIO mode prompt (>>>).
`HALT`	When restart control is set to HALT, the system halts and displays the CIO mode prompt (>>>) after power on or a system crash.

In most cases, you will want to configure restart control so that system availability is automatically restored. If your system has memory battery backup, set the restart control to RESTART/BOOT or enter the command SET HALT RESTART_BOOT (VAX) or SET AUTO_ACTION RESTART (Alpha); otherwise, set it to BOOT.

If you have applications that require manual recovery procedures after a system crash or power failure, you may need to set restart control to either RESTART/HALT or HALT (depending on whether or not you have battery backup). When either HALT option is selected, the power-on action is to halt and display the console mode prompt (>>>). This allows you to boot the system manually and temporarily prevent user access while you perform recovery procedures.

You might want to disable automatic booting when intermittent hardware failures begin to occur. By forcing the system to halt, your hardware service vendor can diagnose hardware problems because the state of the system immediately following the failure is preserved. This technique is most useful when hardware problems are so severe that a crash dump is not created.

The specific terminal control mechanisms for each processor are detailed in appendix C.

4.4 Configuring a Boot Device

OpenVMS exists as a series of executable image files that reside on a system disk. Before OpenVMS is loaded, the system can perform only extremely limited functions, such as loading general CPU registers and reading specific files from disk into memory. Booting essentially involves three steps: locating a valid system disk, loading OpenVMS image files into memory, and transferring control to the operating system.

Most boot configuration steps involve specifying the OpenVMS system disk from which you want to boot. For example, you might want to boot from one of the following sources:

- Local disk
- Local tape (for VAX stand-alone backup); tape bootstraps are not available on Alpha
- CI- or DSSI-attached disk storage (or CI- or DSSI-attached tapes on VAX systems)
- Local-area disk (LAD) communications with an InfoServer or with an OpenVMS system running the host-based version of the InfoServer software
- Remote (served) access to a boot and disk server

In addition, within an OpenVMS cluster, a system disk can contain multiple system roots—one for each member of the cluster (e.g., [SYS0], [SYS1]) as described in chapter 3. Each root contains the configuration files and startup procedures specific to its associated cluster member. To boot a system into a cluster, you must configure boot parameters to locate a valid system disk and specify the appropriate system root.

4.4.1 Processors with Nondedicated Console Subsystems

On processors with nondedicated console subsystems, you configure a default boot disk and system root by establishing values for the following nonvolatile boot registers:

- Default boot device

- Default boot control flags

On most Alpha systems, you configure these using the following SRM console commands:

```
>>> SET BOOTDEV_DEF device
>>> SET BOOT_OSFLAGS boot-root,boot-flags
```

The boot-flags setting is defined in table 4.3.

Table 4.3 *Alpha Boot Control Flags*

boot-flags Bit Position	Purpose
<31:1>	Not applicable
<0:0>	Conversational boot (0 = No, 1 = Yes)

For example, to configure an Alpha system to boot conversationally (the conversational boot is discussed in section 4.5.4) from the device DKA100: and system root [SYS5], you issue the following console commands:

```
>>> SET BOOTDEV_DEF DKA100
>>> SET BOOT_OSFLAGS 5,1
```

On a VAX 4000 model 200, you configure these registers using the following console commands:

```
>>> SET BOOT device
>>> SET BFLG boot-flags
```

Boot control flags must be specified as a 32-bit hexadecimal number. As illustrated in table 4.4, the upper four bits specify the system root (0-F) and the lowermost bit is used to select a conversational boot (discussed later in this chapter).

Thus, to configure the above system to boot from the device DUA1 and system root [SYS1], you issue the following console commands:

Table 4.4 *VAX Boot Control Flags (Register R5)*

Register R5 Bit Position	Purpose
<31:28>	System root (0-F)
<27:1>	Not applicable
<0:0>	Conversational boot (0 = No, 1 = Yes)

```
>>> SET BOOT DUA1
>>> SET BFLG 10000000
```

The console commands required to configure the default boot device and default boot control flags for other processors are detailed in appendix C.

4.4.2 VAX Systems with Dedicated Console Subsystems

On VAX processors with dedicated console subsystems, the default boot device and boot control flags are configured with boot command procedures located on the console load device. When a system in this category boots, it executes either the boot procedure DEFBOO.COM or DEFBOO.CMD.

The commands within the DEFBOO load processor registers R0 to R4 specify the path to a valid system disk; load register R5 specifies the desired system root (see table 4.4). Specifically, the function of each processor register is as follows:

- R0 Boot device type code
- R1 Boot device bus address
- R2 Boot device controller information
- R3 Boot device unit number
- R4 Logical block number (LBN) of boot block on disk; rarely used
- R5 Boot control flags (table 4.4)

When booting from a locally attached disk, registers R0 to R2 specify the local disk controller. The required values depend on the type of controller (e.g., MASSBUS, Unibus, BI). To determine the required values, review the template boot procedures for each controller type included on the console device of your system. The tables in appendix C list the template procedures for each processor.

For example, boot procedure DU0BOO.CMD exists on the VAX 8600 console disk and contains the following commands:

```
! DU0BOO.CMD—Boot from UDA50-attached disk
!
DEPOSIT R0      11
DEPOSIT R1      5
DEPOSIT R2      0103F468
DEPOSIT R3      disk unit #
```

To boot from device DUA1, system root [SYS9], create a DEFBOO.CMD that uses the same values for R0 to R2, but substitute appropriate values for R3 and R5 as follows:

```
! DEFBOO.CMD—Default boot (copied from DU0BOO.CMD)
!
DEPOSIT R0      11
DEPOSIT R1      5
DEPOSIT R2      0103F468
DEPOSIT R3      1
DEPOSIT R5      90000000! [SYS9], not conversational
```

When booting from a hierarchical storage controller like a HSC or HSJ attached disk, registers R0 and R1 specify the CI controller, and R2 specifies the HSC node number. As indicated in appendix C, the template boot procedure to boot from the CI from a VAX 8600 is as follows:

```
! CIBOO.CMD—Boot from HSC-attached disk
!
DEPOSIT R0      20
DEPOSIT R1      E
DEPOSIT R2      HSC NODE #
DEPOSIT R3      disk unit #
```

For instance, to boot from the device DUA1, attached to HSC node #3, system root [SYS9], you create a DEFBOO.CMD that uses the same values for R0 and R1, but substitute appropriate values for R2, R3, and R5 as follows:

```
! CIBOO.CMD—Boot from HSC-attached disk
!
DEPOSIT R0      20
DEPOSIT R1      E
DEPOSIT R2      03
DEPOIST R3      1
DEPOSIT R5      90000000
```

If HSC- or HSJ-attached disks are connected to two controllers, you should adjust register R2 to include both nodes. For example, to specify HSJ nodes #3 and #4, include the following command in your boot procedure:

```
DEPOSIT R2      0304
```

4.4.3 Editing VAX Boot Command Files

Boot command files are stored on the console device and are not directly accessible from OpenVMS. The procedures for modifying boot command files are processor-specific:

VAX-11/725/730/750/751/780/782/785, VAX 8600/8650, VAX 8200/8300/8250/8350

Use the OpenVMS EXCHANGE utility to copy boot command files from the console device to OpenVMS, modify them with any OpenVMS editor, then copy them back to the console device as follows:

```
$ RUN SYS$SYSTEM:SYSGEN
SYSGEN> CONNECT CONSOLE
$
$ EXCHANGE
EXCHANGE> COPY CSA1:DEFBOO.CMD *.*
EXCHANGE> EXIT
$ EDIT DEFBOO.CMD
```

```
[make changes]
^Z
$ EXCHANGE
EXCHANGE> COPY DEFBOO.CMD CSA1:
EXCHANGE> EXIT
```

You can also use the CONSCOPY utility to copy the console media. You will want to use CONSCOPY to create one or more backup copies of your console media, and you will want to maintain an online copy of your console media on one of your OpenVMS disks.

VAX8500/8530/8550/8700/8800/8810/8820N

The Nautilus Pro console subsystem (usually a Pro350 or Pro380 system running a variant of RSX-11 known as P/OS) has a DCL-like interface (PRODCL) that includes an editor similar to EDT, the OpenVMS text editor. To edit a boot file, issue the following console commands:

```
>>> QUIT
$ EDIT/EDT filename
[make changes]
^Z
$ RUN CONTROL or
$ RUN CONSOLE
```

VAX 8820/8830/8840

The PolarStar console subsystem consists of a MicroVAX II running OpenVMS. You edit boot files by accessing OpenVMS on the console and using the standard OpenVMS editor. This is accomplished using the following console commands:

```
PS-OS-0> QUIT
System Power is ON, are you sure?> Y
> EDIT DEFBOO.CMD
[make changes]
^Z
> POLARIS
```

4.4.4 Alpha Boot Sequence

Once a system boot is initiated, the following events occur:

- General-purpose CPU registers R0 to R5 are loaded on the basis of either default values stored in the BOOT_OSFLAGS console environment variable stored in NVRAM or explicit specification of the console BOOT command.
- The system disk is located on the basis of the BOOTDEV_DEF environment variable or explicit specification of the device on the console BOOT command. The APB.EXE primary bootstrap image is located based on the boot block of the OpenVMS Alpha system disk. APB.EXE loads the secondary bootstrap program, SYSBOOT, from the system-disk file, SYS$SYSTEM:SYSBOOT.EXE.
- SYSBOOT loads the system parameters from the file SYS$SYSTEM:ALPHAVMSSYS.PAR. Next, SYSBOOT checks the boot control flags to see if a conversational boot has been requested. If the low-order bit is set, the boot procedure stops and the SYSBOOT> prompt is displayed on the console terminal. Otherwise, SYSBOOT proceeds to load the OpenVMS executable, including SYS$SYSTEM:SYS$BASE_IMAGE.EXE, and transfers control to the routine EXE$INIT.
- EXE$INIT executes in system context, configuring key OpenVMS data structures and initializing process scheduling and memory management. Next, the SWAPPER process is created, and process context is enabled.
- SWAPPER initiates system-startup procedures (see chapter 5). Once startup procedures are complete, users can log in to the system.

4.4.5 VAX Boot Sequence

Once a system boot is initiated, the following events occur:

- General-purpose CPU registers R0 to R5 are loaded on the basis of either default values stored in NVRAM qualifiers appended to a BOOT command or values set by explicit DEPOSIT register commands in boot command files.

- The system disk is located on the basis of the contents of registers R0 to R4. VMB.EXE is loaded from either console-attached media (disk or tape), from ROM, or from the OpenVMS VAX system disk by way of the boot block. More recent versions of VMB load the secondary bootstrap program, SYSBOOT, from the file SYS$SYSTEM:SYSBOOT.EXE located on the system disk.
- SYSBOOT loads the system parameters from the file SYS$SYSTEM:VAXVMSSYS.PAR. Next, SYSBOOT checks the boot control flags to see if a conversational boot has been requested. If the low-order bit is set, the boot procedure stops and the SYSBOOT> prompt is displayed on the console terminal. Otherwise, SYSBOOT proceeds to load the OpenVMS executable, including SYS$SYSTEM:SYS.EXE, and transfers control to the routine EXE$INIT.
- EXE$INIT executes in system context, configuring key OpenVMS data structures, and initializing process scheduling and memory management. Next, the SWAPPER process is created, and process context is enabled.
- SWAPPER initiates system site-specific startup procedures. This topic is described in detail in chapter 5.
- Once startup procedures are complete, users can log in to the system.

4.5 Boot Methods

The following sections describe each of the most important booting methods and the conditions under which they are invoked. The procedures for configuring and invoking each are detailed in appendix C.

4.5.1 Automatic Boot

The system automatically boots under the conditions listed in table 4.5.

Table 4.5 *Automatic Boot Conditions*

Condition	Restart Control Setting
Initial system power-on or power-failure recovery	BOOT or RESTART/BOOT (if restart attempt fails)
Fatal OpenVMS crash	BOOT or RESTART/BOOT
Shutdown requested automatic reboot	Don't care

You must configure restart control to BOOT or RESTART/BOOT if you want systems to perform an automatic boot after initial power on, power-failure recovery, or a system crash. However, an automatic boot is always initiated whenever one is optionally requested during an orderly system shutdown or after forcing a system crash directly with OPCCRASH. System shutdown and OPCCRASH are discussed in chapter 6.

4.5.2 Manual Boot

If a system does not perform an automatic boot (because of restart control settings), you must interactively enter boot commands from the console terminal and initiate a manual boot. These commands should specify which disk to boot from and set boot control flags as necessary.

In general, you use manual boot procedures to select alternative boot methods, such as the following:

- Default boot
- Conversational boot
- Stand-alone backup boot
- Alternative system-disk boot

Before you can initiate a manual boot, you must switch the console terminal into console mode. This can be accomplished with one of the following two techniques:

1. If OpenVMS is currently booted, perform an orderly system shutdown, but do not request an automatic reboot. After the shutdown is complete, enable console-mode switching and enter the appropriate switch sequence, depending on the architecture (e.g., <CTRL/P>, <BREAK> key, or press the <HALT> button).
2. If the system is not currently powered on, enter console mode by first setting the processor's restart control mechanism to HALT or RESTART/HALT, then apply power. After power-on diagnostics are complete, the console mode prompt (>>>) is displayed.

4.5.3 Default Boot

You initiate a default boot by issuing the console BOOT command (without any qualifiers or parameters) as follows:

```
>>> BOOT
```

The default boot actions for each processor are described in appendix C. On most systems, a default boot performs the same steps as an automatic boot. However, carefully review appendix C for your model because this is not always the case.

4.5.4 Conversational Boot

A conversational boot allows you to adjust system parameters interactively during the booting process by invoking the SYSBOOT utility before system-startup procedures are initiated. You need to perform a conversational boot whenever any of the following conditions occur:

- All passwords to privileged accounts are lost
- Incorrect system-parameter settings prevent booting
- Changes to system-startup procedures prevent booting

The procedures for initiating a conversational boot for each processor are discussed in appendix C. SYSBOOT is discussed in more detail in section 4.6.

4.6 SYSBOOT Options

Before you use the following procedures, you must perform a conversational boot using the processor-specific procedure described in appendix C. Once you initiate a conversational boot, the booting process invokes the SYSBOOT utility just before executing system-startup procedures. You can then enter a series of commands at the SYSBOOT prompt as follows:

```
SYSBOOT>
```

When you have finished entering commands, enter CONTINUE so that the boot process will proceed.

From SYSBOOT you can perform the following functions:

- Perform minimal system startup (prevent execution of SYSTARTUP_VMS.COM)
- Bypass system startup (prevent execution of STARTUP.COM)
- Select an alternative UAF
- Adjust system parameters

Most of these functions involve changing system parameters. By default, parameters changed with SYSBOOT are permanently written to the system parameter file (that is, VAXVMSSYS.PAR for VAX systems and ALPHAVMSSYS.PAR for Alpha systems). If you want changes to be temporary, you should set the parameter WRITESYSPAR to 0 after changing the other system parameters. This prevents changes from being written to the system parameter file.

4.6.1 Minimal Startup

When performing system maintenance, or when boot problems occur, you may want to perform a minimal startup. A minimal startup prevents the main site-specific startup command file, SYS$MANAGER:SYSTARTUP_VMS, from being executed. This can be useful if you do not want the full system activated or want to save time during reboots. You may also need to perform a minimal startup prior to installing an OpenVMS upgrade.

To initiate a minimal startup (on a VAX in the example below), respond to the SYSBOOT prompt as follows:

```
>>> B/E0000000 DUA0
SYSBOOT> SET STARTUP_P1 "MIN"
SYSBOOT> CONTINUE
```

The computer continues to boot. Only system logins from the console are permitted. After logging in (any username and password is accepted), you must manually reset STARTUP_P1 as follows before the next system reboot:

```
$ RUN SYS$SYSTEM:SYSGEN
SYSMAN> PARAMETERS USE CURRENT
SYSMAN> PARAMETERS STATRUP_P1 ""
SYSMAN> PARAMETERS WRITE CURRENT
SYSMAN> EXIT
```

On most Alpha systems, an example boot command would look like this:

```
>>> BOOT -FLAGS 0,1 DKA0
```

The next step would be to fix the problem using AUTHORIZE, SYSMAN, and such, as illustrated in the following sections. The AUTHORIZE, SYSBOOT, and SYSMAN commands are identical on both architectures. Since the system is not fully operational at this point, it should be shut down in the normal way and rebooted normally. The normal shutdown command is

```
$ @SYS$SYSTEM:SHUTDOWN
```

This procedure assures you have fixed the problems and the system will boot normally.

4.6.2 Bypass Startup

If you experience system-startup problems that extend beyond SYSTARTUP_VMS.COM, you can bypass the execution of all startup procedures with the following SYSBOOT commands:

```
SYSBOOT> SET/STARTUP OPA0:
SYSBOOT> CONTINUE
```

The computer continues to boot. In this case no login dialog is presented. Instead the DCL prompt ($) is displayed when the system finishes booting. From that point you can enter commands to research the problem. However, you must first enter the SET NOON command to disable the default DCL error handler. Otherwise, if you enter a command that results in a severe or fatal error, your process is terminated and you have to reboot the system.

```
$ SET NOON
```

When you have finished debugging, and editing the necessary files, you can invoke normal system-startup procedures as follows. Executing this script also logs you out.

```
$ @SYS$SYSTEM:STARTUP
```

Then you must log in again to correct the startup parameter so that a normal boot will be performed the next time, as in the following example:

```
$ SET DEFAULT SYS$SYSROOT:[SYSEXE]
$ RUN SYS$SYSTEM:SYSMAN
SYSMAN> PARAMETERS USE CURRENT
SYSMAN> PARAMETERS SET/STARTUP SYS$SYSTEM:STARTUP.COM
SYSMAN> PARAMETERS WRITE CURRENT
```

As in the previous section, you may want to shutdown the system, then reboot it to assure yourself that all necessary changes have been made.

4.6.3 Bypass Password Checking

If you lose passwords to all privileged accounts, you can force OpenVMS to log you in using the following SYSBOOT commands. This technique only works on VT-like terminals, not on graphics terminals (e.g., Motif). To do the equivalent on graphics terminals, see section 4.6.6.

```
SYSBOOT> SET UAFALTERNATE 1
SYSBOOT> CONTINUE
Username: <Return>
Password: <Return>
Password: <Return>
```

These commands allow the OpenVMS bootstrap to complete. Now log in on the console terminal. No username or password is required. Then issue the commands to change the SYSTEM password.

```
$ DEFINE/SYSTEM/EXECUTIVE_MODE SYSUAF SYS$SYSTEM:SYSUAF.DAT
$ SET DEFAULT SYS$SYSTEM
```

```
$ RUN AUTHORIZE
AUTHORIZE> MODIFY SYSTEM/PASSWORD=MUMBLE
AUTHORIZE> EXIT
```

The next series of commands restores *xxx*VMSSYS.PAR to its original state.

```
$ RUN SYS$SYSTEM:SYSMAN
SYSMAN> PARAMETERS USE CURRENT
SYSMAN> PARAMETERS SET WINDOW_SYSTEM 1
SYSMAN> PARAMETERS SET UAFALTERNATE 0
SYSMAN> PARAMETERS WRITE CURRENT
SYSMAN> EXIT
```

Now the system is shutdown.

```
$ @SYS$SYSTEM:SHUTDOWN
```

The system is presumably rebooted so it will run in a normal state. The next time you log in to SYSTEM, you will have to change the password.

4.6.4 Adjust SYSGEN Parameters

You can use SYSBOOT to change any system parameter before booting as follows:

```
SYSBOOT> SET EXPECTED_VOTES 3
SYSBOOT> SET VOTES 1
SYSBOOT> CONTINUE
```

You should use this mechanism only in an emergency. Otherwise, change system parameters with the AUTOGEN utility, as discussed in chapter 18.

4.6.5 Reverting to OLD Parameters

When you change system parameters with AUTOGEN, the previous settings are saved in the files VAXVMSSYS.OLD and ALPHAVMSSYS.OLD.

If the system does not boot because of a system parameter problem, you can return to the previous parameter settings as follows:

```
SYSBOOT> USE VAXVMSSYS.OLD  (or ALPHAVMSSYS.OLD)
SYSBOOT> CONTINUE
```

If returning to previous parameters still does not allow you to boot, you can revert to DEFAULT parameters as follows:

```
SYSBOOT> USE DEFAULT
SYSBOOT> CONTINUE
```

The default parameters are designed to allow any system to boot. However, you may not want to select the default values for all parameters. For instance, OpenVMS cluster parameters such as SCSNODE default to blank spaces. If you want to boot as an OpenVMS cluster member, you must first manually set these parameters to their proper values.

4.6.6 An Alternative Method

If your console terminal is a graphics device rather than a VT-like terminal, another command sequence is shown below. This situation occurs on most hobby systems where the owner does not opt for two terminals and prefers to use the Motif interface.

Although HP reserves the use and meaning of WRITESYSPARAMS, this definition is unlikely to change. If WRITESYSPARAMS is 1 (which is the default), OpenVMS will write VAXVMSSYS.PAR or ALPHAVMSSYS.PAR back to disk in STARTUP.COM. When WRITESYSPARAMS is 0, no write takes place. Thus, by setting WRITESYSPARAMS to 0, temporary changes to *xxx*VMSSYS.PAR in SYSBOOT can be made. These changes do not have to be removed later. This results in a simpler dialog and can be used on either terminal type.

To see how this technique works, compare the following example to the command sequence in section 4.6.3.

```
SYSBOOT> SET/STARTUP OPA0:
SYSBOOT> SET WRITESYSPARAMS 0
SYSBOOT> CONTINUE
```

These commands allow the OpenVMS bootstrap to complete. Now when the $ prompt is displayed, no USERNAME prompt is issued. Next, enter your correction sequence. For instance, to set the system password, enter the following commands and reboot the system:

```
$ SPAWN @SYS$SYSTEM:STARTUP
$ SET DEFAULT SYS$SYSTEM:
$ RUN AUTHORIZE
UAF> MODIFY SYSTEM/PASSWORD=NewPassword
UAF> EXIT
$ @SHUTDOWN
```

Of course, whenever you change a password in this way, the next time you log in, you will be prompted to change it again. See the description of the AUTHORIZE qualifier /FLAG=DISFORCE_PWD_CHANGE to change this behavior.

4.7 Interrupt Priority C

WARNING: Use of the Availability Manager or the AMDS tools—both are distributed with OpenVMS—is strongly recommended over use of the IPC tool. Availability Manager and AMDS are distributed and licensed with OpenVMS, though are separately installed. The IPC tool is no longer the preferred quorum interface, is not particularly reliable, and is mentioned here solely for historical purposes.

If a cluster hangs because of loss of quorum, you can manually restore quorum by invoking the IPC utility as follows:

Enter console I/O mode on console terminal with <CTRL/P> or <BREAK>

```
>>> HALT
>>> D/I 14 C           ! Set Interrupt Priority Level 12
>>> CONTINUE
IPC> Q                 ! recalculate quorum
IPC> ^Z                ! exit IPC
```

The IPC Q command bypasses the standard quorum calculation formula and restores quorum by setting its value equal to the current number of votes present.

WARNING: IPC is extremely dangerous. Quorum is meant to prevent a single cluster from partitioning into multiple unsynchronized clusters. If a cluster loses quorum because of a hardware failure, do not restore quorum with IPC—cluster-accessible disks may become corrupted. You should only use IPC when you know quorum was lost because one or more members shut down.

4.8 Conclusion

Normally, booting OpenVMS is a simple process; however, you should understand all booting options. Otherwise, when emergencies occur, you will waste precious minutes trying to decide what to do. You should thoroughly test all booting methods so that you know they will work when you need them.

4.9 Additional References

1. *OpenVMS Cluster Systems* discusses cluster booting.
2. *OpenVMS Programming Concepts Manual* includes symmetric multiprocess (SMP) boot and a description of boot errors.
3. *OpenVMS System Manager's Manual* defines the various conversational boot methods in more detail.

5

System-Startup Procedures

5.1 Chapter Objectives

- Increase system availability by developing system-startup procedures that are clear and concise and follow commonly practiced standards
- Demonstrate techniques that will reduce system-boot time
- Discuss aspects of DCL error processing that are important to system-startup procedures
- Provide techniques for automatically detecting and reporting system-startup errors
- Provide a fully developed set of template startup procedures to tailor your system

5.2 Introduction

System startup is a continuation of the system-initialization process initiated by a system boot. For the purpose of this book, system startup involves all system-initialization steps that occur in the context of a process, rather than in system context. Chapter 4 only presents booting steps performed in system context; thus, this chapter elaborates on the rest of the boot sequence.

Sometimes system-startup procedures fail because of procedure bugs or hardware problems. By default, system-startup errors and messages are displayed on the console terminal. Unless you read and understand every line displayed on the console, you will miss key messages indicating startup errors. You need a more reliable method of identifying them.

System startup is an involved process—about 50 different command procedures are executed. To minimize downtime, you should thoroughly understand when, where, and why each procedure is executed. In addition, many startup procedures depend on the successful completion of prior procedures. You should understand system-startup dependencies so that you preserve the correct startup order when you make modifications.

5.3 System-Startup Sequence

System startup involves the execution of two general sets of command procedures:

1. Site-independent startup procedures
2. Site-specific startup procedures

Site-independent startup procedures are DCL command procedures (also called *scripts*) supplied by HP. These procedures are the same for every OpenVMS system and should not be modified. Any changes made to site-independent procedures will probably be overwritten during future OpenVMS upgrades. Site-independent procedures perform functions such as initializing OpenVMS data structures, loading portions of the OpenVMS executive, defining logical names, and opening primary page, swap, and dump files. At certain points within site-independent startup procedures, site-specific procedures are invoked.

Site-specific procedures perform functions that depend on your hardware and software configuration and the needs at your site. For example, site-specific startup procedures perform the following: mount disks, configure terminal ports, establish print and batch queues, start layered products, and start applications. HP supplies template procedures, but you must customize them to reflect the configuration at your site.

The following sections detail how, where, and when major startup procedures are executed.

5.3.1 SWAPINIT Phase

The final step of the boot process (described in chapter 4) is to create the SWAPPER detached process. A *detached process* is one that cannot be attached to a terminal. It is also called a *symbiont,* or, in UNIX terms, a *daemon.* SWAPPER is the first process created in the life of an OpenVMS system. During normal OpenVMS operation, SWAPPER performs memory-management functions; however, during system startup, SWAPPER performs the following startup-related functions:

- Initializes of paged pool
- Invokes of OpenVMS executive initialization routines
- Initializes of the logical-name database
- Creates of the SYSINIT detached process
- Branches to the main SWAPPER loop and begins normal memory-management functions

5.3.2 SYSINIT Phase

The SYSINIT process then performs the following startup functions:

- Loads portions of the OpenVMS executive
- Performs OpenVMS cluster initialization if applicable
- Opens primary page, swap, and dump files
- Activates Files-11 extended QIO processor (XQP)
- Loads system-message files
- Defines key OpenVMS logical names (e.g., SYS$SYSROOT, SYS$SYSCOMMON)
- Creates the STARTUP process

5.3.3 STARTUP Phase

The STARTUP process begins by executing the primary site-independent startup procedure as specified in the system-parameter database. By default, this primary startup file is SYS$SYSTEM:STARTUP.COM. You can verify this by issuing the following commands:

```
$ RUN SYS$SYSTEM:SYSMAN
SYSMAN> STARTUP SHOW OPTIONS
Current startup options on node MILLER:
    DCL verification mode is: PARTIAL
    Startup log will be written to SYS$SYSTEM:STARTUP.LOG
    Checkpointing messages are disabled
```

When errors occur during the startup process, you may need to temporarily disable the execution of STARTUP.COM. This is accomplished by invoking a conversational bootstrap, as discussed in chapter 4. STARTUP.COM subsequently invokes the remaining site-independent startup procedures as specified in the *startup database*. The startup database consists of three files contained in the SYS$STARTUP directory. They are described by the three logical names listed below. *Logical names* are synonyms for filenames and created with the DEFINE command.

1. STARTUP$PHASES
2. STARTUP$STARTUP_VMS
3. STARTUP$STARTUP_LAYERED

The following sections detail the contents of these files.

STARTUP$PHASES

The PHASES data file defines the names and order of the system-startup phases:

```
INITIAL
DEVICES
PRECONFIG
CONFIG
BASEENVIRON
LPBEGIN
LPMAIN
LPBETA
END
```

STARTUP$STARTUP_VMS

STARTUP_VMS contains a list of site-independent command procedures to be executed by STARTUP.COM. Several of these procedures invoke the site-specific startup procedures located in the SYS$MANAGER directory. Table 5.1 lists the order in which site-independent command procedures are executed and indicates when and where site-specific startup procedures are invoked.

Table 5.1 *Site-Independent and Site-Specific Startup Procedures*

Startup Phase	Site-Independent Procedure (in SYS$STARTUP)	Site-Specific Procedure (in SYS$MANAGER)
INITIAL	VMS$INITIAL-050_VMS.COM VMS$INITITAL-050_LIB.COM VMS$INITIAL-050_CONFIGURE.COM	None
DEVICES	VMS$DEVICE_STARTUP.COM	==> SYSCONFIG.COM ==> SYLOGICALS.COM ==> SYPAGSWPFILES.COM
PRECONFIG	IPC$STARTUP.COM	None
CONFIG	VMS$CONFIG-050_VMS.COM VMS$CONFIG-050_ERRFMT.COM VMS$CONFIG-050_CACHE_SERVER.COM VMS$CONFIG-050_CSP.COM VMS$CONFIG-050-OPCOM.COM VMS$CONFIG-050_AUDIT_SERVER.COM VMS$CONFIG-050_JOBCTL.COM VMS$CONFIG-050_LMF.COM VMS$CONFIG-050_SHADOW_SERVER.COM	==> SYSECURITY.COM
BASEENVIRON	VMS$BASEENVIRON-050_VMS.COM VMS$BASEENVIRON-050_SMISERVER.COM VMS$BASEENVIRON-050_LIB.COM LICENSE_CHECK.EXE DECDTM$STARTUP.COM	None
LPBEGIN	VMS$LPBEGIN-050_VMS.COM VMS$LPBEGIN-050_STARTUP.COM	==> SYSTARTUP_VMS.COM
LPMAIN	None	None
LPBETA	None	None
END	None	None

You might have noticed that -050- is commonly used in the filenames in table 5.1. I am guessing that this file-naming scheme was introduced in VMS v5.0 and never changed as VMS was rereleased.

STARTUP$STARTUP_LAYERED

The logical name STARTUP$STARTUP_LAYERED locates the file that contains layered product-startup procedures. By default, this file is empty, but when you install some HP products with VMSINSTAL, the startup procedure for the product is automatically inserted in STARTUP_LAYERED. These entries are usually designated to be executed during the LPMAIN startup phase.

The STARTUP sequence begins by setting the current phase to the first phase listed in STARTUP$PHASES (i.e., INITIAL). Then, all command procedures listed in STARTUP$STARTUP_VMS with a phase that matches the current phase are executed. Next, all procedures in STARTUP$STARTUP_LAYERED that match the current phase are executed. Finally, the current phase is set to the next phase listed in STARTUP$PHASES, and the process repeats until the last phase is completed (i.e., END).

A standard structure for organizing site-specific startup procedures has never been specified; as a result, most system managers locate site-specific startup commands in SYSTARTUP_VMS and related files. A mechanism for automatically adding startup procedures into the SYSMAN utility database is of interest to HP and to customers, but the interdependencies among products make this an exceedingly complex problem. You can manually migrate site-specific startup procedures into the STARTUP_LAYERED database using the SYSMAN utility (see the *OpenVMS System Manager's Utility Manual*).

5.4 Site-Specific Startup Procedures

Table 5.2 lists the five site-specific startup procedures in the order in which they are invoked. When OpenVMS is initially installed, each site-specific startup file is identical to its respective HP-supplied template file. The site-specific startup procedures must be customized to reflect the needs of the site. Retain the template files in their original form for reference and because the files may be changed during future OpenVMS upgrades.

Table 5.2 *Site-Specific Startup Procedures and Templates*

Site-Specific Startup File	HP-Supplied Template File
SYS$MANAGER:SYCONFIG.COM	SYS$MANAGER:SYCONFIG.TEMPLATE

Table 5.2 *Site-Specific Startup Procedures and Templates (continued)*

Site-Specific Startup File	HP-Supplied Template File
`SYS$MANAGER:SYLOGICALS.COM`	`SYS$MANAGER:SYLOGICALS.TEMPLATE`
`SYS$MANAGER:SYPAGSWPFILES.COM`	`SYS$MANAGER:SYPAGSWPFILES.TEMPLATE`
`SYS$MANAGER:SYSECURITY.COM`	`SYS$MANAGER:SYSECURITY.TEMPLATE`
`SYS$MANAGER:SYSTARTUP_VMS.COM`	`SYS$MANAGER:SYSTARTUP_VMS.TEMPLATE`

The following sections describe the purpose of each of the site-specific startup files and strategies for customizing them. Strategies for coordinating these startup procedures and system data files are discussed later in this chapter.

5.4.1 SYCONFIG.COM

SYCONFIG.COM configures hardware devices that are not automatically recognized by OpenVMS and that are not included in the device database. If you have third-party equipment that requires manual configuration via DCL, SYSCONFIG should contain the commands listed in your hardware documentation; otherwise, SYCONFIG.COM should be empty.

5.4.2 SYLOGICALS.COM

The function of SYLOGICALS.COM is to define site-specific system logical names. The SYLOGICALS.COM supplied by HP includes code that defines system logical names appropriate for a variety of systems. For example, logical names $DISK1 and $DISK2 are defined as the first and second disk drives on smaller systems. This book suggests logical names that are more appropriate for large-scale OpenVMS systems. If you wish to use the conventions in this book, start with an empty SYLOGICALS startup file instead of using HP's template file. Table 5.3 lists the logical names you may want to define in SYLOGICALS.COM.

Table 5.3 *Logical Names Defined in SYLOGICALS.COM*

Purpose	Logical Name	Related Chapter
System announcement messages	SYS$ANNOUNCE	11
	SYS$WELCOME	11

Table 5.3 *Logical Names Defined in SYLOGICALS.COM (continued)*

Purpose	Logical Name	Related Chapter
System login command procedure	SYS$SYLOGIN	11
Default system print and batch queue	SYS$BATCH	8
	SYS$PRINT	8
Cluster-common files	SYSUAF	9
	RIGHTSLIST	9
	VMSMAIL_PROFILE	9
	VMS$OBJECTS	
	QMAN$MASTER	8
DECnet	NETSERVER$TIMEOUT	8
	NETPROXY	9
	NET$PROXY	9
	NETNODE_REMOTE	8
OPCOM logical names	OPC$LOGFILES_CLASSES	15
	OPC$LOGFILES_ENABLE	15
	OPC$LOGFILE_NAME	15
	OPC$OPA0_CLASSES	15
	OPC$OPA0_ENABLE	15
Shutdown	SHUTDOWN$INFORM_NODES	6
	SHUTDOWN$MINIMUM_MINUTES	6
	SHUTDOWN$DISABLE_AUTOSTART	6
Other data files	ACCOUNTING (accounting data file)	

By convention, disks are usually mounted in SYSTARTUP_VMS.COM. However, if you need certain disks mounted earlier in the startup process, you may want to mount them in SYLOGICALS. An example would include a disk that contains the system-authorization database.

Regardless of your system configuration, system-startup procedures should define logical names that designate the location for each database file. For example, to establish a shared security database on DISK$COMMON:, define the logical names in SYLOGICALS.COM. SYS$MANAGER:SYLOGICALS.TEMPLATE is supplied with every installation and reproduced here in part. The best management philosophy is to copy it to SYLOGICALS.COM, read its in-line documentation, and edit the file to suit your site's needs. This assures the logicals are spelled correctly, that none are missing, and that you have considered all the implications. As you will see by reading the following, the documentation is quite good.

```
$!
$! SYLOGICALS.COM/SYLOGICALS.TEMPLATE
$!
$  Set NoOn  ! continue execution if error encountered
$!
$! This command procedures defines site-specific logical names.  The
$! first sections defines names for devices on small MicroVAX systems
$! which are not part of OpenVMS Clusters.  A later section (search
$! for the asterisks) contains space for user-defined logical names.
$!
$! ------------------------------------------------------------------
$!
$! Regarding the Correct Use of Cluster-Wide Logical Names:
$!
$!   OpenVMS Engineering recommends that all use of Cluster-Wide
$!   logical names (available in OpenVMS V7.2 and later) be deferred
$!   until the SYSTARTUP_VMS.COM procedure.
$!
$!   The initialization of the cluster-wide logical name database
$!   performed by the Cluster Server Process (CSP) may not complete
$!   before SYLOGICALS.COM procedure is executed.
$!
$!   If you must use cluster-wide logical names anywhere in the
$!   OpenVMS system startup prior to the invocation of the
$!   SYSTARTUP_VMS.COM procedure, then you will want to use the
$!   following tests as a guideline:
$!
$!      1. The OpenVMS system must be a member of an OpenVMS Cluster:
$!         e.g., F$GETSYI("CLUSTER_MEMBER") is TRUE
$!      2. The OpenVMS system must not be booted MINIMUM:
$!         e.g., F$GETSYI("STARTUP_P1") is "     "
$!      3. The CSP initialization is complete:
```

```
$!        e.g., F$GETSYI("CWLOGICALS") is TRUE
$!
...
$!
$!   End of SYLOGICALS.COM
$!
```

5.4.3 SYPAGSWPFILES.COM

The purpose of SYPAGSWPFILES is to install *secondary* page and swap files. This is in contrast to *primary* page and swap files installed during site-independent startup procedures. Chapter 18 discusses page and swap files in more detail. If you have not already mounted the disk containing your secondary page files, you should mount it in SYPAGSWPFILES.

5.4.4 SYSECURITY.COM

The function of SYSECURITY.COM is to configure the security events you want to audit. Default security-event auditing is automatically enabled by site-independent startup procedures, and all events are journaled to SYS$MANAGER:SECURITY.AUDIT$JOURNAL.

Chapter 17 discusses additional security events you may want to audit. Enable them by adding appropriate commands to SYSECURITY. If your system has a high volume of security events, causing excessive disk activity on your system disk, you can specify an alternative location for the audit-journal file.

5.4.5 SYSTARTUP_VMS.COM

Most site-specific startup tasks are contained in the file SYSTARTUP_VMS.COM. If your site is large or complex, SYSTARTUP_VMS.COM may contain hundreds of DCL commands, making it difficult to follow. Table 5.4 lists each of the important tasks performed in SYSTARTUP_VMS. Whenever a task requires more than a few DCL commands, move them from SYSTARTUP_VMS into a separate command procedure and include a line in SYSTARTUP_VMS that invokes the new command procedure. Names for these procedures are suggested in the right column of table 5.4.

Table 5.4 *Modularized SYSTARTUP_VMS.COM*

SYSTARTUP_VMS Function	Invokes
Mount disks	STARTUP_MSCPMOUNT
Start DECnet, TCP/IP Services	START/NETWORK
Configure devices and terminals	STARTUP_SETTERM
Initialize print and batch queues	STARTUP_QUEUES
Install images shareable	STARTUP_SHARE
Analyze crash-dump file	STARTUP_SDA
Start layered products	STARTUP_PRODUCTS
Start applications	STARTUP_APPLICATIONS
Define interactive login limit	Executed within SYSTARTUP
Notify users of system availability	Executed within SYSTARTUP

For example, if you need to mount more than one or two disks, put all your mount commands in a file such as

```
STARTUP_MSCPMOUNT.COM
```

for example:

```
$! STARTUP_MSCPMOUNT.COM
$! See SYS$EXAMPLES:MSCPMOUNT.COM for details
$ mount...
$ mount...
.
.
```

Then, configure SYSTARTUP_VMS to invoke MSCPMOUNT as follows:

```
$! SYSTARTUP_VMS.COM
$!
$ @SYS$STARTUP:MSCPMOUNT        ! Mount Disks
.
.
```

Note that the names of the command procedures in table 5.4 all begin with "STARTUP_". This allows you to locate startup-related command procedures quickly by issuing the following command:

```
$ DIRECTORY SYS$STARTUP:STARTUP*.COM
```

Refer to appendix E to obtain the source code for the startup files listed in this chapter.

5.5 Cluster Startup Procedures

You must give special consideration to coordinating system-startup procedures within an OpenVMS cluster environment. Tightly integrated clusters (i.e., *common-environment*) generally share a single system disk, offer the same applications, start the same print and batch queues, and for the most part appear to the user as a single system. Yet, each node in the cluster may also have local disks that have to be mounted. Less-integrated clusters that use multiple system disks or offer different applications on each cluster member are referred to as *multiple-environment* clusters. Because members within a common-environment cluster offer a similar environment, you can generally maintain a single set of startup procedures. Within a multiple-environment cluster you may need to maintain a separate set of startup procedures for each system. Therefore, each of the startup scripts will be laced with statements such as

```
$ if (f$getsyi("nodename") .eqs. "EAGLE")
$ then
$! . . . EAGLE-specific commands
$ endif
```

Alternatively, you may want to set up startup scripts that are node-specific instead. Thus, SYSTARTUP_VMS.COM may contain statements such as

```
$ @STARTUP_APPLICATIONS_''f$getsyi("nodename")'
```

to execute STARTUP_APPLICATIONS_EAGLE.COM on the EAGLE node and STARTUP_APPLICATIONS_LOON.COM on the LOON node, for instance.

A third option is to store these startup scripts in the site-specific directory. Regardless of whether a system is a member of a cluster, its system disk has a cluster structure—that is, it has a system-specific root and a cluster-common root. All startup procedures are located by the SYS$STARTUP logical name; however, SYS$STARTUP is defined in terms of the search list SYS$SYSROOT as follows:

```
SYS$STARTUP
   |
   ==> SYS$SYSROOT:[SYS$STARTUP]
   |    |
   |    | ==> SYS$SPECIFIC:[SYS$STARTUP]
   |    |
   |    ====> SYS$COMMON:[SYS$STARTUP]
   |
   ==> SYS$SYSROOT:[SYSMGR]
        |
        | ==> SYS$SPECIFIC:[SYSMGR]
        |
        ====> SYS$COMMON:[SYSMGR]
```

The structure of an OpenVMS system disk and system logical-name definitions are discussed in more detail in chapter 3.

Figure 5.1 illustrates the SYS$STARTUP organization for a three-node common-environment cluster booting from a common system disk. Chapter 3 discusses OpenVMS system-disk organization in more detail.

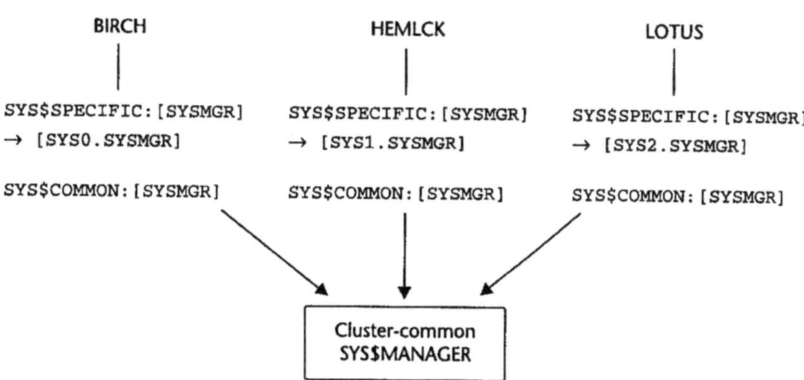

Figure 5.1 *OpenVMS System Disk Organization*

Depending on the size and complexity of your configuration, you locate system-startup files in either the system-specific or cluster-common root. The following sections suggest specific strategies for typical environments.

5.5.1 Stand-Alone System

On a stand-alone system, you need only one set of startup files, which you should locate in SYS$COMMON:[SYS$STARTUP], as illustrated by table 5.5. Locating startup files in the common root makes it easier to convert the system to a cluster.

Table 5.5 *Startup File Organization for a Stand-Alone System*

Member	BIRCH
System disk	1DUA0:
Directory	SYS$COMMON:[SYSMGR]
System-startup files	SYCONFIG
	SYLOGICALS
	SYPAGSWPFILES
	SYSECURITY
	SYSTARTUP_VMS
	. . .

5.5.2 Common-Environment OpenVMS Cluster (Simple)

If you maintain a simple common-environment cluster with few differences between the environments offered by cluster members, you can also maintain a single set of startup procedures in the common root, as illustrated in table 5.6.

Table 5.6 *System-Startup Procedures for a Simple Common-Environment Cluster*

Member	BIRCH	LOTUS	HEMLCK	ALL
Common system disk	1DUA0:	1DUA0:	1DUA0:	1DUA0:
Directory	SYS$SPECIFIC: [SYSMGR]	SYS$SPECIFIC: [SYSMGR]	SYS$SPECIFIC: [SYSMGR]	SYS$COMMON: [SYSMGR]

Table 5.6 *System-Startup Procedures for a Simple Common-Environment Cluster (continued)*

Member	BIRCH	LOTUS	HEMLCK	ALL
System-startup files	None	None	None	SYCONFIG SYLOGICALS SYPAGSWPFILES SYSECURITY SYSTARTUP_VMS, etc.

To reiterate, even in a common-environment cluster, some aspects of system startup are always system-specific (e.g., each system must have dedicated page and swap files). To handle these situations, add IF-THEN statements for conditional execution of system-specific procedures. For example, you might modify SYPAGSWPFILES.COM as follows:

```
$!
$! SYPAGSWPFILES.COM
$!
$ node = f$getsyi("SCSNODE")
$!
$ if node .eqs. "BIRCH"
$ then
$! ... Install BIRCH page files
$ endif
$!
$ if node .eqs. "LOTUS"
$ then
$! ... Install LOTUS page files
$ endif
$! etc.
```

5.5.3 Common-Environment OpenVMS Cluster (Complex)

In a common-environment cluster with many systems, adding DCL conditional statements for each system might be too cumbersome. In these situations, you can establish a system-specific startup procedure for each system (in the SYS$SYPECIFIC:[SYSMGR] root) and invoke it from the common procedure (table 5.7).

Table 5.7 *System-Startup Procedures for a Complex Common-Environment Cluster*

Member	BIRCH	LOTUS	HEMLCK	COMMON
System disk	1DUA0:	1DUA0:	1DUA0:	1DUA0:
Directory	SYS$SPECIFIC: [SYSMGR]	SYS$SPECIFIC: [SYSMGR]	SYS$SPECIFIC: [SYSMGR]	SYS$COMMON: [SYSMGR]
System startup files	SYCONFIG_BIRCH	SYCONFIG_LOTUS	SYSCONFIG_ HEMLCK	SYCONFIG
	SYLOGICALS_ BIRCH	SYSLOGICALS_ LOTUS	SYSLOGICALS_ HEMLCK	SYSLOGICALS
	SYPAGSWPFILES_ BIRCH	SYPAGSWPFILES_ LOTUS	SYSPAGSWPFILES _HEMLCK	SYPAGSWPFILES
	SYSECURITY_ BIRCH	SYSECURITY_ LOTUS	SYSECURITY_ HEMLCK	SYSECURITY
	SYSTARTUP_ BIRCH	SYSTARTUP_ LOTUS	SYSTARTUP_ HEMLCK	SYSTARTUP_Vxx
	. . .	. . .	. . .	. . .

Note that the node name for each system is appended to the system-specific procedures (e.g., SYLOGICALS_BIRCH). This reduces the chance of confusing the startup procedures of one system with those of another and allows you to invoke each procedure more easily; for example:

```
$!
$! SYLOGICALS.COM    (Cluster Common)
$!
$! Execute system-specific SYLOGICALS
$!
$ @SYS$MANAGER:SYLOGICALS_''f$getsyi("SCSNODE")'
$!
$! Define cluster-common logicals
$!
$ DEFINE/SYSTEM ....
```

Do not automatically create a system-specific file for every startup procedure—you will quickly have dozens of command procedures, and they will be difficult to manage. You should create system-specific procedures only when absolutely necessary.

5.5.4 Multiple-Environment OpenVMS Cluster

In a multiple-environment cluster in which each system boots from a different system disk and offers very different environments, you can use the same strategy as you would for a stand-alone system, except you maintain multiple sets of startup procedures (one for each cluster member). For example, in a three-member cluster (BIRCH, LOTUS, and HEMLCK), you might organize system-startup files as shown in table 5.8.

Table 5.8 *System-Startup Procedures for a Multiple-Environment Cluster*

Member	BIRCH	LOTUS	HEMLCK
System disk	`$1$DUA0:`	`$1$DUA1:`	`$1$DUA2:`
Directory	`SYS$COMMON:[SYSMGR]`	`SYS$COMMON:[SYSMGR]`	`SYS$COMMON:[SYSMGR]`
System-startup files	`SYCONFIG`	`SYCONFIG`	`SYCONFIG`
	`SYLOGICALS`	`SYLOGICALS`	`SYLOGICALS`
	`SYPAGSWPFILES`	`SYPAGSWPFILES`	`SYPAGSWPFILES`
	`SYSECURITY`	`SYSECURITY`	`SYSECURITY`
	`SYSTARTUP_VMS`	`SYSTARTUP_VMS`	`SYSTARTUP_VMS`
	...	...	...

If you have a multiple-environment cluster with a common system disk, you can use the same strategy as above, except locate all startup files in SYS$SPECIFIC:[SYSMGR] rather than SYS$COMMON.

5.6 Coordinating Shareable System Files

Within an OpenVMS cluster environment, you must coordinate the contents of the system data files. This task includes coordinating the UIC and identifier binary values across all cluster members. Typically, this requirement is met via a single set of shared files, though a requirement for node-specific process quotas may require you to maintain separate, node-specific SYSUAF files. Table 5.9 lists the system files that can be shared.

To share files among cluster members, you should first ensure that each file is located in the common root of its associated directory. For example, ensure that SYSUAF.DAT is located in SYS$COMMON:[SYSEXE]. Next,

Table 5.9 *OpenVMS Cluster Sharable Data Files*

Sharable File	Function
SYS$SYSTEM	
NETNODE_PROFILE.DAT	DECnet remote-node database
NET$PROXY.DAT	DECnet proxy database
NETOBJECT.DAT	DECnet object database
NETPROXY.DAT	DECnet proxy database
QMAN$MASTER.DAT	Queue master file
RIGHTSLIST.DAT	System-rights identifiers
SYS$QUEUE_MANAGER.QMAN$JOURNAL	Queue-journal file
SYS$QUEUE_MANAGER.QMAN$QUEUES	Queue database file
SYS$TIMEZONE.DAT	Time zone database
SYSALF.DAT	Automatic Login Facility database
SYSUAF.DAT	UAF
SYSUAFALT.DAT	Alternative UAF
TCPIP$HOST.DAT	TCP/IP address database
TCPIP$PROXY.DAT	TCP/IP proxy database
VMS$OBJECTS.DAT	Security-object database
VMS$PASSWORD_HISTORY.DATA	Password history file
VMSMAIL_PROFILE.DATA	Mail profiles
SYS$MANAGER	
NETNODE_UPDATE.COM	Local-area cluster database
VMS$AUDIT_SERVER.DAT	Audit-server database
SYS$LIBRARY	
VMS$PASSWORD_DICTIONARY.DATA	Unacceptable-password list

during system startup (in SYLOGICALS.COM) you should define system-wide logical names specifying the location of each shared file. For example, to share all UAFs, add the following commands to SYLOGICALS:

```
$!
```

```
$! Logicals for System Data Files
$!
$ DSE:=DEFINE/SYSTEM/EXECUTIVE
$!
$ DSE NETPROXY SYS$COMMON:[SYSEXE]NETPROXY.DAT
$ DSE NET$PROXY SYS$COMMON:[SYSEXE]NET$PROXY.DAT
$ DSE RIGHTSLIST SYS$COMMON:[SYSEXE]RIGHTSLIST.DAT
$ DSE SYSUAF SYS$COMMON:[SYSEXE]SYSUAF.DAT
$ DSE VMS$PASSWORD_HISTORY SYS$COMMON:[SYSEXE]VMS$PASSWORD_HISTORY.DATA
$ DSE VMS$PASSWORD_DICTIONARY SYS$COMMON:[SYSLIB]VMS$PASSWORD_DICTIONARY.DATA
$ DSE VMSMAIL_PROFILE SYS$COMMON:[SYSEXE]VMSMAIL_PROFILE.DATA
```

On the other hand, to maintain a separate copy of each of the above files, locate the files in the SYS$SPECIFIC root of each directory and define the logical names in the SYLOGICALS.COM startup file for each cluster member as follows:

```
$!
$! Logicals for System Data Files
$!
$ DSE:=DEFINE/SYSTEM/EXECUTIVE
$!
$ DSE NETPROXY SYS$SPECIFIC:[SYSEXE]NETPROXY.DAT
$ DSE NET$PROXY SYS$SPECIFIC:[SYSEXE]NET$PROXY.DAT
$ DSE RIGHTSLIST SYS$SPECIFIC:[SYSEXE]RIGHTSLIST.DAT
$ DSE SYSUAF SYS$SPECIFIC:[SYSEXE]SYSUAF.DAT
$ DSE VMS$PASSWORD_HISTORY SYS$SPECIFIC:[SYSEXE]VMS$PASSWORD_HISTORY.DATA
$ DSE VMS$PASSWORD_DICTIONARY SYS$SPECIFIC:[SYSLIB]VMS$PASSWORD_DICTIONARY.DATA
$ DSE VMSMAIL_PROFILE SYS$SPECIFIC:[SYSEXE]VMSMAIL_PROFILE.DATA
```

With the exception of the queue database files, you can specify the location of the other system data files listed in table 5.9 by defining similar logical names. Coordinating queue database files requires additional steps that are discussed in chapter 8. Although these logical names are required only for OpenVMS cluster environments, you should consider defining them even on stand-alone systems. This facilities conversion to a clustered environment should that ever by necessary.

The following system files cannot be shared among cluster members because they are CPU-specific:

```
SYS$SYSTEM:VAXVMSSYS.PAR          ! VAX System Parameters
SYS$SYSTEM:ALPHAVMSSYS.PAR        ! Alpha System Parameters
```

```
SYS$MANAGER:OPERATOR.LOG               ! Operator Log File
SYS$MANAGER:ACCOUNTNG.DAT              ! Resource Accounting File
SYS$SYSTEM:NETNODE_LOCAL.DAT           ! Local DECnet Configuration
SYS$MANAGER:SECURITY.AUDIT$JOURNAL     ! Security Audit Events
SYS$ERRORLOG:ERRORLOG.SYS              ! System Error Log File
SYS$SYSTEM:PAGEFILE.SYS                ! Page Files
SYS$SYSTEM:SWAPFILE.SYS                ! Swap Files
SYS$SYSTEM:DUMPFILE.SYS                ! System dump file
```

5.7 Miscellaneous Startup Issues

Other dependencies are implicit in the SYSTARTUP_VMS.TEMPLATE, a skeleton supplied by HP. For instance, DECnet should be started before TCP/IP. The order of the commands is particularly important and described below. If you are creating a system disk for the first time, you should work from this file rather than create your own from scratch. Incidentally, the internal documentation in the template is very good and should be studied as well.

5.7.1 Dependency Issues

When you establish the order of startup procedures, remember the following startup dependencies:

- Disks must be mounted before the applications stored on them are started
- Terminal ports must be configured before printers are configured to them
- DECnet Phase IV must be the first network product started (e.g., start DECnet Phase IV before Local-Area Transport [LAT])
- LAT must be started and configured before LAT print queues can be configured
- TCP/IP must be configured and started before Telnet print queues can be used.

5.7.2 Handling System-Startup Errors

By default, a DCL command procedure aborts when an error or severe error is encountered. This behavior may be appropriate for some DCL command procedures, but not for startup procedures. Many errors are not severe enough to warrant terminating startup procedures. For example, if you have a hardware problem with terminal port TXA0:, and your startup procedures issue a $SET TERMINAL TXA0:, a severe error is generated, and the startup procedure aborts. You can eliminate this problem by disabling the default DCL error handler with the following command inserted at the beginning of each site-specific startup procedure:

```
$ SET NOON              ! Disable error checking
```

When the error handler is disabled, OpenVMS continues processing the remaining commands in each startup procedure, even after errors are encountered. Make certain that this behavior is acceptable for your particular startup procedures.

5.8 Optimizing System Startup

The following sections discuss several techniques for reducing system-startup time, including:

- Console logging
- Using startup batch jobs

5.8.1 Console Logging

Throughout the startup process, status, informational, and error messages are displayed on the console terminal. Even if you have a hard-copy console, a vast number of startup messages can easily span several printed pages. With a video terminal, startup messages quickly disappear from the screen. In either case, you can easily miss important information and critical error messages.

Even if you do notice errors during startup, it is difficult to pinpoint exactly where in the startup process the error occurred. You can facilitate troubleshooting by including the DCL SET VERIFY command in all your startup procedures, or by setting the system parameter STARTUP_P2 to TRUE using SYSMAN (or SYSBOOT). However, this causes every line of every procedure to be displayed on the console terminal during startup. Even if you have a video console terminal, your total system-startup time will dramatically increase while you wait for output to be echoed to the terminal.

Redirecting console output during system startup is simplified with the console logging facility. Instead of having to add commands to each startup procedure, you can redirect output to a file by issuing the following commands:

```
$ RUN SYS$SYSTEM:SYSMAN
SYSMAN> STARTUP SET OPTIONS/OUTPUT=FILE/CHECKPOINTING
```

The /OUTPUT=FILE qualifier causes startup output to be written to the file SYS$SYSTEM:STARTUP.LOG rather than to the console terminal. You can optionally add the /CHECKPOINTING qualifier to force time stamps to be written to the log file. Time stamps help locate specific lines in the log file. Finally, modify STARTUP_CHECK (shown below) to scan STARTUP.LOG for error messages.

An example STARTUP_CHECK is as follows:

```
$! STARTUP_CHECK.COM
$!
$ set default SYS$SYSTEM
$ search/match=or/exact/window=6/output=STARTUP_CHECK.TMP -
   STARTUP.LOG "-W-","-E-","-F-"
```

The /WINDOW=6 qualifier forces the search utility to display the six lines that surround any matches. This helps identify the context of the error message. STARTUP_CHECK could be submitted as a batch job at the end of SYSTARTUP_VMS to check each boot automatically.

5.8.2 Using Startup Batch Jobs

If there are many components in your startup procedures that can be executed independently of each other, you may be able to speed system startup by submitting the procedures as multiple batch jobs that execute simultaneously. This technique yields the most pronounced results when used on HP's more powerful processors, especially systems with multiple processors, because these scripts can execute in parallel.

For example, using the startup procedures discussed earlier in this chapter, assume that STARTUP_PRODUCTS and STARTUP_APPLICATIONS do not depend on each other. Instead of directly executing these command procedures, modify SYSTARTUP_VMS.COM to submit them as batch jobs:

```
$!
$! SYSTARTUP_VMS.COM
$!
$ ...
$ ...
$ submit/noprint/notify SYS$MANAGER:STARTUP_PRODUCTS
$ submit/noprint/notify SYS$MANAGER:STARTUP_APPLICATIONS
$ synchronize STARTUP_PRODUCTS
$ synchronize STARTUP_APPLICATIONS
```

The SYNCRHONIZE command is used to force the execution of SYSTARTUP to pause until both STARTUP_PRODUCTS and STARTUP_APPLICATIONS are complete. This ensures that all system-startup procedures are complete before users are allowed to log in.

5.9 Tools

Several startup tools and skeleton scripts are described in appendix E. These are listed in table 5.10. Many files prefixed with "SY" (e.g., SYCONFIG.COM) are already provided by HP and are present in both a .COM and .TEMPLATE form. They are well documented. The examples provided here are to show how you might want to modify them for your site.

Table 5.10 *Startup Tools*

Procedure Name	Function
SYCONFIG.COM	Configure devices example
SYPAGSWPFILES.COM	Install page/swap files example
SYSECURITY.COM	Configure security example
STARTUP_MOUNT.COM	Mount disks
STARTUP_NETWORK.COM	Start network components
STARTUP_SETTERM.COM	Configure terminal devices
STARTUP_QUEUES.COM	Set up queues

Table 5.10 *Startup Tools*

STARTUP_SHARE.COM	Install images
STARTUP_SDA.COM	Analyze crash dump
STARTUP_PRODUCTS.COM	Start vendor products
STARTUP_APPLICATIONS.COM	Start in-house applications

5.10 Conclusion

Startup procedures for larger systems can be as complex as a small software application, so you should apply standard application-change-management strategies to startup procedures. This includes developing consistent documentation standards and release procedures. For example, you may want to centralize development of all startup procedures on a single development system. Then, you make all changes on the development system, test them, and distribute them to one or more production systems. Using this technique you can deploy changes to multiple systems easily with a simple DCL COPY command.

For more complex environments, you might consider using a formal code-management system such as HP's code-management system (CMS) or the CMS-based OpenVMS Development Environment (VDE) freeware. CMS also allows you to retrieve all prior versions of a piece of code no matter how many times it has been changed. Also, every time you make a change, CMS requests comments that are automatically added to a history journal. Further, you can use the CMS reference directory mechanism to maintain the live copies of the startup files.

5.11 Additional References

1. *OpenVMS Cluster Systems* describes the system directory structure and cluster-wide logicals.
2. *OpenVMSSystem Management Utilities Reference Manual: M–Z* describes the STARTUP command in detail.

6

System Shutdown

6.1 Chapter Objectives

- Minimize accidental system shutdowns
- Ensure continuity of OpenVMS cluster operations when individual members are shut down
- Achieve data integrity by ensuring that application-specific shutdown procedures are performed
- Explore the shutdown process in detail
- Use DCL procedures to automate common system-shutdown methods

6.2 Introduction

The following are typical situations that require a system shutdown:

- After a software installation or upgrade
- After changing nondynamic system parameters
- Before a power shutdown
- Before performing special booting procedures (e.g., system-disk backup)

There are two basic shutdown techniques:

1. Orderly shutdown
2. Emergency shutdown

An orderly shutdown removes installed images and dismounts all disks. These steps ensure that any critical operations in progress are allowed to complete before the system is actually halted. This reduces the risk of data-file and disk corruption. An emergency shutdown halts the system in a more abrupt manner. It is still better than simply turning the system off, but because cached data can be lost, you should use emergency procedures only when orderly shutdown procedures fail or if you need to force a system crash dump (discussed later in this chapter).

6.3 Orderly Shutdown Procedures

Before you actually activate SHUTDOWN, you may want to perform the following steps:

- Disable future logins
- Check for system activity
- Send a shutdown-notification message

6.3.1 Disable Future Logins

Although the shutdown process automatically disables system logins, you may want to disable them earlier to prevent users from logging in before the shutdown. Remember, disabling logins has no effect on users already logged in. In addition, users who are authorized for the OPER privilege can continue to log in. Use the following command to disable logins on a single system, or use SYSMAN to perform the same command on multiple systems in an OpenVMS cluster configuration:

```
$ SET LOGINS/INTERACTIVE=0
%SET-T-INTSET, login interactive limit=0, current interactive value=5
```

or

```
$ RUN SYS$SYSTEM:SYSMAN
SYSMAN> SET ENVIRONMENT/CLUSTER
SYSMAN> DO SET LOGINS/INTERACTIVE=0
```

6.3.2 Check for System Activity

No matter how much you advertise a shutdown, some users do not get the message or forget that it is scheduled. Before you start the shutdown, use the MONITOR and SHOW utilities to check for system activity. First check for interactive and batch logins:

```
$ SHOW USERS/NODE
      OpenVMS User Processes at 22-MAR-2003 15:34:25.34
    Total number of users = 5, number of processes = 15
Username       Node      Interactive     Subprocess     Batch
SIMPSONB       BIRCH          1
SIMPSONM       BIRCH          1
.
.
.
```

Then, check for network jobs:

```
$ SHOW SYSTEM/NETWORK
OpenVMS V7.3-1  on node MILLER   8-MAR-2003 10:57:06.64  Uptime  0 00:34:24
  Pid     Process Name     State  Pri    I/O       CPU        Page flts  Pages
0000008E  EVL              HIB    6       57   0 00:00:01.88       344      52  N
00000091  FAL_8194         LEF    4      109   0 00:00:03.80       435     400  N
```

Only the standard network jobs such as EVL and NETACP should be listed. If there are processes named FAL_*xxxx*, network file transfers may be in progress, and you should investigate further before initiating the shutdown.

To see if any existing processing is active, use MONITOR as follows:

```
$ MONITOR PROCESSES/TOPCPU
                              OpenVMS Monitor Utility
                               TOP CPU TIME PROCESSES
                                   on node BIRCH
                              13-MAR-2003 06:24:14.07
                                  0         25         50         75        100
                                  + - - - - + - - - - + - - - - + - - - - - -+
000000A2 DB_UPDATE          58    ***********************
                                  |         |          |         |          |
0000003D SYSTEM              8    ***
                                  |         |          |         |          |
00000021 SWAPPER             1
```

```
                                        |        |        |        |        |
          00000029 JOB_CONTROL
                                        |        |        |        |        |
          00000028 AUDIT_SERVER
          ...
```

If you find a process and want to know exactly what it is doing, use the SHOW PROCESS command as follows:

```
$ show process/id=3d
 8-MAR-2003 11:25:20.92   User: SYSTEM           Process ID:    0000003D
                          Node: BIRCH            Process name: "_FTA6:"
Terminal:            FTA6:
User Identifier:     [SYSTEM]
Base priority:       4
Default file spec:   Not available
Number of Kthreads: 1
Devices allocated:   MILLER$FTA6:
Soft CPU Affinity: off
```

Again, if you see activity you do not expect, investigate before proceeding with the shutdown.

6.3.3 Send Shutdown Notification

Although shutdown procedures issue shutdown-notification messages, you might want to send your own messages manually as follows:

```
$ REPLY/ALL/BELL/SHUTDOWN/NODE=node -
_$ "System shutting down now, please log-off.  Call extension 1234 for assistance."
```

If you are shutting down only one node in a cluster, use the /NODE qualifier to restrict the message to just that node.

6.3.4 Shutdown Example

Once you are satisfied it is safe to begin shutdown, invoke the SHUTDOWN script. After invoking SHUTDOWN, you are prompted to enter several shutdown options. Some prompts display a default response enclosed in square brackets ([]). To select the default value, press

<RETURN> or key in your selection. Each of these options is discussed in detail in section 6.4.

The following example is performed on a nonclustered OpenVMS/Alpha from a remote terminal—TNA devices are Telnet sessions. Naturally, different options and different software configurations will produce different messages. This example is only meant to indicate the general nature of the shutdown process.

```
$ @sys$system:shutdown
SHUTDOWN -- Perform an Orderly System Shutdown
            on node MILLER
Do you really want to shutdown node MILLER [NO]? y
```

Since the manager is not shutting down from the console, the above query is made to double-check the manager's intention.

If the computer is clustered, two additional queries about the cluster status are presented. These are listed and discussed in section 6.3.5.

```
How many minutes until final shutdown [0]: <RETURN>
Reason for shutdown [Standalone]: <RETURN>
Do you want to spin down the disk volumes [NO]? <RETURN>
Do you want to invoke the site-specific shutdown procedure [YES]? <RETURN>
Should an automatic system reboot be performed [NO]? yes
When will the system be rebooted [shortly via automatic reboot]: <RETURN>
Shutdown options (enter as a comma-separated list):
 REBOOT_CHECK        Check existence of basic system files
 SAVE_FEEDBACK       Save AUTOGEN feedback information from this boot
 DISABLE_AUTOSTART   Disable autostart queues
 POWER_OFF           Request console to power-off the system
Shutdown options [NONE]: reboot_check
```

The query above is the last. All the following are status and progress messages.

```
%SHUTDOWN-I-BOOTCHECK, performing reboot consistency check...
%SHUTDOWN-I-CHECKOK, basic reboot consistency check completed
%SHUTDOWN-I-OPERATOR, this terminal is now an operator's console
%SHUTDOWN-I-DISLOGINS, interactive logins will now be disabled
%SET-I-INTSET, login interactive limit = 0, current interactive value = 6
```

```
%%%%%%%%%%%  OPCOM   8-MAR-2003 15:21:03.88  %%%%%%%%%%%
Operator _MILLER$TNA2: has been enabled, username SYSTEM
%%%%%%%%%%%  OPCOM   8-MAR-2003 15:21:03.94  %%%%%%%%%%%
Operator status for operator _MILLER$TNA2:
CENTRAL, PRINTER, TAPES, DISKS, DEVICES, CARDS, NETWORK, CLUSTER, LICENSE,
OPER1, OPER2, OPER3, OPER4, OPER5, OPER6, OPER7, OPER8, OPER9, OPER10, OPER11,
OPER12
%SHUTDOWN-I-STOPQUEUES, the queues on this node will now be stopped
```

The following message is sent to all interactive sessions. Notice that the message is tailored according to the responses in the dialog above.

```
SHUTDOWN message on MILLER from user SYSTEM at _MILLER$TNA2:   15:21:04
MILLER will shut down in 0 minutes; back up shortly via automatic reboot.  Please
log off node MILLER.
Standalone
2 terminals have been notified on MILLER.
%SHUTDOWN-I-SITESHUT, the site-specific shutdown procedure will now be invoked
DFG$TRANSFERSIZE DEASSIGNED
The POLYCENTER File Optimizer for OpenVMS has been shut down on MILLER
%SHUTDOWN-I-STOPUSER, all user processes will now be stopped
%SHUTDOWN-I-STOPACMESRV, the ACME server will now be shut down
%SHUTDOWN-I-STOPAUDIT, the security auditing subsystem will now be shut down
%SHUTDOWN-I-STOPSECSRV, the security server will now be shut down
%SHUTDOWN-I-QUIESCING, quiescing remaining non-system processes
%SHUTDOWN-I-REMOVE, all installed images will now be removed

%%%%%%%%%%%  OPCOM   8-MAR-2003 15:21:10.00  %%%%%%%%%%%
Message from user SYSTEM on MILLER
%SECSRV-I-CIASHUTDOWN, breakin detection and evasion processing is shutting down

%%%%%%%%%%%  OPCOM   8-MAR-2003 15:21:10.06  %%%%%%%%%%%
Message from user SYSTEM on MILLER
%SECSRV-I-PROXYSHUTDOWN, proxy processing is shutting down

%%%%%%%%%%%  OPCOM   8-MAR-2003 15:21:10.41  %%%%%%%%%%%
Message from user SYSTEM on MILLER
%SECSRV-I-SERVERSHUTDOWN, security server shutting down
%SHUTDOWN-I-DISMOUNT, all volumes will now be dismounted

%%%%%%%%%%%  OPCOM   8-MAR-2003 15:21:11.68  %%%%%%%%%%%
```

```
Message from user SYSTEM on MILLER
_MILLER$TNA2:, MILLER shutdown was requested by the operator.
%%%%%%%%%%%  OPCOM   8-MAR-2003 15:21:11.72  %%%%%%%%%%%
Logfile was closed by operator _MILLER$TNA2:
Logfile was MILLER::SYS$SYSROOT:[SYSMGR]OPERATOR.LOG;321
%%%%%%%%%%%  OPCOM   8-MAR-2003 15:21:11.79  %%%%%%%%%%%
Operator _MILLER$TNA2: has been disabled, username SYSTEM
```

At this point OpenVMS stops communicating with external terminals. A few messages will be displayed on the system console, and then the reboot sequence is started. After reboot, knowledge of this remote session is lost of course. All users must log in again.

6.3.5 Shutdown with SYSMAN

Alternatively, you may perform a system shutdown using the SYSMAN SHUTDOWN NODE command. SYSMAN invokes SYS$SYSTEM:SHUTDOWN to perform the actual shutdown, but qualifiers (rather than a dialog) have been added so you can initiate a system shutdown with a single command line, rather than having to follow an interactive script. You can also use the SYSMAN SET ENVIRONMENT command to select and shut down multiple systems or an entire cluster with a single command.

In general, you can only invoke SHUTDOWN.COM from the system console. Generally, if SHUTDOWN is requested on a terminal session connected via any network protocol, the connection will be broken before shutdown is complete. Thus, the SYSMAN mechanism is of particular use when shutting down a system via a network connection. Particularly on older versions of OpenVMS using Telnet, or DECnet connections, the manager should request a standard system shutdown only via the SYSMAN SHUTDOWN mechanism.

The syntax of the SYSMAN SHUTDOWN command is as follows:

```
$ RUN SYS$SYSTEM:SYSMAN
SYSMAN> SHUTDOWN NODE /qualifiers
```

Table 6.1 illustrates valid SHUTDOWN qualifiers, the corresponding SHUTDOWN.COM question, and the parameter number.

Table 6.1 *SYSMAN SHUTDOWN Qualifiers*

Qualifier	SHUTDOWN.COM Question	Parameter
/MINUTES_TO_SHUTDOWN=minutes	How many minutes until final shutdown?	P1
/REASON="Text"	What is the reason for the shutdown?	P2
/REBOOT_TIME="Text"	When will the system be rebooted?	P5
/[NO]SPIN_DOWN_DISKS	Do you want to spin down the disk volumes?	P3
/[NO]AUTOMATIC_REBOOT	Should an automatic system reboot be performed?	P6
/INVOKE_SHUTDOWN	Do you want to invoke the site-specific shutdown?	P4
/REBOOT_CHECK	Option: REBOOT_CHECK	P7
/CLUSTER_SHUTDOWN	Option: CLUSTER_SHUTDOWN	P7
/REMOVE_NODE	Option: REMOVE_NODE	P7
/SAVE_FEEDBACK	Option: SAVE_FEEDBACK	P7
/DISABLE_AUTOSTART=minutes	Option: DISABLE_AUTOSTART=minutes	P7

Another advantage of SYSMAN SHUTDOWN is that, by default, it executes in a spawned subprocess, leaving you free to monitor the system while you wait for the shutdown to complete. Therefore, make sure you do not log off after starting a shutdown; otherwise, your subprocess will be deleted and the pending shutdown will be aborted. You can prevent this behavior by forcing the shutdown to execute as an independent, detached process rather than as a spawned process. This occurs whenever you use the SET ENVIRONMENT command to select one or more cluster members. If you want to shut down only the local system, use the following command:

```
$ RUN SYS$SYSTEM:SYSMAN
SYSMAN> SET ENVIRONMENT/NODE=local_node
SYSMAN> SHUTDOWN NODE /qualifiers
```

6.4 Orderly Shutdown Details

The HP-supplied DCL command procedure SYS$SYSTEM:SHUTDOWN.COM is the primary mechanism for performing an orderly shutdown. You can also use the SYSMAN SHUTDOWN command (which in turn uses the SHUTDOWN script). These two are invoked in the following ways:

```
$ @SYS$SYSTEM:SHUTDOWN
```

or

```
$ RUN SYS$SYSTEM:SYSMAN
SYSMAN> SHUTDOWN NODE
```

The following privileges are required to perform a shutdown: AUDIT, CMKRNL, EXQUOTA, LOG_IO, NETMBX, OPER, SECURITY, SYSNAM, SYSPRV, TMPMBX, WORLD. If you want to prevent users or operators from initiating an orderly shutdown, you should ensure that they are not authorized for any of these privileges.

SYSMAN SHUTDOWN provides the same functionality as SHUTDOWN.COM, except shutdown options are selected using command qualifiers rather than through an interactive scripting process. The following sections discuss the procedures for using SHUTDOWN.COM. SYSMAN SHUTDOWN is discussed later in this chapter.

The SHUTDOWN script prompts you to select and configure the following shutdown options:

- Shutdown-notification messages
- Disk spin down
- Site-specific shutdown procedures
- Automatic system reboot
- Other shutdown options

6.4.1 Shutdown-Notification Messages

SHUTDOWN allows you to broadcast system messages to all users, reminding them that the system will soon be shut down. Your responses to three SHUTDOWN questions determine the length of the notification period, advertised reboot time, and reason for the shutdown; for example:

```
How many minutes until final shutdown [0]: 10
When will the system be rebooted [later]: at 4:00 p.m.
Reason for shutdown [Standalone]: Performing Maintenance
```

The above responses would force a 10-minute notification period and the following message to be sent to all logged in users:

```
SHUTDOWN message on BIRCH from user SYSTEM at _BIRCH$OPA0: 14:10:07
BIRCH will shut down in 10 minutes; back up at 4:00 p.m.
Please log off node BIRCH
Performing Maintenance
```

The shutdown message is rebroadcast throughout the notification period at decreasing time intervals. Once the notification period is over, the system shutdown begins. If you select a zero-minute notification period (the default), SHUTDOWN sends only a single notification message and immediately begins a system shutdown. Unless you know that no one is using the system, you should always select at least a 5- or 10-minute notification period. Try to be as descriptive and accurate as you can in choosing text for the reboot time and shutdown reason. That way, users will know what is going on and when they can reasonably expect the system to become available.

You can enforce a minimum shutdown notification period by assigning a value to the systemwide logical name SHUTDOWN$MINIMUM_MINUTES. For example, to enforce a 10-minute minimum, issue the following command:

```
$ DEFINE/SYSTEM/EXECUTIVE SHUTDOWN$MINIMUM_MINUTES 10
```

If system shutdowns are usually performed by operations staff, you should establish a minimum shutdown-notification period. To make your choice permanent, add the logical-name definition to your system-startup procedures (see chapter 5).

By default, shutdown-notification messages are sent to users clusterwide even if only a single system is being shut down. Users can become confused when they receive notification messages that really do not affect them. You can restrict shutdown-notification messages to affected nodes by defining the logical name SHUTDOWN$INFORM_NODES for each cluster member as follows:

```
$ DEFINE/SYSTEM SHUTDOWN$INFORM_NODES "node"
```

Again, to make this choice permanent, add the definition to the system-startup procedures (see chapter 5). A complete list of SHUTDOWN logicals is found in table 6.2.

Table 6.2 *SHUTDOWN Logical Names*

Logical Name	Meaning
SHUTDOWN$DECNET_MINUTES	Defines the number of minutes remaining before DECnet is shut down; must be defined with the /SYSTEM qualifier. The default is 6 minutes.
SHUTDOWN$DISABLE_AUTOSTART	Specifies the number of minutes between the time autostart is disabled for queues and the time the system is shut down; must be defined with the /SYSTEM qualifier.
SHUTDOWN$INFORM_NODES	Specifies a list of OpenVMS cluster nodes to be notified when the system is shutting down.
SHUTDOWN$MINIMUM_MINUTES	Defines the minimum number of minutes you can specify as the number of minutes until shutdown (e.g., if your users require 30 minutes' notice before a system shutdown, define this logical name as 30. This logical must be defined with the /SYSTEM qualifier).
SHUTDOWN$QUEUE_MINUTES	Defines the number of minutes remaining before shutdown when shutting down queues; must be defined with the /SYSTEM qualifier. The default is 1 minute.
SHUTDOWN$TIME	Defines the absolute time of the shut down; must be defined with the /SYSTEM qualifier.
SHUTDOWN$VERBOSE	If defined to any string, specifies that the shutdown command procedure is to list each disk as it is dismounted.

6.4.2 Disk Spin Down

You can request that all disk drives—excluding the system disk—be spun down as part of the shutdown process by responding yes to the following SHUTDOWN question:

```
Do you want to spin down the disk volumes [NO]:
```

Normally, you only need to select this option when you want to power off the entire system and its peripherals. Some disk drives, specifically SCSI disks, do not support this option.

6.4.3 Site-Specific Shutdown Procedures

If you respond yes to the following question, SHUTDOWN executes the site-specific shutdown procedure SYS$MANAGER:SYSHUTDWN.COM before stopping user processes:

```
Do you want to invoke the site-specific shutdown [YES]?
```

By default, OpenVMS simply deletes all active processes as part of the normal shutdown process. If you have applications that continuously update data files, such an abrupt action can cause file corruption. To prevent this, many applications and layered products have associated shutdown procedures that perform an orderly application shutdown. You should carefully review documentation for all HP, third-party, and in-house applications and include appropriate shutdown commands in SYSHUTDWN; for example:

```
$! SYSHUTDWN.COM
$!
$ @SYS$MANAGER:RMONSTOP      ! Oracle Rdb shut down
$ @SYS$MANAGER:ACCT_SHUT     ! Local Software Package
```

If you do not have application-specific shutdown procedures, create an empty SYSHUTDWN.COM. This way, you can let it be invoked (the default SHUTDOWN option), but because it is empty, no commands are executed.

In OpenVMS cluster environments, shutdown procedures may have to be tailored further when all systems do not run the same applications. This is similar to SYSTARTUP_VMS.COM, and several techniques for doing this are discussed in chapter 5. For example, if only cluster members BIRCH and LOTUS run Oracle Rdb, SYSHUTDWN might look as follows:

```
$! SYSHUTDWN.COM
$!
$ NODE = F$GETSYI ("SCSNODE")
$ IF (NODE .EQS. "LOTUS") .OR. (NODE .EQS. "BIRCH")
$ THEN
$  @SYS$MANAGER:RMONSTOP       !Oracle Rdb shut down
$ EndIf
$ @SYS$MANAGER:ACCT_SHUT       !Local Software Package
```

In complex cluster environments, it might be easier to establish a separate shutdown procedure for each cluster member; for example:

```
$! SYSHUTDWN.COM—Cluster Common Shutdown
$!
$ NODE = F$GETSYI ("SCSNODE")
$ LOCAL_SYSHUTDWN = "SYS$MANAGER:SYSHUTDWN_" + NODE
$ IF F$SEARCH(LOCAL_SYSHUTDWN) .NES. ""
$ THEN
$    @'LOCAL_SHUTDWN'     !Execute node-specific shut down
$ ELSE
$    WRITE SYS$OUTPUT "No local shut down for node " + Node
$ ENDIF
$!
$! Common Shut down Procedures
$!
$ @SYS$MANAGER:DB_SHUTDOWN           !Database Application
$ @SYS$MANAGER:ACCT_SHUT             !Financial Management System
```

6.4.4 Automatic Reboot

If you want the system to reboot immediately after the shutdown, respond with a yes to the following shutdown question:

```
Should an automatic system reboot be performed [NO]?
```

If you do not request an automatic reboot, the following message will be displayed on completion of the shutdown process:

```
SYSTEM SHUTDOWN COMPLETE—USE CONSOLE TO HALT SYSTEM
```

You can then halt the system and issue manual boot commands (e.g., to boot stand-alone backup) as described in chapter 4.

6.4.5 SHUTDOWN Options

The following SHUTDOWN question allows you to select one or more additional shutdown options:

```
Shutdown options (enter as a comma-separated list):
REMOVE_NODE             Remaining nodes in the cluster should adjust quorum
CLUSTER_SHUTDOWN        Entire cluster is shutting down
REBOOT_CHECK            Check existence of basic system files
SAVE_FEEDBACK           Save AUTOGEN feedback information from this boot
DISABLE_AUTOSTART       Disable autostart queues
POWER_OFF               Request console to power-off the system
Shutdown options [NONE]:
```

REMOVE_NODE

An important issue to consider when performing a system shutdown is cluster quorum continuity. By default, when a cluster member is shut down, its contributed votes are removed, but quorum is not automatically recalculated. Therefore, after you shut down one or more voting members, the number of contributed votes eventually falls below the calculated quorum value, causing loss of quorum and suspension of user activity—or a *cluster hang*. Table 6.3 demonstrates cluster hang for a four-member cluster in which each member contributes one vote.

Table 6.3 *Default Cluster Quorum Adjustment after SHUTDOWN*

Event	Votes Present	Expected Votes	Quorum	Cluster State
Cluster booted	4	4	3	OK
Shutdown member #1	3	4	3	OK
Shutdown member #2	2	4	3	Hung

This behavior can be avoided by selecting the REMOVE_NODE option during system shutdown. REMOVE_NODE forces a SET CLUSTER/EXPECTED_VOTES command to be issued just before the member is shut down. SET CLUSTER/EXPECTED_VOTES forces expected votes to be set to the current number of available votes and forces quorum recalculation.

However, when the SET CLUSTER command is issued, the node being shut down is still contributing its VOTES. Therefore, the quorum recalculation does not take into consideration the loss of votes about to occur from the node being shut down. For example, in table 6.4, after shutdown of the first cluster member, EXPECTED_VOTES is still four; therefore, quorum is still calculated as three. Only when the second cluster member is shut down is the quorum reduced to two.

Because of this delayed quorum recalculation, you cannot successfully perform a REMOVE_NODE when only two cluster members remain. In table 6.4, when the third cluster member is being shut down, EXPECTED_VOTES is adjusted to two, but this leaves quorum at two. As soon as the shutdown of the third node completes, only one remaining vote is present, and therefore the cluster hangs. At this point, the only way to resume the cluster is to force quorum recalculation manually using the IPC utility (see chapter 4).

Table 6.4 *Quorum Adjustment with REMOVE_NODE Option Selected*

Action	Votes Present	Expected Votes	Quorum	Cluster State
Cluster booted	4	4	3	OK
Shutdown #1 (REMOVE_NODE)	4	4	3	OK
After shutdown #1	3	4	3	OK
Shutdown #2 (REMOVE_NODE)	3	3	2	OK
After shutdown #2	2	3	2	OK
Shutdown #3 (REMOVE_NODE)	2	2	2	OK
After shutdown #3	1	2	2	Hung
Invoke IPC on #4	1	1	1	OK

CLUSTER_SHUTDOWN

The CLUSTER_SHUTDOWN option is presented only if the system being shut down is an OpenVMS cluster member. When a cluster member is shut down, a state-transition occurs, and the remaining members negotiate a new cluster configuration. This behavior can cause problems when shutting down all cluster members at the same time. By default, a state-transition occurs after each member is shut down. Eventually, too few cluster members remain to constitute quorum, forcing the cluster to hang without ever completing the shutdown.

When you shut down an entire cluster, specify the CLUSTER_SHUTDOWN option on all members. This forces each to shut down to a point at which it is still considered a cluster member. When all nodes are shut down to this common point, the cluster connection manager forces all nodes to complete the shutdown process simultaneously.

REBOOT_CHECK

The REBOOT_CHECK option forces the SHUTDOWN procedure to perform a reboot consistency check by confirming that key system files exist. If they exist, the shutdown process is allowed to continue; otherwise, the shutdown aborts. If you suspect that system files may have been manipulated, select this option. For example, if the file SYSGEN.EXE did not exist and you initiated a REBOOT_CHECK, you would get the following error messages during a system shutdown:

```
$ @SYS$SYSTEM:SHUTDOWN
...
Shutdown options [NONE]: REBOOT_CHECK
...
%SHUTDOWN-E-OPENIN, Error opening SYS$SYSTEM:SYSGEN.EXE as input
%SHUTDOWN-E-NOREBOOT, The system will be unable to reboot
%SHUTDOWN-E-NOREBOOT, Correct above errors before shutting down
```

SAVE_FEEDBACK

During system operation, performance-feedback data is stored in main memory. By default, this information is discarded after a system shutdown. If you select SAVE_FEEDBACK during shutdown, feedback data is written to the following file:

```
SYS$SYTEM:AGEN$FEEDBACK.DAT
```

See chapter 18 for details on using AUTOGEN with old feedback data.

DISABLE_AUTOSTART=minutes

With the queue manager, all AUTOSTART queues are closed when the DISABLE AUTOSTART/QUEUES command is issued, preventing additional jobs from being submitted. Active jobs in closed queues can continue processing until a STOP/QUEUES/ON_NODE command is executed. At that point, active jobs either abort or fail-over to designated fail-over queues.

By default, the DISABLE_AUTOSTART/QUEUES command is executed as soon as the shutdown process begins, and the STOP/QUEUES/ON_NODE is executed just before final shutdown. The DISABLE_AUTOSTART option allows you to delay the execution of the DISABLE_AUTOSTART/QUEUES command. For example, if you specified a 60-minute shutdown notification period, you might want to use the DISABLE_AUTOSTART=10 option. Then, autostart queues would not be closed until 10 minutes before shutdown.

You can force a default value for DISABLE_AUTOSTART by defining a system logical name as follows:

```
$ DEFINE/SYSTEM/EXECUTIVE SHUTDOWN$DISABLE_AUTOSTART "10"
```

To be effective, the number of minutes specified for the shutdown notification period must be greater than the number of minutes specified with the DISABLE_AUTOSTART option. The queue manager is described in more detail in chapter 8.

POWER_OFF

Turn off the computer after shutdown. Only a few hardware models support this option.

6.5 Emergency Shutdown Procedures

If normal shutdown procedures fail or cannot be invoked, you can use the following emergency shutdown procedures.

6.5.1 OPCCRASH

During the last step of an orderly shutdown, SYS$SYSTEM:OPCCRASH.EXE is executed, which dismounts the system disk and halts the system (or initiates a reboot if requested). Normally, OPCCRASH receives the results of the shutdown dialog via the logicals shown in table 6.5.

Table 6.5 *OPCCRASH Logicals*

OPCCRASH Logical	SHUTDOWN Query
OPC$UNLOAD	Do you want to spin down the disk volumes
OPC$REBOOT	Should an automatic system reboot be performed
OPC$NODUMP	(Always passed as TRUE meaning no DUMPFILE generation)

Table 6.5 *OPCCRASH Logicals (continued)*

OPCCRASH Logical	SHUTDOWN Query
OPC$CLUSTER_SHUTDOWN	SHUTDOWN option: CLUSTER_SHUTDOWN
OPC$NODE_REMOVE	SHUTDOWN option: REMOVE_NODE
OPC$POWER_OFF	SHUTDOWN option: POWER_OFF

If an orderly shutdown fails, you may be able to force a shutdown by manually invoking OPCCRASH as follows:

```
$ RUN SYS$SYSTEM:OPCCRASH
```

OPCCRASH also examines the logical name OPC$NODUMP. If OPC$NODUMP is clear (the default), a crash-dump file is created. During an orderly shutdown, OPC$NODUMP is set to TRUE, preventing a crash dump every time you perform a shutdown.

6.5.2 Forcing a Crash Dump

If you cannot even invoke OPCCRASH (e.g., the system is completely hung), you can manually force a system crash dump by using console commands. The following paragraphs summarize the console procedures for most HP OpenVMS systems.

OpenVMS/Alpha Systems

```
! Set system control switch, if applicable, to LOCAL/ENABLE
^P, <BREAK>, or HALT button     ! Key sequence to switch to console mode
>>> CRASH                    ! Available on Most Alpha SRM consoles
```

or

```
>>> E -N 1E R0
>>> E PS
>>> E PC
>>> D PC FFFFFFFF00000000  ! Put invalid address in Program Counter
>>> D PS 1F00              ! Raise IPL to 31
```

```
>>> C                          ! Jump to invalid address
                               ! at high IPL, thus forcing
                               ! invalid exception on interrupt
                               ! stack bug-check, and
                               ! subsequent crash dump
```

OpenVMS/VAX Systems

```
!Set system control switch, if applicable, to LOCAL/ENABLE
^P, <BREAK>, or HALT button    ! Key sequence to switch to console mode
>>> @CRASH                     ! On processors with boot command files
```

or

```
>>> D/G F FFFFFFFF             ! Put invalid address in Program Counter
>>> DEPOSIT PSL 041F0000       ! Raise IPL 31 on Interrupt Stack,
                               ! (>>>D P 041F0000) on some systems
>>> CONTINUE                   ! Jump to invalid address
                               ! at high IPL, thus forcing
                               ! invalid exception on interrupt
                               ! stack bugcheck, and
                               ! subsequent crash dump
```

6.6 System Dump-File Considerations

The manager has several options regarding the dump file SYSDUMP.DMP. Since it can be larger than all of the physical memory, the resulting file may occupy a considerable amount of disk space.

6.6.1 Sizing the System Dump File

When a crash dump occurs, the system attempts to copy the entire contents of physical memory and error log buffers to the system dump file (SYS$SYSTEM:SYSDUMP.DMP). To ensure a complete crash dump, you should size your crash-dump file.

The easiest approach available for sizing the system dump file (and the page file and swap file, as well) involves the use of the SWAPFILE.COM script:

```
$ @SYS$UPDATE:SWAPFILES.COM
To leave a file size at its current value type a
carriage return in response to its size prompt.
Current file sizes are:
Directory SYS$SPECIFIC:[SYSEXE]
PAGEFILE.SYS;4           172000
SYSDUMP.DMP;3            121551
SWAPFILE.SYS;7             4600
Total of 3 files, 298151 blocks.
There are 2271076 available blocks on SYS$SYSDEVICE.
Enter new size for paging file: <RETURN>
Enter new size for system dump file: <RETURN>
Enter new size for swapping file: <RETURN>
```

Normally AUTOGEN will calculate the required file sizes, but to size the file manually, you can use one of the following formulas:

- OpenVMS/Alpha Systems:

  Dump-file size (blocks) = physical-memory (in pagelets) + (ERRORLOGBUFFERS × ERLBUFFERPAGES) + 10
- OpenVMS/VAX Systems:

  Dump-file size (blocks) = physical-memory (pages) + (ERRORLOGBUFFERS × ERLBUFFERPAGES) + 1

You can determine the number of pages of physical memory using the SHOW MEMORY command.

```
$ SHOW MEMORY/PHYSICAL
System Memory Resources on  8-MAR-2003 16:11:47.16
Physical Memory Usage (pages):      Total        Free      In Use    Modified
  Main Memory (80.00MB)             10240         607        8795         838
Of the physical pages in use, 3170 pages are permanently allocated to OpenVMS.
```

On OpenVMS Alpha systems, SHOW MEMORY displays the number of Alpha pages. To calculate the number of 512-byte pagelets required, multiply the number of pages by the number of blocks per Alpha page as follows:

```
$ BLKS_PER_PG = F$GETSYI("PAGE_SIZE")/512
$ PAGELETS = BLKS_PER_PG * Pages
$ SHOW SYMBOL PAGELETS
```

The system page size on an Alpha system can vary from 8 KB to 64 KB, depending on the Alpha platform and the OpenVMS version. The system page size on a VAX system is always 512 bytes.

You can determine the number of error log buffers and their corresponding size by examining the system parameters ERRORLOGBUFFERS and ERLBUFFERPAGES. Once you have calculated the required dump-file size, you may use the SWAPFILES script shown above or create it with SYSGEN as follows:

```
$ RUN SYS$SYSTEM:SYSGEN
SYSGEN> CREATE SYS$SYSTEM:SYSDUMP.DMP/SIZE=size
```

If your system has substantial physical memory configured, you may not want to reserve system-disk storage sufficient to support a full crash dump. In this case, set the system parameter DUMPSTYLE to 1 to configure the system for selective crash dumps. Alternatively, you can configure your system for a dump file, or DOSD, off the system disk. When the system performs a selective crash dump, it copies only the most critical parts of memory, thus requiring a smaller crash-dump file.

To force AUTOGEN to calculate the proper dump-file size, add the following lines to MODPARAMS.DAT and execute AUTOGEN:

```
$ EDIT MODPARAMS.DAT
! MODPARAMS.DAT
...
DUMPSTYLE=1! Selective dump
...
!DUMPFILE=0                 ! Full dump
!DUMPSTYLE=4                ! DOSD - Dump off System Disk
!DUMPFILE_DEVICE=DKA100     ! DOSD disk name
!DUMPSTYLE=8                ! Compressed dump (alpha only)
[exit and save changes]
$ @SYS$UPDATE:AUTOGEN SAVPARAMS TESTFILES
```

AUTOGEN sizes the dump file to be approximately equal to the number of pages allocated to the system, plus a fraction of pages allocated to processes (10% to 50%). This usually results in a dump file that is 40 to 70 percent of physical memory. As an alternative, you can use these guidelines and manually size your dump file using SYSGEN.

Although a selective dump requires less disk space, a selective dump may not contain enough information to determine the cause of the crash. OpenVMS will copy the core data structures and what are normally most interesting processes into the dump file first.

6.6.2 Using the Page File As the System Dump File

To conserve system-disk space you can optionally use the primary page file as a dump file. If there is no crash-dump file, OpenVMS copies dump information to the primary page file (SYS$SYSTEM:PAGEFILE.SYS). Normally, the page file is initialized after each system boot, potentially invalidating the earlier crash dump. To use the page file as a dump file, you have to prevent this behavior by setting the system parameter SAVEDUMP to 1. This preserves the crash-dump pages written to the page file until they are manually copied or released.

Because much of the page file is unusable after a crash dump, you should make the page file large enough to hold a dump and add several thousand pages to allow the system to boot. Once a system boots after a crash dump, you can release allocated crash-dump pages as follows:

```
$ ANALYZE/CRASH SYS$SYSTEM:PAGEFILE.SYS
SDA> COPY $DISK2:[TEMP]SYSDUMP.TMP
```

If you have no place to copy the dump, perform analysis and release pages as follows:

```
$ ANALYZE/CRASH/RELEASE SYS$SYSTEM:PAGEFILE.SYS
```

6.6.3 Establishing a Common Dump File

Normally, each system requires a dedicated system dump file. Even in a modestly sized OpenVMS cluster, it is usually impossible to allocate enough system-disk space to support a full crash dump for all cluster members. As an alternative, you can establish a shared common-dump file as follows:

1. Rename one dump file to the common root. Make sure it is large enough to support a full dump of any single cluster member. You must not name it SYSDUMP.DMP.

```
$ RENAME SYS$SYSDEVICE:[SYS0.SYSEXE]SYSDUMP.DMP –
SYS$COMMON:[SYSEXE]SYSDUMP-COMMON.DMP
```

2. Rename the dump files on the existing cluster members so that they will not be used.

```
$ RENAME SYS$SYSDEVICE:[SYS1.SYSEXE]SYSDUMP.DMP SYSDUMP.TMP
$ RENAME SYS$SYSDEVICE:[SYS2.SYSEXE]SYSDUMP.DMP SYSDUMP.TMP
```

3. Create an alias file entry in each system root that points to the common dump file.

```
$ SET FILE/ENTER=SYS$SYSDEVICE:[SYS0.SYSEXE]SYSDUMP.DMP –
  SYS$COMMON:[SYSEXE]SYSDUMP-COMMON.DMP
$ SET FILE/ENTER=SYS$SYSDEVICE:[SYS1.SYSEXE]SYSDUMP.DMP -
  SYS$COMMON:[SYSEXE]SYSDUMP-COMMON.DMP
$ SET FILE/ENTER=SYS$SYSDEVICE:[SYS2.SYSEXE]SYSDUMP.DMP -
  SYS$COMMON:[SYSEXE]SYSDUMP-COMMON.DMP
```

4. Reboot the entire cluster.
5. Delete the old dump files.

```
$ DELETE SYS$SYSDEVICE:[SYS0.SYSEXE]SYSDUMP.TMP;
$ DELETE SYS$SYSDEVICE:[SYS1.SYSEXE]SYSDUMP.TMP;
$ DELETE SYS$SYSDEVICE:[SYS2.SYSEXE]SYSDUMP.TMP;
```

To prevent corruption, OpenVMS maintains an open I/O channel to the most recent system dump file at all times. Do not delete the old dump files until after you perform a system reboot. If you should erroneously delete a dump file, OpenVMS will retain the I/O channel and the existing file. You will subsequently want to use the ANALYZE/DISK/REPAIR utility (sometime after the next reboot) to free up the disk storage that remains allocated to the former dump file.

Very old OpenVMS releases did not hold open the dump file, and an errant deletion followed by a system crash could lead to the corruption of the files written to the same areas of the disk that were formerly occupied by the dump file.

6.7 Automating Shutdown

Although shutdown procedures depend on system configuration (e.g., clustered as opposed to stand-alone), each system is usually shut down using the same procedures each time. Once you have determined the shutdown methods you commonly use, you can create automated procedures to streamline the process. The goal is not to make it easier to initiate a shutdown, but to ensure that systems are consistently shut down using the correct procedures.

In the same way that SYSMAN SHUTDOWN passes parameters to SHUTDOWN.COM, you can create your own DCL command procedures that use the same technique. Parameters are passed to SHUTDOWN.COM using the standard DCL parameters P1 through P7 indicated in table 6.1.

Next, you can create a simple DCL menu system that allows you to select the most common shutdown types you perform; for example:

```
                     SHUTDOWN MENU
1 - RETURN          - Return to previous menu
2 - REBOOT          - Shutdown now with immediate reboot
3 - REBOOT5         - Shutdown in 5 minutes, with immediate reboot
4 - NORMAL          - Shutdown now without reboot
5 - NORMAL5         - Shutdown in 5 minutes, without reboot
6 - POWEROFF        - Shutdown, prepare for shutoff power (spin down disks)
Enter choice:
```

Within the DCL menu procedure, option 2 could execute the following command:

```
$ @SYS$SYSTEM:SHUTDOWN 0 REBOOT NO YES LATER YES NONE
```

or

```
$ SYSMAN:==$SYSMAN
$ SYSMAN SHUTDOWN NODE/MINUTES=0/REASON="REBOOT"-
  /NOSPIN_DOWN_DISKS/INVOKE_SHUTDOWN/REBOOT_TIME="LATER"/AUTOMATIC_REBOOT
```

The DCL command procedure SHUTDOWN_MENU.COM provides an example of a shutdown menu with several preconfigured automated shutdown options. The source code for this command procedure is located on the diskette included with this book (see appendix E).

6.8 Tools

One shutdown command procedure is listed in table 6.6 and described in appendix E. This script displays a menu to select one of several shutdown options.

Table 6.6 *Shutdown Tool*

Procedure Name	Function
SHUTDOWN_MENU.COM	Shut down system

A freeware program, WATCHER, available at http://vms.process.com/fileserv-software.html, is a powerful tool that will automatically log out inactive tasks. It can be configured to look at either specific users or classes of users. The manager can specify the definition of inactive by selecting how to measure inactivity.

6.9 Conclusion

Proper shutdown preparation is as essential as the shutdown procedures themselves. All shutdowns should be scheduled as far in advance as possible so that users are accommodated. Once a shutdown is scheduled, it should be communicated so that even infrequent users will receive notification. You do not want to schedule downtime weeks in advance only to have to reschedule because someone did not know.

Users should be notified by OpenVMS mail and login announcement messages. Chapter 16 discusses how to establish mail distribution lists that facilitate sending mail messages to many users. Chapter 5 describes the system logical name SYS$ANNOUNCE, which establishes a login announcement message.

Once you initiate a shutdown, you should give users 5 to 10 minutes' notice with notification messages. These messages are sent as broadcasts to all users using REPLY broadcast messages. However, users' terminals must be configured to receive these messages. If terminal ports have the SET

TERMINAL/NOBROADCAST characteristic or have disabled broadcast reception via the SET BROADCAST command, broadcast messages will not be delivered. You must set all interactive terminal ports to /BROADCAST during system startup (see STARTUP_SETTERM.COM in chapter 5). Also, watch for applications that disable broadcast messages after system startup.

Many problems can occur during system shutdown or after a subsequent system reboot. You should always schedule adequate time to resolve problems. The most common unscheduled downtime occurs as a result of underestimating scheduled downtime requirements. A good rule of thumb is to schedule enough downtime to perform at least two or three complete boot cycles (on many systems this can be 30 to 45 minutes each).

6.10 Additional References

1. *OpenVMS Alpha System Analysis Tools Manual* contains the SDA manual for Alpha systems.
2. *OpenVMS System Manager's Manual, Volume 1: Essentials.*
3. *OpenVMS System Manager's Manual, Volume 2: Tuning, Monitoring, and Complex Systems.*
4. *OpenVMS VAX System Dump Analyzer Utility Manual* is the SDA manual for VAX systems.

7

License Management

7.1 Chapter Objectives

- Promote a better understanding of HP's software-licensing practices and policies
- Provide methods for selecting license types and optimizing their use
- Discuss HP's various license-type offerings
- Ensure system availability through proper management of software licenses

7.2 Introduction

As a system manager, you are responsible for installing, upgrading, and managing the software products on the systems you support. Consequently, you must ensure that these products are used in accordance with the terms and conditions of associated software license agreements; otherwise, you or your organization could face severe civil and criminal penalties.

Starting with the advent of consolidated-distribution CD-ROM media, OpenVMS products incorporate a product authorization key (PAK), shown in figure 7.1, whenever you purchase a software license. Before a product can be activated, the PAK for the product must be registered and loaded on the system or OpenVMS cluster for which it is designated. Every time access to a product is attempted, the product checks to see if a corresponding and currently valid PAK has been loaded. If it has, access is granted; otherwise, access is denied.

PAKs are required for the OpenVMS operating system, TCP/IP Services, and DECnet networking products. General system users are not even able to log in to the system if the necessary PAKs are not registered and

Figure 7.1 *Sample License Product Authorization Key*

DIGITAL EQUIPMENT CORPORATION

LICENSE PAK

(PRODUCT AUTHORIZATION KEY)

This License PAK must be registered as part of the VMS installation or upgrade procedures.

Product: VAX FORTRAN

ISSUER:	DEC
AUTHORIZATION NUMBER:	XYZ123456
PRODUCT NAME:	FORTRAN
PRODUCER:	DEC
NUMBER OF UNITS:	100
VERSION:	
PRODUCT RELEASE DATE:	
KEY TERMINATION DATE:	14-APR-1993
AVAILABILITY TABLE CODE:	?
ACTIVITY TABLE CODE:	
KEY OPTIONS:	MOD_UNITS
PRODUCT TOKEN:	
HARDWARE I.D.:	
CHECKSUM:	1-ABCD-EFGH-IJKL-MNOP

© COPYRIGHT DIGITAL EQUIPMENT CORPORATION, 1993

loaded correctly. Similarly, when you perform system-configuration changes, you may need to update existing PAKs; otherwise, products can accidentally be deactivated. As you can see, system availability depends heavily on proper license management.

Some of the more common license PAKs and their associated products are listed in table 7.1.

Table 7.1 *License PAKs and Corresponding Product Name*

Product	PAK
DECnet Phase IV, DECnet-Plus	DVNETEND, DVNETRTG, DVNETEXT, NET-APP-SUP*
TCP/IP Services	UCX, NET-APP-SUP*
OpenVMS Alpha	OPENVMS-ALPHA, OPENVMS-ALPHA-USER
OpenVMS VAX	VAX-VMS
OpenVMS Galaxy	OPENVMS-GALAXY
OpenVMS cluster (Alpha)	VMSCLUSTER, NET-APP-SUP*
OpenVMS cluster (VAX)	VAXCLUSTER, NET-APP-SUP*
DECprint Services (DCPS)	Any valid license for OpenVMS
AMDS, Availability Manager	Any valid license for OpenVMS

As should be obvious from the list, a single NAS (NET-APP-SUP*) license PAK can authorize a variety of client- or server-oriented products and capabilities. The upper-end NAS license PAKs will enable more capabilities than the lower-end licenses. Most OpenVMS systems are packaged with a NAS license. Remember that some of the products listed in the table can have both a client and a full-function variant. For specific details on product licensing and options, please check the software product description (SPD) associated with the product.

7.3 HP Software Licenses

You generally do not purchase HP software—you purchase a license that grants you the right to use the software under specific terms and conditions. The following are some of the key points of HP's software licensing terms and conditions. For more detailed information, refer to the license-management documentation.

7.3.1 Licensed Version

HP software licenses grant the right to use a specific version of a product (e.g., OpenVMS Alpha v7.3) and prior versions. If you want to use future versions (e.g., OpenVMS Alpha v7.3-1), you must either purchase ongoing software support that includes the right to use new versions, or you must purchase an updated license.

7.3.2 Product Categories

HP licenses products in two general categories

1. System-integrated products (SIPs)
2. Layered products

7.4 System-Integrated Products

SIPs are integrated into the operating system. For example, OpenVMS, Volume Shadowing, and the OpenVMS cluster software are SIPs because they are tightly integrated with and distributed with the OpenVMS operating-system software.

SIPs are generally licensed using only traditional licenses, which are priced on the basis of the processing power of the system and allow unlimited use of the licensed product on that system only. Some SIPs, such as Volume Shadowing, do offer other licensing options. In the case of Volume Shadowing, per-disk licensing is also available.

Layered Products

Most other HP products, such as C, FORTRAN, and TCP/IP Services, are classified as layered products because they provide layered, rather than integral, functionality, and are "layered" onto the operating system. Some of these products may have portions that are system-integrated, but are considered to be layered products. For example, DECwindows has both a layered-product installation component and a system-integrated component. Third-party products are also often referred to as layered products.

Layered products are licensed using one or more of the major license types: traditional, clusterwide, personal use, and concurrent use. Other types are available for specific products, and not all license types are available for every product. For details on available licenses, see the SPD for the particular product.

7.4.1 Transferability

HP software licenses are either *relicensable* or *nonrelicensable*. SIPs and operating system are generally relicensable, and layered products are generally nonrelicensable.

Relicensable products can be transferred outside your organization; however, they must be transferred with the hardware systems with which they were initially licensed. All transfers must be approved by HP. You can apply for approval by submitting a relicense request.

Nonrelicensable products cannot be moved outside your organization; however they can be transferred within your organization as long as the legal entity does not change. Licenses can be transferred from one system to another (although an upgrade fee may be required). You can transfer nonrelicensable products without notifying HP.

In the event of a hardware failure, HP software licenses typically permit the use of the licensed product on another system. This use is permitted during the repair of the licensed system. Put another way, the licenses are deliberately not tied to a particular hardware system serial number or similar construct.

7.5 License Types

The following sections present the four license types offered by HP and discuss their costs in a variety of situations. The prices listed in this book illustrate the general cost differences between license types—they do not represent current HP prices. For current pricing data, refer to HP's software price list.

Traditional

Traditional licenses allow unlimited use of a software product on a single processor. The cost of the license is somewhat proportional to the CPU power of the system. For example, table 7.2 is a listing for an OpenVMS cluster license. The exact part number varies according to the CPU type.

Table 7.2 *Licenses for VMS Clusters*

Description	Part Number	License Name
VAXcluster server	QL-VBRA*-AA	VAXCLUSTER
VMScluster server	QL-MUZA*-AA	VMSCLUSTER
VMScluster client	QL-3MRA*-AA	VMSCLUSTER-CLIENT

Because they lack the flexibility of other license types, traditional licenses are usually less desirable; however, various HP products are licensed only with traditional licenses.

Clusterwide

Clusterwide licenses are available for either a single stand-alone system or for a VMScluster that consists of several systems. Each clusterwide license has an associated *license-unit value* (e.g., 100, 200, 300) that specifies the amount of use the license provides. Each processor has an associated *license-unit requirement* that specifies the number of license units required for a product to be used on that system.

You can view the license-unit requirements for a system by executing the following command:

```
$ SHOW LICENSE/UNIT_REQUIREMENTS
VMS/LMF Charge Information for node MILLER
This is a AlphaStation 200 4/233, hardware model type 1151
Type: A, Units Required: 12      (VAX/VMS Capacity or OpenVMS Unlimited or Base)
Type: B, * Not Permitted *       (VAX/VMS F&A Server)
Type: C, * Not Permitted *       (VAX/VMS Concurrent User)
Type: D, * Not Permitted *       (VAX/VMS Workstation)
Type: E, * Not Permitted *       (VAX/VMS System Integrated Products)
Type: F, * Not Permitted *       (VAX Layered Products)
Type: G, * Not Permitted *       (Reserved)
Type: H, Units Required: 1050    (Alpha Layered Products)
Type: I, Units Required: 1050    (Layered Products)
```

For a stand-alone system to load a clusterwide license successfully, the license-unit value must be greater than or equal to the license-unit requirements of the system. Once you load the license, the product can be used without limit on that system. For example, the AlphaStation above has a license-unit requirement of 1,050 units. Thus, to load and activate a

FORTRAN license successfully, the license must provide at least 1,050 license units.

To use a product on several nonclustered systems, you must purchase a separate clusterwide license for each system.

To use a product on several systems in the same OpenVMS cluster, purchase a license that has a license-unit value equal to or greater than the total license-unit requirements of all systems in the cluster. For example, to run FORTRAN on a cluster of three AlphaStation systems, purchase a license that has 3,150 (3 × 1,050) license units.

You do not have to license a product to run on all members of an OpenVMS cluster configuration. In the foregoing example, to license two of the three AlphaStation systems for FORTRAN, you need to purchase only one 2,100-unit license. When loaded, the licenses would be assigned to specific nodes in the cluster. Clusterwide licenses are most appropriate when a large number of users needs access to a product on one or more cluster members.

Concurrent Use

A concurrent-use license allows a specific number of users to use a product concurrently on a single processor or on any member of an OpenVMS cluster. For example, a four-user concurrent-use Notes license allows up to four users simultaneous access to the Notes product. You might have a total of 10 people who want to use the product, but only 4 can use it at the same time. Concurrent-use licenses are ideal when a large user group needs infrequent access to a product.

Personal Use

Personal-use licenses allow a specifically named user (based on OpenVMS username) unlimited access to a product. When assigned to a stand-alone system, a personal-use license allows unlimited use by the named user on that system. When assigned to a VMScluster, a personal-use license allows the named user unlimited access to the product from any member of the cluster. They are ideal when you have a specific set of users who need access to a product, especially if you need the flexibility to move users frequently from one system to another.

7.6 License-Management Facility

You manage HP licenses with the license-management facility (LMF), which consists of LMF tools and the license database.

7.6.1 License Database

The license database is an electronic representation of the paper PAKs that you receive from HP when you purchase a software license. There are three components to the license database.

Permanent Database

By default, OpenVMS assumes that the permanent database is stored in the file SYS$COMMON:[SYSEXE]LMF$LICENSE.LDB. Normally, you can define the system logical name LMF$LICENSE to locate the permanent, clusterwide database as follows:

```
$ DEFINE/SYSTEM/EXEC LMF$LICENSE SYS$COMMON:[SYSEXE]LMF$LICENSE.LDB
```

When you issue LICENSE commands, operations are performed on the default license database. To specify an alternative license database, add the /DATABASE qualifier to the LICENSE command.

If you maintain a common-environment OpenVMS cluster configuration, you should define LMF$LICENSE so that all cluster members reference a common permanent database. If you maintain a multiple-environment cluster and cannot establish a shared license database, you can maintain multiple databases; however, they should be exact duplicates of each other.

Volatile Database

Each system maintains an in-memory, volatile database that contains all the licenses that were successfully loaded from LMF$LICENSE either at system startup or manually with the LICENSE LOAD command. When you attempt to access a product, the product checks for a valid license in the volatile database—not in the permanent database.

Clusterwide Database

Within a cluster, clusterwide data structures are maintained that track license usage by cluster members. This is the primary reason why you must ensure that all cluster members load exactly the same licenses.

Consider a two-member, multiple-environment cluster (BIRCH and LOTUS) in which each system maintains its own LMF$LICENSE file. Assume that each system requires 100 units to run FORTRAN. Also assume that you register one 100-unit license in the license database of each system. When you attempt to load the license on BIRCH, LMF confirms that the number of units provided (100) meets the unit requirements of the system. LMF loads the license successfully and updates the clusterwide database to reflect 100 units of use.

When you later attempt to load the FORTRAN license on LOTUS, LMF confirms that the license provides 100 units (enough to satisfy the unit requirements of the system); however, it also detects that the clusterwide database shows that 100 units are already being used by BIRCH, and the load attempt fails.

To avoid this particular licensing problem, you must ensure that the LMF$LICENSE database-file contents are identical across all cluster members. In this example, both 100-unit FORTRAN PAKs should be loaded in the license databases of both cluster members.

7.6.2 LMF Tools

You perform LMF functions with either the LICENSE and SHOW LICENSE commands or with the VMSLICENSE.COM command procedure. The remaining examples in this chapter focus on using DCL commands. However, you can also perform most of the same functions by invoking the equivalent option from the VMSLICENSE menu.

LICENSE and SHOW LICENSE Commands

The DISK1 command has the following basic syntax:

```
$ LICENSE command product /qualifiers
```

For example,

```
$ LICENSE REGISTER OPENVMS-ALPHA-USER -
_$ /ISSUER=DEC -
_$ ...
```

Table 7.3 summarizes each of the LICENSE commands.

Table 7.3 *LICENSE Commands*

Command	Function
CANCEL	See MODIFY/TERMINATION=date
COPY	Copy a license from one license database to another, and disable the license in the source database

Table 7.3 *LICENSE Commands (continued)*

Command	Function
CREATE	Create a new (empty) license database in the directory specified by the /DATABASE qualifier
DELETE	Permanently delete a license from the license database
DISABLE	Prevent a license from loading at system startup or manually with the LOAD command
ENABLE	Allow a license to load at system startup or manually with the LOAD command
ISSUE	Create a PAK replica of a license
LIST	Display the contents of the license database
LOAD	Activate a license on the current node
MODIFY	Modify a license: include or exclude list, reservation list, termination date, or units
MOVE	Copies a license from one license database to another, but deletes the license from the source database
REGISTER	Adds a license to the license database and enables it; when PAK generation is authorized on the host (on OpenVMS v7.2 and later), this command is also used to initially generate the new PAK
START	Activates all registered and enabled licenses on the current node (subject to include and exclude lists); is automatically performed during site-independent startup procedures
UNLOAD	Deactivates a license on the current node

If your license database contains multiple licenses for the same product, you must add one or more of the following qualifiers to all LICENSE commands to specify the license uniquely.

```
/AUTHORIZATION=string
/ISSUER=string
/PRODUCER=string
```

In addition to the LICENSE commands, you can use the DCL command SHOW LICENSE to perform several additional license functions as follows:

```
$ SHOW LICENSE /qualifiers
```

For instance, to display the license-unit requirement table (LURT) for your system, issue the following command:

```
$ SHOW LICENSE/UNIT_REQUIREMENTS
```

You can list any active license that will terminate within 1,000 days as follows:

```
$ SHOW LICENSE/WARNING_INTERVAL=1000
```

Fields of a License PAK

Table 7.4 summarizes the fields of a license PAK.

Table 7.4 *LICENSE Fields*

Field	Meaning
Issuer	The unique identity of the organization that generated the license. Usually the same as the producer value. Maximum of 31 characters.
Authorization	A text field whose contents are determined by the issuer and which allows the issuer to assign a unique identifying value to each license PAK. Maximum of 31 characters.
ProductName	An abbreviated name for the licensed product. Maximum of 24 characters.
Producer	The name of the legal owner of the product. Maximum of 24 characters. Assigned by HP.
Units	An arbitrary measure. Must be a value between zero and two billion, inclusive. A zero here indicates an unlimited number of units.
Version	The highest product version authorized by the PAK. The version number must be in the format *nn.nn*, where n is a digit. Optional. Incompatible with the release-date field. Can be combined with the termination date. The value 7.10 authorizes 7.10, 7.09, and all previous versions.

Table 7.4 *LICENSE Fields (continued)*

Field	Meaning
ReleaseDate	A date encoded within a product. All products with this or an earlier date are authorized. Optional. Incompatible with the version value. Can be combined with the termination date. Specified as an OpenVMS-format date: dd-mm-yyyy.
TerminationDate	The last system date on which the license is valid. Can be combined with either the version or the release-date specification. If not specified, the license will not expire. Specified as an OpenVMS-format date: dd-mm-yyyy.
Availability	In combination with the activity-code setting, determines how many units are required to make the license available for the product. Can be specified as a letter code that indicates the units will be determined by the licensing algorithm associated with the letter code in conjunction with the hardware on which the software executes, or as a specific CONSTANT unit value. If there is no charge against the pool of units to make the license available, use CONSTANT=0.
Activity	The number of units to reserve from the available pool each time the product is activated; the per-user charge for the license. Can be specified by a letter code or by a constant value. If no units are to be charged per use, specify ACTIVITY=0.
KeyOptions	Various keywords used to specify specific behaviors. Common keywords are MOD_UNITS and NO_SHARE.
ProductToken	An arbitrary value determined by the issuer and available to the licensed software package. Can be used to contain the same text value as the termination date for use as a display by the software package. With the PAKGEN PAK, this field determines the authorized issuer and producer values.
HardwareID	This field is not used by HP licenses. Intended for use as a serial number for those products that contain a customized licensing scheme.

VMSLICENSE

The command procedure VMSLICENSE.COM allows you to perform the same functions as the DCL commands described above, but from a simple menu system. To invoke VMSLICENSE, enter the following command:

```
$ @SYS$UPDATE:VMSLICENSE
VMS License Management Utility Options:
        1. REGISTER a Product Authorization Key
        2. AMEND an existing Product Authorization Key
        3. CANCEL an existing Product Authorization Key
        4. LIST the Product Authorization Keys
        5. MODIFY an existing Product Authorization Key
        6. DISABLE an existing Product Authorization Key
        7. DELETE an existing Product Authorization Key
        8. COPY an existing Product Authorization Key
        9. MOVE an existing Product Authorization Key
       10. ENABLE an existing Product Authorization Key
       11. SHOW the licenses loaded on this node
       12. SHOW the unit requirements for this node
       99. EXIT this procedure
    Type '?' at any prompt for a description of the information
    requested.  Press Ctrl/Z at any prompt to return to this menu.
Enter one of the above choices [1]:
```

The function of each of the foregoing options is discussed in the previous section. AMEND and CANCEL are no longer valid LICENSE commands, however.

7.6.3 Installing a PAK

To make a license available to a system, you must perform the following steps:

- Register the PAK for the product into the permanent license database (LMF$LICENSE)
- Ensure that the registered license is not disabled; ensure that the PAK can be loaded from the permanent database into the volatile database
- Ensure that only the appropriate PAKs are loaded for the product when multiple PAKs exist for a product
- Load the license into the volatile database of the system

The following two commands demonstrate the process of installing a NO-SUCH-PROD license:

```
$ LICENSE REGISTER NO-SUCH-PROD -
/ISSUER=DEC -
/AUTHORIZATION=ALL-WM-92098-2106 -
/PRODUCER=DEC -
/UNITS=0 -
/TERMINATION_DATE=14-APR-2005 -
/ACTIVITY=CONSTANT=100 -
/CHECKSUM=2-AFKJ-EMCN-NEHP-WXYS
$ LICENSE LOAD NO-SUCH-PROD
```

If you have many licenses, you should consider registering PAKs by creating DCL command procedures, rather than entering them interactively. For example, you could put the LICENSE REGISTER command in a file called REGISTER_NO-SUCH-PROD.COM. To register the PAK, execute the command procedure as follows:

```
$ @REGISTER_NO-SUCH-PROD
```

By creating command procedures, you can easily reregister PAKs in the event the license database becomes corrupted, and you can register new PAKs simply by copying a command procedure for a similar PAK and making a few edits.

7.6.4 Enabling and Disabling PAKs

PAKs registered in the permanent database are either *enabled* or *disabled.* All newly registered PAKs are automatically enabled. Enabled PAKs are automatically loaded into the volatile database during system startup. Disabled PAKs are not loaded.

To temporarily disable automatic loading of a PAK, select DISABLE PAK or ENABLE PAK from the VMSLICENSE Main Menu, or enter the following DCL commands:

```
$ LICENSE DISABLE NO-SUCH-PROD
$ LICENSE ENABLE NO-SUCH-PROD
```

7.6.5 Loading a PAK

All enabled PAKs contained in the permanent database are automatically loaded into the volatile database of each system at boot during system startup. You can manually load and unload PAKs after system startup using the following commands:

```
$ LICENSE LOAD NO-SUCH-PROD
$ LICENSE UNLOAD NO-SUCH-PROD
```

If you need to load or unload PAKs on several systems in an OpenVMS cluster, use the SYSMAN utility as follows:

```
$ RUN SYS$SYSTEM:SYSMAN
SYSMAN> SET ENVIRONMENT/CLUSTER
SYSMAN> DO LICENSE LOAD NO-SUCH-PROD
```

You will generally want to maintain DCL command procedures containing the authorized PAKs, as this permits you to load or reload licenses as required easily. These procedures also allow you to disable or unload license PAKs and delete expired or terminated licenses easily.

7.6.6 Issuing a PAK

If your software license agreement authorizes it, you can extract a license PAK from the specified license database and then relocate the license to another system. To extract the license, use LICENSE ISSUE command. Specify the output file for the PAK, either as a text format or as a DCL command procedure.

The LICENSE ISSUE/PROCEDURE command can be used to create a command procedure containing licenses for existing PAKs, loaded and unloaded. This is convenient for extracting a registered license. If the /PROCEDURE qualifier is not present, the output simulates a PAK.

```
$ LICENSE ISSUE/AUTH=ALL-WM-92098-2106  NO-SUCH-PROD
Software Product Authorization Key Replica
Issued by SYSTEM
Issued on 16-MAR-2003 13:42
-----------------------------------
Issuer:             DEC
Authorization:      ALL-WM-92098-2106
Product Name:       NO-SUCH-PROD
Producer:           DEC
```

```
Units:              0
Activity:           CONSTANT=100
Checksum:           2-AFKJ-EMCN-NEHP-WXYS
```

7.6.7 Deleting a PAK

If you receive a temporary PAK that you later replace with a new one, you may want to remove the old PAK from the license database permanently as follows:

```
$ LICENSE DELETE NO-SUCH-PROD
```

No confirmation of this action is displayed. You should ensure that you have a backup of the PAK in case for some reason you need to reregister it.

7.6.8 Restricting Product Access

In an OpenVMS cluster environment, you may need to restrict loading of PAKs to specific systems. By default, during system startup, OpenVMS attempts to load all PAKs contained in the permanent database. If the license units of a PAK are insufficient to meet the requirements of the entire cluster, some systems display the following error message during system startup:

```
%LICENSE-W-NOLOAD, license was not loaded for PRODUCT
-LICENSE-F-EXCEEDED, attempted usage exceeds active license limits
```

For example, if you have an OpenVMS cluster containing three Alpha systems, a FORTRAN PAK providing 3,150 license units is required to support the entire cluster. But, if you have a PAK that provides only 2,100 units, you will receive error messages when you boot the third system.

In this case, if it is important to provide FORTRAN access on two specific systems, specify an INCLUDE or EXCLUDE list for the PAK. For example, if you want FORTRAN activated only on nodes LOTUS and MANGO, use the following command:

```
$ LICENSE MODIFY/INCLUDE=(LOTUS, MANTO) FORTRAN
```

If you use concurrent-use PAKs, you may have problems when unauthorized users access a product and prevent access by authorized users. To solve this problem, you can restrict access to the product to a specific set of users by establishing a RESERVE list as follows:

```
$ LICENSE MODIFY/RESERVE=(username1, username2, etc.) product-name
```

For instance, the command might read:

```
$ LICENSE MODIFY/RESERVE=(SIMPSONB, SIMPSONH) FORTRAN
```

If you use personal-use licenses, you must establish a RESERVE list for the specific users who are licensed to use the product. Once you have established a RESERVE list, you can add and remove names using the following commands:

```
$ LICENSE MODIFY/RESERVE=(SIMPSONB)/REMOVE FORTRAN
$ LICENSE MODIFY/RESERVE=(SIMPSONM)/ADD FORTRAN
```

License PAK Generation

If you have the PAKGEN license PAK, you can use the OpenVMS LICENSE command to generate license PAKs for the issuer and producer specifically authorized by the PAKGEN PAK. This is an undocumented feature.

To generate a license, use the following sequence:

```
$ LICENSE REGISTER/GENERATE/ISSUER=issuer/PRODUCER=producer...
$ LICENSE ISSUE...
```

When using the LICENSE REGISTER/GENERATE command, you must specify all qualifiers associated with the license being generated, except the /CHECKSUM qualifier. The LICENSE ISSUE command then extracts the newly generated license from the local database, creating a copy of the license, including the appropriate checksum. The LICENSE ISSUE command is typically used to create a text file or a DCL command procedure containing the PAK.

Use of this feature requires a PAKGEN PAK with a producer of "DEC," and OpenVMS v7.2 or later. The producer and issuer values specified must match those specified in the PAKGEN PAK *product token* field. (The PAKGEN PAK *token* field uses the format PRODUCER~ISSUER.)

As only one PAKGEN license can be loaded at any time, you can generate only licenses for a particular issuer and producer pair at any one time. To generate licenses for other PRODUCER~ISSUER pairs, you must unload the current, and then reload the appropriate PAKGEN license PAK.

7.7 Conclusion

DEC/Compaq/HP licensing policy has changed many times over the lifetime of OpenVMS. I would not be surprised to find that this chapter is out of date before it is published. This fluctuation has caused much confusion in the community.

Before making any licensing decisions, contact knowledgeable HP technical assistance to determine the following:

- Which license class best fits your needs
- How those needs fit in with existing licenses

You might find, for instance, that one of your existing licenses can be used to offset the cost of the new license for which you are looking.

7.8 Additional References

1. *OpenVMS License Management Utility Manual* is the definitive authority.
2. *OpenVMS System Manager's Manual, Volume 1: Essentials* provides additional examples of common LICENSE usage.

8

Queue Management

8.1 Chapter Objectives

- Present methods for configuring and naming print and batch queues
- Focus on the centralized queue manager
- Provide guidelines for configuring queues and the queue manager to ensure proper fail-over
- Discuss procedures for defining forms and device control libraries

8.2 Introduction

Many changes have been made to the queue-management subsystem over the last several years, and it can be difficult to remember what features are available in each OpenVMS version. To clarify this, table 8.1 summarizes queue-management changes that have occurred between VMS/VAX 5.4 and OpenVMS 6.0.

Table 8.1 *Summary of Queue-Management Changes*

Feature	VMS/VAX A5.5, OpenVMS Alpha v1.0, pre-VAX/VMS v5.5	OpenVMS v5.5, OpenVMS/Alpha v1.5	OpenVMS/VAX v6.0 and later, OpenVMS/ Alpha v6.1 and later
Queue manager	Distributed	Centralized	Centralized
Queue manager fail-over	No	Yes	Yes
Queue autostart and fail-over	No	Yes	Yes

Table 8.1 *Summary of Queue-Management Changes (continued)*

Feature	VMS/VAX A5.5, OpenVMS Alpha v1.0, pre-VAX/VMS v5.5	OpenVMS v5.5, OpenVMS/Alpha v1.5	OpenVMS/VAX v6.0 and later, OpenVMS/ Alpha v6.1 and later
Multiple queue managers	No	No	Yes

The first set of queue-management changes was introduced in VAX/ VMS v5.5. At the same time, Digital provided a vA5.5 that was equivalent to v5.5, less the queue-management changes. This was to provide a smoother migration path for sites that needed v5.5 functionality, but required additional time to make changes to queue configurations. In terms of queue management, VMS/VAX v5.4 and earlier and A5.5 are identical. Since this changeover is more than 10 years old, version-specific features are not discussed further in this chapter. Only post-v6 features are described.

8.3 Queue Types

The OpenVMS queue-management subsystem allows printers and computer resources to be shared using two types of queues.

8.3.1 Print Queues

To share a printer among several users or systems, establish a print queue and associate it with a physical printer. After users submit jobs (one or more files) to the queue, the jobs are sent to the associated printer. In this way, print queues allow multiple users to submit jobs simultaneously to a single printer and continue working on the other tasks while the jobs print.

Print queues can be designated as either *generic* or *output*. An output print queue has an associated physical printer to which jobs are directed. A generic print queue serves only as a logical queue and directs jobs to one or more associated output queues. You can use generic queues to load-balance print jobs among several printers and as a method to provide better printer availability.

For example, if you had three LP37 line printers in a shipping department, you could configure a single generic queue to feed three output queues as follows:

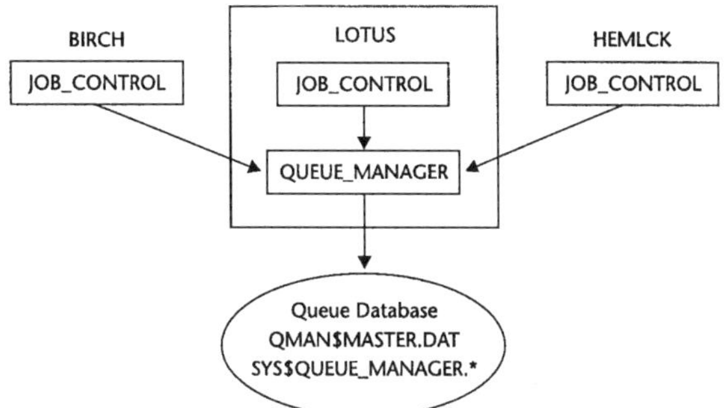

Figure 8.1 *Post-OpenVMS 5.5 Queue Manager*

```
LP37_SHIPPING                  (Generic Print Queue)
|                Device
=>  LP37_SHIPPING_1 =>    TXA0:  (Output Print queue)
=>  LP37_SHIPPING_2 =>    TXA1:         "
=>  LP37_SHIPPING_3 =>    TXA2:         "
```

When many print jobs are submitted to the generic queue (LP37_SHIPPING), they are evenly distributed for printing to the three output queues. If one of the printers fails, print jobs are directed to the remaining printers.

Printed output is frequently critical to the operation of an organization (e.g., checks, documents, invoices, and reports). Within this context, some printer failures can have a business impact as great as a complete system failure. As a result, you should give careful consideration to printer-availability requirements at your site and implement an appropriate print-queue strategy.

8.3.2 Batch Queues

Batch queues provide a mechanism to schedule, coordinate, and share access to the computer resources of a system. Users or applications submit jobs (DCL command procedures) to a batch queue. When a job is ready for execution, a process is created, and the job is executed on the system associated with the queue.

Batch queues can be designated as either *generic* or *execution* queues. Jobs submitted to an execution queue are directed to execute on the system designated by the queue. Generic batch queues direct submitted jobs to one or more associated execution queues. In this way, generic batch queues provide load-balancing and high-availability capabilities for batch execution queues.

For example, consider an OpenVMS cluster (FIRE), consisting of three AlphaServer GS320 systems (FDNY, MASON, and LAFD). You could configure a clusterwide generic batch queue (FIRE_GENERAL) to direct jobs to separate execution queues on each cluster member as follows:

```
FIRE_GENERAL             System    (Generic Batch Queue)
|
=>   FDNY_GENERAL =>     FDNY::    (Execution Batch Queue)
=>   MASON_GENERAL =>    MASON::       "
=>   LAFD_GENERAL =>     LAFD::        "
```

Batch jobs submitted to FIRE_GENERAL are directed to the execution queue on the system that is least busy. If one system fails, batch jobs can continue to be processed by the remaining execution queues.

Depending on your system configuration, you may use applications that rely heavily on batch queues. The failure of a single batch queue can render an application unavailable, even though the system as a whole is operational. As with print queues, you should carefully consider the batch-queue-availability requirements of your site.

8.4 Queue Manager

The queue manager handles batch- and print-queue-management functions such as creating, starting, and stopping queues and manipulating jobs.

The queue manager is designed using a centralized model consisting of a single, clusterwide QUEUE_MANAGER process that performs all queue-management functions. Users and the JOB_CONTROL processes on each system communicate with the QUEUE_MANAGER process by means of a shared interprocess communication (IPC) link. Because only the single QUEUE_MANAGER process accesses the queue database, contention and locking overhead are minimized, allowing better performance within environments with heavy queue activity.

8.4.1 Queue Database

The queue database stores queue and form definitions, job information, and fail-over information. This data is stored in different files as indicated in table 8.2.

Table 8.2 *Queue Database Files*

Database Item	Filename
Defined queue names	`QMAN$MASTER.DAT`
Form definitions	`QMAN$MASTER.DAT`
Queue characteristics	`SYS$QUEUE_MANAGER.QMAN$QUEUES`
Job information	`SYS$QUEUE_MANAGER.QMAN$JOURNAL`
Queue and journal names	`QMAN$MASTER.DAT`
Lists of fail-over nodes	`QMAN$MASTER.DAT`
Fail-over/recovery data	`SYS$QUEUE_MANAGER.QMAN$JOURNAL`

Within a common-environment OpenVMS cluster, a single copy of the files in table 8.2 is normally shared among cluster members and located in the directory SYS$COMMON:[SYSEXE]. Within a mixed-environment OpenVMS cluster, each cluster member typically maintains its own copy of the files, each system locating its copy in SYS$SPECIFIC:[SYSEXE].

OpenVMS supports multiple queue managers, which results in additional queue and journal files. For example, if you add a queue manager named PRINT_MGR, two additional files are created to contain queue and job information for that queue manager as follows:

```
PRINT_MGR.QMAN$QUEUES    ! Queue characteristics
PRINT_MGR.QMAN$JOURNAL   ! Job characteristics
```

8.5 Controlling the Queue Manager

Before any print- and batch-queue functions can be initiated, the queue manager must be started using the following command:

```
$ START/QUEUE/MANAGER
```

This is confirmed with the command

```
$ SHOW QUEUE/MANAGER/FULL
Master file: SYS$SYSROOT:[SYSEXE]QMAN$MASTER.DAT;
Queue manager SYS$QUEUE_MANAGER, running, on MILLER::
 /ON=(*)
 Database location: SYS$COMMON:[SYSEXE]
```

Once the queue manager is started, its state is recorded in the queue database. When you boot the system, OpenVMS checks the previous state of the queue manager and automatically returns it to its previous state. Thus, as long as the queue manager is started when you perform a system shutdown, you need not include a START/QUEUE/MANAGER command in system-startup procedures.

If your system disk is heavily used, you can move the queue-manager master file to another disk by defining a system logical name as follows:

```
$ DEFINE/SYSTEM/EXEC QMAN$MANAGER DISK$USER1:[SYSFILES]
```

To make this change permanent, add the above command to the startup procedure SYLOGICALS.COM, as discussed in chapter 5.

Likewise, the queue and journal files can be located in an alternative directory (not necessarily the same location as the master file). This is accomplished by adding a directory specification when you start the queue manager as follows:

```
$ START/QUEUE/MANAGER DISK$USER1:[SYSFILES]
```

Once you issue this command, the directory you specify is permanently stored in the queue master file; you do not have to specify it again. Table 8.3 summarizes the DCL commands you use to manage the queue manager.

8.5.1 Queue Manager Cluster Fail-Over

If the computer fails, is removed from a cluster, or is stopped, all queues serviced by that queue manager on that computer are stopped—unless the queue manager is configured for automatic fail-over. You ensure proper fail-over by specifying a fail-over-candidate list when you start the queue manager. In the following example, the preferred queue-manager node is designated as FDNY with MASON as a fail-over candidate.

Table 8.3 *Queue Manager Command Summary*

DCL Command	Behavior
START/QUEUE/MANAGER /NEW_VERSION	Creates a new queue database (use this command with extreme care because creating a new queue database deletes any previously defined queues, forms, or printer characteristics)
START/QUEUE/MANAGER	Starts the queue manager for the first time
START/QUEUE/MANAGER/ADD/NAME=SECOND	Starts another queue manager called SECOND
SHOW QUEUE/MANAGER/FULL	Displays the queue manager's status, the master-file location, and the database location
STOP/QUEUE/MANAGER	Stops the queues on the local system
STOP/QUEUE/MANAGER /CLUSTER	Stops the queue manager even on nonclustered systems

```
$ START/QUEUE/MANAGER/ON=(FDNY,MASON)
```

You can specify that all members of an OpenVMS cluster are valid fail-over candidates, as in the following example. This is the default condition.

```
$ START/QUEUE/MANAGER/ON=(*)
```

You may also want to specify a preferred queue manager and that remaining cluster members act as fail-over candidates as follows:

```
$ START/QUEUE/MANAGER/ON=(FDNY,*)
```

8.5.2 Multiple Queue Managers

In environments where there is an extremely high job-submission rate, that is, where many jobs are submitted per second, you may want to consider creating multiple queue managers. You can establish up to five queue managers per cluster. This allows you to spread the overhead generated by the queue manager among several OpenVMS cluster members. For example, in a two-node cluster consisting of members FDNY and MASON, you could establish the default queue manager on FDNY to handle all cluster batch queues, then create a second queue manager on MASON to handle all cluster print queues.

The following command establishes a second queue manager named PRINT_MGR on node MASON.

```
$ START/QUEUE/MANAGER/ADD/NAME=PRINT_MGR/ON=(MASON::,*) -
$_ DISK$USER1:[SYSFILES]
```

Presuming the above is starting a second queue manager, the following command shows the characteristics of both sharing a common database.

```
$ SHOW QUEUE/MANAGER/FULL
Master file: DISK$1USER1:[SYSFILES]QMAN$MASTER.DAT;
Queue manager PRINT_MGR, running, on MASON::
  /ON=(MASON,*)
  Database location: DISK$USER1:[SYSFILES]
Queue manager SYS$QUE_MANAGER, running, on FDNY::
  /ON=(FDNY,*)
  Database location: DISK$USER1:[SYSFILES]
```

To create queues on a specific queue manager, add the

`/NAME_OF_MANAGER`

qualifier to queue initialization commands; for example:

```
$ INITIALIZE/QUEUE/ON=LOUTS::TXA1:/NAME=PRINT_MGR SALES_LN03_2
```

There is one restriction regarding multiple queue managers. Queues running on one manager cannot reference queues running on a different queue manager. For example, generic queues and their associated execution queues must be started on the same queue manager. This means you cannot requeue a job from one queue manager to another.

8.6 Queue Naming Conventions

Once one or more queue managers are established, one or more queues must be associated with each.

You should carefully develop a queue naming convention before you begin configuring queues. Frequently, queue names are assigned with the intent of renaming them later. However, you will quickly find that so many users depend on the temporary names that changing them becomes impossible.

Queue names should be consistent, and it should be easy for users to associate a queue name with a queue. Regarding printers, users are primarily concerned with the printer type and its location. Therefore, one possible strategy is to form printer queue names with the printer *type* and *location*, separated by an underscore (_), such as *LOCATION_TYPE.*

You may want to specify location in terms of a department name, rather than a physical building or room identifier. For example, use ACCT, HR, and SHIP to specify the departments accounting, human resources, and shipping, respectively. Choose a naming convention that will not have to change as people, departments, or equipment move. Otherwise, you will spend all your time changing queue names. You can specify printer type in terms of the printer make or model (e.g., LN03, HP4P, LG31) or in a more general sense (e.g., LASER, LINE, or LABEL).

When you have multiple printers at the same location, add a sequential number or letter at the end of the queue name. If a generic queue feeds several output queues, give it the same name as the output queues, but omit the letter or number at the end of the name; for example:

```
BILLING_LP37_A     ! LP37 Line Printer in Billing Dept.
SALES_LN03_2       ! LN03 Laser Printer in Sales Dept.
HR_HPLASER_1       ! first HP Laser Printer in Human Resources
HR_HPLASER_2       ! second HP Laser Printer in Human Resources
HR_HPLASER         ! Human Resources generic queue
```

Regarding batch queues, one possible strategy is to define queue names based on the *function* of the queue and its associated *node name*, such as *NODENAME_FUNCTION.* Function might specify GENERAL, BACKUPS, BIG, MEDIUM, or SMALL for general jobs, system backups, or big, medium, and small batch jobs, respectively; for example:

```
MASON_BACKUPS   ! Queues of MASON:: for running system backups
FDNY_BIG        ! Batch queue for BIG jobs on node FDNY::
MASON_GENERAL   ! General Batch queue on node MASON::
FIRE_GENERAL    ! Cluster-wide generic queue
```

8.7 Configuring Printer Devices

Several steps are required to set up a printer, and the specific commands depend on how the printer is connected to the computer. The following list is representative:

- Terminal device (e.g., TXA0:, TTA0:)
- LAT device (e.g., LTA1:)
- Dedicated printer controller (e.g., LPA0:, LRA0:)

The following sections will examine the specific commands for each of these classes.

8.7.1 Configuring a Terminal Device

Before you can use a terminal device with a print queue, you have to configure it using the SET TERMINAL command as follows:

```
$ SET TERMINAL/qualifiers device-name
```

Depending on the device type, you may need to specify the qualifiers summarized in table 8.4.

Table 8.4 *SET TERMINAL Qualifiers*

Qualifier Keyword	Meaning
/DEVICE=*device-type*	LA34, LA100, LA210, LN03, UNKNOWN, etc.
/SPEED=*baud-rate*	1,200, 2,400, 4,800, 9,600, etc.
/NOBROADCAST	Disable system broadcast messages
/PAGE=*page-length*	Set lines per page

Table 8.4 *SET TERMINAL Qualifiers (continued)*

Qualifier Keyword	Meaning
/WIDTH=*page-width*	Set characters per line
/NOTYPE_AHEAD	Disables interactive logins
/WRAP	Wrap lines greater than *page-width* to next line
/NOWRAP	Truncate lines greater than *page-width*
/PERMANENT	Make these settings permanent

Each *device-type* has associated default characteristics for /PAGE, /WIDTH, and the like. When you issue the SET TERMINAL/DEVICE command, any characteristics you do not specify are taken from the device defaults. See SET TERMINAL documentation in the *OpenVMS DCL Dictionary* for the defaults for about 50 characteristics on approximately 25 predefined terminals; for example:

```
$ SET TERMINAL/DEVICE=LA120 TXA0:  ! Defaults to /WIDTH=132/PAGE=66
$ SET TERMINNL/DEVICE=LN03 TXA0:   ! Defaults to /WIDTH=80/PAGE=66
```

You should set /NOBROADCAST on all terminal devices used for print queues; otherwise, system broadcast messages are printed on the printer. For security purposes, you may also want to set /NOTYPE_AHEAD. This prevents someone from replacing a printer with a terminal and attempting an interactive login.

Once you have determined the appropriate SET TERMINAL commands, add them to your site-specific startup procedures. You should also add the /PERMANENT qualifier so that terminal settings stay in effect until the system is rebooted. As discussed in chapter 5, place these commands in a command procedure like STARTUP_SETTERM.COM; for example:

```
$! STARTUP_SETTERM.COM
$!...
$ SETTERM_PRT:=SET TERMINAL/PERMANENT/NOBROADCAST/WRAP/NOTYPE_AHEAD
$ SETTERM_PRT/SPEED=9600/DEVICE=LN03  TXA0:
$ SETTERM_PRT/SPEED=9600/DEVICE=LA100  TXA1:
```

8.7.2 Configuring a LAT Device

Print queues can be configured to use printers attached to ports on terminal servers or remote hosts using LAT, a proprietary protocol.

8.7.2.1 Configure the Terminal Server Port

The port on the LAT terminal server must be configured to be used by a printer rather than an interactive terminal. To configure a terminal server port, you must have access to an interactive terminal attached to the server, or initiate a connection to the server maintenance port using the OpenVMS Network Control Program (NCP).

To access the server from NCP, issue the following commands:

```
$ RUN SYS$SYSTEM:NCP   ! Run Network Control Program (NCP)
NCP> CONNECT NODE TS001 ! TS001 = terminal server name
                        ! enter terminal server password
                        ! by default, "ACCESS"
```

If you have a locally attached terminal, start from this point:

```
Local> SET PRIVILEGE  ! Enable privileged mode
Password:             ! enter privilege password
                      ! by default, "SYSTEM"
```

To connect to a server, NCP must know the server's Ethernet hardware address (the 12-digit number printed on the server chassis). If the server is not defined, you can define it manually as follows:

```
$ RUN SYS$SYSTEM:NCP
NCP> DEFINE NODE 1.100 NAME TS001 HARDWARE ADDR 08-00-2B-A1-83-BE
NCP> SET NODE 1.100 ALL
```

If you prefer not to define the node, you can explicitly specify the hardware address with the connect command as follows:

```
NCP> CONNECT VIA circuit PHYSICAL ADDRESS 08-00-2B-A1-83-BE
```

where *circuit* is the name of the Ethernet circuit for the system (e.g., BNA-0, QNA-0). Next, configure the ports to which you want to connect a printer as follows:

```
Local> DEFINE PORT 1 ACCESS REMOTE ENABLED SPEED 4800 -
    BROADCAST DISABLE NAME "PORT_1"
Local> DEFINE PORT 2 ACCESS REMOTE ENABLED SPEED 4800 -
    BROADCAST DISABLE NAME "PORT_2"
Local> LOGOUT PORT 1    ! copy permanent to volatile database
Local> LOGOUT PORT 2    ! copy permanent to volatile database
```

Table 8.5 summarizes each of the foregoing settings.

Table 8.5 *DEFINE PORT Settings*

Keyword	Purpose
REMOTE ENABLED	Configures port for printer use
SPEED 4800	Set device speed to 4,800 baud
BROADCAST DISABLE	Disable system broadcast messages
NAME ‘ ’	Name used to reference server port

If you plan to establish print queues on multiple systems that will all reference the same terminal server port, you should add the QUEUE ENABLE option to the foregoing defining statements. Terminal server port settings are saved even if the terminal server loses power. However, ports must be reconfigured if the server is replaced or reset to factory settings.

8.7.2.2 Create LAT Device

Next, use the LAT Control Program (LATCP) to create a LAT device that points to the desired terminal server and port as follows:

```
$ RUN SYS$SYSTEM:LATCP
LATCP> CREATE PORT LTA100:
LATCP> MODIFY PORT LTA100:/NODE=TS001/PORT="PORT_1"
LATCP> CREATE PORT LTA101:
LATCP> MODIFY PORT LTA101:/NODE=TS001/PORT="PORT_2"
```

Configure Device

Finally, use SET TERMINAL to configure other device characteristics not controlled at the terminal server level

```
$ SETTERM_PRT:=SET TERMINAL/PERMANENT/NOBROADCAST/WRAP/NOTYPE_AHEAD
$ SETTERM_PRT/DEVICE=LN03   LTA100:
$ SETTERM_PRT/DEVICE=LA100  LTA101:
```

As discussed in chapter 5, these commands should be added to site-specific startup procedure (e.g., STARTUP_SETTERM.COM).

8.7.3 Configuring a Local Printer Device

When print queues are established to locally connected (non-networked) printer devices, such as LPA0: or LRA0:, configure the device using the SET PRINTER command as follows:

```
$ SET PRINTER/qualifiers printer-device
```

You may need to specify one or more of the qualifiers summarized in table 8.6.

Table 8.6 *SET PRINTER Qualifiers*

Qualifier Keyword	Meaning
Printer Type	
/LP11	LP printer type (default)
/LA11	LA printer type
/LA180	LA180 printer
/UNKNOWN	Other printer type
Page Formatting	
/PAGE=*page-length*	Set lines per page (default=64)
/WIDTH=*page-width*	Set characters per line (default=132)
/UPPERCASE	Print all uppercase letters (default)
/NOUPPERCASE	Print upper and lowercase

Table 8.6 *SET PRINTER Qualifiers (continued)*

Qualifier Keyword	Meaning
/WRAP	Wrap lines greater than *page-width* to next line
/NOWRAP	Truncate lines greater than *page-width* (default)
Parallel printer communications	
/POLL	Controls the parallel port polling

For example, to configure printer device LPA0:, issue the following command:

```
$ SET PRINTER/PAGE=60/WIDTH=132/WRAP LPA0:
```

As discussed in chapter 5, add the foregoing commands to site-specific startup procedures (e.g., STARTUP_SETTERM.COM).

8.7.4 Enabling Spooling

The second step in establishing a print queue is to define spooling characteristics. When you establish a print queue and associate it with a device, all output sent to the device should originate from the queue. If you attempt to bypass the queue and send output directly to the device, the queue may fail. If you have applications that send printer output directly to a device that has an associated print queue, you should enable spooling on the device as follows:

```
$ SET DEVICE/SPOOL=(queue-name, device) printer-name:
```

For example:

```
$ SET DEVICE/SPOOL=(SALES_LN03_2, SYS$SYSDEVICE) TXA0:
```

When output is sent directly to the device TXA0:, the output is redirected to a temporary spool file on the device specified. When output is completed, the spool file is submitted as a job to the print-queue specified. In other words, spooling forces all output to a print queue. Add all spool commands to site-specific startup procedures (e.g., STARTUP_SETTERM.COM).

Spooled devices buffer files copied directly to the specified device using hidden files on the specified disk device. If you regularly copy large print jobs directly to a spooled device, you will want to ensure that sufficient free storage exists on the disk device.

8.8 Creating and Starting Print Queues

The final step is to create and start queues. Use the INITIALIZE/QUEUE and START/QUEUE commands. Specify the /NAME_OF_MANAGER command to establish or start a queue associated with an alternative queue manager.

The following sections discuss how to create and start various batch and output queues.

8.8.1 Autostart Execution Queues

Execution queues can be configured as either *autostart* or *nonautostart*. The autostart feature allows you to start and stop all autostart-enabled queues with a single command:

```
$ ENABLE AUTOSTART/QUEUES
$ DISABLE AUTOSTART/QUEUES
```

This feature greatly simplifies system-startup procedures. You may include a START/QUEUE command for each queue in the SYSTARTUP_VMS.COM procedure, but by using the autostart feature, you can replace potentially hundreds of commands with a single ENABLE AUTOSTART/QUEUES command.

Autostart queues also provide enhanced fail-over capabilities. Autostart batch queues can be configured to fail-over to an alternate cluster member if the current member fails. Similarly, autostart print queues that use LAT devices or network printers can be configured to fail-over to an alternative system and device if the current system fails. To take advantage of these features, you should configure queues for autostart whenever possible.

The following command creates an autostart print queue on node FDNY:

```
$ INITIALIZE/QUEUE/AUTOSTART_ON=FDNY::TTA1: SALES_LN03_2
```

The following command creates an autostart batch queue on node FDNY:

```
$ INITIALIZE/QUEUE/BATCH/AUTOSTART_ON=FDNY:: FDNY_GENERAL
```

Once you create a queue, its configuration is stored in the queue database—you do not have to execute the INITIALIZE command in system-startup procedures.

8.8.1.1 Starting Autostart Queues

Autostart queues are automatically started during system startup. However, if you manually stop a queue, you can restart it with the following command:

```
$ START/QUEUE queue-name
```

To manually restart all autostart queues enter the following command:

```
$ ENABLE AUTOSTART/QUEUES
```

8.8.2 Standard (Nonautostart) Execution Queues

Nonautostart queues are configured in nearly the same manner as autostart queues, except the /ON qualifier is used in place of the /AUTOSTART_ON qualifier. In addition, nonautostart queues must be individually started with a START/QUEUE or INITIALIZE/QUEUE/START command and must be explicitly started during system startup. Because this process increases the complexity of system-startup procedures, you should use standard queues only when you do not want queues to start automatically during system startup.

For example, to create a nonautostart batch queue (FDNY_GENERAL), issue the following command:

```
$ INITIALIZE/QUEUE/BATCH/ON=FDNY::FDNY_GENERAL
```

Once you create the queue, start it with the following command:

```
$ START/QUEUE FDNY_GENERAL
```

To start the queue automatically after a system reboot, add the above command to the site-specific startup procedures (e.g., STARTUP_QUEUES.COM). You can optionally add the /START qualifier to the INTIALIZE/QUEUE command, which eliminates the need for the START/QUEUE command:

```
$ INITIALIZE/QUEUE/BATCH/START/ON=FDNY:: FDNY_GENERAL
```

To create a nonautostart print queue, use the INITIALIZE/QUEUE/ON= command. For example, to create a queue SALES_LN03_2 on device TXA1 use the following command:

```
$ INITIALIZE/QUEUE/ON=FDNY::TXA1: SALES_LN03_2
```

Once the queue is created, start it with the following command:

```
$ START/QUEUE SALES_LN03_2
```

To start the queue automatically after a system reboot, add the above command to the site-specific startup procedures (e.g., STARTUP_QUEUES.COM). You can optionally add the /START qualifier to the INITIALIZE/QUEUE command, which eliminates the need for the START_QUEUE command:

```
$ INITIALIZE/QUEUE/START/ON=FDNY::TXA1: SALES_LN03_2
```

8.8.3 Generic Queues

Generic queues allow you to load-balance print and batch jobs among several printers or systems. Normally, you must use the autostart feature to configure queues for automatic fail-over. However, if you cannot configure a queue as autostart, you can achieve some level of queue fail-over capability by using generic queues.

8.8.3.1 Load-Balancing Print Queues

For example, to load-balance incoming jobs to three LP37 printers in a shipping department, create the following queues:

```
$ INITIALIZE/QUEUE/START/ON=FDNY::TXA1: LP37_SHIPPING1
$ INITIALIZE/QUEUE/START/ON=FDNY::TXA2: LP37_SHIPPING2
$ INITIALIZE/QUEUE/START/ON=FDNY::TXA3: LP37_SHIPPING3
$ INITIALIZE/QUEUE/START /GENERIC= -
_$ (LP37_SHIPPING1, LP37_SHIPPING2, LP37_SHIPPING3) LP37_SHIPPING
```

8.8.3.2 Load-Balancing Batch Queues

For example, to load-balance batch jobs among three OpenVMS cluster members, perform the following:

```
$ INITIALIZE/QUEUE/BATCH/START/ON=FDNY:: FDNY_GENERAL
$ INITIALIZE/QUEUE/BATCH/START/ON=MASON:: MASON_GENERAL
$ INITIALIZE/QUEUE/BATCH/START/ON=LAFD:: LAFD_GENERAL
$ INITIALIZE/QUEUE/START/GENERIC= -
_$ (FDNY_GENERAL,MASON_GENERAL,LAFD_GENERAL) FIRE_GENERAL
```

8.8.3.3 Automatic Fail-Over with Nonautostart Queues

To create a clusterwide print queue with automatic fail-over, create the following queues:

```
$ INITIALIZE/QUEUE/PROCESSOR=LATSYM/ON=(FDNY::LTA100)
SALES_LN03_2_FDNY
$ INITIALIZE/QUEUE/PROCESSOR=LATSYM/ON=(MASON::LTA100)
SALES_LN03_2_MASON
$ INITIALIZE/QUEUE/PROCESSOR=LATSYM/ON=(LAFD::LTA100)
SALES_LN03_2_LAFD
$ INITIALIZE/QUEUE/START/GENERIC= -
_$ (SALES_LN03_2_FDNY, SALES_LN03_2_MASON, SALES_LN03_2_LAFD)
SALES_LN03_2
```

8.8.3.4 Automatic Fail-Over with Autostart Queues

Configuring automatic fail-over with autostart queues is much simpler than it is with nonautostart queues. The following single queue accomplishes the same level of fail-over for which nonautostart queues require four queues:

```
$ INITIALIZE/QUEUE/PROCESSOR=LATSYM/AUTOSTART_ON= -
_$ (FDNY::LTA100:, MASON::LTA100:, LAFD::LTA100:) SALES_LN03_2
```

8.8.4 Default Print and Batch Queue Logical Names

By default, print and batch jobs are submitted to the queues SYS$PRINT and SYS$BATCH, respectively. Because of the implicit logical-name translation performed, you need not create queues named SYS$PRINT and SYS$BATCH. Rather, you can use queue names as descried in this chapter and define logical names to redirect print or batch submissions to the specified queues:

```
$ DEFINE/SYSTEM/EXEC SYS$BATCH FDNY_GENERAL
$ DEFINE/SYSTEM/EXEC SYS$PRINT SALES_LN03_2
```

The procedures for defining these logical names during system startup and system login are discussed in chapters 5 and 11.

8.8.5 Other Queue Characteristics

In addition to the qualifiers already discussed, several other qualifiers may be specified when creating queues. Some qualifiers are specific to batch queues, others are specific to print queues, and the rest are applicable to both, as illustrated in table 8.7.

Table 8.7 *Print and Batch Queue Characteristics*

Qualifier	Function
BATCH and PRINT	
/BASE_PRIORITY	Establishes base priority for batch jobs or base priority of symbiont process (print queues)
/WSDEFAULT /WSQUOTA /WSEXTENT	Specifies working-set parameters for batch jobs or for symbiont process (print queues)
/CHARACTERISTCS	Associates printer characteristics with queue
/DESCRIPTION	Uses text to describe queue
/RETAIN	Retains jobs in queue after processing
/OWNER_UIC	Displays owner user-identification code of queue (see chapter 17)

Table 8.7 *Print and Batch Queue Characteristics (continued)*

Qualifier	Function
/PROTECTION	Provides protection mask on queue (see chapter 17)
BATCH Only	
/CPUDEFAULT	Defaults maximum CPU time a job can use
/CPUMAXIMUM	Shows maximum CPU time a job can request
/DISABLE_SWAPPING	Prevents batch jobs from swapping
/JOB_LIMIT	Limits number of concurrent jobs being executed
PRINT Only	
/BLOCK_/LIMIT	Shows maximum allowed print-job size
/DEFAULT	Defaults flag, form, and burst pages
/DEVICE	Specifies either printer, server, or terminal
/FORM_MOUNTED	Shows mounted form being used
/LIBRARY	Provides device control library containing setup modules
/PROCESSOR	Shows printer symbiont type
/RECORD_BLOCKING	Sends individual job records in larger blocks
/SEPARATE	Controls separation pages between files and jobs
/SCHEDULE	Allows scheduling of jobs by size

These qualifiers are described in more detail in the *OpenVMS Systems Manager's Manual: Essentials* and in the *DCL Dictionary.*

8.9 Device Control Libraries

Use device control libraries to include special character sequences (escape sequences) at the beginning or end of a print job. These characters configure printer characteristics, such as the following:

- Page orientation (landscape or portrait)
- Printer font (Times Roman, Courier)
- Character point size
- Character lines per inch

A device control library contains a series of *setup modules*. Each setup module is a text file that contains escape sequences to perform certain printer functions. When you want to activate a printer function you request that the setup module be sent to the printer.

8.9.1 Create Setup Modules

You create a setup module by creating text files that contain printer programming sequences

```
$ SET DEFAULT DISK$SYS1:[SYSFILES.SETUP.LN03]
$ EDIT LANDSCAPE.TXT    ! LN03—Select Landscape Orientation
<ESC>]?21J
$ EDIT PORTRAIT.TXT     ! LN03—Select Portrait Orientation
<ESC>]?20J
$ EDIT LN03_RESET.TXT   ! LN03—Reset
<ESC>C
```

The *escape* character (<ESC>) cannot normally be entered directly and must be input using editor-specific command mechanisms, including the special insert function within EDT and compatible editors. The following sequence requires pressing the Gold key (<PF1> key on Digital keyboards), entering "27" (the ASCII code for the escape character), pressing the Gold key again, and pressing the "3" key on the terminal keypad.

```
<GOLD>27<GOLD><KEYPAD 3>
```

8.9.2 Creating a Device Control Library

Create a separate device control library for each printer type as follows:

```
$ LIBRARY/CREATE/TEXT SYS$LIBRARY:LN03_DEVCTL.TLB
```

8.9.3 Adding Modules

Add the modules as follows:

```
$ LIBRARY/INSERT/TEXT SYS$LIBRARY:LN03_DEVCTL.TLB –
_$ DISK$USER1:[SYSFILES.SETUP.LN03]*.TXT
```

8.9.4 Using Device Control Libraries

Before a setup module can be sent to a print queue, the queue must be assigned to a device control library using the /LIBRARY qualifier as follows:

```
$ INITIALIZE/QUEUE/LIBRARY=LN03_DEVCTL/SEPARATE=RESET=SOFT_RESET -
_$ SALES_LN03_2
```

The /SEPARATE qualifier forces the SOFT_RESET module to be sent to the printer after each print job. This forces the printer to reset to its default configuration, preventing one job from setting printer characteristics that conflict with future jobs. Once the queue is configured properly, include a setup module when printing a job:

```
$ PRINT/SETUP=setup-module filename
```

For example, to print a file in landscape mode, use the following:

```
$ PRINT/SETUP=LANDSCAPE filename
```

You can also associate a set module with a form definition as follows:

```
$ DEFINE/FORM LANDSCAPE 1/SETUP=LANDSCAPE
```

When you submit a print job with a form that has an associated setup module, the module is sent to the printer before the job as follows:

```
$ PRINT/FORM=LANDSCAPE filename
```

8.10 Print Forms

Print forms perform the following functions:

- Format page output (margins, page length, and page width)
- Facilitate printing on multiple paper stock

8.10.1 Creating Forms

Forms are defined using following command:

```
$ DEFINE/FORM/qualifiers form-name form-number
```

A form has the following characteristics:

```
form-name          ! form name (1-31 characters long)
form-number        ! form number (0–2 million)
```

The DEFINE/FORM qualifiers are summarized in table 8.8.

Table 8.8 *DEFINE/FORM Qualifiers*

Qualifier Keyword	Meaning
/MARGIN=	
BOTTOM=*lines*	Bottom margin
TOP=*lines*	Top margin
LEFT=*characters*	Left margin
RIGHT=*characters*	Right margin
/STOCK=*stock-name*	Paper stock that form requires (e.g., 8.5 × 11, 11 × 14)
/WRAP	if *line-width* is greater than *page-width*, then wrap to next line
/NOWRAP	if *line-width* is greater than *page-width*, then truncate
/WIDTH=*page-width*	Page width
/LENGTH=*page-length*	Page length
/SETUP=*setup-module*	Set up module to send before each job
/PAGE_SETUP=*setup-module*	Set up module to send before each page
/SHEET_FEED	For sheet-fed printers only

Table 8.8 *DEFINE/FORM Qualifiers (continued)*

Qualifier Keyword	Meaning
/DESCRIPTION="*text*"	Description of form

You can view the forms defined on your system by issuing the following command:

```
$ SHOW QUEUE/FULL/ALL/FORM
```

HP supplies the system default form (DEFAULT), which has the following characteristics:

```
Form name         Number       Description
---------         ------       -----------
DEFAULT            0        System-defined default
 /MARGIN=(BOTTOM=6) / STOCK=DEFAULT /TRUNCATE /WIDTH=132
 /LENGTH=66
```

The following commands are used to create several example forms:

```
$ DEFINE/FORM LETTERHEAD 2 -
_$ /STOCK=8_5X11/MARGIN=(TOP=10,BOTTOM=5,LEFT=10)/WIDTH=80/LENGTH=66) -
_$ /NOWRAP/DESCRIPTION="Corporate Letterhead"
$ DEFINE/FORM PLAIN 3 -
_$ /STOCK=8_5X11/MARGIN=(TOP=2,LEFT=5)/WIDTH=80/LENGTH=66)/NOWRAP -
_$ /DESCRIPTION="Plain paper"
$ DEFINE/FORM LABEL1 4 -
_$ /STOCK=1X4LABEL/MARGIN=(TOP=1,LEFT=1)/WIDTH=40/LENGTH=6) -
_$ /NOWRAP/DESCRIPTION="1 x 4 Label"
```

When you define forms, specify a stock name that represents the physical type of paper used (e.g., 8.5 × 11).

8.10.1.1 Printing Jobs Using Forms

When you create a queue, you establish the *mounted form* for the queue using the following command:

```
$ INITIALIZE/QUEUE/FORM_MOUNTED=form-name queue-name
```

By default, the mounted form for a queue is the system default form (named DEFAULT). A queue also has an associated *mounted stock* that matches the stock of the mounted form. The DEFAULT form has an associated stock also named DEFAULT.

To specify a different default mounted form (and stock) for a queue, create the queue as follows:

```
$ INITIALIZE/QUEUE/DEFAULT=FORM=form-name queue-name
```

When you submit a print job, specify its printed form using the following command:

```
$ PRINT/FORM=form-name filename
```

When a job is submitted to a queue without a specified printed form, the printed form for the job is set to the default form for the queue. Print jobs are accepted into a queue regardless of their printed form. However, a queued job can print only when the stock of the printed form matches the stock of the mounted form. When there is a stock mismatch, the queued job remains in a pending state until one of the following conditions occurs:

1. The mounted form for the queue is changed (after the correct paper stock is loaded) to a form with a stock that matches the stock for the printed job as follows:

   ```
   $ SET QUEUE/FORM_MOUNTED=form-name queue-name
   ```

2. The printed form for the job is changed to a form with stock that matches the stock of the mounted form as follows:

   ```
   $ SET ENTRY/FORM=form-name entry-number
   ```

8.11 Configuring PostScript Printers with DCPS

Compaq DECprint Supervisor (DCPS) supports approximately 100 PostScript printers manufactured by HP, Apple, Compaq, GENICOM, Lexmark, Tektronix, and Xerox. DCPS permits users to print files on PostScript level 1, 2, and 3 devices. Furthermore it will translate several other file types to PostScript, including the following:

- Printer Control Language (PCL) 4 generated for printing on HP LaserJet IID devices
- Proprinter generated for printing on IBM Proprinter XL24 devices
- ReGIS graphics (monochrome output only)
- TEKTRONIX generated for printing on TEKTRONIX 4010/4014 devices
- ASCII text to be printed with line numbers, page headers, and alternating groups of gray and white bars
- Digital Document Interchange Format (DDIF) bitonal images

Detection of the specific file type is automatic or can be directed by the user. For instance to force a ReGIS file to be translated, the user would issue the following command:

```
$ PRINT/PARAMETER=DATA_TYPE=REGIS PICTURE.REG
```

Several other options are available to control page orientation, pages per side of paper (usually four), double-sided printing, printer-tray selection, pages to print, and sheet size. These are more fully described in the Help topic called PRINT_PARAMETER and in the *Compaq DECprint Supervisor (DCPS) for OpenVMS—User's Guide.*

DCPS queues are managed as described in sections 8.8, 8.9, and 8.10, including forms and device control libraries management. Actually, DCPS is a print symbiont that sits between the job controller (and queue manager) and the device, see Figure 8.1, DCPS sends and receives printer control sequences and data.

DCPS does not support Telnet or LPD protocols. See section 8.11.1.3 to set up networked printers and section 8.12 for non-PostScript TCP/IP printer support.

8.11.1 Setting Up a PostScript Printer

DCPS will support the following non-print-server bidirectional connections:

- Serial port on the computer
- Centronics parallel port on the computer
- Raw TCP/IP, LAT, or AppleTalk

8.11.1.1 Serial Port

DCPS expects to transmit eight-bit, nonparity data streams at the fastest possible baud rate supported by the computer's serial interface device and the printer's serial port. The printer parameters must be set manually, usually from its front panel. Setting the DCPS device baud rate is described below in parameter six of the DCPS$EXECUTION_QUEUE script.

8.11.1.2 Parallel Port

The computer's parallel port must be set up with a SET PRINTER command as described in section 8.7.3. Then, the DCPS$EXECUTION_QUEUE script is used to start the queue.

8.11.1.3 Networked Connections

Raw TCP/IP, LAT, and AppleTalk connections are specified in parameter two of the DCPS$EXECUTION_QUEUE script shown in section 8.11.2. A LAT interface must be set up prior to executing the script. That procedure is described above in section 8.7.2. AppleTalk setup is beyond the scope of this book and only pertains to OpenVMS/VAX systems.

The specific protocol is called out in parameter two of the DCPS$EXECUTION_QUEUE script described in section 8.11.2. The general syntax of this parameter is as follows:

```
node::"interconnect/interconnect_specific_device_address"
```

where

- *node::* is the name of the OpenVMS cluster member on which the queue executes. If the OpenVMS system is not a member of a cluster, then *node::* can be omitted.
- *interconnect* specifies the interconnect type. You can use one of the types listed in table 8.9.

Table 8.9 *Valid DCSP Interconnects*

Purpose	Interconnect
Printers that connect through raw TCP/IP sockets	IP_RAWTCP
Printers that connect directly or through	LAT SERIAL
Print-server printers using CPAP and DECnet	DECNET
Print-server printers using CPAP and TCP/IP	IP_CPAP
Printers that connect through EtherTalk and LocalTalk protocols	APPLETALK

- *interconnect_specific_device_address* is the actual address of the printer.

  Table 8.10 shows examples of common usage.

Table 8.10 *Common DCSP Interconnect Examples*

P2 Value	Purpose
"IP_RAWTCP/199.7.45.7:9100"	Raw TCP/IP Sockets
"SERIAL/LTA101"	LAT connection unit number 101
"SERIAL/TTA0"	Direct serial connection to TTA0
"IP_CPAP/16.128.144.11"	Print-server printer on a TCP/IP network
"DECNET/MILLER"	Print-server printer on a DECnet network
"APPLETALK/Steve's Printer@MRO"	Printer on an AppleTalk network

8.11.1.4 Digital Print-Server Connections

Both TCP/IP and DECnet print servers must be running and have valid addresses assigned to them before creating a print queue with the SYS$STARTUP:DCPS$EXECUTION_QUEUE script. The operation specifics of any print server are beyond the scope of this book.

8.11.2 Creating a PostScript Print Queue

The print queue is created with a script called SYS$STARTUP:DCPS$EXECUTION_QUEUE. However, there are several prerequisites, and the easiest way to assure the correct initialization is to copy SYS$COMMON:[SYS$STARTUP]DCPS$STARTUP.TEMPLATE and edit it to meet site-specific requirements. Then, insert a call to the edited file in SYSTARTUP_VMS.COM. The .TEMPLATE file also contains limited documentation. DCPS$EXECUTION_QUEUE has eight parameters, which are briefly described in table 8.11.

Table 8.11 *DCPS$EXECUTION_QUEUE Parameters*

Parameter	Limitations	Description
P1	31 characters maximum	Unique queue name, the name of the printer
P2	See section 8.11.1.3	Interconnect protocol and device names
P3		Logical name for library(ies)
P4		Default queue parameters
P5		Default queue qualifiers (as in INITIALIZE/QUEUE)
P6	Serial only	Communication speed for serial interface only
P7	Serial only	Device characteristics (as in SET DEVICE)
P8	0 or 1	0=SET NOVERIFY, 1=SET VERIFY

8.11.3 Creating a PostScript Generic Queue

DCPS supports generic queues, which were defined in section 8.8.3. The SYS$COMMON:[SYS$STARTUP]DCPS$STARTUP.TEMPLATE contains an example script for setting up a generic queue called SYS$STARTUP:DCPS$GENERIC_QUEUE.COM. This script has five parameters, which are described in table 8.12.

Table 8.12 *DCPS$GENERIC_QUEUE Parameters*

Parameter	Limitations	Description
P1	31 characters maximum	Unique queue name
P2		Execution queue name(s)

Table 8.12 *DCPS$GENERIC_QUEUE Parameters (continued)*

Parameter	Limitations	Description
P3		Default queue parameters
P4		Default queue qualifiers (see INITIALIZE/QUEUE)
P5	0 or 1	0=SET NOVERIFY, 1=SET VERIFY

8.12 Configuring TCP/IP Printers

Most modern printers can incorporate a network interface card (NIC) and a network controller, so OpenVMS can use IP network protocols to transfer print jobs to these printers. Most older printers can be retrofitted to use an external NIC and a serial or parallel connection to the printer.

Examples of IP packages available for OpenVMS include the HP TCP/IP Services product and third-party packages such as Process Software Corporation's MultiNet package. The examples shown here assume the use of the HP TCP/IP Services package; the requirements and capabilities of other IP packages can vary.

HP TCP/IP supports three methods of communicating with a networked printer:

- TELNETSYM
- LPR/LPD
- PC-NFS

8.12.1 Configuring the Printer

Printer requirements will vary, so consult your printer documentation for specific details and settings. A few details are required for any IP-based printer: the IP address of the printer, the port, and the protocol to use. In the latter case, LPR/LPD, Telnet, and raw TCP are the most common protocol choices. The protocol choice is generally arbitrary, although you may encounter particular printers with problems with either LPR/LPD or Telnet printing. HP printers are quite commonly used with OpenVMS and with other platforms.

8.12.2 Configuring TELNETSYM

The TELNET print symbiont is quite easy to use because it is based on the queue manager discussed in the majority of this chapter. Print queues set up with this scheme are managed like any other print queue.

TELNETSYM can be configured to startup when TCP/IP is started using the TCP$CONFIG script. It can also be started and stopped independently using the scripts TCPIP$TELNETSYM_STARTUP and TCPIP$TELNETSYM_SHUTDOWN.

Two new qualifiers are required in the INITIALIZE/QUEUE command to specify this symbiont and the printer's address; for instance:

```
$ INITIALIZE /QUEUE /PROCESSOR=TCPIP$TELNETSYM -
_$ /ON="printserver.HP4_7.com:4242" HP_ACCOUNTING
```

Defining TELNETSYM logicals prior to starting the symbiont will modify its behavior. If the logical is defined, the option is ON; otherwise, it is OFF. The logicals and their meanings are described in table 8.13.

Table 8.13 *TELNETSYM Logicals*

Logical Name	Meaning
TCPIP$TELNETSYM_RAW_TCP	Suppresses all TELNET-type modifications of the print output stream
TCPIP$TELNETSYM_SUPPRESS_FORMFEEDS	Suppresses form feeds between jobs
TCPIP$TELNETSYM_VERBOSE	Turns on the logging of TELNETSYM diagnostics to the file TCPIP$TELNETSYM.LOG
TCPIP$TELNETSYM_NO_OPCOM	Stops TELNETSYM from sending messages to the operator console
TCPIP$TELNETSYM_DEBUG	Used with TCPIP$TELNETSYM_VERBOSE, tells TELNETSYM which diagnostic message types to log
TCPIP$TELNETSYM_LOG_KEEP	Limits the number of log files saved
TCPIP$TELNETSYM_SCRATCH	Changes the default directory (SYS$SPECIFIC:[TCPIP$LPD]) for one or all TELNETSYM queues
TCPIP$TELNETSYM_KEEPALIVE	Controls KEEPALIVE processing

Table 8.13 *TELNETSYM Logicals (continued)*

Logical Name	Meaning
TCPIP$TELNETSYM_DROPTIME	Controls how long a connection should be maintained
TCPIP$TELNETSYM_PROBETIME	Controls the PROBE timer
TCPIP$TELNETSYM_SNDBUF	Specifies the size of the socket send buffer that TELNETSYM uses
TCPIP$TELNETSYM_RETRY_INTERVAL	Defines the time for TELNETSYM to wait between link establishment retries, when link establishment has failed
TCPIP$TELNETSYM_IDLE_TIMEOUT	Defines the length of time to wait before terminating an inactive link
TCPIP$TELNETSYM_STREAMS	Defines the number of execution queues handled by each TELNETSYM process; the default is 16

8.12.3 Configuring LPR/LPD

As with UNIX systems, LPR provides printer services on remote hosts running the LP daemon (LPD). In HP TCP/IP, LPR is included within LPD. Both are supported by HP TCP/IP, but these services are only partially supported by the OpenVMS print symbiont as indicated in table 8.14.

Table 8.14 *LPR/LPD Commands*

Command	Meaning
PRINT	Submits a print job to a remote printer whose queue is managed by the LPD symbiont
LPRM	Removes (cancels) a pending print job previously spooled
LPQ	Views the queue of pending jobs for a remote printer

8.12.3.1 LPR/LPD Setup

Before configuring the first printer, you must enable the LPR/LPD service. This creates the necessary directories and templates. This is done in the following example. The point is that since the LPR/LPD service is disabled, it must be enabled. This example then shows what is checked and created if necessary in the TCPIP$LPD directory.

```
$ @tcpip$config
            TCP/IP Network Configuration Procedure
    This procedure helps you define the parameters required
    to run Compaq TCP/IP Services for OpenVMS on this system.
    Checking TCP/IP Services for OpenVMS configuration database files.
    Compaq TCP/IP Services for OpenVMS Configuration Menu
    Configuration options:
         1 - Core environment
         2 - Client components
         3 - Server components
         4 - Optional components
         5 - Shutdown Compaq TCP/IP Services for OpenVMS
         6 - Startup Compaq TCP/IP Services for OpenVMS
         7 - Run tests
         A - Configure options 1 - 4
        [E] - Exit configuration procedure
Enter configuration option: 3
Compaq TCP/IP Services for OpenVMS Server Components Configuration Menu
 Configuration options:
  1 - BIND       Disabled Stopped   12 - NTP        Disabled Stopped
  2 - BOOTP      Disabled Stopped   13 - PC-NFS     Disabled Stopped
  3 - DHCP       Disabled Stopped   14 - POP        Disabled Stopped
  4 - FINGER     Disabled Stopped   15 - PORTMAPPER Disabled Stopped
  5 - FTP        Disabled Stopped   16 - RLOGIN     Enabled Started
  6 - IMAP       Disabled Stopped   17 - RMT        Disabled Stopped
  7 - LBROKER    Disabled Stopped   18 - SNMP       Disabled Stopped
  8 - LPR/LPD    Disabled Stopped   19 - TELNET     Enabled Started
  9 - METRIC     Disabled Stopped   20 - TFTP       Disabled Stopped
  10 - NFS       Disabled Stopped   21 - XDM        Disabled Stopped
  11 - LOCKD/STATD Disabled Stopped

  A - Configure options 1 - 21
  [E] - Exit menu
Enter configuration option: 8
LPD Configuration
Service is not defined in the SYSUAF.
Service is defined in the TCPIP$SERVICE database.
 Application proxy is enabled.
By default, Compaq TCP/IP Services for OpenVMS configures
services to require proxies for remote access. If this
restriction is removed, any host on the network will have
```

```
unrestricted access to LPD.
 Nonprivileged user access is not enabled.
By default, Compaq TCP/IP Services for OpenVMS configures
LPD such that nonprivileged users cannot modify queue entries.
Service is not enabled.
Service is stopped.
    LPD configuration options:
         1 - Enable service on this node
         2 - Proxy access not required
         3 - Enable & Start service on this node
        [E] - Exit LPD configuration
Enter configuration option: 3
%TCPIP-I-INFO, TCPIP$AUX identifier (uic=[3655,*]) already exists
 Creating template SYS$SPECIFIC:[TCPIP$LPD]TCPIP$LPD_CONF.TEMPLATE
    Compaq TCP/IP Servics for OpenVMS supports Line Printer Daemon
    Protocol (see RFC 1179)
    LPD requires the following:
      - Name of the local queue
      - Name of the remote queue
      - Name of the remote host
      - Spooling directory for the local queue
    To add or delete printers in the TCPIP PRINTCAP database use the
    $RUN SYS$SYSTEM:TCPIP$LPRSETUP command
%TCPIP-I-INFO, image SYS$SHARE:TCPIP$LPD_SHR.EXE installed
%TCPIP-I-INFO, image SYS$SYSTEM:TCPIP$LPD_RCV.EXE installed
%TCPIP-I-INFO, logical names created
%TCPIP-I-INFO, inbound service queues started
%TCPIP-I-INFO, utility service queues started
%TCPIP-I-INFO, service enabled
%TCPIP-S-STARTDONE, TCPIP$LPD startup completed
Press Return to continue ...
```

The next step is to define the printer, as in the following example:

```
$ RUN SYS$SYSTEM:TCPIP$LPRSETUP
TCPIP Printer Setup Program

Command < add delete view help exit >: add
Adding printer entry, type '?' for help.

Enter printer name to add : LOCAL1
```

```
Enter the FULL name of one of the following printer types:
remote local : local
Enter printer synonym:

Enter full file specification for spool directory
SPOOLER DIRECTORY 'sd' : [SYS$SPECIFIC:[TCPIP$LPD.LOCAL1]] ?
Enter full file specification for printer log file.
printer error log file 'lf' [SYS$SPECIFIC:[TCPIP$LPD]LOCAL1.LOG] ?
Enter the name of the printcap symbol you want to modify. Other
valid entry is :
    'q' to quit (no more changes)

The names of the printcap symbols are:

 sd for the printer spool directory
 lf for the printer error log file
 lp for the name of the local printer
 ps for the LPD PrintServer extensions flag
 rm for the name of the remote host
 rp for the name of the remote printer
 fm for the printer form field
 pa for the /PASSALL flag
 nd for the /NODELETE flag
 cr for the cr flag
 p1-p8 for the /PARAMETER=(p1,...,p8) field

Enter symbol name: q
                  Symbol type value
                  ------ ---- -----
Error log file :  lf     STR  /SYS$SPECIFIC/TCPIP$LPD/LOCAL1.LOG
Printer Queue  :  lp     STR  LOCAL1
Spool Directory : sd     STR  /SYS$SPECIFIC/TCPIP$LPD/LOCAL1

Are these the final values for printer LOCAL1 ? [y]
Adding comments to printcap file for new printer, type '?' for help.
Do you want to add comments to the printcap file [n] ? :

    ***********************************************
    * TCPIP$LPD_SYSTARTUP.COM  TCPIP$LPD_PRINTCAP *
    *  and TCPIP$LPD_SYSHUTDOWN.COM               *
    * have been updated for this printer          *
```

```
*                                              *
* Set up activity is complete for this printer*
************************************************

Command < add delete view help exit >: exit
```

8.12.3.2 LPR/LPD Logicals

Several logicals control the behavior of LPR/LPD. Normally, they are set up when TCP/IP is started, but you may want to modify this symbiont. The logicals are summarized in table 8.15.

Table 8.15 *LPR/LPD Logicals*

Logical Name	Meaning
TCPIP$LPD_CLIENT_ENABLE	Enables the LPD client
TCPIP$LPD_PRINTCAP	Locates TCPIP$PRINTCAP.DAT
TCPIP$LPD_SPOOL	Specifies the main spooling directory
TCPIP$LPD_LOGFILE	Specifies the name of the log file for the TCPIP$LPD_QUEUE
TCPIP$LPD_KEEPALIVE	Periodically checks the other end of a link that appears to be idle; disabled by default
TCPIP$LPD_DROPTIME	Indicates how long a connection should be maintained before closing the connection
TCPIP$LPD_VMS_FLAGPAGES	Enables the OpenVMS flag-page print options on the PRINT command
TCPIP$LPD_DEBUG	Writes diagnostics to the LPD queue log file
TCPIP$LPD_RCV	Writes diagnostics to the receiver log file, TCPIP$LPD_RCV_LOGFILE.LOG

8.12.4 Configuring PC-NFS

The PC-NFS server provides authentication and print services for personal computers running PC-NFS. Users on a PC can associate the name of the PC printer with an OpenVMS print queue and, thus, print files to the associated queue.

8.12.4.1 PC-NFS Setup

PC-NSF is part of HP TCP/IP. In the example in section 8.12.3.1, note that option 13 is used to configure, start, and stop PC-NSF. The following is a portion of that dialog:

```
$ @tcpip$config
. . .
PCNFS Configuration

Service is not defined in the SYSUAF.
Service is not defined in the TCPIP$SERVICE database.
Service is not enabled.
Service is stopped.

    PCNFS configuration options:
         1 - Enable service on this node
         2 - Enable & Start service on this node
        [E] - Exit PCNFS configuration

Enter configuration option: 2

%TCPIP-I-INFO, TCPIP$AUX identifier (uic=[3655,*]) already exists
Creating PCNFS Service Entry
%TCPIP-I-INFO, image SYS$SYSTEM:TCPIP$PCNFSD.EXE installed
%TCPIP-I-INFO, service enabled
%TCPIP-S-STARTDONE, TCPIP$PCNFS startup completed

    The portmapper service is not configured to be enabled

    WARNING: PC-NFS will not function if the portmapper
         service is disabled

    You will be asked to configure the portmapper
Press Return to continue ...

PORTMAPPER Configuration

Service is not defined in the SYSUAF.
Service is not defined in the TCPIP$SERVICE database.
Service is not enabled.
```

```
Service is stopped.

    PORTMAPPER configuration options:
         1 - Enable service on this node
         2 - Enable & Start service on this node
        [E] - Exit PORTMAPPER configuration

Enter configuration option: 2

Creating PORTMAPPER Service Entry
%TCPIP-I-INFO, image SYS$SYSTEM:TCPIP$PORTMAPPER.EXE installed
%TCPIP-I-INFO, service enabled
%TCPIP-S-STARTDONE, TCPIP$PORTMAPPER startup completed
Press Return to continue ...
```

Once configured, PC-NSF will start with TCP/IP. However, it can be manually started with SYS$STARTUP:TCPIP$PCNFS_STARTUP.COM and stopped with SYS$STARTUP:TCPIP$PCNFS_SHUTDOWN.COM, if necessary.

8.12.4.2 PC-NSF Printers

To configure PC-NFS print services, you must create and export a spool directory and define two system logical names. Follow these steps when configuring your print server for printing by PC-NFS clients:

1. If one does not already exist, create a spool directory.
2. In TCP/IP, map the OpenVMS device to the spool directory path name; for example:

   ```
   TCPIP> MAP "/PC_PRINT/WORK" DSA31:
   ```

3. In TCP/IP, make the path available with the ADD EXPORT command as follows:

   ```
   TCPIP> ADD EXPORT "/PC_PRINT/WORK" /HOST=* /
   OPTIONS=TYPELESS_DIRECTORIES
   ```

4. Create or edit the SYS$STARTUP: TCPIP$PCNFS_SYSTARTUP.COM file to include the following logical-name definitions:

```
$ DEFINE /SYSTEM TCPIP$PCNFSD_SPOOLDEV DSA31:
$ DEFINE /SYSTEM TCPIP$PCNFSD_SPOOLEXPORT "/PC_PRINT/WORK"
```

The logical name TCPIP$PCNFSD_SPOOLDEV specifies the device name for the spool device. The logical name TCPIP$PCNFSD_SPOOLEXPORT specifies the exported spool directory.

8.13 Tools

For hobby and smaller systems with PC printers, a shareware tool called Mocha W32 LPD will provide an LPD on a PC. This permits ASCII printing from OpenVMS to a PC printer using LPR. See http://www.mochasoft.dk for details.

OpenVMS Management Station software provides a graphical user interface (GUI) for queue and printer management. A PC client is connected to an OpenVMS server via TCP/IP. With this package you may do the following:

- Create a printer and its queues
- Monitor printers
- Modify printer, queue, and job attributes
- Delete a printer and its queues
- Rename a printer
- Stop, start, or restart a printer or queue

8.14 Conclusion

I think the topic of printers is the most confusing part of OpenVMS; of course, it is a very complex problem. DCPS tools are probably best for rectifying this situation. However, this only applies to PostScript printers. DCPS is constantly evolving to keep up with changing printer offerings. DCPS is released in between OpenVMS releases, so pay close attention to keep up with the latest version.

8.15 Additional References

1. *OpenVMS System Manager's Manual, Volume 1: Essentials* discusses forms and device control libraries with several examples.
2. *Compaq DECprint Supervisor (DCPS) for OpenVMS* contains several volumes: *System Manager's Guide, User's Guide, Installation Guide,* and *Release Notes*. There are also separate manuals for Xerox printers.
3. *OpenVMS Management Station Overview and Release Notes* is designed to get you started.

9

Managing User Accounts

9.1 Chapter Objectives

- Standardize username formats
- Establish account groups to facilitate access control
- Ensure minimum password content standards
- Create templates for frequently added accounts
- Automate account-management functions

9.2 Introduction

The user account is the primary mechanism that the system uses to control system access and resource usage. Before a user can access the system, you must create an account for the user and assign the account sufficient resources for the user's applications.

9.3 User-Authorization Database

Account information is contained in the user-authorization database, which consists of the files in table 9.1. Logical assignments are made when the system is booted via the SYLOGICALS.COM script and are fully discussed in chapter 5.

Table 9.1 *Files in the Authorization Database*

Filename	Logical Name	Purpose
SYSUAF.DAT	SYSUAF	System UAF (user-account entries)

Table 9.1 *Files in the Authorization Database (continued)*

Filename	Logical Name	Purpose
RIGHTSLIST.DAT	RIGHTSLIST	Rights-identifier database file (all defined identifiers and holders)
NETPROXY.DAT	NETPROXY	DECnet network proxy database file (old)
NET$PROXY.DAT	NET$PROXY	DECnet network proxy database file (new)
TCPIP$PROXY.DAT	TCPIP$PROXY	TCP/IP network proxy database file

The SYSUAF file contains most of the information usually associated with an account. The RIGHTSLIST file contains the definitions for all identifiers and tracks to whom they have been granted. The NETPROXY and NET$PROXY files contain proxy definitions used to determine access from remote DECnet users, the latter being accessed by DECnet-Plus and the proxy database system services. (NET$PROXY was added in OpenVMS/VAX v6.1 and later, and in OpenVMS/Alpha v6.2 and later.) Finally, TCPIP$PROXY contains proxy definitions used to determine access from remote TCP/IP and Network File System (NFS) users. The TCP/IP command ADD PROXY manages this database. All of these files nominally reside in the SYS$SYSTEM directory, although through the use of a logical, they may be in any directory.

This chapter focuses on managing the SYSUAF file, not on TCP/IP. The procedures for managing identifiers and DECnet proxies are discussed in chapter 17.

As discussed in chapter 5, you must coordinate access to the user-authorization database files within an OpenVMS cluster environment. In a common-environment cluster, a single database is shared among cluster members and is (by default) located in a common directory: SYS$COMMON:[SYSEXE], not SYS$SPECIFIC:[SYSEXE]. In a multiple-environment cluster, the authorization database files are typically located in a device and directory that is accessible to all cluster members. This could be located in a common area on one of the system disks or on another shared disk. If multiple parallel copies of the authorization database are required on specific cluster members, the necessary copies of the SYSUAF and RIGHTSLIST files are generally located in either SYS$SPECIFIC:[SYSEXE] or SYS$COMMON:[SYSEXE].

A single authorization database greatly simplifies account administration. For example, if you have a six-member cluster that shares a single authorization database, you only have to create and maintain a single account for each user. On the other hand, with a multiple-file authorization database, a cluster with six systems would need up to six separate (and parallel) database entries for each user.

You manage entries in the SYSUAF file using the OpenVMS AUTHORIZE utility as follows:

```
$ SET DEF SYS$SYSTEM
$ RUN AUTHORIZE
UAF>
```

By default, AUTHORIZE attempts to locate the authorization database by translating the logical names discussed above. If the logical names are not defined, AUTHORIZE searches the current default directory. You should define logical names for the three database files so you will not have to set your default directory manually to SYS$SYSTEM before invoking AUTHORIZE.

You can further simplify access to AUTHORIZE by defining a symbol in your login command procedure as follows:

```
$ UAF:== $SYS$SYSTEM:AUTHORIZE    ! Define symbol
$ UAF                             ! Invoke Authorize
UAF>
```

You can simplify this using the DCL$PATH mechanism. You need to define an order and a sequence of directories to search; then, you can enter the name of a DCL command procedure or an executable image to be found within the list of directories. DCL$PATH is typically defined in the LOGIN.COM command procedure.

```
$ DEFINE DCL$PATH SYS$DISK:[],SYS$LOGIN:,SYS$SYSTEM:
$ AUTHORIZE
```

Warning: If you should mistype a command with DCL$PATH defined, and the misspelling happens to match the name of a DCL procedure or an image, you will invoke it. If you should happen to enter a command verb containing an asterisk or a percent character, you will invoke the first matching command procedure or image located. Beware the asterisk character.

Refer to chapter 11 for more information on developing login command procedures.

If you choose to maintain multiple authorization files, you must maintain the UIC values and binary values of all identifiers. While entries can be omitted, it is preferable to include all username entries in all files, with differences in the flags (e.g., DISUSER) or quota settings as required. Failure to maintain consistent UICs and identical binary identifier values across all parallel authorization files can easily lead to security lapses.

9.4 Account Characteristics

Each user account has a number of characteristics that you configure depending on the user's requirements. The following output shows the characteristics for a sample account:

```
UAF> show SROSSELET
I.      Username: SROSSELET                  Owner:  SUE ROSSELET
        Account:  CS_Fac                     UIC:    [30,2] ([SROSSELET])

II.     CLI:      DCL                        Tables: DCLTABLES
        Default:  FACULTY:[SROSSELET]
        LGICMD:   LOGIN

III.    Flags:
        Primary days:   Mon Tue Wed Thu Fri
        Secondary days:                       Sat Sun
        Primary   000000000011111111112222  Secondary 000000000011111111112222
        Day Hours 012345678901234567890123  Day Hours 012345678901234567890123
        Network:  --------#########------             --------#########------
        Batch:    --------#########------             --------#########------
        Local:    --------#########------             --------#########------
        Dialup:   --------#########------             --------#########------
        Remote:   --------#########------             --------#########------
        Expiration:            (none)    Pwdminimum:  6   Login Fails:     0
        Pwdlifetime:         90 00:00    Pwdchange:  20-MAR-1998 10:20
        Last Login: 20-MAR-1998 14:44 (interactive),
                    21-MAR-1998 10:14 (non-interactive)

IV.     Maxjobs:          0  Fillm:       100  Bytlm:         64000
        Maxacctjobs:      0  Shrfillm:      0  Pbytlm:            0
        Maxdetach:        0  BIOlm:       150  JTquota:        4096
        Prclm:            8  DIOlm:       150  WSdef:          2000
        Prio:             4  ASTlm:       250  WSquo:          4000
```

```
        Queprio:          4  TQElm:        10  WSextent:      16384
        CPU:         (none)  Enqlm:      2000  Pgflquo:       50000
V.      Authorized Privileges:
          NETMBX        TMPMBX
        Default Privileges:
          NETMBX        TMPMBX
VI.     Identifier               Value              Attributes
          PRODX_READ             %X80010002
```

Account characteristics are grouped in the following six major categories. The Roman numerals refer to the listing above.

I. User identification

II. Account defaults

III. Login attributes

IV Quotas and limits

V Privileges

VI Identifiers

9.4.1 User Identification

Username

The account *username* is a string containing between 1 and 12 alphanumeric characters, including the dollar sign ($) and underscore (_) characters. This rule follows the rule for On-Disk Structure (ODS-2) filenames. The account username provides a mechanism for the system to identify a user in a textual way. Before users can log in, they must identify themselves by supplying their username in response to the Username: login prompt; for example:

```
Username: SROSSELET
```

Each user account must have a unique username. Normally, you derive usernames by combining characters from the user's first and last names. A common strategy is to truncate the user's last name to 11 (or fewer) characters and append the first letter of the user's first name. For example, Sue Rosselet would be assigned the username SROSSELET. If the resulting username is already in use, you can add more letters from the first name until you obtain a unique username; for example:

```
SROSSELET, SUROSSLET, SUEROSSELET
```

If your site has a large number of users, you may have users with exactly the same first and last names. In that case, you may want to append characters from the user's middle name or append a sequential number. In any case, it is wise to have a systematic policy for generating usernames.

Every account and every UIC should be assigned to and used by one person. Avoid creating shared accounts like BILLING for use by several billing clerks. Individual accounts ensure that you can locate a specific person in the event of a problem or identify an individual in the event of a security breach. OpenVMS provides other powerful mechanisms for data sharing that are far preferable to overloading accounts.

User-Identification Code

Each OpenVMS file (and other system objects) has an associated owner. The user-identification code (UIC, pronounced "you-ick") is a concept inherited from RSX-11, which was a PDP-11 operating system on which OpenVMS was based. One form of the UIC is alphabetic as described in the alphanumeric UIC paragraph below. The other form is numeric. A UIC is associated with each user account and is used to determine access to and ownership of system objects, such as files, directories, devices, and queues. Refer to chapter 17 for more information on UIC-based access control.

The numeric form consists of a group number, a comma, and a member number, all enclosed in square brackets as follows:

```
[group number, member number]
```

You specify group and member numbers using octal (base 8) notation, limited to the following ranges:

```
Group: 1—37,776
Member: 0—177,776
```

Selecting appropriate UICs is one of the most important aspects of account administration. Even though the username and password control initial access, UICs determine which system objects users can access after they log in. Although it is not required, each user account should be assigned a unique UIC. If you assign the same UIC to multiple accounts, each is considered the same account in terms of access control.

Avoid using low UIC group numbers. UIC groups between one and the system parameter MAXSYSGROUP are granted system access. The MAX-

SYSGROUP setting defaults to 8, which will be displayed as 10 octal in the UIC. UIC group 1 and groups between 300 and 377 (octal) are reserved for use by HP and HP layered products. Some layered products create account with four-digit UICs.

You should organize user accounts with similar access requirements into the same UIC group; for instance, all engineering accounts should have the same group number. By grouping users in this way, you can use UIC-based protection to establish access control, rather than having to implement a more complicated access control list (ACL)–based protection scheme (see chapter 17). In a more elaborate example, you might want to organize user accounts into the UIC groups described in table 9.2.

Table 9.2 *Example UIC Assignments*

UIC Group	Organization
[100,*]	Executive staff
[200,*]	Billing department
[400,*]	Human resources
[500,*]	Shipping department
[600,*]	Data-center staff

When you add an account, specify a UIC using the following AUTHORIZE qualifier:

```
/UIC=[group, member]
```

If you maintain parallel authorization databases across multiple computers, ensure that you have parallel UIC values. Failure to maintain identical UIC-username mappings across all authorization databases can lead to unexpected access or unexpected access denial due to skewed protection masks across cluster members.

Alphanumeric UIC

An alphanumeric UIC can be specified as a synonym for the numeric UIC of an account. The alphanumeric identifier provides a more convenient way of specifying a UIC value. Alphanumeric UIC identifiers are automatically created when you add an account. By default, the alphanumeric group identifier is the username, and the alphanumeric user identifier is the username for the account enclosed in square brackets. For example, the UIC identifier for SROSSELET is listed in parentheses next to the numeric UIC for the account as follows:

```
Username: SROSSELET
...           UIC [30, 2] ([SROSSELET])
```

When you add the first account in a particular UIC group, and you specify an account name (using the /ACCOUNT qualifier), a group identifier is typically created; for example:

```
UAF> ADD SIMPSONM/ACCOUNT=HR/UIC=[400,1]
%UAF-I-ADDMSG, user record successfully added
%UAF-I-RDBADDMSGU, identifier SIMPSONM value: [000400,0000001] added ...
%UAF-I-RDBADDMSGU, identifier HR value: [000400,177777] added ...
```

The UIC group identifier is not created if the specified account field should match an existing identifier, such as an existing group identifier or an existing username-based identifier.

To explicitly add a UIC group identifier to an existing UIC group, or to rename one, use the following syntax:

```
UAF> ADD/IDENTIFIER/VALUE=UIC=[400,*] HR
%UAF-I-RDBADDMSGU, identifier HR value: [000400,177777] added ...
UAF> RENAME/IDENTIFIER HR HUM_RES
%UAF-I-RDBMDFYMSG, identifier HR modified
```

When there is a UIC group identifier, it is included in the UIC identifiers for all accounts in that same group; for example:

```
Username: SIMPSONM
...          UIC [400, 1] ([HUM_RES,SIMPSONM])
```

You can view the UIC identifier and UIC group identifiers for an account as follows:

```
UAF> SHOW/IDENTIFIER SIMPSONM
Identifier    Value     Attributes
```

```
SIMPSONM    [000400,000001]
UAF> SHOW/IDENTIFIER HUM_RES
Identifier   Value      Attributes
CHILD      [000400,177777]
```

Note that the member UIC value of the identifier HUM_RES is greater than the maximum number allowed for numeric UICs (177,776). When an identifier has a member number of 177,777, it is a group UIC identifier.

Passwords

Each account contains no passwords, a primary password, or both a primary and a secondary password. Each password can be a sequence of 0 to 31 alphanumeric characters, including the dollar sign ($) and underscore (_).

Specify password options using the following AUTHORIZE qualifiers:

```
/PASSWORD=(primary-pwd, secondary-pwd)
```

For instance:

```
/NOPASSWORD
/PASSWORD=1IS_BETTER_THAN_NONE
/PASSWORD=(NOT_SO_EASY, EVEN_HARDER1$TO_GUESS)
```

You should encourage users to include random characters or phrases, numbers, the dollar sign ($), and the underscore (_) in their passwords, to make password guessing difficult. Users should also be educated to avoid the use of names of family members, or pets, or birthdays, or sequences (e.g., helen01, helen02) or other similar information.

The secondary password mechanism should only be used on usernames that require two users present to log in. This option might occur for reasons of trusted access, as a single user possessing both passwords provides no additional security over a single password. A double-password username can only be used for local access, not for remote access.

Owner Name

The account owner is the person responsible for the account. Enter the owner name as a character string containing 1 to 31 alphanumeric characters as follows:

```
/OWNER="owner-name"
```

For instance:

```
/OWNER="Sue Rosselet"
```

If you have more than a few accounts, it is critical for good management that you set the account owner name to the full name of the user who is responsible for the account.

Incidentally, an account with two passwords has only a single username.

Account Name

Although the name is misleading, the *account* field is used to indicate the group or department with which a user is associated. It may contain 1 to 8 alphanumeric characters and is specified as follows:

```
/ACCOUNT="account-name"
```

for instance:

```
/ACCOUNT="PAYROLL"
```

9.4.2 Account Defaults

This section describes login file default fields.

9.4.2.1 Default Login Directory

The line labeled "Default:" is actually set by two qualifiers, *default device* and *default directory*, and is the default directory used after execution of system login procedures. The device name should always be expressed in a logical name, such as DISK$USER1. This allows you to move default directories from one physical disk to another without having to modify account information.

This information is configured using the following qualifiers:

```
/DEVICE=device-name:
```

For instance:

```
/DEVICE=DISK$USER1:
```

```
/DIRECTORY=[dir-name]
```

For instance:

```
/DIRECTORY=[SROSSELET]
```

9.4.2.2 Default User Login Command Procedure (LGICMD)

The default login procedure indicates the name of the DCL command procedure to be executed after the system login procedure (which is SYS$MANAGER:SYLOGIN.COM). It is specified using the following qualifiers:

```
/LGICMD=device:[directory]command-procedure
```

For instance:

```
/LGICMD=LOGIN
```

If the command procedure specified does not include a device and directory specification, this specification is taken from the default login device and directory for the account. If no login procedure is specified, LOGIN.COM is executed, if it exists. If no file extension is specified on the login file, the default file extension associated with the command-line interpreter (CLI) is used. Login command procedures are discussed in more detail in chapter 11.

9.4.2.3 Command-Line Interpreter

The CLI parameters select the default CLI the account will use. In most cases, select DCL as follows:

```
/CLI=DCL
```

The tables refer to a database used by the CLI to parse commands. Normally, this is SYS$COMMON:[SYSLIB]DCLTABLES.EXE, specified as follows:

```
/CLITABLES=DCLTABLES
```

9.4.3 Login Attributes

This section refers to Roman numeral III in the previous example. Each account has a number of characteristics that specify the following attributes.

9.4.3.1 Flags

Account flags control specific account constraints as described in table 9.3. When the qualifier is prefixed with NO, the meaning of the qualifier is complemented. For instance, /DISUSER disables the account and /NODISUSER enables the account. This double negative convention is sometimes confusing.

Table 9.3 *Account Flags*

Flag Qualifier	Meaning
Mail Attributes	
/FLAG=DISMAIL	Prevents account from receiving mail
/FLAG=DISNEWMAIL	Suppresses new mail message count at login
Login Message Restrictions	
/FLAG=DISREPORT	Suppresses login time and failure messages at login
/FLAG=DISWELCOME	Suppresses login welcome message at login
Password Attributes	
/FLAG=NODISFORCE_PWD_CHANGE	Forces password change when expired
/PWDEXPIRED	Pre-expires password
/FLAG=PWD_EXPIRED	Expires primary password
/FLAG=PWD2_EXPIRED	Expires secondary password
/FLAG=LOCKPWD	Prevents user from changing password
/FLAG=GENPWD	Forces generated passwords
/PWDMINIMUM=*min-length*	Forces password length to greater than or equal to min-length

Table 9.3 *Account Flags (continued)*

Flag Qualifier	Meaning
/PWDLIFETIME=*delta-time*	Forces regular password change
Other Security Attributes	
/FLAG=AUDIT	Enables full security auditing for the account
/FLAG=AUTOLOGIN	Restricts logins from auto login terminals (ALF)
/FLAG=DEFCLI	Forces use of default CLI and tables
/FLAG=DISUSER	Disables account
/FLAG=CAPTIVE	Configures accounts as captive account
/FLAG=DISCTLY	Disables <CTRL/Y> interrupts during the login process
/FLAG=DISIMAGE	Prevents user from being able to issue RUN command
/FLAG=RESTRICTED	Configures accounts as a restricted account
/FLAG=DISRECONNECT	Prohibits reconnect to disconnected process

Most of these characteristics are security related and are discussed in more detail in chapter 17.

9.4.3.2 Access Restrictions

The access restriction qualifiers listed in table 9.4 determine the time of day and days of the week when an account may access the system. These restrictions also specify the login mode, e.g., interactive, an account must use.

Table 9.4 *UAF Account Access Restrictions*

Access Qualifier	Controls
/ACCESS=*access-times*	Access for all login modes
/BATCH=*access-times*	Access for batch logins
/DIALUP=*access-times*	Access from dial-up terminals
/INTERACTIVE=*access-times*	Access for all interactive logins
/LOCAL=*access-times*	Access for all local logins of directly connected terminals

Table 9.4 *UAF Account Access Restrictions*

/NETWORK=*access-times*	Access for network batch logins using SET HOST
/REMOTE=*access-times*	Access for interactive remote logins using SET HOST

For example:

```
/ACCESS=(PRIMARY, 7-18)  ! Allow any access 7 A.M. to 6 P.M. (M-F)
/ACCESS=(7-19)           ! Allow any access 7 A.M. to 7 P.M. (M-S)
/NOBATCH=(7-18)        ! Prohibit batch access 7 A.M to 6 P.M. (M-S)
```

9.4.3.3 Login Statistics

Finally, login statistics and password controls are displayed. Some of these are not controllable, while others are, as described in table 9.5.

Table 9.5 *Login Statistics*

Displayed Field	Qualifier	Meaning
Expiration	/EXPIRATION	Expiration date/time; usually computed by system
Pwdminimum	/PWDMINIMUM	Minimum password length; default of six characters
Pwdlifetime	/PWDLIFETIME	Delta-time of password lifetime; default of 90 days
Pwdchange		Date of last password change
Last Login		Date of most recent login, both interactive and noninteractive (e.g., batch)

9.4.4 Quotas and Limits

Account quotas and limits restrict the amount of system resources available to users. Refer to the documentation for each application you use at your site to determine the settings they require. These quotas and limits are summarized in table 9.6.

Scheduling priority controls how and when processes are scheduled to receive CPU time. Higher-priority processes are executed first. Accounts

Table 9.6 *Quota Qualifiers*

UAF Display Title	Qualifier Name	Meaning
ASTlm	/ASTLM	Maximum outstanding asynchronous system traps
BIOlm	/BIOLM	Maximum outstanding buffered I/O requests
Bytlm	/BYTLM	Maximum byte count of outstanding buffered I/Os
CPU	/CPUTIME	Maximum amount CPU time used per session
DIOlm	/DIOLM	Maximum number of outstanding direct I/O requests
Enqlm	/ENQLM	Maximum number of locks process can own
Fillm	/FILLM	Maximum number of simultaneous files process can open
JTquota	/JTQUOTA	Bytes allocated for JOB logical names
Maxacctjobs	/MAXACCTJOBS	Maximum interactive, batch, detached processes
Maxdetach	/MAXDETACH	Maximum detached processes
Maxjobs	/MAXJOBS	Maximum interactive, batch, detached processes, and network jobs (not counting first four)
Prclm	/PRCLM	Maximum number of subprocesses
Shrfillm	/SHRFILLM	Maximum number of shared files that can be open
TQElm	/TQELM	Maximum number of outstanding timer queue entries

used for interactive purposes usually are assigned a base-scheduling priority of four. The priority qualifiers are presented in table 9.7.

Next, a number of attributes control working-set sizes, that is, the processing paging algorithm. These are shown in table 9.8.

Process priority and working sets are discussed in more detail in chapter 18.

Table 9.7 *Priority Qualifiers*

Display Title	Qualifier Name	Meaning
Prio	/PRIORITY	Default base-scheduling priority
Queprio	/QUEPRIO	Reserved for future use

Table 9.8 *Paging Control Qualifiers*

Display Title	Qualifier Name	Meaning
Pgflquo	/PGFLQUOTA	Page-file quota in pages
Wsdef	/WSDEF	Working-set default limit
Wsextent	/WSEXTENT	Working-set extent limit
Wsquo	/WSQUOTA	Working-set quota limit

9.4.5 Privileges

Account privileges extend user access and resource-usage capabilities. Each account has associated *authorized* (in the UAF) and *default* (activated at login time) privilege(s). The system manager may choose to authorize certain privileges, but not automatically activate (default) them when the user logs in. A user may activate authorized privileges after login using the following command:

```
$ SET PROCESS/PRIVILEGE=(privilege,privilege,...)
```

Thus, when users log in, their associated default privileges are automatically activated. Default and authorized privileges are configured using the following authorize qualifiers:

```
/DEFPRIVILEGE=(privilege,privilege,...)
/PRIVILEGE=(privilege,privilege,...)
```

Executable images can also be installed with privileges. This is a much safer alternative to granting privileges. Refer to chapter 17 and appendix D for more information on OpenVMS privileges.

9.4.6 Identifiers

Identifiers are used in conjunction with ACLs to provide greater flexibility in determining access to system objects. Typically, a user account is granted an identifier that either provides or restricts access to a file, queue, or other system object. Identifiers can also be associated with executable images, using the subsystem identifier mechanism. Identifiers and ACLs are discussed in detail in chapter 17.

9.5 Creating Template Accounts

HP supplies a predefined account named DEFAULT, UIC=[200,200] that automatically determines the default account attributes for newly created accounts. When you add an account and do not specify a particular account attribute, attributes are copied from the DEFAULT account. You should configure the DEFAULT account so that its attributes match those you most commonly use. This minimizes the number of account characteristics you must explicitly specify. Do not assign the DEFAULT account to any user. The out-of-the-box DEFAULT account looks as follows:

```
UAF> sho default
Username: DEFAULT                          Owner:
Account:                                   UIC:    [200,200] ([DEFAULT])
CLI:       DCL                             Tables: DCLTABLES
Default:   [USER]
LGICMD:
Flags:   DisUser
Primary days:    Mon Tue Wed Thu Fri
Secondary days:                      Sat Sun
No access restrictions
Expiration:            (none)    Pwdminimum:  6   Login Fails:      0
Pwdlifetime:         90 00:00    Pwdchange:      (pre-expired)
Last Login:            (none) (interactive),           (none) (non-interactive)
Maxjobs:             0  Fillm:        100  Bytlm:         64000
Maxacctjobs:         0  Shrfillm:       0  Pbytlm:            0
Maxdetach:           0  BIOlm:        150  JTquota:        4096
Prclm:               8  DIOlm:        150  WSdef:          2000
Prio:                4  ASTlm:        250  WSquo:          4000
Queprio:             4  TQElm:         10  WSextent:      16384
CPU:            (none)  Enqlm:       2000  Pgflquo:       50000
Authorized Privileges:
```

```
  NETMBX         TMPMBX
Default Privileges:
  NETMBX         TMPMBX
```

Notice that the default Flags is DisUser, which means no one can log in to this account. It is important to leave that field unchanged, or you might compromise your system to hackers, because this account is on all OpenVMS systems.

As an example of possible changes you may want to make to DEFAULT, you may decide that most of your accounts should have the following default attributes:

- Minimum password length of eight characters
- Password lifetime of 60 days
- Access time of Monday through Friday (8 A.M. to 7 P.M.), no weekend access

Modify the DEFAULT account as follows:

```
UAF> MODIFY DEFAULT –
      /PWDLIFETIME= "60-00:00"/PWDMINIMUM=8/ACCESS=(PRIMARY,8-19)
```

If you frequently add accounts, you should create other, more detailed template accounts for each major user group or application; for example:

```
UAF> ADD TMPL_BILLING/ACCOUNT=BILLING/FILLM=30/PGFLQUO=25000 –
     /DEVICE=USR$BILLING/FLAG=DISUSER
UAF> ADD TMPL_HR/ACCOUNT=HR/WSDEF=1000/WSQUOTA=2000/WSEXTEN=5000 –
     /DEVICE=USR$HR/UIC=[400,1]/FLAG=DISUSER
```

9.6 Managing Accounts

Now that the basic account-management tool has been described, you need to know the rest of the steps required to create an account. You must also know what is involved in deleting accounts from the database. There are also some management tricks that are convenient to use from time to time.

9.6.1 Adding New Accounts

To add a new account, perform the following steps:

- Choose a username, UIC, initial password, and default directory.
- Select the template account that most closely matches your needs.
- Determine additional qualifiers not included in the selected template.
- If you selected the DEFAULT template, simply use the authorize ADD command with any other required qualifiers; for example:

```
UAF> ADD SROSSELET/OWNER="Sue Rosselet"/UIC=[200,2] –
_UAF> /ACCOUNT="KIDS"/PASSWORD=VERY2HARD/DIR=[SROSSELET]/FLAG=NODISUSER
```

- If you selected a different template account, you must add the account by using the authorize COPY command; for example:

```
UAF> COPY DEF_BILLING SIMPSONM/OWNER="Mary Simpson" –
_UAF> /UIC=[300,2]/PASSWORD=DIFFICULT9/DIRECTORY=[SIMPSONM] /FLAG=NODISUSER
```

- Add a disk-quota entry if quotas are enabled on the user's default device (see chapter 10).
- Create the user's default directory; for example:

```
$ CREATE /DIRECTORY DISK$USER1:[SROSSELET]/OWNER=[SROSSELET]
```

  This step assumes the logical DISK$USER1 is defined and the disk is initialized. This is discussed in chapter 10.

- Create default user-login command procedures (see chapter 11). The user may choose to modify that file, so make sure the privileges are properly set.
- Add the user to mail distribution lists (see chapter 16). If your users are novices, for instance in a university environment, you may also want to create a mail folder. This is done by running a batch job in the user's account. The batch job executes a MAIL command setting the proper variables; for example:

```
$ submit/noprint/user="SROSSELET" SYS$MANAGER:MAIL_DEFAULTS
```

An example of MAIL_DEFAULTS.COM would be as follows:

```
$ MAIL
set editor EDT
set nomail_directory
set mail_directory [.MAIL]
set noforward
quit
$ EXIT
```

9.6.2 Disabling and Enabling Accounts

To enable and disable a user account temporarily, issue the following command:

```
UAF> MODIFY username/FLAG=NODISUSER ! enable account
UAF> MODIFY username/FLAG=DISUSER   ! disable account
```

NODISUSER is the default operational setting. DISUSER prohibits the user from logging in, even if the password is known. This option could be used for employees that leave the company when you do not want to delete the employee's account and all its files. The account's directory tree may contain valuable public files. You may need to move the files eventually, but do not have time in your schedule to do it immediately. Another possibility is that an employee may take an extended leave of absence, and you need to protect the account from unauthorized access, yet you want to leave the account in place.

If you DISUSER an account, it is also a good idea to disable the mail as well, so that the mailbox does not overflow. This is done with either of the following commands:

```
UAF> MODIFY username/FLAG=DISMAIL           ! disable mail delivery
UAF> MODIFY username/FLAG=(DISUSER,DISMAIL) ! disable account & mail
```

9.6.3 Deleting Accounts

To remove a user account permanently, perform the following steps:

- Archive user's files (if necessary):

```
$ BACKUP/VERIFY –
_$  DISK$USER1:[SROSSELET...]*.*;* -
_$  ARCH$DIR:SROSSELET.BCK/SAVE_SET
```

  This assumes that ARCH$DIR is a logical name pointing to a device and directory that serves as a temporary holding area for archived accounts.

- Delete default directory and subdirectories:

```
$ DELETE DISK$USER1:[SROSSELET...]*.*;*
```

  Repeat the above command until all subdirectories are deleted; then, delete the home directory:

```
$ DELETE DISK$USER1:[000000]SROSSELET.DIR;1
```

- Remove the disk-quota entry (see chapter 10) based on the UIC, not the username:

```
SYSMAN> DISKQUOTA REMOVE [SROSSELET]/DEVICE=DISK$USER1
```

- Disable the username using MODIFY/FLAG=DISUSER:

```
UAF> MODIFY SROSSELET/FLAG=DISUSER
```

  Leaving the entry in the database preserves the UIC identifier values for display purposes—should there be objects owned by the UIC—and avoids reissuing the UIC and the username to another user. It also eases re-enabling the user, should that become necessary. This is a conservative policy.

  Should you decide to remove the user account entirely, use the AUTHORIZE utility's REMOVE command:

```
UAF> REMOVE SROSSELET
```

- Remove the username from the mail profile so that e-mail can no longer be received:

```
$ MAIL
MAIL> SHOW REMOVE/USER=SROSSELET
```

- Locate all objects (e.g., files, queues, devices) with ownership or an ACL containing the user's UIC or user-specific identifiers, and any username, UIC, or identifier references stored within site-specific application databases. Remove the references. There is no tool to help with this activity. However, these identifiers are all deleted when the account is deleted, so the danger posed by dangling references is minimal.

In general, the removal of an account is difficult due to the need to locate and remove all existing references. Failure to remove these references can lead to unintended access or access-denial problems should the UIC, binary identifier value, or even the username associated with the deleted account be reused later. Often, it is simpler and more secure to leave the username and the references in place, marking the entry /FLAG=(DISUSER,DISMAIL). This also means it is far easier to reactivate the username should that later become necessary or appropriate.

9.6.4 User-Account Reporting

The following command generates a report listing all user accounts:

```
UAF> LIST [*,*] /FULL    ! Detail report sorted by UIC
UAF> LIST [*,*] /BRIEF   ! Brief report by UIC
UAF> LIST * /FULL       ! Detail report sorted by Username
UAF> LIST * /BRIEF      ! Brief report by Username
```

By default, the report is written to SYS$SYSTEM:SYSUAF.LIS. However, if you have a lot of users, this report can obvious become quite large.

9.7 Copying SYSUAF to Another System

The format and contents of the SYSUAF file are compatible across OpenVMS versions and OpenVMS platforms because it and all related files must be fully shareable across all nodes in an OpenVMS cluster. This compatibility also means you can generally copy the SYSUAF and related files to any OpenVMS system running the same or a later version. In rare instances, you may need to run a conversion tool—the details of any conversion requirements are included in the OpenVMS upgrade documentation.

Copying the RIGHTSLIST file is rather more interesting, as you must align the existing binary identifier values associated with security-relevant objects (files, queues, logical-name tables, global sections, etc.) on the target system with the binary identifier values stored in the source RIGHTSLIST. Failure to match the binary values correctly can result in unexpected access to objects or unexpected object-protection errors.

The details of copying the SYSUAF and RIGHTSLIST files closely parallel the requirements for merging the files when creating an OpenVMS cluster. The details of these procedures are included in the OpenVMS documentation set.

9.8 Tools

Several account-database-manipulation command procedures are listed in table 9.9 and described in appendix E. These are conveniently controlled with a menu. These command procedures demonstrate techniques to automate the account-management tasks discussed in this chapter.

Table 9.9 *Account-Management Tools*

Procedure Name	Function
ACCT_ADDUSER.COM	Adds new user account
ACCT_REMUSER.COM	Removes user account
ACCT_UAFRPT.COM	Produces UAF report
ACCT_MENU.COM	Provides menu to access ACCT functions

HP supplies a script in SYS$EXAMPLES called ADDUSER.COM, which can be modified to suit site requirements.

A freeware package called LAST is available at http://vms.process.com/fileserv-software.html; it provides information about when users last logged into the system. This is an extremely valuable tool for identifying inactive accounts, especially on systems with many users. LAST has several options which can be used to limit the search with various criteria (e.g., time, group, interactive only).

Another freeware package called MAILUAF, also available at http://vms.process.com/fileserv-software.html, provides a much cleaner interface to the mail profile than MAIL does. For instance:

```
MAILUAF> show SROSSELET/full
User SROSSELET subdirectory is [.MAIL]
User SROSSELET has 2 new messages
User SROSSELET has not set a forwarding address
User SROSSELET personal name is "Sue Rosselet"
User SROSSELET has not set an editor
User SROSSELET has cc prompting disabled
User SROSSELET has automatic copies to self disabled
User SROSSELET has automatic deleted message purge enabled
User SROSSELET default print queue is MCSLASER
User SROSSELET has not set a default print form
```

The OpenVMS Management Station software provides a GUI interface for account management. A PC client is connected to an OpenVMS server via TCP/IP. With this package you may do the following:

- Create user accounts
- Modify user accounts
- Delete user accounts
- Rename user accounts
- Display user accounts

9.9 Conclusion

The OpenVMS account database is quite complex and several tools are required to manage it; there is no simple shortcut for good management. In my experience, rather than learn how to manage users properly, novice managers simply give all users all privileges. This is not an intelligent choice. Obviously, this opens the door to abuses. It also makes the system vulnerable to mistakes and accidents.

The responsible manager should take the time to design the account database to accommodate all the users without compromising system security.

9.10 Additional References

1. *OpenVMS Guide to System Security* is the authority for the account database.
2. *OpenVMS System Manager's Manual, Volume 1: Essentials* contains many examples of the use of AUTHORIZE.
3. *OpenVMS Management Station Overview and Release Notes* is designed to get you started.

10

Disk-Space Management

10.1 Chapter Objectives

- Prevent application downtime resulting from insufficient disk space
- Stabilize disk-space use
- Encourage automatic disk-space reclamation by OpenVMS and users

10.2 Introduction

Users depend heavily on the availability of disk space to create new files and extend existing ones. If a disk completely runs out of space, applications can fail, and the OpenVMS system itself may hang. To prevent application downtime, proper disk-space management is essential.

An effective disk-space-management strategy should consider the following issues:

- Current and future storage requirements and technologies
- Backup strategy
- Disk cluster size
- Purging files
- File version limits
- Disk quotas
- File expiration dates
- Volume rebuilds
- System log file archiving

- Bad blocks

Users may also monitor disk usage using commands described in this chapter and in chapter 11.

10.3 Current and Future Storage Requirements

Typically, applications grow as they are improved. This means that you must plan for the addition of storage, in particular for the addition or the replacement of existing storage devices with newer storage devices. This can also involve controller and cabinetry upgrades as storage technologies change. You will also often need to plan for the off-line or near-line archiving of older data and for the migration of existing data to newer storage.

As an example of technology upgrades, older DSSI disks and cabinetry were replaced with SCSI disks, then with Fast SCSI or with UltraSCSI disks, and then with Fibre Channel or other disk storage. These upgrades provide far faster disk access, far denser storage, and far better device lifetimes. Not surprisingly, these upgrades can also lower hardware maintenance costs.

As an example of data archiving considerations, older data was often archived to nine-track magnetic tape, then to cartridge media or CD-R media. Subsequently, the oldest archival data were relocated onto newer media as the archival devices were themselves retired and replaced. Failure to move the data forward to newer media can render it unreadable or inaccessible, either due to simple media degradation or due to the retirement of the associated archival media devices.

10.4 Backup Strategy

A robust backup strategy is an important component of any disk-space-management strategy. If users do not feel comfortable with your backup strategy, they may perform their own backups by storing duplicate versions of their files. Refer to chapter 13 for a detailed discussion of backup strategies.

10.5 Disk Cluster Size

When you initialize a disk for the first time, you establish its cluster size using the following command, although normally OpenVMS defaults to the most efficient size:

```
$ INITIALIZE/CLUSTER_SIZE=n disk-name disk-label
```

A disk's cluster size specifies its minimum unit of allocation (in blocks). For example, if the cluster size of a disk is three, the size of the smallest file that can be created on that disk is three blocks, where a block is 512 bytes. Then, when the file is extended, it grows in increments of three blocks.

If you do not explicitly specify a cluster size when you initialize a disk, a default value is calculated based on the volume size and on the (version-specific) size limit of the volume storage bitmap. The permissible size of the disk volume storage bitmap was increased in OpenVMS v7.2, permitting smaller disk cluster factors to be selected than was otherwise possible with earlier versions.

A large cluster can potentially increase application file performance, but at the expense of disk space. On average, wasted space, technically called *internal fragmentation,* can be estimated by multiplying one-half the cluster factor by the number of files present. For example, a disk with a cluster size of four will have two allocated (but unused) blocks per file on average. Therefore, if you expect a disk to contain mostly small files, set its cluster size to the minimum allowed for the disk. On the other hand, if a disk has only a few large files, a larger cluster size can potentially help performance when the file is extended.

Use of the file extension size mechanism is often preferable to the use of the volume cluster factor. The file extension size can be determined on a systemwide or a volume-, file-, user-, or application-specific basis. By default, the extension size is five blocks, rounded up to the next multiple of the volume cluster factor. For users or applications that are commonly extending files, select an appropriate extension size value to reduce file fragmentation. These two values, cluster size and extend quantity, may be displayed for a particular disk with the following command:

```
$ show device/full dka0:
Disk MILLER$DKA0:, device type RZ29B, is online, mounted, file-oriented device,
   shareable, available to cluster, error logging is enabled.
```

```
   Error count                   0    Operations completed             93100
   Owner process                ""    Owner UIC                     [SYSTEM]
   Owner process ID       00000000    Dev Prot           S:RWPL,O:RWPL,G:R,W
   Reference count             348    Default buffer size                512
   Total blocks            8380080    Sectors per track                  113
   Total cylinders            3708    Tracks per cylinder                 20
   Volume label         "ALPHASYS"    Relative volume number               0
   Cluster size                  9    Transaction count                  379
   Free blocks             5943384    Maximum files allowed           419004
   Extend quantity               5    Mount count                          1
   Mount status             System    Cache name      "_MILLER$DKA0:XQPCACHE"
   Extent cache size            64    Maximum blocks in extent cache  594338
   File ID cache size           64    Blocks in extent cache          594126
   Quota cache size             64    Maximum buffers in FCP cache       205
   Volume owner UIC          [1,1]    Vol Prot    S:RWCD,O:RWCD,G:RWCD,W:RWCD
  Volume Status:  ODS-2, subject to mount verification, protected subsystems
      enabled, write-through caching enabled.
```

10.6 OpenVMS Purge Utility

By default, when you create new versions of a file, prior file versions are not deleted. This treatment is unique to OpenVMS. If you update a file frequently, you quickly accumulate many versions of the same file, perhaps needlessly consuming valuable disk space. For example, after changing the file LETTER.TXT 10 times, the following versions exist:

```
$ DIR LETTER.TXT/DATE=MODIFIED/SIZE
Directory DISK$USER1:[SIMPSONB]
LETTER.TXT;10   195   28-MAR-2003 11:34
LETTER.TXT;9    180   28-MAR-2003 11:23
LETTER.TXT;8    175   28-MAR-2003 11:04
LETTER.TXT;7    170   28-MAR-2003 10:51
LETTER.TXT;6    160   28-MAR-2003 09:54
LETTER.TXT;5    155   27-MAR-2003 19:12
LETTER.TXT;4    125   27-MAR-2003 18:32
LETTER.TXT;3    125   27-MAR-2003 18:10
LETTER.TXT;2    105   27-MAR-2003 18:02
LETTER.TXT;1    100   27-MAR-2003 13:59
Total of 10 files, 1490 blocks.
```

To delete all but the most recent version, use the DCL PURGE command as follows:

```
$ PURGE LETTER.DOC
$ DIR LETTER.DOC/DATE=MODIFIED/SIZE
Directory DISK$USER1:[SIMPSONB]
LETTER.DOC;10  100  28-FEB-2003 10:10
Total of 1 file, 100 blocks.
```

More generally, to delete all but the most recent *n* versions, use

```
$ PURGE LETTER.DOC/KEEP=n
```

If a disk contains many unneeded duplicate file versions, purge the entire disk as follows:

```
$ PURGE DISK$USER1:[000000...]*.*
```

Warning: Use PURGE with extreme caution—remember you are deleting files, and OpenVMS has no UNDELETE utility. Some users or applications may need to maintain multiple file versions. To purge while retaining the last *n* versions of each file, perform the following command:

```
$ PURGE/KEEP=n DISK$USER1:[000000...]*.*
```

Extensive file purging has a severe effect on system performance because of I/O requirements. Identify disks or directories that require regular purging, assemble appropriate PURGE commands into a DCL command procedure, and submit the procedure to run as a batch job during off hours. Refer to chapter 12 for more information on creating automated batch jobs.

10.7 File Version Limits

Every file has a version limit attribute, which specifies the maximum number of file versions that can exist at any one time. By default, files are assigned a version limit of zero, allowing an unlimited number of versions. Once you have established version limits, you do not have to perform a PURGE, because files are automatically purged each time a new version of the file is created. Some managers establish directory version limits when creating new accounts.

File version limits are established as follows:

```
$ SET FILE/VERSION_LIMIT=2 LETTER.DOC;*
$ DIR LETTER.DOC/DATE=MODIFIED/SIZE
Directory DISK$USER1:[SIMPSONB]
LETTER.DOC;2    100  28-FEB-2003
LETTER.DOC;1    100  01-JAN-2003
Total of 2 files, 200 blocks.
```

If a new version of LETTER.DOC (v3) is created, LETTER.DOC (v1) is automatically deleted:

```
$ CREATE LETTER.DOC
TEST
^Z
$ DIR LETTER.DOC/DATE=MODIFIED/SIZE
Directory DISK$USER1:[SIMPSONB]
LETTER.DOC;3      1  15-MAR-2003
LETTER.DOC;2    100  28-FEB-2003
Total of 2 files, 200 blocks.
```

Notice that v3 contains only four characters, and only one block is used, not 100 blocks like v2.

To view a file's current version limit, issue the following command:

```
$ DIR/FULL LETTER.DOC
Directory DISK$USER1:[SIMPSONB]
LETTER.DOC;2
.
.
File attributes:   Allocation: 6, Extend: 0, Global buffer
count: 0
            === >  Version limit: 2
.
.
```

Even if you carefully control the number of versions in a directory, the version number will never exceed 32,767. This is an OpenVMS file system (ODS-2) limitation. Unfortunately, when an attempt to create version 32,768 has been made, OpenVMS diagnostics are less than precise. Therefore, you must monitor for this condition. When you find a file approaching this limit, a solution is as follows:

```
$ PURGE/KEEP=3 filename.ext
$ RENAME filename.ext;-2 filename.ext;1
$ RENAME filename.ext;-1 filename.ext;2
$ RENAME filename.ext;0  filename.ext;3
```

A more elegant solution that is independent of the number of versions follows. This is easily converted to a script with one argument, the filename.

```
$! find all occurrences of filename.ext and rename them TEMP.LOG
$! Do this oldest first, i.e. ;-0 , so that the oldest version
$! of filename.ext becomes TEMP.LOG;1
$!
$loop1:
$  xfile = f$search("filename.ext;-0")
$  if xfile .eqs. "" then goto loop2
$  rename 'xfile temp.log
$  goto loop1
$endloop:
$!
$! Now rename all the TEMP.LOG back to filename.ext again,
$! oldest first, so the versions stay in the correct order
$! And TEMP.LOG;1 becomes filename.ext;1, etc.
$!
$loop2:
$  xfile = f$search("temp.log;-0")
$  if xfile .eqs. "" then goto endloop
$  fname =  "filename.ext"
$  rename 'xfile 'fname
$  goto loop2
$!
$endloop:
```

OpenVMS creates files periodically in the normal course of operation. These files are listed in table 10.1. Depending on what layered products you have installed, there may be others. Therefore you must also examine system files to see if the version numbers are approaching the 32,767 limit.

Table 10.1 *OpenVMS Files Periodically Updated*

Filename
[*]$MAIN.TPU$JOURNAL

Table 10.1 *OpenVMS Files Periodically Updated (continued)*

Filename
[*]LSE$WORK.TPU$WORK
[SYS0.SYSCOMMON.DFG$DATABASE]DFG$node.LOG
[SYS0.SYSCOMMON.SYSMGR]DECW$SM.LOG
[SYS0.SYSCOMMON.SYSMGR]SECURITY.AUDIT$JOURNAL
[SYS0.SYSERR]ERRLOG.SYS
[SYS0.SYSEXE]STARTUP.LOG
[SYS0.SYSMGR]ACCOUNTNG.DAT
[SYS0.SYSMGR]ACME$SERVER.LOG
[SYS0.SYSMGR]CLUE$STARTUP_node.LOG
[SYS0.SYSMGR]DECW$SERVER_0_ERROR.LOG
[SYS0.SYSMGR]EVL.LOG
[SYS0.SYSMGR]LAN$ACP.LOG
[SYS0.SYSMGR]OPERATOR.LOG
[VMS$COMMON.SYSEXE]SYS$TIMEZONE.DAT

10.7.1 Default File Version Limits

When you create files and directories, version limits are assigned as follows:

- When a new version of an existing file is created, its version limit is copied from the previous version of the file.
- When a new file is created, the version limit is copied from the default version limit for that directory (specified by the parent directory).
- When a new directory is created, its version limit is copied from the default version limit of its parent directory.

10.7.2 Default Directory Version Limit

Initially, directories are assigned a default version limit of zero, implying unlimited versions. You can view a directory's default version limit by issuing the following command:

```
$ DIR DKA0:[FACULTY]DMILLER.DIR/FULL
```

The version limit indicated when you issue a DIR/FULL command does not apply to the directory itself. You can view the directory version limit only by using DUMP/HEADER.

10.7.3 Establishing Version Limits

When you want to establish version limits for new directories, or directories that do not yet contain files, issue a SET DIRECTORY/VERSION_LIMIT command:

```
$ SET DIRECTORY/VERSION_LIMIT=n [.dir-name]
Directory DKA0:[FACULTY]
DMILLER.DIR;1                  File ID:  (4575,9,0)
Size:            20/27         Owner:    [DMILLER]
.
.
File attributes:    Allocation: 27, Extend: 0, Global buffer count: 0
             === >  Default version limit: 10, Contiguous, MoveFile disabled
                    Directory file
.
.
```

To establish version limits on an existing file, you must do so explicitly. For example, to establish a version limit of two on all files and subdirectories within the directory tree rooted at DISK$USER1:[SIMPSONB], do the following:

1. Ensure that users are not accessing files in the directories you want to manipulate. If users have open files, you will not be able to establish version limits.
2. Set the directory version limit of the top-level directory and all subdirectories:

   ```
   $ SET DIRECTORY/VERSION_LIMIT=2 DISK$USER1:[SIMPSONB...]
   ```

3. Set the file version limit on the most recent version of each file:

```
$ SET FILE/VERSION_LIMIT=2 DISK$USER1:[SIMPSONB...]*.*;
```

4. Use PURGE to delete extra file versions created before version limits were enabled, because setting a version limit does not delete any files:

   ```
   $ PURGE DISK$USER1:[SIMPSONB...]*.*
   ```

10.8 Disk Quotas

Left unchecked, users can consume all available space on any disk to which they have write access. By establishing disk quotas, you can restrict space usage to a specific number of blocks per user. When they exceed their allocations, users cannot use additional space; instead, they must reduce their current usage below their quota.

Disk quotas encourage users to manage their own space usage actively. Every time they approach their quota, they are forced to immediately purge or delete files. Without quotas, the manager must become more involved in policing users' disk space.

10.8.1 Disk-Quota Tools

Disk quotas are managed with the SYSMAN utility. You can also use the DISKQUOTA utility, although it is considered a retired product. SYSMAN is the preferred interface.

Disk-quota commands issued from SYSMAN have the following format:

```
$ RUN SYS$SYSTEM:SYSMAN
SYSMAN> DISKQUOTA disk-quota-command/qualifiers
```

Some commonly performed activities using DISKQUOTA are discussed in the following sections.

10.8.2 Enabling Disk Quotas

Disk quotas are enabled and disabled on a disk-by-disk basis, not at the user level. To activate disk quotas, you must first create a quota file as follows:

```
$ RUN SYS$SYSTEM:SYSMAN
SYSMAN> DISKQUOTA CREATE/DEVICE=disk-name
```

When you enter the above command, the following occurs:

- The file *disk-name:*[000000]QUOTA.SYS is created. It contains disk-quota entries and current disk-usage statistics.
- The default quota entry ([0,0], which is the same as [000000]) is added to the quota file. It determines default quotas assigned when they are not explicitly specified.
- Quota entries are added for existing users. Any user who has existing files on the disk is given a default quota.
- Disk quotas are enabled on the specified disk.

If a disk contains a QUOTA.SYS file, disk quotas are automatically enabled when the disk is mounted. Therefore, exercise care when creating a QUOTA.SYS file. Even if you manually disable quotas, they will automatically be enabled when the disk is mounted or when the system is next booted.

To enable and disable disk quotas manually, issue the following command:

```
$ RUN SYS$SYSTEM:SYSMAN
SYSMAN> DISKQUOTA ENABLE/DEVICE=disk-name
SYSMAN> DISKQUOTA DISABLE/DEVICE=disk-name
```

Anyone may use the following command to determine his or her quota and current usage:

```
$ SHOW QUOTA
  User [DMILLER] has 125982 blocks used, 74018 available,
  of 200000 authorized and permitted overdraft of 100 blocks on FACULTY
```

10.8.3 Rebuilding the Quota File

If disk quotas are disabled for a period of time, or if you suspect the quotas are wrong, you must issue a REBUILD command to update the space usage statistics recorded in the quota file:

```
$ RUN SYS$SYSTEM:SYSMAN
SYSMAN> DISKQUOTA REBUILD/DEVICE=disk-name
```

Warning: While you are rebuilding the quota file, users will not be able to allocate new space on the device. Therefore, you should only perform a rebuild when user activity is minimal. Also, be aware that disk quotas are automatically enabled after a rebuild.

10.8.4 Managing Quota Entries

After you enable disk quotas, you must manage quota entries for each user. Each entry has an associated *permanent* and *overdraft* quota specified in blocks. Users can continue to allocate disk space as long as the total space used is less than their permanent quota. Users may exceed their permanent quota to append to an existing file until the additional space used exceeds their overdraft limit.

The following illustrates disk-quota enforcement:

```
$ SHOW QUOTA
  User [SIMPSONB] has 6435 blocks used, 5 available,
  of 6440 authorized and permitted overdraft of 10000 blocks on DISK$USER1
```

This user has only five blocks of permanent disk quota available. If the user attempts to create a new file larger than five blocks, the user's disk quota will be exceeded, and the operation will not be allowed to complete:

```
$ DIRECTORY/SIZE=ALL T.TMP
Directory DISK$USER1:[SIMPSONB]
T.TMP;2                     17/18
Total of 1 file, 17/18 blocks.
$ COPY T.TMP T.TMP
%COPY-E-OPENOUT, error opening DISK$USER1:[SIMPSONB]T.TMP; as output
-RMS-E-CRE, ACP file create failed
-SYSTEM-F-EXDISKQUOTA, disk quota exceeded
%COPY-W-NOTCOPIED, DISK$USER1:[SIMPSONB]T.TMP;2 not copied
```

However, consider the following user who attempts to edit and save a file when he is nearly out of disk quota:

```
$ SHOW QUOTA
  User [SIMPSONB] has 6435 blocks used, 5 available,
  of 6440 authorized and permitted overdraft of 10000 blocks on DISK$USER1
```

```
$ EDIT T.TMP
    1 ***********************************************************
*EXIT
DISK$USER1:[SIMPSONB]T.TMP;3 100 lines
$ SHOW QUOTA
  User [SIMPSONB] has 6454 blocks used, 14 OVERDRAWN,
  of 6440 authorized and permitted overdraft of 10000 blocks on $DISK1
```

This operation was successful because the OpenVMS editor initially allocates a small file and then appends to it during the EXIT operation. Because the user had available overdraft quota, the operation was allowed to complete; thus, edits were not lost.

10.8.4.1 Adding Quota Entries

Add disk-quota entries using the following command:

```
$ RUN SYS$SYSTEM:SYSMAN
SYSMAN> DISKQUOTA ADD [uic-value]/PERMANENT=blocks /OVERDRAFT=blocks –
_SYSMAN> /DEVICE=disk-name
```

The uic-value you specify should be either the UIC or UIC alphabetic identifier (as listed in the UAF). For example, a user has the following account information:

```
Username:        SIMPSONB
UIC:           [150, 1]
UIC Identifier:   [SIMPSONB]
```

You may add a quota entry by specifying a uic-value of either [150,1] or [SIMPSONB]. You can also specify SIMPSONB. However, remember that this works because SIMPSONB is an abbreviated form of the full UIC identifier. Disk-quota entries are managed by UIC, not by username.

10.8.4.2 Listing Quota Entries

To list an existing quota entry, use the following command:

```
$ RUN SYS$SYSTEM:SYSMAN
SYSMAN> DISKQUOTA SHOW [SIMPSONB] /DEVICE=SYS$SYSDEVICE
```

```
%SYSMAN-I-QUOTA, disk quota statistics on device DISK$USER1 --
Node MILLER
     UIC                   Usage        Permanent Quota   Overdraft Limit
[SIMPSONB]                   125982        200000              100
```

To list all quota entries use the following command:

```
$ RUN SYS$SYSTEM:SYSMAN
SYSMAN> DISKQUOTA SHOW [*,*] /DEVICE=SYS$SYSDEVICE
%SYSMAN-I-QUOTA, disk quota statistics on device MILLER$DKA0: --
Node MILLER
     UIC                   Usage        Permanent Quota   Overdraft Limit
[0,0]                        0             1000                100
[1,1]                        408852        1000000             100
[SYSTEM]                     1883096       3000000             100
[DMILLER]                    125982        200000              100
[UCX$AUX,UCX$FTP]            130           1000                100
[UCX$AUX,UCX_SMTP]           50            1000                100
[UCX$AUX,UCX_LPD]            189           1000                100
[NML$SERVER]                 70            1000                100
[PHONE$SERVER]               40            1000                100
[FAL$SERVER]                 110           1000                100
[MAIL$SERVER]                90            1000                100
[376,375]                    20            1000                100
[DECNET]                     80            1000                100
[TCPIP$AUX,TCPIP$FTP]        20            100000              1000
[TCPIP$AUX,TCPIP$TFTP]       30            40000               1000
[TCPIP$AUX,TCPIP$LPD]        20            40000               1000
[TCPIP$AUX,TCPIP$PCNFS]      40            40000               1000
[TCPIP$AUX,TCPIP$PORTM]      30            40000               1000
```

Notice that certain layered products create accounts when they are installed and, therefore, are subject to the same quota rules that users follow. Therefore, it is possible for a layered product to fail because it has exceeded its disk quota.

10.8.4.3 Removing Quota Entries

To remove a disk-quota entry, use the following command:

```
$ RUN SYS$SYSTEM:SYSMAN
SYSMAN> DISKQUOTA REMOVE [uic-value]/DEVICE=disk-name
```

This operation should be included in the list of tasks that must be performed when an account is deleted.

10.8.5 Soft Disk Quotas

Enforced disk quotas are not appropriate for every situation. If users are unsophisticated or you cannot afford to risk that an application will exhaust disk quota, you may want to consider using soft disk quotas.

Soft disk quotas are established by means of the same procedures discussed in the previous sections, except each user is given a permanent quota equivalent to the disk size. This way, users can never exceed their quotas. Although soft quotas do not directly limit disk-space usage, the advantage is that now you can use the SYSMAN utility as a monitoring tool. For example, by periodically generating usage reports, you can track overall usage trends and identify which users are consuming space at the highest rate.

To generate a usage report for a particular device, use the following commands:

```
$ RUN SYS$SYSTEM:SYSMAN
SYSMAN> DISKQUOTA SHOW [*,*]/DEVICE=disk-name
```

Frequently, users do not bother deleting files simply because they do not realize just how much space they are using. With soft quotas enabled, you can add commands to system login procedures to let users know just how much they are using; for example:

```
$! SYLOGIN.COM
$!
.
.
$ SHOW QUOTA
  User [SIMPSONB] has 6443 blocks used, 93557 available,
  of 100000 authorized and permitted overdraft of 10000 blocks on
DISK$USER1
```

Another way of doing this is presented in chapter 11. Since nearly everyone overlooks informational messages, a better way to catch the user's eye is to display a report only when quota is low or exceeded. DQ.MAR is a tool you can use to perform this task.

10.8.6 Resource Identifiers

If you require a common shared storage area for a project, or if you require a shared scratch area, you can create a resource identifier and add a disk-quota entry for it. The storage requirements for files created in a directory owned by a resource identifier are charged to the resource identifier. Identifiers are described in detail in chapter 17.

10.9 Using File Expiration Dates

Each file has an associated file expiration date that can be used to determine when a file can be deleted or archived. By default, the file expiration date of each file is set to none, indicating that the file has no expiration date. To establish expiration dates, issue the following command:

```
$ SET FILE/EXPIRATION=expiration-date file-name
```

A file is considered expired when its expiration date is earlier than the current date. OpenVMS does not initiate any action when files become expired (e.g., the file is not deleted). Expired files can, however, be manipulated using date-selection qualifiers or utilities such as COPY, DELETE, DIRECTORY, and BACKUP. For example, to archive all expired files to tape and delete them from disk, issue the following command:

```
$ BACKUP/EXPIRED/SINCE=TODAY/DELETE –
      DISK$USER1:[000000...]*,*;* -
      MKA0:ARCH.BCK/SAVE_SET
```

Warning: Files that have no expiration date are considered expired (because "none" is always considered to be before the current date).

To establish expiration dates automatically for all files on a specific disk, you must enable *volume retention* by specifying a minimum and maximum retention time, using the following command:

```
$ SET VOLUME/RETENTION=(minimum-time, maximum-time) disk-name
```

The retention times must be expressed in the OpenVMS delta-time format. For example, to establish a minimum retention time of 30 days and a maximum retention time of 60 days, issue the following command:

```
$ SET VOLUME/RETENTION=("30-","60-") DISK$USER1
```

When volume retention is enabled on a disk, newly created files are assigned an expiration date equal to the sum of the current date and the maximum retention time. Then, each time a file is accessed, the sum of the current date and the minimum retention time is calculated. If this sum is a date later than the current expiration date of the file, a new expiration date is set to the sum of the current date plus the maximum retention time.

With a minimum retention time of 30 days and a maximum of 60 days, a file when it is first created or accessed is assigned an expiration date of the current time plus 60 days. Then, any accesses over the next 30 days would not cause the expiration date to be updated. If the file is accessed after the thirtieth day, its expiration date would again be set 60 days in the future. By selecting a minimum retention time that is sufficiently large, you minimize the amount of system overhead required to maintain expiration dates.

For the purposes of volume retention, only accesses with EDIT, TYPE, OPEN, or COPY constitute a file access. Although BACKUP and DIRECTORY commands access a file, they do not cause file expiration dates to be modified. For example, the following code uses BACKUP and DIRECTORY:

```
$ DIR/DATE=(MODIFIED, EXPIRED) T2.TMP
Directory DISK$USER1:[SIMPSONB]
T2.TMP;1        18-FEB-2003 13:09:14.08 19-MAY-2003 14:00:17.53
Total of 1 file.
$ BACKUP T2.TMP T3.TMP
$ DIR/DATE=(MODIFIED, EXPIRED) T2.TMP
Directory DISK$USER1:[SIMPSONB]
T2.TMP;1         18-FEB-2003 13:09:14.08 19-MAY-2003 14:00:17.53
Total of 1 file.
```

The expiration date of the file does not change. However, when COPY is used, the date does change:

```
$ SHOW TIME
  20-APR-2003 15:21:29
$ COPY T2.TMP T3.TMP
$ DIR/DATE=(MODIFIED,EXPIRED) T2.TMP
Directory DISK$USER1:[SIMPSONB]
T2.TMP;1       18-FEB-2003 13:09:14.08 19-JUN-2003 15:21:46.21
Total of 1 file.
```

Because volume retention requires several calculations and an I/O operation to update the file header, updates resulting from frequent file accesses will be folded into fewer header updates. While this will reduce the accuracy of the modification date, it will also reduce the disk I/O activity.

Enabling volume retention provides a very powerful tool for managing disk space. When files expire, you know that they have not been accessed in at least 30 days (or the minimum retention time you specify). Once you identify files that have not been accessed recently, you can ask users whether you can archive or delete their expired files. To identify the amount of disk space used by expired files, issue the following command:

```
$ DIRECTORY/EXPIRED/BEFORE=TODAY/SIZE=ALL disk-name:[000000...]
```

10.9.1 Establishing Volume Retention

When you enable volume retention, expiration dates are set only when you create or access a file. For example, enable volume retention on DISK$USER1 with the following command:

```
$ SET VOLUME/RETENTION=("30-","60-") DISK$USER1
```

The expiration dates are not automatically set, as can be seen in the following code:

```
$ DIRECTORY T.TMP/DATE=EXP
Directory DISK$USER1:[SIMPSONB]
T.TMP;6 <None specified>
T.TMP;5 <None specified>
Total of 2 files.
```

You must first access the file as follows:

```
$ SHOW TIME
  18-FEB-2003 13:05:34
$ TYPE T.TMP;*
$ DIR/DATE=(MODIFIED,EXPIRED) T.TMP
Directory DISK$USER1:[SIMPSONB]
T.TMP;6    18-FEB-2003 13:06:40.93    18-APR-2003 13:06:40.93
T.TMP;5    18-FEB-2003 13:06:41.05    18-APR-2003 13:06:41.05
Total of 2 files.
```

Note that the file expiration date is set to the current time plus the maximum retention time of 60 days. When the file is accessed 1 month (30 days) later, its expiration date is again set to the current time plus the maximum retention time of 60 days:

```
$ SHOW TIME
  20-MAR-2003 14:00:01
$ TYPE T2.TMP
ASDF
$ DIR/DATE=(MODIFIED,EXPIRED) T2.TMP
Directory $DISK1:[USER.BALDWIN]
T2.TMP;1        18-FEB-2003 13:09:14.08  19-MAY-2003 14:00:17.53
```

To force expiration dates to be updated on an entire volume, copy the entire disk to the NULL device when no files are open on the disk as follows:

```
$ COPY DISK$USER1:[000000...]*.*;* NL:
```

10.9.2 Other Selection Commands

The following are additional commands for manipulating expired files. Substitute DELETE or BACKUP for DIRECTORY to perform other functions:

```
$ DIRECTORY/BEFORE=TODAY/EXPIRED      ! list all expired files
$ DIRECTORY/SINCE="-30-"/EXPIRED      ! files that expired in the last 30 days
$ DIRECTORY/SINCE="30-"/BEFORE="59-"/EXPIRED ! all files accessed today
```

10.10 Volume Rebuild

Periodically, the amount of disk space reported by SHOW DEVICE does not indicate the correct amount of space in use. This problem occurs because space-allocation information is stored in memory and is not written to disk when disks are dismounted improperly (e.g., after a system crash). For example:

```
$ SHOW DEVICE DISK$USER1
Device     Device     Error   Volume      Free    Trans   Mnt
Name       Status     Count    Label    Blocks    Count   Cnt
DUA0:      Mounted        0    USER1     17324      118     1
```

To correct the problem issue the following command:

```
$ SET VOLUME/REBUILD DISK$USER1
$ SHOW DEVICE DISK$USER1
Device     Device     Error   Volume      Free    Trans   Mnt
Name       Status     Count    Label    Blocks    Count   Cnt
DUA0:      Mounted        0    USER1     18356      118     1
```

By default, disks are mounted with the /REBUILD option, which performs the same function as SET VOLUME/REBUILD. If you mount disks at system-startup time with the /REBUILD option, you do not need to issue a manual rebuild. However, because volume rebuilds can take a long time, many system managers mount disks with the /NOREBUILD option so that systems can recover from a crash much faster. If you use this technique (see STARTUP_MOUNT in chapter 5), you should make sure you manually rebuild each disk after a system crash using SET VOLUME/REBUILD.

Warning: Exercise care in performing volume rebuilds when users are accessing the system. Rebuilds can degrade performance on the volume being rebuilt.

10.11 Archiving System Log Files

OpenVMS maintains the log and data files listed in table 10.2, which can consume a great deal of disk space if not archived or deleted on a regular basis.

Table 10.2 *OpenVMS Log and Data Files*

Data Filename	Purpose
ACCOUNTNG.DAT	Resource accounting data
SECURITY.AUDIT$JOURNAL	Security-audit database
OPERATOR.LOG	Operator log file
ERRORLOG.SYS	Device-error log file

The following procedures restart the appropriate process, which starts a new file, then copies the old files to archive area TASM$ARCHIVE. Once all files are moved to the archive area, you can use the backup utility to archive files to tape.

Accounting Data File: ACCOUNTNG.DAT

```
$ SET ACCOUNTING/NEW_FILE
$ BACKUP/DELETE SYS$SPECIFIC:[SYSMGR]ACCOUNTNG.DAT;-1  -
_$      TASM$ARCHIVE:ACC_mmm_yy.DAT
```

Security-Audit Journal File: AUDIT$SECURITY.JOURNAL

```
$ SET AUDIT/SERVER=NEW_LOG
$ BACKUP/DELETE SYS$COMMON:[SYSMGR]SECURITY_AUDIT.AUDIT$JOURNAL,-1  -
_$      TASM$ARCHIVE:SEC_mmm_yy.DAT
```

System-Error Log File: ERRORLOG.SYS

```
$ BACKUP/DELETE SYS$SPECIFIC:[SYSERR]ERRORLOG.SYS; -
_$        TASM$ARCHIVE:ERR_mmm_yy.DAT
```

Operator Log File: OPERATOR.LOG

```
$ REPLY/ENABLE=ALL
$ REPLY/LOG
$ BACKUP/DELETE SYS$COMMON:[SYSMGR]OPERATOR.LOG;-1 -
_$      TASM$ARCHIVE:OPER_mmm_yy.DAT
```

10.12 Bad Blocks

All disk devices are eventually prone to developing bad blocks: bad areas or sectors of the disks. These bad blocks can no longer be used reliably.

SCSI disk devices typically do not provide a reliable way to recover the data from a failed disk block—from a bad block. Most SCSI disk devices will provide an indication that an error has occurred and some guess at the contents of the failed disk block.

When OpenVMS receives notification of a SCSI disk block error, the file is marked as containing an error (FORCEDERROR), and OpenVMS will not reuse the block. When the block is next rewritten, OpenVMS, the controller, and the device will together revector the data to a new block and will permanently reserve the bad block. This provides the appearance of a logically perfect disk. Unfortunately, OpenVMS may or may not be able to retrieve the original contents of the failed disk block, meaning the contents of the file may or may not be consistent.

If you do not wish to have to recover the disk data from failing blocks from available BACKUP, you will want to use the OpenVMS Volume Shadowing product or controller-based RAID. Both Volume Shadowing and controller-based RAID products are designed to mirror copies of each disk block across multiple disk volumes, reducing the exposure to a device failure or particularly to a bad block. Volume shadowing further allows the disks to be located across multiple hosts within an OpenVMS cluster.

Volume shadowing and controller-based RAID can be used together.

10.13 Tools

Two disk-management tools are listed in table 10.3.

Table 10.3 *Tools to Manage Disk Usage*

Name	Function
CUTTER.COM	Archives system log files
CHECK_DISKS.COM	Monitors disk usage

CUTTER

A DCL command procedure called CUTTER is located on the Digital Press site (see appendix E). It automatically archives system log files, as discussed in the previous sections.

CHECK_DISKS

No matter how robust your space-management strategy, some user or application will still unintentionally consume all of the disk space. Therefore, in addition to implementing the strategies discussed in this chapter, you should also deploy an automated monitoring system that notifies you when space gets low. Such a tool, CHECK_DISKS, is presented in chapter 15.

The OpenVMS Management Station software provides a GUI interface for disk management. A PC client is connected to an OpenVMS server via TCP/IP. With this package you may do the following:

- Create a volume
- Monitor volume storage
- Modify volume and device attributes
- Delete a volume and move its devices to the unassigned list
- Mount or dismount a volume
- Add or remove a volume set member

10.14 Conclusion

The manager is ultimately responsible for all data on the disks and for efficient utilization of disk resources. Even when users make mistakes, managers are often faulted for data loss. Every available tool should be used to its maximum capability to assure data integrity.

Chapter 11 discusses tools that may be used to assess disk utilization.

10.15 Additional References

1. *OpenVMS System Manager's Manual, Volume 1: Essentials* contains many examples of common uses of the commands cited in this chapter.
2. *OpenVMS System Management Utilities Reference Manual* contains detailed description of SYSMAN.
3. *OpenVMS Management Station Overview and Release Notes* is designed to get you started using this PC tool.

11

Login Command Procedures

11.1 Chapter Objectives

- Create organized login procedures
- Minimize login time
- Develop a simple menu system

11.2 Introduction

Login *command procedures* (or *scripts*) are files consisting of DCL commands that are executed during the login process. The purpose of these procedures is to customize a user's environment to facilitate a simpler user interface. Not all users have the same requirements, so you may need to establish several levels of login procedures. For example, you may need to establish a systemwide login procedure that everyone executes, a group login procedure for each major user group, and a user login procedure for each user. If you maintain an OpenVMS cluster, you may need to establish system login procedures for each cluster member.

Normally, after login procedures execute, users receive the DCL prompt and can enter DCL commands until they log out. If you have users who are unfamiliar with DCL, you can establish a login procedure that provides a menu interface with DCL. You may want to restrict access to DCL altogether by creating a captive login procedure.

Login procedures usually define symbols, logical names, and keys strokes that allow users to access their applications easily. When login procedures fail, users may not be able to access their applications. Therefore, you must be extremely careful to test changes whenever you modify login procedures.

11.3 Login Sequence

Login procedures are executed immediately after a user enters a valid username and password combination. The following steps are followed for each interactive login:

1. The logical SYS$ANNOUNCE is translated, and that message is displayed on the terminal. SYS$ANNOUNCE has two formats. Out of the box, it is defined in SYSTARTUP_VMS as follows:

```
$ DEFINE /SYSTEM SYS$ANNOUNCE -
  "Welcome to OpenVMS (TM) ''ARCH_NAME' Operating System, Version  ''F$GETSYI("VERSION")'"
```

   This displays a message like the following:

```
Welcome to OpenVMS (TM) Alpha Operating System, Version V7.3-1
```

   In this format, the message is limited to 63 characters. Messages longer than 63 characters and multiline messages must be put in a file, and the logical definition made to resemble the following:

```
$ DEFINE /SYSTEM SYS$ANNOUNCE "@ANNOUNCE.TXT"
```

2. OpenVMS then prompts the user for his or her account name and password:

```
Username: SIMPSONB
Password: password
```

   (password does not echo, nothing is displayed)

3. If the username and password are valid, the logical SYS$WELCOME is translated and displayed. Using the SYS$ANNOUNCE @-sign convention, SYS$WELCOME may also contain long messages.

4. The name of the systemwide login procedure is defined by the logical name SYS$SYLOGIN, SYS$MANAGER:SYLOGIN.COM, by default. If SYS$SYLOGIN is not defined, no system login file is executed, even if SYS$MANAGER:SYLOGIN.COM exists. This logic is not affected by the presence of /COMMAND and / NOCOMMAND on the Username prompt.

5. The user login procedure is executed next. The name of this procedure is established by the UAF SYSUAF (see chapter 9) parameters on a per-user basis. Normally, your LOGIN.COM is located in your default directory:

```
/LGICMD=default-user-login-procedure-file-name
/DEVICE=default-login-device
/DIRECTORY=default-login-directory
```

   If LGICMD is undefined, OpenVMS will execute LOGIN.COM by default if that file is present. LGICMD may be set to NL: to prohibit execution of any script.

6. Finally, OpenVMS will display the DCL prompt (unless you have modified the prompt in your LOGIN.COM script), which is the dollar sign ($).

When running DECwindows/Motif, the rules above are altered because the logical DECW$SESSIONCOM is translated; by default, it is SYS$MANANGER:DECW$STARTUSM.COM. This script will execute after the SYS$SYLOGIN and LOGIN.COM scripts. Several other DECwindows-specific scripts are executed as well. However, DECwindows is beyond the scope of this book.

The following sections discuss system- and user login procedures in more detail.

11.4 System Login Command Procedures

All login scripts are executed in the context of and with the privileges of the user's process. That is, before any script is executed, the user privileges (stored in the UAF) are assigned to the executing process. Therefore, these scripts must be executable for all users. Usually that means they have World Executable privilege.

The system login procedure is located by the system logical name SYS$SYLOGIN, which is typically defined in system-startup procedures (e.g., SYSTARTUP_VMS.COM) as follows:

```
$ DEFINE/SYSTEM/EXEC SYS$SYLOGIN SYS$COMMON:[SYSMGR]SYLOGIN.COM
```

The purpose of SYLOGIN.COM is to define frequently used DCL symbols. OpenVMS does not support systemwide symbols and systemwide logical names should be defined during system startup (see chapter 5). Groupwide logical names should be established during system startup by invoking a batch job or a detached process under the target UIC group.

Typically, SYLOGIN.COM performs the following functions:

- Disable control/Y interrupts so the user is unable to abort execution of the login scripts
- Execute mode-specific (interactive, batch, etc.) login procedures
- Configure terminal type
- Define special keys
- Define symbols
- Assign a default system printer
- Possible set default file protection
- Execute group login procedures if any
- Execute clusterwide or node-specific login procedures
- Permit or deny access to a particular cluster member.

11.4.1 Disable Interrupts

To avoid aborting the execution of system login procedures, you can temporarily disable <CTRL/Y> interrupts in SYLOGIN.COM as follows:

```
$! 'f$verify(0)'  ! silently disable DCL verification
$! SYLOGIN.COM
$!
$! Start of procedure
$ OLDCTL = F$ENVIRONMENT("CONTROL")
$ SET NOCONTROL=Y      ! Disable Interrupts  <== this is the key
$ ...Body of procedure
$! End of procedure
$ SET CONTROL='OLDCTL'      ! re-establish interrupt setting
```

However, even if you disable interrupts in this way, users can still abort the system login procedure by pressing <CTRL/Y> immediately after entering their password, before the script is started. To more effectively disable interrupts, set the UAF RESTRICTED flag on each user account as follows:

```
$ SET DEFAULT SYS$SYSTEM
$ RUN AUTHORIZE
UAF> MODIFY username /FLAGS=RESTRICTED
```

The RESTRICTED flag disables <CTRL/Y> interrupts from the moment a login is initiated, through the completion of both system and user login procedures (see chapter 9 for more information about AUTHORIZE).

11.4.2 Execute Mode-Specific Login Procedures

The system login procedure is executed not only for interactive logins, but also for network and batch logins. Network and batch jobs do not have an associated terminal; therefore, you must design login procedures so that noninteractive jobs bypass interactive-specific commands. For example, a batch job shouldn't execute a SET TERMINAL/INQURE.

To detect this, use the F$MODE lexical function to skip over inappropriate parts of your login procedure, as show in the following skeleton SYLOGIN.COM:

```
$ GOTO 'F$GETJPI("MODE")'
$!
$INTERACTIVE:
$! ... commands for interactive mode only
$ GOTO COMMON
$!
$BATCH:
$! ... commands for batch mode only
$ GOTO COMMON
$!
$NETWORK:
$! ... commands for network mode only
$ GOTO COMMON
$!
$OTHER:
$! ... commands for all modes
$COMMON:
$! ... commands in common to all modes
$ EXIT
```

11.4.2.1 Set Terminal Type

OpenVMS, most layered products, and other applications format output to terminals differently, depending on terminal type. During system startup (see chapter 5), the device characteristics for physically attached terminal ports (e.g., TXA0: and TTA0:) are configured in system-startup procedures (e.g., STARTUP_SETTERM.COM) as follows:

```
$ SET TERMINAL/DEVICE=VT300/PERMANENT TXA0:
$ SET TERMINAL/DEVICE=VT400/PERMANENT TXA1:
. . .
```

However, when users log in from the network, a terminal server, or a modem, you never know what type of terminal is being used until after they log in. Thus, in these cases terminal characteristics must be set at login. This is accomplished using the following command:

```
$ SET TERMINAL/INQUIRE
```

When the above command is issued, OpenVMS queries the terminal to send its device type, and the terminal responds by sending back a special sequence of characters. Then, OpenVMS issues the equivalent of a SET TERMINAL/DEVICE=*terminal-type*. There are two disadvantages to this inquiry mechanism:

- It can take as long as five seconds to complete.
- It requires support from the login device for the inquiry sequence.

If minimizing login time is important, you should design your login procedures so that SET TERMINAL/INQUIRE is executed only when absolutely necessary. For instance, you can pretty much assume that all logins are from VT100-supported devices.

11.4.3 Define Special Keys

To make entering commands even easier, define special keys for the most commonly used commands as follows:

```
$ DEFINE/KEY PF1 "DIRECTORY"/TERMINATE/ECHO
$ DEFINE/KEY PF2 "SET DEFAULT"/TERMINATE/ECHO
```

These two commands define the <PF1> key (on the keypad of a Digital keyboard) to echo the DIRECTORY command in a single keystroke. Likewise the <PF2> key will echo SET DEFAULT. This feature is available on all terminals and terminal emulators. However, if your users normally use PC keyboards, this convention may be a little confusing.

11.4.4 Define Global Symbols

If users execute certain DCL commands frequently, you can create symbols to make it easier for them to key; for example:

```
$ LS       :== DIRECTORY/DATE/SIZE=ALL
$ LO*GOUT  :== LOGOUT/FULL
$ LP       :== PRINT/NOTIFY
$ HOME     :== SET DEFAULT SYS$LOGIN
$ CD       :== SHOW DEFAULT
$ RM       :== DELETE/CONFIRM
```

When entering the key sequence on the left of the :==, OpenVMS executes the DCL command on the right. For instance, when RM *file.name* is keyed, OpenVMS will execute (without echoing) the DELETE/CONFIRM *file-name* command.

However, you must choose your substitutions carefully. If you choose a symbol that matches a command, you override the meaning of that command. For example, if you defined DELETE (or DEL*ETE) as a symbol for DELETE/CONFIRM, the symbol DELETE will also conflict with the use of other related DCL verbs such as DELETE/SYMBOL. That is, if you create the following symbol

```
$ DEL*ETE :== DELETE/CONFIRM
```

then when you enter

```
$ DEL/SYMBOL XYZ
```

you are actually saying

```
$ DEL/COMFIRM/SYMBOL XYZ
```

which is an illegal syntax. You will get an error message.

For this reason, the above example uses common UNIX shell commands (rm, cd, ls) instead of OpenVMS commands.

11.4.5 Assign Default System Printer

As discussed in chapter 8, when users send print jobs without explicitly specifying a print queue, that is PRINT, not PRINT/QUEUE=*name*, the jobs are sent to the queue defined by the logical name SYS$PRINT. System-startup procedures define the system logical name SYS$PRINT that defines the default system printer. However, during the login process, you can define a SYS$PRINT job logical to define a default print queue for each specific user.

In general, there are user characteristics that you may capture during the login process from which you can determine a default print queue or any other characteristic. To extract this information, add the following commands to the SYLOGIN.COM procedure:

```
$ uic_group =  f$getjpi("0","GRP")          ! UIC group
$ account =    f$getjpi("0","ACCOUNT")      ! UAF Account name
$ terminal =   f$getjpi("0","TERMINAL")     ! Terminal name
$ term_serv =  f$getdvi(terminal,"TT_ACCPORNAM")  ! remote port name
$!
$! Establish default printer based on user characteristics
$!
$ if uic_group .EQ. 150 then DEFINE/JOB SYS$PRINT SALES_LN03
$ if uic_group .EQ. 160 then DEFINE/JOB SYS$PRINT HR_LN03
$ if account .EQ. "SHIPPING" then DEFINE/JOB SYS$PRINT SHIPPING_LP37
. . .
```

For example, if all users in the sales department have the same UIC group number ([150,*]), you could automatically assign their default print queue as SALES_LN03. Alternatively, you could define SYS$PRINT in the groupwide logical-name table in SYSTARTUP_VMS as shown below:

```
$ DEFINE/TABLE=LNM$GROUP_000150 SYS$PRINT SALES_LN03
$ DEFINE/TABLE=LNM$GROUP_000160 SYS$PRINT ...
```

Of course, this assumes you have carefully assigned UICs as we encouraged you to do in chapter 9.

11.4.6 Set Default File Protection

OpenVMS establishes a default protection mask during login based on the value of the system parameter RMS_FILEPROT (use SYSMAN PARAM SHOW RMS_FILEPROT). By default, RMS_FILEPROT specifies the following protection mask:

```
(S:RWED, O:RWED, G:RE, W:)
```

When users create new files, the file is assigned the user's default protection mask. If the standard default mask specified by RMS_FILEPROT is not acceptable for your site, you should either modify RMS_FILEPROT (see chapter 17) or add a SET PROTECTION command to the login procedures. For example, to remove group read and execute protection, add the following command:

```
$ SET SECURITY/PROTECTION=(S:RWED,O:RWED,G,W)/DEFAULT
```

11.4.7 Establish Group Login Procedures

This concept is an extension of establishing printer defaults based on groups discussed in section 11.4.5. You may want to establish group login procedures to configure symbols, logical names, or both, specific to a particular set of users. For example, you could create a login procedure for the sales, human resources, and shipping groups as follows:

```
LOGIN_SALES.COM
LOGIN_HR.COM
LOGIN_SHIPPING.COM
```

Then, add conditional statements to the system login procedure to execute the appropriate group login procedure as follows:

```
$! SYLOGIN.COM
$! ...
$ uic_group = f$getjpi("0","GRP")
$ if uic_group .EQ. %o150 then @SYS$MANAGER:LOGIN_SALES
$ if uic_group .EQ. %o160 then @SYS$MANAGER:LOGIN_HR
$ if uic_group .EQ. %o170 then @SYS$MANAGER:LOGIN_SHIPPING
```

Keep in mind that the UICs you assigned in AUTHORIZE is octal. For constancy, the F$GETJPI value must be compared to an octal number, hence the %o prefix. Alternatively, you could use the account name directly, using the following construct. This is much less error prone and more flexible to expansion.

```
$! SYLOGIN.COM
$! ...
$ account = f$getjpi("0","ACCOUNT")
$ if f$search("SYS$MANAGER:LOGIN_''account'.COM") .nes. ""
$ then
$    @sys$manager:login_'account'.COM
$ endif
```

11.4.8 Establish Cluster Login Procedures

If your systems are stand-alone or members of a common-environment cluster, you can maintain a single common set of system login command procedures. On the other hand, if you maintain a multiple-environment cluster or if there are some differences in the applications available throughout the cluster, you may need a common login procedure and one or more system specific login procedures.

This can be accomplished by using the same basic strategy as for system-startup procedures (see chapter 5). If there are few differences between cluster members, you may want to maintain a common login procedure, but surround member-specific commands with IF-THEN statements; for example:

```
$! SYLOGIN.COM
$!
$ NODE = F$GETSYI("NODENAME")
$ ...
$ ... common login procedure
$ ...
$ IF NODE .EQS. "FDNY"
$ THEN
$... FDNY-specific login procedures
$ ENDIF
$ IF NODE .EQS. "MASON"
$ THEN
$ ... MASON-specific login procedure
$ ENDIF
. . .
```

On the other hand, if there are many differences between cluster members, you may want to have a common system login procedure that invokes a member-specific login procedure for each system; for example:

```
$! SYLOGIN.COM
$!
$ NODE = F$GETSYI("NODENAME")
$ ...
$ ... common login procedures
$ ...
$ if f$search("SYS$MANAGER:SYLOGIN_''NODE'.COM") .nes. ""
$ THEN
$ @SYS$MANAGER:SYLOGIN_'NODE'.COM  ! Execute system-specific procedures
$ ENDIF
$!
$! SYLOGIN_FDNY.com
$ ...
$ ...  FDNY-specific login procedure
$ ...
$!
$! SYLOGIN_MASON.COM
$ ...
$ ... MASON-specific login procedures
$ ...
```

11.4.9 Establish Template System Login Procedures

The following is an example SYLOGIN.COM that implements the techniques discussed in the previous sections:

```
$! SYLOGIN.COM       - Common login procedure
$!
$ SET NOCONTROL=Y               ! Disable interrupts
$!
$ NODE = F$GETSYI("NODENAME")
$ GOTO 'F$GETJPI("MODE")'
$! ---------------------------------------------------------
$! Perform login commands appropriate for Interactive only
$! ---------------------------------------------------------
$INTERACTIVE:
$ terminal = f$getjpi("0","TERMINAL")               ! String
```

```
$ term_serv = f$getdvi(terminal, "TT_ACCPORNAM")    ! String
$!
$! Set terminal type (unless TT or TX port)
$!
$ term_type = f$extract(0,2,f$getjpi("0","TERMINAL"))
$ dialup = f$getdvi(terminal,"TT_DIALUP")
$ if dialup
$ then
$ SET TERMINAL/INQUIRE
$ else
$ if (term_type .NES. "TX" .and. term_type .NES. "TT" then –
  SET TERMINAL/INQUIRE
$ endif
$!
$! Set DCL prompt
$!
$ SET PROMPT="''NODE'$ "
$!
$! Define Special Keys
$!
$ DEFINE/KEY PF1 "DIRECTORY"/TERMINATE/ECHO
$ DEFINE/KEY PF2 "SET DEFAULT"/TERMINATE/ECHO
$ GOTO COMMON
$! ------------------------------------------------
$! Perform login commands appropriate for BATCH only
$! ------------------------------------------------
$BATCH:
$ GOTO COMMON
$OTHER:
$ GOTO COMMON
$NETWORK:
$ GOTO COMMON
$!
$! -----------------------------------------------------
$! Perform login commands appropriate for all login modes
$! -----------------------------------------------------
$COMMON:
$ uic_group = f$getjpi("0","GRP")        ! Integer
$ account =   f$getjpi("0","ACCOUNT")    ! String
$!
$! Define system-wide symbols
```

```
$!
$ LS       :==DIRECTORY/DATE/SIZE=ALL
$ LO*GOUT :==LOGOUT/FULL
$ LPR      :==PRINT/NOTIFY
$ HOME     :==SET DEFAULT SYS$LOGIN
$ CD       :==SHOW DEFAULT
$ RM       :==DELETE/CONFIRM
$!
$! Set default file protection
$ SET SECURITY/PROTECTION=(S:RWED,O:RWED,G,W)/DEFAULT
$!
$! Execute Group Login procedure
$!
$ if f$search("SYS$MANAGER:LOGIN_''account'.COM") .nes. ""
$ then
$   @sys$manager:login_'account'.COM
$ endif
$!
$ SET CONTROL=Y          ! Enable interrupts
$!
$! Execute system-specific login procedures
$!
$ IF F$SEARCH("SYS$MANAGER:SYLOGIN_''NODE'.COM") .nes. ""
$ THEN
$   @SYS$MANAGER:SYLOGIN_'NODE'.COM
$ ENDIF
$ exit
```

When OpenVMS is installed, it conveniently writes SYS$MANAGER:SYLOGIN.TEMPLATE. This is well documented and is intended as a first cut for your version. You would do well to read the latest version on your system.

11.4.10 Develop a Disk-Quota Test

If disk quotas for the user's disk are enabled, current usage may be tested and low quotas flagged at login time. The following Macro32 program does this test. If there is enough disk quota, no message is displayed; if there are problems with the quota, the user's attention is drawn to that fact. One of two messages is displayed:

```
"***** Warning, Your disk quota has only !UL blocks remaining *****"
```

or

```
***** Warning, You have OVERDRAWN your disk quota *****
```

You may adjust the warning limit (at label 37$) as indicated below:

```
        .TITLE  DQ
; From: MX%"gessling@angelo.amd.com" 26-JAN-1995 19:51:49.30
; Subj: Check for quotas in login.com
;
...
37$:
;
;    adjust the following constant (500) to your site's policy
;
  SUBL3   #500,LEFT,LTHN           ; see if it's more than tolerance
  BGTR    50$                      ; no message if above limit
  $FAO_S  CTRSTR=FAODes, -         ; Format the output string
                OUTLEN=LENGTH, -         ; Length of output string
                OUTBUF=FAODO, -          ; Output string descriptor
                P1=<LEFT>
  BLBS    R0, 40$
  BRW     ERROR
40$:
...
ERROR:                                   ; End up here on exit and error
        $EXIT_S R0
        .END DiskQuota
```

To make an executable, enter the following two lines

```
$ MACRO DQ
$ LINK DQ
```

This routine is further discussed in section 11.9 at the end of the chapter. A RUN DQ line would be included in SYLOGIN.COM. The source code for DQ.MAR can be found on the Digital Press site.

11.5 User Login Command Procedures

After the system login procedure is executed, OpenVMS determines if a user login procedure should be executed. To determine the name of this file,

OpenVMS checks the user's UAF record. If the UAF LGICMD attribute contains a complete file specification that includes device, directory, and filename, that command procedure is executed. However, LGICMD normally contains only a filename, such as LOGIN or nothing at all. In this case, the user's default login device and directory are used to generate the complete file specification, and the extension is determined by the CLI. LGICMD may also contain the null device, NL:, which is interpreted to mean "no login file specified."

For example, if a user account has the following UAF parameters

```
LGICMD:       LOGIN
DEVICE:       DISK$USER1
DIRECTORY:    [SMITH]
CLI:          DCL
CLITABLES:    DCLTABLES
```

the default user login procedure would be

```
DISK$USER1:[SMITH]LOGIN.COM
```

As long as you design your system login procedures correctly, most users should need very few commands in their login procedures. However, more experienced users may add commands to define personal symbols, logical names, and keys to suit their needs.

It is possible to override the LGICMD specified when logging in using the following syntax:

```
Username: DMILLER/NOCOMMAND
```

This skips the execution of LOGIN.COM (but not SYLOGIN.COM). This is useful if the user makes a serious error in coding his or her login script. By not executing it, the user can still log in and then examine the file for errors. Adding a SET VERIFY at the top of the LOGIN.COM is another useful method of debugging. SET VERIFY causes all statements in the script to be displayed as they are executed.

The user may have alternative login scripts. He or she may select a specific one with the following login command:

```
Username: DMILLER/COMMAND=PAYROLL
```

This executes the PAYROLL.COM script instead of LOGIN.COM (or whatever was specified in LGICMD).

11.6 Reducing Login Time

If users experience unacceptably long login times, you should begin by identifying exactly where most of the time is being spent. You should first identify if most of time is spent in system login procedures (e.g., SYLOGIN.COM) or in user login procedures (e.g., LOGIN.COM). Start by timing the entire login process for a given user. Next, temporarily rename the user's login procedure to prevent it from executing, then time the login process again. If login time decreases considerably, you know to focus your efforts on the user login procedure; otherwise, focus on the system login procedure.

Once you isolate the problem to either the user or system procedure, the next step is to identify exactly which statements within the procedures are taking the most time. The SET PREFIX command is intended to enable checkpointing. In the following example, the 12 specifies the field width and !%T specifies that time is to be entered into the field. Notice also that the SET VERIFY is required to display the results. Output is sent to a file, not to the screen to remove I/O time from the experiment. This produces output as follows:

```
$ SET PREFIX "<!12%T>"
$ SET VERIFY
$ @SYLOGIN/OUTPUT=SYLOGIN.LOG
$ SET NOVERIFY
$ TYPE SYLOGIN.LOG
<16:33:22.11 >$! SYLOGIN.COM—Common login procedure
<16:33:22.11 >$!
<16:33:22.12 >$ SET NOCONTROL=Y          ! Disable interrupts
<16:33:22.13 >$!
<16:33:22.14 >$ NODE = F$GETSYI("NODENAME")
<16:33:22.15 >$ IF F$MODE() .EQS. "INTERACTIVE" THEN GOTO INTERACTIVE
<16:33:22.20 >$INTERACTIVE:
<16:33:22.20 >$ terminal = f$getjpi("0","TERMINAL")          ! String
<16:33:22.22 >$ term_serv = f$getdvi(terminal,"TT_ACCPORNAM") !String
<16:33:22.25 >$!
```

```
<16:33:22.26 >$! Set terminal type (unless TT or TX port)
<16:33:22.26 >$!
<16:33:22.27 >$ term_type = f$extract (0,2,fgetjpi("0","TERMINAL"))
<16:33:22.30 >$ dialup = f$getdvi(terminal, "TT_DIALUP")
......
<16:33:23.32 >$ SET NOPREFIX! turn off prefixing
```

An alternative to the SET PREFIX command can be simulated by adding the following command to key areas of your login procedures:

```
$ WRITE SYS$OUTPUT "''F$TIME()'"
```

To reduce login time focus on the following:

- Execute only the procedures that are absolutely needed. Use the F$MODE and F$GETJPI lexical functions to identify the type of user logging in and execute only the login procedures he or she needs.
- Remove duplication between user login procedures and system procedures. Make sure users don't unnecessarily add commands to their own login procedures that are already executed in system or group login procedures.
- Remove extensive comments from the execution stream. Comments take time to execute! If the procedure is extensively commented, place comments at the end of the command procedure after an EXIT statement, or code a GOTO around them.
- Use system- or group-level logical names or shared logical-name tables when appropriate. If all users need the same logical name, define a system- or group-level logical name during system-startup procedures.
- Evaluate the need to rewrite login procedures in a compiled language (see section 11.6.1).

11.6.1 Compiled Login Procedures

If you define many symbols or logical names in login procedures (and are using an older and slower VAX system), you may find that these commands contribute substantially to login time. In these cases, you may want to recode symbol and logical-name definitions using a compiled language (e.g., C, FORTRAN, or Macro).

The following is a sample Macro32 program that defines a number of global symbols using the run-time library routine LIB$SET_SYMBOL. This same strategy can be used for logical names using the routine LIB$SET_LOGICAL.

```
; DEFINE_SYMB.MAR
;
; Procedure to define global symbols
;
     .TITLE DEFINE_SYMB
$SSDEF                                    ; System status values
;+
; Declare external routines
;-
    .EXTRN LIB$SET_SYMBOL
    .SBTTL RO_DATA - Read Only DATA
    .PSECT RO_DATA RD,NOWRT,NOEXE
; Declare definitions and their symbols in pairs
SYMBOLS:
    .ASCID "SET DEFAULT"                  ; Symbol Value
    .ASCID "CD"                           ; Symbol Name
    .ASCID "$AUTHORIZE"
    .ASCID "UAF"
    .ASCID "$SYSMAN"
    .ASCID "SYSMAN"
    .ASCID "REPLY/STATUS"
    .ASCID "STATUS"
    ; add more definitions here
    ; ....
    .LONG 0                              ; End of list
; The following routine accesses the definitions above and runs them through
; LIB$SET_SYMBOL to define each symbol.
GLOBAL_SYM:.LONG LIB$K_CLI_GLOBAL_SYM    ; Select Global symbols tbl
    .SBTTL CODE—Start of program
    .PSECT CODE RD,NOWRT,EXE
    .ENTRY DEFINE_SYMB ^M<>
    MOVAQ SYMBOLS,R3             Start w/ first symbol
10$:
    TSTL (R3)                    ; Check for end of table
```

```
    BEQL 20$                        ; If 0, done
    PUSHAL GLOBAL_SYM               ; Make it a GLOBAL symbol
    PUSHL R3                        ; Push address of symbol name
                                    ; Compute address of symbol value
    ADDW (R3),R3                    ; + length of symbol name
    ADDL #8,R3                      ; + 8 more bytes to skip descriptor
    PUSHL R3                        ; Push address of symbol value
    CALLS #3,G^LIB$SET_SYMBOL       ; Define it
    ADDW (R3),R3                    ; Move to next symbol name
    ADDL #8,R3                      ; + 8 bytes to skip descriptor
    BRB 10$                         ; do it again
20$: RET
    .END DEFINE_SYMB
```

Create the foregoing program using any Compaq editor and add your site-specific symbols. Then, compile and link it as follows:

```
$ MACRO DEFINE_SYMB
$ LINK DEFINE_SYMB
```

To see how it works, first see if SYSMAN is defined (normally, it is not). Now, run the program with RUN DEFINE_SYMB and check SYSMAN again. Now it is defined.

```
$ SHOW SYMBOL/GLOBAL SYSMAN
%DCL-W-UNDSYM, undefined symbol—check validity and spelling
$ RUN DEFINE_SYMB
$ SHOW SYMBOL/GLOBAL SYSMAN
  SYSMAN == "$SYSMAN"
```

As you can see, after DEFINE_SYMB is executed, the symbol SYSMAN is defined. To use this technique, remove equivalent DCL commands from the SYLOGIN.COM script and replace them with the RUN command; for example:

```
$! SYLOGIN.COM
$!
$! ....
$ RUN SYS$MANAGER:DEFINE_SYMB
$ ...
```

Using a compiled language as in the above example provides several advantages over using DCL. First, compiled code generally executes faster than comparable DCL statements as long as you need to define more than a few symbols. Starting up an executable image consumes some overhead, so using this technique with fewer than five symbols is not recommended. Second, with a compiled language, you compile symbol definitions into an executable image (e.g., DEFINE_SYMB.EXE) and install it as shareable using the OpenVMS Install utility. Once the definitions are installed, multiple users who execute the image simultaneously share the same copy in memory, reducing memory usage and image-activation time. To install it, add the following line to SYSTARTUP_VMS:

```
$ INSTALL ADD SYS$MANAGER:DEFINE_SYMB.EXE/SHARE/OPEN/HEADER
```

The main disadvantages of using compiled code are that you must recompile source code after every change. Also, debugging compiled code can be much more difficult than debugging DCL. The source code for DEFINE_SYMB.MAR is located on the Digital Press site.

11.7 Establishing Menus

If you have users who are unfamiliar with DCL, you may want to configure their user login procedure as a menu command procedure. The following command procedures demonstrate this technique:

```
$! SYS$MANAGER:MENU.COM
$!
$! A simple menu system to select one of four applications
$!
$! NOTE: The symbols "123" & "WP" are defined in system login procedures
$ say:=write sys$output
$!
$DISP_MENU:
$ say "1—Word Processing"
$ say "2—Application"
$ say "3—Mail"
$ say "4—Logout"
$ say ""
$ read sys$command inp /prompt="Enter Selection (1-4): "
$!
```

```
$ if inp .lt. 1 .or. inp .gt. 4
$ then
$ read sys$command inp –
  /prompt="Invalid command, press <RETURN> to continue."
$ goto DISP_MENU
$ endif
$!
$ if inp .EQ. 1
$ then
$   DEFINE/USER SYS$INPUT SYS$COMMAND
$   WP
$   GOTO DISP_MENU
$ endif
$!
$ if inp .EQ. 2
$ then
$   DEFINE/USER SYS$INPUT SYS$COMMAND
$   RUN UserApplication
$   GOTO DISP_MENU
$ endif
$!
$ if inp .EQ. 3
$ then
$   DEFINE/USER SYS$INPUT SYS$COMMAND
$   MAIL
$   GOTO DISP_MENU
$ endif
$!
$ if inp .EQ. 4 then LOGOUT
```

To activate the menu for a particular user, modify the UAF record as follows:

```
$ UAF
UAF> modify username /LGICMD=SYS$MANAGER:MENU.COM
```

More sophisticated menu systems can be found on http://vms.process.com/fileserv-software.html, including MENU, OMI, and ZMENU.

11.8 Captive Login Procedures

In some cases, you may want to prevent a user from accessing DCL completely and instead provide the user with a menu interface. This can be accomplished by developing a captive login command procedure and specifying it as the default login command procedure for the account as follows:

```
$ UAF
UAF> modify username /LGICMD=device:[directory]CAPTIVE.COM -
_UAF>        /FLAG=(CAPTIVE,DISCTLY)
```

The procedures for creating captive command procedures are discussed in chapter 17.

11.9 Tools

Two tools were discussed in this chapter. These are listed in table 11.1.

Table 11.1 *LOGIN tools*

Procedure Name	Function
DEFINE_SYMB.MAR	Macro code to define DCL symbols
DQ.MAR	Macro code to test disk quota

- DEFINE_SYMB.MAR: This is compiled Macro (assembly) code that will create symbols faster than DCL scripts.
- DQ.MAR: This is compiled Macro code that will alert users at login time to pending disk-quota problems.

These two tools may be downloaded from the Digital Press site and tailored to your specific policies.

11.10 Conclusion

Providing the proper environment for the user is essential to keeping the user community happy. This chapter dovetails with chapter 9 because setting up accounts will directly determine your login script plan. A haphazard assignment in the UAF will make your life miserable. You must pay particular attention to account name and UIC to make login scripting easier.

11.11 Additional References

1. *OpenVMS DCL Dictionary: A–M* describes the uses of lexicals, in particular F$GETJPI.
2. *OpenVMS Programming Concepts Manual* describes how to program correctly, making the most of OpenVMS-provided utilities.
3. *OpenVMS RTL Library (LIB$) Manual* describes the uses and arguments of all LIB$ routines.
4. Sherlock's *Using DECwindows Motif for OpenVMS* is the authority describing the specifics of this version of X Windows.
5. Anagnostopoulos and Hoffman's *Writing Real Programs in DCL, Second Edition,* discusses scripting in detail.

12

Automating System Management

12.1 Chapter Objectives

- Use Digital Command Language (DCL) batch jobs to schedule routine system-management tasks
- Develop error handling and restart capabilities for automated procedures

12.2 Introduction

A number of system-management tasks must be performed on a regular basis. Rather than leaving these tasks to chance, you should create batch jobs that are automatically submitted at the required time. For example, system log files (see chapter 10) should be closed and archived on a regular basis. Instead of performing this task manually, create a batch job and schedule it to run automatically once a month.

An automated batch procedure must be more robust than a DCL command procedure that you run interactively. When executing a procedure interactively, you constantly watch for error messages and decide how to proceed. Because batch jobs do not automatically notify you when there is a problem, you need to include additional code to handle error reporting and recovery. You should also include code to mail error messages to SYSTEM to assure the problem does not go unnoticed.

This chapter also discusses the process of incorporating error handling and job restart capabilities into DCL command procedures.

12.3 Error Handling

Every time you execute a DCL command, OpenVMS returns a *severity level* and stores it in the symbol $SEVERITY. Table 12.1 summarizes the different severity levels that indicate the completion status of the executed command.

Table 12.1 *DCL Error Severity Levels*

Severity Level	Completion Status	Description
0	WARNING	A noncritical error or unusual condition
1	SUCCESS	Normal completion
2	ERROR	Unsuccessful completion
3	INFORMATIONAL	Normal completion with alternate condition
4	SEVERE_ERROR	Termination with fatal error
5–7	(reserved)	Reserved by HP for future use

You can confirm this behavior by issuing the following series of commands:

1. Enter a valid command and examine the result code:

```
$ SHOW TIME
  28-FEB-2001 19:11:00
$ SHOW SYMBOL $SEVERITY
  $SEVERITY == "1"
```

2. Enter an invalid command and examine the result code:

```
$ XYZ
%DCL-W-IVVERB, unrecognized command verb—check validity and spelling
\XYZ\
$ SHOW SYMBOL $SEVERITY
  $SEVERITY == "0"
```

3. Examine the code resulting form another error, referencing an invalid device:

```
$ COPY T.TMP DKA9999:
%COPY-E-OPENOUT, error opening DKA9999:[SYSMGR].; as output
-RMS-F-DEV, error in device name or inappropriate device type for
operation
$ SHOW SYMBOL $SEVERITY
  $SEVERITY == "2"
```

Notice also that $SEVERITY is a string, not an integer. However, you may test it with either string (e.g., .EQS.) or integer (e.g., .EQ.) operators.

In addition to $SEVERITY, another symbol, $STATUS, is created for each command. $STATUS contains a much more elaborate error code. In particular, the low-order three bits of $STATUS contain the $SEVERITY code. Table 12.2 summarizes $STATUS definitions.

Table 12.2 *$STATUS Code Definitions*

Bits	Field Name	Description
0–2	$SEVERITY	Severity code described in table 12.1
3–14	Message Number	Specific status code for this facility
15	Facility Specific	Indicator that message is shared by multiple facilities
16–26	Facility Number	Software application identifier
27	Customer Facility	Third-party message
28	Inhibit Display	Inhibit the EXIT message display
29–31	Reserved	

12.3.1 Default Error Handler

By default, when a command within a command procedure generates an error with an ERROR or FATAL severity level, a message is displayed, and the command procedure immediately aborts. On the other hand, if the severity level is WARNING or INFORMATIONAL, the command procedure continues and displays an informational message. If a command generates a severity of SUCCESS, the command procedure continues without displaying a message.

This behavior is inappropriate for many automated jobs because you do not want a job to abort every time an error is encountered. If possible, you want to trap these errors and take an appropriate recovery action. In addition, some errors classified as WARNING may actually be very serious. By default, a command procedure continues executing no matter how many warnings are generated. To avoid these problems, your automated job should include a customized error handler.

12.3.2 Customized Error Handling

Establish a customized error handler by adding the following DCL command near the beginning of your command procedure:

```
$ ON severity-level THEN command
```

Then, if a command within the procedure generates an error with a severity level that is equal to or greater than the specified severity level, the specified command is executed. If you specify more than one ON severity-level command, only the last is used. If you do not explicitly issue an ON ERROR THEN statement, the default error handler is in effect and is equivalent to the following command:

```
$ ON ERROR THEN EXIT
```

To perform more elaborate error handling, you can establish a subroutine as follows:

```
$! Start of command script
$ ERROR_STATUS = 1              ! Set to normal completion, by default
$ ON WARNING THEN GOSUB ERROR_CHECK
$!
$! [command procedure]
$!
$! End of procedure
$ EXIT ERROR_STATUS             ! Exit and return last error status
$!
$ERROR_CHECK:
$ ERROR_STATUS = $STATUS        ! Save error status
$ ON WARNING THEN GOSUB ERROR_CHECK
$ RETURN
```

In the foregoing, the ON WARNING statement causes the procedure to branch to an error handler, ERROR_CHECK, whenever an error occurs. The error handler saves the latest error status so that it can be later passed as a parameter to the EXIT statement, indicating the final completion status of the command procedure. The ON WARNING statement is included in the subroutine because you must reestablish a customized error handler every time it is triggered; otherwise, the default error handler is in effect again. By default, when a command procedure exits, it returns the status of the last command executed. By designing your command procedures using the foregoing strategy, your command procedures will return the last error status.

Instead of trapping errors, you can disable error handling altogether by adding the following line to the beginning of your command procedures:

```
$ SET NOON                          ! Set NO ON_ERROR
```

Disabling the error handler prevents command procedures from aborting due to errors; however, it is up to you to add appropriate recovery procedures to deal with the errors. If you completely disable the error handler, you should carefully review all batch-job log files either manually or using the OpenVMS SEARCH utility (see CHECK_STARTUP.COM in chapter 5) for error messages.

12.4 Restart Handling

Batch jobs can be submitted so that they automatically restart after a system crash or other events that cause jobs to terminate abnormally. If you want batch jobs to be restartable, you must submit them, either manually or within the script, with the following command:

```
$ SUBMIT/RESTART command-procedure
```

The job will then be automatically restarted if it is interrupted by any of the following events:

- The system crashes and queue manager fail-over is not possible.
- STOP/QUEUE/MANAGER/CLUSTER is executed.
- STOP/QUEUE/RESET is executed.

- SET ENTRY/RESTART is executed.

When a restart occurs, the command procedure is started over from the beginning, and the symbols listed in table 12.3 are defined. To make a batch job restartable, add commands to the beginning of your command procedure that test the value of the $RESTART symbol. If $RESTART is TRUE, jump to the label stored in the BATCH$RESTART symbol. For BATCH$RESTART to be set properly, you must include SET RESTART_VALUE commands at the beginning of each major step.

Table 12.3 *Batch-Job Restart Symbols*

Symbol	Value
$RESTART	Set to TRUE, which indicates a restart has occurred.
BATCH$RESTART	Set to the value of the job step that was in progress when the job aborted. The job step is established from the last SET RESTART_VALUE=*step command executed before the abort.*

For example, suppose the command procedure BACKUP.COM performs a backup of DISK1, DISK2, and DISK3 and is submitted as follows:

```
$ SUBMIT/NOPRINT/RESTART BACKUP.COM
```

If the backup is interrupted because of a system crash, the script automatically restarts whichever backup was in progress when the crash occurred:

```
$! BACKUP.COM
$!
$ IF $RESTART
$ THEN
$     IF F$TYPE(BATCH$RESTART) .NES. ""
$     THEN
$          REQUEST/TO=CENTRAL "RESTARTING JOB AT STEP ''BATCH$RESTART'"
$          GOTO 'BATCH$RESTART
$     ENDIF
$ ELSE
$     REQUEST/TO=CENTRAL "NO RESTART VALUE - STARTING FROM BEGINNING"
```

```
$ ENDIF
.
.
.
$DISK1:
$ SET RESTART_VALUE=DISK1
$ BACKUP/REWIND/IMAGE DISK$USR1: MKA0:USR1.BCK/SAVE
$!
$DISK2:
$ SET RESTART_VALUE=DISK2
$ BACKUP/REWIND/IMAGE DISK$USR2: MKA0:USR2.BCK/SAVE
$!
$DISK3:
$ SET RESTART_VALUE=DISK3
$ BACKUP/REWIND/IMAGE DISK$USR3: MKA0:USR3.BCK/SAVE
$ EXIT
```

When the above command procedure first executes, it checks to see if $RESTART is set. Because $RESTART is not defined, the command procedure proceeds to the label DISK1:. Next, the procedure sets the restart value to DISK1 and begins a backup of the first disk. Assume that halfway through the backup of the first disk, the system crashes and automatically reboots. Because the batch job was submitted with the /RESTART qualifier, the script is automatically restarted from the beginning, the symbol $RESTART is set to TRUE and BATCH$RESTART is defined and set to DISK1 (the last restart value set). When the command procedure begins executing for the second time, it detects that $RESTART is set to TRUE, indicating that the procedure has been restarted. Next, the F$TYPE function is used to verify that the BATCH$RESTART symbol exists so it does not attempt to perform an illegal GOTO. If BATCH$RESTART exists, the procedure issues an informational operator broadcast message and branches to the label stored in the BATCH$RESTART symbol. Because the value of this symbol is DISK1, the procedure branches to the DISK1: label and restarts the backup of DISK1.

12.5 Synchronizing Batch Jobs

In some cases, you may have automated batch procedures that depend on one another. For example, you may have a backup job that should run immediately after a disk purging job completes. Batch job dependencies like this can be handled with the DCL SYNCHRONIZE command as follows:

```
$! NIGHTLY_BACKUP.COM
$!
$ SYNCHRONIZE NIGHTLY_PURGE    ! Wait for NIGHTLY_PURGE.COM to complete
$!
$! Backup disk 1
$!
$!...
$ EXIT
$!
$! NIGHTLY_PURGE.COM
$!
$ ERROR_STATUS = 1             ! Set to normal completion, by default
$ ON WARNING THEN GOSUB ERROR_CHECK
$!
$ PURGE ...
$ PURGE ...
$ PURGE ...
$!
$! End of procedure
$ EXIT ERROR_STATUS            ! Exit and return last error status
$!
$ERROR_CHECK:
$ ERROR_STATUS = $STATUS        ! Save error status
$ ON WARNING THEN GOSUB EPROR_CHECK
$ RETURN
```

Then, submit the two jobs as follows from another command procedure, DAILY_PROCESSING, as follows:

```
$!
$! DAILY_PROCESSING.COM
$!
$! Procedure to perform daily automated tasks-invoked by SCHEDULER
$!
$! ...
$ SUBMIT NIGHTLY_PURGE.COM ...
$ SUBMIT NIGHTLY_BACKUP.COM ...
```

```
$! ...
$ EXIT
```

When the two jobs are submitted, both begin executing immediately, assuming the batch queue is set up for multiple jobs. However, when NIGHTLY_BACKUP reaches the SYNCHRONIZE command it enters a wait state until the NIGHTLY_PURGE job completes. The SYNCHRONIZE command also returns the final exit status from the target job as its own status value, permitting the job to act upon the value.

12.6 Scheduling Batch Jobs

Once you develop robust command procedures, you need a tool that automatically submits jobs at the required frequency. SCHEDULER.COM is a command procedure that allows you to submit jobs automatically that must be run on a daily, weekly, or monthly basis. SCHEDULER submits itself every morning at 12:10 A.M. and then executes one or more of the following command procedures, if appropriate:

```
DAILY_PROCESSING   ! If the current day is Monday through Friday
WEEKLY_PROCESSING  ! If the current day is a Sunday
MONTHLY_PROCESSING ! If the current day is the first day of the month
```

The source code for SCHEDULE is as follows:

```
$! SCHEDULER.COM
$!
$! Note: Define the following logicals in SYLOGICALS.COM:
$!
$! SCHED$DIR:
$!        Directory that contains the command procedures
$!        Referenced in this procedure
$!
$!
$ SCHED_SUBMIT := SUBMIT/RESTART/NOPRINT/USER=SYSTEM
$ SCHED_HOUR == F$CVTIME(,,"HOUR")
$ SCHED_WKDY == F$CVTIME(,,"WEEKDAY")
$ SCHED_MTHDY == F$CVTIME(,,"DAY")
$ SCHED_MONTH == F$CVTIME(,"ABSOLUTE","MONTH") ! Use DD-MMM-YYYY format
$ SCHED_YEAR == F$CVTIME(,,"YEAR")
$!
$! See if we're being restarted
```

```
$!
$ IF $RESTART
$ THEN
$  IF F$TYPE(BATCH$RESTART) .NES. ""
$  THEN
$   REQUEST/TO=CENTRAL "RESTARTING SCHEDULER AT STEP ''BATCH$RESTART'"
$   GOTO 'BATCH$RESTART
$  ENDIF
$  ELSE
$  REQUEST/TO=CENTRAL "RESTARTING SCHEDULER FROM BEGINNING."
$ ENDIF
$!
$ SET RESTART=RESUBMIT
$!
$! Re-submit for tomorrow
$!
$ SCHED_SUBMIT/AFTER="TOMORROW+00:10" SCHED$DIR:SCHEDULER
$!
$! Perform Daily Processing
$!
$DAILY:
$ SET RESTART=DAILY
$ SCHED_SUBMIT SCHED$DIR:DAILY_PROCESSING
$!
$! If Saturday, perform Weekly Processing
$!
$WEEKLY:
$ SET RESTART=WEEKLY
$ IF SCHED_WKDAY .EQS. "Saturday" THEN SCHED_SUBMIT SCHED$DIR:WEEKLY_PROCESSING
$!
$! If 1st day of Month, perform Monthly Processing
$!
$MONTHLY:
$ SET RESTART=MONTHLY
$ IF SCHED_MTHDY .EQS. "01" THEN SCHED_SUBMIT SCHED$DIR:MONTHLY_PROCESSING
$!
$ EXIT
```

The command procedure above makes extensive use of the lexical function F$CVTIME to extract the components of the current date and time to determine when to execute the daily, weekly, and monthly procedures. For more information on the F$CVTIME function, refer to the *OpenVMS DCL Dictionary*.

The example MONTHLY_PROCESSING.COM, available on the Digital Press site, moves key system log files to a directory located by the logical name TASM$ARCHIVE. For example, on August 1, 2002, this procedure moves and renames the following files:

```
SYS$MANAGER:ACCOUNTNG.DAT        ==> TASM$ARCHIVE:ACC_AUG_2002.DAT
SYS$MANAGER:SECURITY_AUDIT.AUDIT$JOURNAL.DAT  ==>
                                     TASM$ARCHIVE:SEC_AUG_2002.DAT
SYS$ERRORLOG:ERRORLOG.SYS        ==> TASM$ARCHIVE:ERR_AUG_2002.DAT
SYS$MANAGER:OPERATOR.LOG         ==> TASM$ARCHIVE:OPER_AUG_2002.DAT
```

Finally, on a periodic basis (e.g., quarterly or yearly), you can archive the files to tape or delete them if they are no longer needed.

12.7 Tools

Several sample scripts are included on the Digital Press site. These were partially described in the chapter and are summarized in table 12.4.

Table 12.4 *Chapter 12 Tools*

Procedure Name	Function
SCHEDULER.COM	Main scheduler
DAILY_PROCESSING.COM	Daily tasks
WEEKLY_PROCESSING.COM	Weekly tasks
MONTHLY_PROCESSING.COM	Monthly tasks

A number of vendors offer automated job-scheduling products that provide functionality necessary for production-oriented environments. Among the features offered in many of these products are the following:

- Menus for adding, changing, and removing jobs
- Automatic error detection
- Exception checking (e.g., late start time, late end time)
- Customizable fiscal calendars
- Programmable job dependencies

Table 12.5 is a partial list of commercially available job schedulers. See appendix A for vendor contact information.

Table 12.5 *Job Schedulers*

Vendor	Product
Freeware	Kronos
Computer Associates	CAscheduler
Target Systems	Target->Batch

A freeware package called BAT is available from http://vms.process.com/fileserv-software.html. BAT is designed to submit a series of commands, entered from the keyboard, to a batch queue. BAT eliminates the need for the user to create a command procedure manually for every batch submission.

12.8 Conclusion

These few examples show possibilities and present working examples of useful management scripts. It is unlikely that you will be able to use these examples as they are presented; instead, you should apply the principles presented and modify the examples to suit your needs.

If you have not done so already, read chapter 9 for tips and scripts to periodically monitor disk utilization.

12.9 Additional References

1. *OpenVMS DCL Dictionary: A–M* describes the uses of lexicals, in particular F$CVTIME.
2. Anagnostopoulos and Hoffman's *Writing Real Programs in DCL, Second Edition,* discusses scripting in detail, especially the fine art of error handling.

13

OpenVMS BACKUP/RESTORE Considerations

13.1 Chapter Objectives

- Develop and implement backup strategies that meet service-level objectives
- Minimize risks associated with online backups
- Automate backups with DCL command procedures
- Optimize OpenVMS BACKUP performance

13.2 Introduction

Data backup, when viewed from a larger perspective, is saved for the following reasons:

- For data safety
- For business or statutory reasons

To meet cost and resource needs, data saved to near-line or offline storage can be deleted to make more online storage space available. In this chapter we discuss data backup primarily from the safety standpoint.

Your system contains valuable data stored on disk. To prevent data from being lost, you should perform regular backups by copying files to some type of removable media (usually magnetic tape). If files become damaged or lost, you can recover them from backups and restore the system to a usable state.

Performing backups is very time-consuming, but like many forms of insurance, you realize its value when a problem occurs. If your home or car were destroyed and you did not have insurance, the financial impact could be devastating. Similarly, performing anything other than robust backups might save you some time and money now, but will financially ruin you or your organization in the long run. Backups are one of your most important responsibilities; give them the attention they deserve.

Backups provide protection against the following three types of failures:

1. *Hardware failures:* Although computer systems are relatively reliable, individual components can and do eventually fail. When failures occur, files or entire disks may be damaged or left in an inconsistent state, requiring recovery from backups. Usually, the most severe and most frequent failures involve disk devices.
2. *Software failures:* Data corruption can be caused by bugs in software, including OpenVMS, layered products, or in-house applications. You must perform backups so that you can restore disks to the state in which they were before corruption.
3. *User errors*: Although usually less severe, data loss can occur if users accidentally delete files or perform incorrect updates. In such cases, you may need to perform a partial restore of one or more files from backups.

13.2.1 Security

Accidental file deletions can be disruptive enough. Some intentional corruption can be exceedingly difficult to detect and then equally difficult to resolve. Other attacks can be obvious and massive. Conscientious system backups with the retention of an extensive archive can be instrumental in the resolution of intentional system attacks.

As an alternative to regular full backups, consider operating your vulnerable or critical applications and even the OpenVMS operating system partially or fully on read-only media (e.g., CD-ROM or DVD). This approach allows you to concentrate on protecting and archiving your writeable data.

13.3 Backup Requirements

Business requirements dictate when backups can be performed, what must be backed up and how frequently, when backups should be stored off-site, and how quickly recovery must occur. These requirements must be developed by collaborating with users and managers and considering the following issues:

- Backup window
- Backup frequency
- Recovery time
- Retention requirements
- Off-site rotation

13.3.1 Backup Window

The backup window is the time period during which it is acceptable for backups to be performed. This is necessary because backups require resources and because it is best to back up a quiescent database. For users to specify this requirement, you should make them aware of the following issues:

- When backups are performed, system performance may be severely degraded.
- Some applications require that user access be restricted during backups.
- You may not be able to perform backups while application-related production jobs are processing.

Once you have derived an acceptable backup window, record it in terms of the exact hours of each day that backups can be performed. For example:

- *Weekdays:* 00:00–06:00, 20:00–24:00
- *Weekends:* 00:00–24:00

Some applications may permit no window, typically meaning that application-specific backup tools must be used rather than the OpenVMS tool, BACKUP. An example of this involves the use of the Oracle Rdb RMU command.

13.3.2 Backup Frequency

The data contained on a disk is an asset with an associated value. As data is manipulated, its value increases by the cost of the manipulation. For example, consider an Accounts Receivable department with 20 data-entry clerks each making $15 per hour. On a normal day, clerks enter billing information and generate invoices totaling $10,000,000. If this data were lost and had to be reentered, the cost would be as follows:

20 clerks × 8 hours × $15/hour = $2,400

The value of data is also affected by the business impact of its loss. For example, if the disk containing the aforementioned invoices failed, it might take a day to repair the disk and another day to reenter the invoices. Because the invoices would be mailed late, the business would receive payment two days later, resulting in the following loss (assuming 10 percent interest):

$10,000,000 × (10%/365) × 2 days = $5,479

Therefore, the total value of a day's data in this example is $7,879. The more quickly the value of the data increases, the more frequently users require backups.

If the vulnerable data contains online customer order information, the costs can be significant. Most obviously, the value of the orders can be lost. Additionally, the customer relationship is risked when the orders are not fulfilled when expected, if the orders are not lost completely.

13.3.3 Recovery Time

You should discuss with users the different system failures that might occur and agree on how quickly you must be able to recover from each of them. When you calculate total recovery time, include the time to perform each of the following steps:

- Detect failure
- Determine appropriate action

- Wait for service vendor to arrive
- Diagnose problem
- Locate replacement parts
- Repair equipment
- Retrieve backups (especially if off-site)
- Restore backups
- Perform postrecovery procedures

In this analysis, be sure to include every step that must be performed before users can access the system. Do not forget to include postrecovery procedures such as rerunning production jobs.

13.3.4 Archive Requirements

Backups allow you to recover the system to a previous state. However, exactly which prior states must you be able to recover to? For example, users may need to recover to specific dates in the past, such as key month-end, quarter-end, or year-end closing dates. You should coordinate your backups with these events and retain each backup long enough to meet recovery requirements.

13.3.5 Off-Site Rotation

Off-site rotation provides protection against local disasters that might damage disks and any backups stored on-site. You should determine the maximum data loss allowed in such a disaster and rotate backups off-site at an appropriate interval to meet those requirements. You should also ensure that you have the ability to retrieve backup media from off-site fast enough to meet disk-recovery time requirements. Finally, you need to develop mechanisms to rotate backup media back on-site when retention periods expire so you can reuse the media.

13.4 Developing a Backup Strategy

The OpenVMS BACKUP utility provides the three following major backup types:

1. Image backups
2. Physical backups
3. File backups

To develop a backup strategy, consider the backup requirements for your organization and combine backup techniques that meet those requirements. For example, if file volatility is very high and the business requires a maximum data loss of one day, you can perform daily full backups. On the other hand, if file volatility is low, you can perform weekly full backups and daily cumulative incremental backups.

Table 13.1 lists a number of common backup strategies and the circumstances under which they might be appropriate.

Table 13.1 *Common Backup Strategies*

Backup Strategy	File Volatility	Backup Window/ Capacity	Backup Time	Maximum Data Loss	Recovery Time
Daily full only	Very high	Unlimited/very high	Very high	1 day	Very low
Weekly full, daily cumulative incremental	Low	Limited/moderate	Moderate	1 day	Moderate
Weekly full, daily differential	Moderate	Very limited/low	Low	1 day	High
Monthly full, weekly cumulative, daily cumulative	Very low	Very limited/low	Moderate	1 day	Very high
Weekly full only	Very low	Very limited/moderate	Low	1 week	Very high
Monthly full, weekly cumulative incremental	Very low	Very limited/low	Low	1 week	Moderate
Monthly full, weekly differential	Very low	Very limited/very low	Moderate	1 week	Very high
Monthly full only	Very low	Very limited/very low	Low	1 month	Very low

13.4.1 Image Backups

An image backup saves the entire contents of a disk to backup media, including volume initialization information and, in the case of system disks, bootstrap programs. Because image backups allow you to completely restore a disk, they are considered full backups. The major limitation of image backups is that you must back up the entire contents of a disk. However, you may selectively restore from an image backup.

Of the three techniques, only an image backup and restore eliminates disk fragmentation. However, OpenVMS includes a disk file optimizer (DFO) tool, which will operate on an online disk.

One very nice feature of the BACKUP utility is that you can check its progress anytime with <CTRL/T>. It will show a three-line display similar to the following. <CTRL/T> under any other circumstances will display only the first line.

```
<CTRL-T>
MILLER::_FTA6: 11:59:27 BACKUP    CPU=00:01:55.75 PF=1798 IO=61502 MEM=220
 Restoring file: DKA0:[BAE.SRC]PROCESS_MSG.OBJ;288
 Saveset volume:1, saveset block:20060 (32256 byte blocks)
```

13.4.2 Physical Backups

A physical backup ignores the file structure of a disk and makes an exact copy of the disk on a block-by-block basis, including unused blocks. Normally, a physical backup of a full disk takes less time than an image backup. However, if the disk is nearly empty, a physical backup will probably take longer, because it must still copy unused disk blocks.

Physical backups have several disadvantages. You cannot selectively restore files. When you restore a physical backup, every block must restore perfectly; otherwise, the target disk will not be usable—with modern disks, automatic bad-block replacement support will substitute a spare, good disk block for any disk block found to be failing. If you perform a physical disk backup and restore, the resulting disk structure will be exactly as it was before the backup, including any disk fragmentation.

Because of the serious limitations of physical backups, this chapter focuses on image and file backups.

13.4.3 File Backups

In contrast to an image backup, a file backup allows you to selectively copy one or more files from disk to backup media. Similarly, a file restore allows you to copy one or more files from backup media to disk.

You can perform a file backup of an entire disk (a full backup) by selecting all files on the disk. However, full file backups do not contain volume initialization information. You can completely restore a disk from a file backup, but you must manually initialize the disk before performing the restore. For this reason, it is usually more convenient to use image backups to perform full backups.

A special type of file backup is known as an *incremental file backup*. An incremental backup selectively copies all files that have changed since a previous backup. If you have disks with low file volatility, you can save considerable backup time by performing frequent incremental backups and less frequent full backups. When file volatility is high, incremental backups are not useful because an incremental backup may take as long as a full backup, and the restoration can involve increased time and complexity.

File volatility measures the total size of all files modified during a particular period. For example, the collective size of all files that change on a daily basis might total as little as a few megabytes or as much as several hundred megabytes.

To calculate the daily file volatility for a particular disk, execute the following command over a period of several days:

```
$ DIR/SIZE=ALL/TOTAL/MOTIFIED/SINCE="-1-" ddcu:[000000...]*.*;*
```

The resulting total indicates the total size and number of files that changed on the disk during the previous 24 hours. Depending on file volatility, you may want to perform one of the two following types of incremental backups.

13.4.3.1 Cumulative Incrementals

With cumulative incremental backups, you back up all files that have been modified since the last full backup. For example, you might perform a full backup on Saturday and then cumulative incremental backups Monday through Friday evening. The Monday night backup would contain all files changed between the full backup on Saturday and Monday night. The Tuesday night backup would contain all files changed between the full backup on Saturday and Tuesday night, and so on.

To restore a disk using cumulative incremental backup, first restore the latest full backup then the most recent cumulative incremental. For example, if you used the backup strategy just described, you would restore the most recent Saturday full backup and then the cumulative incremental backup from the previous night. When file volatility is very low, a cumulative incremental backup takes much less time than a full backup. However, recovery time is longer because you must restore both the full backup and the incremental backup.

13.4.3.2 Differential Backup

With differential backups, you back up all files changed since either the last full backup or the last differential backup. For example, you might perform a full backup on Saturday and a differential Monday through Friday evening. The Monday night backup would contain all files changed between the full backup on Saturday and Monday night. The Tuesday night backup would contain all files changed since the Monday night backup, and so on.

To restore a disk using this backup technique, first restore the most recent full backup, then restore every differential backup created since the full backup. For example, if a disk failed on Thursday morning, you would first restore the full backup from the previous Saturday, then restore the Wednesday, Tuesday, and Monday differential backups (in that order). When file volatility is moderate, differential backups require less backup time. However, recovery can take much longer because you may need to perform many incremental restore operations.

13.4.4 Backup Mode

When you perform a backup, its mode is either *online* or *offline.* A backup is considered online if the source disk is publicly mounted and user activity can possibly occur. A backup is considered offline when the source disk is mounted privately to the backup process, preventing any user activity, or when all applications that are referencing the device are known to be quiescent.

A *stand-alone* backup refers to the system disk and involves performing a system shutdown and booting an alternate operating system disk such as the CD-ROM installation media (OpenVMS Alpha or OpenVMS VAX), or booting Standalone BACKUP (OpenVMS VAX only). When backups are performed from another system disk or from Standalone BACKUP, users cannot access any disks, ensuring an offline backup.

13.4.4.1 Minimizing the Risks of Online Backups

Backup integrity can be absolutely assured only when you perform offline backups; however, this may not be possible due to system utilization. If you perform online backups, you run the risk of a user writing to a file at the exact moment it is being backed up or that there will be inconsistencies between the data in the cache and the data on the disk. When this occurs, the backup of the file may be left in a stale, an inconsistent, or an unrecoverable state. If you need to restore that particular file, it may be unusable.

Unfortunately for many sites, offline backups are simply not practical because of system uptime requirements. As long as you use the correct BACKUP commands, you can back up files while users are reading from them. You only have to be concerned with files that are open for writing access. If recovering these files is not essential, online backups may be acceptable. However, if one file of a larger database does not restore properly, the entire database may be left in an inconsistent state.

You should be especially careful when performing online backups of an OpenVMS system disk. Most activity to a system disk is read access to executable program files, which does not affect the integrity of the backup. However, some system files are written to on a regular basis, such as the error log file, accounting file, operator log file, user authorization file, audit journal file, and queue database. You can reduce the risk of inconsistent backups of these files by minimizing the following activities during online backups:

- System logins
- Adding/modifying user accounts
- Process termination of any kind (interactive, batch, network, subprocess, detached)
- Any batch or print job activity or submissions
- Activities that generate security alarms

You should use the following procedure to make backup copies of the queue database files before performing an online system disk backup:

```
$ CONVERT/SHARE SYS$SYSTEM:QMAN$MASTER.DAT *.TMP
$ CONVERT/SHARE SYS$SYSTEM:SYS$QUEUE_MANAGER.QMAN$QUEUES *.TMP
```

13.4.4.2 System Disk Backup (OpenVMS VAX)

Because OpenVMS requires constant access to the system disk, you cannot dismount the system disk and subsequently perform an offline backup. To perform an offline backup of the system disk, you must use an alternate system disk or (on OpenVMS VAX only) the Standalone BACKUP utility. Invoke BACKUP by first performing a system shutdown and then booting the system from a minimal OpenVMS root, from distribution media, or from an OpenVMS VAX Standalone BACKUP kit previously created on disk or on tape.

When OpenVMS is bootstrapped from the distribution kit or from a minimal or an alternate system disk, BACKUP and other standard OpenVMS commands and utilities are available. This permits the direct restoration of an entire disk or of individual files on a disk and permits repairs to the contents of the target disk.

When bootstrapped from Standalone BACKUP, the VAX system is running a minimal version of OpenVMS VAX that allows you to perform only image backup and restore functions from the console terminal. (OpenVMS VAX V7.2 distributions and later do include a full bootable OpenVMS VAX root, in addition to the stand-alone root.) Users cannot access the system, nor can they execute standard DCL commands. Because Standalone BACKUP can process only image backups, make sure you have full image backups of your system disk. You cannot restore a system disk from full file backups using Standalone BACKUP. Standalone BACKUP commands have the same syntax as online OpenVMS BACKUP commands, but you can only perform image backup and restore operations.

If your system disk fails, you will not have access to OpenVMS or the OpenVMS BACKUP utility on the failed disk. You must use another copy of BACKUP to perform any required restoration.

The procedures for creating bootable minimal OpenVMS system roots and for creating Standalone BACKUP kits and the associated console bootstrapping commands are discussed in section 13.6.

13.4.4.3 System Disk Backup (OpenVMS Alpha)

OpenVMS Alpha provides a bootable environment on the distribution media. This environment is a bootable version of OpenVMS akin to what is possible with recent OpenVMS VAX releases, and it permits the system manager to MOUNT, COPY, INITIALIZE or perform any other activities.

This environment also permits the system manager to use the BACKUP command.

The manager may optionally create a bootable environment on other disks using a provided tool described in section 13.5.6.

13.5 Backup Tools

The primary tool used to perform backups is the OpenVMS BACKUP utility. An example invocation follows:

```
$ BACKUP/qualifiers input output:save-set
```

When you perform a backup, the *input* is the disk being backed up and the *output* is the name of a tape drive followed by a *save-set* name. For example:

```
$ BACKUP/IMAGE DUA1: MUA300:IMAGE.SAV
```

A save-set is a special file used by BACKUP to serve as a container for all files selected by the backup. When you perform a restore, you simply reverse the order of the input and output parameters as follows:

```
$ BACKUP/IMAGE MUA300:IMAGE.SAV DUA1:
```

The more general syntax of the BACKUP command is as follows:

```
$ BACKUP/command-qualifiers input/input-qualifiers output/
output-qualifiers
```

The following sections detail the importance of each of the optional BACKUP qualifiers.

13.5.1 BACKUP Command Qualifiers

/IGNORE=INTERLOCK

This qualifier overrides and disables the file OpenVMS interlocks that normally prevent data inconsistencies. If you use this qualifier, BACKUP attempts to copy files even if they are open. Usually you must select this option when you perform online backups. If you do not use this qualifier and a file is open, BACKUP skips the file. Files that are open when backed up will probably fail the /VERIFY check.

CAUTION: The use of /IGNORE=INTERLOCK may result in one or more unrecoverable files. The best policy is to mount the disk privately so no files are open.

/IGNORE=LABEL

When you select this qualifier, BACKUP does not perform tape label processing. This instructs BACKUP to use a tape regardless of the current label name. If you do not include this option, BACKUP expects the tape label to be equal to the first six characters of the input or output save-set or the label specified with the /LABEL qualifier. If there is a label mismatch, BACKUP generates an operator message requesting further instructions.

/IMAGE

Use the /IMAGE qualifier to perform a full image backup or restore, as discussed earlier.

/INCREMENTAL

When you perform an incremental restore operation you must include this qualifier to indicate that the input save-set is an incremental backup.

```
/LABEL=label-name
```

As discussed above, this qualifier instructs BACKUP to expect the loaded tape to contain the specified label name. This option is often used with /EXACT_ORDER or /IGNORE=LABEL.

/LIST=listing-file

This qualifier causes BACKUP to generate a file containing a complete list of all files written during the backup. By using this qualifier, you can create a database of listing files that itemize the contents of each of your backups. You can then use the OpenVMS SEARCH command to scan all or some of the listing files to find which backup contains the file for which you are looking.

/RECORD

This qualifier forces the backup date to be written to all files processed by BACKUP. You must use the /RECORD qualifier during full backup if you later wish to perform incremental backups (see /SINCE=BACKUP).

If you use the /RECORD qualifier only when you perform full backups, each incremental backup is a cumulative incremental backup. If you use the /RECORD qualifier when you perform full backups and with each incremental backup, each incremental backup is a differential backup.

/RELEASE_TAPE

This qualifier notifies BACKUP to dismount and deallocate a tape device as soon as it is finished writing it to the tape. Use this qualifier to cause BACKUP to automatically dismount the last tape of a backup operation (by default, you must manually dismount it). If you specify this qualifier with the /RECORD qualifier, BACKUP frees the tape drive as soon as the backup date writing pass begins, rather than waiting for the entire backup to complete.

/VERIFY

This qualifier causes BACKUP to perform a verification pass after a backup or restore operation. During a backup verification pass, the output save-set is reread and compared with the backup source disk. During a restore verification, the input save-set is reread and compared with the restored disk.

Although backup verification doubles the amount of time it takes to complete a backup, it is the most reliable method of ensuring backup integrity. HP strongly recommends using /VERIFY on all backups. However, you may want to avoid using /VERIFY when performing online backups because you will receive many verification errors regarding files that change during the backup.

If the save-set requires multiple tapes, each one will have to be remounted during this operation.

13.5.2 BACKUP Input Qualifiers

/SINCE=BACKUP

Use this qualifier to perform incremental file backups as discussed in section 13.4.2 (see also /RECORD).

13.5.3 BACKUP Output Qualifiers

/REWIND

The /REWIND qualifier is very misleading. This qualifier causes the backup media to be rewound and to be initialized. When you reuse a tape that contains a previous backup, you normally use the /REWIND qualifier. Otherwise, BACKUP skips to the end of the backup media and appends to it. You should think of /REWIND as INITIALIZE TAPE, and /NOREWIND as APPEND TO TAPE.

To perform a backup to a medium that has never been initialized, you must use the /REWIND qualifier. If a backup requires more than one medium, subsequent media are automatically initialized. To store multiple backups on a single backup medium (such as a DLT tape), use the /REWIND qualifier for the first backup and the /NOREWIND qualifier for subsequent backups.

/TAPE_EXPIRATION=expiration-date

By specifying a tape expiration date you can prevent backups from being improperly overwritten. You should establish a tape expiration date on the basis of the desired retention period for the backup. For example, when you perform a backup that should be retained for one year, specify a tape expiration date one year in the future. If you attempt to use the tape before its expiration date, you receive an error message. The /TAPE_EXPIRATION qualifier is valid only when used with the /REWIND qualifier.

13.5.4 Automatic Tape Handling

When you use a tape device you normally perform the following steps:

1. Allocate the device to prevent other processes from accessing the device.
2. Initialize the tape with a label, if necessary.
3. Mount the tape.
4. Perform read/write operations.
5. Dismount the tape.
6. Deallocate the device when you are finished.

When performing a backup, you can explicitly issue ALLOCATE, INITIALIZE, MOUNT, DISMOUNT and DEALLOCATE commands, or you can allow BACKUP to perform most of these functions for you. When you create a backup that requires more than one tape, the BACKUP utility can mount and dismount each tape. However, the last tape is not automatically dismounted, unless you use the /RELEASE-TAPE qualifier. Table 13.2 lists the syntax and function of these commands. The examples in this chapter allow BACKUP to perform these functions automatically.

Table 13.2 *Tape Handling Commands*

OpenVMS Command/Qualifier	Function
ALLOCATE *device-name*	Allocates a device to your process, preventing other processes from using the device.
INITIALIZE *device-name label*	Prepares a disk or tape for initial use by OpenVMS. To initialize a device, a disk or tape medium must be loaded and online, but not mounted. The initialization process clears a disk or tape of existing data. New media must be initialized before they can be used by OpenVMS. When invoked, INITIALIZE writes an alphanumeric label to the medium. Labels for tape devices can be six characters in length. Disk labels may be 12 characters long.
MOUNT *device-name label log-name*	Makes a volume available on a device. When a volume is mounted, OpenVMS first compares the supplied label with the actual label of the medium (as written during initialization). If the labels match, the medium is mounted, and a logical name is defined that equates with the device name of the medium. By default, when you mount a tape device, it is mounted as a ODS-2 formatted device. That is, you can use DIR and COPY commands to manipulate the drive.
/FOREIGN	Mounts a volume in foreign mode for use by OpenVMS BACKUP.

Table 13.2 *Tape Handling Commands (continued)*

OpenVMS Command/Qualifier	Function
DISMOUNT *device-name*	Performs the reverse of a MOUNT. By default, when volumes are dismounted they are also taken offline and unloaded. Before a volume can be remounted it must be reloaded and put online by manual operator intervention.
/NOUNLOAD	Prevents the volume from being unloaded after dismount. The volume can then be subsequently remounted without operator intervention.

OpenVMS also supports "foreign" tapes, that is, tape formats that do not follow OpenVMS file conventions. Foreign tapes are not supported by BACKUP. In particular, the UNIX tar format is different from BACKUP format.

13.5.5 Booting OpenVMS/Alpha from CD-ROM

You can bootstrap from the OpenVMS Alpha distribution media to perform a system disk backup and restore when OpenVMS Alpha is not operating. Before you bootstrap the environment, you must have a distribution kit CD-ROM.

When you boot from the CD, the OpenVMS Alpha system used is built into the [SYS0] system root. Therefore, you specify a value of 0 for the first field of the bootstrap flags (BOOT_OSFLAGS). For example:

```
>>> BOOT -flag 0,0 disk-device
```

For instance:

```
>>> BOOT -flag 0,0 DKA400
```

Alternatively, set the flags using a separate command. For example:

```
>>> SET BOOT_OSFLAGS 0,0
>>> BOOT DKA400
```

Once booted, a menu is presented which looks like this:

```
OpenVMS (TM) Alpha Operating System, Version 7.3-1
Copyright (c) 2002 -- All rights reserved.
. . .
Please choose one of the following:

1) Upgrade, install or reconfigure OpenVMS Alpha Version 7.3-1
2) Display products and patches that this procedure can install
3) Install or upgrade layered products and patches
4) Show installed products
5) Reconfigure installed products
6) Remove installed products
7) Execute DCL commands and procedures
8) Shut down this system

Enter CHOICE or ? for help: (1/2/3/4/5/6/7/8/?)
```

Select option 7 and you will receive a $$$ prompt. Enter MOUNT and BACKUP commands and then enter LOGOUT to get back to this menu so you can shut the system down using option 8.

13.5.6 Booting OpenVMS/Alpha from an Alternate Disk

If your OpenVMS Alpha system disk fails, you must restore your system backups using the bootable environment. As stated in section 13.5.5, you can use an OpenVMS Alpha distribution kit on CD. However, depending on the speed of your CD drive, this can be a time-consuming process. To create the equivalent bootable environment on separate disk you can use following command:

```
$ @SYS$SYSTEM:AXPVMS$PCSI_INSTALL_MIN DKA200:

DEC AXPVMS OPENVMS V7.3-1: OpenVMS and related products platform
COPYRIGHT (c) 14-MAY-2002 -- All rights reserved
Compaq Information Technologies Group, L.P.

Execution phase starting ...
The following product will be installed:

DEC AXPVMS VMS V7.3-1
Portion Done: 0%..10%..20%..30%..40%..50%..60%..70%..80%..90%..100%
```

```
The following product has been installed:
DEC AXPVMS VMS V7.3-1
.
.
.
The installation of minimum OpenVMS Alpha is now complete.
Use the following command to boot minimum OpenVMS:
BOOT -FLAGS E,0 device-name
(Your system may require additional parameters to boot.)
```

This command creates a copy of the OpenVMS Alpha operating system on the specified target disk and makes it bootable. However, you will want to build this bootable environment on a disk other than your system disk—on a disk that does not already contain a copy of the OpenVMS Alpha operating system.

You boot this disk with the following command because SYSE is the root directory on this system:

```
>>> BOOT –flag E,0 DKA200
```

Once booted, no system password is required. You will get the $$$ prompt to remind you that you're on the minimum system. No licenses are active on this system.

Using the bootable environment, you have full access to standard OpenVMS commands and can quickly perform a restoration of your primary system disk (DKA0: in the example below) from the first save-set present on a magnetic tape (loaded in the MKA300:) tape drive as follows:

```
$$$ MOUNT/FOREIGN MKA300:          ! Mount the tape media
$$$ MOUNT/FOREIGN DKA0:            ! Target must be /FOREIGN
$$$ BACKUP/IMAGE  MKA300:/SAVE DKA100:
```

13.5.7 Booting OpenVMS/VAX from CD-ROM

You may have noticed that when you initially installed OpenVMS/VAX by booting from the CD-ROM distribution disk, you landed in Standalone BACKUP. To refresh your memory, this is in beginning of the installation dialog:

```
>>> boot dka400

-DKA400
%SYSBOOT-I-SYSBOOT Mapping the SYSDUMP.DMP on the System Disk
%SYSBOOT-W-SYSBOOT Can not map SYSDUMP.DMP on the System Disk
%SYSBOOT-W-SYSBOOT Can not map PAGEFILE.SYS on the System Disk

   OpenVMS (TM) VAX Version X7G7 Major version id = 1 Minor version id = 0

%WBM-I-WBMINFO Write Bitmap has successfully completed initialization.
PLEASE ENTER DATE AND TIME (DD-MMM-YYYY  HH:MM)  28-APR-2003 18:04

Configuring devices . . .

Available device  DKA400:                 device type SONY CD-ROM CDU-5
Available device  DKB100:                 device type RZ28B
Available device  MKB300:                 device type TK86

%BACKUP-I-IDENT, Stand-alone BACKUP T7.2; the date is 28-APR-2003 18:05:31.41
$
```

When at the $ prompt, the only acceptable command is BACKUP. This can be used to backup the system disk as described throughout this chapter. No MOUNT commands are necessary because BACKUP mounts both devices. Simply enter the following:

```
$ BACKUP/IMAGE/VERIFY DKB100: MKB300:FULL.SAV/REWIND/LABEL=FULL
```

13.5.8 Booting Standalone BACKUP from Disk

There is no provision to build a VAX bootable environment as done in the previous section for the Alpha. Instead, a bootable system supporting only BACKUP can be created on most any device. This is called the Standalone Backup utility. Standalone BACKUP is invoked by issuing special boot commands described below. So, instead of booting OpenVMS, you boot Standalone BACKUP from the system disk, an alternative disk, the console device, or tape.

If you have a small spare disk, you should consider establishing it as the Standalone BACKUP disk. You can create this disk either by making an exact copy of your current system disk using OpenVMS BACKUP or by installing a minimal OpenVMS kit using the OpenVMS/VAX VMSKITBLD command procedure as illustrated below. Once this disk is established, you have the ability to boot Standalone BACKUP and then save and restore your system disk.

Standalone BACKUP is actually a minimal version of the OpenVMS/VAX operating system. Before you can boot Standalone BACKUP from disk, you have to create the system on a device that is accessible during system boot.

Invoke VMSKITBLD with the following command:

```
$ @SYS$UPDATE:VMSKITBLD
```

This script prompts the user as follows:

```
* Operation [BUILD,ADD,COPY]? BUILD
```

where BUILD means to build OpenVMS on another disk in SYS0. This disk will be initialized prior to build. ADD means to create an alternate system root directory (SYSE) on a system disk without initializing it. COPY means to copy the OpenVMS files to another system disk without deleting the existing files on that disk, thus creating an alternate system root directory (SYSE).

The dialog continues to determine the source and target devices as follows:

```
* Enter mounted SOURCE disk name (ddcu:): SYS$SYSDEVICE:
* Enter SOURCE top level system directory [default = SYS0]:
* Enter TARGET disk name (ddcu:): DUA200:
* Enter TARGET disk top level system directory [default = SYS0]:
```

The dialog continues and the specific prompts depend on the [BUILD,ADD,COPY] option you selected. To make sure it is doing the right thing. The confirmation message below is displayed:

```
The target disk will be initialized.
Target disk, _DUA200:, ready to be initialized? (Y/N): Y
```

Finally, the script displays progress messages:

```
%MOUNT-I-MOUNTED, VAXVMS mounted on _DUA200:
Creating system specific directories ...
Creating cluster common directories ...
Creating SYSGEN files ...
%SYSGEN-I-CREATED, _DUA200:<SYS0.SYSEXE>SWAPFILE.SYS;1 created
%SYSGEN-I-CREATED, _DUA200:<SYS0.SYSEXE>PAGEFILE.SYS;1 created
%SYSGEN-I-CREATED, _DUA200:<SYS0.SYSEXE>SYSDUMP.DMP;1 created
Copying files from source disk ...
Copying DECwindows file from source disk ...
Writing a boot block ...
System disk complete.
```

If you built a Standalone BACKUP on an existing system disk, an additional system root [SYSE] is created; that is, the files necessary to boot Standalone BACKUP are created in the SYSE root. The build procedure actually uses alias directory entries to point to existing system directories, so there is really only one physical copy of each file. For this reason, building the kit on a system disk uses very little disk space.

To boot from the SYSE root directory, the following command is used:

>>> **B/E0000000** ***disk-device***

For example, on MicroVAX systems this is accomplished as follows:

>>> **B/E0000000 DUA0**

On the other hand, when you build a Standalone BACKUP on a nonsystem disk, it is built into the [SYS0] system root. Therefore, you specify a value of 0 for the upper four bits of the boot control flags (register R5). On MicroVAX systems, 0 is the default value for the boot control flags, so you can simply enter the standard boot command followed by the name of the device containing the Standalone BACKUP:

>>> **B** ***disk-device***

for example:

>>> **B DUA1**

Or

```
>>> B tape-device
```

for example:

```
>>> B MUA300
```

The specific procedures for booting Standalone BACKUP for each processor are presented in appendix C.

13.6 Implementation

Once you develop a backup strategy, the next step is to determine the exact DCL commands necessary to implement your strategy. The following sections present details for performing the different backup types discussed throughout this chapter.

13.6.1 Full Backups

Full backups can be implemented by performing either a full file backup or full image backup as follows:

Full (online) File Backup

[load unused tape and place online]

```
$ MOUNT/FOREIGN MUA300:

$ BACKUP/REWIND/LABEL=S01W2/IGNORE=INTERLOCK -
      /VERIFY/LIST=TASM$BACKUPS:S01W2_FILEU1.LIS/RECORD -
      DISK$USER1: MUA300:FILEU1.BCK
```

Full (online) Image Backup

[load unused tape and place online]

```
$ MOUNT/FOREIGN MUA300:

$ BACKUP/IMAGE/REWIND/LABEL=S01W1/IGNORE=INTERLOCK -
      /VERIFY/LIST=TASM$BACKUPS:S01W1_IMAGEU1.LIS/RECORD -
      DISK$USER1: MUA300:IMAGEU1.BCK
```

The subtle difference between these two commands is the /IMAGE qualifier. /IMAGE is required only for bootable disks. In both of these cases, the disk to be backed up is presumed to be mounted and accessible by the user. The tape, mounted with the /FOREIGN qualifier, will be initialized by BACKUP so any data on it beforehand will be lost. /IGNORE=INTERLOCK is specified so that any open files will be copied—if this is not specified, open files will not be copied. The /LIST qualifier specifies a file in which the names of all files will be placed. This is for accurate record keeping. The /RECORD qualifier forces BACKUP to put the date and time into the file's directory entry. Again, this is for record keeping. For instance, to find out when a file was last backed up, you can enter the command:

```
$ dir/date=backup systartup_vms.com;0

Directory SYS$COMMON:[SYSMGR]

SYSTARTUP_VMS.COM;3
                                   8-MAY-2003 09:36:41.82
```

If the disk to be backed up is offline, it must be mounted before performing the backup operation. Presumably, it would be mounted so that only BACKUP could access it—it would not be mounted so that others may access it, thus opening files on it.

13.6.2 Incremental Backups

13.6.2.1 Cumulative Incremental Backup

Before you perform a cumulative incremental backup, you must first perform a full backup. During the full backup (either an image or full file backup), use the optional /RECORD qualifier. This forces the date and time of the backup to be written into the backup date field of each file after the BACKUP completes. For example:

[Monday (online) Full Image Backup]

```
$ MOUNT/FOREIGN MUA300:
$ BACKUP/IMAGE/REWIND/LABEL=S01W1/IGNORE=INTERLOCK -
      /VERIFY/LIST=TASM$BACKUPS:S01W1_IMAGEU1.LIS/RECORD -
      DISK$USER1: MUA300:IMAGEU1.BCK
```

Then perform the cumulative incremental backups.

[Tuesday (online) Cumulative Incremental]

```
$ MOUNT/FOREIGN MUA300:
$ BACKUP/REWIND/LABEL=S01D2/IGNORE=INTERLOCK -
      /VERIFY/LIST=TASM$BACKUPS:S01D2_INCRU1.LIS -
      DISK$USER1:[000000...]*.*;*/SINCE=BACKUP -
      MUA300:INCRU1.BCK
```

Notice the above command does not include the /RECORD modifier; thus, the backup time on the file is not changed—it remains the date of Monday. Thus, the Tuesday, Wednesday, and so forth, backups each contain all files created since Monday. That is, the backup save-set grows each day.

[Wednesday (online) Cumulative Incremental]

```
$ MOUNT/FOREIGN MUA300:
$ BACKUP/REWIND/LABEL=S01D3/IGNORE=INTERLOCK –
      /VERIFY/LIST=TASM$BACKUPS:S01D3_INCRU1.LIS –
      DISK$USER1:[000000...]*.*;*/SINCE=BACKUP -
      MUA300:INCRU1.BCK
```

The above command only differs from the Tuesday command because the names of the label and list file are unique to the day of the week. This is done to help manage the save-sets.

13.6.2.2 Differential Backup

The syntax for a differential backup is similar to that of a cumulative incremental backup, except each incremental backup uses the /RECORD qualifier to force an update of the file backup date.

[Monday (online) Full Image Backup]

```
$ MOUNT/FOREIGN MUA300:
$ BACKUP/IMAGE/REWIND/LABEL=S01W1/IGNORE=INTERLOCK -
      /VERIFY/LIST=TASM$BACKUPS:S01W1_IMAGEU1.LIS/RECORD -
      DISK$USER1: -
      MUA300:IMAGEU1.BCK
```

[Tuesday (online) Differential Backup]

```
$ MOUNT/FOREIGN MUA300:
```

```
$ BACKUP/REWIND/LABEL=S01D2/IGNORE=INTERLOCK -
     /VERIFY/LIST=TASM$BACKUPS:S01D2_INCRU1.LIS -
     DISK$USER1:[000000...]*.*;*/SINCE=BACKUP/RECORD -
     MUA300:INCRU1.BCK
```

[Wednesday (online) Differential Backup]

```
$ MOUNT/FOREIGN MUA300:
$ BACKUP/REWIND/LABEL=S01D3/IGNORE=INTERLOCK -
     /VERIFY/LIST=TASM$BACKUPS:S01D3_INCRU1.LIS -
     DISK$USER1:[000000...]*.*;*/SINCE=BACKUP/RECORD -
     MUA300:INCRU1.BCK
```

Note that the /RECORD qualifier is used on every backup. Again, the label and list file names are unique.

13.6.3 Standalone BACKUP

You have several Standalone BACKUP options as summarized in table 13.3. If you have not done so already, read section 13.5 for building and using these options.

Table 13.3 *Stand-alone Boot Options*

Architecture	Typical Boot Command	Description
Alpha	BOOT DKA400	Boot OpenVMS/Alpha distribution CD
Alpha	BOOT -flags E,0 DKA500	Boot alternate system disk*
VAX	B DKA400	Boot OpenVMS/VAX distribution CD
VAX	B/R5:E0000000 DKA200	Boot Standalone BACKUP kit*

* Alternates and kits must be built by the manager before use.

Before you can boot a minimal OpenVMS system or a Standalone BACKUP system, you must first perform a system shutdown (see chapter 6 for details), as follows:

```
$ @SYS$SYSTEM:SHUTDOWN
```

During the shutdown process, do not request an automatic reboot. When the shutdown completes, force the console terminal into console mode by pressing the key sequence appropriate to the hardware model (e.g., type <CTRL/P>, <BREAK> or press the console <HALT> button). After you receive the console boot prompt, enter the specific console command required to boot the desired backup disk as outlined in table 13.3.

The exact command necessary to bootstrap a CPU is processor- and platform-specific. Refer to appendix C to determine the commands for your system.

After you enter the correct boot command on OpenVMS/Alpha, you then enter the following BACKUP commands. The $$$ prompt indicates that the CD-ROM distribution has been booted.

```
$$$ MOUNT/FOREIGN MKA300:
$$$ MOUNT/OVER=ID DKA200:
$$$ BACKUP/REWIND/IMAGE/VERIFY DKA200: MKA300:IMAGEA0.BCK/SAVE
```

After you enter the correct boot command on OpenVMS/VAX, you then can enter the following BACKUP commands. The VAX CD-ROM distribution has only a single $ prompt and BACKUP is the only valid command; MOUNT is unnecessary.

```
$ BACKUP/REWIND/IMAGE/VERIFY DKA0: MKA300:IMAGEA0.BCK/SAVE
```

Similar commands would be used to restore the system disk.

13.6.4 Full Image Restore with Incremental Backup

The following is a sample restore of DKA200: using the latest cumulative incremental backup created in the previous examples.

[Full Image Restore]

[load S01W1 into the tape drive]

```
$ MOUNT/FOREIGN DKA200:
$ MOUNT/OVER=ID MKA300:
$ BACKUP/IMAGE/VERIFY/LOG MKA300:IMAGEU1.BCK/SAVE DKA200:
```

[Restore Cumulative Incremental]

[load S01D3 into tape drive]

```
$ MOUNT/OVER=ID MKA300:
$ BACKUP/INCREMENTAL/VERIFY/LOG MKA300:INCRU1.BCK DKA200:[*]
```

[Remount drive for public use]

```
$ MOUNT/SYSTEM DKA200: USER1 DISK$USER1
```

To restore a backup that consists of multiple incremental differential backups, first restore the full image backup. Then, restore each incremental backup, starting with the latest and ending with the earliest.

13.6.5 BACKUP and Volume Shadowing

HP's OpenVMS Volume Shadowing product allows you to bind two or more physical disks together and logically view them as a single device called a *shadowset.* When you write to a shadowset, the change is applied to every member of the set. In this way, the contents of all shadow members remain identical. If one members fails, it is removed from the shadowset, and users can continue accessing the remaining members without interruption.

Volume shadowing provides extra protection against drive failures and particularly against data loss due to bad blocks; however, it is not a backup technique because it does not account for deleted files. Volume shadowing does provide protection specifically against disk failure and disk block failures and (when operating in a cluster) against the failure of a host system. Shadowing does not protect against failure of all members of a shadowset, against cluster hardware failures, software failures, or user error. Even if all your disks are shadowed, you should still perform regular image or file backups.

Although volume shadowing itself is not a backup strategy, it does provide additional backup options. As on any other disk, you can perform an online backup of a shadowset, but you must consider the usual warnings regarding online backups, as discussed earlier in this chapter. Another option is to remove one member from a shadowset and perform an offline backup of that member, then add the disk back into the shadowset. Using this technique, you can ensure consistent backups and maintain high data availability.

The following procedure demonstrates how to back up a user's shadowset member. This procedure does not apply to shadowed system disks. A system disk should be backed up with a stand-alone system as explained earlier.

[Mount two disks as a shadowset during startup]

```
$ MOUNT/SYSTEM DSA8:/SHADOW=($1$DGA1:, $1$DGA2:) USR1
%MOUNT-I-MOUNTED, USR1 mounted on _DSA8:
%MOUNT-I-SHDWMEMSUCC, _$1$DGA1: (USR1) is now a valid shadowset member
%MOUNT-I-SHDWMEMSUCC, _$1$DGA2: (USR1) is now a valid shadowset member
```

[Prepare to backup. Dissolve the shadowset, then recreate it less DGA2:]

```
$ DISMOUNT/SYSTEM DSA8:
$ MOUNT/SYSTEM DSA8:/SHADOW=($1$DGA1:) USR1
```

[Mount the tape and DGA2: locally and privately. Back it up as described above]

```
$ MOUNT/FOREIGN MKA400:
$ MOUNT $1$DGA2: USR1
%MOUNT-W-VOLSHDWMEM, mounting a shadowset member volume write locked
$ BACKUP/VERIFY $1$DGA2: MKA400:D2USR1/SAVE
```

[After the backup, add it into the shadowset, where it will be synchronized with the online disk]

```
$ MOUNT/SYSTEM DSA8:/SHADOW=($1$DGA1:, $1$DGA2:) USR1
%MOUNT-I-SHDWMEMSUCC, _$1$DGA2: (USR1) added to shadowset with a copy operation
```

To ensure a consistent backup, you must dissolve the entire shadowset, then recreate the shadowset less one member. You cannot use this technique with the BACKUP /RECORD qualifier (e.g., for incremental backups), because when you add the member back to the shadowset, the backup date information is overwritten by the shadow copy operation.

You must also take special steps when restoring a shadowset, because when the disks are synchronized, you could lose the backup. The correct procedure requires that the target disk of a restore operation be mounted foreign. HP does not support mounting a shadowset foreign; thus, you must manually mount the target disk using the following commands:

[Dismount shadowset and mount DGA1: foreign. Also mount the tape]

```
$ DISMOUNT/SYSTEM DSA8:
$ MOUNT/FOREIGN/OVERRIDE=SHADOW_MEMBERSHIP $1$DGA1:
$ MOUNT/OVER=ID MKA400:
```

Then, restore the disk, as follows:

[Restore as described above]

```
$ BACKUP/VERIFY MKA400:D2USR1/SAVE $1$DGA1:
```

[Recreate shadowset. DGA1: must be on the left and DGA2: will be synchronized to it.]

```
$ MOUNT/SYSTEM DSA8:/SHADOW=($1$DGA1:, $1$DGA2:) USR1
%MOUNT-I-MOUNTED, USR1 mounted on _DSA8:
%MOUNT-I-SHDWMEMSUCC, _$1$DGA1: (USR1) is now a valid shadowset member
%MOUNT-I-SHDWMEMSUCC, _$1$DGA2: (USR1) added to shadowset with a copy operation
```

When you mount the shadowset, 1DGA1: is considered more current (because of the restore operation); thus, the shadow software initiates a shadow copy from 1DGA1: to 1DGA2:.

13.6.6 Media Labeling

Even if you retain tapes for a moderate amount of time you can easily accumulate a backup tape inventory containing hundreds of tapes. For even the smallest site, you will need to adopt a tape-labeling scheme that allows you to quickly locate and identify each tape. Each tape should have a written label and a unique electronic label. To keep things simple, you should make the written label the same as the electronic label. Tape labels should indicate when the backup was created and its contents. Alternatively, the tape labels may be six-digit numbers and a log book system may be used to keep track of the detailed history and status of the tape. Electronic tape labels can be only six characters long.

The sample backup procedures presented at the end of this chapter use labels by concatenating a backup set name, the backup type, and a sequential number, as follows:

"Backup-set-name + Backup-type + Sequence-number"

3 characters + 1 character + 2 characters = 6 characters

For example:

Label	Description
S0lW4	Weekly Backup #4 of Set S01
S02D2	Daily Backup #2 of Set S02
S0lY2	Yearly Backup #2 of Set S01

The backup set describes the set of disks contained on the tape. Some system managers include the device name in the tape label. This strategy will not work if you want to back up multiple devices onto a single tape. For example, you might organize disks into the following backup sets:

- Backup Set: "S01"

  ```
  DISK$USER1—DKA200
  DISK$USER2—DKA300
  ```

- Backup Set: "S02"

  ```
  DISK$SCR1—DKA0
  ```

To specify the backup type, this strategy uses a single letter, as follows:

D—Daily

W—Weekly

M—Monthly

Q—Quarterly

Y—Yearly

The last two characters of the tape label are sequential numbers to make the tape labels unique.

13.6.7 Locating Backup Media

You can facilitate locating backup media by creating OpenVMS backup listing files as indicated in the examples above. When you perform backups, you should use the /LIST qualifier to create a list of all files written during the backup.

In the earlier examples, all backup listing files were created in the directory TASM$BACKUPS and included the tape label and the backup save-set, as follows:

```
S01W4_IMAGEU1.LIS ! Listing file for DISK$USER1
S01W4_IMAGEU2.LIS ! Listing file for DISK$USER2
S02D2_IMAGES1.LIS ! Listing file for DISK$SCR1
```

Thus, if a user requests a specific file named XXY.DAT, you could search all DISK$USER2 image backups for that name, as follows:

```
$ SEARCH TASM$BACKUPS:*IMAGEU1.LIS "XXY.DAT"
```

Once located in the list file, you will know which save-set (or sets) contains the specific file. Then, you can perform the restore of that specific file.

13.7 OpenVMS BACKUP Performance

For the best OpenVMS BACKUP performance, you must set two system parameters and six user account values correctly.

First, you must ensure that the system parameters are set as follows. You cannot change the user's account in SYSUAF until the system parameters are corrected.

```
CHANNELCNT 128 ! Must be >= 128 (FILLM)
WSMAX 16384    ! Must be >= 16,384 (WSQUOTA)
```

Use SYSMAN to examine these values; for instance:

```
$ MCR SYSMAN PARAMETER SHOW CHANNELCNT
%SYSMAN-I-USEACTNOD, a USE ACTIVE has been defaulted on node VAX
Node VAX:    Parameters in use: ACTIVE
Parameter Name          Current     Default     Minimum     Maximum Unit  Dynamic
--------------          -------     -------     -------     ------- ----  -------
CHANNELCNT                  128         128          31        2047 Channels
```

If you must change them, edit them into SYS$SYSTEM:MODPARAMS.DAT and run AUTOGEN with the REBOOT parameter; for example:

```
$  @SYS$UPDATE:AUTOGEN GETDATA REBOOT FEEDBACK
```

Next, you must properly configure the user account as summarized in table 13.4. If you use the SYSTEM account to perform backups, changes should be made to that account. Two databases must be checked and possibly changed.

Table 13.4 *Recommended Account Values for Optimal BACKUP Performance*

AUTHORIZE parameter	SET/SHOW WORKING_SET *name*	Recommended Value
WSQUOTA	/Quota	16,384
WSEXTENT	/Extent	at least WSQUOTA
AUTHORIZE *parameter*	**SHOW PROCESS/QUOTA *name***	**Recommended Value**
PGFLQUO	Paging file quota	32,768
FILLM	Open file quota	128
DIOLM	Direct I/O limit	4,096
ASTLM	AST quota	4,096
BIOLM	Buffered I/O limit	128
BYTLM	Buffered I/O byte count quota	65,536
ENQLM	Enqueue quota	256

When logged into the account, use SHOW WORKING_SET to examine WSQUOTA and WSEXTENT. Then, use SET WORKING_SET to change these variables. Any changes made to these working-set variables are permanent.

Still in the account, use SHOW PROCESS/QUOTA to examine the other six variables and AUTHORIZE to change them if necessary. The SHOW PROCESS/QUOTA data resembles the following. Unfortunately, this display and the AUTHORIZE display variables (see next example) are labeled differently.

```
$ show process/quota

 9-MAR-2003 12:28:27.02   User: SYSTEM          Process ID:   00000036
                          Node: VAX           Process name: "SYSTEM"

Process Quotas:
 Account name: SYSTEM
 CPU limit:                      Infinite  Direct I/O limit:       4000
 Buffered I/O byte count quota:     63872  Buffered I/O limit:      150
 Timer queue entry quota:              30  Open file quota:         300
 Paging file quota:                 62448  Subprocess quota:         10
 Default page fault cluster:           64  AST quota:              4094
```

```
Enqueue quota:                    200  Shared file limit:        0
Max detached processes:             0  Max active jobs:          0
```

Since some variables need adjustment in this account, AUTHORIZE must be used; for example:

```
$ MCR AUTHORIZE
UAF> MODIFY SYSTEM /ENQLM=256
```

Once in AUTHORIZE you can confirm the settings with the following command:

```
UAF> SHOW SYSTEM
. . .
Maxjobs:          0  Fillm:        300  Bytlm:        64000
Maxacctjobs:      0  Shrfillm:       0  Pbytlm:           0
Maxdetach:        0  BIOlm:        150  JTquota:       4096
Prclm:           10  DIOlm:       4000  WSdef:         2000
Prio:             4  ASTlm:       4096  WSquo:        16000
Queprio:          0  TQElm:         30  WSextent:     16000
CPU:         (none)  Enqlm:        256  Pgflquo:      64000
. . .
```

Refer to chapter 18 for more detailed information on system-performance issues and procedures for changing system parameters.

13.8 Enterprise Backup Solutions

The focus of this chapter has been on the primary OpenVMS backup/restore tool called BACKUP. For 24/7 systems and for multiterabyte databases, HP has more extensive layered products available.

13.8.1 Archive Backup System

Archive Backup System (ABS) is a software product that allows you to save and restore data in a heterogeneous environment. ABS provides you with the ability to perform anything from full system backup operations to user-requested or user-created backup operations. ABS ensures data safety and integrity by providing a secure environment for save and restore operations.

ABS uses various backup agents to save and restore data. The backup agent is determined by the type of data, such as OpenVMS files, Oracle Rdb databases, Oracle Rdb storage areas, UNIX files, or NT files. The specific backup agent is responsible for the actual data movement operation, while ABS is responsible for invoking the correct backup agent and recording the information about the save operation in the ABS database. ABS supports the following backup agents:

- OpenVMS BACKUP utility—For OpenVMS files
- RMU BACKUP utility—For Oracle Rdb databases and storage areas
- gtar—For UNIX and NT files (tape archiver).

ABS supports systems that have Hierarchical Storage Management (HSM) installed. HSM is described in the next section. ABS and HSM can be configured together to permit HSM to perform shelving or preshelving of an OpenVMS file data, while nightly backups under ABS will copy only the file system metadata. This cooperative configuration is referred to as *backup via shelving.*

ABS works in conjunction with Media and Device Management Services (MDMS) described below.

13.8.2 Hierarchical Storage Management (HSM)

HSM software is an extension of the OpenVMS file system that allows you to manage your dormant data efficiently. It moves your dormant data from primary storage (where your active data is usually kept) to shelf storage. This frees the space in primary storage for use, while the dormant data remains available on lower-cost media. The movement of your dormant data to shelf storage is called *shelving.*

In the HSM model, data exists in one of three categories:

1. *Active:* data that you access frequently. You want virtually immediate access to this data.
2. *Dormant:* data that you access less frequently. You are willing to wait a short time to access this data.

3. *Inactive:* data that you do not expect to access again, but must keep. Generally, this type of data is kept in an archive for legal or business purposes.

HMS works in conjunction with MDMS described below.

13.8.3 Storage Library System for OpenVMS

There are three kinds of computer users that work with Storage Library System (SLS):

1. *Storage administrators:* responsible for designing and implementing storage-management policies
2. *Operators:* responsible for controlling media and devices to save and restore data
3. *Users:* responsible for managing their own data, which includes requesting information be saved and restored

In any given operating environment, these kinds of users may not be distinguishable. However, SLS provides menus and presumes particular responsibilities are appropriate for each.

13.8.4 Media and Device Management Services

MDMS is an integral part of SLS, providing for customized media management and device control. MDMS serves as an information repository for media and device configurations. MDMS reflects the physical and logical design of your storage devices (tape and optical drives) and the volumes on which you store data. It is important to note that MDMS provides media and device management services. Storage-management tasks, such as backup and restore activities, are managed by the layered applications you use with this product.

13.8.5 Save-Set Manager

Compaq Save-Set Manager for OpenVMS (SSMgr) is a layered software product that reduces user time spent on save-set operations. SSMgr reduces operational time spent during OpenVMS backup operations by providing an avenue for offline save-set validation, copy, and save-set merge functions.

13.9 Tools

Table 13.5 lists several example BACKUP command procedures that are contained with the scripts associated with the book (see appendix E).

Table 13.5 *Example BACKUP Command Procedures*

Command Procedure	Description
BCK CALC_LABEL.COM	Calculate tape label to use
BCK ERRORS.COM	Backup error codes
BCK MENU.COM	Main backup menu
BCK NIGHTLY.COM	Main backup program
BCK RESTORE_FILE.COM	Perform file restore
BCK SELECT_FILE.COM	Select file to restore
BCK SETS.COM	Defines backup sets and attributes

13.10 Conclusion

Saving and restoring the system's data is quite easily done with OpenVMS's BACKUP command. It will format disks and tapes, backup and restore the data, mark the files, and record the names of the files upon which these operations are performed. Unlike other systems, notably UNIX, one command does it all.

However, it is incumbent on the system manager to formulate a policy and process to assure that data is backed up regularly and correctly. The policy should include considerations for restoring data, for coordinating the backup with the site's workload, and for off-site disaster plans.

13.11 Additional References

1. *Disk File Optimizer for OpenVMS* can be scheduled or run manually on online disks.
2. *Hierarchical Storage Management for OpenVMS*

3. *Archive Backup System for OpenVMS*
4. *Storage Library System for OpenVMS*

14

OpenVMS Support and Documentation

14.1 Chapter Objectives

- Present strategies for organizing site documentation
- List OpenVMS online and offline documentation sources
- Discuss HP's support offerings
- Identify other support resources

14.2 Introduction

Sometimes, when you are working on a difficult problem, you reach a point where your progress halts and you become frustrated. This usually happens because you do not completely understand some aspect of the problem. More specifically, there is something you do not know or something you once knew, but have forgotten. This something prevents you from being able to develop a solution. At this point, you have two options:

1. Continue to work on the problem and become even more frustrated.
2. Try to find help.

The ability to recognize when you do not know something is important. Even more important is knowing where to find the information you need. This chapter helps you identify the resources at your disposal and better use your own knowledge by organizing information into site documentation.

14.3 Developing a Site Guide

There is no such thing as a generic data center. Each data center is unique because network equipment, customized startup files, applications, user accounts, system-management tools, batch queues, printers, and terminals are added. This nongeneric site cannot be managed by just anyone. It requires a system manager who knows all the aspects of the site that differentiate it from a generic site.

Ideally, site documentation should describe all nongeneric site attributes. If available, this information allows you and your successors to better understand the environment and to resolve problems quickly. Unfortunately, collecting and organizing this information is difficult and time-consuming. This chapter offers several suggestions for putting your site documentation together.

To get you started, a sample site guide outline is provided in appendix B. As you scan each item in the outline, think about the configuration of your particular site. The information that comes to mind is what should be in the site guide. For each item ask yourself the following questions:

- Why is it there?
- What does it do?
- Who uses it?
- How do I manage it?
- How do I monitor it?

At first you may want simply to assemble information into a three-ring binder. However, as you gather more and more information, you will probably want to make your site guide available online. To facilitate this process, a DCL command procedure named SYSDOC is described in appendix E. SYSDOC allows you to store documentation as standard OpenVMS text files and access them from a simple DCL menu system.

Although there is a large amount of information to document, you do not have to create an entire site guide all at once. Remember that even the simplest documentation can be extremely helpful. First consider compiling a phone list of all support resources (external and internal) and the system components they support. For internal resources, include office, pager, home, and manager phone numbers. This document might take a few hours to assemble, but it will save you an enormous amount of time. More importantly, such a document is essential during emergencies, when saving a few minutes is critical. Of course, accuracy is paramount, so this list must be carefully maintained.

To expand on this idea, think of the information that will save you the most amount of time. Then allocate 15 to 30 minutes each day to work on those items. Gradually, you will find your site guide evolving into a document that you depend on.

14.4 HP Documentation

The next few sections discuss various forms of documentation provided by HP, including the following:

- OpenVMS Help utility (VMSHELP)
- Modifying OpenVMS Help
- OpenVMS Message Help utility (MSGHLP)
- Example code SYS$EXAMPLES and SYS$ETC
- Release notes
- OpenVMS documentation (hard copy)
- CD-ROM documentation

14.4.1 VMSHELP

VMSHELP is a utility that provides access to OpenVMS online documentation. This is usually the quickest way to get answers to simple command syntax questions.

The HELP command invokes the HELP facility to display information about a command or topic. In response to the Topic? prompt, you can do the following:

- Type the name of the command or topic for which you need help.
- Type "INSTRUCTIONS" for more detailed instructions on how to use HELP.
- Type "HINTS" if you are not sure of the name of the command or topic for which you need help.

- Type "/MESSAGE" for help with the HELP/MESSAGE utility.
- Type a question mark (?) to redisplay the most recently requested text.
- Press the <RETURN> key one or more times to exit from HELP.

You can abbreviate any topic name, although ambiguous abbreviations result in all matches being displayed.

Invoke VMSHELP using the following command:

```
$ HELP
. . .

Additional information available:

  :=          =           @           ACCOUNTING ACL_Editor ALLOCATE   ANALYZE
  APPEND      ASSIGN      ATTACH      AUTHORIZE  AUTOGEN    BACKUP_API
  BACKUP_Command          BAT         CALL       CANCEL     CC         CDSA
  CLI_Routines            CLOSE       CMS        CONFIGURE  CONNECT    CONTINUE
  CONV$_Routines          CONVERT     COPY       CPML       CQUAL_Routines
  CREATE      CRTL        CXX         CXXDEMANGLE           CXXL       CXXLINK
  CXXLSTD     DCL_Tips    DCX_Routines           DEALLOCATE DEASSIGN   DEBUG
  DECdts      DECevent    DECK        DECset     DECthreads DECTPU     DEFINE
  DEFRAGMENT DELETE       DEPOSIT     DIAGNOSE   DIFFERENCES           DIRECTORY
  DISABLE     DISCONNECT DISMOUNT     DPML       DSR        DUMP       EDIT
  EDT_Routines            ENABLE      ENDSUBROUTINE         EOD        EOJ
  Errors      EXAMINE     EXCHANGE    EXIT       Ext_File_Specs        F77
  F90         FDL_Files   FDL_Routines           FINGER     FONT       FORTRAN
  FTP         GENCAT      GKS         GOSUB      GOTO       GZIP       HELP
  Hints       ICONV       IF          INITIALIZE INQUIRE    INSTALL
  Instructions            JAVA        JOB        KERBEROS   LANCP      LAST
  LATCP       LBR_Routines            LDAP       Lexicals   LGI_Routines
  LIBRARY     LICENSE     Line_editing           LINK       LMCP       LOCALE
  LOGIN       LOGOUT      LPQ         LPRM       LSEDIT     MACRO
  MAIL_Command            MAIL_Routines          MERGE      MESSAGE    MIBCOMP
  MIME        MMK         MMS         MONITOR    MOUNT      Multimedia NCP
  NCS_Command             NCS_Routines           NFS        NOTICE     ON
  OPEN        PASCAL      PASSWORD    PATCH      PCX        Perf_Meter PHIGS
  PHONE       PIPE        POLYCENTER POSIX_Threads          PPPD       PRINT
  PRINT_Parameter         PROBE       PRODUCT    PSM_Routines          PURGE
  Queues      RCP         READ        RECALL     RECOVER    RENAME     REPLY
  REQUEST     RETURN      REXEC       RLOGIN     RMS        RPC        RPCGEN
  RSH         RTL_Routines            RUN        RUNOFF     SCACP      SEARCH
  SET         SHOW        SMB_Routines           SMTP       SORT
```

```
  SOR_Routines          SPAWN      SPELL      START      STOP       SUBMIT
  SUBROUTINE Symbol_Assign         SYNCHRONIZE           SYSGEN     SYSMAN
  System_Services       Sys_Files  Sys_Parameters        TCPIPTRACE
  TCPIP_Services        TCPTRACE   TELNET     TFF        TN3270     TYPE
  UIL         UNLOCK    UNZIP      UNZIPSFX   V731_Features
  V73_Features          VERB       VIEW       VMSTAR     WAIT       WRITE
  WWPPS       XGCP      ZIP

Topic?
```

At the prompt, you can request more information on any of the topics presented (e.g., PRINT, SHOW).

14.4.2 OpenVMS HINTS

If you are not sure which utility or command you need information about, use the hints facility as follows:

```
$ HELP HINTS

HINTS

Type the name of one of the categories listed below to obtain a list of
related commands and topics. To obtain detailed information on a topic,
press the <RETURN> key until you reach the Topic? prompt and then type the
name of the topic. Topics that appear in all upper case are DCL commands.
The following additional information is information:

Batch_and_print_jobs     Command_procedures       Contacting_People
Creating_processes       Developing_programs      Executing_programs
Files_and_directories    Logical_names            Operators_in_expressions
Physical_devices         Security                 System_management
Terminal_environment     User_environment

HINTS Subtopic?
```

At the prompt, enter the topics about which you want more information. You will be presented with a list of commands and utilities related to the topic you selected. Finally, return to the main help menu and request help on the utilities suggested.

14.4.3 Modifying the HELP library

The HELP library, HELPLIB.HLP, is easily modified to meet your site's needs. An alternative approach to VMSDOC described in section 14.3 is to add one or more entries to the library.

As an example, suppose you would like to add a subject entitled "Emergencies" to HELP. The first step is to create an ASCII file called EMERGENCIES.HLP with any editor. It could look like the following:

```
$ type emergencies.hlp

1 EMERGENCIES

The following categories contain contact numbers for various
emergencies.  Remember that 911 should be used for any medical
emergency day or night.

2 AIR_CONDITIONING

If the air conditioning fails - the blowers stop - in the
machine room, it is imperative that it is fixed quickly or the
computers will overheat.  You have approximately one hour
before the room becomes too hot to safely operate the
computers.

Week Days:
Week Evenings:
Week Nights:
Weekends any time:

2 ELECTRICAL_FAILURE

Mumble, mumble.

2 SERVER_CRASH

Etc., etc.
```

Next the .HLP is added to HELPLIB.HLB with the following command.

```
$ LIBRARY/REPLACE/HELP SYS$HELP:HELPLIB.HLB EMERGENCIES.HLP
```

Then, it can be used as follows:

```
$ help emer

EMERGENCIES

  The following categories contain contact numbers for
  various emergencies.  Remember that 911 should be
  used for any medical emergency day or night.

  Additional information available:

  AIR_CONDITIONING    ELECTRICAL_FAILURE    SERVER_CRASH

EMERGENCIES Subtopic? air

EMERGENCIES

  AIR_CONDITIONING


  If the air conditioning fails - the blowers stop -
  in the machine room, it is imperative that it is fixed
  quickly or the computers will overheat.  You have
  approximately one hour before the room becomes too hot
  to safely operate the computers.

    Week Days:
    Week Evenings:
    Week Nights:
    Weekends any time:


EMERGENCIES Subtopic?
```

Some caution must be used in generating the .HLP file. Since HELP indents, the .HLP file should not extend all the way to column 80. I stop at column 60 to be safe. Any number in column 1 defines a subcategory head-ing. I make it a practice to indent all my prose and use column 1 exclusively for subcategories. Subcategories should not contain blanks. This facilitates the use of HELP because it will not permit the following.

14.4.4 Other HELP Libraries

By default, the HELP command accesses the main OpenVMS help library, which consists of the file SYS$HELP:HELPLIB.HLB. There are a number of separate help libraries for more complex utilities (e.g., AUTHORIZE), which you can list using the following command:

```
$ DIR SYS$HELP:*.HLB

Directory SYS$COMMON:[SYSHLP]

ACLEDT.HLB;1          ANALAUDIT$HELP.HLB;1                          ANLRMSHLP.HLB;1
BKM$HELP.HLB;1        CMS$DW_HELP.HLB;1     DBG$HELP.HLB;1          DBG$UIHELP.HLB;1
DECSET$ENVMGR.HLB;1   DECW$DXMHELP_HELP.HLB;1                       DECW$HELPHELP.HLB;1
DECW$PRINTWGT.HLB;1   DEFRAGMENT.HLB;1      DFG$DW.HLB;3            DISKQUOTA.HLB;1
DTEHELP.HLB;1         DTSDTR.HLB;1          EDFHLP.HLB;1            EDTHELP.HLB;2
ESS$LADCP.HLB;1       ESS$LASTCPHELP.HLB;1                          EVE$HELP.HLB;1
EVE$KEYHELP.HLB;1     EXCHNGHLP.HLB;1       HELPLIB.HLB;7           INSTALHLP.HLB;1
KRB$ADMIN_HELP.HLB;1                        KRB$USER_HELP.HLB;1     LAN$HELP.HLB;1
LANCP$HELP.HLB;1      LATCP$HELP.HLB;1      LSE$CLIHELP.HLB;1       LSE$HELP.HLB;1
LSE$KEYPAD.HLB;1      LSE$MENU.HLB;1        MAILHELP.HLB;1          MAILUAF.HLB;1
MIME$HELP.HLB;1       MMS$DW_HELP.HLB;1     MNRHELP.HLB;1           NCPHELP.HLB;1
PCX_HELPLIB.HLB;1     PE$HELP.HLB;1         PHONEHELP.HLB;1         PPPD$HELP.HLB;1
REGCP$HELP.HLB;1      SCACP$HELP.HLB;1      SDA.HLB;1               SHWCLHELP.HLB;1
SYSGEN.HLB;2          SYSMANHELP.HLB;2      TCPIP$FTP_HELP.HLB;1
TCPIP$NSLOOKUP_HELP.HLB;1                   TCPIP$SDA.HLB;1
TCPIP$TELNET_HELP.HLB;1                     TCPIP$UCP_HELP.HLB;1
TECO.HLB;1            TFF$TFUHELP.HLB;1     TPUHELP.HLB;2           UAFHELP.HLB;2
UCM$HELP.HLB;1        WP.HLB;1              WWPPSHLP.HLB;1          XFC$SDA.HLB;1

Total of 63 files.
```

To access one of the foregoing libraries, specify the library name using the /LIBRARY qualifier, as follows:

```
$ HELP/LIBRARY=SYS$HELP:UAFHELP.HLB

HELP
```

```
    Displays information concerning the use of AUTHORIZE, including
    formats and explanations of commands, parameters, and qualifiers.

    Format

      HELP  [keyword[,...]]

  Additional information available:

  ADD         AUTHORIZE  Command_Summary       COPY        CREATE      DEFAULT
  EXIT        GRANT      HELP         LIST     MODIFY      REMOVE      RENAME
  REVOKE      SHOW       Usage_Summary         Using_AUTHORIZE

Topic?
```

This is, of course, identical (except for the introduction) to what you would see if you entered HELP to the UAF prompt as shown below:

```
$ MCR AUTHORIZE

UAF> HELP

  Information available:

  ADD         AUTHORIZE  Command_Summary       COPY        CREATE      DEFAULT
  EXIT        GRANT      HELP         LIST     MODIFY      REMOVE      RENAME
  REVOKE      SHOW       Usage_Summary         Using_AUTHORIZE

Topic?
```

14.4.5 MSGHLP

You can use MSGHLP to receive context-sensitive help after receiving an error message. For example:

```
$ XYZ          ! Type and invalid command
%DCL-W-IVVERB, unrecognized command verb – check validity and spelling
\XYZ\
$ HELP/MESSAGE
IVVERB, unrecognized command verb – check validity and spelling
```

```
Facility:     CLI, Command Language Interpreter (DCL)

Explanation: The first word on the command is not a valid DCL command or a
symbol name equated with a command. The rejected portion of the command is
displayed between backslashes.


User Action: Check the spelling of the command name or symbol name, then
reenter the command.
```

You can also use MSGHLP at any time to display information about a specific system message, as follows:

```
$ HELP/MESSAGE NOSUCHFILE
```

MSGHLP will also translate a hexadecimal status code to an English message:

```
$ HELP/MESS/STAT=%xC

ACCVIO,   access violation, reason mask='xx', virtual
           address='location', PC='location', PSL='xxxxxxxx'

  Facility:      SYSTEM, System Services

  Explanation:   An image attempted to read from or write to a memory
                 location that is protected from the current mode. This
                 message indicates an exception condition and is followed by
                 a register and stack dump to help locate the error. The
                 reason mask is a longword whose lowest 5 bits, if set,
                 indicate that the ...
```

This facility is very powerful and more information can be obtained with the following command. In particular several other qualifiers are available.

```
$ HELP HELP/MESSAGE
HELP

  /MESSAGE
```

```
   Displays descriptions of system messages.

   Format

     HELP/MESSAGE  [/qualifier [...]] [search-string]

Additional information available:

Parameter  Qualifiers
/BRIEF     /DELETE    /EXTRACT   /FACILITY  /FULL     /INSERT
/LIBRARY   /OUTPUT    /PAGE      /SECTION_FILE        /SORT      /STATUS
/WORD_MATCH           /WORK_FILES
Examples
```

If your site is creating applications, MSGHLP can be used to extend its database of messages. Then the application error messages would be presented in the same way and in the same format as any other OpenVMS error message. HELP/MESSAGE would be supported as well. This is a good human-engineering practice.

14.4.6 SYS$EXAMPLES and SYS$ETC

DEC, Compaq, and HP engineers have contributed several examples, usually for programmers, over the years. These two directory trees contain many of them. Release notes, installation notes, and so forth may refer to some of them. But mostly the manager and programmers must simply dig through them for nuggets. The listing of the files in this tree is huge. A display of the directory tree should be enough to convince you that this is a valuable source of information.

```
$ tree SYS$EXAMPLES
Directory SYS$SYSROOT:[SYSHLP.EXAMPLES]

 GKS
 APPDEV+
       +COMMON
       +GUI
       +NOM
       +OBB
       +RPC
       +SOCKETS
```

```
CDSA+
    +DES
    +MDS
CRTL
CXX
DCE+
   +TOOLS
DCPS
DECCHART
DECW+
    +UTILS
DECWRITE+
        +FONTS
GKS
KRB
LSE
MMOV+
    +AUDIO
    +COMMON
    +SAMPLE
    +VIDEO
MMS
PASCAL
PHIGS+
     +ADA
     +BATTLEZONE
     +DEMO
     +DEVELOPERS-GUIDE
     +GETTING-STARTED
     +MISC
     +UTILS
PPPD+
    +DOC
TCPIP+
     +IPV6+
          +BIND
     +RPC
     +SNMP
UCX
XDPS
Grand total of 48 subdirectories
```

TREE is a freeware tool, not part of the supported OpenVMS system.

14.4.7 Release Notes

Each time a product is installed in OpenVMS, release notes are copied into SYS$HELP. To find them, enter the following command:

```
$ dir SYS$HELP:*.release_notes

Directory SYS$COMMON:[SYSHLP]

ADX072.RELEASE_NOTES;1                  ALPBASE01_071.RELEASE_NOTES;1
ALPBASE02_071.RELEASE_NOTES;1           ALPCLUSIO01_062.RELEASE_NOTES;3
ALPCPU02_062.RELEASE_NOTES;1            ALPDCL01_071.RELEASE_NOTES;1
ALPF11X03_071.RELEASE_NOTES;1           ALPIPC01_071.RELEASE_NOTES;1
ALPLAD01_071.RELEASE_NOTES;1            ALPLAN04_062.RELEASE_NOTES;1
ALPLAT02_071.RELEASE_NOTES;1            ALPLAT03_062.RELEASE_NOTES;1
ALPLMF01_062.RELEASE_NOTES;1            ALPLOGI07_071.RELEASE_NOTES;1
ALPMAIL02_071.RELEASE_NOTES;1           ALPMANA02_070.RELEASE_NOTES;1
ALPMOTF02_U4012.RELEASE_NOTES;1         ALPMOTF03_U4012.RELEASE_NOTES;1
ALPMOUN04_071.RELEASE_NOTES;1           ALPMTAA01_070.RELEASE_NOTES;1
ALPOPCO01_070.RELEASE_NOTES;1           ALPRMS02_062.RELEASE_NOTES;1
ALPRMS02_071.RELEASE_NOTES;1            ALPRMS03_071.RELEASE_NOTES;1
ALPRTPA01_062.RELEASE_NOTES;1           ALPSCSI04_071.RELEASE_NOTES;1
ALPSCSI05_062.RELEASE_NOTES;1           ALPSYS06_070.RELEASE_NOTES;1
ALPSYS08_070.RELEASE_NOTES;1            ALPSYS09_071.RELEASE_NOTES;1
ALPSYS15_071.RELEASE_NOTES;1            ALPSYSB02_071.RELEASE_NOTES;1
AXPPHIGS050.RELEASE_NOTES;1             CC056.RELEASE_NOTES;2
CC065.RELEASE_NOTES;1                   CMS039.RELEASE_NOTES;2
CXX065.RELEASE_NOTES;2                  DCPS013.RELEASE_NOTES;1
DCPS021.RELEASE_NOTES;1                 DECAXPGKS065.RELEASE_NOTES;1
DECSET122.RELEASE_NOTES;2               DECW$MOTIFU6012.RELEASE_NOTES;1
DECWRITE031.RELEASE_NOTES;1             DFG023.RELEASE_NOTES;3
DFG026.RELEASE_NOTES;1                  DTM038.RELEASE_NOTES;2
ENVMGR012.RELEASE_NOTES;2               FORRTL.RELEASE_NOTES;1
FORTRAN.RELEASE_NOTES;1                 HGFTP031.RELEASE_NOTES;1
LSE045.RELEASE_NOTES;2                  MGFTP024.RELEASE_NOTES;2
MMOV-V2_0.RELEASE_NOTES;1               MMS032.RELEASE_NOTES;2
MX042.RELEASE_NOTES;3                   NETLIB020.RELEASE_NOTES;1
NETLIB022.RELEASE_NOTES;2               NETLIB023.RELEASE_NOTES;1
PASCAL058.RELEASE_NOTES;1               PCA045.RELEASE_NOTES;2
```

```
SCA045.RELEASE_NOTES;2                      TCPIP053.RELEASE_NOTES;1
TCPIP53ECO02.RELEASE_NOTES;1                TNT032.RELEASE_NOTES;1
UCX042.RELEASE_NOTES;1                      VMS731_F11X-V0100.RELEASE_NOTES;1
VMS731_FIBRE_SCSI-V0100.RELEASE_NOTES;1 VMS731_RMS-V0200.RELEASE_NOTES;1
VMS731_SYS-V0200.RELEASE_NOTES;1            VMS731_SYS-V0300.RELEASE_NOTES;1

Total of 70 files.
```

In the example above you will notice the system I am using dates back quite a way. It also includes release notes from several patches I have installed along the way. In other words, this is one way to determine what is installed on the system.

Installation of layered products and patches is further discussed in chapter 20.

14.4.8 OpenVMS Help Text Files

HP provides the option to copy several help-related text files onto your system disk during an OpenVMS upgrade or installation. By default, these files are created in the directory specified by the logical name SYS$VMSDOC_TEXT. You can list these files and search them with the OpenVMS Search utility, as follows:

```
$ SET DEFAULT SYS$VMSDOC_TEXT

$ DIR/SIZE

Directory SYS$COMMON:[SYSHLP.VMSDOC]

VMSDOC_GLOSSARY.TXT;1          622
VMSDOC_MASTER_INDEX.TXT;1     5843
VMSDOC_OVERVIEW.TXT;1          180

Total of 3 files, 6645 blocks.
```

For example, if you want to know what an accounting file is, you could issue the following command:

```
$ SEARCH/WINDOW=10 VMSDOC_GLOSSARY.TXT "ACCOUNTING FILE"
```

```
accounting file

A file that contains information about system resource use. The
information is stored in binary format: you cannot print it with the
PRINT command or type it with the TYPE command. To process the
accounting file, use the Accounting utility. See current accounting
file.
...
```

Then, if you want to find out which manual discusses the ACCOUNTING utility, you could issue the following command:

```
$ SEARCH/WINDOW=10 VMSDOC_MASTER_INDEX.TXT "ACCOUNTING"
```

The /WINDOW=10 qualifier tells the SEARCH utility to list the 10 lines of text surrounding any matches.

14.4.9 OpenVMS Manuals

Like that of many operating systems, the OpenVMS manual set is huge. The *OpenVMS System Manager's Manual* is a must read. The *OpenVMS User's Manual* is a good starting place for those who are just learning about OpenVMS. If you will be writing applications for OpenVMS, you must have *OpenVMS Programming Concepts Manual* handy.

You should also make sure that you have all the documentation necessary to support the third-party products installed at your site. Frequently, these manuals address product-specific system-management tasks. Without updated manuals, you will not be able to support these products adequately.

Manuals are available in both hard-copy and electronic versions. The electronic manuals may be served to your user community either from a personal computer (PC)–based network or from OpenVMS itself. Installation instructions accompany the CD-ROMs.

14.4.10 CD-ROM Documentation

HP distributes documentation on CD-ROM as a product called *Consolidated On-Line Documentation* (ConOLD). These disks contain the entire extended documentation set and the documentation for many of the HP layered products. This amounts to more than 50,000 pages of documentation. Current documentation uses HTML and Adobe PDF formats for files and is, thus, readable on OpenVMS and a variety of other platforms. Older versions of the ConOLD and older documentation require an X Windows display (such as DECwindows) and the BNU or BOOKREADER application to view CD-ROM documentation. (BNU is included on ConOLD and permits access to both HTML and BOOKREADER documentation.) Freeware tools such as MGBOOK and other tools are available for reading BOOKREADER-format documentation on character-cell terminals. Another benefit of ConOLD is that you can view all documentation on the disks, even for products you have not licensed.

You can purchase CD-ROM distribution service as part of your software support agreement and receive a new ConOLD disk set every few months. If you have many people who need access to OpenVMS documentation, CD-ROM documentation can save you a lot of time and money.

14.4.11 Hard-Copy Documentation

If you would rather have hard copies of the documentation, the order number is published on the title sheet of each document in the ConOLD.

OpenVMS itself is available in a base documentation set or a full documentation set. The base set includes the most commonly used OpenVMS manuals, and it addresses the needs of general users and system managers of small, stand-alone systems. Manuals such as the *Release Notes, New Features,* and the *DCL Dictionary* are included in the base set.

Order numbers are also published in the SPD, which accompanies every HP product. In addition, the SPD contains order numbers for the product's media, license, and support service.

14.5 HP Support

HP offers four basic software support products:

1. Software Support Service (SSS)
2. Software Node Service (SNS)
3. Layered Product Support (LPS)
4. Media and Documentation Distribution Service (MDDS)

14.5.1 SSS

When you purchase SSS for a specific HP system, it provides support for system-integrated products associated with that system. System-integrated products typically include the following:

- OpenVMS
- DECnet
- VMScluster Software

SSS provides the support services described in the following sections.

14.5.1.1 Telephone Support

Telephone support allows three named individuals within your organization to make unlimited telephone support calls to HP customer support centers (CSCs) 24 hours a day, 7 days a week.

14.5.1.2 Advanced Electronic Support

Support Technical Notes

When many customers log support calls concerning a similar problem, HP technicians publish technical notes providing a detailed solution or workaround. Upon request, HP will mail or fax these notes to you.

Software Patches

Sometimes software bugs are discovered in the operating system and layered products. If the impact is severe enough, HP issues a patch kit. These patch kits are deployed only to customers who log a support call that exhibits the symptoms repaired with the patch. Sometimes you may experience the impact of a software bug, but because you do not describe the symptoms exactly, a patch is never suggested. If you suspect such a problem, it helps to ask if patches exist for components of your problem. As you hear what patches are available, it may become obvious that you need them.

HP provides a list of mandatory patch kits for all supported versions of the operating systems. You will want to install these kits.

HP also offers a notification service; you can subscribe to a service that will send you e-mail whenever new patch kits are released.

Patch kits are often called an engineering change order (ECO) kits. The terms are used interchangeably. Many of the ECO kits are available for downloading, in particular OpenVMS ECOs, but ECOs for many layered products are available also. Installation of ECOs is discussed in chapter 20. The best online site for ECOs is http://ftp.support.compaq.com.au/ecos.phtml. This site maintains ECOs for several generations of software.

Right to Use New Versions

Right to Use New Versions provides you with an ongoing license granting you the right to use new versions of OpenVMS and system-integrated products. When you first purchased OpenVMS, you were granted a license to use only the then-current version of OpenVMS. These and other software-licensing issues are discussed in more detail in chapter 7.

14.5.2 SNS

SNS is a stripped-down version of SSS. Again, it applies only to support of OpenVMS and system-integrated products. SNS provides only the right to use new versions (as described above). In general, you purchase SSS for one system at your site (to receive telephone support) and SNS for the remaining systems (to keep your OpenVMS licenses updated). You do not need to purchase telephone support for every system.

14.5.3 LPS

LPS is a service purchased on a per-product basis to extend software support to layered products. For example, if you wanted software support for the following products, you would have to purchase LPS for each one:

- Compaq C — C Compiler
- DECforms — Forms Management System
- CMS — DECset Code Management System

The services to which LPS entitles you depend on the level of software support you have on the system itself. If you purchased SSS for your system, LPS provides the following services:

- Telephone support
- Advanced electronic support
- Right to use new versions

On the other hand, if you have only SNS, LPS provides only the right to use new versions. You cannot purchase LPS unless you have either SSS or SNS.

14.5.4 MDDS

SSS, SNS, and LPS provide you with the right to use new versions of OpenVMS and layered products, but they do not provide you with the actual software to perform the upgrades. You must purchase media and documentation for each product. To receive the media and documentation kits for new product versions automatically, subscribe to HP's MDDS.

If you have a large number of layered products, consider using HP's CD-ROM distribution service. For a considerably lower cost, you receive on compact disks media and documentation for nearly every HP product.

14.5.5 Self-Maintenance

Self-maintenance means you have no software support agreement with HP. This raises important licensing issues. If you do not subscribe to software support, you do not receive the right to use new versions of HP products. If you wish to upgrade a product, you must purchase an update license to use a new version and obtain a media and documentation kit.

This policy has considerable impact on hobbyists, who can afford neither the licenses nor the support contracts. Fortunately HP (and their predecessors) have addressed this issue and provide free licenses for OpenVMS and many layered products. Media may be purchased for a nominal fee, currently $30. However, if the hobbyist has access to HP CD-ROMs, he or she may use them without any fee. Hobbyist considerations are discussed in appendix A.

14.5.6 HP Support Centers

Various HP CSCs provide hardware and software technical support. Several are located in the United States.

HP hardware and software support is referred to as HP Services and is reached by calling a single number: (800) 354-9000. After you place your call, your request is routed to the proper support center.

To place a support call, perform the following steps:

1. Before you even think about placing a support call, you must be prepared to describe the nature of the problem clearly. If you receive a specific error message, write down the exact syntax of that message. If you are experiencing a general problem, record the exact set of steps that produced the problem. If at all possible, you should be able to duplicate the problem consistently.
2. Determine if you have a hardware or a software problem. If you are not sure, guess. If you have a hardware problem, first locate the serial number of the system. If you have a software problem, you will need your software support access number. This is the number given to you by your local HP contract administrator when you established a software support contract.
3. Place a call to HP services at (800) 354-9000. You will be greeted by a call handler, who will ask you for your access number or serial number. Call handlers are trained to log your call and determine which support team your call should be dispatched to. Call handlers are not technicians. Be prepared to provide the following information:

   - Whether the problem is with OpenVMS or a layered product
   - Your name and phone number
   - OpenVMS version and product version
   - Problem statement
   - Hardware type (if applicable)

It is critical that you convey your problem in brief, yet precise, terms; otherwise, you will not be directed to the correct support team.

Once the call is logged and assigned to a team, the call handler checks to see if anyone on the team is available. When someone is available, you are connected immediately. When all members of the team are busy, your problem is queued to the team. You are asked to leave your phone number so that a team member can call you back. Before you hang up, make sure you verify your phone number.

Usually within 30 to 60 minutes, a technician returns your call. When you begin speaking to the technician, give a complete description of the problem. Statements such as "My machine won't boot," "It doesn't work," or "How soon can you fix it?" are not helpful and can serve solely to delay resolution of your problem. You need to tell the technician what error messages you are receiving, what may have recently occurred on the system, and how frequently the problem has been occurring. For example: "I begin to boot the machine. During the startup procedures the message '%SYSTEM-F-NOGBL—insufficient global pages' is displayed. The start-up continues, but hangs with a blank screen several minutes later."

Your call may be handled by a technician who is immediately familiar with the problem and can begin helping you troubleshoot the it. Unfortunately, many problems will require searching HP's extensive trouble database for specific key words or for the error messages that you have mentioned.

If you believe a technician does not understand your problem, suggest that he or she get help. If that does not work, ask to speak to the duty manager, and request that the call be reassigned. If you place a call and do not receive a response within a reasonable amount of time, contact the duty manager and request that the call be escalated. Continue to call back and escalate the call until you get results. You should use these tactics only when you need immediate response, such as when your system is down.

You do not necessarily have to wait until you have a specific problem before you place a support call. You can call just to ask a question or to learn more about a utility or command. If you place such calls though, let the call handler know that it is a low priority.

14.6 Encompass

Encompass is a volunteer organization of HP users throughout the world. The purpose of Encompass is to promote the exchange of information among users of HP products. Membership is free and open to anyone interested. Encompass is by far the most comprehensive and cost-effective way to keep abreast of HP's technology. The following sections discuss aspects of the Encompass organization in detail. To learn more about Encompass, refer to the hobbyist information contained in appendix A.

14.6.1 Local Users Groups

There are several Encompass local users groups (LUGs) throughout the United States and elsewhere. LUG activities vary widely; most groups have monthly meetings and provide a newsletter. At each meeting, speakers (other Encompass members, HP employees, or third-party vendors) present technical information on topics that members of the LUG have requested.

The LUG is meant to be your primary local resource. By attending LUG meetings you can gain valuable information and meet other HP users in your neighborhood with whom you can share problems and solutions.

14.6.2 Symposia

Encompass organizes various symposia around the world, usually one per year per country. During a symposium, Encompass members, many of whom are senior HP engineers, give technical presentations on topics relating to HP equipment. The larger symposia include many hundreds of hours of presentations and can have thousands of attendees. Most presentations are 60 to 80 minutes long, with a question and answer period at the end. Presentations vary in depth and quality, but with so many sessions to choose from, it is hard not to learn something that makes the trip worthwhile.

Considering the amount of information available and the reasonable cost, Encompass is by far the best training value for the money. Many system managers consider yearly symposium attendance mandatory. The symposia, however, should be thought of as supplements to, not replacements for, formal training. Presentations are relatively unstructured, and you cannot expect to learn what you might in a focused five-day training class.

The symposia are preceded by presymposium seminars that do provide one- and two-day focused presentations on specific topics. The seminars are frequently abbreviated formats of standard HP training classes, taught by the same instructors, but at a considerably lower cost.

Digital Equipment Corporation Users Society (DECUS) sponsors local seminars and regional conferences in major metropolitan areas throughout the year. The topics discussed are similar to the content of the presymposium seminars.

14.6.3 Encompass Software Library

Encompass maintains an extensive library of public-domain software developed by Encompass members and other organizations. For a detailed listing of available packages, visit the Encompass Web site or contact the Encompass office directly. Software from the Encompass library may be purchased from Encompass and can often be downloaded from the Encompass Web site.

14.6.4 ENCOMPASServe

ENCOMPASServe is an online electronic conferencing system which allows one-on-one discussions with Encompass users from across the United States. Hundreds of very specific topics are discussed, such as performance, third-party products, and terminal server tips.

14.7 Tools

Table 14.1 lists one command procedure referenced in this chapter. It is further discussed in Appendix E.

Listing 14.1 *Example Documentation Command Procedure*

Procedure Name	Function
SYSDOC.COM	On-line site guide

14.8 Conclusion

You have extensive support resources at your disposal: books, magazines, HP, and Encompass. You pay a lot of money for some of them—use them and use them often.

The average person forgets more in a day than he or she learns. To make use of past knowledge, you must record it before it is forgotten. Documentation allows members of a system-management team to share information and provides a permanent resource to their successors. Even the best system manager with the most elaborate tools is not truly effective without good site documentation.

14.9 References

1. *OpenVMS System Messages: Companion Guide for Help Message Users*
2. *OpenVMS Master Index* is a huge index containing references to about 30 common OpenVMS documents.
3. *OpenVMS Glossary* is an older (1993) document containing definitions of several hundred OpenVMS terms.

4. The Encompass home page is located at

   `www.encompassus.org.`

5. The home page of all OpenVMS SPDs is located at

   `www.compaq.com/info/spd.`

6. The comp.os.vms FAQs are located at

   `www.openvms.compaq.com/wizard/openvms_faq.html.`

7. The HP-sponsored Ask The Wizard is an extension-companion to the FAQs and is located at

   `www.openvms.compaq.com/wizard.`

8. The URL of ECOs, both current and for older systems, is

   `http://ftp.support.compaq.com.au/ecos.phtml.`

15

OpenVMS Integrity Monitoring

15.1 Chapter Objectives

- Detect system problems before they affect users
- Explore HP's error-analysis tools
- Monitor disks for low space and device errors
- Receive automatic notification when queues are stopped or stalled

15.2 Introduction

Many problems that occur within a system are not preventable, for example, disks that run out of space, hardware failures, and stalled print queues. When any one of these events occurs, applications may become unstable or unavailable. Many of these problems do not just happen spontaneously; they develop over time. Through vigilant monitoring of system integrity, you can often detect a developing problem before it becomes critical. You should process problems proactively, not simply react to the symptoms.

This chapter discusses system events that are clues to pending problems. A number of DCL command procedures that provide automatic problem detection and reporting are included with this book.

15.3 Monitoring Hardware Errors

Whenever hardware errors occur, the OpenVMS error formatter (ERRFMT), a detached process, writes an error record to the system error log file. The location of the error log file, ERRLOG.SYS, is specified by the logical name SYS$ERRORLOG, which by default is defined as SYS$SPECIFIC:[ERRORLOG].

The error log file contains a record of all system and device errors that occurred since the log file was created. Unfortunately, ERRFMT does not send a notification message when device errors occur. Therefore, you must monitor hardware errors using one or more of the following utilities.

15.3.1 SHOW ERROR

The SHOW ERROR command displays a count of all device errors that occurred since the last system boot, as follows:

```
$ SHOW ERROR

Device          Error Count
JTA0:              1
MKA0:              9
DKA100:            3
```

The results of SHOW ERROR can be misleading—some devices will normally register a specific error count. These errors are not actual errors, but normal controller initialization messages that occur during system startup. For example, the foregoing error for JTA0: is only an initialization message. You must become familiar with your system environment and will want to include a SHOW ERROR during or immediately after a system boot or SYSTEM login—this will permit you to become familiar with which devices will log initialization events.

If you see error counts increasing for a device, you should contact your hardware service vendor to see if repairs are necessary. Sometimes even a single error can indicate a serious problem that requires immediate attention. At other times and with other devices, increasing errors can simply indicate a failing storage cartridge or a dirty read-write head, such as the errors shown against the device MKA0: in the above example.

15.3.2 ANALYZE/ERROR

The OpenVMS ANALYZE utility is a tool for reporting errors contained in the error log file. The syntax for the ANALYZE utility is as follows:

```
$ ANALYZE/ERROR/qualifiers
```

where *qualifiers* are one or more of the following:

/SINCE=date

The error log file may contain device errors for many months or even years. To reduce the length of a report, use the standard date-selection qualifiers as follows:

```
$ ANALYZE/ERROR/SINCE=YESTERDAY
$ ANALYZE/ERROR/SINCE=01-Feb-2002
```

/SUMMARY

By default, a full page (or more) of information is presented for each error log entry. This level of detail is mainly for HP service personnel. For instance, to get a brief report, use the following command:

```
$ ANALYZE/ERROR/SUMMARY/NOFULL/SINCE=TODAY

Error Log Report Generator
Version V7.1

 SUMMARY OF ALL ENTRIES LOGGED BY SID 0A000005

       SYSTEM START-UP                          1.
       TIME-STAMP                               1.
       VOLUME MOUNT                             1.

       DATE OF EARLIEST ENTRY   23-MAY-2003 08:57:12.08
       DATE OF LATEST ENTRY      3-MAY-2003 11:08:01.35

 PROCESSED ENTRIES HOUR-OF-DAY HISTOGRAM LOGGED BY SID
0A000005

       00:00      0.
       01:00      0.
       02:00      0.
       03:00      0.
       04:00      0.
       05:00      0.
       06:00      0.
       07:00      0.
       08:00      2. **
       09:00      0.
```

```
10:00       0.
11:00       1. *
12:00       0.
13:00       0.
14:00       0.
15:00       0.
16:00       0.
17:00       0.
18:00       0.
19:00       0.
20:00       0.
21:00       0.
22:00       0.
23:00       0.
```

/INCLUDE=component

To report errors on a specific system component, use the following commands:

```
$ ANALYZE/ERROR/INCLUDE=MEMORY
$ ANALYZE/ERROR/INCLUDE=DUA0
```

/OUTPUT=filename

It is usually helpful to send the results of ANALYZE/ERROR to a file, as follows:

```
$ ANALYZE/ERROR/OUTPUT=ERROR.RPT
```

15.3.3 Other ANALYZE Functions

ANALYZE is actually a common user interface to several OpenVMS tools and, therefore, appears to have several additional functions. These are listed below, but not described in any detail:

- /AUDIT—Invoke the Audit Analysis utility to extract selective information from the system security audit journal.
- /CRASH_DUMP—Invoke the System Dump Analyzer (SDA) to examine the specified dump file.
- /DISK_STRUCTURE—Invoke the ANALYZE/DISK_STRUCTURE utility to examine disk volumes.

- /ERROR_LOG—Invoke the Errorlog Report Formatter to selectively report the contents of an error log file.
- /IMAGE—Describe the contents of an image file or shareable image file.
- /MEDIA—Invoke the Bad utility to find disk blocks that cannot be used to store data.
- /OBJECT—Describe the contents of an object file.
- /PROCESS_DUMP—Invoke the OpenVMS debugger for analysis of a process dump file.
- /RMS_FILE—Analyze the internal structure of an Record Management Services (RMS) file.
- /SYSTEM—Invoke the SDA to examine the running system.

15.3.4 DIAGNOSE

The DIAGNOSE command calls the DECevent utility, an event-management utility that provides the interface between a system user and the operating system's event log files on the OpenVMS/Alpha system. DECevent allows system users to produce ASCII reports derived from system event entries. The format and content of the ASCII reports depend on the specifics of the command parameters. DECevent also provides for the analysis and interpretation of data contained in event log files, SYS$ERRORLOG:ERRLOG.SYS. It translates the contents of one or more event log files for inclusion in a report. DECevent produces five types of reports: full (default), brief, terse, summary, and FSTERR. These report types are mutually exclusive when selected within a command; no combinations are allowed. DECevent also provides for the analysis and interpretation of that data.

On Alpha DS, ES, and GS systems (other than the AlphaServer GS60 and GS140 systems) running OpenVMS, use the Web-Based Enterprise Services (WEBES) instead. This tool includes the Compaq Analyze, the Compaq Crash Analysis Tool (CCAT), and the Revision and Configuration Management (RCM) tools. You can find WEBES and its documentation on the Compaq System Tools CD-ROM, which is included in the OpenVMS Version 7.3-1 CD-ROM package. You cannot use WEBES on the AlphaServer GS60 or the AlphaServer GS140. DECevent and the WEBES tools can be used together in a cluster.

These tools are updated asynchronously with OpenVMS releases. The most up-to-date service tool information is available at

`http://www.support.compaq.com/svctools.`

15.3.5 VAX System Integrity Monitor

VAX System Integrity Monitor (VAXsim) Plus is an older utility that facilitates hardware error analysis and notification. HP distributed VAXsim free of charge to customers who had an HP hardware-maintenance agreement. If you are covered by such an agreement, you may already have the VAXsim tools installed. VAXsim components include the following.

15.3.5.1 VAXsim Analyzer

The VAXsim Analyzer provides an interactive, graphical interface to your system error log file. When you invoke the analyzer, boxes that represent system devices are drawn on the screen. Devices with error counts that exceed predefined thresholds are highlighted. When you select a specific device, you are given a single-line message indicating the type and quantity of errors for the device. This is much easier then reading a full-page output from ANALYZE/ERROR. In a VMScluster environment VAXsim displays the hardware errors for the entire cluster.

15.3.5.2 VAXsim Fault Manager

The VAXsim Fault Manager consists of a detached system process, VAXSIMV.VVV (where V.VVV is the VAXsim version), which continuously monitors and analyzes errors as they occur. If error rates on a device exceed predefined thresholds, a fault notification message is dispatched. A component of the Fault Manager is a notification database, which indicates which OpenVMS users should be notified when faults occur. These messages are sent either by OpenVMS MAIL or as broadcast messages via the REPLY command.

15.3.5.3 VAXsim Repair Manager

The Repair Manager is used to keep track of repairs made by HP. Whenever a device is repaired, you or your hardware service technician should make an entry into the repair database. The repair log not only helps you track when repairs were made, but also affects VAXsim error analysis.

15.4 Monitoring Disks

Even when disk space is carefully managed, disks run out of space. This can occur if a user accidentally creates a large file or when a software problem creates a large log file. Running out of disk space has a severe effect on users. Users trying to save documents might lose their work, or other key system tasks might fail in the middle of a large process, leaving files or databases in corrupted states.

To prevent these problems, you should periodically monitor disk space using the SHOW DEVICE command. In the example below, all devices starting with "D" are displayed. This is the convention for disk drives.

```
$ sho dev d

Device                   Device          Error    Volume         Free  Trans Mnt
 Name                    Status          Count     Label        Blocks Count Cnt
$1$DKA0:       (MILLER)  Mounted             0  ALPHASYS       2950398   394   1
$1$DKA400:     (MILLER)  Mounted alloc       0  ALPHA0731       181494     1   1
                         wrtlck
$1$DVA0:       (MILLER)  Online              0
$2$DKA0:          (VAX)  Mounted             0  OVMSVAXSYS     1671462     1   2
$2$DKA100:        (VAX)  Online              0
$2$DKA400:        (VAX)  Mounted wrtlck      0  VAXVMS073         6237     1   1
$2$DKB200:        (VAX)  Online              0
```

If you see disk space drop below 10 percent of available space, you should take immediate action to reclaim space as discussed in chapter 10. You should also give special attention to any OpenVMS system disks—if your system disk runs out of space, the OpenVMS systems bootstrapped from the disk can hang.

An example command procedure named CHECK_DISKS, which automates disk space monitoring, is discussed at the end of this chapter. Another tool, DISK, produces a graphical representation of current disk utilization as shown below:

```
$ disk

Disk Device         --------------------------------------------------
RRD43 ALPHA0731     ||||||||||||||||||||||||||||||||||||||||||86%
RZB29 ALPHASYS      ||||||||||||||||||||||||||||||||64%
DKX00 OVMSVAXSYS    |||||||||18%
DKX00 VAXVMS073      ||||||||||||||||||||||||||||||||||||||||||||||||||99%
```

In this example, the CD-ROM drives are seen to be near capacity, as one would expect.

15.5 Monitoring Processes

A number of system detached processes should always exist (e.g., JOB_CONTROL, OPCOM, ERRFMT). Sometimes OpenVMS bugs cause these jobs to fail, and you have to manually restart them. Even the failure of JOB_CONTROL is not immediately apparent—users cannot log in, and batch jobs cannot be submitted, but other processing continues unaffected. It might take hours before you notice that a problem has occurred.

You should periodically use the SHOW SYSTEM command to verify that key system processes are running, as follows:

```
$ show system
OpenVMS V7.3-1  on node MILLER  23-MAY-2003 15:46:37.81  Uptime  0 09:23:42
  Pid    Process Name    State  Pri     I/O       CPU       Page flts  Pages
20200041 SWAPPER          HIB     16       0   0 00:00:03.15         0      0
20200046 CLUSTER_SERVER   HIB     12      21   0 00:00:00.08        57     73
20200047 CONFIGURE        HIB     10      38   0 00:00:00.09        52     35
20200048 LANACP           HIB     13      70   0 00:00:00.13       101    122
2020004A ERRFMT           HIB      8    1101   0 00:00:01.97       105    106
2020004B CACHE_SERVER     HIB     16       4   0 00:00:00.01        26     35
2020004C OPCOM            HIB      8      44   0 00:00:00.13        78     36
2020004D AUDIT_SERVER     HIB     10      83   0 00:00:00.16       118    147
2020004E JOB_CONTROL      HIB     10      65   0 00:00:00.09        58     79
20200050 QUEUE_MANAGER    HIB     10     242   0 00:00:00.47       127    157
20200051 SECURITY_SERVER HIB      10      66   0 00:00:00.81       388    336
20200052 ACME_SERVER      HIB      9     110   0 00:00:00.46       412    457 M
20200054 SMISERVER        HIB      9      49   0 00:00:00.16       152    168
20200056 NETACP           HIB     10      68   0 00:00:00.22        54     92
20200057 EVL              HIB      6      66   0 00:00:00.18       183     97 N
20200058 REMACP           HIB      8      10   0 00:00:00.03        28     14
20200059 LATACP           HIB     12       8   0 00:00:01.08        77     59
2020005A TCPIP$INETACP    HIB      8     135   0 00:00:00.26       218    128
2020005B CANNON           HIB      5     169   0 00:00:00.31       296    157
2020005C LPD_IN_MILLER_1 HIB       5     137   0 00:00:00.43       277    132
2020005D DFG$MILLER       LEF      6     173   0 00:00:00.63       293    236
2020005E MGFTP Listener   HIB      4      34   0 00:00:00.15       131    137
20200060 DECW$SERVER_0    HIB      8    1272   0 00:00:50.98       769    813
20200061 DECW$SESSION     LEF      6     813   0 00:00:02.57      1420    664
20200063 DECW$MWM         LEF      4     336   0 00:00:02.61      1175    327
20200064 VUE$SYSTEM_2     LEF      4     534   0 00:00:01.51      1332     91
20200065 VUE$SYSTEM_3     LEF      4     243   0 00:01:01.61       514    292 S
```

```
20200066 VUE$SYSTEM_4     LEF       5      340    0 00:00:03.31        990      485
20200067 DECW$TE_0067     LEF       6      283    0 00:00:09.48        780      661
20200068 _FTA5:           HIB       6    13397    0 00:00:13.42       1601      125
2020006A SYSTEM           CUR       4      442    0 00:00:00.82        744      157
2020006B _FTA6:           LEF       7      733    0 00:00:01.84       1875       70
```

The node MILLER is a cluster member running LAN, DECnet IV, and TCP/IP, with Motif installed and active. Many of the sessions are hosted by TELNET.

Sometimes bugs occur in products or applications that cause processes to loop forever. Such a problem can go undetected for hours, even days, consuming huge amounts of system resources and having a severe impact on system performance and response time. Detecting this condition is difficult because you must be able to differentiate between excessive and normal system usage. Unfortunately, you probably cannot automate this process, but you should periodically use the Monitor utility as follows:

```
$ MONITOR PROCESS/TOPCPU

                                   TOP CPU TIME PROCESSES
                                        on node MILLER
                                   23-MAY-2003 16:07:22.40

                                           0         25         50         75        100
                                           + - - - - + - - - - + - - - - + - - - - -+
 20200085   HOG                         79 ≠≠≠≠≠≠≠≠≠≠≠≠≠≠≠≠≠≠≠≠≠≠≠≠≠≠≠≠≠≠≠≠
                                           |         |          |         |         |
 20200067   DECW$TE_0067                 1
                                           |         |          |         |         |
 20200060   DECW$SERVER_0                1
                                           |         |          |         |         |
 2020006A   KERMIT
                                           |         |          |         |         |

                                           |         |          |         |         |

                                           |         |          |         |         |

                                           |         |          |         |         |

                                           + - - - - + - - - - + - - - - + - - - - -+
```

If you see a particular process that seems to be using an inordinate amount of CPU resources (e.g., HOG), you can investigate that process in more detail, as follows:

```
$ SHOW/PROCESS/CONT/ID=20200085

                          Process HOG                               16:15:05


   State               COM                Working set                     80

   Cur/base priority   4/4                Virtual pages                10403

   Current PC          804836A0           CPU time            0 00:00:46.80

   Current PSL         0000000A           Direct I/O                   64972

   Current user SP     7AEB9AF0           Buffered I/O                   104

   PID                 20200085           Page faults                    451

   UIC                 [SYSTEM]           Event flags               C0000001
                                                                    80000000
```

When you issue the SHOW PROCESS/CONTINUOUS command, the information is displayed and is updated every second. Whenever the process runs an executable image, the name of the image is displayed at the bottom of the screen. In this case, HOG is not executing an image—DCL is doing all the processing. You can also monitor the CPU time, direct input-output (I/O), and page faults counter to gauge demand of the process for CPU, disk I/O, and memory resources. Also, if you notice that the current program counter (PC) frequently indicates the same addresses, you might suspect that the process is in some kind of infinite loop.

You can further gauge what a process is doing by listing all the files opened by the process using the SDA utility, as follows:

```
$ analyze/system

OpenVMS (TM) Alpha system analyzer
```

```
SDA> show summary

Current process summary
-----------------------
 Extended Indx Process name    Username  State   Pri PCB/KTB   PHD     Wkset
-- PID -- ---- --------------- --------- ------- --- -------- -------- ------
 20200041 0001 SWAPPER         SYSTEM     HIB     16 810CF1C0 810CEC00      0
 20200085 0005 HOG             SYSTEM     COM      5 81683C00 821AA000     84
 20200046 0006 CLUSTER_SERVER  SYSTEM     HIB     12 8151C3C0 82014000     73
 20200047 0007 CONFIGURE       SYSTEM     HIB     10 8151E840 82030000     35
 20200048 0008 LANACP          SYSTEM     HIB     13 81522700 8203E000    122
 2020004A 000A ERRFMT          SYSTEM     HIB      8 815B1880 8205A000    106
 2020004B 000B CACHE_SERVER    SYSTEM     HIB     16 815B3A80 82068000     35
. . .
```

To select the HOG process, specify its index from the above list, as follows:

```
SDA> set process/index=5
```

You can then use the following command to view all the files HOG has open:

```
SDA> sho process/channel

Process index: 0005   Name: HOG               Extended PID: 20200085
--------------------------------------------------------------------

                            Process active channels
                            -----------------------

Channel    CCB     Window   Status Device/file accessed
-------    ---     ------   ------ --------------------
  0010  7FF8E000  00000000         $1$DKA0:
  0020  7FF8E020  8169A2C0         $1$DKA0:[SYSCOMMON.SYSMGR.BALDWIN]HOG.COM;7
  0030  7FF8E040  8169A080 Busy    $1$DKA0:[SYSCOMMON.SYSMGR.BALDWIN]HOG.TXT;1
  0050  7FF8E080  8159F640         $1$DKA0:[SYSCOMMON.SYSEXE]DCL.EXE;1
  0060  7FF8E0A0  81590280         $1$DKA0:[SYSCOMMON.SYSLIB]DCLTABLES.EXE;362
  0080  7FF8E0E0  00000000         FTA11:
  0090  7FF8E100  00000000         FTA11:

Total number of open channels : 7.
```

HOG appears to be executing a DCL command procedure (HOG.COM) and sending output to a log file (HOG.TXT).

Now exit SDA and use other monitor commands to watch for processes performing inordinate disk I/O activity. For example, the following display indicates that HOG is issuing 24 disk I/O operations per second:

```
$ MONITOR PROCESS /TOPDIO

                              OpenVMS Monitor Utility
                           TOP DIRECT I/O RATE PROCESSES
                                  on node MILLER
                              23-MAY-2003 16:32:10.49

                                   0         5         10        15         20
                                   + - - - - + - - - - + - - - - + - - - - -+
 20200085  HOG                 24  ≠≠≠≠≠≠≠≠≠≠≠≠≠≠≠≠≠≠≠≠≠≠≠≠≠≠≠≠≠≠≠≠≠≠≠≠≠≠≠≠≠≠
                                   |         |         |         |          |

                                   |         |         |         |          |

                                   |         |         |         |          |

                                   |         |         |         |          |

                                   |         |         |         |          |

                                   |         |         |         |          |

                                   |         |         |         |          |

                                   + - - - - + - - - - + - - - - + - - - - -+
```

If this activity (heavy CPU and disk utilization) continues for more than a few minutes, you can use SHOW PROCESS and ANALYZE/SYSTEM to determine exactly what images or command procedures the activity is executing.

Unfortunately, there really are no absolute guidelines for detecting excessive system activity. You should regularly monitor your system to define normal activity. When you detect activity that exceeds your own norms, you should investigate individual processes in detail, using the techniques discussed in this section.

15.6 Operator Communications Process

The Operator Communications (OPCOM) detached process is the primary facility used by OpenVMS and by applications to notify the operator of key system and application events. When an event occurs, OpenVMS (or the application) formats a message and requests that OPCOM deliver it. To receive OPCOM messages, you must be at a terminal enabled as an operator. By default, only the system console terminal (OPA0:) is enabled as an operator terminal. However, you can manually enable any terminal by using the following command:

```
$ REPLY/ENABLE

%%%%%%%%%%%  OPCOM  23-MAY-2003 17:11:24.74  %%%%%%%%%%%
Operator _MILLER$TNA2: has been enabled, username SYSTEM

%%%%%%%%%%%  OPCOM  23-MAY-2003 17:11:24.74  %%%%%%%%%%%
Operator status for operator _MILLER$TNA2:
CENTRAL, PRINTER, TAPES, DISKS, DEVICES, CARDS, NETWORK, CLUSTER, SECURITY,
LICENSE, OPER1, OPER2, OPER3, OPER4, OPER5, OPER6, OPER7, OPER8, OPER9, OPER10,
OPER11, OPER12
```

The following command reverses the REPLY/ENABLE and displays status once again.

```
$ REPLY/DISABLE

%%%%%%%%%%%  OPCOM  23-MAY-2003 17:13:35.45  %%%%%%%%%%%
Operator _MILLER$FTA13: has been disabled, username SYSTEM
```

You may want to include the RELPY/ENABLE command in your LOGIN.COM so that any terminal to which you log in is automatically enabled to receive OPCOM messages.

You can control operator messages on another terminal through a series of DCL commands. The following example disables OPCOM messages on the system console (OPA0:) terminal:

```
$ DEFINE/USER SYS$COMMAND OPA0:
$ REPLY/DISABLE
```

Because OPCOM sends notifications using broadcast messages, you must also ensure that your terminal is broadcast enabled by issuing the following commands:

```
$ SET TERMINAL/BROADCAST
$ SET BROADCAST=OPCOM
```

You can show the status of a terminal with either of the following commands:

```
$ show broadcast
Broadcasts are enabled for all classes

$ show terminal
Terminal: _TNA2:      Device_Type: VT200_Series  Owner: KERMIT
                                              Username: SYSTEM
Remote Port Info: Host: LAPTOP Port: 1145

   Input:     9600     LFfill:  0      Width:  80      Parity: None
   Output:    9600     CRfill:  0      Page:   24

Terminal Characteristics:
   Interactive         Echo                Type_ahead          No Escape
   Hostsync            TTsync              Lowercase           Tab
   Wrap                Scope               No Remote           Eightbit
   Broadcast           No Readsync         No Form             Fulldup
   No Modem            No Local_echo       No Autobaud         Hangup
   No Brdcstmbx        No DMA              No Altypeahd        Set_speed
   No Commsync         Line Editing        Overstrike editing  No Fallback
   No Dialup           No Secure server    No Disconnect       No Pasthru
   No Syspassword      No SIXEL Graphics   No Soft Characters  Printer port
   Numeric Keypad      ANSI_CRT            No Regis            No Block_mode
   Advanced_video      Edit_mode           DEC_CRT             DEC_CRT2
   No DEC_CRT3         No DEC_CRT4         No DEC_CRT5         No Ansi_Color
   VMS Style Input
```

15.7 Tools

Table 15.1 lists the several system-integrity command procedures that are fully described in appendix E.

Table 15.1 *Tools for System-Integrity Monitoring*

Command Procedure	Function
CHECK_QUEUES.COM	Uses the Get Queue Information lexical function (F$GETQUI) to scan active print and batch queues. When queues are found to be in a stopped, stalled, or paused state, broadcast messages are sent to the operator console.
CHECK_PROCESSES.COM	Uses the Get Job Process Information lexical function (F$GETJPI) to monitor for the existence of a set of expected processes. You control which processes are scanned by creating a text file that contains a list of process names (e.g., JOB_CONTROL, OPCOM). When a process contained in the list you specified is no longer detected, broadcast messages are sent to the operator console terminal.
CHECK_DISKS.COM	Uses the Get Device Information lexical function (F$GETDVI) to determine the available free space and error count for each disk you specify. When free space or error counts reach the thresholds you specify, broadcast messages are sent to the operator console.
DISK.COM	Presents a graphical display of current disk utilization.

15.8 Conclusion

Obviously you cannot watch a monitor screen all day long to make sure the system is performing well and automated tools are the reasonable alternative. Even so, you have monitor the tools regularly. Another possibility is to code the tool to send a mail message to a special account, which, in turn, dials your pager when mail arrives. Although not discussed, this is a rather simple solution to the notification procedure.

Sometimes identifying the reason an image crashes or loops is more of an art than a science. The techniques presented only brush the surface of this problem. However, the tools presented (MONITOR, ANALYZE/SYSTEM, ANALYZE/ERROR, SHOW PROCESS) are primary when looking for problems. You should become familiar with their capabilities. MONITOR, for instance, has more than 20 major subcategories.

There are many more OpenVMS tools to monitor system integrity than those described in this chapter. Investigate SHOW (e.g., AUDIT, MEMORY, SYSTEM, USER, CLUSTER, DEVICES, INTRUSION) to see others.

15.9 References

1. ANALYZE/SYSTEM documentation is well hidden. On the VAX, look for *OpenVMS VAX System Dump Analyzer Utility Manual;* on the Alpha, it is called *OpenVMS Alpha System Analysis Tools Manual.*
2. MONITOR is described in *OpenVMS System Management Utilities Reference Manual.* The *OpenVMS System Manager's Manual* contains many examples.
3. REPLY and its companion, REQUEST, are documented in *OpenVMS DCL Dictionary: N–Z,* and many examples are sprinkled throughout the *OpenVMS System Manager's Manual.*

16

OpenVMS MAIL Management

16.1 Chapter Objectives

- Identify critical OpenVMS MAIL components
- Configure mail logical names
- Compress user mail files
- Fix message count mismatch problems
- Create and maintain distribution lists

16.2 Introduction

This chapter focuses on OpenVMS MAIL system-management tasks and techniques for using MAIL as a system-management tool. In environments where mail is heavily utilized, you must perform a number of mail-management tasks on a regular basis. Otherwise, system performance suffers, and excessive disk space is consumed.

16.3 System Profile Database

The system profile database contains an entry for each OpenVMS MAIL user that describes how mail options are configured and the user's new message count. You can view a user's entire profile only by executing the SHOW ALL command from the user's account as follows:

```
MAIL> show all
Your mail file directory is FACULTY:[DMILLER.MAIL].
Your current mail file is FACULTY:[DMILLER.MAIL]MAIL.MAI.
No folder is currently selected.
```

```
The wastebasket folder name is WASTE.
Mail file FACULTY:[DMILLER.MAIL]MAIL.MAI
        contains 24415 deleted message bytes.

You have 0 new messages.

You have not set a forwarding address.
You have not set a personal name.
Your editor is defined by the file SYS$LOGIN:MAIL_EDIT.COM.
CC prompting is disabled.
Automatic copies to yourself are disabled.
Automatic deleted message purge is enabled.
Your default print queue is SYS$PRINT.
You have not specified a default print form.
```

As awkward as it may seem, this cannot be done from the SYSTEM account. A freeware tool is available that will allow the manager not only to access, but modify, any parameter in any user's profile. The interface is very much like the AUTHORIZE interface and, therefore, is easy to use. For instance, MAILUAF would present the same information as above like this:

```
$ MAILUAF
MAILUAF> show/full dmiller
User DMILLER subdirectory is [.MAIL]
User DMILLER has 0 new messages
User DMILLER has not set a forwarding address
User DMILLER has not set a personal name
User DMILLER has not set an editor
User DMILLER has cc prompting disabled
User DMILLER has automatic copies to self disabled
User DMILLER has automatic deleted message purge enabled
User DMILLER has not set a default print queue
User DMILLER has not set a default print form
```

To change the profile, you would do this:

```
MAILUAF> modify dmiller /personal="David Miller"
User DMILLER modified
```

In some ways, MAILUAF is superior to MAIL because it is more powerful. For instance, MAIL will not permit the following command, and MAILUAF will permit the equivalent.

```
MAIL> SET EDITOR EDT /USER=DMILLER
```

Normally, the logical VMSMAIL_PROFILE is defined to point to the mail profile. By default, the mail profile database is located on the system disk as follows:

```
SYS$SYSTEM:VMSMAIL_PROFILE.DATA
```

Depending on your configuration, the profile database should be located in either the SYS$SPECIFIC or SYS$COMMON component of SYS$SYSTEM. On a stand-alone system, VMSMAIL_PROFILE.DATA should be located in the SYS$COMMON:[SYSEXE]. Within a VMS cluster you can maintain a single profile database for the entire cluster or a separate database for each cluster member (in SYS$SPECIFIC:[SYSEXE]). However, because mail profiles are directly associated with user accounts, you should use the same configuration that you established for your user authorization database (see chapter 9); that is, the mail profile should be in the same directory tree as the SYSUAF.DAT.

You should define a systemwide logical name to explicitly select one of the paths. For example, to establish a single common profile database, create the following logical name in SYLOGICALS.COM:

```
$ DEFINE/SYSTEM/EXECUTIVE VMSMAIL_PROFILE -
      SYS$COMMON:[SYSEXE]VMSMAIL_PROFILE.DATA
```

If your system disk is heavily utilized, you may wish to locate the profile database to an alternative disk as follows:

```
$ DEFINE/SYSTEM/EXECUTIVE VMSMAIL_PROFILE -
      DISK$USER1:[SYSFILES]VMSMAIL_PROFILE.DATA
```

Wherever you choose to locate the profile database, change the logical name definition to the startup procedure SYLOGICALS.COM (see chapter 5).

16.4 User Mail Database

The text of mail messages is stored in each user's personal mail database, which by default is located in the user's default login directory. The user's mail database consists of a MAIL.MAI file and possibly a number of files of the format MAIL$*xxxx*.MAI. Short mail messages (fewer than 2,000 characters) are stored in the file MAIL.MAI. Longer messages are stored in separate MAIL$*xxxx*.MAI files (where *xxxx* is a unique character string).

As users receive messages, their default login directory tends to fill up with mail-related files. To minimize file clutter, you may want to move each user's mail database to a subdirectory as follows:

[from user's account]

```
$ SET DEFAULT SYS$LOGIN
$ MAIL
MAIL> SET MAIL_DIRECTORY [.MAIL]
MAIL> EXIT
```

When a user deletes a long message, its associated MAIL$*xxxx*.MAI file is automatically deleted. However, when smaller messages (those stored in MAIL.MAI) are deleted, space in MAIL.MAI is not automatically reclaimed. To reclaim this space you must periodically compress each user's mail file, as follows:

```
MAIL> COMPRESS DSK$SYST:[SIMPSONB]MAIL.MAI

%MAIL-S-CREATED, DSK$SYST:[SIMPSONB]MAIL_0070_COMPRESS.TMP;1 created

%MAIL-S-COPIED, DSK$SYST:[SIMPSONB]MAIL.MAI;1 copied to
     DSK$SYST:[SIMPSONB]MAIL_0070_COMPRESS.TMP;1 (2 records)

%MAIL-S-RENAMED, DSK$SYST:[SIMPSONB]MAIL.MAI;1 .renamed to
     DSK$SYST:[SIMPSONB]MAIL.OLD;1
%MAIL-S-RENAMED, DSK$SYST:[SIMPSONB]MAIL_0070_COMPRESS.TMP;1 renamed to
     DSK$SYST:[SIMPSONB]MAIL.MAI;1

MAIL> EXIT
```

When compression is completed, the old MAIL.MAI file is renamed to MAIL.OLD. If the compression was successful, delete the MAIL.OLD file, as follows:

```
$ DELETE DSK$SYST:[SIMPSONB]MAIL.OLD;*
```

Since users are not very good at doing this sort of thing, you may want to consider running a command file script occasionally. See the section 16.12 for a sample command procedure, MAIL_COMPRESS, that compresses every mail file on a specific disk.

16.5 Managing Mail Profiles

Like the SYSUAF.DAT, the VMSMAIL_PROFILE.DAT needs to be managed occasionally. I have found that it is easier to correct a user MAIL mistake than it is to tell the user what to do. One of the most common problems I have found is circular forwarding addressing.

16.5.1 Viewing Profiles

With the proper privileges enabled (SYSPRV), you can use the MAIL utility to view or modify any user's forwarding address and personal name, as follows:

```
$ MAIL
MAIL> SHOW FORWARD/USER=username
MAIL> SET FORWARD/USER=username
MAIL> SHOW PERSONAL_NAME/USER=username
```

However some other profile attributes can be modified only from the user's account.

Additionally, you can use wild cards to view multiple profiles, as follows:

```
MAIL> SHOW FORWARD/USER=*/ALL
Username                 Forwarding address
BALDWIN                  None
DSN$SERVER               None
SMITH                    SYSTEM
SYSTEM                   BALDWIN
TEMP1                    None
```

16.5.2 Adding Profiles

A mail profile is automatically added for each user the first time he or she invokes the MAIL utility; thus, it is not normally necessary to add profiles manually. However, you may want to add profiles for nonexistent users to provide automatic forwarding to existing mail accounts or to provide transparent forwarding to remote systems.

Normally, to send mail to users on a remote system, you must precede the username with the remote DECnet node name. For example, to send a message from node BIRCH to node MASON, you must do the following:

```
MAIL> SEND
To: MASON::KRIEGER
Subj: Yo, Boris!
^Z
```

This process can be simplified by establishing a dummy profile on node BIRCH:: for user KRIEGER. Even though KRIEGER does not have an account on node BIRCH, a mail profile can be added with a forwarding address to the BIRCH profile, as follows:

```
$ MAIL
MAIL> SET FORWARD/USER=KRIEGER MASON::KRIEGER
```

Now, any user on node BIRCH can send mail to KRIEGER without having to specify the remote DECnet node name.

This capability is also handy for setting up duplicate names without creating accounts. For instance to create POSTMASTER on BIRCH and forward mail to SYSTEM, you would enter

```
$ MAIL
MAIL> SET FORWARD/USER=POSTMASTER SYSTEM
```

16.5.3 Removing Profiles

When you remove a user account with the AUTHORIZE utility, the profile is left intact. You should also remove the user's mail profile eventually, as follows:

```
$ UAF
UAF> REMOVE username

$ MAIL
```

```
MAIL> REMOVE username
```

Warning: Make sure you delete the mail profile entry when you delete an account from SYSUAF. Otherwise, if an account with the same name is ever added, it may inherit the previous mail profile settings.

16.6 Mail Logical Names

The system logical name MAIL$SYSTEM_FLAGS is used to customize aspects of the mail system in VMScluster environments. MAIL$SYSTEM_FLAGS can be set to a value between 0 and 31, as shown in table 16.l.

Table 16.1 *Setting MAIL$SYSTEM_FLAGS*

Flag Value	Effect
1	Deliver mail directly to cluster accessible disk, rather than using DECnet
2	Broadcast "new mail" messages clusterwide
4	Include message deliver time in new mail broadcast messages
8	Use DECnet IV address syntax if DECnet-Plus is installed (not recommended)
16	Use DECnet-Plus address syntax (always recommended)

Define the logical name to equate to the sum of the options you want to activate. For example, to activate all options, define the following logical name:

```
$ DEFINE/SYSTEM/EXECUTIVE MAIL$SYSTEM_FLAGS 23
```

To make this change effective permanently, add the command to the site specific startup procedure SYLOGICALS.COM (see chapter 5).

16.7 Forcing Message Count Synchronization

Sometimes a user's new mail message count indicates that there is new mail when actually there is not. This problem occurs when the system profile database (VMSMAIL_PROFILE) is out of synchronization with one or more user mail databases (MAIL.MAI). This phenomenon occurs when the system and user mail databases are on separate disks and a disk failure occurs. For example, if a user disk fails on Friday and is restored from backups that were taken on Monday, the system profile database reflects the number of new mail messages that existed on Friday, not on Monday.

To resolve this problem, have any affected users read all new mail until there are no new messages. Then have them issue the following commands:

```
$ MAIL

You have 1 New mail message.

MAIL> READ/NEW
```

16.8 Managing Mail Distribution Lists

A distribution list is a text file with a file extension of .DIS that contains a list of OpenVMS MAIL addresses. You can then specify a distribution list in response to the standard Mail To: prompt, instead of having to enter each address manually. When you create a distribution list, enter valid usernames (or other distribution lists) each on a separate line, as follows:

```
$ EDIT MAIL_LISTS:ALLTECHS.DIS            ! MAIL_LISTS is a logical name
!
! Exclamation points (!) are for comments
!
! ALLTECHS.DIS – all technical staff
!
@MAIL_LISTS:ALLOPS                        ! All operations staff
! Others Misc.
JONESB
SMITHJ
TORESSA
```

To send a message to all users on the distribution list, issue the following commands:

```
$ MAIL
MAIL> send
To: @MAIL_LISTS:ALLTECHS.DIS
```

```
Subj: Hello
^Z
```

You can further simplify this process by creating a systemwide logical name in SYLOGICALS.COM as follows:

```
$ DEFINE/SYSTEM/EXEC    DIS_ALLTECHS     "@MAIL_LISTS:ALLTECHS.DIS"
```

Once the logical name is defined, enter DIS_ALLUSERS in response to the To: prompt. Start all mail distribution list logical names with a common prefix (e.g., DIS_) so that you can view all distribution lists easily, as follows:

```
$ SHOW LOGICAL DIS_*
```

16.9 Using MAIL As a Management Tool

The OpenVMS MAIL utility can be used as a simplistic trouble-tracking system as follows. Establish a dummy mail profile, PROBLEM, which is forwarded to your account as follows:

```
$ MAIL
MAIL> SET FORWARD/USER=PROBLEM BALDWINL
MAIL> EXIT
```

Then notify users to send mail to PROBLEM whenever they need help. Any mail they send will be forwarded to your mail account.

When you receive problem requests from users, the requests are added to your Newmail folder. Create the following folders, which you can use to set your schedule:

- Reviewed problems you have reviewed, but not scheduled
- Critical problems you need to resolve as soon as possible
- Today problems to resolve today
- Thisweek problems to resolve this week
- Thismonth problems to resolve this month

After you read a new message, issue the following command to file it into the appropriate scheduling folder:

```
MAIL> READ/NEW
MAIL> FILE folder name
```

To read messages in a particular folder, issue the following commands:

```
MAIL> SELECT folder-name
MAIL> READ
```

Create the following distribution lists for groups of people to whom you frequently send mail:

- DIS_OPERATORS
- DIS_PROGRAMMERS
- DIS_SYSMGR

For example, mail is sent to the DIS_SYSMGR list after system startup (see chapter 5) to indicate problems with startup procedures. Similarly, the system monitoring utilities in chapter 15 send mail to DIS_SYSMGR.

16.10 Multipurpose Internet Mail Extension

Multipurpose Internet Mail Extension (MIME) is supported as utility in OpenVMS and is not built into MAIL. To enable this feature, you should include the following line in SYLOGIN.COM:

```
$ MIME :== $SYS$SYSTEM:MIME
```

You should also create two files, MIME$MAILCAP.DAT and MIME$FILETYPES.DAT, in SYS$MANAGER. Sample files can be found by entering the following commands:

```
$ MIME
MIME> HELP SHOW CONTENT EXAMPLE
```

16.11 Mail Exchange

Mail Exchange (MX) is a robust SMTP mailer accessed via the MAIL command. However, MX has several features not included in HP's TCP/IP SMTP product. MX is released as a hobbyist product (version 4.2) and as a licensed and formally supported product (version 5.*x*). Historically, MX was a substitute for HP's version of SMTP, a product that was delivered late and was quite buggy. The MX manager also has a good set of tools to log and monitor all internal and external e-mail traffic. MX seamlessly supports SMTP, X25, DECnet, UUCP and Jnet protocols to provide a uniform user interface for e-mail. MX is cluster-aware, so its functions (hence, its computing resource requirements) may be distributed across all nodes in the cluster.

Even today HP does not support any form of a mailing list/file server (MLF), and sites that need that feature must turn to another source.

An MLF, also called a list server, supports discussion groups. A member subscribes to a discussion group and then posts messages to that group and receives all messages posted to that group by anyone else. This is a very convenient way to set up Intranet and Internet special-interest groups. Unlike news groups, the messages are propagated to members as they are posted. MX also supports daily digests—a collection of all messages posted in a 24-hour period sent as a single message.

Hunter Goatley, the creator of MX, pointed out another feature:

> The MX Site interface, which allows a DCL command procedure to be run to process a message (which literally means anything can be done with that message). For example, we use the MX Site interface to completely automate the generation and mailing of Hobbyist license PAKs for MultiNet and TCPware. Forms are submitted by mail to MX Site, and various command procedures authenticate the request, generate the PAK, e-mail the PAK to the requesting user, and automatically add the user to a hobbyist announcement mailing list.

16.12 Tools

Table 16.2 lists three example MAIL command procedures that are contained with the scripts associated with the book (see appendix E).

Table 16.2 *Example MAIL Command Procedures*

Command Procedure	Description
MAIL_COMPRESS.COM	Compresses all MAIL.MAI files contained on a particular disk
MAIL_DEFAULTS.COM	When adding a new user, creates a user [.MAIL] and initializes the user's profile
MAIL_EDIT.COM	Prefixes each line of a mail message with ">" and adds the user's signature.

MAIL_EDIT.COM was contributed to the OpenVMS community by Harry Flowers.

Another e-mail freeware tool is called DELIVER. Unlike the MX Site interface, DELIVER is user specified and controlled. Each user may configure DELIVER to filter and optionally process every message, based on sender, subject keywords, and other criteria. The user may write personal processors or use DELIVER's default actions.

16.13 Conclusion

For the most part MAIL manages itself pretty well and automatically. However, that does not mean you will never have any problems with it. If you have a special problem or special requirement, you will have to study this chapter carefully. In particular, you must manually remove accounts from the mail profile to assure system integrity.

16.14 References

1. *OpenVMS User's Manual* describes both MAIL and MIME. However, many management examples are provided throughout the *OpenVMS System Manager's Manual.*
2. MX 4.2 can be downloaded from ftp://ftp.madgoat.com/mx.

17

OpenVMS Security Management

17.1 Chapter Objectives

- Ensure system access to authorized users
- Enforce password content standards
- Understand UIC-based and ACL-based object protection
- Identify security-related system parameters
- Consider network-security requirements
- Review procedures for auditing security events

17.2 Introduction

Like performing backups (chapter 13), security management is a system-management task that is easily neglected. Because a system that is not secure will still operate, it is easy to focus your efforts on more pressing tasks. The increase in publicized system break-ins and computer virus incidents has increased sensitivity to security matters, but these events tend to encourage a dictatorial approach to security management (e.g., "This is my system and thou shalt not enter").

Although a large part of an effective security-management policy is to restrict, you have to be careful not to lose sight of the service objectives of your organization. You want to deny access to unauthorized users, but you also want to ensure access to authorized users. However, even authorized users must be restricted, if only so they do not accidentally inflict damage on one another. OpenVMS security features are summarized in table 17.1.

Table 17.1 *OpenVMS Security Features*

Feature	Description
Security domain distributed clusterwide	Changes to the security attributes of a device or volume are automatically distributed to all cluster members.
Security templates	Default security attributes for system objects are user-modifiable security templates. Security templates eliminate the need to reapply ACLs on some system objects after every system boot.
SET SECURITY command	This single command configures all security and other attributes for system objects.
ALARM_JOURNAL	Access control entry (ACE) is used to generate an OPCOM security alarm and an audit event in the audit journal file.
Audit server data file	This file that defines the configuration for the AUDIT_SERVER process is named VMS$AUDIT_SERVER.DAT.
Auditable events	These include any object access, use of privileges, network connections, system-parameter changes, use of identifiers, use of process control system services, UAF database changes, system time changes.
Protected subsystems	These allow users to acquire identifiers temporarily while running an executable image

17.3 Controlling System Access

The nominal installation of OpenVMS results in, arguably, the most secure system available; it is certainly more secure than any version of UNIX. However, there are certain additional steps the system manager may take to make OpenVMS even more secure.

Before anyone can access an OpenVMS system, a username and password must be presented and validated against the UAF, as discussed in chapter 9. Thus, the UAF is your first line of defense against unauthorized access. To ensure that user accounts are not compromised, you should consider the following:

- Password content and length

- Access restrictions
- Captive accounts

17.3.1 Password Considerations

OpenVMS passwords are encoded using a one-way hashing scheme and stored in the SYSUAF.DAT file. Anyone with read access to SYSUAF.DAT can view the hashed passwords. However, OpenVMS does not require that anyone, except the system manager, have any privileges to SYSUAF.DAT. To confirm this, enter the following command:

```
$ dir/security sysuaf

Directory SYS$COMMON:[SYSEXE]

SYSUAF.DAT;1          [SYSTEM]
(RWE,RWE,,)

Total of 1 file.
```

While we are on the subject, RIGHTSLIST.DAT should not be accessible to other users either, as shown below.

```
$ dir/s rightslist

Directory SYS$COMMON:[SYSEXE]

RIGHTSLIST.DAT;1      [SYSTEM]
(RWED,RWED,,)

Total of 1 file.
```

There is no way to decrypt passwords directly; there is no system tool capable of decryption. There are only two ways you can learn someone else's account password:

- If the account owner reveals it, which is called *social hacking*
- By repeatedly trying all possible password combinations until a match is found, which is called *brute-force hacking*

Therefore, to prevent user accounts from being compromised, you must ensure that passwords are difficult to guess, and you must minimize the likelihood that users will reveal their passwords to others. Unfortunately, these two requirements conflict with each other, requiring a strategy that achieves a careful balance. Passwords must be difficult to guess, but not so difficult that users must write them down to remember them. When developing a password-protection strategy, you should consider the following issues.

17.3.1.1 Multiple Passwords

You can configure user accounts so that they require both a primary and a unique secondary password, as follows:

```
$ UAF
UAF> MODIFY username/PASSWORD=(primary-pwd, secondary-pwd)
```

When a user initiates a login that requires multiple passwords, the login proceeds as follows:

```
Username: SIMPSONB
Password: primary-pwd
Password: secondary-pwd
```

Secondary passwords are designed primarily for those accounts that require that two users be present to log in.

17.3.1.2 Minimum Password Length

To make passwords difficult to guess, you should ensure that all passwords are at least six characters long. This is defined in the DEFAULT account, [200,200], as follows:

```
$ mcr authorize
UAF> show default

Username: DEFAULT                          Owner:
Account:                                   UIC:    [200,200] ([DEFAULT])
. . .
Expiration:          (none)    Pwdminimum:  6   Login Fails:     0
Pwdlifetime:       90 00:00    Pwdchange:      (pre-expired)
. . .
```

However, by default, the minimum password length for system accounts is eight. To increase the number of combinations, you also should encourage users to include numeric digits in their passwords. As you can see from table 17.2, there are more than two billion possible combinations for a password six characters long (when numbers and digits are used).

Table 17.2 *Number of Password Combinations*

Password Length	Using A–Z	Using A–Z, 0–9
1	26	36
2	676	1,296
3	17,576	46,656
4	456,976	1,679,616
5	11,881,376	60,466,176
6	308,915,776	2,176,782,336

The underscore, "_", and the dollar sign, "$", are also permitted. The password is not case sensitive. Passwords are limited to 32 characters.

You should not specify a password length shorter than the default. To increase password length, use the following AUTHORIZE command:

```
UAF> MODIFY username/PWDMINIMUM=min-length
```

To increase the password length for all user accounts created in the future, modify the DEFAULT account, too.

Incidentally, there is no OpenVMS check for one-up passwords, like MUMBLE01, MUMBLE02, . . . MUMBLE50. If this form of password concerns you, you must write a VMS$PASSWORD_POLICY to look for this case. This procedure is discussed in section 17.3.1.8.

17.3.1.3 Password Lifetime

The password lifetime for an account determines how frequently the password must be changed. For example, if the password lifetime for an account is 90 days, the password must be changed at least once every 90 days. You should configure accounts with password lifetimes of no more than 30 to 90 days. The default password lifetime in DEFAULT is 90 days. The SYS-

TEM account default is 30 days. To change the password lifetime for an account (e.g., to 60 days), issue the following command:

```
UAF> MODIFY username/PWDLIFETIME="60-"
```

In the example above, the trailing dash is required. To prevent a password from expiring, enter the word "NONE" instead of a number.

If the password expires before the user has a chance to change it, the next time the user logs in he or she will be forced into a SET PASSWORD dialog immediately after logging in. The user will not be permitted to do anything else until the password is changed.

17.3.1.4 Locked Passwords

If you must ensure that passwords adhere to strict content standards, use locked passwords. With locked passwords, only the system manager can set passwords with the AUTHORIZE utility. It is usually not practical to enable locked passwords for too many accounts because you have to change passwords every time they expire. Locked passwords are most appropriate for accounts shared by many users because you do not want one person changing the password and potentially locking out other users.

To configure accounts for locked passwords, use the following command from AUTHORIZE:

```
UAF> MODIFY/FLAG=LOCKPWD username
```

17.3.1.5 Generated Passwords

Another method of enforcing password content is to use generated passwords. When an account is configured with generated passwords, users must select a new password from a list generated by OpenVMS. Generated passwords comprise a variable number of semirandom alphabetic characters and are at least as long as the minimum password length for an account. Generated passwords do not form words, but they are constructed so that they can be pronounced.

To enable generated passwords for a specific account, issue the following command:

```
UAF> MODIFY username /FLAG=GENPWD
```

If a user is restricted to generated passwords, and the user attempts to change the password, the user receives the following prompts:

```
$ SET PASSWORD
Old password:                       ! Enter old password
               (Pronunciation)
cehokbej       ce-jok-bej
eajhaumda      eaj-haum-da
vufholid       vuf-ho-lid
elfnawwra      elf-naw-wra
nacseavwoa     nacs-eav-woa

Choose a password from this list, or press RETURN to get a new
list

New Password:
```

Even if generated passwords are not required, the user may choose to generate passwords with the following command:

```
$ SET PASSWORD/GENERATE
```

Although they defeat password guessing, generated passwords almost guarantee that users will write down their passwords, because the passwords are nearly impossible to remember. As a result, forcing generated passwords can actually increase the risk of a security breach. If your site requires strict password content, consider implementing a custom password filter in place of generated passwords, as discussed in section 17.3.1.8.

17.3.1.6 Password History

By default, OpenVMS maintains a history of the passwords previously used by each account and prevents them from being used again for a certain period of time. Password history data is stored in the file

```
SYS$SYSTEM:VMS$PASSWORD_HISTORY.DATA.
```

The logical VMS$PASSWORD_HISTORY should be defined to point to this database.

By default, OpenVMS tracks up to the last 60 passwords used by each user (history limit) and retains each password for 365 days (history lifetime). If a user enters more passwords than can be stored in the history file, the user is forced to use generated passwords.

You can modify the values for history limit and history lifetime by adding the following logical names to system startup procedures:

```
$ DEFINE/SYSTEM/EXEC SYS$PASSWORD_HISTORY_LIMIT "50"
$ DEFINE/SYSTEM/EXEC SYS$PASSWORD_HISTORY_LIFETIME "120"
```

The LIMIT maximum is 2,000 and the LIMETIME maximum is 28,000. You can disable password history checking for a specific user, using the following command:

```
UAF> MODIFY username /FLAG=DISPWDHIS
```

17.3.1.7 Password Dictionary

By default, users cannot select passwords contained in the HP-supplied password dictionary. The password dictionary contains about 50,000 words and is stored in the file SYS$LIBRARY:VMS$PASSWORD_DICTIONARY.DATA.

You may want to add to the system password dictionary and include local words of significance. The following shows you how to add words to the system dictionary. This procedure retains the existing dictionary and creates a file with the passwords that you consider unacceptable.

First, create a file containing passwords you would like to add to the dictionary. Each password should be left justified on a separate line and in lowercase, as follows. You can use any editor to create this file.

```
$ CREATE LOCAL_PASSWORD_DICTIONARY.DATA
somefamous
localheroes
Ctrl/Z
```

Then merge your local additions into the HP-supplied database:

```
$ CONVERT/MERGE/PAD LOCAL_PASSWORD_DICTIONARY.DATA -
_$ SYS$LIBRARY:VMS$PASSWORD_DICTIONARY.DATA
```

You can disable dictionary checking for a specific user account by using the following AUTHORIZE command. However, this is not a recommended policy.

```
UAF> MODIFY username/FLAG=DISPWDDIC
```

17.3.1.8 Custom Password Filter

You can use any high-level language (e.g., C or FORTRAN) to implement a custom password filter that forces users to select passwords that meet specific criteria. To accomplish this you must define a function POLICY_PLAINTEXT that receives a username and a password as parameters. Within your function, you can verify that passwords meet the requirements for your site (e.g., must have at least one numeric character, cannot be an anagram of the username). You can also use the $GETUAI (get user account information) system service to read parameters from the UAF and perform additional checks.

To enable a password filter, perform the following steps for a filter written in C. This must be done on all nodes in the cluster. In particular, VMS$PASSWORD_POLICY must be installed each time a node is booted.

```
$ CC VMS$PASSWORD_POLICY
$ @SYS$EXAMPLE:VMS$PASSWORD_POLICY_LNK
$ COPY VMS$PASSWORD_POLICY.EXE SYS$LIBRARY:
$ INSTALL ADD SYS$LIBRARY:VMS$PASSWORD_POLICY/OPEN/HEAD/SHARE

$ RUN SYS$SYSTEM:SYSMAN
SYSMAN> PARAMETER USE ACTIVE
SYSMAN> PARAMETER SET LOAD_PWD_POLICY 1
SYSMAN> PARAMETER WRITE ACTIVE
SYSMAN> EXIT
```

To make the change permanent, modify MODPARAMS.DAT and use AUTOGEN to change the LOAD_PWD_POLICY parameter.

Several example password filters are included with OpenVMS and located in the SYS$EXAMPLES directory (VMS$PASSWORD_POLICY.*). The source code for an expanded password filter (VMS$PASSWORD_POLICY.C) and the link script (VMS$PASSWORD_POLICY_LNK.COM) is described in appendix E.

Warning: If you do not need custom password filters, verify that LOAD_PWD_POLICY is disabled. Otherwise, this mechanism can be used by hackers to trap and record valid username and password combinations.

17.3.1.9 System Passwords

Normally, when users initiate a login, they immediately receive the standard Username: and Password: prompts. However, you may need an additional level of protection for some terminals, for instance, for dial-up lines or uncontrolled public terminals. You can add more protection by establishing a system password, as follows:

```
$ UAF
UAF> MODIFY/SYSTEM_PASSWORD=XYZZY
```

Or, equivalently, with the dialog started with

```
$ SET PASSWORD/SYSTEM
```

This latter technique is node-specific and must be repeated on all nodes in the cluster.

Next, configure each terminal device that you want to protect with the system password by adding the following command(s) to system startup procedures (e.g., STARTUP_SETTERM.COM):

```
$ SET TERMINAL/PERMANENT/SYSPASSWORD TXA0:
$ SET TERMINAL/PERMANENT/SYSPASSWORD TXA1:
etc.
```

When a terminal port is enabled for the system password, an interactive login proceeds as follows:

```
<RETURN>          ! User presses <RETURN> key
<BELL>            ! System responds with an audible bell ONLY
XYZZY<RETURN>     ! User must enter system password (which is not echoed)
```

If system password is valid, normal login begins as usual:

```
Username:
Password:
```

You can enable system passwords on all terminal devices, including LAT and remote terminals, by setting bit 19 of the SYSGEN parameter TTY_DEFCHAR2, as follows. First, determine the current value of TTY_DEFCHAR2.

```
$ RUN SYS$SYSTEM:SYSMAN
SYSMAN> PARAMETER SHOW TTY_DEFCHAR2

Parameter Name          Current
--------------          -------
TTY-DEFCHAR2            4098
SYSMAN> EXIT
```

Now compute the new value of TTY_DEFCHAR2

```
$ TEMP = 4098           ! Save current value
$ TEMP[19,1] = 1        ! Set Bit 19
$ SHOW SYMBOL TEMP      ! Display new value
TEMP = 528386   Hex = 00081002 ...
```

Finally, change the value of TTY_DEFCHAR2 to the calculated value by modifying MODPARAMS.DAT using AUTOGEN, as discussed in chapter 18. This would have to be done on every node on the cluster.

The system password has limited value. First, every user must know it; hence, it is public knowledge within the user community. Furthermore, most terminals are not hardwired to the computer these days. Instead they are connected via TCP/IP, LAT and/or DECnet, and therefore, a SET TERMINAL command is not possible. Instead, the TTY_DEFCHAR2 technique (which restricts all terminals) must be used.

17.3.2 Access Restrictions

You can restrict certain types of system access to specific days of the week or specific times during each day. For example, you can prevent interactive logins on weekends or dial-up access during the evening. You enforce these restrictions on an account-by-account basis, and since this is part of the SYSUAF database, it applies across the cluster.

To use access restrictions you must first define the primary and secondary days of the week for each user account, as follows:

```
UAF> MODIFY username/PRIMEDAYS=(day1, day2, day3 ...)
```

To indicate a day as a primary day, enter "MONDAY," "TUESDAY," etc. To configure a day as a secondary day, enter "NOMONDAY," "NOTUESDAY," etc. By default, all user accounts are configured so that Monday through Friday are primary days and Saturday and Sunday are secondary days, as follows:

```
/PRIMEDAYS=(MONDAY, TUESDAY, WEDNESDAY, THURSDAY, FRIDAY,
NOSATURDAY, NOSUNDAY)
```

This can be verified by displaying the DEFAULT account:

```
$ MCR AUTHORIZE
UAF> show default

Username: DEFAULT                              Owner:
Account:                                       UIC:     [200,200]
([DEFAULT])
. . .
Primary days:   Mon Tue Wed Thu Fri
Secondary days:                     Sat Sun
No access restrictions
. . .
```

Once you define the primary days, grant or restrict access to each account using the following AUTHORIZE qualifiers:

- /ACCESS
- /BATCH
- /DIALUP
- /INTERACTIVE
- /LOCAL

- /NETWORK
- /REMOTE

For example,

```
UAF> MODFIY username/access-restriction
```

Examples of access-restriction are shown in table 17.3.

Table 17.3 *Access-Restriction Examples*

Access-Restriction	Meaning
/ACCESS=(PRIMARY, 7-18)	Allow any access 7 A.M. to 6 P.M. (Monday–Friday)
/ACCESS=(7-19)	Allow any access 7 A.M. to 7 P.M. (Monday–Sunday)
/NOBATCH=(7-18)	Prohibit batch access 7 A.M. to 6 P.M. (Monday–Sunday)
/NODIALUP=(SECONDARY)	Prevent dial-up access on weekends (Saturday–Sunday)

17.3.3 Captive Accounts

Captive accounts allow you to restrict users to running a particular DCL command procedure (a captive command procedure) without the ability to access the DCL. In this way, you can restrict users to the functions you provide within the captive procedure and no others.

To make an account captive, set the CAPTIVE login flag and establish a captive login command procedure, as follows:

```
$ UAF
UAF> MODIFY user-account -
_UAF> /FLAGS=CAPTIVE/LGICMD=device:[directory]CAPTIVE_MENU.COM
```

When a user logs into a captive account, the following rules are in effect:

- <CTRL/Y> interrupts or errors force an immediate logout.
- The INQUIRE command is disabled.
- The SPAWN command is disabled.

To prevent automatic logout, a captive login command procedure must include a customize error and interrupt handler, as follows:

```
$ ON ERROR THEN GOTO label
$ ON CONTROL_Y THEN GOTO label
```

In writing the captive menu script, you must use the READ command instead of INQUIRE because the latter cannot be used in a captive login procedure. The following is an example of a captive menu display that implements a simple menu system. It is described in appendix E:

```
1 - Word Processing
2 - Transactions
3 - Mail
4 - Logout

Enter Selection (1-4): 3

You have 1 new message.

MAIL>exit
1 - Word Processing
2 - Transactions
3 - Mail
4 - Logout

Enter Selection (1-4): 4
```

17.4 Object Protection

After a user successfully performs a login, object protection mechanisms provide the next layer of access control. With object protection, a *subject,* a process acting on behalf of a user, attempts access to an *object,* for example, a file. Access is granted if the protection of the object allows it; otherwise, access is denied.

The following commonly used object protection mechanisms are discussed in this section:

- Volumes (magnetic tape, disk)

- Devices (disk drive, magnetic tape drive, terminals)
- Files and directories
- Queues
- Security classes

For information on the other objects (capabilities, common event flag clusters, global sections, logical name tables, and resource domains), refer to the OpenVMS manuals listed at the end of this chapter.

You protect objects using either of the following object protection types:

- UIC-based protection
- ACL-based protection

By default, access to all system objects is controlled solely by UIC-based protection. To enable ACL-based protection, you have to add ACLs manually to each object. When an object is protected by both UIC- and ACL-based mechanisms, the following precedents are in effect:

- ACLs take priority over UIC-based protection.
- If an ACL grants access, access is granted, and UIC-based protection is not evaluated.
- If an ACL explicitly denies access, access is denied, unless UIC-based protection grants access through the SYSTEM or OWNER access categories.

Access categories are discussed in the following sections.

17.4.1 UIC-Based Protection

With UIC-based protection, the following three factors determine access.

17.4.1.1 Subject Owner

After a user obtains access to the system by performing a login, a process is created on the user's behalf. The user's process acts as the subject. The subject *owner* is the UIC of the process attempting access. For example, after a user logs into the account SIMPSONB, a process is created and assigned the UIC value [SIMPSONB] from the user's SYSUAF account record. Any object accessed by the user is considered to have been initiated by the subject owner, [SIMPSONB].

Depending on how the user's account is configured, the subject owner's UIC may be expressed in one or more of the formats listed in table 17.4.

Table 17.4 *Valid UIC Formats*

UIC Type	Format	Example
Number UIC	[*group-number, member-number*]	[100,2]
Alphanumeric UIC	[*group-name, member-name*]	[BILLING, SIMPSONB]
Alphanumeric UIC	[*member-name*]	[SIMPSONB]
Alphanumeric UIC	*member-name*	SIMPSONB

To determine the valid UIC formats for a specific user, view the user's account entry using the AUTHORIZE utility, as follows:

```
UAF> SHOW SIMPSONB
Username: SIMPSONB
...                        UIC: [100, 2] ([SIMPSONB])
```

Either value listed to the right of UIC: can be used as UIC values. If the account has an alphanumeric UIC, it can be used without the square brackets ([]).

Another way to determine UIC, when logged into your account, is by use of the following command. There is no SHOW UIC command.

```
$ show process

31-MAY-2003 14:01:21.46   User: SIMPSONB          Process ID:    2020003A
                          Node: VAX               Process name:  "_FTA6:"

Terminal:            FTA6:
User Identifier:     [SIMPSONB]
Base priority:       4
. . .
```

17.4.1.2 Object Owner

Every object has an associated owner, as specified by a UIC value. For example, the file T.TMP (a file object) might be owned by [SIMPSONB], as indicated by the following command:

```
$ DIRECTORY/OWNER T.TMP

Directory DISK$USER1:[SIMPSONB]

T.TMP;1          [SIMPSONB]

Total of 1 file.
```

The SHOW SECURITY command can be used in place of the DIRECTORY command, as follows:

```
$ show security reset.txt

FACULTY:[DMILLER]RESET.TXT;3 object of class FILE
     Owner: [DMILLER]
     Protection: (System: RWED, Owner: RWED, Group: RE, World)
     Access Control List: <empty>
```

17.4.1.3 Object Protection Mask

Each object has an associated protection mask that specifies how and by whom the object can be accessed. A protection mask lists four access categories (SYSTEM, OWNER, GROUP, and WORLD) and specifies the type of access that is allowed to each category. Protection masks are formatted as a list of access categories and access types (Read, Write, Execute, Delete) separated by a colon character (:), as follows:

- *Full format:*

  (SYSTEM:*rwed*, OWNER:*rwed*, GROUP:*rwed*, WORLD:*rwed*)

- *Abbreviated format:*

  (S:*rwed*, O:*rwed*, G:*rwed*, W:*rwed*)

For example, a file might have an associated protection mask, as follows:

```
$ dir/protection reset.txt

Directory FACULTY:[DMILLER]

RESET.TXT;3          (RWED,RWED,RE,)

Total of 1 file.
```

In the foregoing example, the characters RWED specify read, write, execute, and delete access types. A fifth access mode, CONTROL, is not explicitly specified in the protection mask, but is implicitly granted if one or more of the following conditions are met:

- The subject holds the SYSPRV privilege.
- The subject's UIC is a system UIC, [1,1]...[MAXSYSGROUP,*x*]. MAXSYSGROUP is a parameter whose default is 8 (or 10 octal).
- The subject's UIC exactly matches object's UIC.
- The subject holds the GRPPRV privilege, and the subject's UIC group matches the object's.

When a subject accesses an object, it qualifies for one or more access categories based on the relationship between the subject's UIC and the object's UIC, as illustrated in table 17.5.

Table 17.5 *UIC-Based Access Categories*

Example Subject UIC	Example Object UIC	Relationship	Qualified Access Categories
[1,4]	Any	Subject UIC is a system UIC	SYSTEM, WORLD
[100,2]	[100,2]	Same UICs	OWNER, GROUP, WORLD
[100,27]	[100,-]	Same UIC group	GROUP, WORLD
[100,2]	[300,-]	Different UICs	WORLD

If a subject qualifies for more than one access category, it receives the benefit of the access types from each category.

The actual meaning of each access type depends on the object being manipulated. For example, WRITE access to a directory means you can add files to the directory. However, WRITE access to a queue means you can submit jobs to the queue. Some objects have different access types (e.g., logical and physical); thus, protection masks for those devices use different characters (e.g., L and P). If a subject holds certain privileges, access capabilities may be amplified.

Access types have been named to reflect their function. For example, the WRITE access type for queues has been called SUBMIT. As a result, you should specify the "S" character to allow SUBMIT access to a queue.

17.4.2 ACL-Based Protection

The most important limitation of UIC-based protection is that access to only four general categories can be controlled (SYSTEM, OWNER, GROUP, and WORLD). If you have more complex access control requirements, ACL-based protection provides flexibility to a specific user or an arbitrary set of users.

With ACL-based protection, the two following factors determine access:

1. Rights identifiers held by the subject
2. ACLs associated with an object

Subjects are identified by the rights identifiers they hold. Object ACLs then grant or restrict access to subjects holding given rights identifiers.

17.4.2.1 Rights Identifiers

The three following types of rights identifiers are used with ACL-based object protection:

1. UIC identifiers
2. General identifiers
3. Environmental identifiers
4. UIC identifiers

By default, a process holds the UIC identifiers associated with its account entry. For example, a process created by the account SIMPSONB holds the numeric UIC identifier [100,2] and alphanumeric UIC identifier [SIMPSONB].

```
UAF> SHOW SIMPSONB

UIC: [100, 2] ([SIMPSONB])
...                              UIC: [100,2] ([SIMPSONB])
```

17.4.2.2 General Identifiers

The real power of ACL-based protection centers on general identifiers, arbitrary names containing 1 to 31 characters with at least one alphabetic character. They are created as follows:

```
$ UAF
UAF> ADD/ID ANNUAL_REPORT
UAF> ADD/ID BILLING_DATA
UAF> ADD/ID CORP_OFFICER
```

You make users holders of a general identifier by granting them the AUTHORIZE utility, as follows:

```
UAF> GRANT/ID identifier username
UAF> GRANT/ID CORP-OFFICER SIMPSONB
```

General identifiers can also have several associated attributes, which are listed in table 17.6.

Table 17.6 *General Identifier Attributes*

Identifier Attribute	Function
RESOURCE	Allows a holder of the identifier to charge disk space usage to the identifier
DYMANIC	Allows the identifier to be dynamically enabled or disabled after login with the DCL SET RIGHTS command

Table 17.6 *General Identifier Attributes (continued)*

Identifier Attribute	Function
NO_ACCESS	Prevents identifier from affecting access; used to allow disk space to be charged to an identifier
HOLDER_HIDDEN	Prevents users from displaying holders of an identifier, unless they themselves hold the identifier
NAME_HIDDEN	Prevents users from displaying an identifier name, unless they themselves hold the identifier
SUBSYSTEM	Allows holders to create and maintain a protected subsystem (see section 17.6)

To enable attributes, specify them when you create the identifier and when you grant it; for example:

```
UAF> ADD/ID/ATTRIBUTE=(RESOURCE,DYNAMIC) CORP_OFFICER
UAF> GRANT/ID/ATTRIBUTE=(RESOURCE,DYNAMIC) CORP_OFFICER SIMPSONB
```

17.4.2.3 Environmental Identifiers

A number of environmental identifiers are predefined and automatically associated with a process depending on its login mode. A few of these are listed in table 17.7 to illustrate this class of identifiers.

Table 17.7 *Several Environmental Identifiers*

Identifier	Meaning
BATCH	Held by any batch process
DIALUP	Held by any dial-up process; attached via dial-up port
INTERACTIVE	Held by any interactive process
LOCAL	Held by any process attached to local terminal ports
NETWORK	Held by any network process
REMOTE	Held by any process created by SET HOST or TELNET

The complete database can be displayed with the following AUTHORIZE command:

```
UAF> SHOW/ID *
```

You may examine your process rights with the following command:

```
$ show process/rights
. . .
Process rights:
 SYSTEM
 INTERACTIVE
 REMOTE
```

It is important to distinguish between identifiers and rights, because the two are often confused. An identifier is simply an alphanumeric name without a place to go. The process (via the user) is assigned that identifier name; hence, it becomes a right of the process.

17.4.2.4 ACLs

You establish ACL-based access control to an object by associating an ACL with the object. An ACL consists of one or more Access Control Entries (ACEs) enclosed in parentheses, as follows:

```
(ACE)
(ACE)
(ACE)
. . .
```

For example, a directory might have the following associated ACL:

```
$ DIRECTORY/ACL T.TMP

Directory DISK$USER1:[SIMPSONB]

T.TMP;1
(IDENTIFIER=CHILD,ACCESS=READ+WRITE+EXECUTE+DELETE)
(DEFAULT_PROTECTION,S:RWED,O:RWED,G:RE,W)
(ALARM, ACCESS=WRITE+DELETE+FAILURE)

Total of 1 file.
```

The foregoing example also demonstrates three of the six types of ACEs:

- Identifier
- Default protection
- Alarm (and Audit)

We will discuss these in greater detail in the rest of the section. We will not discuss:

- Creator
- Subsystem

Identifier ACE

An Identifier ACE grants or restricts access to subjects who hold specific rights identifiers, using the following format:

```
(IDENTIFIER=identifier, [OPTIONS=option,] ACCESS=access-type)
```

An identifier can be any rights identifier, including the following:

- UIC identifier (e.g., [SIMPSONB])
- General identifier (e.g., CORP_OFFICER)
- Environmental identifier (e.g., BATCH)

For example, to grant full access to the file REPORT.TXT to users who hold the general identifier ANNUAL_REPORT, perform the following steps:

1. Create and grant a general identifier using authorize.

```
$ UAF
UAF> ADD/ID ANNUAL_REPORT
UAF> GRANT/ID ANNUAL_REPORT SIMPSONB
UAF> GRANT/ID ANNUAL_REPORT SIMPSONH
```

2. Associate an ACE with the file granting access to the identifier.

```
$ SET SECURITY/ACL= -
(IDENTIFIER=ANNUAL_REPORT,ACCESS=READ+WRITE+EXECUTE+DELETE)REPORT.TXT
```

With these two steps you have associated an ID with a file and then named the users that are permitted access to that file.

You can deny access to REPORT.TXT (located in account REPORTS) from dial-up users, by adding the following ACE at the bottom of the list. The default is to add ACLs to the top of the list.

```
$ SET SECURITY/ACL=(IDENTIFIER=DIALUP,ACCESS=NONE) -
_$ /AFTER=(IDENTIFIER=ANNUAL_REPORT,ACCESS=READ+WRITE+EXECUTE+DELETE) -
_$ REPORT.TXT

$ DIRECTORY/ACL REPORT.TXT

Directory DISK$USER1:[REPORTS]

REPORT.TXT;1
(IDENTIFIER=ANNUAL_REPORT,ACCESS=READ+WRITE+EXECUTE+DELETE) ! <== ACE #2
(IDENTIFIER=DIALUP,ACCESS=NONE)                             ! <== ACE #1
Total of 1 file.
```

When you add ACEs that deny access, you have to make sure that you order them to produce the desired effect. OpenVMS scans ACEs from top to bottom to determine if the resource can be accessed. As soon as it encounters an ACE that grants access, it grants access and stops scanning. Similarly, as soon as it finds an ACE that denies access, it denies access and stops scanning. The ACL in the example does not deny access to all dial-up users. Users who access the file from dial-up and who hold the ANNUAL_REPORT identifier are granted access because OpenVMS encounters that ACE first. If you wanted to deny access to all dial-up users, the DIALUP ACE would have to be placed before the ANNUAL_REPORT ACE, as in the following example:

```
$ DIRECTORY/ACL REPORT.TXT

Directory DISK$USER1:[REPORTS]
```

```
REPORT.TXT;1
(IDENTIFIER=DIALUP,ACCESS=NONE)                              ! <== ACE #1
(IDENTIFIER=ANNUAL_REPORT,ACCESS=READ+WRITE+EXECUTE+DELETE) ! <== ACE #2

Total of 1 file.
```

When specifying UIC identifiers within ACLs, you can grant or deny access to several users by using wildcard formats, such as the following:

Format	Meaning
[*,*]	Any UIC
[200,*]	All UICs in group 200
[PARENTS,*]	All UICs in PARENTS group

Default Protection ACE

A default protection ACE specifies the default protection for each file as it is created. It can only be associated with directory objects.

Default protection ACEs have the following format:

```
(DEFAULT_PROTECTION, [OPTIONS=option,] S:rwedc,O:rwedc,G:rwedc,W:rwedc)
```

The *rwedc* options correspond to UIC-based access modes (READ, WRITE, EXECUTE, DELETE, and CONTROL). Unlike UICs, the CONTROL access type can be specified explicitly for all four access categories.

Use default protection ACEs when you want to ensure that files within a directory are created with a specific protection mask. Normally, the protection of newly created files is taken from the default protection of the process creating the file. This can cause security problems if users change their default protection to an unacceptable value. For example, users do not require any special privileges to perform the following command:

```
$ SET PROTECTION=(W:RWED)/DEFAULT
```

Now, the user's default protection is set for world full access. Any new file this user creates could be fully accessible by all users on the system. If a directory has an associated default protection ACE, any new files created in the directory are assigned the protection mask specified in the ACE, thus overriding the default protection of the creating process.

For example, to force all files created in DISK$USER1:[SIMPSONB] to have no WORLD access, perform the following command:

```
$ SET SECURITY/ACL=(DEFAULT_PROTECTION,S:RWED, O:RWED, G:RE, W:) -
_$ DISK$USER1:[000000]SIMPSONB.DIR
```

Audit and Alarm ACEs

Use security ACEs to generate audit events and security alarms whenever users access an object. When a security ACE is triggered, the audit event is written to the security audit file (see section 17.8) and a security alarm is displayed (using OPCOM) on all enabled security operator consoles. These ACEs have the following formats:

```
(ALARM=SECURITY, [OPTIONS=option,] ACCESS=access-type) ! Alarm ACE
(AUDIT=SECURITY, [OPTIONS=option,] ACCESS=access-type) ! Audit ACE
```

To generate an audit event or alarm you must specify one or more of the standard object access modes (READ, WRITE, EXECUTE, DELETE, CONTROL) and indicate whether successful (SUCCESS) or failed (FAILURE) accesses are to be audited. For example, to add a security ACE to the SYSUAF file that generates a security alarm whenever a failed write access occurs, enter the following command:

```
$ SET SECURITY -
_$  /ACL=(ALARM JOURNAL=SECURITY, ACCESS=WRITE+FAILURE) -
_$  SYS$SYSTEM:SYSUAF.DAT
```

After execution, the directory listing for SYSUAF.DAT becomes

```
$ dir/security sysuaf

Directory SYS$COMMON:[SYSEXE]

SYSUAF.DAT;1    [1,1]        (RWED,RWED,,)
   (ALARM=SECURITY,ACCESS=WRITE+FAILURE)

Total of 1 file.
```

Now, if an unauthorized user attempts to open SYSUAF.DAT, via AUTHORIZE, the following message is displayed:

```
%%%%%%%%%%% OPCOM 1-JUN-2003 13:26:41.51 %%%%%%%%%%%
Message from user AUDIT$SERVER on MILLER
Security alarm (SECURITY) on MILLER, system id: 8981
Auditable event:   Object access
Event information:  file access request (IO$_ACCESS or IO$_CREATE)
Event time:    1-JUN-2003 13:26:41.51
PID:       2020006D
Process name:     DMILLER
Username:      DMILLER
Process owner:    [DMILLER]
Terminal name:    RTA1:
Image name:     $1$DKA0:[SYS0.SYSCOMMON.][SYSEXE]AUTHORIZE.EXE
Object class name:  FILE
Object owner:     [1,1]
Object protection:  SYSTEM:RWED, OWNER:RWED, GROUP:, WORLD:
File name:     _$1$DKA0:[SYSCOMMON.SYSEXE]SYSUAF.DAT;1
File ID:     (570,2,0)
Access requested:   READ,WRITE
Sequence key:     0000E5EA
Status:      %SYSTEM-F-NOPRIV, insufficient privilege or
       object protection violation
```

ACE Options

ACEs can have one or more associated options, which modify the characteristics of the ACE. See table 17.8.

Table 17.8 *ACE Options*

ACE Option	Function
DEFAULT	Indicates that an ACE is to be included in the ACL of any files created within a directory. When the entry is propagated, the DEFAULT attribute is removed from the ACE of the created file. This attribute is valid for directory files only.
HIDDEN	Users need the SECURITY privilege to display a hidden ACE with the DCL commands SHOW SECURITY or DIRECTORY/SECURITY. SECURITY privilege is also required to modify or delete a hidden ACE with the DCL command SET SECURITY.

Table 17.8 *ACE Options (continued)*

ACE Option	Function
PROTECTED	Protects the ACE against casual deletion. The following commands do not delete protected ACEs: SET SECURITY/ACL/DELETE, SET SECURITY/LIKE, and SET SECURITY/DEFAULT.
NOPROPAGATE	Prevents ACE from being automatically propagated. For example, prevents directory ACEs from propagating to new subdirectories. Similarly, prevents file ACEs from propagating to new file versions.
NONE	Specifies that ACE has no options. Behaves like OPTIONS=NONE.

17.4.3 Device Protection

Within the context of system management, device protection primarily controls the ability to initialize, mount, and dismount volumes on a device and to change device protection attributes. Table 17.9 lists the access required to perform each of these functions. In this table the column headers have the following meaning:

- Read is the right to read data from the device.
- Write is the right to write data to the device.
- Physical is the right to perform physical I/O operations to the device.
- Logical is the right to perform logical I/O operations to the device.
- Control is the right to change the protection elements and owner of the device.

Table 17.9 *Disk Device Access Requirements*

Function	Required Access				
	Read (R)	Write (W)	Physical (P)	Logical (L)	Control (C)
Perform physical I/O operation (e.g., SET TERM, /SYSPASSWORD, /PERMANENT)			Yes		
Perform logical I/O operation (e.g., SET TERM, /PERMANENT)				Yes	

Table 17.9 *Disk Device Access Requirements (continued)*

Function	Required Access				
Mount/dismount device local	Yes	Yes			Yes
Mount/dismount device /GROUP GRPNAM	Yes	Yes			Yes
Mount/dismount device /SYSTEM SYSNAM	Yes	Yes			Yes
Change device protection					Yes

The physical and logical access types allow a process to perform low level I/O operations using the queued I/O ($QIO) system service. Most applications that access file-structured devices do not issue direct $QIOs, but rather interface with HP's RMS and, thus, do not require this level of access. However, physical and logical access is required to modify certain terminal device characteristics, as indicated in table 17.9.

Table 17.10 describes the device protection defaults and management commands.

Table 17.10 *Device Protection Defaults and Commands*

Device Operation	Protection Default
Default ownership	[SYSTEM]
Default protection	Disk: (S:RWPL, O:RWPL, G:R, W:) Tape: (S:RWPL, O:RWPL, G:R, W:) Term: (S:RWPL, O:RWPL, G:, W:)
Change defaults	SET SECURITY *device-type* /CLASS=SECURITY /PROTECTION=*mask* /OWNER=*uic* /ACL=*(acl)* (where *device-type*=DISK, TAPE, or TERMINAL)
Change ownership	SET SECURITY/CLASS=DEVICE/OWNER=*uic device*
Change protection	SET SECURITY/CLASS=DEVICE/PROTECTION=*mask device*
Add ACLs	SET SECURITY/CLASS=DEVICE/ACL=*(acl) device*

Some characteristics of these defaults are worth noting:

- Default disk device protection matches default tape device protection.
- Templates are used to establish default protection for disk and tape devices.
- Devices are controlled with nearly identical commands.

17.4.4 Volume Protection

Before you can access files on a volume, you must first have appropriate access to the volume that contains the files. Table 17.11 lists the volume access required to perform various file operations and to change volume protection. To perform file operations on the volume, you must also meet the access requirements of individual files or directories, as discussed in the next section. Notice that WRITE access implies READ access and that DELETE access implies READ and WRITE access. For magnetic tape volumes, only READ and WRITE access is meaningful.

For instance, your system disk will have the following attributes:

```
$ show security/class=volume dka0:

ALPHASYS object of class VOLUME
     Owner: [1,1]
     Protection: (System: RWCD, Owner: RWCD, Group: RWCD, World: RWCD)
     Access Control List: <empty>
```

Table 17.11 *Volume Access Requirements*

Function	Required Access			
	Read (R)	Write (W)	Delete (D)	Control (C)
Read, list, copy, and print files	Yes			
Modify or append files	Yes	Yes		
Create files	Yes	Yes		
Delete files	Yes	Yes	Yes	
Change volume protection or ownership				Yes

Table 17.12 summarizes the device protection defaults and management commands. These defaults can be overridden by using the /PROTECTION and /OWNER qualifiers with the DCL INITIALIZE and MOUNT commands.

Table 17.12 *Volume Protection Defaults and Commands*

Volume Operation	Protection Default
Default ownership	UIC of creating process
Default protection	Disk and tape: (S:RWCD, O:RWCD, G:RWCD, W:RWCD)
Change defaults	SET SECURITY VOLUME /CLASS=SECURITY /PROFILE= TEMPLATE /PROTECTION=*mask* /OWNER=*uic* /ACL=*(acl)*
Change ownership	SET SECURITY/CLASS=VOLUME /OWNER=*uic device* To change ownership of a tape volume, you must reinitialize it.
Change protection	SET SECURITY/CLASS=VOLUME /PROTECTION=*mask device* To change protection of a tape volume, you must reinitialize it.
Add/Delete ACLs	SET SECURITY/CLASS=VOLUME/ACL=(*acl*)

17.4.4.1 Volume High-Water Marking and Erase on Delete

You need to consider the following two additional factors in relation to disk volume security protection.

1. *High-water marking:* By default, when you delete a file, disk blocks are deallocated from the file, but the actual data remains intact on the disk. High-water marking prevents you from reading data contained in previously deallocated disk blocks. When you create or extend a file, it may map disk blocks that were used by a file that was recently deleted. If high-water marking is enabled, OpenVMS records the point at which you write data to the new file and lets you read only up to that point.

   If this level of security is not required, you should disable high-water marking by using the following command:

   ```
   $ SET VOLUME/NOHIGHWATER disk-name
   ```

The next time you mount the disk, high-water marking is disabled. A system reboot is required to disable high-water marking on the system disk.

2. *Erase on delete:* Erase on delete causes OpenVMS to physically overwrite each block of a file when it is deleted. This prevents someone from reading deallocated disk blocks using special disk scavenging software/hardware techniques. If this mechanism is not required by your site, disable it as follows:

```
$ SET VOLUME/NOERASE_ON_DELETE disk-name
```

To determine the status of a volume, use the following command:

```
$ show device $1$dka0: /full

Disk $1$DKA0: (MILLER), device type RZ29B, is online, mounted,
    file-oriented device, shareable, served to cluster via MSCP Server,
    error logging is enabled.

    Error count                0  Operations completed                12023
    Owner process             ""  Owner UIC                        [SYSTEM]
    Owner process ID    00000000  Dev Prot              S:RWPL,O:RWPL,G:R,W
    Reference count          392  Default buffer size                   512
    Total blocks         8380080  Sectors per track                     113
    Total cylinders         3708  Tracks per cylinder                    20
    Allocation class           1

    Volume label      "ALPHASYS"  Relative volume number                  0
    Cluster size               9  Transaction count                     399
    Free blocks          2811402  Maximum files allowed              419004
    Extend quantity            5  Mount count                             1
    Mount status          System  Cache name             "_$1$DKA0:XQPCACHE"
    Extent cache size         64  Maximum blocks in extent cache     281140
    File ID cache size        64  Blocks in extent cache              60372
    Quota cache size          64  Maximum buffers in FCP cache          205
    Volume owner UIC       [1,1]  Vol Prot    S:RWCD,O:RWCD,G:RWCD,W:RWCD

  Volume Status:  ODS-2, subject to mount verification, protected
      subsystems enabled, write-through caching enabled.
```

17.4.5 File Object Protection

To access a file, you must first have access to the volume containing the file, as discussed in the pervious section. Next, you need EXECUTE (E) access to all directories (just directories, not files) between the master file directory (MFD—[000000]) and the directory that contains the file. Finally, depending on the requested access, you need a combination of access types to the file and the immediate parent of the file.

Table 17.13 summarizes which access modes are required for every file operation. In the table, DELETE (D) is required only when creating a new file would cause a version of the same file to be deleted (due to file version limits).

Table 17.13 *File Access Modes*

File Operation	Access Required (F=file, D=parent directory). You also must have EXECUTE access to every directory back to the root [000000].				
	Read (R)	Write (W)	Execute (E)	Delete (D)	Control (C)
List named file			D		
Read, type, print, or view attributes of named file	F		D		
List files using wildcard specification	D				
Read, type, print, or view attributes using wildcard specification	D,F				
Write, modify, append file	D,F	D,F			
Execute named file			D,F		
Create brand-new file	D	D			
Create new version of file	D	D,F		D	
Delete or rename file	D,F	D		F	
Change file attributes	D,F	D,F	F		
Change file ownership and protection	D,F	D,F			
All operations	D,F	D,F		F	F

For example, the file DISK$USER1:[USER.SIMPSONB]T.TMP has the following associated directory structure:

```
DISK$USER1:          ! [1,4]      (S:RWED,O:RWED,G,W:RWED)   ! Volume Protection
DISK$USER1:[000000] ! [1,4]        (S:RWE,O:RWE,G,W:E)      ! MFD Protection
USER.DIR             ! [1,4]      (S:RWE,O:RWE,G,W:E)        ! Intervening Dir
SIMPSONB.DIR         ! [200,200] (S:RWE,O:RWE,G,W:RW)        ! Immediate Parent
T.TMP                ! [200,200] (S:RWE,O:RWE,G,W:RWED)      ! File
```

If user SIMPSONB (UIC [200,200]) wanted to delete the file T.TMP, the user would need the following access:

- DELETE access to the volume DISK$USERI
- EXECUTE access to the MFD, USER.DIR, and SIMPSONB.DIR
- READ access to T.TMP and SIMPSONB.DIR
- WRITE access to SIMPSONB.DIR
- DELETE access to T.TMP

Because all these requirements are met, the user can successfully delete the file. Table 17.14 shows the file protection defaults and management commands.

Table 17.14 *File Protection Defaults and Commands*

File Operation	Protection Default
Default ownership	Usually inherits UIC of creating process
Default protection	(S:RWED, O:RWED, G:RE, W:)
Change defaults	Same as OpenVMS 5.5
Change ownership	SET SECURITY/OWNER=uic file
Change protection	SET SECURITY/PROTECTION=mask file
Display security attributes	DIR/OWNER file DIR/PROTECTION file DIR/ACL file DIR/SECURITY file SHOW SECURITY file
SYSPRV privilege	Allows access via the SYSTEM access category, regardless of subject's UIC

Table 17.14 *File Protection Defaults and Commands (continued)*

File Operation	Protection Default
GRPPRV privilege	Allows access via the SYSTEM access category if the subject's UIC group matches the object's UIC group
READALL privilege	Allows READ access, regardless of subject's UIC
BYPASS privilege	Allows subject to bypass UIC-based protection completely
Add ACLs	SET SECURITY/ACL=(*acl*) file

17.4.5.1 Default File Ownership

By default, when a new directory is created, its ownership is established as follows:

- If the creating process has CONTROL access to the parent directory, the UIC owner of the new directory is set to the UIC of the parent directory.
- Otherwise, the UIC of the new directory is set to the UIC of the creating process.

By default, when a new file is created, ownership is established as follows:

1. When a new version of an existing file is created, it is assigned the UIC owner of the previous version of the file only if the creating process has CONTROL access to the file.
2. When a new file is created, it is assigned the UIC owner of the parent directory only if the creating process has CONTROL access to the parent directory.
3. If the creating process does not have CONTROL access, the UIC of the created file is set to the UIC of creating process.

17.4.5.2 Default File Protection

When you create a directory, its protection is established from the parent directory. When you create a directory in the MFD (e.g., DISK$USER1:[USER]), the protection for the directory is established from the MFD

[000000]. By default, the protection of the MFD is as follows: (S:RWE, O:RWE, G:RE, W:E).

When you create a new file, its protection is set to the default protection of the creating process. The default protection of a process is established during system login with the following command:

```
$ SET PROTECTION=(S:rwed, O:rwed, G:re, W:)/DEFAULT
```

You can examine the current default with the following command:

```
$ show protection/default
  SYSTEM=RWED, OWNER=RWED, GROUP=RE, WORLD=NO ACCESS
```

If you do not explicitly set default protection with the SET PROTECTION command, default protection is set to the value specified by the system parameter RMS_FILEPROT. The default value for RMS_FILEPROT (64,000 decimal) translates to a protection mask as follows:

S:RWED	O:RWED	G:RE	W:	Operation
0000	0000	0101	1111	0 = set, 1 = not set
1111	1010	0000	0000	Invert bits from left to right
F	A	0	0	Hexadecimal for 64,000

When you create a new version of an existing file, its default protection is set to the protection of the previous version of the file.

17.4.6 Queue Object Protection

Table 17.15 summarizes the queue protection defaults and DCL commands.

Table 17.15 *Queue and Job Access Requirements*

Queue Operation	Protection Default
Default ownership	[SYSTEM]
Default protection	(SYSTEM:M, OWNER:D, GROUP:R, WORLD:S)

Table 17.15 *Queue and Job Access Requirements (continued)*

Queue Operation	Protection Default
Change defaults	SET SECRUITY QUEUE /CLASS=SECURITY /PROTECTION=*mask* /OWNER=*uic* /ACL=*(acl)*
Change Ownership	SET SECURITY /CLASS=QUEUE /PROTECTION=*mask queue*
OPER Privilege	Provides EXECUTE access to all queues
SYSNAM Privilege	Stops and starts the queue manager
Add ACLs	SET SECURITY /CLASS=VOLUME /ACL=(*acl*) queue

Table 17.16 summarizes the access modes required to perform various queue and job operations.

Table 17.16 *Queue and Job Access Requirements*

File Operation	Access Required (Q=queue, J=job)				
	Read (R)	Submit (S)	Manage (M)	Delete (D)	Control (C)
Submit jobs to queue		Q			
Control queue			Q		
View job information	J		Q		
Delete a job			Q	J	

Characteristics of a queue can be displayed with the command:

```
$ show queue/full cannon
Server queue CANNON, idle, on MILLER::, mounted form DEFAULT
 /BASE_PRIORITY=4 /DEFAULT=(FEED,FORM=DEFAULT) Lowercase /OWNER=[SYSTEM]
 /PROCESSOR=TCPIP$LPD_SMB /PROTECTION=(S:M,O:D,G:R,W:S) /RETAIN=ERROR
```

Security settings of a queue can also be displayed with the command:

```
$ SHOW SECURITY/CLASS=QUEUE CANNON

CANNON object of class QUEUE
     Owner: [SYSTEM]
     Protection: (System: M, Owner: D, Group: R, World: S)
     Access Control List: <empty>
```

17.5 Security Class Object Protection

You need appropriate access to the security class object as indicated in table 17.17 to modify default object security templates using the commands listed in the previous sections (e.g., SET SECURITY *object*/CLASS=SECURITY).

Table 17.17 *Security Class Access Requirements*

Security Operation	Required Access		
	Read	Write	Control
Display a security template	Yes		
Modify a security template		Yes	
Change the protection of the security class object			Yes

By default, the security class object has the following protection:

```
$ SHOW SECURITY/CLASS=SECURITY SECURITY_CLASS

SECURITY_CLASS object of class SECURITY_CLASS
     Owner: [SYSTEM]
     Protection: (System: RW, Owner: RW, Group: R, World: R)
     Access Control List: <empty>

  Template: DEFAULT
     Owner: [SYSTEM]
     Protection: (System: RW, Owner: RW, Group: R, World: R)
     Access Control List: <empty>
```

17.6 Protected Subsystems

Sometimes users need elevated access when they execute a particular application (e.g., to access associated data files). One solution is to create a general identifier, grant it to selected users, and add ACLs to the necessary data files granting access to identifier holders. This strategy allows access from the application; however, there is no mechanism to prevent knowledgeable users from manipulating data files directly using DCL commands.

Another option is to install the executable image with the elevated privileges using the INSTALL utility, as follows:

```
$ INSTALL ADD DISK$TOOLS:TASM.EXE/PRIVILEGE=SYSPRV
```

This technique temporarily elevates a user's access privilege, but enabling powerful privileges such as SYSPRV may create additional security exposure.

To resolve these problems, OpenVMS includes a protected subsystem mechanism that effectively allows you to associate an identifier (rather than a privilege) with an executable image. When a user activates an image that has an associated subsystem identifier, the identifier is temporarily enabled for the user's process. When the user exits the application, the identifier is disabled. By applying ACLs to subsystem objects, you can allow users to access objects only when they are executing within the subsystem.

To use protected subsystems, you must enable the processing of subsystem ACLs on a volume-by-volume basis. By default, the system disk is automatically enabled. To enable additional disks mount them during system startup with the /SUBSYSTEM qualifier, as follows:

```
$ MOUNT/CLUSTER/SUBSYSTEM $2$DKA100: USER1
$ SET VOLUME/SUBSYSTEM $2$DKA100:      ! If device is already mounted
```

To demonstrate the use of protected subsystems, consider an application called XYZ that consists of an executable image XYZ.EXE and a number of data files XYZ1.DAT, XYZ2.DAT, etc. Assume that when users are executing XYZ.EXE, they should have full access to the associated data files.

The first step is to create a subsystem identifier with the AUTHORIZE utility, as follows:

```
UAF> ADD/ID/ATTRIBUTES=(SUBSYSTEM, RESOURCE) SYSTEM_XYZ
```

Grant the identifier to yourself or to the person who will be configuring subsystem objects. This is necessary because to add subsystem ACLs, you must hold the identifier.

```
UAF> GRANT/ID/ATTRIBUTES=(SUBSYSTEM, RESOURCE) SYSTEM
```

Then, add a subsystem ACL to XYZ.EXE:

```
$ SET SECRUTIY/ACL=(SUBSYSTEM, IDENTIFIER=SYSTEM_XYZ, -
_$     ATTRIBUTES=RESOURCE) XYZ.EXE
```

Next, add normal ACLs to the database files that allow access to holders of the SYSTEM_XYZ identifier.

```
$ SET SECURITY/ACL=(IDENTIFIER=SYSTEM_XYZ, ACCESS=READ+WRITE) XYZ*.DAT
```

To prevent access from any users outside the subsystem, you should remove UIC-based group and world access, make SYSTEM_XYZ the owner, and add an identifier to deny access to users who have not acquired the SYSTEM_XYZ subsystem identifier.

```
$ SET SECURITY/PROTECTION=(G,W)/OWNER=SYSTEM_XYZ -
/ACL=(IDENTIFIER=*, ACCESS=NONE)-
/AFTER=(IDENTIFIER=SYSTEM_XYZ, ACCESS=READ+WRITE) XYZ*.DATE

$ DIR/SECURITY XYZ1.DAT

Directory SYS$SYSROOT:[SYSMGR]

XYZ1.DAT;1       SYSTEM_XYZ       (RWED,RWED,,)
  (IDENTIFIER=SYSTEM_XYZ,ACCESS=READ+WRITE)
  (IDENTIFIER=*,ACCESS=NONE)

Total of 1 file.
```

Now, anyone who executes XYZ.EXE will temporarily acquire the SYSTEM_XYZ identifier, allowing that user to read and write to the XYZ data files. This is demonstrated by the following:

```
$ SPAWN/NOWAIT/OUT=T.TMP RUN XYZ
%DCL-S-SPAWNED, process SYSTEM_1 spawned

$ SHOW PROCESS/RIGHTS SYSTEM_1

26-MAY-1995 14:20:16:12  User: SYSTEM    Process ID: 00000052
                         Node: BIRCH     Process ID: "SYSTEM_1"

Process rights:

INTERACTIVE
LOCAL

Subsystem rights:
 SYSTEM XYZ                ! <=== SUBSYSTEM rights ARE enabled

System rights:
 SYS$NODE_BIRCH
```

17.7 Security-Related Login Parameters

Several login parameters (each prefixed with LGI_) control a variety of OpenVMS login security mechanisms. To modify these parameters use AUTOGEN as discussed in chapter 18. These several parameters can be displayed with the following command:

```
$ mcr sysman
SYSMAN> parameter show /lgi
%SYSMAN-I-USEACTNOD, a USE ACTIVE has been defaulted on node MILLER
Node MILLER:   Parameters in use: ACTIVE
Parameter Name     Current     Default     Minimum     Maximum Unit   Dynamic
--------------     -------     -------     -------     ------- ----   -------
LGI_CALLOUTS             0           0           0         255 Count        D
LGI_BRK_TERM             1           1           0           1 Boolean      D
LGI_BRK_DISUSER          0           0           0           1 Boolean      D
LGI_PWD_TMO             30          30           0         255 Seconds      D
```

```
LGI_RETRY_LIM          3         3         0        255 Tries      D
LGI_RETRY_TMO         20        20         2        255 Seconds    D
LGI_BRK_LIM            5         5         1        255 Failures   D
LGI_BRK_TMO          300       300         0    5184000 Seconds    D
LGI_HID_TIM          300       300         0 1261440000 Seconds    D
```

17.7.1 LGI_CALLOUTS

LGI_CALLOUTS specifies the number of installation-security-policy callout modules to be invoked at each login. LGI_CALLOUTS must be set to 0 unless callout modules are present.

17.7.2 LGI_BRK_TERM

When set to 1, login failures by the same username from multiple terminals are counted separately. The default setting is acceptable if logins are initiated only from direct terminal ports (TT or TX devices). However, if users log in from terminal servers, you should seriously consider setting LGI_BRK_TERM to 0 so that login failures are tracked by username only.

For example, if LGI_BRK_TERM is set to 1, and a single user generates nine login failures from a terminal server using LAT, the failures are counted as follows:

```
$ SHOW INTRUSION

Intrusion       Type      Count  Expiration     Source
   TERM_USER    SUSPECT     3    14:43:50.22    _LTA160:SIMPSONB
   TERM_USER    SUSPECT     3    14:44:19.72    _LTA158:SIMPSONB
   TERM_USER    SUSPECT     3    14:44.32.62    _LTA159:SIMPSONB
```

After every three login failures (LGI_RETRY_LIM), the terminal session is terminated by OpenVMS (see LGI_RETRY_LIM). When the user reconnects, the terminal name changes from LTA159: to LTA160:. Because the username and terminal are tracked separately, OpenVMS does not combine the total login failures. Therefore, LGI_BRK_LIM is not exceeded, and the login failures are considered SUSPECT, rather than as bona fide break-ins.

When LGI_BRK_TERM is set to 0, OpenVMS tracks login failures by username only. The same nine login failures would be counted as follows:

```
$ SHOW INTRUSION

Intrusion       Type      Count  Expiration     Source
   TERM_USER    INTRUDER   6     13:05:36.61    _OPA0:SIMPSONB
```

Note that the intrusion type is INTRUDER, indicating that a break-in has been detected and evasion action is in progress. Further logins from that source are disabled, until the intrusion record expires. As an alternate, you can delete an intrusion record manually, as follows:

```
$ DELETE/INTRUSION _OPA0:SIMPSONB    ! Spell the source EXACTLY
$ SHOW INTRUSION
%SHOW-F-NOINTRUDERS, no intrusion records match specification
```

When connecting via TCP/IP, that is TELNET or FTP, the intruder is detected earlier because the TELNET or FTP server is more persistent. That is, the source name is not changed every three tries.

17.7.3 LGI_BRK_DISUSER

If this parameter is set to 1 and a break-in attempt occurs, the user account named as the source of the attempt is disabled by setting the account's DISUSER login flag in the SYSUAF. To reactivate the account, you must manually remove the DISUSER flag with the AUTHORIZE utility.

By default, LGI_BRK_DISUSER is not set. Therefore, accounts are not automatically disabled when they are involved in break-in attempts. If you set this parameter to 1, break-in evasion is more effective. However, you run the risk that all accounts will be disabled by a hacker generating login failures to every valid username.

17.7.4 LGI_RETRY_LIM

This procedure specifies the maximum number of failures that can occur during a dial-up, network, or terminal server login. If the limit is exceeded, the current connection is terminated, requiring the user to redial, reissue a SET HOST, or reconnect from terminal servers.

The purpose of LGI_RETRY_LIM is to increase the amount of time it takes to repetitively guess passwords. By default, a person guessing passwords via a dial-up line would have to redial after every three failed login attempts.

17.7.5 LGI_RETRY_TWO

This procedure specifies the login time-out period. By default, if after receiving the username or password prompt you do not respond within 20 seconds, a login time-out failure occurs.

Once you receive a login prompt, OpenVMS has already created a process to handle the anticipated login. LGI_RETRY_TWO helps conserve system resources by terminating a login and deleting any associated processes if the login is not completed within a reasonable amount of time.

17.7.6 LGI_PWD_TMO

This procedure indicates the amount of time users have to enter the system password, if that feature is enabled, when performing a login. If the time-out period is exceeded, a login time-out failure occurs.

17.7.7 LGI_BRK_LIM

This procedure specifies the maximum number of login failures that can occur from a specific source before the failures are considered a break-in attempt. This means the intrusion type changes from SUSPECT to INTRUDER in the example above. When the first login failure occurs, it is set to expire in LGI_BRK_TMO seconds. If additional login failures occur before the expiration time, the expiration time is extended to the current time plus LGI_BRK_TMO seconds. By default, if five or more failures occur before the count expires, OpenVMS assumes a break-in attempt is in progress and begins evasive action; no one is permitted to log in on the terminal, not even SYSTEM with the correct password.

17.7.8 LGI_BRK_TMO

See LGI_BRK_LIM.

17.7.9 LGI_HID_TIM

Once a break-in has been detected, OpenVMS initiates evasive action for the period of time specified by LGI_HID_TIM. During the evasion period, OpenVMS rejects even valid usernames and passwords from any account. Thus, it hides the system from all users.

17.8 Network Security

When your systems are part of a DECnet network, or if you use terminal servers, you should carefully consider the following network security issues:

- Terminal server passwords
- Default DECnet access
- DECnet proxy access

17.8.1 Terminal Server Passwords

Most terminal servers have an associated *server password* and a *privilege password.* The following discussion illustrates management of a typical server. However, not all servers are alike so you should consult your server's documentation for details.

17.8.1.1 Privilege Password

The terminal server privilege password controls access to server-management functions such as testing ports and changing the server configuration.

By default, the privilege password is set to SYSTEM. To prevent malicious users from changing your server configurations, you should establish new privilege passwords as follows:

```
Local> SET PRIVILEGE
Password: old-password
Local> SET SERVER PRIVILEGE PASSWORD new-password
Local> DEFINE SERVER PRIVILEGE PASSWORD new-password
```

17.8.1.2 Server Password

The server password works much like the OpenVMS system password in that it is enabled on a port-by-port basis. If users attempt to connect to a port when a server password is enabled, they receive the # prompt and must enter the server password before they can continue.

The factory default server password is ACCESS. You should take care to change this password and enable server passwords on dial-up ports (at a minimum). Change the server password as follows:

```
Local> SET PRIVILEGE
Password: privilege-password
Local> SET SERVER PASSWORD password
Local> DEFINE SERVER PASSWORD password
```

To enable a port to require a server password, perform the following procedure:

```
Local> SET PRIVILEGE
Password: privilege-password
Local> DEFINE PORT n PASSWORD ENABLED
Local> LOGOUT PORT n
```

17.8.2 Default DECnet IV Access

This discussion is limited to DECnet IV. If you are running DECnet-Plus (also called DECnet V), the principals are the same, but the implementation is different.

When you initially configured DECnet on your system, you may have established a default DECnet account. The purpose of this account is to allow remote DECnet users minimal access to your system without requiring standard username and password authentication.

To verify if you have a default DECnet account, execute the following commands:

```
$ RUN SYS$SYSTEM:NCP
NCP> SHOW EXECUTOR CHARACTERISTICS
.
.
Nonprivileged user id       = DECNET
Nonprivileged password      = FOOBAR
Default access              = incoming and outgoing
. . .
```

You must be enabled for BYPASS privilege to see the nonprivileged password, if it is set. If something like the foregoing is displayed, and the user ID specified exists in your UAF, a default DECnet account is enabled.

If you have a default DECnet account, ensure that its UAF parameters are set as follows:

- Does not have system UIC
- Has only TMPMBX and NETMBX privileges
- Is restricted to network access only

At a minimum, users from remote nodes can copy files to and from the default login directory of the DECnet account. For example, if the user is on node LOTUS, he or she may perform the following from a nonprivileged user account:

```
$ COPY T.TMP BIRCH::
$ DIR BIRCH::

Directory of BIRCH::SYS$SPECIFIC:[DECNET]

T.TMP;1

Total of 1 file.
```

A potential problem with default DECnet accounts is that remote users can copy large files to your system and cause disk space to be exhausted.

The biggest concern, however, is that remote users have access to all files on your system via the WORLD access category. If this is a concern, you should restrict access to the WORLD category or disable default DECnet access.

17.8.3 DECnet Proxy Access

DECnet proxy access provides another means of facilitating access by remote users. A proxy allows a remote user access to the local system without having to specify a username and password.

The most common use of proxies is when a user has several user accounts on different (unclustered) DECnet nodes. Without proxies, the user would have to specify a username and password when transferring files between systems. Assume user SIMPSONL has accounts on node BIRCH and node LOTUS and wants to copy a file from LOTUS:: to BIRCH::. This would require the following command on LOTUS:

```
$ COPY T.TMP BIRCH"SIMPSONL password"::
```

To eliminate the need to add the username and password in the COPY command, you should create a proxy entry on node BIRCH::, as follows:

```
UAF> ADD/PROXY LOTUS::SIMPSONL SIMPSONL/DEFAULT
```

The foregoing proxy allows any remote DECnet requests originating from node LOTUS and user SIMPSONL to use the local user account SIMPSONL without a password. The /DEFAULT option specifies that the proxy entry be used to determine default access by the specified user, thus superseding the default DECnet account (if one exists). The LOTUS copy could then be performed as follows:

```
$ COPY T.TMP BIRCH::
```

Proxy entries to privileged accounts should be carefully considered. Without them, the account and password is transmitted unencrypted with the request. On the other hand, malicious users on remote nodes outside your control could gain full access to your system if they have accounts.

Often the system manager will enter the following proxy:

```
UAF> ADD/PROXY LOTUS::* */DEFAULT
```

This command permits all users on LOTUS to access their accounts on BIRCH, if they have one.

To examine the entire proxy database, enter the command:

```
UAF> SHOW/PROXY *
```

17.8.4 TCP/IP Proxy Access

OpenVMS TCP/IP proxy database is define by the logical TCPIP$PROXY, which is normally equated to SYS$COMMON:[SYSEXE]TCPIP$PROXY.DAT. This database performs the same function as the UNIX files .hosts in the user's directory and /etc/hosts.equiv, namely to list trusted users and hosts.

The command used to manage this database is

```
$ TCPIP
TCPIP> ADD PROXY user /HOST=host /REMOTE_USER=user
```

However, this subject is quite involved because TCP/IP includes so many services (e.g., NSF, rlogin, PPP, lpd), and each must be dealt with separately. These variations are beyond the scope of this book.

17.9 OpenVMS Security Auditing

Robust implementation of the OpenVMS security mechanisms discussed in this chapter is only the first step of good management. You should also perform regular system auditing to ensure that security mechanisms are effective.

During system startup, OpenVMS creates the audit server process (AUDIT_SERVER). When active, the audit server logs select security events by sending security broadcast messages (via OPCOM) and by writing audit records to the audit log file. By default, the audit login file is SYS$MANAGER:SECURITY.AUDIT$JOURNAL.

Depending on your security requirements, you can enable auditing for a variety of events, as listed in table 17.18.

Table 17.18 *Auditable OpenVMS Events*

Audited Event	Audit Option
General object access	ACCESS=*condition*
Objects with alarm ACEs	ACL
Audit modifications	AUDIT
Authorization database modified (SYSUAF, RIGHTSLIST, NETPROXY)	AUTHORIZATION
Break-in detected	BREAKIN
Connection from DECnet, DECwindows, $IPC, or SYSMAN	CONNECTION
Object creation	CREATE
Object deaccess	DEACCESS
Object deletion	DELETE
Use of identifier	IDENTIFIER
Installed image added or removed	INSTALL
Login failures	LOGFAILURE=*keyword*
Specified logins	LOGIN=*keyword*

Table 17.18 *Auditable OpenVMS Events (continued)*

Audited Event	Audit Option
Specified logouts	LOGOUT=*keyword*
Device mounts	MOUNT
Modification of NCP (DECnet database)	NCP
Use of privilege	PRIVILEGE=*keyword*
Process control functions (e.g., create process, delete process)	PROCESS=*keyword*
System parameter modification	SYSGEN
System time modification	TIME

To enable an audit, use

```
$ SET AUDIT/ENABLE=event
```

To enable an alarm, that is, to display an audit on the operator's console, use

```
$ SET AUDIT/ALARM/ENABLE=event
```

To list the events that are enabled on your system, use

```
$ SHOW AUDIT

System security alarms currently enabled for:
  ACL
  Authorization
  Breaking: dialup,local,remote,network,detached
  Logfailure: batch,dialup,local,remote,network,subproces,detached

System security audits currently enabled for:
  ACL
  Authorization
  Breakin: dialup,local,remote,network,detached
  Logfailure: batch,dialup,local,remote,network,subprocess,detached
```

If an event is enabled for an alarm, it generates only a security broadcast to the console. To generate an entry in the audit log file, you must also enable the event for audits.

You should choose the events you audit carefully and select only those you really need. Excessive auditing can easily generate thousands of audit events per minute (or more), which will seriously degrade system performance. By default, only the operator console is enabled to receive security alarms. To receive alarms at other terminals, you should add the following command to your login procedure:

```
$ REPLY/ENABLE=SECURITY
```

17.9.1 Generating Audit Reports

Once you enable the events you want to audit, you can generate reports using the ANALYZE/AUDIT facility. On a daily basis you should generate a summary report that indicates the number of audit records generated for each event type, as follows:

```
$ ANALYZE/AUDIT/SUMMARY/SINCE=TODAY/OUT=SUMMARY.RPT SYS$MANAGER

Total records read:     263    Records selected:    8
Record buffer size:     917
Successful logins:        0    Object creates:          0
Successful logouts:       0    Object accesses:         0
Login failures:           0    Object deaccesses:       0
Breakin attempts:         0    Object deletes:          0
System UAF changes:       0    Volume (dis)mounts:      0
Rights db changes:        3    System time changes:     0
Netproxy changes:         0    Server messages:         0
Audit changes:            5    Connections:             0
Installed db changes:     0    Process control audits:  0
Sysgen changes:           0    Privilege audits:        0
NCP command lines:        0    Persona
```

If you see any records for UAF, audit, installed images, SYSGEN, or network control program (NCP) changes, you should investigate them further, unless you can account for them. Login failures and break-in attempts are more difficult to analyze, because if you have a large user population, you will receive many such audit events each day. To deal with these events, you should record the typical number of login failures and break-in attempts that you normally receive and explore further if record counts exceed these norms.

To get a little more information, you can generate a brief audit report, as follows:

```
$ ANALYZE/AUDIT/BRIEF/SINCE=TODAY/OUT=BRIEF.RPT SYS$MANAGER
$ TYPE BRIEF.RPT

Date / Time          Type    Subtype          Node   Username  Term
------------------------------------------------------------------------------
 7-JUN-2003 06:17:00 AUDIT   AUDIT_INITIATE   MILLER SYSTEM
 7-JUN-2003 06:19:03 LOGFAIL LOCAL            MILLER <login>   _WSA1:
 7-JUN-2003 06:27:00 AUDIT   AUDIT_TERMINATE  MILLER SYSTEM
 7-JUN-2003 06:30:04 AUDIT   AUDIT_INITIATE   MILLER SYSTEM
 7-JUN-2003 12:09:51 LOGFAIL REMOTE           MILLER DMILLER  Host:LAPTOP Port:1060
 7-JUN-2003 12:09:59 LOGFAIL REMOTE           MILLER DMILLER  Host:LAPTOP Port:1060
 7-JUN-2003 12:10:04 LOGFAIL REMOTE           MILLER DMILLER  Host:LAPTOP Port:1060
 7-JUN-2003 12:10:12 LOGFAIL REMOTE           MILLER DMILLER  Host:LAPTOP Port:1061
. . .
```

In analyzing the above report, you should look for suspect events, such as the following:

- Many login failures from the same source
- Excessive login attempts during evenings or weekends
- Any changes by unfamiliar usernames
- Newly installed images, especially if added with privileges

If you see any changes that look suspect, for example the LOGFAIL changes in the foregoing listing, you can produce a full report on just those events by using the /EVENT qualifier, as follows:

```
$ ANALYZE/AUDIT/FULL/SINCE=TODAY/EVENT_TYPE=LOGFAIL/OUT=FULL.RPT -
      SYS$MANAGER
$ TYPE FULL.RPT

Security alarm (SECURITY) and security audit (SECURITY) on MILLER,
   system id: 8981
Auditable event:          Local interactive login failure
Event time:                7-JUN-2003 06:19:03.79
PID:                      20200061
Process name:             DECW$LOGINOUT
```

```
Username:                  <login>
Terminal name:             _WSA1:
Status:                    %LOGIN-F-NOSUCHUSER, no such user
. . .
```

As the foregoing report indicates, an unknown user attempted to log in at 6:19 A.M. from DECwindows (the terminal name is WSA). Probably I spelled my user name wrong. Further on in the report, the following entry appeared:

```
. . .
Security alarm (SECURITY) and security audit (SECURITY) on MILLER,
   system id: 8981
Auditable event:           Remote interactive login failure
Event time:                 7-JUN-2003 12:09:51.79
PID:                       20200083
Process name:              _TNA3:
Username:                  DMILLER
Terminal name:             TNA3:, _TNA3:, Host: LAPTOP Port: 1060
Remote nodename:           LAPTOP
Remote node id:            3367113159 (4.455)
Remote username:           TELNET_C711B2C8
Status:                    %LOGIN-F-INVPWD, invalid password
. . .
```

This entry was caused by DMILLER entering an invalid password when attempting to log in from a remote location (LAPTOP) using TCP/IP (the terminal is TNA). If audit reports indicate events with which you are not familiar, you should investigate further.

17.10 Tools

One tool was presented in this chapter, and it is further discussed in appendix E. It is listed in table 17.19.

Table 17.19 *A Password Policy Sample Program*

File	Purpose
VMS$PASSWORD_POLICY.C	A sample program that enforces a "one numeric" policy
VMS$PASSWORD_POLICY_LNK.COM	A script to link VMS$PASSWORD_POLICY
CAPTIVE_MENU.COM	Captive login procedure

17.11 Conclusion

OpenVMS contains a number of security tools. Many consider it an unhackable system. The default installation of OpenVMS activates many of these tools to enforce a generic secure system. For instance, the DEFAULT account is already set up to limit password lifetime to 90 days. The system manager must review the default conditions and be prepared to modify various security databases to meet his or her site's specific needs.

However, if the manager does not use the tools effectively, or if he or she does not monitor the security reports regularly, these tools are useless.

17.12 References

1. *OpenVMS Guide to System Security* is the primary reference for this chapter.
2. *OpenVMS DCL Dictionary: N–Z* describes SET/SHOW SECURITY, in part.
3. *OpenVMS System Management Utilities Reference Manual: A–L* contains a surprising amount of information regarding the six ACE types in the section titled "Access Control List Editor."
4. There are a dozen TCP/IP documents available. Depending on which layered products you intend to install and manage, you must select the security model that is available.

18

OpenVMS Performance Management

18.1 Chapter Objectives

- Achieve performance requirements dictated by service-level objectives
- Monitor and analyze application performance
- Identify and eliminate resource bottlenecks
- Adjust system parameters using SYSMAN and AUTOGEN

18.2 Introduction

An OpenVMS system consists of three major resources: CPU, memory, and disk. Every application uses each of these resources to varying degrees. For example, a statistical analysis application might rely mostly on the CPU and less on memory and disk. On the other hand, a database update might perform many disk operations while requiring only moderate amounts of CPU and memory resources.

CPU, memory, and disk resources are interrelated. Disk I/O affects a physical disk, but it also requires CPU time to set up and complete the request. Similarly, requests for pages of memory require CPU time and may require disk I/O if the requested pages are no longer located in physical memory. Figure 18.1 illustrates how various application requests affect each of the major system resources.

Some performance-management approaches focus solely on monitoring each system resource, detecting when they become saturated, and tuning or load-balancing them until utilization seems acceptable. This approach relies on the assumption that as long as a resource is not overutilized, user application response time will be acceptable. Unfortunately, this is not necessarily the case. For example, an application might issue I/O requests to a

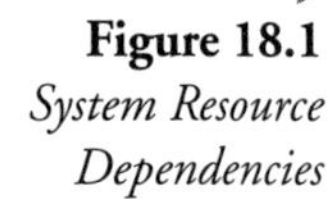

Figure 18.1
System Resource Dependencies

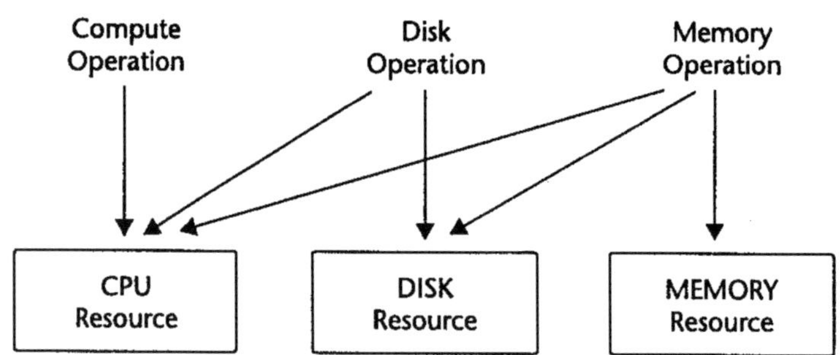

dedicated disk at a rate less than 10 percent of the capacity of the drive. However, just because a drive is underutilized does not mean its response time is acceptable. Similarly, it certainly is not a good sign if the CPU of your system is always 85 percent busy, but it is not that important if application response times are consistently twice as fast as service-level objectives. Users do not care how well the system performs; they only care how well their applications perform. This type of objective-based methodology is illustrated in figure 18.2 and forms the basis of the approach detailed in this chapter.

With this approach you start by identifying performance objectives for each application in terms of response time. Then, you consistently monitor application performance to ensure that objectives are met. If response times become unacceptable, focus on the system resource on which the application is most dependent. Finally, attempt to load-balance, tune, and expand (in that order) the bottlenecked resource until response time returns to an acceptable level. Each of these steps is detailed in the sections that follow.

18.3 Identifying Performance Objectives

Objectives are the most important input to the performance-management process. Before you can begin to address or even identify a problem, you must understand exactly what level of performance is considered acceptable. Reasonable objectives should be developed by consulting with users and management. These objectives guide your performance-management activities and assist you in reconciling performance trade-offs between one application and another.

Performance objectives should indicate how quickly the system should process and respond to particular user requests or activities. This can be difficult to specify for applications that involve many different functions, but you do not necessarily have to establish and track response times for every

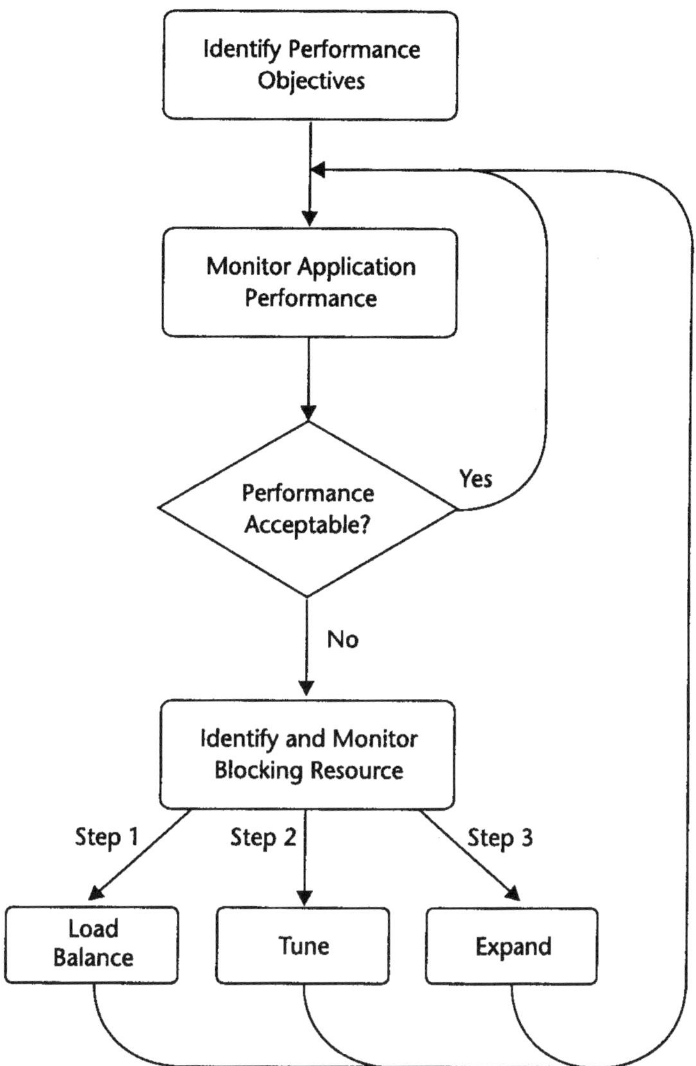

Figure 18.2 *Objective-Based Performance Management*

activity. To approximate overall response time, focus on key activities or on activities that seem to be representative of overall use. For example, for a word-processing application, you might want to measure the time required to invoke the application, or the time to perform a spell-check on an average-sized document. On the other hand, for a batch job that performs a database update, you might want to measure only the total elapsed time it takes to perform the update.

Application objectives should also include an estimated number of concurrent uses. By documenting this estimate, you will be better prepared to explain and deal with deteriorating performance when the number of users accessing an application mysteriously increases from 30 to 60. Finally, no OpenVMS system can produce a particular response time 100 percent of the time, because of unpredictable events such as VMScluster state transitions and hardware errors. To weed out these extremes, you should decide on a consistency factor that specifies the percentage of time you expect to meet response-time objectives. For example, if you agree on a 95 percent consistency factor, discard the worst 5 percent of the response times you sample. Once you agree on performance objectives, formalize them in writing, as illustrated in table 18.1.

Table 18.1 *Sample Application Performance Objectives*

Application	Average Uses	Activity	Response Time	Consistency (%)
Text processing utility (TPU)	20	Start TPU editor	00:00:10	95
Login	100	Get DCL prompt	00:00:15	95
WORDPERFECT	30	Spell-check 4K document	00:01:30	95
DB_UPD	1	Perform database update batch job	01:30:00	95

18.4 Monitoring Application Performance

After you have identified performance objectives, you should regularly monitor whether application performance goals are being satisfied. On a weekly or monthly basis you should summarize response times and publish the results to users or management. Such a report also becomes a historical record of response times, which is immensely helpful in analyzing performance over a longer term.

18.4.1 Monitoring Batch Jobs

You can monitor resource usage and response times for batch jobs simply by reviewing the resource-accounting information included at the end of the log file for each batch job. To ensure that this information is retained, include the /KEEP and /LOG qualifiers when jobs are submitted. By default, a log file is created in the job owner's default directory. The log file is given the same name as the command procedure that submitted it with a file extension of .LOG. For example:

```
$ SUBMIT/KEEP/NOPRINT DB_UPD.COM
. . .
$ TYPE DB_UPD.LOG
. . .

SYSTEM     job terminated at 20-SEP-2003 10:28:10.17

Accounting information:
Buffered I/O count:           1545   Peak Working set size:     912
Buffered I/O count:           1034   Peak page file size:     11134
Direct I/O count:             8512   Mounted Volume:              1
Charged CPU time:    0 00:20:00.46   Elapsed time:      0 01:04:25.59
```

When you review the log file, you should record the following information:

- *Direct I/O count:* Usually an indication of disk I/O activity
- *Page faults:* Number of requests for pages of memory
- *Charged CPU time:* Total amount of CPU time used
- *Elapsed time:* Total wall-clock time to complete job

The procedures for analyzing these statistics are discussed later in this chapter.

18.4.2 Monitor Interactive jobs

Measuring interactive activity is difficult because the system does not normally record resource-usage statistics until a user logs out. You can gather more timely statistics using one or more of the following techniques.

18.4.2.1 SHOW PROCESS

You can monitor the resource utilization of an active process by using the following command:

```
$ SHOW PROCESS/CONTINUOUS/ID=process-id
```

```
$ SHOW PROCESS/CONTINUOUS/ID=28

Process AUDIT_SERVER        17:58:30
State                          HIB   Working set                651
Cur/base priority             10/8   Virtual pages             3207
Current PC                7FFEDF8A   CPU Time        000:00:00:03.34
Current PSL               03C00000   Direct I/O                  75
Current user SP           7FF8C8F8   Buffered I/O                39
PID                       00000028   Page faults                504
UIC                       [SYSTEM]   Event faults          E0000001
                                                      80000000

BIRCH$DUA1 : [SYSO.SYSCOMMON.] [SYSEXE]AUDIT_SERVER.EXE;1
```

After you issue the command, resource-usage statistics are displayed and continuously updated once a second. You can get a general idea of how much CPU, memory, and disk resources the process is using by watching the CPU time, page faults, and direct I/O statistics. However, because statistics are constantly updated, it is difficult to collect precise data with this method.

18.4.2.2 ACCOUNTING Utility

By periodically enabling image-level accounting, you can force the system to record resource-utilization statistics after every image termination. Enable image-level accounting using the following command:

```
$ SET ACCOUNTING/ENABLE=IMAGE
```

Warning: If your normal system workload involves frequent image activations, the overhead of image-level accounting may substantially degrade system performance. Therefore, you should enable image accounting for only brief periods of time.

To disable image accounting use the following command:

```
$ SET ACCOUNTING/DISABLE=IMAGE
```

Once you have collected image accounting data, you can produce a summary report using the command following this paragraph. The commands assume that your default directory is set to SYS$MANAGER or that you have defined a systemwide logical (ACCOUNTING) that specifies the location of your accounting data file, as discussed in chapter 5. The following report provides the same basic data as SHOW PROCESS, except you can also determine the percentage of page faults that require a disk I/O (a hard fault) by referring to the Page I/O Reads statistics. The procedures for analyzing these statistics are discussed later in this chapter.

```
$ ACCOUNTING /TYPE=IMAGE/SUMMARY=(IMAGE)/OUTPUT=IMAGE.RPT -
_$ /REPORT=(RECORDS,PROCESSOR,ELAPSED,FAULTS,PAGE_READS,DIRECT_IO) ACCOUNTING
$ TYPE IMAGE.RPT

From:  7-JUN-2003 12:50 VAX/VMS Accounting Report To: 7-JUN-2003 12:52

Image Name    Total         Elapsed Time       Page             Page I/O  Direct  I/O
              Processor                        Time             Faults    Reads
              Records
-----------------------------------------------------------------------------------
ACC             4        0 00:00:01.86    0 00:00:06.76    260        63      19
DELETE          1        0 00:00:00.28    0 00:00:00.81     59         5       5
DIRECTORY       2        0 00:00:00.48    0 00:00:01.07    127         4       5
HARD            6        0 00:00:00.13    0 00:00:00.19    140         6       0
SET             2        0 00:00:00.08    0 00:00:00.73     51         4       0
SHOW            1        0 00:00:00.17    0 00:00:00.38     50         2       0
TPU             4        0 00:00:10.07    0 00:00:16.77   6836        13      28
```

18.4.2.3 Get Job/Process Information Function (F$GETJPI)

To measure the performance of a specific activity without enabling image-level accounting, you can use the lexical function Get Job/Process Information (F$GETJPI). Lexicals are callable from DCL and, therefore, can be used in scripts. This lexical is able to extract over 100 variables from a specified process. Its general form is

```
$ value = F$GETJPI(pid, "item")
```

where *pid* is the process ID and *item* is the name of the variable you wish to extract.

An example of F$GETJPI is presented in DCL command procedure BENCH.COM to gather usage statistics before and after a specific function is performed. BENCH then calculates total elapsed time and resource utilization for the activity. BENCH is available for downloading; see appendix E.

Unfortunately, there is no way to extract hard page fault statistics using F$GETJPI; thus, BENCH executes a small macro program, HARD.MAR, also available for downloading. HARD.MAR is only coded to execute on the VAX.

When the BENCH procedure is executed on a VAXstation 2000 to test the activation time of the Text Processing Utility (TPU), the following is displayed:

```
$ @BENCH/OUTPUT=BENCH.LOG
$ TYPE BENCH.LOG

Cpu: 589      Dio: 11     SF:  928     HF: 170     ET: 5528
Cpu: 522      Dio: 12     SF: 1081     HF: 103     ET: 4649
Cpu: 532      Dio: 12     SF: 1062     HF: 100     ET: 4941
```

And on a VAXstation 3100, the following is displayed:

```
Cpu: 141      Dio: 10     SF: 1925     HF:  11     ET:  212
Cpu: 147      Dio:  9     SF: 1925     HF:  11     ET:  203
Cpu: 147      Dio:  9     SF: 1925     HF:  11     ET:  206
```

The abbreviations in the foregoing output represent the following:

- CPU—CPU time used in 1/100 of a second (e.g., 528 = 5.28s)
- DIO—Number of disk I/O operations
- SF—Total number of page faults
- HF—Total number of hard page faults
- ET—Elapsed time in 1/100 of a second (e.g., 4,941 = 49.41s)

As you can see on the VAX 2000, elapsed time (response time) to invoke the TPU on this system ranges from 49.41 to 55.28 seconds, which does not meet the objective of 10 seconds listed in table 18.1. The remaining sections in this chapter analyze the results of this example and present techniques for achieving the required time.

18.5 Identifying Resource Dependencies

After you identify a performance problem, you have to decide which system resource to focus on. Ideally, you should focus on the resource for which users spend most of their time waiting. The procedures for roughly estimating CPU, memory, and disk dependency from the usage statistics that you have collected are discussed in the following sections.

18.5.1 Estimating Memory Dependency

Available memory on an OpenVMS system is organized as a linked list of pages known as the *free-page list.* When a process requests memory, pages are removed from the head of the free list and assigned to the process.

Each process has an associated working-set list that specifies the pages of memory resident in physical memory and that the process can immediately access. The maximum size of the working-set list of a process is generally configured with AUTHORIZE parameters (e.g., WSQUOTA, WSEXTENT). By restricting working-set sizes to a few hundred or a few thousand pages, you can ensure that no one process consumes all the physical memory of a system.

When a process attempts to access more pages of memory than its working-set list will allow, *page replacement* occurs. Replacement involves removing older pages from the working set and replacing them with the newly accessed pages. When a page containing read-only structures (e.g., executable code) is replaced, it is placed at the end of the free list. Replaced pages are likely to remain on the free-page list for some time before being allocated for another use; as a result, they act as a read-only page cache. When a page containing writable structure (e.g., a data page) is replaced, it is placed on a second list known as the *modified-page list.* The modified-page list can grow to contain several hundred or even several thousand pages (depending on the configuration of system parameters) and, thus, acts as a modified-page cache. If the size of the modified list exceeds its configured limits, groups of pages are written to the page file contained on disk.

Most of the strain on the memory resource occurs when a process attempts to access a page of memory that is not currently contained in its working set. This event is referred to as a *page fault* and is categorized as either a *hard fault* or a *soft fault,* depending on whether disk I/O is required to resolve the fault. Hard faults are resolved either by reading a page from an image file on disk (e.g., *XX*.EXE) or from a page file. Soft faults are resolved by accessing either the free-page or the modified-page list. Figure 18.3 summarizes the transition of memory pages from one location to another.

When a process activates an executable image, hard page faults occur as

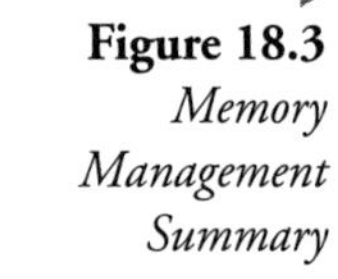

Figure 18.3 *Memory Management Summary*

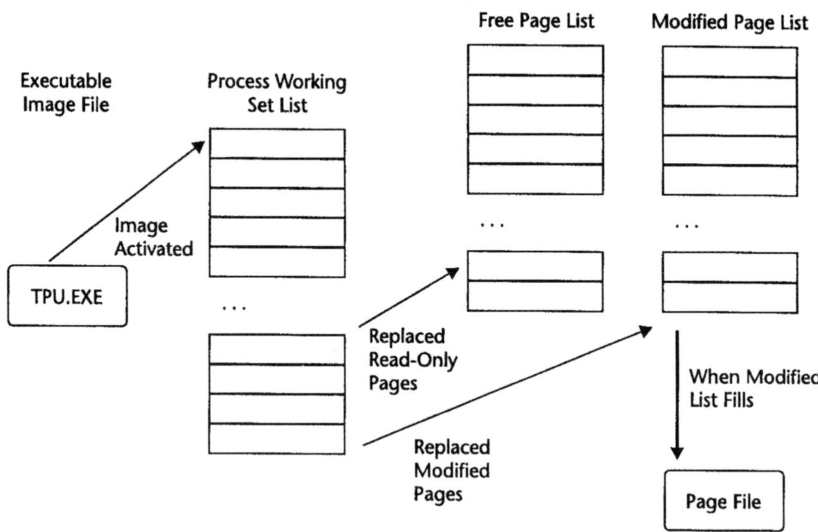

an image is loaded from an image file on disk. As the process begins to execute the image, it typically requests memory to store data. This generates soft page faults that are resolved by allocating pages from the free list to the working set of the process. Eventually, the working set of the process reaches its maximum size, forcing read-only pages, data pages, or both to be removed from the working set and placed on the free list and modified list, respectively.

If the process later accesses a replaced read-only page while the page is still on the free list, it is soft-faulted back into the working set of the process. If the replaced page is no longer on the free list, the page is hard-faulted back into the working set by being read from the original image file. When a process accesses a replaced data page that is still on the modified list, the page is soft-faulted back into the working set of the process. However, if the replaced page has already been removed from the modified list and written to a page file, a hard fault occurs, and the page must be read from the page file on disk.

Because soft faults do not require disk I/O, the time to process them depends largely on the CPU. Hard faults depend mostly on the response time of the disk that contains the image file or page file to which the faults occur. You can use the following formula to estimate the amount of elapsed time an activity spends waiting for memory operations:

```
Memory wait time = soft-fault rate × soft-fault CPU time +
                   hard-fault rate × hard-fault wait time
```

The amount of time it takes to process a soft page fault (soft-fault CPU time) depends on the speed of the processor. According to *Guide to OpenVMS Performance Management* (May 1993), HP indicates that it takes approximately 0.0005 seconds to process a soft fault on a VAX 11/780, a processor defined to have 1.0 VAX units performance (VUP). VUP ratings for all VAX processors is included in appendix C.

You can extrapolate the time it takes to process as follows:

```
Soft-fault CPU time
     = soft-fault rate × 0.0005 sec. × (1/processor VUP ratings)
Soft-fault CPU time
     = soft-fault rate × 0.0005 sec. × (1/12)
     = soft-fault rate × 0.00004 sec. (on a 12 VUP VAX)
```

Because a hard page fault requires disk I/O, the time to process a hard fault is roughly equal to the service time of the device. The procedure for calculating disk service time is discussed in the next section.

18.5.2 Estimating Disk I/O Dependency

Again, using values from the *Guide to OpenVMS Performance Management*, you can calculate the amount of time an activity spends waiting for disk operations to be completed by using the following formula:

```
Disk wait time = I/O count × disk service time
```

Disk service time varies from one device to another, but you can approximate a value (in milliseconds) using the following formula:

```
Disk service time (ms)
  = (Average queue length/average operation rate) × 1,000
```

Measure the operation rate and queue length for the disk during a time you believe represents normal usage, as follows:

```
$ MONITOR DISK/ITEM=ALL/BEGIN=0/END="+0-00:03:00"/NODISPLAY -
_$ /SUMMARY=DISK.SUM
$ TYPE DISK.SUM
                         OpenVMS Monitor Utility
                           DISK I/O STATISTICS
                             on node MILLER       From:  8-JUN-2003 12:51:02
                                SUMMARY           To:    8-JUN-2003 12:54:02

I/O Operation Rate                         CUR       AVE       MIN       MAX

$1$DKA0:      (MILLER) ALPHASYS           0.00     12.91      0.00    101.66


                               SUMMARIZING




                         OpenVMS Monitor Utility
                           DISK I/O STATISTICS
                             on node MILLER       From:  8-JUN-2003 12:51:02
                                SUMMARY           To:    8-JUN-2003 12:54:02

I/O Request Queue Length                   CUR       AVE       MIN       MAX

$1$DKA0:      (MILLER) ALPHASYS           0.00      0.12      0.00      1.00


                               SUMMARIZING
```

Then, estimate service time by using the average operation rate and queue length. For example, the estimated response times for DKA0: is as follows:

```
DKA0: (0.12/12.91) × 1,000 = 93 ms
```

Use the estimated response times for disks containing page files to calculate hard-fault wait time.

18.5.3 Estimating CPU Dependency

The following two factors account for elapsed time when processing CPU requests:

1. Time waiting for the CPU to become available
2. Actual time performing computer operations

When a process is scheduled to receive CPU time, it receives an allocation of CPU time based on the system parameter QUANTUM. On many systems QUANTUM is set to a default value of 20, which represents 0.2 seconds. Once a process begins using its quantum, it is allowed to continue until one of the following events occurs:

- Another process with a higher priority becomes computable.
- The process enters a voluntary wait state (e.g., issues an I/O request).
- The process has consumed its entire quantum.

Once a process consumes its quantum (reaches quantum end), another computable process with the same or higher scheduling priority is given a quantum. If there are no computable processes, a single process can continue to receive a new quantum after each quantum end. As you can see, if there is a large number of computable processes, the amount of time a single process has to wait to use the CPU can be considerable. For example, if quantum is 200 ms and there are 10 computable processes, each process has to wait 2 seconds (10 × 200 ms) each time it needs to use the CPU.

You can calculate average CPU waiting time at a given time using the following formula:

CPU wait time = (average computable processes – 1) × quantum

You can measure the average number of computable processes by noting the average compute queue length using MONITOR, as follows:

```
MONITOR>MONITOR STATES/ALL

                     OpenVMS Monitor Utility
                         PROCESS STATES
                          on node MILLER
                      4-JUN-2003 13:38:56

                                     CUR      AVE      MIN      MAX
   Collided Page Wait               0.00     0.00     0.00     0.00
   Mutex & Misc Resource Wait       0.00     0.00     0.00     0.00
   Common Event Flag Wait           0.00     0.00     0.00     0.00
   Page Fault Wait                  0.00     0.05     0.00     1.00
   Local Event Flag Wait            0.00     0.11     0.00     1.00
   Local Event Flag (Outswapped)    0.00     0.00     0.00     0.00

   Hibernate                        6.00     4.94     3.00     6.00
   Hibernate (Outswapped)           5.00     6.05     5.00     8.00
   Suspended                        0.00     0.00     0.00     0.00
   Suspended (Outswapped)           0.00     0.00     0.00     0.00
   Free Page Wait                   0.00     0.00     0.00     0.00
==>Compute                          2.00     2.00     1.00     2.00
   Compute (Outswapped)             0.00     0.00     0.00     0.00
   Current Process                  1.00     1.00     1.00     1.00
```

From the foregoing output, the average CPU wait time (per quantum) is as follows:

```
CPU wait time = (2.00 – 1.00) × 0.200 sec. = 0.200 sec.
```

The total time spent waiting for the CPU during a particular activity is the average wait time multiplied by the total number of quanta needed. This can be roughly calculated as follows:

```
Total CPU wait time
= CPU wait time × total quanta used
= CPU wait time × [(total CPU time/QUANTUM) + hard faults + disk I/Os]
```

Hard faults and disk I/Os are added because they force an immediate quantum end. Last, you estimate the time the activity spends performing other computer operations as follows:

CPU compute time = total CPU time – soft-fault CPU time

18.5.4 Resource Dependency Example

In an earlier section we said that invoking the TPU on a VAXstation 2000 used the following resources:

Cpu: 532 Dio: 12 SF: 1062 HF: 10 ET: 4941

Using the formulas that have been presented, you can estimate the waiting times for each resource.

```
Total soft-fault CPU time
= Soft-fault-rate × 0.0005 sec. × (1/processor VUP rating)
= 1,062 × 0.0005 × (I/O.75)(VS2000 = 0.75 VUPs)
= .708 sec.

Total hard-fault wait time
= hard-fault count × disk service time
= 100 × 0.049 sec.(RD54 disk)
= 4.9 sec.

Total disk wait time
= I/O count × disk service time
= 12 × .049 sec.
= 5.88 sec.
```

```
Total CPU wait time
= CPU wait time × [(total CPU time/QUANTUM) + Hard faults + Disk I/Os]
= 0.200 × [(5.32/0.00) + 12 + 100]
= 27.72 sec.
```

```
CPU compute time
= total CPU time – soft-fault CPU time
= 5.32 sec. – 0.708 sec.
= 4.612 sec.
```

The results for the TPU example are summarized in table 18.2.

Table 18.2 *Example Resource Dependency Analysis*

System Resource	Calculated Wait Time (sec.)	Percentage
Memory		
Soft faults	0.708	1.6
Hard faults	4.900	11.2
Disk	5.880	13.4
CPU		
Wait time	27.720	63.3
Compute time	4.612	10.5
Total	43.820	100.0

As you can see, the blocking resource is the CPU, which accounts for nearly 75 percent of the total elapsed time, 63 percent of which is spent simply waiting to use the CPU. As a result, the only way to achieve a 10-sec. response time is to focus on reducing CPU wait time.

You will notice that the total calculated wait time (43.820 sec.) does not exactly match the actual elapsed time recorded by BENCH (49.41 sec.). This is because the formulas presented in the previous sections are only rough approximations. However, if you find that the calculated and actual elapsed times vary dramatically, you should verify all calculations.

18.6 Load Balancing

When you have a performance problem and you have identified the blocking resource, the next step is to consider load-balancing options. Load-balancing activities include the following:

- Distributing load among systems in a VMScluster

- Shifting high-priority interactive activities to lower-priority batch jobs
- Delaying processing until off-peak periods (e.g., night or weekends)

Many computer systems sit idle from 5 P.M. to 9 A.M. This idle time represents more than 60 percent of the total potential capacity of a system. While you certainly cannot expect users to wait until midnight to edit an important document, you should carefully identify less critical system activities that can be performed during off hours as batch jobs. This will free scarce resources for users during normal business hours.

If you have multiple stand-alone systems or a VMScluster, you should ensure that user workloads are distributed as evenly as possible across available systems. You may have one system that is fully utilized and another system that is only 50 percent utilized. By distributing the load equally, you can increase overall responsiveness. If you do not have multiple systems to distribute load or if your systems are already load-balanced, skip to the sections of this chapter on tuning.

The following sections discuss techniques for load balancing each of the major system resources.

18.6.1 Load-Balancing Memory

To load-balance memory you should try to ensure that page faulting and memory use are distributed proportionally among available systems. Monitor memory use on each system (during peak times) using the following command:

```
$ MONITOR PAGE/BEGIN=0/END="+0-00:03:00"/NODISPLAY/SUMMARY=FAULT.SUM

$ TYPE FAULT.SUM

                            OpenVMS Monitor Utility
                          PAGE MANAGEMENT STATISTICS
                               on node MILLER        From:  8-JUN-2003 13:53:43
                                 SUMMARY             To:    8-JUN-2003 13:56:43

                                      CUR        AVE        MIN        MAX

   Page Fault Rate                   0.00       1.72       0.00      57.00
```

```
Page Read Rate                    0.00      0.91      0.00     43.66
Page Read I/O Rate                0.00      0.36      0.00     17.33
Page Write Rate                   0.00      0.00      0.00      0.00
Page Write I/O Rate               0.00      0.00      0.00      0.00

Free List Fault Rate              0.00      0.12      0.00      4.66
Modified List Fault Rate          0.00      0.10      0.00      4.66
Demand Zero Fault Rate            0.00      0.71      0.00     26.33
Global Valid Fault Rate           0.00      0.41      0.00     22.33
Wrt In Progress Fault Rate        0.00      0.00      0.00      0.00
System Fault Rate                 0.00      0.00      0.00      0.00

Free List Size                 6827.00   6797.76   6642.00   6998.00
Modified List Size              872.00    871.33    866.00    872.00

                           SUMMARIZING
```

If one system consistently has more free memory (free-list size) than another, you might shift memory-intensive users or batch jobs to that system. Similarly, if one system incurs considerably more page faults than another, you might want to try to equalize faulting among available systems.

18.6.2 Load-Balancing Disk I/O

Most HP disks can handle at least 20 to 60 I/Os per second. If you exceed the capacity of a drive, disk queue lengths and service times increase. If you have an I/O-bound application that is performing poorly and the disk it is accessing has a large queue length, you should consider distributing I/O to less utilized disks.

Because of the large number of files on the system disk, it is frequently overutilized. If you experience this problem, you can migrate OpenVMS data and log files to alternative disks, including the following:

- Queue database
- System authorization file
- Security audit journal
- Resource accounting database

The procedures for locating these files on alternative disks are discussed in detail in chapter 5.

18.6.3 Load-Balancing CPU

To gauge CPU activity use MONITOR as follows:

```
$ MONITOR MODES/ALL

                         OpenVMS Monitor Utility
                         TIME IN PROCESSOR MODES
                              on node MILLER
                          8-JUN-2003 14:00:40.38

                                   CUR        AVE        MIN        MAX

  Interrupt State                 1.33       2.69       1.33       4.00

  MP Synchronization              0.00       0.00       0.00       0.00

  Kernel Mode                     5.00       9.23       2.33      16.00

  Executive Mode                  0.00       0.03       0.00       0.33

  Supervisor Mode                 0.00       0.00       0.00       0.00

  User Mode                       7.33       8.56       2.00      25.66

  Compatibility Mode              0.00       0.00       0.00       0.00

  Idle Time                      86.33      79.47      67.66      91.33
```

Here an average idle time of 80 percent indicates the CPU is not very busy. For batch-oriented systems, idle times near zero are acceptable (if not desirable). However, to yield consistent response on time-sharing systems, HP recommends that you maintain no less than 30 percent idle time. If you have some systems that are mostly idle and others that are mostly busy, you should move system activity from busy systems to systems that are relatively idle.

To balance the CPU load generated by batch jobs, you can establish execution batch queues on each system and have those queues fed by a single clusterwide or networkwide generic queue. This process is discussed in detail in chapter 8.

To balance interactive CPU load, you should try to balance logins across multiple systems. This can be difficult if users log in from direct terminal ports (e.g., TXAO). However, if you use terminal servers, you can have OpenVMS perform automatic load-balancing using LAT service ratings and VMScluster alias node names. With this technique, you establish an alias node name for the cluster. The LAT software running on the cluster continuously determines which system is more utilized than the other. When users connect to the alias service, they are attached to the cluster member that is least busy. For more information on establishing a VMScluster alias name, consult the OpenVMS networking manuals.

18.7 Tuning Memory

If you have determined that the memory resource is a performance bottleneck, and you have considered load-balancing options, the next step is to tune the memory subsystem.

18.7.1 Introduction

VAX systems typically have between 4 and 512 MB of physical memory. OpenVMS allocates memory in pages of 512 bytes each. You can translate megabytes to pages by multiplying by 2,048. For example, a system with 16 MB of memory has approximately 32,000 pages. With the introduction of OpenVMS 6.0, OpenVMS supports up to 3.5 GB of physical memory on the VAX 6600, 7600, and 10000 systems.

OpenVMS/Alpha systems use a different page size than OpenVMS/VAX systems. An Alpha page size can be either 8K, 16K, 32K, or 64K, however, all current systems use an 8K page. To maintain compatibility with VAX systems, Alpha systems define a unit of page measurement called a *pagelet*, which equals one VAX page. For example, on an Alpha system with an 8K page, 1 Alpha page equals 16 pagelets.

On an Alpha system, usually all references to a quantity of pages are displayed and evaluated in both of pagelets and pages (e.g., GBLPAGES, PGFLQUOTA), for instance:

```
$ mcr sysgen
SYSGEN> SHOW GBLPAGES

Parameter Name          Current    Default      Min.       Max.     Unit  Dynamic
--------------          -------    -------    -------    -------    ----  -------
GBLPAGES                 400000      65536      10240            -1 Pagelets   D
 internal value           25000       4096        640            -1 Pages      D
```

On the other hand, all references to physical memory are displayed and evaluated in terms of Alpha pages (e.g., SHOW MEMORY).

18.7.2 Excessive Hard Page Faults

A high hard-fault rate is strong evidence that either your memory subsystem is severely mistuned or an application is poorly designed. An excessive hard-page-fault rate could be caused by one or more of the following problems.

18.7.2.1 Excessive Image Activation

When a process activates an image, hard faults occur as the executable image is read from the image file into memory. Because the execution of many DCL commands results in an image activation, complex DCL command procedures can easily generate hundreds of image activations per minute. If you have such procedures, you should consider streamlining them, or if possible, implement them with high-level language.

You can also reduce image-activation overhead by installing images shareable with the OpenVMS INSTALL utility. When an executable image is installed as shareable, only the first process to access it incurs hard page faults as it reads the image and sets up global sharing structures. Subsequent processes accessing the image concurrently incur global soft page faults because they can access the same pages already mapped into memory by the previous process. To determine which images to install as shareable, you can use image-level accounting to identify frequently activated images, as follows:

```
$ ACCOUNTING/TYPE=IMAGE/SUMMARY=IMAGE/OUTPUT= -
       IMAGE.LIS/REPORT=(RECORDS,PAGE_READS) ACCOUNTNG

$ TYPE IMAGE.LIS

From: 1-JUN-2003 21:04          VAX/VMS Accounting Report
To:    1-JUN-2003 22:21
```

```
Image name      Total     Page I/O
                Records   Reads
------------------------------------------
ACC             1         14
CREATE          3         21
DELETE          2         13
DIRECTORY       1         11
EDT             5         31
LINK            4         39
LOGINOUT        14        109
MACRO32         5         144
MONITOR         5         138
QUEMAN          3         35
SET             5         40
SETPO           2         6
SHOW            12        66
SUBMIT          7         71
SYSGEN          2         45
TPU             35        212
TYPE            9         61
VMSHELP         1         42
```

The images with the most activations (total records) and the most hard faults (page I/O reads) are the best shareable image candidates. In this case, TPU is one possible candidate.

Bear in mind that an executable image may also access shareable libraries that could benefit from being installed. You can identify the shareable libraries associated with an image by performing the following command:

```
$ ANALYZE/IMAGE/OUT=T.TMP TPU.EXE
$ SEARCH T.TMP/WINDOW=(0,10) "Shareable Image List"

Shareable Image List

                0)  "TPUSHR"
                1)  "LIBOTS"
                2)  "LIBRTL"
                3)  "DPML$SHR" Shareable Image List
```

You may also want to use the undocumented SET WATCH command to see other types of files that are accessed when you invoke an image, as follows:

```
$ SET WATCH FILE/CLASS=ALL
$ EDIT/TPU
...
%XQP, Thread #0, Directory scan for: TPU$CCTSHR.EXE;0,
Status:00000000
...
%XQP, Thread #0, Directory scan for:
EVE$SECTION.TPU$SECTION;0, Status:00000000
...
$ SET WATCH FILE/CLASS=NONE
```

As you can see, SET WATCH uncovers two additional files that are accessed when TPU is invoked. These files are thus potential INSTALL candidates.

To install an image or library as shareable, use the INSTALL utility as follows:

```
$ INSTALL ADD SYS$SYSTEM:TPU.EXE/OPEN/SHARE
$ INSTALL ADD SYS$LIBRARY:TPUSHR.EXE/OPEN/SHARE
```

Some of the foregoing libraries may already be installed by OpenVMS. To make these changes permanent, you should add the foregoing commands to your system startup procedures, as discussed in chapter 5 (e.g., STARTUP_SHARE.COM).

To install a shareable image you need sufficient global pages and global sections. To determine the number available, perform the following steps:

```
$ INSTALL LIST/GLOBAL/SUMMARY

        Galaxy Group Global Sections


   516 Global Sections Used,  139984/260016 Global Pagelets Used/Unused
```

```
$ RUN SYS$SYSTEM:SYSMAN
SYSMAN> PARAMETER SHOW GBLSECTIONS

%SYSMAN-I-USEACTNOD, a USE ACTIVE has been defaulted on node MILLER
Node MILLER:   Parameters in use: ACTIVE
Parameter Name            Current    Default    Minimum    Maximum Unit  Dynamic
--------------            -------    -------    -------    ------- ----  -------
GBLSECTIONS                   700        250         80      65535 Sections
```

To determine the number of available global sections, you must subtract the number in use from the system parameter GBLSECTIONS. In the foregoing example there are 184 free global sections (700 – 516). If you do not have many free global pages or global sections, you should add more using AUTOGEN (discussed later in this chapter).

18.7.2.2 Image File I/O

If you have applications that do not warrant being installed as shareable (e.g., there is little concurrent access), users may generate disk I/O to the image file during or even after image activation. This can be caused by one or more of the following problems:

- Insufficient free-list cache size
- Insufficient working-set size

If a user's working sets are too small, code pages are frequently replaced and are placed on the free list. If the free-list cache is not large enough, these cached pages are quickly allocated to other processes before they are faulted back into the user's working sets. If a MONITOR PAGE indicates a small free-list size and a low free-list fault rate, you should consider adjusting the following system parameters:

- FREELIM: Specifies the minimum allowable size of the free list. When the number of pages on the free list falls below FREELIM, OpenVMS attempts to reclaim memory from processes until FREEGOAL pages are on the free list.
- FREEGOAL: Specifies the target free-list size.

Because FREELIM specifies the minimum size of the free list, it also represents the minimum number of read-only pages cached. You should increase FREELIM to a value that provides efficient caching of read-only pages. As an alternative, if only a few specific processes are experiencing high hard-fault rates, you might achieve better results by increasing their individual working sets (see the following sections).

18.7.2.3 Page File I/O

Another reason for high hard-page-fault rates is faulting modified pages from a page file. The MONITOR PAGE command allows you to monitor all hard-fault activity based on the Page Read I/O statistic. Unfortunately, there is usually no easy way to determine exactly what portion of the I/Os is reading from files versus reading from page files. However, if your page files are located on dedicated disks, you can gauge page-file activity by reviewing the results of MONITOR DISK statistics.

You can reduce hard faults resulting from page-file reads by increasing the maximum allowable size of the modified-page list. The modified-page list size and other attributes are configured with the system parameters shown in table 18.3.

Table 18.3 *Modified Page Writer (MPW) System Parameters*

Parameter	Description
MPW_WAITLIMIT	This parameter forces processes into a wait state if they attempt to add pages to the modified list when it contains more than MPW_WAITLIMIT pages. Such processes are not allowed to continue until the MPW completes writing pages.
MPW_HILIMIT	This parameter specifies the number of pages that can accumulate on the modified list before OpenVMS begins writing modified pages to the page file. After pages are written to the page file, they are returned to the end of the free list.
MPW_THRESH	This parameter specifies the minimum number of pages that must be contained on the modified list for OpenVMS to consider writing modified pages to the page file.
MPW_LOWAITLIMIT	Processes that are forced into a wait state because of modified-page writing are allowed to resume when the number of pages on the modified list drops below MPW_LOWAITLIMIT.
MPW_LOLIMIT	When OpenVMS determines that it is necessary to write pages from the modified list to the page file, it continues until only MPW_LOLIMIT pages remain. In this way, MPW_LOWLIMIT specifies the minimum size for the modified-list cache.

Warning: Before you increase the size of the modified list, be certain that there are no processes whose working sets are configured so low that they generate the majority of modified pages.

18.7.2.4 Establishing Page File Sizes

When pages are written from the modified list, OpenVMS must locate a contiguous area within the page file. If a contiguous area cannot be located, OpenVMS attempts to write pages in several smaller operations. When the page file becomes full, OpenVMS incurs considerable overhead trying to locate page-file space, during which time, processes trying to add pages to the modified list may be placed in a wait state. If the situation becomes severe enough, the entire system can hang. As a result, HP recommends that you maintain page files with at least 50 percent free space to minimize page-file fragmentation.

Alpha

You examine the page-file allocation with the following command:

```
$ SHOW MEMORY/FILE
            System Memory Resources on  8-JUN-2003 15:57:34.13

Swap File Usage (8KB pages):                   Index         Free         Size
  DISK$ALPHASYS:[SYS0.SYSEXE]SWAPFILE.SYS
                                                   1          280          280

Paging File Usage (8KB pages):                 Index         Free         Size
  DISK$ALPHASYS:[SYS0.SYSEXE]PAGEFILE.SYS
                                                 254        12496        12496
  Total committed paging file usage:                                       4903
```

VAX

You examine the page-file allocation with the same command as the Alpha, but the display is different:

```
$ SHOW MEMORY/FILE
System Memory Resources on 13-JUN-2003 08:27:00.52

Paging File Usage (pages):                      Free  Reservable         Total
  DISK$OVMSVAXSYS:[SYS0.SYSEXE]SWAPFILE.SYS
                                                1008        1008          1008
  DISK$OVMSVAXSYS:[SYS0.SYSEXE]PAGEFILE.SYS
                                                3554      -36216          4296
```

Note the number of reservable pages indicated by the SHOW MEMORY command. If your system has multiple page files, OpenVMS uses the reservable-page count to determine page-file assignment. When a process is created, OpenVMS examines the reservable-page count of each page file. The process is assigned an allocation of up to 2,048 pages (the default value of the system parameter RSRVPAGCNT) in the page file that has the most reservable pages. If a process uses up its allocation, OpenVMS examines the reservable pages a second time and gives the process another allocation in the page file that has the most available pages. As a process continues to use its allocations, it can be assigned to up to four different page files. Thus, if you experience extremely heavy page-file activity, you can increase performance by creating several page files on different disks.

On many systems the number of reservable pages is frequently negative. This occurs when many small processes are given an allocation of 2,048 pages, but only use a small portion of it. In the foregoing example, the reservable-page count was about –36,000 because there were approximately 20 active processes.

On either the VAX or the Alpha, if you see that free space is less than 50 percent of total space, you should increase the page-file size. There are two ways to do this. If you know what changes you would like to make, use SYSGEN as follows:

```
$ RUN SYS$SYSTEM:SYSGEN
SYSGEN> CREATE SYS$SPECIFIC:[SYSEXE]PAGEFILE.SYS/SIZE=6000
%SYSGEN-I-EXTENDED, SYS$SPECIFIC:[SYSEXE]PAGEFILE.SYS;1 extended
```

A second method is to allow AUTOGEN to compute and change these files. AUTOGEN is discussed in section 18.12.2.

18.7.3 Excessive Soft Page Faults

Excessive soft faults are of less concern than hard faults because they are resolved 100 times faster. However, if your applications are generating many hundreds of soft faults per second, you might be able to increase performance by tuning working-set-related system parameters.

You must consider the following three mechanisms when tuning working sets:

1. Working-set sizes
2. Automatic working-set adjustment (AWSA)
3. Memory reclamation

18.7.3.1 Establishing Working-Set Sizes

The purpose of the OpenVMS working-set mechanism is to limit the amount of physical memory any one process can control. The *working-set list* of a process is an array of pointers that describes the physical pages of memory that a process can access without incurring a page fault. Working-set list size is controlled by the following three parameters:

1. Working-set default (also called working-set limit)
2. Working-set quota
3. Working-set extent

Current process settings are displayed with the command:

Alpha

```
$ show working_set
  Working Set (pagelets) /Limit=2000  /Quota=4000  /Extent=90112
  Adjustment enabled     Authorized Quota=4000  Authorized Extent=90112

  Working Set (8Kb pages) /Limit=125  /Quota=250  /Extent=5632
                         Authorized Quota=250  Authorized Extent=5632
```

VAX

```
$ show working_set
  Working Set      /Limit=21195   /Quota=21195    /Extent=21195
  Adjustment enabled     Authorized Quota=21195  Authorized Extent=21195
```

When a process activates an image, its working-set list size is set to the default value. As the process generates page faults and maps physical pages, its working-set list size can increase to the quota value. The working-set list of the process can expand further, up to the extent value, but only if sufficient free memory is available.

When a process needs to reference more pages than can be mapped by its working set, pages must be removed from the working set. The removed pages migrate to the free list (as described earlier). If migrated pages are referenced again, they are faulted back into the working set, forcing the replacement of other pages. When the actual working-set size of a process is configured far below what it actually requires, pages are faulted back and forth between the working set and the system page caches. If you detect an application that faults heavily, you should try to expand its working set until page-fault rate levels off.

The mechanisms used to configure working sets depend on process type, as follows.

Interactive Processes

Working-set limits are established from the SYSUAF, as follows:

/WSDEFAULT	Working-set default
/WSQUOTA	Working-set quota
/WSEXTENT	Working-set extent

The limit will never be set lower than the following system parameters. These may be adjusted with the SYSMAN PARAMETER command.

PQL_MSDEFAULT	Minimum working-set default
PQL_MWSQUOTA	Minimum working-set quota
PQL_MWSEXTENT	Minimum working-set extent

Detached Processes

Working-set limits are established from the following system parameters and are adjusted with the SYSMAN PARAMETER command.

PQL_DWSDEFAULT	Default working-set default
PQL_DWSSQUOTA	Default working-set quota
PQL_DWSEXTENT	Default working-set extent

These limits will not be set lower than corresponding PQL_M* system parameters.

Batch Processes

Batch queues may be configured with working-set characteristics using the INITIALIZE/QUEUE and START/QUEUE commands with the following qualifiers:

/WSDEFAULT=*pages*	Working-set default
/WSQUOTA=*pages*	Working-set quota
/WSEXTENT=*pages*	Working-set extent

If these queue characteristics are not specified, then working-set parameters are set to the working-set limits established in the account's SYSUAF, subject to the limits of the PQL_D and PQL_M system parameters.

In general, the standard working-set parameters are set much too small for the average application. The default values are set in account DEFAULT, [200,200]. Table 18.4 contains some guidelines for establishing working-set parameters. Values in table 18.4 should be multiplied by at least two for Alpha systems.

Table 18.4 *VAX Working-Set Parameters Guidlines*

Working Set	Small Jobs	Medium Jobs and DECwindows	Large Jobs
Default	512	512	1,024
Quota	768	1,024	2,048
Extent	1,024	2,048	4,096

If a system has ample free memory, you can increase working sets to sizes substantially greater than those indicated in table 18.4. Ideally, you should distribute available memory to applications that will most benefit from it. Generally, these are applications that exhibit the highest page-fault rates.

DECwindows Motif requires considerably more resources and requires a significantly different algorithm to determine SYSUAF parameters and system parameters. You should pay careful attention to the DECwindows installation manual to configure your system properly.

If you manage a mixed architecture (VAX and Alpha) cluster, this difference in working-set sizes makes it difficult to use a common SYSUAF. Of course, this problem is caused by the underlying page size of the two architectures, 512 bytes versus 8,192 bytes.

18.7.3.2 AWSA

After a process invokes an image, working-set size adjustments are controlled by the AWSA mechanism. AWSA behavior is determined by the configuration of the system parameters listed in table 18.5.

Table 18.5 *Working-Set Adjustment*

Parameter	Description
AWSTIME	The interval at which working-set adjustment occurs
AWSMIN	The lowest number of pages to which a working-set limit can be decreased by AWSA
PFRATH	Minimum page-fault rate necessary to justify a working-set size increase
WSINC	WSINC > 0 triggers AWSA algorithm. Amount by which working-set size is increased when PFRATH is triggered
PFRATL	PFRATL > 0 triggers AWSA based on fault rate; forces working-set size decrease if page-fault rate drops below specified value
WSDEC	Amount by which working-set size is decreased when PFRATL is triggered
BORROWLIM	The minimum number of pages that must exist on the free list for working-set list size of a process to be expanded above its quota value
GROWLIM	The minimum number of pages that must exist on the free list for a process to map additional pages of memory into a working set larger than the working-set quota of the process
QUANTUM	Used together with AWSTIME to determine the paging data sampling rate

By default, every 200 ms (AWSTIME), AWSA is triggered, and OpenVMS calculates a page-fault rate for a process. If the fault rate is greater than the system parameter PFRATH, the working-set size of the process is increased by WSINC entries. The working-set size of a process can increase up to its working-set quota value without regard to free memory. However, working-set size can increase beyond its quota (up to its extent) only if there are at least BORROWLIM pages on the free list. In addition, a process can map more pages than its working-set quota only if there are at least GROWLIM pages on the free list.

You can enable AWSA as an optional feature to automatically decrease working-set list sizes by setting the system parameters PFRATL and WSDEC to nonzero values. When AWSA is enabled, the working-set size of a process is decremented if its page-fault rate drops below PFRATL. However, automatic working-set decrementing generally causes undesirable working-set size oscillation and is therefore not normally enabled.

18.7.4 Memory Reclamation

Up to this point, we have discussed how OpenVMS allocates memory to processes by increasing their working-set sizes. Once memory becomes scarce, OpenVMS uses the following mechanisms to reclaim memory from idle processes and processes that have exceeded their working-set quotas:

- SWAPPER Trimming
- Proactive memory reclamation

18.7.4.1 SWAPPER Trimming

When the number of pages on the free list drops below the system parameter FREELIM, the SWAPPER process attempts to reclaim memory by initiating SWAPPER trimming. The SWAPPER calculates the number of pages that must be recovered to establish FREEGOAL pages on the free list. It then begins first-level trimming by reducing process working sets to their quota values until enough pages are reclaimed.

If first-level trimming does not free enough pages, the SWAPPER initiates second-level trimming and trims selected process working sets back to the value of the system parameter SWPOUTPGCNT until sufficient pages are reclaimed. Finally, if trimming efforts do not yield enough free memory, the SWAPPER swaps selected processes to the swap file, making all the remaining pages available in the process. The SWAPPER first trims processes that are least likely to become computable, thereby freeing memory for more active processes.

SWAPPER trimming is generally desirable because it allows you to maximize use of the system memory. However, if you detect excessive trimming or swapping of active processes, you probably do not have enough physical memory to support existing working-set sizes; thus, you should consider decreasing these working sets.

18.7.4.2 Proactive Memory Reclamation

This mechanism is designed to reclaim memory more aggressively before a memory deficit is detected. Proactive memory reclamation (PMR) targets reclamation from the following two types of processes whenever the number of pages on the free list drops below FREEGOAL.

- Long-waiting processes
- Periodically waking processes

Processes that have been in wait states (hibernate and local event flag wait) for longer than LONGWAIT seconds are swapped. Unlike SWAPPER trimming, the working-set sizes of outswapped processes are not reduced. Therefore, when the process is swapped back in, it is able to begin executing more quickly, without excessive page faulting.

SWAPPER trimming is ineffective at reclaiming memory from periodically waking processes because such processes still consume some amount of CPU time and are never considered idle. PMR monitors for periodically waking processes whenever the number of pages on the free list drops below two times FREEGOAL. It locates processes that have been idle for more than 30 seconds and that are idle 99 percent of the time. When such processes are identified, 25 percent of their pages are trimmed from their working sets; however, process working-set sizes are not reduced.

18.8 Tuning I/O

If you determine that disk I/O is constraining an application or the system as a whole, use the strategies discussed in the following sections to improve I/O performance.

18.8.1 Disk Defragmentation

When a disk is first initialized, its available free space is contained in one large contiguous area. When files are created, they are allocated from this contiguous pool and, thus, are also contiguous. As more files are created, deleted, and extended, available free space becomes more fragmented.

Eventually, files must be allocated to space made up of multiple fragments located in different physical regions of a disk. When users perform an I/O operation to a fragmented file, OpenVMS may be forced to break a single operation into two or more operations—a split I/O—to read the multiple fragments.

A file is made up of one or more *extents*. Each extent describes each fragment of a file. A contiguous file has only a single extent, whereas a severely fragmented file might have several hundred extents. OpenVMS can access only a limited number of extents within a file at one time. By default, this limit is defined by the system parameter ACP_WINDOW, which has a default value of 7. If a file has more than seven fragments, and a user attempts to access a fragment not described by the current window, OpenVMS must perform a *window turn* and retrieve information about the unmapped fragment. An excessive window-turn rate is an indication of a severe fragmentation problem.

You can monitor the systemwide split I/O rate by issuing the following command and reviewing split transfer rate:

```
$ MONITOR IO/BEGIN=0/END="+0-00:03:00" /NODISPLAY/SUMMARY=IO.SUM
$ TYPE IO.SUM
                       OpenVMS Monitor Utility
                        I/O SYSTEM STATISTICS
                          On node MILLER          From: 3-JUN-2003 12:05:52
                             SUMMARY               To: 3-JUN-2003 12:08:53

                              CUR          AVE         MIN          MAX

Direct I/O Rate              1.98         2.05        0.33         3.65
Buffered I/O Rate            0.99         3.33        0.33         6.64
Mailbox I/O Rate             0.00         0.00        0.00         0.00
Split Transfer Rate          0.00         0.00        0.00         0.33
Log Name Translation Rate    1.98        14.94        0.66        35.09
File Open Rate               0.33         0.53        0.00         0.99

Page Fault Rate            214.56       318.44       80.79       572.18
Page Read Rate               0.00         3.67        0.00        12.95
Page Read I/O Rate           0.00         1.59        0.00         3.98
Page Write Rate              0.00         1.99        0.00        39.86
Page Write I/O Rate          0.00         0.01        0.00         0.33
Inswap Rate                  0.00         0.00        0.00         0.33
```

```
Free List Size            2537.00      2935.03     2070.00     3854.00
Modified List Size         403.00       312.53      191.00      435.00
                                    SUMMARIZING
```

Monitor the systemwide window-turn rate by using the following command and reviewing the window-turn rate:

```
$ MONITOR FCP/BEGIN=0/END="+0-00:03:0"/NODISPLAY/SUMMARY=FCP.SUM
$ TYPE FCP.SUM

                         OpenVMS Monitor Utility
                        FILE PRIMITIVE STATISTICS
                              On node BIRCH     From:    3-JUN-2003 12:09:14
                                 SUMMARY           To:    3-JUN-2003 12:12:14

                              CUR          AVE          MIN          MAX
FCP Call Rate                2.29         1.87         0.32         2.95
Allocation Rate              0.00         0.18         0.00         0.65
Create Rate                  1.00         0.64         0.00         1.63

Disk Read Rate               0.00         0.01         0.00         0.98
Disk Write Rate              0.00         1.26         0.00         2.95
Volume Lock Wait Rate        1.00         0.00         0.00         0.00

CPU Tick Rate                1.31         1.89         0.32         3.93
File Sys Page Fault Rate     0.00         0.28         0.00         0.98
Window Turn Rate             0.32         0.18         0.00         0.65

File Lookup Rate.            1.63         0.73         0.00         1.63
File Open Rate               0.65         0.53         0.00         0.98
Erase Rate                   0.00         0.04         0.00         0.32

                               SUMMARIZING
```

Unfortunately, you will need performance-monitoring tools (e.g., DECamds) to monitor the split I/O and window-turn rates of individual disks.

If your applications depend heavily on access to a specific file, you can determine the number of fragments contained in the file using the DUMP utility as follows:

```
$ DUMP/HEADER/BLOCK=COUNT:0 CHECK_PROCESSOR.IDX/OUT=T.TMP
$ SEARCH T.TMP "Count"

     Count:     39          LBN:       24027
```

Because only one extent is listed (containing 39 blocks), this file is contiguous. If there is sufficient contiguous space on a disk, you can defragment a file using the COPY command as follows:

```
$ COPY/CONTIGUOUS filename.ext newfile.ext
```

However, to defragment an entire disk you must perform an image backup and then restore the disk. Alternative you may use a disk fragmentation optimizer (DFO) or a similar third-party tool on a running system.

When installed, DFO may be invoked from either the DCL prompt (with DEFRAG) or from DECwindows. For instance, to display a fragmentation summary of a disk, the following command would be entered:

```
$ defrag
Disk File Optimizer for OpenVMS DFG V2.6
Copyright C Compaq Computer Corp. 1991,2001.   All rights reserved
DFO>show/statistics/volume dka0:

                   F r a g m e n t a t i o n   R e p o r t

DISK$ALPHASYS                                        13-JUN-2003 11:20:30.72

The fragmentation index is 23.3
      1 - 20.9 is excellent
     21 - 40.9 is good
     41 - 60.9 is fair
     61 - 80.9 is poor
     81 - 100 indicates a badly fragmented disk
Approximately 3.3 (out of 80.0 possible) is due to file fragmentation
Approximately 20.0 (out of 20.0 possible) is due to freespace fragmentation
Freespace Summary:
        Total free space:       2937861 blocks
        Percentage free:             35 (rounded)
        Total free extents:         571
        Maximum free extent:    1760166 blocks, LBN: 6619914
```

```
        Minimum free extent:          9 blocks, LBN: 3094929
        Average free extent:       5145 blocks
        Median free extent:          36 blocks


File Fragmentation Summary:
        Number of files (with some allocation):  23032
        Total file extents on the disk:          23354
        Average number of file extents per file: 1.013981
        Median number of file extents per file:  1

Most Fragmented File:
        [SYSCOMMON.SYSEXE]SYS$QUEUE_MANAGER.QMAN$JOURNAL;1 (87 extents)
```

18.8.2 Adjust Volume Characteristics

By default, when you delete a file, its disk blocks are deallocated, but not erased. Sophisticated users can create a new file that allocates previously deallocated blocks and access another user's deleted data. The volume attributes /HIGHWATER and /ERASE-ON-DELETE prevent this access, but result in additional overhead to create and delete files. To examine the status of the volume, use SHOW DEVICE/FULL.

If potential security disadvantages are acceptable, you can increase disk performance by disabling these characteristics on all disk volumes, as follows:

```
$ SET VOLUME/NOHIGHWATER device
$ SET VOLUME/NOERASE_ON_DELETE device
```

To make the change effective you must dismount and then mount the volume again. To make the change effective on a system disk you must reboot the system. The security implications of disabling these parameters are discussed in more detail in chapter 17.

18.8.3 Adjust ACP (Ancillary Control Process) Caches

OpenVMS maintains caches of file, directory, and extent structures. If these caches are not large enough, unnecessary I/O is incurred. You can determine the effectiveness of the caches by monitoring cache bit rates using MONITOR, as follows:

```
$ MONITOR FILE/BEGIN=0/END="+0-00:03:00"/NODISPLAY/SUMMARY=FILE.SUM
$ TYPE FILE.SUM
                         OpenVMS Monitor Utility
                     FILE SYSTEM CACHING STATISTICS
                              on node MILLER       From: 13-JUN-2003 11:26:30
                                 SUMMARY           To:   13-JUN-2003 11:29:30

                                       CUR        AVE        MIN        MAX

    Dir FCB     (Hit %)               0.00     100.00       0.00     100.00
                (Attempt Rate)        0.00       0.01       0.00       0.66
    Dir Data    (Hit %)               0.00      33.33       0.00      33.00
                (Attempt Rate)        0.00       0.01       0.00       1.00
    File Hdr    (Hit %)               0.00      50.59       0.00      70.00
                (Attempt Rate)        0.00       8.80       0.00      98.66
    File ID     (Hit %)               0.00       0.00       0.00       0.00
                (Attempt Rate)        0.00       0.00       0.00       0.00

    Extent      (Hit %)               0.00       0.00       0.00       0.00
                (Attempt Rate)        0.00       0.00       0.00       0.00
    Quota       (Hit %)               0.00       0.00       0.00       0.00
                (Attempt Rate)        0.00       0.00       0.00       0.00
    Bitmap      (Hit %)               0.00       0.00       0.00       0.00
                (Attempt Rate)        0.00       0.00       0.00       0.00

                                SUMMARIZING
```

HP recommends that you attempt to maintain at least a 75 percent hit ratio to all caches that have a nonzero attempt rate. If you need to increase the size of cache, adjust the following system parameters:

- ACP-SYSACC DIR FCB
- ACP-DINDXCACHE Dir FCB
- ACP-DIRCACHE Dir Data
- ACP-HDRCACHE File Hdr
- ACP-FIDCACHE File ID
- ACP-EXTCACHE Extent
- ACP-EXTLIMIT Extent

- ACP-QUOCACHE Quota
- ACP-MAPCACHE Bitmap

You can also use the AUTOGEN facility to adjust cache sizes automatically based on feedback information (see the AUTOGEN section at the end of the chapter).

18.8.4 I/O Cache

A disk cache stores the most recently accessed disk blocks in memory. When an application accesses the same disk block more than once, subsequent requests are satisfied from the cache, rather than from the physical disk.

You can activate the virtual I/O cache (VIOC) on a VAX and either VIOC or extended file cache (XFC) on an Alpha to improve disk performance. XFC has better performance than VIOC in the following areas:

- Read-ahead caching
- Automatic resizing of the cache
- Larger maximum cache size
- No limit on the number of closed files that can be cached
- Control over the maximum size of I/O that can be cached
- Control over whether cache memory is static or dynamic

VIOC cache on a VAX is controlled by setting a system parameter as follows:

```
VBN_CACHE_S = 0 ! disable
VBN_CACHE_S = 1 ! enable
```

VIOC and XFC cache on an Alpha are controlled by setting a system parameter as follows:

```
VCC_FLAGS = 0    ! disable
VCC_FLAGS = 1    ! enable VIOC
VCC_FLAGS = 2    ! enable XFC
```

Both cache techniques can also be used within a VMScluster, with the following restrictions:

- To enable caching you must enable it on every cluster member.
- Caching is disabled for any file that is opened for write access by two or more members.

To monitor the status of the VIOC, use the following command:

```
$ SHOW MEMORY/CACHE/FULL
```

On a VAX, the following is displayed:

```
   System Memory Resources on 2-JUN-2003 17:02:08.51

Virtual I/O Cache
Total Size (pages)    544      Read IO Count            4622
Free Pages            0        Read Hit Count           1814
Pages in Use          544      Read Hit Rate            39%
Maximum Size (SPTEs)  715      Write IO Count           85
Files Retained        36       IO Bypassing the Cache   0
```

On an Alpha with XFC enabled, the following is displayed:

```
   System Memory Resources on 13-JUN-2003 12:06:38.10

Extended File Cache  (Time of last reset: 12-JUN-2003 18:35:05.36)
  Allocated (MBytes)           49.85    Maximum size (MBytes)          88.00
  Free (MBytes)                 0.00    Minimum size (MBytes)           3.12
  In use (MBytes)              49.85    Percentage Read I/Os             96%
  Read hit rate                  67%    Write hit rate                    0%
  Read I/O count               11183    Write I/O count                 378
  Read hit count                7522    Write hit count                   0
  Reads bypassing cache          157    Writes bypassing cache            0
  Files cached open              381    Files cached closed             468
  Vols in Full XFC mode            0    Vols in VIOC Compatible mode      1
  Vols in No Caching mode          0    Vols in Perm. No Caching mode     0

I/O Statistics - Distributions (MAX_IO_SIZE: 127)
```

```
-------------------------------------------------
Transfer Size:        Reads  Read Hits    Writes
   1 Block IO:         2999       2450        65
   2 Block IO:          511        283        37
. . .
 118 Block IO:            1          0         0
 123 Block IO:            1          0         0

>127<256 Block IO:        9                    0
>255     Block IO:       16                    0
-------------------------------------------------
Totals:               11051       7522       378
```

The foregoing statistics indicate the current size of the cache, the number of free pages, and maximum possible size of the cache. Another important statistic is the read hit rate. According to HP, a 50 percent hit rate is the point at which the performance gains from caching exceed the overhead required to maintain the cache.

18.9 Tuning CPU

If you have determined that the CPU is the major resource hampering application or system performance, and you have verified that the CPU overhead incurred by the I/O and memory subsystems has been minimized, you should review the following:

- Process scheduling
- Priority boosting
- Adjust quantum
- Decompressing system libraries

18.9.1 Process Scheduling

Within an OpenVMS environment, processes share access to the CPU based on the OpenVMS process-scheduling algorithm. The most important aspect of this algorithm is the *scheduling priority* of a process. Scheduling priority for interactive users is initially established based on the priority specified in the users' AUTHORIZE record. Batch-job priority is set to the default base priority established with the INITIALIZE/QUEUE/

BASE_PRIORITY command. In general, various processes are assigned the following priorities, where 1 is lowest:

- 1–3 Batch jobs
- 4–7 Interactive users (usually 4)
- 8–6 VMS system processes (SWAPPER, etc.)
- 16–32 Real-time processes

Internally, priorities on Alpha/VMS range from 0 to 63 in compliance with POSIX threads. OpenVMS always gives precedence to the computable process with the highest priority. Processes with the same priority are serviced in a round-robin manner. It is important to understand that a CPU-intensive process at priority 5 completely blocks the CPU from all priority 4 processes. As a result, all interactive users should be set to the same priority (generally priority 4). Batch jobs can be assigned priorities between 1 and 3, depending on which are more time critical. However, priorities are not static, as is explained in section 18.9.2.

If you suspect that the CPU is not being shared equitably among interactive users, use the MONITOR utility to identify processes that are capitalizing the CPU:

```
$ MONITOR PROCESS/TOPCPU
                              OpenVMS Monitor Utility
                               TOP CPU TIME PROCESSES
                                  on node MILLER
                              13-JUN-2003 14:28:54.45

                                  0         25        50        75        100
                                  + - - - - + - - - - + - - - - + - - - - -+
 20400062  DECW$SERVER_0       90 ≠≠≠≠≠≠≠≠≠≠≠≠≠≠≠≠≠≠≠≠≠≠≠≠≠≠≠≠≠≠≠≠≠≠≠≠
                                  |         |         |         |          |
 20400082  _FTA6:               5 ≠≠
                                  |         |         |         |          |
 20400069  DECW$TE_0069         3 ≠
                                  |         |         |         |          |
 20400067  VUE$SYSTEM_3

                                  |         |         |         |          |
                                  |         |         |         |          |
                                  |         |         |         |          |
                                  |         |         |         |          |
                                  + - - - - + - - - - + - - - - + - - - - -+
```

Then, use the following command to monitor individual processes:

```
$ SHOW PROCESS/CONT/ID=process-id
```

By default, users cannot increase their priority above the /PRIORITY value *(also called base priority)* established in the SYSUAF (see chapter 9), unless they have the ALTPRI privilege.

18.9.2 Priority Boosting

Each process actually has two priorities, *base priority* and *current priority.* The current priority is used to determine scheduling precedence. By default, the base and current priorities of a process are equal to its default priority. However, OpenVMS temporarily increases the current priority of a process after certain events. The two most important events are disk I/O completion and terminal I/O completion, after which processes receive a priority boost of 2 and 4, respectively,

Priority boosting helps make processes more likely to receive CPU time immediately after I/O completion. Unfortunately, this can cause I/O-bound jobs to capitalize the CPU. Therefore, if you have I/O intensive batch jobs, and you do not want them to interfere with interactive users, you should set their base priority to 1 to disable the effects of priority boosting.

18.9.3 Quantum

When a process is selected to receive CPU time, it is allowed to execute for a set number of milliseconds, defined by the system parameter QUANTUM. By default, QUANTUM is set to 20, representing 200 ms (or 1/5 sec.).

Once a process is executing, it is allowed to continue until one of the following events occurs:

- Another process with a higher priority becomes computable
- The process enters a voluntary wait state (e.g., issues an I/O request)
- The process consumes its entire quantum

The default QUANTUM value is designed to yield acceptable response time in environments with a mix of interactive and batch processing. If your environment mostly consists of interactive users, you might consider using a smaller QUANTUM value. If you are attempting to support a large number of concurrent interactive users, you may even want to set QUANTUM to its minimum value of 2 (representing 20 ms).

If you run many batch jobs, you may be able to reduce process-scheduling overhead by slightly increasing QUANTUM. If your system is used purely for batch processing, you should consider increasing QUANTUM considerably, perhaps by a factor of 2 or 3 to reduce system overhead.

18.9.4 Decompress System Libraries

When you install or upgrade OpenVMS, a number of system libraries is installed in compressed form. Compressed libraries reduce disk-space usage by several thousand blocks. However, if users frequently access OpenVMS Help or use compilers that link to compressed shareable libraries, additional CPU overhead occurs, as the libraries are decompressed as they are accessed. If you believe these libraries are accessed regularly, you should permanently decompress them as follows:

```
$ @SYS$UPDATE:LIBDECOMP
                    OpenVMS Library Decompression Utility
                      Candidate Libraries to be expanded
   (Libraries not present and libraries already expanded are not listed)

     1  ACLEDT.HLB           11  NCPHELP.HLB          21  VAXCRTLT.OLB
     2  BKM$HELP.HLB         12  SDA.HLB              22  VAXCRTLTX.OLB
     3  DBG$HELP.HLB         13  SHWCLHELP.HLB        23  VAXCRTLX.OLB
     4  DBG$UIHELP.HLB       14  LANIDEF.MLB          24  ERFLIB.TLB
     5  EVE$HELP.HLB         15  LIB.MLB              25  LIB_ADA_SUBSET.TLB
     6  EVE$KEYHELP.HLB      16  STARLET.MLB          26  NTA.TLB
     7  EXCHNGHLP.HLB        17  STARLET.OLB          27  STARLETSD.TLB
     8  LANCP$HELP.HLB       18  VAXCRTL.OLB          28  SYS$LIB_C.TLB
     9  LATCP$HELP.HLB       19  VAXCRTLD.OLB         29  SYS$STARLET_C.TLB
    10  MAILHELP.HLB         20  VAXCRTLDX.OLB

        30  VMS$VOLATILE_PRIVATE_INTERFACES.OLB
        31  STARLET_RECENT_ADA_SUBSET.TLB

         A  ALL libraries to be expanded
         H  Display HELP information for LIBDECOMP
         E  EXIT this procedure
* Enter a letter or the number(s) of libraries to be expanded
  (Separate multiple numbers with a comma)
```

18.10 Expanding Capacity

If your load-balancing and tuning efforts do not help increase performance to an acceptable level, your only remaining alternative is to expand system capacity. However, before you purchase additional hardware, you should carefully review the information you have collected concerning individual application and overall system-resource demand. With this information you should be able to determine which resource most needs expansion. If you expand a resource that is not constraining application performance, the affect will be minimal, and you will waste a considerable amount of money.

18.11 Sample Performance Problem

Let us return to the example of invoking TPU. This section uses the techniques discussed in this chapter to rectify the unacceptable response time measured for this particular activity. The results from BENCH have indicated a 49-sec. response time to invoke TPU:

- Cpu: 532 Dio: 12 SF: 1062 HF: 100 ET: 4941

The resource-dependency analysis has indicated that this activity depends mostly on the CPU, most of the time being spent simply waiting because another processes is using the CPU. Consequently, a MONITOR PROCESS/TOPCPU shows the following:

```
$ MONITOR PROCESS/TOPCPU

                    OpenVMS Monitor Utility
                     TOP CPU TIME PROCESSES
                         On node BIRCH
                     4-JUN-2003 17:10:29

                              0        25        50        75       100
                              + - - - -+ - - - - + - - - -+ - - - - -+
00000044 INF LOOP    69       *************************
                              |        |         |        |          |
0000004F BENCH       24       **********
                              |        |         |        |          |
00000030 SYSTEM       2
```

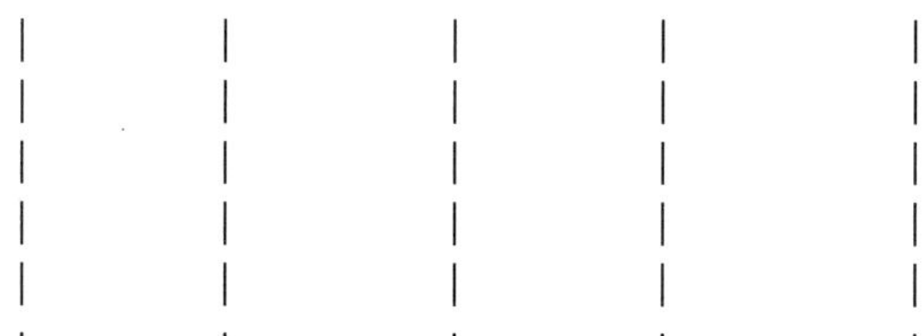

A process INF_LOOP is consuming 69 percent of the CPU, forcing the TPU activity to wait for the CPU. On further investigation you determine that the INF_LOOP process is a broken DCL program that is looping infinitely. After you stop this process, BENCH results are as follows:

- Cpu: 597 Dio: 12 SF: 1031 HF: 201 ET: 1723

The 17-sec. response time is much better, but still does not meet the objective. A new resource dependency analysis indicates that hard-fault wait time represents a large portion of the current response time. To reduce hard faults, TPU and the images it accesses are installed with the /SHARE option. BENCH results are then as follows:

- Cpu: 509 Dio: 12 SF: 2385 HF: 9 ET: 631

  Response time is now 6 seconds, 4 seconds less than the objective!

It is interesting to note that in some cases installing an image with the /SHARE option can reduce hard faults even when the image is not accessed concurrently. In the example, hard faults were reduced even though only a single process was invoking TPU over and over again. When a process exits an image that is not installed, the code pages return to the free list. When the process accesses the image again, it still must hard-fault from the image file, even if the image pages are on the free list from an earlier activation. When a process exits an image that is installed, the code pages return to the free list, but global page structures that describe the installed image remain intact. If the process activates the same image again, it soft faults the image from the free list.

18.12 Managing System Parameters

When you change system parameters, it is important that you modify them using the correct procedures. The following sections describe how to use properly the two utilities designed for this process (SYSMAN and AUTOGEN).

18.12.1 SYSMAN PARAMETER Command

You can manipulate system parameters with either the SYSGEN utility or the SYSMAN PARAMETER command. You should use SYSMAN, however, because it provides additional features and will eventually supersede SYSGEN.

To review system parameters, use SYSMAN as follows:

```
$ RUN SYS$SYSTEM:SYSMAN
SYSMAN> PARAMETER SHOW FREELIM
%SYSMAN-I-USEACTNOD, a USE ACTIVE has been defaulted on node MILLER
Node MILLER:   Parameters in use: ACTIVE
Parameter Name            Current    Default    Minimum    Maximum Unit  Dynamic
--------------            -------    -------    -------    ------- ----  -------
FREELIM                        61         32         16         -1 Pages
```

By default, the SHOW command displays the active settings for the specified parameter. When the system boots, active parameters are loaded from the permanent system-parameter database, referred to as *current parameters*. On a VAX, these parameters are stored in the following file:

```
SYS$SYSTEM:VAXVMSSYS.PAR
```

On Alpha OpenVMS systems, system parameters are stored in the following file:

```
SYS$SYSTEM:AlphaVMSSYS.PAR
```

You can view current parameter values instead of active values by issuing a PARAMETER USE command, as follows:

```
SYSMAN> PARAMETER USE CURRENT
```

Dynamic parameters can be changed after a system boot and are identified by a D in the Dynamic column on the right of the listing. Nondynamic parameters can only be made effective by rebooting the system.

Each parameter has an associated *default, minimum,* and *maximum* value. Parameters cannot be set to values outside their associated minimums and maximums. The HP-established default values allow virtually any system configuration to boot. When you have a system-parameter-configuration problem that prevents your system from booting, you can temporarily force the system to use the default parameters or previously correct parameters by performing a *conversational boot* (see chapter 4).

18.12.2 AUTOGEN Utility

You should use SYSMAN only to display system parameters; changes should be performed using the AUTOGEN utility. Frequently, a change in one parameter requires changes in related parameters. The AUTOGEN utility allows you to specify parameter changes, and it automatically calculates the required changes to related parameters. Furthermore, using AUTOGEN enables you to document changes.

You make parameter adjustments with AUTOGEN by adding or modifying entries in file SYS$SYSTEM:MODPARAMS.DAT. MODPARAM entries have a number of valid formats, as detailed in table 18.6.

Table 18.6 *MODPARAMS.DAT Entry Formats*

Format	Description
Parameter = value	Sets the specified parameter to an absolute value.
ADD_*parameter = delta-value*	Sets the parameter equal to the sum of the default value of the parameter plus any additional amount that AUTOGEN calculates is necessary.
MIN_*parameter = minimum-value*	Forces the parameter to be set to at least the specified minimum value. The parameter is set high if AUTOGEN recognizes it warranted
MAX_*parameter = maximum-value*	Restricts the parameter from being set higher than the specified maximum value.

18.12.2.1 System Parameter Entries

To set a parameter to a specific value, specify the parameter name and value separated with an equal sign (=). For example:

```
QUANTUM=10
```

If you are making an incremental change to a parameter, you should use the ADD_ format. For example, if you plan to install a new application with the /SHARE option and need 1,000 additional global pages, use the following format:

```
ADD_GBLPAGES 1000 ! Installed VAX C 5/1/95
```

By using this type of format, you create an audit trail of parameter changes. If you want to ensure that AUTOGEN establishes a minimum or maximum value for a particular parameter, you can also include a MIN_ and MAX_ entry. For instance:

```
MIN_GBLPAGFIL=4096
```

You will find that installation of some products add entries to MODPARAMS.DAT, the automatically perform the AUTOGEN sequence for the node. DECwindows, cluster configuration, and system upgrades are examples products that do this. Entries made by these products are documented in MODPARAMS.DAT as well.

18.12.2.2 Page-, Swap-, and Dump-File Entries

In addition to entries that control system parameter values, several of special AUTOGEN entries control the size of the page, swap, and dump files. Use the following entries to specify the sizes for the dump file and primary page-swap files:

- PAGEFILE = *size*
- SWAPFILE = *size*
- DUMPFILE = *size*

If you want to manage page and swap files manually, you should disable AUTOGEN sizing by adding the following MODPARAM entries:

- PAGEFILE = 0
- SWAPFILE = 0
- DUMPFILE = 0

To specify the name and size for additional page and swap files, use the following entry formats (where *n* indicates the page- or swap-file number):

- MIN_PAGEFILEN_NAME = *file_name*
- MIN_PAGEFILEN_SIZE = *size*
- MIN_SWAPFILEN_NAME = *file_name*
- MIN_SWAPFILEN_SIZE = *SIZE*

18.12.2.3 Establishing Cluster-Common Parameters

In the VMScluster environment, you may have several system parameters and should have the same value on each cluster member. To simplify management of these parameters, you can establish a cluster-common MODPARAMS file, as follows:

```
$ EDIT SYS$COMMON:[SYSEXE]COMMON-MODPARAMS.DAT

! Cluster Common MODPARAMS.DAT
FREELIM=1000
FREEGOAL=2000
WSMAX=32768
```

Then add an INCLUDE statement to each member-specific MODPARAMS as follows:

```
$ EDIT SYS$SPECIFIC:[SYSEXE]MODPARAMS.DAT
! Include Cluster-common parameters
!
AGEN$INCLUDE_PARAMS SYS$COMMON:[SYSEXE]COMMON-MODPARAMS.DAT
!
! Member-specific parameters
!
. . .
```

When you install the OpenVMS cluster product, it suggests that you use the file, SYS$MANAGER:AGEN$NEW_NODE_DEFAULTS.DAT and puts a line in MODPARAMS.DAT to include it. However, AGEN$NEW_NODE_DEFAULTS.DAT is merely an empty template.

Notice in the foregoing examples that anything to right of a bang (!) is considered to be a comment and is ignored by AUTOGEN.

18.12.2.4 Invoking AUTOGEN

Once you have added the appropriate entries in MODPARAMS, invoke AUTOGEN as follows:

```
$ @SYS$UPDATE:AUTOGEN START-PHASE END-PHASE FEEDBACK-MODE
```

The valid AUTOGEN phases are listed in table 18.7.

Table 18.7 *AUTOGEN Phases*

AUTOGEN Phase	Description
SAVPARAMS	Saves current tuning feedback data to the file AGEN$FEEDBACK.DAT
GETDATA	Gathers information required to calculate proper parameters from MODPARAMS and AGEN$FEEDBACK
GENPARAMS	Generates new system-parameter values
TESTFILES	Calculates page-, swap-, and dump-file sizes Creates AUTOGEN feedback report (AGEN$PARAMS.REPORT)
GENFILES	Creates (or extends) page, swap, and dump files if necessary
SETPARAMS	Copies existing system parameters to VAXVMSSYS.OLD or ALPHAVMSSYS.OLD, then invokes SYSMAN to set parameters
SHUTDOWN	Performs an orderly system shutdown
REBOOT	Performs an automatic system reboot
HELP	Displays extensive documentation

When you are ready to run AUTOGEN, you generally start with the SAVPARAMS phase and end with the SETPARAMS phase, as follows:

```
$ @SYS$UPDATE:AUTOGEN SAVPARAMS SETPARAMS
```

You can optionally extend the end phase to include SHUTDOWN or REBOOT if you want AUTOGEN to perform an automatic shutdown or reboot.

You can get online help with the following command:

```
$ @SYS$UPDATE:AUTOGEN HELP
```

18.12.2.5 AUTOGEN Feedback

During normal system operation, OpenVMS maintains statistics regarding utilization of system resources. By default, AUTOGEN uses this data to determine settings for many system parameters. You can override the default usage of feedback data by specifying the feedback mode as detailed in table 18.8.

Table 18.8 *AUTOGEN Feedback Modes*

Feedback Mode	Description
FEEDBACK	Forces AUTOGEN to use tuning feedback data when calculating system parameter values
NOFEEDBACK	Forces AUTOGEN to ignore feedback data
CHECK_FEEDBACK	Instructs AUTOGEN to use feedback data as long as there is at least 24 hours of data and the data is not more than 30 days old
Blank	The default AUTOGEN action is to use feedback

By default, AUTOGEN uses feedback data to calculate parameter settings. If you prefer to retain control over when and how system parameters are changed, you should force AUTOGEN to ignore feedback, as follows:

```
$ @SYS$UPDATE:AUTOGEN SAVPARANS SETPARAMS NOFEEDBACK
```

You can review the parameter changes that feedback data suggests by generating an AUTOGEN feedback report without changing the .PAR file, as follows:

```
$ @SYS$UPDATE:AUTOGEN SAVPARAMS TESTFILES FEEDBACK

$ TYPE/PAGE SYS$SYSTEM:AGEN$PARAMS.REPORT
```

```
AUTOGEN Parameter Calculation Report on node: MILLER
  This information was generated at  7-JUN-2003 06:26:17.66
  AUTOGEN was run from GETDATA to REBOOT using FEEDBACK

Processing Parameter Data files
-------------------------------

Including parameters from: SYS$SYSTEM:MODPARAMS.DAT

Including parameters from:  SYS$MANAGER:AGEN$NEW_NODE_DEFAULTS.DAT

The following concerns were detected within MODPARAMS.DAT

** Note ** - Multiple MIN values found for MIN_GBLSECTIONS.
        Using MODPARAMS value (700) which is superseding VMS value (600)
. . .

Swap file calculations:

        SWAPFILE information:
        Feedback information.
           Old value was 4600, New value is 4600
           Maximum observed usage: 0
        Override Information - parameter calculation has been overridden.
           The calculated value was 5500.  The new value is 4600.
           SWAPFILE calculation has been set to current size by user.
           SWAPFILE will not be modified. The file size is within 10%.
```

When you perform a system shutdown (as discussed in chapter 6), you can optionally select the SAVE_FEEDBACK shutdown option and force current feedback data be written to the following file:

```
SYS$SYSTEM:AGEN$FEEDBACK.DAT
```

To use the old feedback with AUTOGEN, rename the old AGEN$FEEDBACK.DAT file so that it is the most current feedback file. Then run AUTOGEN starting with the GETDATA phase, as follows:

```
$ @SYS$UPDATE:AUTOGEN GETDATA TESTFILES FEEDBACK
```

By skipping the SAVPARAMS phase, you prevent AUTOGEN from writing current feedback statistics to the AGEN$FEEDBACK.DAT file.

Next, to implement the changes recommended by the feedback report, execute the following command:

```
$ @SYS$UPDATE:AUTOGEN GETDATA REBOOT FEEDBACK
```

Alternatively, you can manually add the suggested changes to the MODPARAMS file, and run AUTOGEN.

18.13 System Health Check

HP provides a performance measurement service called System Health Check (SHC). You can read a full explanation of it at http://www.compaq.com/support/svctools/shc/ and the product, including documentation, can be downloaded from this site. No additional license is required to run it.

SHC is a tool produced by HP Services to analyze a system's configuration, performance, and security status. SHC analysis results are gathered into a series of reports that highlight any problems found on a system and provide suggestions for resolving these problems. The problem data is processed by HP Services and the resulting reports are sent to an HP specialist or technical account manager (TAM). The type and detail of report provided by HP depends on the SHC customer's service contract. SHC Lite Report is free to any user; SHC Professional Report is for HP service professionals.

18.14 Tools

One tool discussed in this chapter and discussed further in appendix E is listed in table 18.9. HARD.MAR will link only on VAX systems.

Table 18.9 *VAX Performance Tool*

Procedure Name	Function
BENCH.COM	Gather resource-usage statistics for an activity
HARD.MAR	Gets hard page-fault count (macro code)

18.15 Conclusion

The OpenVMS paging algorithm is very complex and adjusting its parameters should be done only as a last resort. Even so, carefully record the out-of-the-box settings so, if necessary, you can restore them to a known configuration.

The I/O examples in this chapter were based on older technologies. Disks and I/O paths are many times faster now. Nevertheless, the algorithms presented are still valid.

Memory sizes on the VAX and Alpha are incomparable. For instance my VAX has 16 MB and is running 50 percent utilized with a standard OpenVMS 7.3 installation. My Alpha has 176 MB and is running 60 percent utilized with a standard OpenVMS 7.3-1 installation. Thus, for memory utilization, the rule of thumb is that the Alpha needs 8 to 10 times as much memory as a VAX, simply because of the page size difference.

18.16 References

Many of the following documents are dated and out of print. I include them because this very complicated issue needs as many viewpoints as necessary to thoroughly understand it.

1. *OpenVMS Performance Management* (April 2001) is the current tuning document. It discusses OpenVMS tuning algorithms in great detail.
2. Ruth E. Goldenberg. *OpenVMS Alpha Internals and Data Structures—Memory Management.* Digital Press, 2003.
3. Ruth E. Goldenberg, Denise E. Duman, and Saro Saravanan. *OpenVMS Alpha Internals—Scheduling and Process Control.* Digital Press, 1997.
4. Ruth E. Goldenberg and Lawrence J. Kenah. *VAX/VMS Internals and Data Structures.* Digital Press, 1991. This is the last Goldenberg publication that included VAX structures.
5. James W. Coburn. *OpenVMS Performance Management.* CBM Books, 1994.
6. Bruce Ellis. *The Hitchhikers Guide to VMS.* Professional Press, 1990.

7. *Enterprise Capacity and Performance Suite,* October 2000.

8. *DECwindows Motif for OpenVMS Installation Guide* and *Managing DECwindows Motif for OpenVMS Systems* are required reading if you are using this product.

9. *Guide to OpenVMS Performance Management,* Digital Press, May 1993.

10. *Guide to OpenVMS AXP Performance Management,* Digital Press, March 1994.

11. *OpenVMS System Manager's Manual,* Digital Press, April 2001.

12. *DECamds User's Guide*. Compaq DECamds is a real-time monitoring, diagnostic, and correction tool that assists system managers in improving OpenVMS system availability.

19

OpenVMS Network Management

19.1 Chapter Objectives

- Describe DECnet IV concepts
- Describe DECnet IV management
- LAT concepts
- Describe LAT management

19.2 Introduction

Before the early 1980s, most users interacted with Digital systems using directly connected terminals (figure 19.1). Frequently, systems operated in a stand-alone manner and were not connected to any type of network. To transfer data between systems you had to copy it to magnetic media and physically transport it to another system.

As the installed base of systems and PCs swelled, transporting magnetic media from host to host ("sneaker-net") became impractical—direct file transfer between systems was desperately needed. Users also needed to access more than one host from a single terminal, and many hosts needed to access common printers. Digital developed the DECnet protocol (and its associated applications) to address the file-transfer requirement. Digital later developed the LAT protocol to provide greater flexibility and performance for terminal-based connectivity.

Today, OpenVMS systems can be networked by means of a wide variety of physical connections (e.g., Ethernet, FDDI, Token Ring, serial line). OpenVMS systems can communicate using many other protocols (e.g., TCP/IP, Novell IPX). However, because most Digital users rely on DECnet and LAT protocols on Ethernet, this chapter focuses on that environment.

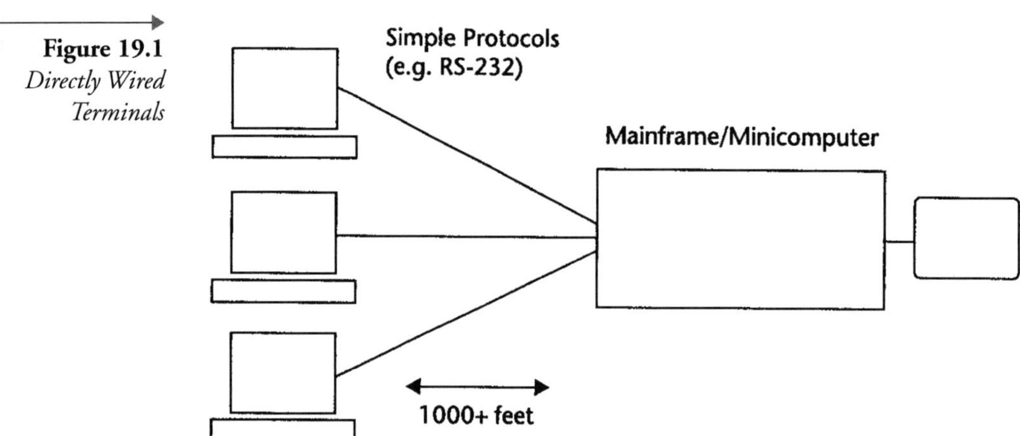

Figure 19.1
Directly Wired Terminals

DECnet-Plus (called DECnet V and DECnet/OSI in the early 1990s) is the preferred product today. This chapter discusses its predecessor, DECnet IV, in detail. The reader is cautioned that some key concepts have changed between the two products. In particular, DECnet IV is managed by NCP, and DECnet V is managed by NCL. If you wish to migrate to DECnet-Plus, HP supplies tools that will handle most configurations. These are described in the DECnet-Plus documents.

19.3 Ethernet Basics

Ethernet was developed in the mid-1970s by Xerox, Digital Equipment Corporation, and Intel. It allows up to 1,023 nodes to be connected by means of inexpensive coaxial or unshielded twisted-pair (UTP) cabling. With additional devices, Ethernet networks can be extended to support tens of thousands of nodes that span several thousand miles. Ethernet also provides a relatively high transfer speed. Because of its low cost and good performance, Ethernet has become the dominant physical infrastructure for Digital local area networks (LANs). Figure 19.2 shows a sample Ethernet network. Bridges, repeaters, and routers are discussed later in this chapter.

19.3.1 Ethernet Addressing

Every node in an Ethernet network has a unique 48-bit address recorded in its adapter. This address is frequently referred to as the physical, datalink, or media-access control (MAC) address of a node. Whenever a node transmits data on an Ethernet network, it places the data and destination address in an Ethernet frame. The beginning of the frame contains the destination MAC

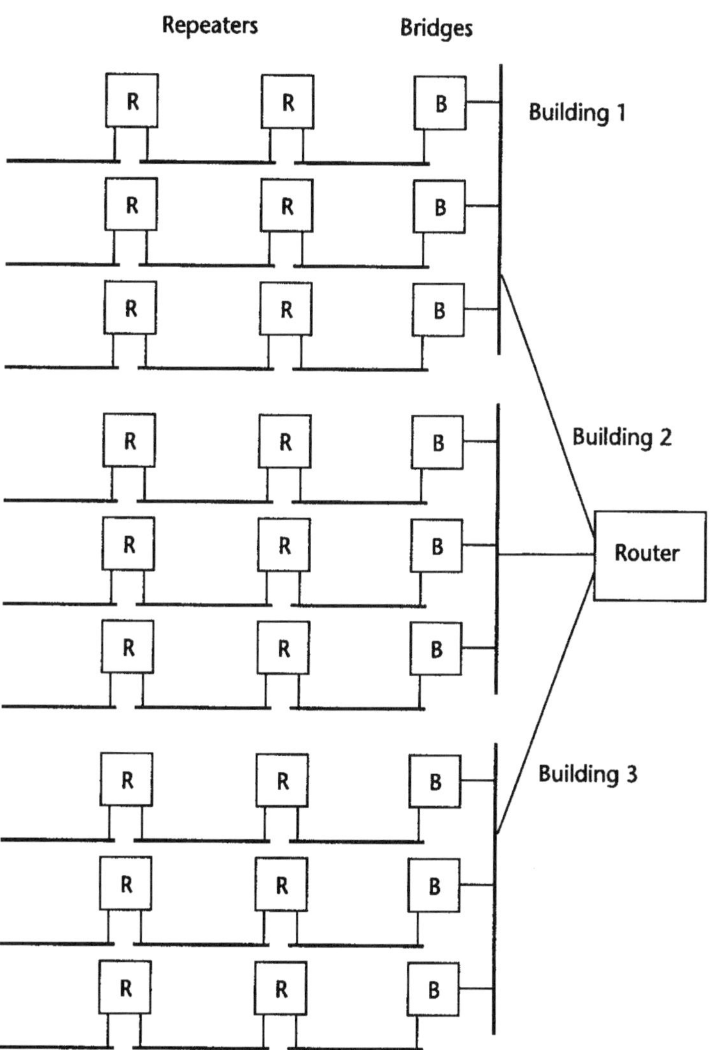

Figure 19.2
Example of an Ethernet Network

addresses of the target node and the MAC address of the source node, followed by the data, and finally ending in a frame checksum, as follows:

- Ethernet preamble:

    00-00-00-00-00-00-00-00[eight-byte synchronization string]

- Ethernet header:

    AA-00-04-00-02-14[Destination datalink address: bytes 0–5]

AA-00-04-00-01-04[Source datalink address: bytes 6–11]

60-03[Protocol type: bytes 12–13]

- Ethernet data:

  Data[Data: 46–1,500 bytes]

- Ethernet trailer:

  00-00-00-00[Checksum: 4 bytes]

The first six bytes are the destination datalink address (dashes are added between each byte for readability). The next six bytes are the source datalink address, followed by a two-byte protocol type. Then, between 46 and 1,500 bytes of data are inserted into the frame. Finally a four-byte packet checksum is put at the end of the frame. An Ethernet frame must contain a minimum of 64 bytes and a maximum of 1,518 bytes. Because Ethernet frames are used by many different protocols, the protocol *type* field helps easily identify which protocol is using the frame. Some common protocol types (in hexadecimal) are listed in table 19.1.

Table 19.1 *Selected Protocol Codes*

Protocol Code	Protocol Name
08-00	IP
08-05	X.25 level 3
08-06	ARP
60-01, 60-02	MOP
60-03	DECnet IV
60-04	LAT
60-07	LAVC (cluster)
80-48	DEC AMDS
80-9B	Appletalk over Ethernet
81-37	IPX–Novell
81-4C	SNMP over Ethernet
81-91	NetBios

19.3.2 Ethernet Terminology

Networking terms such as *node*, *segment*, and *LAN* are frequently used to describe two entirely different entities. The following sections define these terms as they should be interpreted within the context of this chapter.

19.3.2.1 Node

A node is an OpenVMS host, terminal server, PC, or other network device that has an Ethernet datalink address. When a node transmits a frame, all other nodes on the same LAN "hear" the packet. However, the computer's Ethernet adapter (also called the NIC) passes the contents of the frame to higher-level software only if the destination datalink address of the frame matches the adapter's datalink address.

19.3.2.2 Physical Segment

A physical segment is a length of cable with one or more attached nodes. Depending on the type of cable used, segment lengths and maximum attachments are limited as indicated in table 19.2.

Table 19.2 *Ethernet Cable Types*

Cable Type	Maximum Segment Length (m)	Maximum Attachments per Segment
UTP	100	1
Thinwire coaxial (RG58/U)	180	31
Thickwire coaxial	500	100
Fiber Distributed Data Interface (FDDI)	100,000 (62 mi.)	500

The length limits exist because, as the signal travels from one end of a segment to another, it becomes weaker and begins to distort. A repeater can be used to extend the network.

19.3.2.3 Repeater

A repeater is a network device with two or more network interfaces. When attached to two physical segments, a repeater listens to the signal on one segment and immediately retransmits it (one bit at a time) on all its other interfaces. As a repeater retransmits, it reamplifies and retimes the signal so that the signal is strong enough to travel the length the next segment. Repeaters are not nodes, they do not have a datalink address, and they are transparent to the protocol.

A series of physical segments connected by repeaters creates a single *logical segment*, also called a LAN. Ethernet specifications allow a maximum of four repeaters between any two network stations within a LAN. Thus, the maximum diameter of an copper Ethernet LAN is 2,500m (five thickwire segments connected with four repeaters). An FDDI LAN is much larger, as table 19.2 shows.

19.3.2.4 Bridge

The diameter of a LAN is restricted so that a packet can propagate from one side of a LAN to the other in a reasonable amount of time. A bridge is a network device with two or more network interfaces. You use bridges to connect several LANs to create a single *extended LAN*.

A bridge has a datalink address for each Ethernet interface it contains. When a bridge detects the start of a packet on one of its interfaces, it reads the entire packet and stores it in a buffer. Only after it has received the entire packet does it then forward the packet to all its other interfaces. Thus, a bridge propagates packets more slowly than a repeater does. Although bridges are full Ethernet nodes (they have datalink addresses), packets are usually not sent directly to them. Rather, bridges operate in *promiscuous mode*, which allows them to receive and process all packets on a LAN—even when the destination address of a packet does not match the address of the bridge.

Most Ethernet bridges are classified as *transparent learning bridges*. They are termed "learning," because as a bridge receives packets, it examines the source address of each packet and records the interface on which the packet was received. They are called "transparent," because bridges receive and forward packets without changing them in any way (see figure 19.3).

Once a bridge has learned the network address locations, it filters traffic destined for the same LAN from which it was received. For example, if TS001 sends a packet to LISA, the bridge receives it from LAN1 and forwards it to LAN2. However, if TS001 sends a packet to BART, the bridge receives the packet on LAN1, but it notices that its bridge table indicates that BART is connected to LAN1. Thus, the bridge assumes that the packet has already reached its destination and discards the packet. The end result is that any traffic between TS001 and BART does not propagate to LAN2.

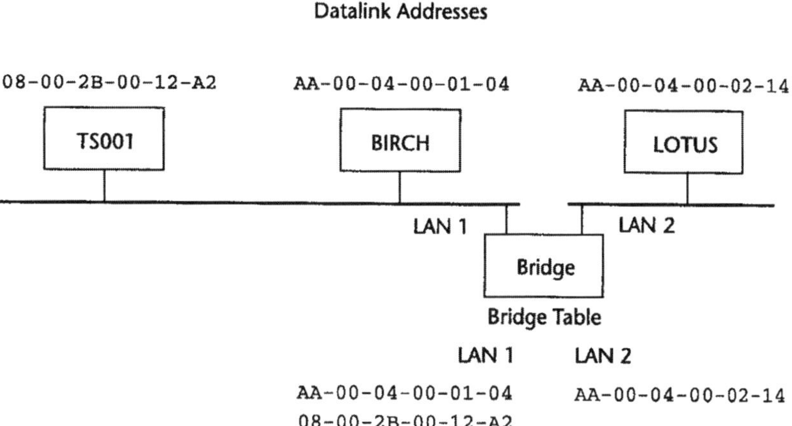

Figure 19.3 *Example of a Learning Bridge*

Although bridges are necessary to extend a LAN, they can also be used to segment traffic.

Many bridges support Ethernet and serial interfaces. Using serial interfaces, modems, and leased phone lines, you can create LANs that extend over many thousands of miles.

19.3.2.5 Router

As the number of nodes in a LAN increases dramatically, bridges become impractical because bridge tables grow excessively large. Bridges must keep track of every datalink address in an entire extended LAN (not just the LANs to which they are attached). If you were to depend on bridges to build a large network, you could easily have bridge tables containing tens of thousands of entries.

Routers resolve this problem by using a second layer of node addressing—a *network address*, not the MAC address. Network address formats are different for every protocol, but in DECnet protocol they consist of two components: a *network number* and a *node number.* Typically, each LAN (or extended LAN) is assigned a unique network number, and each node on that LAN is assigned a unique node number. Routers are then used to interconnect multiple networks to build an *internetwork.* Routers generally only have to keep track of each network within the internetwork (not every node). An example internetwork is shown in figure 19.4.

In figure 19.4, the internetwork consists of 12 extended LANs (networks 1–12) connected by three routers. Each router has four Ethernet interfaces (e1–e4) and two serial interfaces (s0, s1). Unlike configuring

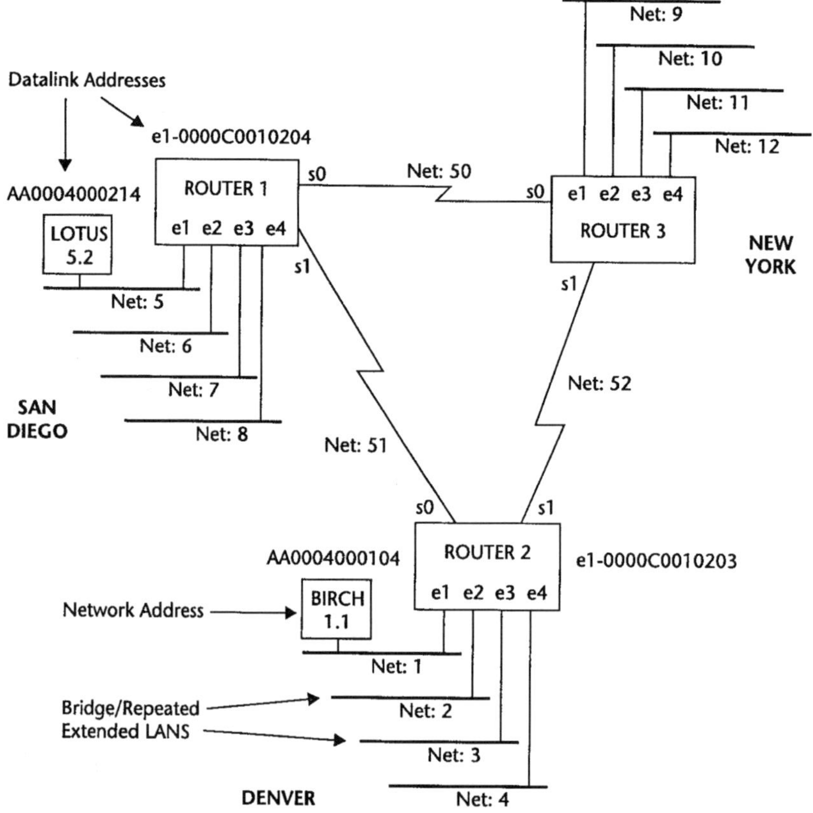

Figure 19.4 *Example of a Routed Internetwork*

bridges, you must configure a router by telling it which network numbers it is attached to. After a router begins operating, it periodically transmits routing update packets describing the networks about which it knows (the networks to which it is directly attached). Other routers listen to these updates and add the information to their routing tables. As routers listen to routing updates and send their own updates, all routers eventually build tables that detail the topology of the entire internetwork. Table 19.3 shows an example of routing tables for ROUTER1.

Table 19.3 *ROUTER1 Routing Tables*

Network Number	Hop Count	Via Interface	Learned From
1, 2, 3, 4	1	s1	ROUTER2
5, 6, 7, 8	0	e1, e2, e3, e4	Self

Table 19.3 *ROUTER1 Routing Tables (continued)*

Network Number	Hop Count	Via Interface	Learned From
9, 10, 11, 12	1	s0	ROUTER3
50	0	s0	Self
51	0	s1	Self
52	1	s1	ROUTER2

Routers may receive routing updates describing several possible paths to the same network. In this case routers use the information that contains the lowest *hop count,* the number of routers that must be traversed to reach a given network.

DECnet uses a routing scheme similar to the one just described. It is described in more detail in the next section.

LAT was designed to work within a LAN or extended LAN only. The main objectives are to deliver quick response time (critical for interactive terminal sessions) with minimal overhead. To meet these objectives, Digital chose not to add a network layer to the LAT protocol. As a result, LAT cannot be routed—it can only be bridged (or repeated).

19.4 DECnet Introduction

Initially, Digital developed the DECnet protocol to allow file transfers between Digital hosts. The early versions of DECnet (Phase I through Phase III) allowed low-speed (e.g., 56 Kbps), point-to-point connections. DECnet (Phase IV), introduced in the early 1980s, enhanced networking capabilities by allowing Digital hosts to participate in Ethernet-based LANs.

DECnet is a communication protocol used by several DECnet applications. Some of the more popular DECnet capabilities are listed below:

- Log into another network node on which you have an account
- Access public directories or databases located on any node on the network
- Display locally the contents of remote directories and files to which you have access

- Copy files from node to node or append files on one node to a file on another node
- Print files at the remote node where they reside, copy them to a remote printing device, or copy them to the local node for printing
- Using an editor, access and edit a file on a remote node
- Create a new file in a remote directory
- With the appropriate access, delete or purge files from directories, search files, and compare the contents of files on different nodes
- Perform sort and merge operations on remote files
- Analyze the structure of files, convert their organization and format, and dump their contents in a specific format
- Back up local files by using a remote save-set on disk
- Create, display, and delete logical names for nodes and devices that are to be included in remote file specifications
- Send and receive e-mail to or from any node
- Communicate in real-time with any logged-on user via PHONE

19.5 DECnet Components

DECnet is designed to operate in a LAN or an internetwork (multiple LANs separated by routers). Like other Ethernet nodes, DECnet nodes address each other (within an extended LAN) by means of datalink addressing. To support internetworking, DECnet nodes also use a 16-bit network address. The first 6 bits represent the *area number* (1 through 63) and the last 10 bits represent the *host number* (1 through 1,023). The area number identifies a distinct extended LAN, and the host number identifies a host within a LAN. As a result, DECnet allows a maximum of 64,449 (63 × 1,023) nodes to participate in a DECnet internetwork.

DECnet networks consist of three types of nodes: end nodes, Level 1(L1) routers, and Level 2 (L2) routers.

19.5.1 End Nodes

End nodes are allowed to have one active network connection. End nodes can have multiple Ethernet adapters or serial DECnet links, but only one can be started at any given time. An end node can communicate directly only with nodes to which it is directly connected (e.g., on the same Ethernet). In most cases the other nodes must also be in the same area. End nodes periodically broadcast hello messages so that L1 routers (see section 19.5.2) know they are still available. End nodes ignore hello messages transmitted by other nodes and, thus, do not keep track of the availability of other end nodes.

19.5.2 L1 Routers

L1 Routers are responsible for tracking the availability of all end nodes within the areas to which they are attached. In figure 19.5, nodes 1.1, 1.2, and 1.9 transmit end node hello messages that are received by L1 router 1.3. Node 1.3 adds those nodes to its routing tables. L1 routers periodically transmits L1 router hello messages so that end nodes can select a designated L1 router. End nodes select an L1 router by selecting the hello message containing the highest router priority. In case of a tie, the router with the highest DECnet node number wins. In figure 19.5, node 1.3 is the designated L1 router for nodes 1.1 and 1.2.

Every few minutes, L1 routers within an area exchange L1 routing tables. The routing tables describe each end node, the number of hops (routers to traverse) to reach the end node, and a path cost. *Path cost* is a routing metric that more accurately describes the shortest path between two points. Two paths might exist to the same destination with a hop count of 2. However, one path might consist of two Ethernet hops and the other of

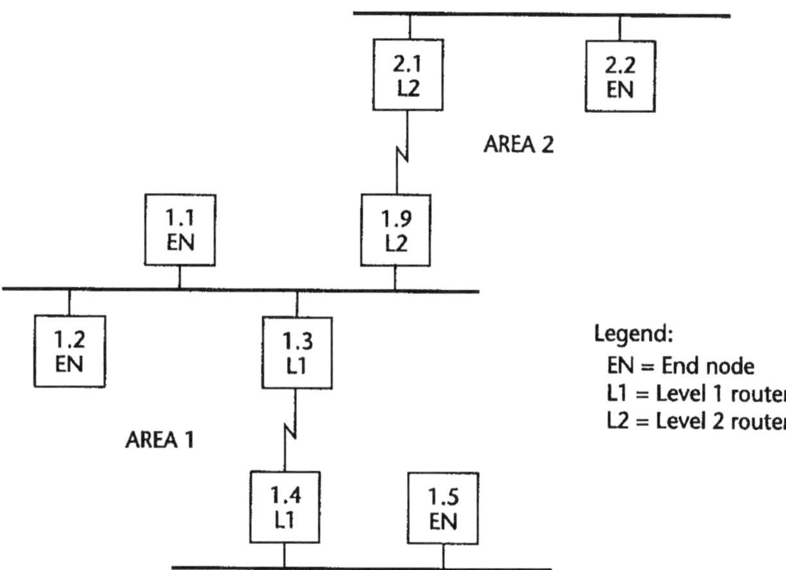

Figure 19.5
Example of a DECnet Internetwork

two 19,200-baud serial links. In a DECnet network, an Ethernet circuit is typically assigned a cost of 4, and a 19,200-baud serial connection is assigned a cost of 10. In the foregoing example, the Ethernet path would have a total cost of 8, as opposed to a cost of 20 for the serial links. By choosing the least-cost path, DECnet tries to assure that the best path is used. When L1 routers receive updates from other L1 routers, they update their routing tables to include the least-cost path to each end node and the address of the routers from which they learned the route. Eventually, every L1 router knows the least-cost path to every end node within its area.

When an end node wants to send data to another end node within the same area, it sends the data to its designated L1 router. The L1 router then checks the availability of the target end node. If the end node is reachable, the L1 router forwards the data to the end node or to the next L1 router in the path to the end node. For example, if end node 1.1 were to send data to end node 1.2, it would first forward the data to the designated L1 router (node 1.3). The L1 router would see that node 1.2 was available and directly accessible; it would thus forward the data directly to node 1.2. In this case the router would have received and forwarded the data on the same Ethernet interface. When this occurs, the router sets a special bit in the frame, known as the *intra-Ethernet bit.*

The intra-Ethernet bit is used to signal the receiving end node that it is attached to the same LAN as the original source node. From this point on, the receiving node knows that it can communicate with the source node directly, without the assistance of a router. On the other hand, if end node 1.2 needed to communicate with end node 1.5, *all* end nodes would be routed through the L1 router node 1.3.

DECnet hosts configured as L1 routers can also perform all end node functions.

19.5.3 L2 Routers

L2 routers are responsible for tracking the availability and path to all other areas (networks) within an entire DECnet internetwork. In figure 19.5, for example, node 2.1 knows that it is directly attached to area 2. It adds an entry in its L2 routing tables indicating that area 2 is zero hops away. Periodically, node 2.1 exchanges routing tables with other L2 routers to which it is directly attached (e.g., node 1.9). When node 1.9 receives a routing update form node 2.1, it adds information concerning area 2. Similarly node 2.1 learns about area 1 from node 1.9.

When an end node forwards traffic to an L1 router and the router determines that the data is destined for a different area, the L1 router forwards the data to the designated L2 router for that area. The L2 router then forwards the data to the next hop in the path to the final destination. This process continues until the data reaches its destination LAN.

OpenVMS systems configured as L2 routers also perform all L1 and end node functions.

19.6 DECnet Management

You manage a DECnet node using three major utilities: NETCONFIG.COM, STARTNET.COM, and NCP. Use NETCONFIG to configure a DECnet node, STARTNET to start DECnet at boot time, and NCP to stop DECnet and to perform other management functions. You invoke NCP using the following command:

```
$ RUN SYS$SYSTEM:NCP
NCP>
```

19.6.1 Assigning Addresses and Host Names

Every DECnet host must have a unique network address and host name. Initially, this limitation was not an issue for most Digital customers, because they had far fewer than 64,000 systems. However, if you integrate PCs into a DECnet network by means of Digital's Pathworks product, you can very easily use all DECnet addresses. As a result, assign DECnet addresses sparingly.

You should try to assign only one area number for each extended LAN. Otherwise, you will need to add area routers to route between the two areas, even though the nodes are in the same extended LAN. However, any VAX or Alpha node can act as an area router.

DECnet host names consist of an alphanumeric string of up to six characters, such as BART and LISA. Names are not case sensitive. You can choose host names that have geographic significance (e.g., LA, NYC, PHIL), but do this only if there is little chance that nodes will move.

19.6.2 Configuring a DECnet Node

Once you have chosen a DECnet network address and host name, you are ready to configure DECnet using the NETCONFIG utility. Log into the node you wish to configure and proceed as follows:

```
$ @SYS$MANAGER:NETCONFIG

    DECnet for OpenVMS network configuration procedure

This procedure will help you define the parameters needed to get DECnet running on
this machine. You will be shown the changes before they are executed, in case you
wish to perform them manually.

What do you want your DECnet node name to be? : BRO
What do you want your DECnet address to be? : 4.1
Do you want to operate as a router? [NO (nonrouting)]: NO
```

NO configures the node as an end node. YES configures the node as a router.

```
The network object database file is SYS$SYSROOT:[SYSEXE]NETOBJECT.DAT;1.

Do you want to purge the object database? [YES]: NO
Do you want a default DECnet account? [NO]: [RETURN]
```

The foregoing procedure allows users on remote nodes to copy files to and from the default directory for the DECnet account on this system. By enabling this account, remote users could consume excessive disk space on this node.

```
Do you want a default account for the MAIL object? [YES]: NO
Do you want a default account for the FAL object? [NO]: [RETURN]
```

If you respond YES, then nonprivileged users can access the FAL$SERVER (file access listener) directory from a remote node. For example:

```
$ DIR BRO::

Directory BRO::SYS$SPECIFIC:[FAL$SERVER]

NETSERVER.LOG;1

Total of 1 file.
```

Without the FAL$SERVER account, remote users get the following error message:

```
$ DIR BRO::
%DIRECT-E-OPENIN, error opening BRO::*.*;* as input
-RMS-E-FND, ACP file or directory lookup failed
-SYSTEM-F-INVLOGIN, login information invalid at remote node

Do you want a default account for the PHONE object? [YES]: [RETURN]
```

The foregoing procedure allows users on remote nodes to contact users on this node using the PHONE utility. See your OpenVMS documentation for more information on the PHONE utility.

```
Do you want a default account for the NML object? [YES]: NO
```

This option enables or disables the network management listener (NML) object. By enabling the NML object on this node, nonprivileged users on remote nodes can use the NCP>TELL command to view network configuration parameters and counters. With the NML listener, a remote user can use the TELL command as follows:

```
NCP>TELL BRO SHOW KNOWN NODES

Known Node Volatile Summary as of 26-MAY-2003 21:15:55

Executor node = 4.5 (BRO)

State = on
Identification = DECnet-VAX V5.5-2, VMS V5.5-2

Node     State     Active     Delay     Circuit     Next node
```

```
Links

@4.1 (FRED) SVA-0 4.2 (LISA)
@4.2 (LISA) SVA-0 4.2 (LISA)
```

Without NML, you would get the following error message:

```
NCP>TELL LISA SHOW KNOWN NODES
%NCP-F-CONNEC, unable to connect to listener
-SYSTEM-F-INVLOGIN, login information invalid at remote node

Do you want a default account for the MIRROR object? [YES]: NO
```

This option enables or disables the MIRROR object. When the MIRROR object is enabled, nonprivileged users on remote nodes can perform a loop-back test (or a PING) to this node. For example, with the MIRROR object enabled, a user on node PEG could perform a successful loop test (e.g., no error message is returned).

```
NCP>LOOP NODE BRO
```

Without the MIRROR object, the following error message would be generated:

```
NCP>LOOP NODE BRO
     %NCP-W-MIRCTF, Mirror connect failed , Access control rejected
     Messages not looped = 1

Do you want a default account for the VPM object? [YES]: NO
```

The Virtual Performance Manager (VPM) object enables users on remote nodes (within a VMScluster) to display performance statistics on this node. This object is typically used when you issue MONITOR/NODES=(*node1*, *node2*, etc) or the MONITOR/CLUSTER command.

```
Here are the commands necessary to setup your system.

PURGE KNOWN CIRCUITS ALL
PURGE KNOWN LOGGING ALL
```

```
PURGE MODULE CONFIGURATOR KNOWN CIRCUITS ALL
$ DEFINE/USER SYS$OUTPUT NL:
$ DEFINE/USER SYS$ERROR NL:
$ RUN SYS$SYSTEM:NCP ! Remove existing entry, if any
PURGE NODE 4.1 ALL
PURGE NODE FRED ALL
$ RUN SYS$SYSTEM:NCP
DEFINE EXECUTOR ADDRESS 4.1
DEFINE EXECUTOR STATE ON
DEFINE EXECUTOR NAME FRED
DEFINE EXECUTOR MAXIMUM ADDRESS 1023
DEFINE EXECUTOR TYPE NONROUTING IV
DEFINE OBJECT TASK NUMBER 0 USER ILLEGAL PASSWORD DISABLED
DEFINE LINE SVA-0 STATE ON
DEFINE CIRCUIT SVA-0 STATE ON COST 4
DEFINE LOGGING MONITOR STATE ON
DEFINE LOGGING MONITOR EVENTS 0.0-9
DEFINE LOGGING MONITOR EVENTS 2.0-1
DEFINE LOGGING MONITOR EVENTS 4.2-13,15-16,18-20
DEFINE LOGGING MONITOR EVENTS 5.0-18
DEFINE LOGGING MONITOR EVENTS 128.0-4

Do you want these commands to be executed? [YES]: [RETURN]

The changes have been made.

If you have not already registered the DECnet-VAX key, then do so now.

After the key has been registered, you should invoke the procedure
SYS$MANAGER:STARTNET.COM to startup DECnet-VAX with these changes.
```

If the key is already registered:

```
Do you want DECnet started? [YES]: [RETURN]
%RUN-S-PROC_ID, identification of created process is 00000097
%RUN-S-PROC_ID, identification of created process is 00000099
```

19.6.3 Starting DECnet

If you want DECnet to be started automatically during a system boot, you should add the following command to your system startup command procedures, SYSTARTUP_VMS.COM:

```
$ @SYS$MANAGER:STARTNET
```

While DECnet is starting up, messages similar to the following will be displayed:

```
%RUN-S-PROC_ID, identification of created process is 00000092
%%%%%%%%%%% OPCOM 14-APR-2003 13:05:52.95 %%%%%%%%%%%
Message from user DECNET
DECnet starting

%%%%%%%%%%% OPCOM 14-APR-2003 13:06:00.48 %%%%%%%%%%%
Message from user DECNET
DECnet event 4.10, circuit up
From node 4.1 (BART), 14-APR-2003 13:05:59.23
Circuit SVA-0

%RUN-S-PROC_ID, identification of created process is 00000094
```

19.6.4 Stopping DECnet

To manually shut down DECnet use the following NCP command:

```
$ RUN SYS$SYSTEM:NCP
NCP> SET EXECUTOR STATE OFF
```

Before you shutdown DECnet, you should use the NCP command SHOW KNOWN LINKS to display active DECnet links. This tells you if remote users have active SET HOST or file-transfer connections to the host you want to shut down.

19.6.5 Basic DECnet Troubleshooting

If you are having trouble getting two DECnet nodes to communicate, perform the following steps:

1. *Identify the designated L1 router.* Log into one of the end nodes and use the DCL SHOW NETWORK command to determine the designated L1 router, as follows:

```
$ SHOW NETWORK/OLD
OpenVMS Network status for local node 4.5 BRO on 26-MAY-2003 20:45:58.60

This is a nonrouting node, and does not have any network information.
The designated router for BRO is node 4.2 LISA
```

Since OpenVMS 7.0, the display will resemble the following:

```
$ SHOW NETWORK
Product:  DECNET     Node:  VAX             Address(es):  8.2
Product:  TCP/IP     Node:  vax.e           Address(es):  199.17.178.190
```

2. *Examine the L1 routing tables.* Log into the designated L1 router and examine its L1 routing tables, as follows:

```
$ SHOW NETWORK/OLD
OpenVMS Network status for local node 4.2 LISA on 4-FEB-2003 08:52:31.14

The next hop to the nearest area router is node 4.1 FRED.

Level 1 Routing Tables

Node         Links    Cost    Hops    Next Hop to Node

@4.2 LISA     0        0       0      (Local) -> 4.2 LISA
@4.1 FRED     0        4       1      SVA-0 -> 4.1 FRED
@4.5 BRO      0        4       1      SVA-0 -> 4.5 BRO

Total of 3 nodes.
```

If the target node is in the same area, it should be listed in the foregoing table. If it is not, then the L1 router is not receiving the hello from the target end node. If the target end node is in a different area, determine the designated L2 router from the output. In this example, node 4.1 (FRED) is the designated L2 router.

3. *Examine the routing tables on the designated L2 router.* Log into the designated L2 router and issue the following command:

```
$ SHOW NETWORK/OLD
OpenVMS Network status for local node   4.1 FRED on    26-MAY-2003    20:56:22.85

Level 2 Routing Tables
Area     Cost     Hops     Next Hop to Area

4        0        0       (Local)     ->     4.1     FRED
5        10       1       TT-0-1      ->     5.1     PEG

Level 1 Routing Tables

Node     Links     Cost     Hops     Next Hop to Node

@4.2     LISA     0    4    1    SVA-0     ->     4.2     LISA
@4.5     BRO      0    4    1    SVA-0     ->     4.5     BRO

Total of 2 nodes.
```

4. *Trace the L2 routing tables.* Identify the next L2 router in the path to the target node (e.g., PEG). Log into that node and continue to trace the path until you reach an L2 router in the target area. Frequently, the problem is that a link is down and the target area is listed as unreachable.

```
$ SHOW NETWORK/OLD

OpenVMS Network status for local node 5.1 PEG on 26-MAY-2003 21:03:07.44

Level 2 Routing Tables

Area     Cost     Hops     Next Hop to Area

4    10    1    TT-0-1 -> 4.1 FRED
5    0    0    (Local) -> 5.1 PEG

Level 1 Routing Tables
```

```
Node     Links    Cost    Hops    Next Hop to Node

@5.1 PEG    0    0    0    (Local) -> 5.1 PEG
```

Once you reach the target area, examine the L1 routing tables of a router in that area. Finally, trace the path to the target end node.

As you trace the path in one direction, you usually stop at the point where the problem is occurring (e.g., a link is down). If the problem is not obvious, try tracing the path in the reverse direction. Ideally, you should use this tracing procedure to map out the entire network before you have a problem. This way, when a problem occurs, you will be able to pinpoint it more easily.

19.7 Managing LAT

To address the need for more flexible terminal and printer connectivity, Digital developed the LAT protocol and several models of terminal servers (e.g., DECserver 100, 200, 300, 500, 700). A terminal server typically has eight or more serial ports and one Ethernet port. In a LAT network, terminals and printers are connected to terminal servers rather then directly wired to a specific host. The Ethernet port on a terminal server is then connected to a LAN. Once the system is configured, a user can log into any LAT host connected to the same extended LAN as the terminal server. Hosts can also direct print queues to printers attached to any terminal server on the same extended LAN. Starting LAT on the host is discussed in section 19.7.5.

For example, in figure 19.6, users attached to terminal servers TS001 and TS002 can log into either node LISA or node BART. Print queues on BART and LISA can be directed to printers attached to either TS001 or TS002.

19.7.1 LAT Components

The following three main entities participate in a LAT network.

1. *Service node:* Service nodes offer one or more service names to the network. In figure 19.6, LISA and BART are service nodes. Frequently, the service node name and service name are the same. However, they are two distinct entities.

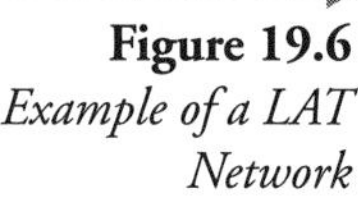

Figure 19.6
Example of a LAT Network

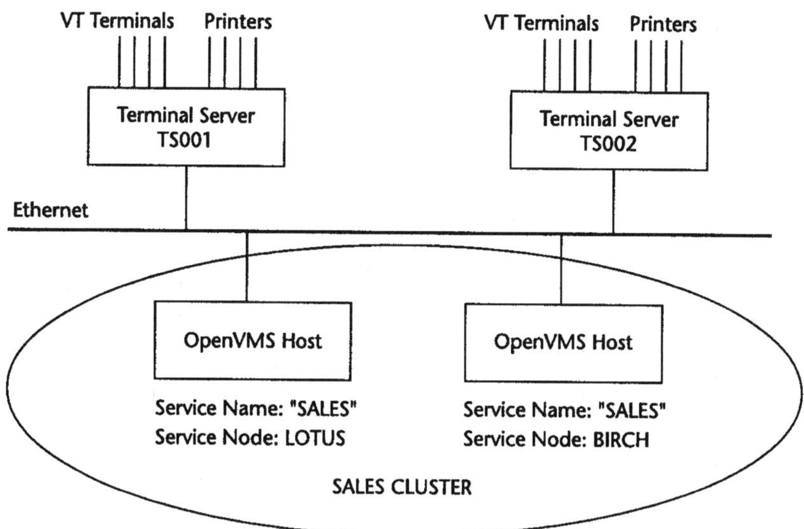

2. *Service name:* Service names represent services available on a service node. Usually, the service is an interactive login offered by one or more OpenVMS nodes.
3. *Terminal server:* Terminal servers (e.g., TS001 and TS002) allow users to initiate interactive terminal sessions to service names. Service nodes also can request that terminal servers establish a connection between a printer port and an OpenVMS print queue.

After LAT is configured and started on an OpenVMS service node, the service node periodically transmits a special packet, called a *service announcement*, onto the network. Service announcements are sent to a special datalink address (LAT multicast) that causes the packet to be processed by all terminal servers on the LAN. Service announcements contain the service node name, a list of services names being offered, and a numeric rating for each service. The following shows a service announcement sent by service node BART offering the service SALES:

```
Ethernet Header:
Destination: 09:00:2b:00:00:0f LAT Multicast [0-5]
Source: 08:00:2b:13:97:2c [6-11]
Protocol Type:6004 DEC LAT [12-13]
DEC LAT - Local Area Transport
Message Type:    10 [14 Mask - fc] Service
```

```
Flags:             0 [14 Mask 03] From host No Response
...
...[irrelevant packet contents omitted]
...
Enabled Groups:    %00000001 [27] ! Only Group 0 enabled
Node Name:    BART [28-32]
Node Description:   Welcome to OpenVMS (TM) Alpha Operating System, Version V7.3-
[33-61]
Number of Services:    1 [62]
Rating:    83 [63]
Service Name:    SALES [64-69]
Service Description: Welcome to OpenVMS (TM) Alpha Operating System, Version V7.3-
[70-98]
Number of Classes:    1 [99]
Service:    1 [100] Remote Terminal Service
Frame Check Sequence: 0x40f3de00 [101-104]
```

Terminal servers constantly listen for service announcements and build a table of known service nodes, service names, and ratings. Users cannot connect to a LAT service until the terminal server to which they are connected receives a service announcement.

You can view the service table of a terminal server by entering the following command on the server:

```
TS001> SHOW SERVICE ALL

Service SALES - Available

Node Name    Status    Rating    Identification

BART    Reachable    83    Welcome to OpenVMS V6.1
LISA    Reachable    83    Welcome to OpenVMS V5.5-2
```

The foregoing output confirms that the terminal server TS001 knows about the service SALES and that it is offered by service nodes BART and LISA. Currently, both BART and LISA are advertising a service rating of 83, indicating that they are both equally available.

19.7.2 Connection Basics

Once services are known to a terminal server, users can request a connection, as follows:

```
TS001> CONNECT SALES

Local -051- Session 1 [SALES] established

Welcome to OpenVMS V6.1 (BART)

Username:
```

When TS001 receives a connection request, it looks in its tables and locates the node offering the highest rating for the SALES service. In the foregoing example, the server chose BART—in case of a tie, the server picks the first node it encounters.

19.7.3 Managing Terminal Servers

The following sections deal with the issues of loading terminal server software, accessing the server console port, and configuring various server parameters. The exact syntax of terminal server commands varies for each server model. For example, some servers do not support the CHANGE command; instead you must use the DEFINE and SET commands to change the permanent and volatile server settings. Refer to your terminal server user's guide for more information on exact command syntax.

19.7.3.1 Loading Server Software

A terminal server is a small computer that runs LAT, TCP/IP and/or IPX software. Some terminal servers have the protocol software built into read-only memory (ROM) or flash memory. Others must down-line load their software from a host before they can begin operating. If your server requires a down-line load, you must install a terminal server load image file on a host. Older Digital terminal servers perform down-line loads from an OpenVMS host using a Maintenance Operation Protocol (MOP). Refer to your terminal server manual for more information on configuring a MOP server, if necessary.

A host does not have to be a MOP server to accept LAT connections. If your terminal servers require MOP downloads, you should configure at least two MOP servers for your network. Otherwise, if your MOP server is down, and a terminal server attempts to boot, it will not be able to load its required software. If you are particularly concerned about system performance, you should choose your MOP servers carefully. If you configure an important host to act also as a MOP server, performance could deteriorate after a wide-scale power outage. When power is restored, hundreds of terminal servers could simultaneously issue MOP load requests and inundate your MOP server.

Because of these management issues, the trend is to use terminal servers with built-in software. Servers with flash memory are the most desirable because you can easily perform upgrades by inserting new flash cards. Servers without flash require that you physically replace a ROM chip on the motherboard of your server.

19.7.3.2 Connecting to the Terminal Server Console Port

After a server is installed and loaded, typically you perform management functions by attaching a terminal to one of its ports. If possible you should connect the terminal to port 1. Port 1 is usually the designated console port, and important diagnostic messages are sometimes sent to that port. If the terminal server is at a remote location, you can connect to the server from a DECnet host using the MOP remote console facility, as follows.

First, log into a DECnet host on the same extended LAN as the terminal server, and execute the following commands:

```
$ RUN SYS$SYSTEM:NCP
NCP>SHOW KNOWN CIRCUITS

Known Circuit Volatile Summary as of 14-JUN-2003 12:48:51

   Circuit          State                   Loopback    Adjacent
                                              Name      Routing Node
  SVA-0             on
```

Next, locate the Ethernet circuit attached to the same extended LAN as the remote terminal server. The datalink (MAC) address of the terminal server should be printed on the back of the terminal server. If you do not know its address, you will have to have someone look at the server. Digital's servers usually start with 08-00-2B. In the following example 00-80-64-06-

01-E2 is a for Wyse terminal server. Use that circuit name and the server datalink address in the following command:

```
NCP>CONNECT VIA SVA-0 PHYSICAL ADDRESS 00-80-64-06-01-E2
Console connected (press CTRL/D when finished)
```

It may be necessary to press <RETURN> a few times to get the server's attention. It should respond with a message and prompt like the following.

```
WN-5104 Terminal Server V4.212
64B Seaside rm: 202

Enter username: BOGUS    ! type anything

Please type HELP for assistance
WN5104 5>
```

Once connected to the terminal server, you can view its configuration as follows. Different servers may present different data, of course.

```
WN5104 5> SHOW SERVER

WN-5104 Terminal Server V4.212    Uptime: 00:47:18

Ethernet: 00-80-64-06-01-e2    Internet: 192.4.4.1
Name: WN5104    Number: 0

Identification: 64B Seaside rm: 202

Console Port: 1    Prompt: "%N %p>%P "
Inactivity Timer: 30    Password limit: 3
Monitor Timer: 3    Session limit: 32
Circuit Timer: 80    Queue limit: 100
Keepalive Timer: 20    Node limit: 200
Multicast Timer: 30    Retransmit limit: 8

Service Groups: 0

Startup File: WN-5104.CFG
```

```
Enabled Characteristics:
Broadcast, Lock, Heartbeat, Announcements
```

Notice that this server will also support TCP/IP connections, although that discussion is beyond the scope of this book.

19.7.3.3 Initial Terminal Server Configuration

Although there are many terminal server parameters that you can configure, the following are the most important.

Server Name

By default, most Digital terminal servers are named LAT_*xxxxxxxxxxxx* where *xxxxxxxxxxxx* is the datalink address of the server. Because this naming system is rather cumbersome, you should consider changing the server name to something more meaningful and easier to type. Remember, you will probably reference this name in many places (e.g., in startup files that create LAT device mappings for printers). Some system managers use server names that indicate a geographic location. Do not do that, however, unless, you are sure you will never need to relocate the server. Otherwise, you will have to change all your system startup procedures. An arbitrary naming scheme is perfectly acceptable, for example TS0001, TS0002 (TS for terminal server). A sample syntax is as follows:

```
> CHANGE SERVER NAME "TS0001"
```

Server Passwords

The following two passwords control access to a terminal server:

- *Access password:* Users must enter the access password when passwords are enabled on a specific port (this is sometimes used for modem ports). More importantly, on most servers you are prompted for the access password when you connect to a server using the MOP remote console facility. By default, most servers are configured with the default access password ACCESS. Thus, by default, any user with access to DECnet can connect to the remote console port of any terminal server in your network. If this is undesirable, change the access password on all your servers.

- *Privilege password:* To change server parameters, you must first enter the SET PRIVILEGE command, followed by the privilege password. By default, nearly all terminal servers use a privilege password of SYSTEM. Unless you change the default privilege password, any user in the network can reconfigure your servers.

The procedures for changing the privilege and access passwords are discussed in chapter 17.

Identification String

You should set the server identification (ID) string to indicate the physical location of the server. This might include a building name, room number, or communication rack. This facilitates locating servers in a large network. By using the ID string, you do not have to worry about naming the server to indicate geographic location. If you later move a server, you can simply change its ID string. The sample syntax for an ID string is as follows:

```
> CHANGE SERVER ID "4TH FLOOR COMM. ROOM"
```

Circuit Timer

When a terminal server transmits information to a LAT host, the server encapsulates the data into an Ethernet packet. An Ethernet LAT packet contains approximately 25 bytes of addressing information and other overhead, leaving a minimum of 39 bytes available for user data. Regardless of how much data a terminal server has to send, it must send at least 64 bytes to meet the design requirements of Ethernet. If necessary, LAT adds null characters (padding) to a packet to meet this requirement. If a terminal server transmitted a packet immediately after a user typed a character, it would have to send 63 bytes of overhead just to send 1 byte of data. To utilize the available space in a packet better, terminal servers buffer characters from all ports for 80 ms before sending a packet. On a terminal server with many active ports to a common host, each transmitted packet usually contains data buffered from many ports.

Although servers buffer characters for 80 ms by default, you can adjust the buffer by changing the value of the server CIRCUIT TIMER parameter. A larger value forces a longer delay and usually reduces network traffic. However, if you increase the buffer too much, users may begin to notice a delay between when they enter a character and when it is displayed on their terminals. In an OpenVMS environment, character echoing is the responsibility of the host. Every character that a user types is first sent to the host, the host optionally echoes the character back to the terminal, and terminal prints it on the screen. This requires some overhead, but it allows the host to suppress character echo when appropriate (e.g., when entering passwords). A sample syntax is as follows:

```
> CHANGE SERVER CIRCUIT TIMER 100
```

Review RETRANSMIT LIMIT Parameter

Many Digital networks have been extended to bridge LAT traffic over relatively low-speed, wide-area network (WAN) connections. Because the speed of these links is usually far lower than that of Ethernet (56 Kbps or 1.5 Mbps versus 10 Mbps), these links are more susceptible to overutilization. When LAT traffic attempts to traverse an overutilized WAN link, packets are frequently dropped.

When a packet is transmitted by a terminal server, it should be acknowledged within 50 to 100 ms. If the original packet never reaches its destination or the returning acknowledgment is lost, the server retransmits the packet. The terminal server continues to retransmit with a 1-sec. delay between retransmissions up to eight times (or the setting of the retransmit limit). If the retransmit limit is exceeded, the terminal server assumes that the connection to the host is no longer reliable and terminates the virtual circuit to that host. This results in termination of all sessions from that terminal server to the host!

If someone performs a large file transfer over a network link that is near its capacity, all LAT sessions using that same link may time out. The default retransmit limit of 8 allows LAT connections to withstand network anomalies of approximately 8 seconds, or 8 × 1 second between retransmits. If you frequently experience LAT time-outs, you may want to consider increasing the retransmit limit to 30 or even 100 in extreme cases. If you use automatic LAT fail-over, a terminal server performs its retransmission cycle before it tries to fail-over to another host. Thus, if you set the retransmit limit to too high, fail-over can take several minutes.

A sample syntax is as follows:

```
> CHANGE SERVER RETRANSMIT LIMIT 50
```

Configure LAT Groups

In a large LAT network, you probably need to use LAT group codes to partition the network. The specific procedures for using LAT groups are discussed later in this chapter.

19.7.4 Configuring Terminal Server Ports

Usually, the default port settings allow interactive terminal connections. Use the SHOW PORT command to view a port configuration, as follows:

```
WN5104 1> SHOW PORT 1

Port 1: B    Name: PORT_01

Character Size: 8    Speed: 9600
Parity: None    Flow Control: XON
Stop Bits: Dynamic    Lines x Columns: 24 x 80

Access: Local    Type: Dynamic
Break Key: Local    Terminal: ansi
Backwards Switch: None    Session Limit: 4
Forwards Switch: None    Prompt: "%N %p>%P "
Local Switch: None    Default Protocol: ANY

Dedicated Service: None
Preferred Service: None

Authorized Groups: 10-20
Current Groups: 10-20

Enabled Characteristics:
Autoprompt, Broadcast, Failover, Lock, Loss Notification,
Message Codes, Command Completion, Verification, Input Flow
Control,
Output Flow Control
```

Of the foregoing parameters, the following are the key settings to allow interactive terminal access:

```
SPEED:       9600    (Set to match terminal speed or Enable AUTOBAUD)
CHARACTER SIZE:    8    (Set to match terminal)
PARITY:      NONE    (Set to match terminal)
ACCESS:     LOCAL    (Specifies access from the server port)
```

In configuring a port for a printer connection, the key difference is that ACCESS must be set to REMOTE. This allows connections from the network (a LAT host) to the port. The procedures for configuring LAT printer ports are discussed in chapter 8.

19.7.4.1 Managing Service Nodes (Hosts)

In a LAT environment, terminal servers are usually considered the master, and hosts are considered slaves. Master nodes dictate the settings to be used for a LAT connection. Thus, settings for many LAT parameters (e.g., CIRCUIT TIMER, RETRANSMIT LIMIT) are specified by the terminal server, leaving few parameters to be configured on the service node.

The following sections address the procedures for configuring the few LAT parameters that must be set on service nodes.

19.7.4.2 Setting LAT Node Name

Each LAT service node can have only one node name. By default, LAT defines its node name during LAT startup based on the setting of the system parameter SCSNODE (the VMScluster node name for the system). You can optionally select a different node name by passing it as a parameter to the LAT startup procedure as follows:

```
$ @SYS$STARTUP:LAT$STARTUP SALES BART
```

The foregoing command starts LAT on the node. It offers the service SALES, and the service node name is BART.

19.7.4.3 Assigning Service Names

You can configure a LAT node to offer one or more service names. By default, LAT hosts offer a service name that is the same as the node name. For example, node BART offers the service name BART.

If you run multiple applications on a single system or VMScluster, you may want to consider creating a service name for each application. For example, consider a cluster consisting of two nodes BART and LISA that provide word-processing, payroll, and sales forecasting applications. You could configure the cluster to offer three different LAT services (WP, PAYROLL, and SALES). You would then tell the respective users of each application to issue CONNECT commands to the appropriate service name. At some future point, you could move these three applications to three physically different systems (e.g., BARNEY, HOMER, and MARGE). You would then disable the WP, PAYROLL, and SALES services on BART and LISA and enable them on the new systems. Because users would still connect to the same service names, the change would be transparent to them.

19.7.4.4 Assigning Service Names on VMSclusters

If you have two or more nodes in a common-environment VMScluster, you probably want to have all cluster members broadcast the same service name. For example, both nodes in a two-node cluster (BART and LISA) offer the same service name (e.g., SALES). This allows users to issue connect requests to SALES and not be concerned about which physical node they are connected to.

Using this kind of service naming strategy greatly simplifies future hardware upgrades or changes. You can easily add a third cluster member and have it offer the same SALES service. You effectively increase capacity without users' knowing it.

As the load on a service node increases, the LAT ratings of the services it offers decrease. In the following example, many users have logged into BART, resulting in a drop in its LAT rating from 83 to 51.

```
TS001> SHOW SERVICE ALL STATUS

Service SALES - Available

Node    Name      Status    Rating    Identification

BART    Reachable     51     Welcome to OpenVMS V6.1
LISA    Reachable     83     Welcome to OpenVMS V5.5-2
```

Because LISA is now more available than BART, any future connections to the SALES service result in a connection to LISA, as follows:

```
TS001> CONNECT SALES
```

```
Local -051- Session 1 [SALES] established

Welcome to OpenVMS V5.5-2 (LISA)

Username:
```

You may want to favor one node over another. For instance if one node is a VAXstation 2000 (VUP = 0.9) and another is a VAXstation 4000/96 (VUP = 46), it would be wise to lower the static rating on the 2000 and raise the static rating on the 4000. Raising the static rating is done with the LATCP command:

```
LATCP> SET SERVICE /STATIC_RATING=200
```

19.7.4.5 Starting LAT

Although DECnet and LAT are independent protocols, they usually share the same Ethernet adapter. DECnet modifies the datalink (MAC) address of the controller when it starts; thus, you must start DECnet before any other protocol. Assuming DECnet is already started, you can start LAT from your system startup procedures, as follows:

```
$ @SYS$STARTUP:LAT$STARTUP
```

The LAT startup procedure executes the following two procedures:

```
SYS$STARTUP:LAT$CONFIG.COM     !  Initialize LAT drivers
SYS$MANAGER:LAT$SYSTARTUP.COM ! Site-specific procedures
```

LAT$STARTUP.COM and LAT$CONFIG.COM are not intended to be modified by the manager. LAT$SYSTARTUP.COM is usually modified to create printer ports, to create services, to change messages, and to change service ratings.

Because of the similarities in name, system managers sometimes inadvertently try to start LAT by executing LAT$SYSTARTUP instead of LAT$STARTUP. When this happens, you get an error message because LAT$CONFIG has not been executed. Make sure you start LAT using LAT$STARTUP.

If you have problems starting DECnet, check to make sure LAT was not started first, as is the case in the following display example from a VAX (the Alpha display is similar):

```
$ ANALYZE/SYSTEM
SDA> SHOW LAN

LAN Data Structures
-------------------
LSB address  = 8084A300
Device state = 0013 Inited,Run,Timer

              -- ESA Unit Summary 14-APR-2003 13:17:40 --

UCB     UCB Addr    Fmt     Value     Client     State
--------------------------------------------------------
ESA0    805AFF40
ESA1    805CED00   Eth    60-07            SCA      0017 Strtn,Len,Uniq,Strtd
ESA4    80691400   Eth    60-03            DECNET   0017 Strtn,Len,Uniq,Strtd
ESA5    8068DA80   Eth    08-00            IP       0015 Strtn,Uniq,Strtd
ESA6    8068FD80   Eth    08-06            ARP      0015 Strtn,Uniq,Strtd
ESA7    8068F880   Eth    86-DD                     0015 Strtn,Uniq,Strtd
ESA8    806A3F80   Eth    60-04            LAT      0015 Strtn,Uniq,Strtd
```

Look for the Ethernet devices (e.g., ESA2, ESA3). If LAT is listed first, you attempted to start LAT before DECnet. To resolve the problem, modify your system startup procedures to start DECnet first and reboot the system.

19.7.4.6 Stopping LAT

Stop LAT using the following command:

```
$ RUN SYS$SYSTEM:LATCP
LATCP> SET NODE/STATE=OFF
```

Warning: If you stop LAT on an active node, all LAT sessions to that host are terminated, and all LAT print queues stop. If all your users access the system from LAT terminal servers, stopping LAT has the same effect as shutting down the system. Do not stop LAT if you are logged into the same host using LAT—you will terminate your own session, and you will not be able to log back in. If you have to restart LAT and your only connection to that host is via LAT, submit your commands to stop and restart LAT as a batch job.

You can tell if any users have LAT connections by using the SHOW USERS/FULL command to look for process names of the form _LTAnn:. However, even if there are no user connections, be aware that LAT print queues do not normally restart automatically when LAT is stopped and restarted. If you use normal (non-AUTOSTART) print queues, you have to manually issue a START/QUEUE for every print queue on your system. If you have a lot of queues, you might be better off rebooting the entire system.

19.7.5 Configuring LAT Groups

In a large LAT network you can easily have hundreds of services offered by a variety of nodes. Some servers (e.g., DECserver 100s) have limited memory and run out of memory as the number of services increases. A large number of services can also be confusing to users. You might want to simplify their view of the network to include only the LAT services to which they need access.

LAT group codes address both of these issues by assigning group codes to service nodes, servers, and server ports. Each of these entities can be assigned one or more group codes consisting of the numbers 0–255. LAT groups are assigned at three layers, as follows:

1. *Service node groups (set on a service node):* By default, service nodes are enabled for group 0 only. When a node sends a LAT service announcement, it sets a bit to indicate each group for which it is enabled. You control service node groups by modifying the contents of SYS$STARTUP:LAT$SYSTARTUP.COM. For example, the following command enables the service node for groups 10 through 15:

```
$ lcp set node /connections=incoming /groups=enable=(10-15)
```

2. *Server groups (set on a terminal server):* By default, server groups are enabled for group 0 only. When a terminal server receives a LAT service announcement, the server compares the group code bits in the packet to its enabled groups. If there is at least one match, the server adds the service (defined in the announcement)

to its tables. If the no group codes match, the server ignores the announcement. In this way terminal servers effectively filter out all services for which they are not group members. You control terminal server groups by entering the following commands on each terminal server:

```
TS001> CHANGE SERVER GROUPS 10-15
```

3. *Port groups (set on terminal server ports):* Service node groups and server groups control which services are added to the tables of a terminals server. Port groups determine which subset of those services individual users attached to each port can access. To access a service known to a server, a port must share at least one group with the service node group. You control port groups by entering the following commands from a terminal server:

```
TS001> CHANGE PORT # AUTHORIZED GROUPS 10-11
( WHERE # = PORT NUMBER)
```

Table 19.4 shows the access that would be allowed by the group configuration indicated in figure 19.7.

Table 19.4 *Restricting Access with LAT Groups*

From Server/Port	Access to BART?	Access to LISA?
TS001	Yes	Yes
TS002	Yes	No
TS001/PORT_1	Yes	Yes
TS001/PORT_2	Yes	No
TS001/PORT_3	No	Yes
TS002/PORT_3	No	No

19.7.6 Troubleshooting LAT

The following are some typical LAT error messages and techniques for resolving them:

- Local -100- Access to service *xxxxx* denied

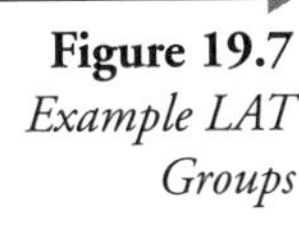

Figure 19.7
Example LAT Groups

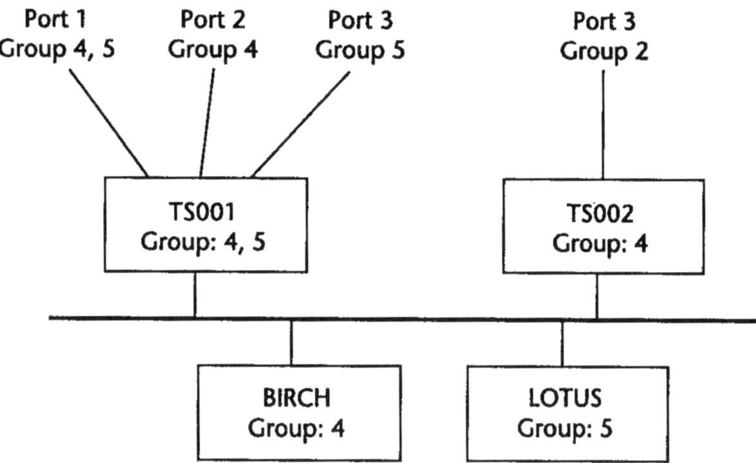

The server knows about the service, but port groups deny access. Compare the enabled port groups with the service node groups.

- Local -030- Unknown service/host "*xxxxxx*"

Server groups may prevent the server from receiving service announcements. Compare server groups with service node groups.

Service announcements may not be reaching the server. Do terminal servers on the same segment as the service node know about the service? If so, then the service node is operating properly and service announcements are probably being dropped by an intervening device (e.g., a bridge).

- Local -012- Session 1 [*xxxx*] disconnected

Session time-outs are a common problem in extended networks that bridge over low-speed links (e.g., 56 Kbps). LAT works well at these speeds, as long as the links are not overutilized. You can decrease the sensitivity of LAT by increasing the retransmit limit parameter on every terminal server in your network, as discussed earlier in this chapter. However, this only masks a larger problem of link overutilization. You should regularly measure bridge link utilization and error counts (e.g., number of dropped packets). Remember, LAT sessions can time out in less than 10 to 15 seconds. The fact that a bridge might indicate that average utilization was only 10 percent over the last 10 minutes is meaningless. If you see a large number of dropped packets with low average utilization, you are probably experiencing short bursts of heavy traffic.

19.8 Tools

One freeware tool that operates in the promiscuous mode and can be used to "snoop" the network is called PROBE. The value of this too is to do the following:

- Identify which protocols are on your network
- Identify which nodes are responsible for network load
- Suggest how to segment your network to reduce traffic

A typical display produced by PROBE is shown below:

```
$ probe/statistics
%PROBE-I-DEFSPEC, using network adapter EWA0 found on system
------------------------------------------------------------------------------
PROBE 2.3B STATISTICS   Elapsed time: 00:00:29.49

Segment                      Node::Device           Rate(hz)  Load(%)  Coll(%)
(local)                    MILLER::EWA0      Max:         18      0.3      0.0
                                              Min:          0      0.0      0.0

                                                                  ------Size------
Category          Frames  Multicasts                     Bytes   Ave    Min   Max

Ethernet:            137          16                     16325   119     64   283
IEEE 802.3:            0           0                         0     0      0     0
Total:               137          16                     16325   119     64   283
Filtered:              0           0                         0
Dropped:               0
                          -Max--Ave-                              ------Size------
Nodes             <Hits>  Rate %Load      Frames         Bytes   Ave    Min   Max

DEC(8.2)
S:  <_______________|____>  17  86.0         102         14045   137     64   283
D:  <_______________|____>   0   0.0           0             0     0      0     0
<multicast>
-:  <_______________|____>   0   0.0           0             0     0      0     0
D:  <_______________|____>   2  12.7          16          2060   128     64   138
------------------------------------------------------------------------------
%PROBE-I-FLUSH, cycle 1 statistics completed at 14-JUN-2003 09:09:53.25
%PROBE-S-SPACEBAR, stop - operator termination command received
```

19.9 Conclusion

Of course, TCP/IP is the protocol of choice these days and there are plenty of books written on the subject. DECnet and LAT are pretty much unique in the DIGITAL/COMPAQ/HP community, and very little is available besides the manufacture's documentation. However, the protocol is published and available for platforms other than those HP sells. TCP/IP concepts are not easily transferred to DECnet and LAT, and you have to pretty much forget about TCP/IP when learning DECnet and LAT.

19.10 References

1. DECnet Phase IV is still licensed and supported by HP, and you can install it instead of DECnet-Plus. However, the documentation is difficult to find; it is not published with current versions of OpenVMS documents.
2. *DECnet for OpenVMS Guide to Networking,* Digital Press, March 1994.
3. *DECnet for OpenVMS Networking Manual,* Digital Press, March 1994.
4. *OpenVMS System Manager's Manual,* Digital Press, March 1994.

20

Installing OpenVMS Software

20.1 Chapter Objectives

- Identify major steps for installing freeware
- Describe how VMSINSTAL is used
- Describe how PRODUCT is used
- Overview OpenVMS installation

20.2 Introduction

Freeware is, of course, a potpourri of installation techniques governed by the whims of the author. However, there are certain steps that all software installations must follow.

PRODUCT is the preferred tool used to install layered products. OpenVMS installation uses PRODUCT as well. The VMSINSTAL script predated PRODUCT and was used for many years for layered product installation. Some products still use VMSINSTAL.

20.3 Installing Freeware

Freeware installation procedures are ragged at best. A few (notably Hunter Goatly's contributions) follow the VMSINSTAL format very well. Furthermore, freeware documentation is very uneven, excepting Hunter's documents, which closely resemble HP's format.

Most packages contain an AAAREADME (or a variation like AAAREAD.ME, README.TXT) or perhaps INSTALL.TXT, which is an ASCII file that describes the installation process. That document should be followed as closely as possible. The following sections describe all steps that could be involved in installing freeware.

Whenever installing freeware, I like to start by creating a SYS$MANAGER subdirectory for the package. This helps me to identify which files are involved easily, reduces the clutter in SYS$MANAGER root, and makes it easy to delete if necessary. However, some packages prefer directories located as a [000000] subdirectory.

Most packages include source files. If you are unsure of the author's reputation you may want to read the source to make sure it will not compromise the system. Although most installations only require that you like the precompiled objects, you may want to recompile from the reviewed source to be doubly sure you know what you are working with.

20.3.1 Downloading and Unziping

Most freeware packages are zipped, although some follow the UNIX convention of GZ and tar. There are freeware packages to deal with all of these formats available on the process.com site. My discussion describes the ZIP format only.

ZIP compresses the package, which in turn reduces download time. A benefit of the ZIP format is that it effectively checksums the files and that assures proper download delivery. If you use any intermediate computers to download a freeware package, do not unzip it until you get to the OpenVMS machine. This preserves the file characteristics and the directory structure. So, transfer the ZIP file to OpenVMS first, and then unzip the freeware in the destination subdirectory.

20.3.2 Compiling and Linking

Normally the compilation step is not necessary. But if you must compile the code, is it commonly stored in a [.SOURCE] or [.SRC] subdirectory. In it you are likely to find a .COM (or perhaps a .MMS file) script containing all the required compilation commands.

Linking is normally necessary so the precompiled objects can be linked with the OpenVMS version-specific run-time libraries. Usually you will find a BUILD.COM, an MMS.COM (MMS is an HP product) or an MMK.COM script file (MMK is freeware contributed by Matt Madison). One of these techniques will do the entire compile and link procedure.

20.3.3 Creating a Command

Some packages require that a command be defined as a symbol, that is a foreign command, and some must be formally defined with a command definition. Foreign commands are defined to look like the following:

```
$ freeware_command :== $SYS$MANAGER:[freeware_dir]freeware.EXE
```

If the command must be created, there will be a .CLD file in the delivery. Typically it must be edited to reference the freeware's subdirectory correctly. As a minimum the IMAGE line of the .CLD file must be modified, but sometimes other lines must be edited as well. After editing, the command is added to the DCLTABLES.EXE with the following utility:

```
$ SET COMMAND freeware.CLD /TABLE=SYS$COMMON:[SYSLIB]DCLTABLES.EXE -
        /OUTPUT=SYS$COMMON:[SYSLIB]DCLTABLES.EXE
```

To activate this new definition, the DCLTABLES must be installed again with the following command,

```
$ INSTALL REPLACE SYS$COMMON:[SYSLIB]DCLTABLES.EXE
```

You must log out and log in again to access this new definition.

Some packages will supply command files to perform all of the above steps, others will not. A good policy is to look for a script before manually doing it.

20.3.4 Modifying Help

Usually an ASCII Help file, *freeware*.HLP, accompanies the application. I find it most convenient to add this information to the OpenVMS help library, HELPLIB.HLB. This is done with the following command:

```
$ LIBRARY/INSERT/HELP SYS$HELP:HELPLIB.HLB freeware.HLP
```

You may also find a *freeware*.HLP help library in the delivery package. This indicates the freeware itself has a help option. Probably, you will be directed to define a logical to define its location. However, the .CLD (if there is one) may point to this library.

20.3.5 Installing the Image

Usually some boot-time installation of the freeware is necessary, particularly if extended privileges are required. Look for a file called *freeware*_STARTUP.COM. Sometimes these files have to be edited to reference the freeware's subdirectory, and sometimes the author will assume this STARTUP script is located in the freeware subdirectory.

Once the *freeware*_STARTUP.COM is modified you can insert a line in SYSTARTUP_VMS.COM to call it. There are several tasks that the freeware script may have to perform:

- Install the package, particularly if elevated privileges are required
- Define one or more systemwide logicals
- Create a command or symbol to call out the freeware easily
- Start a symbiont

Occasionally there is no startup script, just startup instructions in the README. In that case it is a good idea to write your own STARTUP script and, thus, document the process precisely.

20.3.6 Privilege Precautions

Freeware authors are well aware of OpenVMS security arrangements and will, either explicitly or implicitly, address security provisions in the installation instructions. Generally you must be cognizant of the freeware package's intended audience.

If the freeware package is a management tool only, you must take care to protect the .EXE file. Make sure it is not declared to be a public file. If the freeware has a database, make sure it is not public too. To make it more secure, do not start these tools to SYSTARTUP_VMS.COM. Instead, add the startup command to SYSTEM's LOGIN.COM script.

On the other hand, if the freeware package is intended for public use, make sure the .EXE's protection is public or installed with the required privileges and install it via SYSTARTUP_VMS.COM. Make sure the user has access to the package's Help, so that it is used as intended.

20.3.7 In Case of Problems

If you have difficulties with the freeware, courteously contact the author. To help with debugging, include the following:

- The specific freeware command used and the specific error message
- The freeware version number
- The OpenVMS version number
- The hardware model on which the freeware is running

If you do not provided the details, the author will have nothing on which to base his or her analysis of the problem, and both of you will be frustrated. Debugging is a cooperative effort between you and the author.

Some freeware is several years old, and the author may be difficult to contact. If so, try posting a query on the OpenVMS discussion group, comp.os.vms. This is a knowledgeable and active group that is very willing to help anyone interested in OpenVMS.

20.4 Using VMSINSTAL Script

SYS$UPDATE:VMSINSTAL is the legacy product installation script. It operates from BACKUP save-sets suffixed with .A, .B, .C, .D, and so forth. VMSINSTAL is a skeleton script that turns over control to a script called KITINSTAL.COM in the .A save-set.

There is no Help associated with VMSINSTAL. The general form of this command is:

```
@SYS$UPDATE:VMSINSTAL product-list source: [OPTIONS option-list]
[destination] [qualifiers]
```

For example:

```
$ @VMSINSTAL.COM NEWAID021 MTA0: OPTIONS A,N

$ @SYS$UPDATE:VMSINSTAL.COM NEWAID010 CSA1: OPTIONS AWD=DUA2:[INSTALL]
```

The options are described in table 20.1.

Table 20.1 *VMSINSTAL Options*

Letter Choice	Option	Description
A	Autoanswer	Makes it easier to reinstall a product after an upgrade by providing responses to the questions and prompts during the reinstallation (layered products only)
AWD=	Alternate working device	Lets you specify an alternate working device for the temporary working directory (not all products support this option)
C	Callback trace	Traces VMSINSTAL internal subroutine calls
G	Get save-set	Allows you to store product save-sets temporarily on a magnetic tape or in a disk directory (layered products only)
K	Kit debug	Provides kit-specific debug information
L	File log	Logs all file activity to the terminal during installation
N	Release notes	Displays or prints the online release notes file supplied by the layered product
R	Alternate root	Lets you install the product on a system disk other than that of the running system
RSP	Restore save-set and pause	After performing the BACKUP and before the installation takes place, pause with an appropriate message
S	Statistics	Displays various information about the installation

The qualifiers are described in table 20.2.

Table 20.2 *VMSINSTAL Qualifiers*

Qualifier	Explanation
/VERIFY	Compares the contents of the output specifier with the contents of the input specifier after a save, restore, or copy operation completes. If a file does not compare successfully, an error message reporting this fact is displayed.

Table 20.2 *VMSINSTAL Qualifiers (continued)*

Qualifier	Explanation
/LOG	Causes the file specification of each file processed to be displayed at the terminal during the operation. The default is /NOLOG.
/CONFIRM	Displays a prompt on your screen before each file is processed.

When installing any product, it is a good idea to disable user access to the system so VMSINSTAL has exclusive access to all system files. To disable logins, enter the following command:

```
$ SET LOGINS/INTERACTIVE=0
```

However, this command does not log out any users. You will have to identify logged in users and contact them. One convenient way to do this is as follows:

```
$ REPLY/ALL/BELL "SYSTEM GOING DOWN FOR S/W INSTALLATION. PLEASE LOG OFF."
```

VMSINSTAL deletes all global symbols defined by the LOGIN scripts, so usually you must log out and log back in to restore your environment.

20.4.1 VMSINSTAL Example

The following example shows a freeware product installation using the VMSINSTAL. Naturally every product has a different dialog, so the reader is always encouraged to read the installation instructions prior to performing the installation. Since VMSINSTAL is a script, not an executable module, HELP is not found in the usual place. However, any time you are prompted, the "?" is a valid response. To determine the exact name of the product, look at the directory; for instance:

```
SYSMGR.HGFTP? dir/col=1 hgftp*

Directory SYS$COMMON:[SYSMGR.HGFTP]

HGFTP.ZIP;1
HGFTP031.A;1
```

```
HGFTP031.B;1
HGFTP031.C;1
HGFTP031.D;1
HGFTP031.E;1
HGFTP031.F;1
HGFTP031.G;1

Total of 8 files.
```

Now you may enter the VMSINSTAL command:

```
SYSMGR.HGFTP? @SYS$UPDATE:VMSINSTAL HGFTP031 SYS$COMMON:[SYSMGR.HGFTP]


OpenVMS AXP Software Product Installation Procedure V7.3-1

It is 23-MAR-2003 at 16:23.

Enter a question mark (?) at any time for help.

* Are you satisfied with the backup of your system disk [YES]?

The following products will be processed:

  HGFTP V3.1

Beginning installation of HGFTP V3.1 at 16:23

%VMSINSTAL-I-RESTORE, Restoring product save-set A ...
%VMSINSTAL-I-RELMOVED, Product's release notes have been moved to SYS$HELP.

    HGFTP V3.1 Installation

    Copyright © 1994,2002 Hunter Goatley.
    All rights reserved.
    Redistribution for no commercial gain is permitted.

* Do you want to purge files replaced by this installation [YES]?

   NOTE:  This system appears to have a version of MGFTP installed.
   Please note that this release of this software is now packaged
   as HGFTP and all MADGOAT_FTP_* logical names must be changed to
   HG_FTP_* logicals.  Please check your startup procedures for
   definitions of the MADGOAT_FTP_* logicals so that you can
   properly create the HG_FTP_* logicals (it is recommended that
```

```
   you start with HG_ROOT:[COM]FTP_LOGICALS.TEMPLATE as your
   sample source .COM file for defining logicals).

* Please press RETURN to continue this installation [YES]?

    Configuring Base HGFTP Directories and Logicals
    -----------------------------------------------------

    HG software is installed in its own rooted directory to avoid
    mixing HG files with normal VMS files.  The directory can reside
    on any disk.

    THERE ARE NO FILES COPIED TO SYS$SYSTEM, SYS$LIBRARY, etc.  (The only
    file copied to a VMS directory is the Release Notes file, which is
    copied to SYS$HELP.)

* Enter the top-level directory for the HG root directory [SYS$SYSDEVICE:[HG]]:

%VMSINSTAL-I-SYSDIR, This product creates system disk directory
MILLER$DKA0:[HG].
%VMSINSTAL-I-SYSDIR, This product creates system disk directory
MILLER$DKA0:[HG.EXE].
%VMSINSTAL-I-SYSDIR, This product creates system disk directory
MILLER$DKA0:[HG.ALPHA_EXE].

    Selecting HGFTP Components
    --------------------------------
. . . [component selection dialog deleted for brevity]
    No further questions will be asked.  The HGFTP installation will
    now continue for 2 to 15 minutes, depending on your type of media and
    the system configuration.

%VMSINSTAL-I-SYSDIR, This product creates system disk directory
MILLER$DKA0:[HG.COM].
%VMSINSTAL-I-SYSDIR, This product creates system disk directory
MILLER$DKA0:[HG.DATA].
%VMSINSTAL-I-SYSDIR, This product creates system disk directory
MILLER$DKA0:[HG.LOGS].
%VMSINSTAL-I-SYSDIR, This product creates system disk directory
MILLER$DKA0:[HG.DOC].
%VMSINSTAL-I-SYSDIR, This product creates system disk directory
MILLER$DKA0:[HG.HELP].
%VMSINSTAL-I-SYSDIR, This product creates system disk directory
MILLER$DKA0:[HG.SOURCES].
%VMSINSTAL-I-SYSDIR, This product creates system disk directory
MILLER$DKA0:[HG.SOURCES.FTP].
%VMSINSTAL-I-RESTORE, Restoring product save-set E ...
%HGFTP-I-LINKING, Linking image FTP....
```

```
%HGFTP-I-LINKING, Linking image FTP_LISTENER....
%HGFTP-I-LINKING, Linking image FTP_SERVER....

    To install the HGFTP images and define the HG_ROOT logical,
    execute the following command.

    To automate this procedure at system startup, you should also add the
    following line to the system startup command procedure
    (SYSTARTUP_V5.COM or SYSTARTUP_VMS.COM in SYS$MANAGER:).

           $ @MILLER$DKA0:[HG.COM]FTP_STARTUP.COM

    If you do not want to run the HGFTP server, then use this
    command instead:

           $ @MILLER$DKA0:[HG.COM]FTP_STARTUP.COM CLIENT_ONLY

%VMSINSTAL-I-MOVEFILES, Files will now be moved to their target directories...

Installation of HGFTP V3.1 completed at 16:26

    Adding history entry in VMI$ROOT:[SYSUPD]VMSINSTAL.HISTORY

    Creating installation data file: VMI$ROOT:[SYSUPD]HGFTP031.VMI_DATA

VMSINSTAL procedure done at 16:26
```

20.4.2 VMSINSTAL Status

VMSINSTAL leaves a history records in SYS$UPDATE. For instance, the installation above will leave a file that resembles this:

```
SYS$UPDATE? type/page hgftp031.vmi_data

! File: VMI$ROOT:[SYSUPD]HGFTP031.VMI_DATA
! Product:
! Mnemonic: HGFTP    Version: 3.1
! Installation started: 23-MAR-2003 16:23    Completed: 23-MAR-2003 16:26
! Installed by: SYSTEM using node MILLER
! Architecture: OpenVMS AXP
! System Disk Usage (Blocks) -    Net:   2012     Peak:   7024
! Alternate Disk Usage (Blocks) - Net:      0     Peak:      0
!= VMI$ROOT = MILLER$DKA0:[SYS0.SYSCOMMON.]
!= VMI$COMMON = MILLER$DKA0:[SYS0.SYSCOMMON.]
```

```
!= VMI$SPECIFIC = MILLER$DKA0:[SYS0.]
!------------------------------------------------------------------------------
!+ Files provided by installation
! Size      File location
   721   HG_ROOT:[ALPHA_EXE]FTP.EXE;
   171   HG_ROOT:[ALPHA_EXE]FTP_LISTENER.EXE;
   534   HG_ROOT:[ALPHA_EXE]FTP_SERVER.EXE;
     8   HG_ROOT:[COM]ANONYMOUS_LOGIN.TEMPLATE;
     1   HG_ROOT:[COM]FTP_GET_ANONYMOUS_PASSWORD.COM;
     3   HG_ROOT:[COM]FTP_GET_CONNECTION_INFO.COM;
     9   HG_ROOT:[COM]FTP_LOGICALS.TEMPLATE;
     1   HG_ROOT:[COM]FTP_RUN_LISTENER.COM;
     1   HG_ROOT:[COM]FTP_SERVER.COM;
```

Thus, VMSINSTAL leaves a sort of history trail if you use the following command:

```
$ dir/date .vmi* /width=filename=30

Directory SYS$COMMON:[SYSUPD]

ALPBASE01_071.VMI_DATA;1        12-MAY-1998 10:26:33.93
ALPBASE02_071.VMI_DATA;1        23-MAY-1998 13:27:40.01
ALPCLUSIO01_062.VMI_DATA;2      27-APR-1998 15:40:43.23
ALPCPU02_062.VMI_DATA;1         14-MAR-1998 14:41:03.43
ALPDCL01_071.VMI_DATA;1         11-MAY-1998 09:45:24.31
ALPF11X03_071.VMI_DATA;1         7-OCT-1998 11:07:58.79
ALPIPC01_071.VMI_DATA;1         15-MAY-1998 14:18:20.99
ALPLAD01_071.VMI_DATA;1          7-OCT-1998 10:21:37.75
ALPLAN04_062.VMI_DATA;1         14-MAR-1998 12:29:26.97
ALPLAT02_071.VMI_DATA;1         10-MAY-1998 14:33:28.45
ALPLAT03_062.VMI_DATA;1         14-MAR-1998 12:48:23.61
ALPLMF01_062.VMI_DATA;1         14-MAR-1998 13:04:41.31
ALPLOGI07_071.VMI_DATA;1         7-OCT-1998 10:19:00.40
ALPMAIL02_071.VMI_DATA;1         7-OCT-1998 10:16:18.09
ALPMANA02_070.VMI_DATA;1        14-MAR-1998 13:18:18.53
ALPMOTF02_U4012.VMI_DATA;1      10-MAR-1998 21:17:26.81
. . .
```

The installation files should leave tracks in SYS$HELP as well; for instance:

```
SYS$UPDATE? dir sys$help:hg*

Directory SYS$COMMON:[SYSHLP]

HGFTP031.RELEASE_NOTES;1

Total of 1 file.
```

However, a much more reliable method of determining installation status is to examine the VMSINSTAL.HISTORY file; for instance:

```
$ type sys$update:vmsinstal.history

VMSINSTAL Product Installation History File

S = Success    F = Failure    NA = Not Applicable

-------------------------------------------------------------------------------
Product Information            | Installation Information
-------------------------------|-----------------------------------------------
Name | Mnemonic      | Version | Date         | Status| IVP    | Node    | Installer
-------------------------------|-----------------------------------------------
     | DECSET        | 12.2    |   7-MAR-1998 | F     | NA     | MILLER | SYSTEM
     | DECSET        | 12.2    |   7-MAR-1998 | S     | S      | MILLER | SYSTEM
     | CC            |  5.6    |   7-MAR-1998 | S     | S      | MILLER | SYSTEM
     | ALPMOTF02_U4|  1.2    |  10-MAR-1998 | S     | NA     | MILLER | SYSTEM
. . .
     | ALPSCSI04_    |  7.1    | 14-OCT-1998  | S     | NA     | MILLER | SYSTEM
     | NETLIB        |  2.3    |   3-MAR-2003 | S     | NA     | MILLER | SYSTEM
     | HGFTP         |  3.1    | 23-MAR-2003  | S     | NA     | MILLER | SYSTEM
     | CC            |  6.5    |   5-APR-2003 | S     | S      | MILLER | SYSTEM
     | ADX           |  7.2    |   5-APR-2003 | F     | NA     | MILLER | SYSTEM
     | CXX           |  6.5    |   5-APR-2003 | S     | S      | MILLER | SYSTEM
     | PASCAL        |  5.8    |   5-APR-2003 | S     | S      | MILLER | SYSTEM
     | AXPGKS        |  6.5    |   5-APR-2003 | S     | S      | MILLER | SYSTEM
     | AXPPHIGS      |  5.0    |   5-APR-2003 | S     | S      | MILLER | SYSTEM
     | DCPSAXP       |  2.1    |   5-APR-2003 | S     | S      | MILLER | SYSTEM
     | DFG           |  2.6    |   5-APR-2003 | S     | S      | MILLER | SYSTEM
```

20.5 Using PRODUCT

PRODUCT is the successor to VMSINSTAL. However, many layered products have not yet switched to this tool.

The PRODUCT command invokes the POLYCENTER software installation utility to perform the following operations:

- Install, reconfigure, or remove software products
- Display information from the software product database, such as the names of installed products, the names of patches applied, product dependencies, the names of files provided by PRODUCT, and historical information about past operations
- List the software product kits from the source directory that are available for installation
- Create a software product kit in sequential or reference format
- List the contents of a software product kit or extract files from the kit, such as release notes or files you specify
- Perform miscellaneous functions, such as establishing default configuration choices offered by a product, copying a product kit or converting it to a different format, and registering information about a product in the product database

The format of this command follows. This command is well documented in HELP.

```
$ PRODUCT [subcommand product-name [/qualifiers]]
```

I will present an example of PRODUCT in the next section.

PRODUCT also manages a history file to help you manage the configuration layered product and patch installation. With this tool you can easily identify the version number and date of each installation. The following is an example of this tool on a VAX.

```
$ product show history *
----------------------------------- ----------- ----------- --------------------
PRODUCT                             KIT TYPE    OPERATION   DATE AND TIME
```

```
----------------------------------- ----------- ----------- -------------------
DEC VAXVMS SHC V2.2-220             Full LP     Install     23-MAY-2003 12:56:07
DEC VAXVMS TCPIP_ECO V5.1-154       Patch       Install     22-MAY-2003 16:06:40
DEC VAXVMS TCPIP V5.1-15            Full LP     Install     08-MAY-2003 07:33:07
DEC VAXVMS DECNET_PHASE_IV V7.3     Full LP     Install     30-APR-2003 19:17:37
DEC VAXVMS VMS V7.3                 Transition  Reg Product 30-APR-2003 19:16:46
----------------------------------- ----------- ----------- -------------------

5 items found
```

To find out details of the installation, that is, what files were involved, use the PRODUCT LIST tool as follows:

```
$ product
_Operation (INSTALL, SHOW, ...): list
_Product name (* to show list): shc

The following product has been selected:
    DEC VAXVMS SHC V2.2-220                Layered Product

Do you want to continue? [YES]

Files in DSA0:[SYS0.][SYSMGR.SHC]DEC-VAXVMS-SHC-V0202-220-1.PCSI

------------------------------------------------------------------------------
RELATIVE FILE SPECIFICATION
------------------------------------------------------------------------------
[000000]DEC-VAXVMS-SHC-V0202-220-1.PCSI$TLB
[SHC]SHC$DEFAULTS.CFG
[SHC]SHC.RELEASE_NOTES
[SHC]SHCHS.EXE
[SHC]SHCT4.EXE
[SHC]SHC_COLLECT.COM
[SHC]SHC_DEINSTALL.COM
[SHC]SHC_OVMS_USERGUIDE.TXT
[SHC]SHC_README.TXT
[SHC]SHC_START.COM
[SHC]SHC_STATUS.COM
[SHC]SHC_STOP.COM
[SHC]T4_METRICS.LIS
[SHC]UUENCODE_ALPHA.OBJ
[SHC]UUENCODE_VAX.OBJ
[SHC]VERINFO.CFG
[SHC]ZIP-ALPHA.EXE
[SHC]ZIP-VAX.EXE
[SYSUPD]SHC_SETUP.COM
```

```
[000000]DEC-VAXVMS-SHC-V0202-220-1.PCSI$DESCRIPTION
------------------------------------------------------------------------------
```

20.6 Patches

HP provides corrections, also called ECOs or patches, for many of their products online. The most convenient URL is http://ftp.support.compaq.com.au/ecos.phtml. Patches at that site are ordered by version, and within version, by priority. By clicking appropriately, you can download the patch—actually a self-extracting executable, which, when run, generates a file to be installed by PRODUCT or VMSINSTAL.

20.6.1 Example

This example uses PRODUCT to install an ECO. PRODUCT is also used to install most layered products. PRODUCT files are suffixed with .PSCI.

Previously, I downloaded the self-extracting patch file into SYS$COMMON:[SYSMGR.PATCH]. To determine its name, I did the following:

```
$ directory

Directory SYS$COMMON:[SYSMGR.PATCH]

DEC-AXPVMS-VMS731_SYS-V0300--4.;1

Total of 1 file.
```

Now, I execute the file. Notice the .EXE file type is not required to perform this step:

```
$ run dec-axpvms-vms731_sys-v0300--4.

FTSV DCX auto-extractible compressed file for OpenVMS (AXP)
FTSV V3.0 -- FTSV$DCX_AXP_AUTO_EXTRACT
Copyright (c) Digital Equipment Corp. 1993

Options: [output_file_specification [input_file_specification]]

The decompressor  needs to know  the filename to use for the
decompressed file. If you don't specify any, it will use the
```

```
original name of the file before it was compressed, and
create it in the current directory. If you specify a
directory name, the file will be created in that directory.

Decompress into (file specification):

Opening and checking compressed file...
Decompressing (press Ctrl-T to watch the evolution)...
Creating decompressed file...
Original file specification: DISK$TIMA_TOOLS:[TOOLS_DIR]DEC-AXPVMS-VMS73
1_SYS-V0300--4.PCSI;1
Decompressed file specification: SYS$COMMON:[SYSMGR.PATCH]DEC-AXPVMS-VMS
731_SYS-V0300--4.PCSI;1
Successful decompression, decompression report follows:
File Size: 12063.30 Blocks, 6031.65 Kbytes, 6176410 bytes
Decompression ratio is 1 to 1.57 ( 56.51 % expansion )
Elapsed CPU time:     0 00:00:11.17
Elapsed time     :    0 00:00:13.30
Speed : 85160.88 Blocks/min, 42580.44 Kbytes/min, 726706.13 bytes/s
```

When completed, the directory is examined again to discover if the .PCSI file has been created.

```
$ DIR/SIZE/DATE

Directory SYS$COMMON:[SYSMGR.PATCH]

DEC-AXPVMS-VMS731_SYS-V0300--4.;1      12064/12064    8-MAR-2003 09:20:48.14
DEC-AXPVMS-VMS731_SYS-V0300--4.PCSI;1 18880/18880    8-MAR-2003 09:32:24.57

Total of 2 files, 30944/30944 blocks.
```

If there is any confusion about the name or content of this file, the safe procedure to follow is to let PRODUCT examine it:

```
$ product find * /source=[]
----------------------------------- ----------- ----------
PRODUCT                             KIT TYPE    KIT FORMAT
----------------------------------- ----------- ----------
DEC AXPVMS VMS731_SYS V3.0          Patch       Sequential
```

```
---------------------------------- ----------- ----------

1 item found
```

Now it can be installed using PRODUCT.

```
$ product install vms731_sys /source=sys$common:[sysmgr.patch]

The following product has been selected:
    DEC AXPVMS VMS731_SYS V3.0             Patch (maintenance update)

Do you want to continue? [YES]

Configuration phase starting ...

You will be asked to choose options, if any, for each selected product and for
any products that may be installed to satisfy software dependency requirements.

DEC AXPVMS VMS731_SYS V3.0: OpenVMS V7.3-1 SYS V3.0

* This product does not have any configuration options.

    << System Disk Backup >>

    This kit will make functional changes to your system.
    Before installing this kit you should make a backup
    copy of your system disk.  If you do not make a copy
    of your system disk you will not be able to restore
    your system to a pre-kit installation state.

    Do you want to continue? [YES]

    Installing this patch kit requires a reboot.

    Compaq  strongly  recommends that you reboot your system
    immediately after installation  of  this kit.  The images
    in this kit will not fully take effect until the system
    is rebooted.  However, if you do not re-boot immediately
    after kit installation, the system may become unstable and
    may not function as expected.
```

```
    If you have other nodes in your VMS cluster, they must also
    be rebooted in order to make use of the new image(s).  If it
    is not possible or convenient to reboot the entire cluster
    at this time, a rolling re-boot (kit installation and reboot
    on one node at a time) may be performed.

    Do you want to continue? [YES]

Execution phase starting ...

The following product will be installed to destination:
    DEC AXPVMS VMS731_SYS V3.0             DISK$ALPHASYS:[VMS$COMMON.]

Portion done: 0%...10%...20%...30%...40%...50%...60%...70%...80%...90%...100%

The following product has been installed:
    DEC AXPVMS VMS731_SYS V3.0             Patch (maintenance update)

DEC AXPVMS VMS731_SYS V3.0: OpenVMS V7.3-1 SYS V3.0

    VMS731_SYS-V0300 Release notes available

            Release notes for the VMS731_SYS-V0300 kit are available
        at SYS$COMMON:[000000.SYSHLP]

     << PREVIOUS IMAGES RENAMED >>

        The previous versions of the images installed by this
    kit have been renamed to IMAGE_NAME.EXE_OLD, where
    IMAGE_NAME is the actual name of the image.
```

Some patches require a system reboot. Do not even think about ignoring that step. It is critical!

20.7 OpenVMS/Alpha Installation

OpenVMS/Alpha installation is from a CD-ROM. You have three distinct options:

1. Installation onto an empty disk—that is, initializing a disk

2. Preserving, which means upgrade of an existing system disk, preserving all but the system files
3. Performing a rolling upgrade of multiple system disks in a cluster

Furthermore, your firmware may require an update as well. Current OpenVMS/Alpha installation scripts confirm your installed version is compatible with OpenVMS's requirements. If it is incompatible, an error message will be displayed. This is illustrated in the next section.

These are the basic steps:

1. Boot from the installation CD.
2. Selection Option 1 from the menu.

   Patch kits are also supplied on the CD. You may want to apply them or you may want to visit the patch site to determine the latest recommendations. That site is http://ftp.support.compaq.com.au/ecos.phtml. See section 20.6 for a patch discussion.
3. You must select the type of installation, upgrade, or install and, of course, name the target disk.

   Two file systems are available: On-Disk Structure Level 2 (ODS-2) is the legacy system, and ODS-5 is compatible with Windows and UNIX systems.
4. You must supply an initial password for the SYSTEM account.
5. Next the installation script determines which components of OpenVMS you want installed:
   - Cluster
   - Galaxy
   - DECwindows
   - TCP/IP
   - DECnet
6. Next you are presented with a time zone dialog.
7. Licenses may be entered next, although that is not a requirement. You can delay this step until your first login after the installation is complete.

8. When it has determined what is required, the installation begins. PRODUCT is used to install OpenVMS and presents various options and progress reports depending on the product.
9. The installation is complete. The initial menu is presented again. This time you want option 8.
10. Reboot the system for the newly configured disk. Use the SYSTEM password you created in Step 6.

20.7.1 Firmware Installation Example

If you do not have the required version of console firmware, the system displays a message similar to the following when you attempt to install/update OpenVMS:

```
%SYSBOOT-F-FIRMREV, Firmware rev. nnn is below the absolute minimum of nnn.
  Please update your firmware to the recommended revision nnn,
  Alpha Systems Firmware Update Vn.n.
```

If you do not have the recommended version of console firmware, the system displays a message similar to the following:

```
%SYSBOOT-W-FIRMREV, Firmware rev.nnn is below the recommended minimum of nn.
  Please update your firmware to the recommended revision,
  which can be found on the firmware CD labeled:
  Alpha Systems Firmware Update Vn.n.
```

Firmware can be upgraded from either a CD-ROM or a downloaded bootable update. The location of the downloadable updates is ftp://ftp.digital.com/pub/Digital/Alpha/firmware/index.html. This site also includes instructions. You should take the time to read these instructions.

The following examples use the firmware CD-ROM, but the dialogs are similar for the downloaded version. Two updates may be required, the System Reference Manual (SRM) or console firmware and the PCI drivers.

Incidentally, you may see references to ARC firmware. ARC has to do with Windows-NT (WNT), not OpenVMS. Some Alpha computers will support WNT, and you should skip ARC instructions.

20.7.1.1 SRM Update

Insert the firmware CD-ROM and boot from it. The boot logic will determine what Alpha model it is running on and load the appropriate firmware upgrade. There are very few queries or decisions to make. A sample dialog follows:

```
>>> boot dka400
(boot dka400.1.0.1.0)
block 0 of dka400.1.0.1.0 is a valid boot block
reading 989 blocks from dka400.5.0.1000.0
bootstrap code read in
base = 156000, image_start = 0, image_bytes = 7ba00
initializing HWRPB at 2000
initializing page table at 148000
initializing machine state
setting affinity to the primary CPU
jumping to bootstrap code
[Release notes are displayed]
Bootfile: [press enter-key]
*** AlphaStation 250/233 -- Firmware Update V7.2 ***
Use HELP or ? for help
Update
Verify
List
Show
DEbug
NDebug
?
Apu-> update
APU-I ARE YOU READY TO PROGRAM (SRM ) ROM DEVICE ? (Y/N) y
APU-I PRECHARGING (SRM ) ROM DEVICE
APU-I ERASING (SRM ) ROM DEVICE
APU-I PROGRAMMING (SRM ) ROM DEVICE
APU-I VERIFY LOADED (SRM ) ROM IMAGE
APU-I VERIFY LOADED (SRM ) ROM IMAGE DONE
APU-I PROGRAMMING (SRM ) ROM COMPLETED
APU-I PRECHARGING (ARC /AlphaBIOS) ROM DEVICE
APU-I ERASING (ARC /AlphaBIOS) ROM DEVICE
APU-I PROGRAMMING (ARC /AlphaBIOS) ROM DEVICE
APU-I VERIFY LOADED (ARC /AlphaBIOS) ROM IMAGE
```

```
APU-I VERIFY LOADED (ARC /AlphaBIOS) ROM IMAGE DONE
APU-I PROGRAMMING (ARC /AlphaBIOS) ROM COMPLETED
Apu-> exit
```

You must cycle power before the updates will take effect.

20.7.1.2 PCI Update

To update the PCI firmware, you must boot from the firmware CD-ROM once again. However, this time you must know which file to boot, so you must read the release notes for specifics. Shut down your system and reboot as follows:

```
>>> boot -fl 0,A0 dka400
INIT-S-CPU...
AUDIT_CHECKSUM_GOOD
AUDIT_LOAD_BEGINS
AUDIT_LOAD_DONE
BOOTFILE: [ALPHA200]AS200_PCI_V1_4.EXE

*** PCI Loadable Firmware Update Utility V1.4 ***
----------------------------------------------------------------------------
Function    Description
----------------------------------------------------------------------------
Display     Displays the system's configuration table.
Exit        Done exit LFU (reset.)
List        Lists the device, revision, firmware name, and update revision.
Update      Replaces current firmware with loadable data image.
Verify      Compares loadable and hardware images.
? or Help   Scrolls this function table.

UPD-> list
Device Current Revision Filename     Update Revision
fwa0      2.46          dfpaa_fw       2.46
pka0      A06           kzpsa_fw       A07
UPD-> update pka0

Confirm update on:
pka0
[Y/(N)]Y
```

```
WARNING: updates may take several minutes to complete for each device.
DO NOT ABORT!

pka0        Updating to A07... Verifying A07... PASSED.

UPD-> exit
```

You must cycle power on the computer before rebooting.

20.7.2 OpenVMS/Alpha Example Installation

You must boot from the CD-ROM. Depending on your computer's configuration, this can be a lengthy process that will take several minutes. Once booted, the following dialog will be displayed. The example below has been truncated because complete examples are included in the installation manual.

```
>>> BOOT DKA400

OpenVMS (TM) Alpha Operating System, Version 7.3-1
Copyright (c) 2002 -- All rights reserved.
Compaq Information Technologies, L.P.

Installing required known files...
Configuring devices...

****************************************************************

You can install or upgrade the OpenVMS Alpha operating system
or you can install or upgrade layered products that are included
on the OpenVMS Alpha operating system CD-ROM.
You can also execute DCL commands and procedures to perform
"standalone" tasks, such as backing up the system disk.

Please choose one of the following:
1) Upgrade, install or reconfigure OpenVMS Alpha Version 7.3-1
2) Display products and patches that this procedure can install
3) Install or upgrade layered products and patches
4) Show installed products
5) Reconfigure installed products
6) Remove installed products
7) Execute DCL commands and procedures
8) Shut down this system
```

```
Enter CHOICE or ? for help: (1/2/3/4/5/6/7/8/?) 1
```

When you choose the install or upgrade option from the menu, the system asks whether you want to preserve or initialize the system disk. The dialog is similar to the following:

```
There are two choices for Installation/Upgrade:

INITIALIZE - Removes all software and data files that were
previously on the target disk and installs OpenVMS Alpha.

PRESERVE -- Installs or upgrades OpenVMS Alpha on the target disk
and retains all other contents of the target disk.

* Note: You cannot use PRESERVE to install OpenVMS Alpha on a disk on
which OpenVMS VAX or any other operating system is installed.

Do you want to INITIALIZE or to PRESERVE? [PRESERVE]
```

Next, you enter the volume label for the target system disk. If this is a PRESERVE operation, the old label is the default. You will be asked if you want to initialize the target system disk with ODS-2 or ODS-5.

```
Enter volume label for target system disk: [ALPHASYS]

The target system disk can be initialized with On-Disk Structure
Level 2 (ODS-2) or Level 5 (ODS-5). (? for more information)

Do you want to initialize with ODS-2 or ODS-5? (2/5/?) 2
```

Now you must select OpenVMS components to install. The display is similar to the following:

```
You can install the following products along with the OpenVMS operating system:

o DECwindows Motif for OpenVMS Alpha
o DECnet-Plus for OpenVMS Alpha
o DECnet Phase IV for OpenVMS Alpha
o Compaq TCP/IP Services for OpenVMS
```

```
If you want to change your selections, you can do so later in the
installation by answering "NO" to the following question:

"Do you want the defaults for all product options?"

Do you want to install DECwindows Motif for OpenVMS Alpha V1.2-6?
(Yes/No) [YES] y

Do you want to install DECnet-Plus for OpenVMS Alpha V7.3-1?
(Yes/No) [YES] y
```

Note that if you answer no to the prompt to install DECnet-Plus for OpenVMS, you will be prompted to install DECnet Phase IV for OpenVMS. The two protocols are mutually exclusive.

```
Do you want to install Compaq TCP/IP Services for OpenVMS V5.1?
(Yes/No) [YES] y
```

Before you can use the OpenVMS Alpha operating system and its components, you must register all licenses in one of two ways, during installation or after installation with VMSLICENSE. The following query is presented during installation:

```
Do you want to register any Product Authorization Keys? n
```

The system next displays the following message, indicating that the procedure is ready to install the operating system:

```
The following product has been selected:
DEC AXPVMS OPENVMS V7.3-1 Platform (product suite)
Configuration phase starting ...
You will be asked to choose options, if any, for each selected product and for
any products that may be installed to satisfy software dependency requirements.

    DEC AXPVMS OPENVMS V7.3-1: OpenVMS and related products Platform
    COPYRIGHT (c) 27-MAY-2002 -- All rights reserved
    Compaq Information Technologies Group, L.P.
```

After the system displays a series of additional messages, the procedure prompts you to choose the default values for all the options and suboptions for each component included in the operating system. The display is similar to the following:

```
Do you want the defaults for all options? [YES]

Do you want to review the options? [NO]
Execution phase starting ...

The following products will be installed to destinations:
   CPQ AXPVMS CDSA V1.0 DISK$ALPHASYS:[VMS$COMMON.]
   DEC AXPVMS DECNET_OSI V7.3-1 DISK$ALPHASYS:[VMS$COMMON.]
   DEC AXPVMS DWMOTIF V1.2-6 DISK$ALPHASYS:[VMS$COMMON.]
   DEC AXPVMS OPENVMS V7.3-1 DISK$ALPHASYS:[VMS$COMMON.]
   DEC AXPVMS TCPIP V5.1 DISK$ALPHASYS:[VMS$COMMON.]
   DEC AXPVMS VMS V7.3-1 DISK$ALPHASYS:[VMS$COMMON.]

Portion done: 0%..10%..20%..30%..40%..50%..60%..70%..80%..90%..100%

The following products have been installed:
   CPQ AXPVMS CDSA V1.0 Layered Product
   DEC AXPVMS DECNET_OSI V7.3-1 Layered Product
   DEC AXPVMS DWMOTIF V1.2-6 Layered Product
   DEC AXPVMS OPENVMS V7.3-1 Platform (product suite)
   DEC AXPVMS TCPIP V5.1 Layered Product
   DEC AXPVMS VMS V7.3-1 Operating System
The installation is now complete.
```

If you do not want to install layered products or perform any other operations prior to booting the new system disk, choose option 8 from the menu to shut down the system. The system display is similar to the following:

```
Enter CHOICE or ? for help: (1/2/3/4/5/6/7/8/?) 8
Shutting down the system
SYSTEM SHUTDOWN COMPLETE
```

The above example was an upgrade, so all passwords and licenses are intact. When you log in for the first time, use previously active SYSTEM password. However, other reconfigurations may be required. See the Installation Guide and Release Notes for details.

20.8 OpenVMS/VAX Installation

OpenVMS/VAX installation is from either a TK-50 tape or a CD-ROM. This example is from CD-ROM. You have three distinct options:

1. Installation onto an empty disk—that is, initializing a disk
2. Preserving, which means upgrade of an existing system disk, preserving all but the system files
3. Performing a rolling upgrade of multiple system disks in a cluster

Of course, this installation procedure is fully documented in the *Upgrade and Installation Manual,* so the example below is truncated. This section presents an overview and another example of this process. These are the basic steps.

1. Boot from the installation CD. This brings up Standalone BACKUP.
2. Restore the .B save-set to disk. This save-set provides a minimum OpenVMS system required to install or upgrade.
3. Boot from disk. This looks somewhat like a normal OpenVMS boot, except there are no licenses.

   A very important step in the dialog is to identify the location of the CD. I almost missed this question. Of course, OpenVMS needs to know where to find the rest of the save-sets.
4. Next, the installation script determines which components of OpenVMS you want installed.
5. When the installation script has determined what products and options are required, the installation begins. PRODUCT is used to install OpenVMS.
6. When the installation is complete, you must supply passwords for built-in three accounts namely SYSTEM, SYSTEST, and FIELD.
7. Licenses may now be entered, although that is not a requirement.
8. Finally you are presented with a time zone dialog.

9. OpenVMS then performs an AUTOGEN to configure the system to your computer. This requires that OpenVMS reboot.

10. The installation is complete. Use the SYSTEM password you created in Step 7.

20.8.1 Example

You may boot Standalone Backup ($$$ prompt) or a robust version of OpenVMS ($ prompt) from the CD-ROM. To boot OpenVMS, boot from root 1 of the CD-ROM. The exact boot command varies by VAX model. Details are found in appendix C. This is an example command:

```
>>> B/R5:10000000 DKA400:
```

To boot Standalone Backup, use the following command:

```
>>> B DKA400:
```

In either case you must copy the .B save-set to disk, then reboot from disk to start the actual installation.

```
-DKA400
%SYSBOOT-I-SYSBOOT Mapping the SYSDUMP.DMP on the System Disk
%SYSBOOT-W-SYSBOOT Can not map SYSDUMP.DMP on the System Disk
%SYSBOOT-W-SYSBOOT Can not map PAGEFILE.SYS on the System Disk
   OpenVMS (TM) VAX Version X7G7 Major version id = 1 Minor version id = 0
%WBM-I-WBMINFO Write Bitmap has successfully completed initialization.
PLEASE ENTER DATE AND TIME (DD-MMM-YYYY  HH:MM)  28-APR-2003 18:04

Configuring devices . . .

Available device  DKA400:                        device type SONY CD-ROM CDU-5
Available device  DKB100:                        device type RZ28B
%BACKUP-I-IDENT, Stand-alone BACKUP T7.2; the date is 28-APR-2003 18:05:31.41
$$$ backup/verify/image dka400:vms073.b/save dkb100:
%BACKUP-I-STARTVERIFY, starting verification pass
%BACKUP-I-PROCDONE, operation completed.  Processing finished at 28-APR-2003
18:51:20.22
If you do not want to perform another standalone BACKUP operation,
use the console to HALT the system.

If you do want to perform another standalone BACKUP operation,
```

```
ensure the standalone application volume is online and ready.
Enter "YES" to continue:
```

At this point you must halt the system and boot it again, this time from the target disk.

```
>>> b dkb100

-DKB100
%SYSBOOT-I-SYSBOOT Mapping the SYSDUMP.DMP on the System Disk
%SYSBOOT-W-SYSBOOT Can not map SYSDUMP.DMP on the System Disk
%SYSBOOT-I-SYSBOOT Mapping PAGEFILE.SYS on the System Disk
%SYSBOOT-I-SYSBOOT SAVEDUMP parameter not set to protect the PAGEFILE.SYS
   OpenVMS (TM) VAX Version BI73-7G7 Major version id = 1 Minor version id = 0
%WBM-I-WBMINFO Write Bitmap has successfully completed initialization.

           OpenVMS VAX V7.3 Installation Procedure

                        Model: VAXserver 3100
                System device: RZB28 - _DKB100:
                  Free Blocks: 4024044
                     CPU type: 10-04

* Please enter the date and time (DD-MMM-YYYY HH:MM) 30-apr-2003 18:43

*********************************************************
%SYSTEM-W-TZGMT, your local timezone has defaulted to GMT
%SYSTEM-I-SETTZ, to set your local timezone use:

     $ @SYS$MANAGER:UTC$TIME_SETUP.COM

*********************************************************
On MIN or UPGRADE system startup - CLUE is not run.
%%%%%%%%%%%  OPCOM  30-APR-2003 18:43:23.58  %%%%%%%%%%%
Operator _OPA0: has been enabled, username SYSTEM

. . .

%LICENSE-E-NOAUTH, DEC VAX-VMS use is not authorized on this node
-LICENSE-F-NOLICENSE, no license is active for this software product
-LICENSE-I-SYSMGR, please see your system manager
Startup processing continuing...

%SET-I-INTSET, login interactive limit = 1, current interactive value = 0
%SET-I-INTSET, login interactive limit = 0, current interactive value = 0
```

```
    If this system disk is to be used in an OpenVMS Cluster with multiple
    system disks, then each system disk must have a unique volume label.
    Any nodes having system disks with duplicate volume labels will fail
    to boot into the cluster.

    You can indicate a volume label of 1 to 12 characters in length.  If you
    want to use the default name of OVMSVAXSYS, press RETURN in response
    to the next question.

* Enter the volume label for this system disk [OVMSVAXSYS]:
```

The next question is a sleeper. I missed it the first time. You must enter the device name of the CD-ROM so OpenVMS can access the other save-sets during the installation.

```
* Enter name of drive holding the OpenVMS distribution media: dka400:
* Is the OpenVMS media ready to be mounted? [N] y

%MOUNT-I-MOUNTED, VAXVMS073 mounted on _DKA400:
```

Now you are presented with a list of the components and products you may install along with OpenVMS. A dialog follows to select them. If you do not install them now, you can do it later.

```
    Select optional software you want to install.  You can install one
    or more of the following OpenVMS or DECwindows components:

    o OpenVMS library                          -  52200 blocks
    o OpenVMS optional                         -  19000 blocks
    o OpenVMS Help Message                     -  10400 blocks
    o OpenVMS Management Station               -  20000 blocks
    o DECwindows base support                  -   4400 blocks
    o DECwindows workstation support           -  23800 blocks
          -  75 dots per inch video fonts      -    (included)
          - 100 dots per inch video fonts      -   6200 blocks
    o DECnet-Plus networking                   -  80000 blocks
    o DECnet Phase IV networking               -    800 blocks

    Space remaining on system disk:  4023855 blocks

* Do you want to install the OpenVMS library files? (Y/N) y
```

```
    Space remaining on system disk:  3971655 blocks
. . .
```

When the dialog is finished, the results are summarized. If necessary you may modify your selections.

```
    The following options will be provided:

        OpenVMS library
        OpenVMS optional
        OpenVMS Help Message
        DECnet Phase IV

    Space remaining on system disk:  3941455 blocks

* Is this correct? (Y/N) y

    Restoring OpenVMS library save-set ...
%BACKUP-I-STARTVERIFY, starting verification pass

. . .


The following product will be registered:
    DEC VAXVMS VMS V7.3                    DISK$VAXVMSV73:[VMS$COMMON.]

The following product has been registered:
    DEC VAXVMS VMS V7.3                    Transition (registration)

    Installing DECnet Phase IV...
%MOUNT-I-MOUNTED, VAXVMS073 mounted on _DKA400:

The following product has been selected:
    DEC VAXVMS DECNET_PHASE_IV V7.3        Layered Product
```

Depending on which products you selected, there may be additional options and, hence, another dialog.

```
Configuration phase starting ...

You will be asked to choose options, if any, for each selected product and for
any products that may be installed to satisfy software dependency requirements.
```

```
DEC VAXVMS DECNET_PHASE_IV V7.3: DECNET_PHASE_IV

    COPYRIGHT (c)  2-APR-2001 -- All rights reserved

    Digital Equipment Corporation

* This product does not have any configuration options.

    Support addendum to DECnet Phase IV service contract required

    Do you want to continue? [YES]

 Execution phase starting ...

The following product will be installed to destination:
    DEC VAXVMS DECNET_PHASE_IV V7.3        DISK$VAXVMSV73:[VMS$COMMON.]

Portion done: 0%...10%...30%...40%...50%...60%...70%...80%...100%

The following product has been installed:
    DEC VAXVMS DECNET_PHASE_IV V7.3        Layered Product

    You can now remove the distribution kit from DKA400:.

. . .
```

At this point the CD-ROM is no longer needed.

```
    Now we will ask you for new passwords for the following accounts:

        SYSTEM, SYSTEST, FIELD

    Passwords must be a minimum of 8 characters in length.  All passwords
    will be checked and verified.  Any passwords that can be guessed easily
    will not be accepted.

* Enter password for SYSTEM:

* Re-enter for verification:
%UAF-I-MDFYMSG, user record(s) updated
%VMS-I-PWD_OKAY, account password for SYSTEM verified
. . .
```

If you are unfamiliar with VMSclusters, you need to read the installation instructions before answering the following two questions:

```
* Please enter the SCSNODE name: vax

* Please enter the SCSSYSTEMID:  8194
```

The installation instructions contain a list of postinstallation tasks. The following is just a reminder of some of them:

```
   After the installation finishes, you might want to do one or more of the
    following tasks:

    o DECOMPRESS THE SYSTEM LIBRARIES - To save space, many of the system
      libraries are shipped in a data-compressed format.  If you have
      enough disk space, you can decompress the libraries for faster access.
      To data expand the libraries, type:

        $ @SYS$UPDATE:LIBDECOMP.COM

      If you do not decompress these libraries, you will experience
      slower response to the HELP and LINK commands.

    o BUILD A STANDALONE BACKUP KIT - You can build a standalone backup kit
      using the procedure described in the "Backup Procedures" chapter of
      tye upgrade and installation supplement provided for your VAX computer.

    o TAILOR THE SYSTEM DISK - You might want to review the files provided or
      not provided during this installation.  If you find there are files
      you want to remove from the system disk (TAILOR OFF) or files you want
      to add (TAILOR ON), use the following utilities to perform the
      desired tailoring.

          OpenVMS tailoring:           $ RUN SYS$UPDATE:VMSTAILOR

          DECwindows tailoring:        $ RUN SYS$UPDATE:DECW$TAILOR

      NOTE:  The tailor procedure cannot be used to TAILOR ON or TAILOR OFF
             files located on an alternate disk.

================================================================
    Continuing with OpenVMS VAX V7.3 Installation Procedure.

    Configuring all devices on the system ...
```

```
    If you have Product Authorization Keys (PAKs) to register, you can
    register them now.

* Do you want to register any Product Authorization Keys? (Y/N): n

*******************************************************************************

    After the system has rebooted you should register any additional
    Product Authorization Keys (PAKs) you have, or receive in the
    future, by executing the following procedure:

        $ @SYS$UPDATE:VMSLICENSE

    See the OpenVMS License Management Utility Manual for any additional
    information you need.

*******************************************************************************

%UTC-I-UPDTIME, updating Time Zone information in SYS$COMMON:[SYSEXE]

. . .

*******************************************************************************

    Running AUTOGEN to compute the new SYSTEM parameters ...

%AUTOGEN-I-BEGIN, GETDATA phase is beginning.
%AUTOGEN-I-NEWFILE, A new version of SYS$SYSTEM:PARAMS.DAT has been created.
        You may wish to purge this file.
%AUTOGEN-I-END, GETDATA phase has successfully completed.
%AUTOGEN-I-BEGIN, GENPARAMS phase is beginning.
%AUTOGEN-I-NEWFILE, A new version of SYS$MANAGER:VMSIMAGES.DAT has been created.
        You may wish to purge this file.
%AUTOGEN-I-NEWFILE, A new version of SYS$SYSTEM:SETPARAMS.DAT has been created.
        You may wish to purge this file.
%AUTOGEN-I-END, GENPARAMS phase has successfully completed.
%AUTOGEN-I-BEGIN, GENFILES phase is beginning.
%SYSGEN-I-EXTENDED, SYS$SYSROOT:[SYSEXE]PAGEFILE.SYS;1 extended
%SYSGEN-I-EXTENDED, SYS$SYSROOT:[SYSEXE]SWAPFILE.SYS;1 extended
%SYSGEN-I-CREATED, SYS$SPECIFIC:[SYSEXE]SYSDUMP.DMP;1 created
%SYSGEN-I-CREATED, DKB100:[SYS0.SYSEXE]ERRORLOG.DMP;1 created

%AUTOGEN-I-REPORT, AUTOGEN has produced some informational messages which
        have been stored in the file SYS$SYSTEM:AGEN$PARAMS.REPORT.  You may
        wish to review the information in that file.

%AUTOGEN-I-END, GENFILES phase has successfully completed.
```

```
%AUTOGEN-I-BEGIN, SETPARAMS phase is beginning.
%AUTOGEN-I-END, SETPARAMS phase has successfully completed.
%AUTOGEN-I-BEGIN, REBOOT phase is beginning.

    The system is shutting down to allow the system to boot with the
    generated site-specific parameters and installed images.

    The system will automatically reboot after the shutdown and the
    installation will be complete.

        SHUTDOWN -- Perform an Orderly System Shutdown

%SHUTDOWN-I-BOOTCHECK, performing reboot consistency check...
%SHUTDOWN-I-CHECKOK, basic reboot consistency check completed
```

The system is shut down and should automatically reboot. If it does not reboot, you may have to change the reboot options, in particular the default boot device. Again, look at appendix C for the commands specific to your VAX model.

20.9 Conclusion

I thought an overview of freeware installation would be helpful, especially to hobbyists and novices. My intent is to review the most important installation steps, but of course you will be able to find some package that has a special case that I forgot to mention. I hope this description does not throw you off too much.

Although VMSINSTAL and PRODUCT are described in various documents in some detail, this chapter presents a brief overview of these tools. This information can be used as either a precursor to reading the HP documents or as a refresher.

I have not found any formal documentation regarding patches. The best (and only) procedure I have located is in the cover letter that accompanies the patch, and I found that to be cursory and intended only for an experienced manager. Even so, I left out the checksum step, which I never have understood; there is no Help. All I know for sure is that there is a file, SYS$SYSTEM:CHECKSUM.EXE, that can be used to confirm the patch's integrity.

20.10 References

1. *OpenVMS/VAX Version 7.3 Upgrade and Installation Manual, OpenVMS Version 7.3 Release Notes,* and *OpenVMS Version 7.3 New Features and Documentation Overview* constitute the latest installation manuals for VAX. The documentation overview is new with this version, and it is a valuable addition.
2. *OpenVMS/Alpha Version 7.3–1 Upgrade and Installation Manual, OpenVMS Version 7.3-1 Release Notes,* and *OpenVMS Version 7.3-1 New Features and Documentation Overview* constitute the latest installation manuals for Alpha.
3. VMSINSTAL is documented in *OpenVMS System Manager's Manual.*
4. PRODUCT is documented in *OpenVMS System Management Utilities Reference Manual: M–Z.*

Tips for the Hobbyist

Hobbyists have several opportunities to investigate OpenVMS and various layered products. This appendix introduces you to the possibilities and to the available resources. I do not intend to endorse any product or vendor; this information is intended merely to guide the interested hobbyist.

The following steps outline the process to acquire a hobbyist system. Each of these steps is further described in latter section of this appendix.

- Acquire either VAX or Alpha hardware or a PC emulator. Make sure your hardware has a CD-ROM device.
- Apply for an Encompass associate membership.
- After you receive your Encompass membership number and your hardware, go to the Montagar site at www.montagar.com/hobbyist. You can order licenses (delivered immediately via e-mail) and media (delivered in about a week) via online queries. The one tricky question in the dialog is that you must supply your hardware's serial number. It is of the form ABxxxxxxxx (that is, AB followed by a combination of eight alphanumeric characters). There is usually a sticker attached to the back of the hardware box on which is printed the model and serial number.
- Encompass membership must be renewed annually. Likewise, the hobbyist licenses are only good for one year.
- When the media arrives, install OpenVMS, layered products and the licenses. You can download basic installation instructions from Montagar, too.

A.1 Acquiring Hardware

OpenVMS was designed originally for the VAX and later (about 1993) upgraded to run on the Alpha. Both of these computers are readily available on eBay. All you have to do is select a computer to fit your pocketbook.

Any VAX will run OpenVMS, but some are better than others. Look in appendix C for a list of VAXes along with their VUP ratings; higher is better. A VUP = 3 will run OpenVMS okay, but if you plan to use DECwindows, you will be disappointed with the response time if the VUP is less than 10.

Some Alphas were not designed to run OpenVMS; they were intended to run Windows NT only. These are called the Whitebox series. One of these is the Digital Server 3300. However, in some cases, it can be coaxed into booting, as indicated in the OpenVMS FAQ.

Digital also rebadged some MIPS processors to run their version of UNIX (called RISC ULTRIX). This series was called a DECsystem or DECstation. No computer in this series will run OpenVMS.

If there is any question about the box you are planning to buy, look at the SPD for OpenVMS. It lists every hardware model and all hardware peripherals that will support OpenVMS. If you still are confused, post a query on comp.os.vms newsgroup.

There are also several VAX and Alpha resellers in the United States and in Europe. My experience is that older machines are readily available through reputable dealers; often, a small VAX can be acquired for less than $100. If you are lucky you may get one for free. If your budget is over $100, you should lurk on eBay for an Alpha system. A short list of dealers is presented below:

- Building Block Computers: www.bbcusa.com
- Island Computers: www.hpaq.net
- CPU Options: www.cpuoptions.com
- Great Lakes Computers: www.glcomp.com
- MIT, Ltd.: www.mitlimited.com

The system you buy must include a CD-ROM player, and a floppy drive is a sometimes nice to have as well. Most VAX and Alpha systems include an Ethernet NIC, but it is good to double-check that option before buying. At minimum, a VAX should have at least 16 MB of memory and a 1 GB hard drive. An Alpha minimum is 64 MB of memory and a 2 GB hard drive. If you plan to run Motif, you should have more memory on both systems. You may also want to consider buying a 4-mm or 8-mm tape drive with sufficient capacity to backup your disk.

Finally, you will need a monitor. If you do not intend to install Motif, your PC will work fine. Both the VAX and Alpha have a console serial port option (VT100, 9,600 baud, 8 bit, no parity). I use C-Kermit on my PC to connect to a VAX, but there are other terminal emulators available. The C-Kermit site is www.columbia.edu/kermit. The $50 (or so) price tag is a good investment because it includes full documentation and upgrade rights. Kermit can also be used to transfer files between the PC and the VAX/Alpha until you have TCP/IP running. As I recall, VAX/Alpha Kermit is freeware and can be downloaded from the Kermit site.

Monitors for the VAX are a bit tricker. Most VAX graphics cards were sync-on-green, which is not recognized by modern monitors. Special monitors were developed by Digital for the VAX. However, there are converters available from Black Box to deal with this problem. Check the OpenVMS FAQ for details. Alpha graphics cards are easier to adapt to most multisync monitors. If video expertise is not on your resume, look in the FAQ or check with the comp.os.vms membership.

Both the VAX and Alpha have been emulated on Intel xx86 computers. I have no direct experience with these products. The following companies produce VAX and Alpha 8086 emulators, although I am not sure this list is complete:

VAX Emulators

simh—Simulation History is available at http://simh.trailing-edge.com.

Charon-VAX—Software Resources International (SRI) supplies Charon-VAX at www.softresint.com/charon-vax/index.htm. It runs under Windows or Linux on an Intel platform. There is currently no hobbyist license for Charon-VAX. However, it is a robust and supported product.

EVAX—Available at www.forest-edge.net/evax.html, the evax emulator is not complete enough to run VMS, or really any other OS at this writing.

Alpha Emulators

SimOS—This is available at http://simos.stanford.edu.

A.2 Joining Encompass

The next step is to acquire media and licenses. To qualify for a (free) hobbyist license, you must have a (free) associate membership in Encompass. You can do this quickly and easily online. Look at www.encompass.org for an online dialog to apply for membership. Once the necessary form is filled out, it only takes a couple of days for the staff to process your application. Expect to receive your Encompass membership number via e-mail.

A.3 Acquiring Licenses and Media

Both licenses and media are available from www.montagar.com. The licenses are free, and media is only $30. Licenses are issued immediately via e-mail and media takes about a week for delivery. Currently, the OpenVMS/Alpha media include the following:

- OpenVMS Alpha V7.3-1
- DECWindows 1.2.6 (Motif)
- TCP/IP V5.3
- DECnet Phase V and Phase IV
- Compaq C V6.5
- FORTRAN 7.5

As an alternative, if you have access to an OpenVMS CD-ROM set, you may legally use them or copy them for personal use. HP does not control the CD-ROMs, only the product licenses.

Once at the Montagar site, using an online query you may request an OpenVMS/VAX license, an OpenVMS/Alpha license, and licenses for the products listed below. These are full licenses for the software supplied with no capability restrictions. Of course, there is an understanding that the products will only be used by hobbyists, not for commercial endeavors.

Currently there are about 100 products covered by the layered product licenses. The following list of products is copied from the cover letter:

ACMS
ACMS-REM
ACMS-RT
ACMSXP-DEV
ACMSXP-RT
ADA
ADA-PDO
ALLIN1-MAIL-DW-CLIENT
ALLIN1-MAIL-SERVER
ALLIN1-MAIL-SERVER-USER
ALLIN1-MAIL-VT-CLIENT
ALLIN1-MAIL-VT-USER
ALLIN1-MAIL-WAN-SERVER
BASIC
C
CMS
COBOL
CXX-V
DCE-APP-DEV
DCE-CDS
DCE-SECURITY
DCPS-OPEN
DCPS-PLUS
DECDCS-SRV-VA
DECMIGRATE
DECRAM
DECWRITE
DECWRITE-USER
DESKTOP-ACMS
DFS
DFG
DQS
DTM
DTR
DTR-UI-JAPANESE
DVNETEND
DVNETEXT
DW-MOTIF
DW-MOTIF-UI-CESKY
DW-MOTIF-UI-DEUTSC
DW-MOTIF-UI-ESPANO
DW-MOTIF-UI-FRANCA
DW-MOTIF-UI-HANGUL
DW-MOTIF-UI-HANYU
DW-MOTIF-UI-HANZI
DW-MOTIF-UI-HEBREW
DW-MOTIF-UI-ITALIA
DW-MOTIF-UI-JAPANE
DW-MOTIF-UI-MAGYAR
DW-MOTIF-UI-POLSKI
DW-MOTIF-UI-RUSSKI
DW-MOTIF-UI-SLOVEN
DW-MOTIF-UI-SVENSK
DW-SNA-3270-TE-VMS
EXT-MATH-LIB
EXT-MATH-LIB-RT
FMS
FMS-RT-UI-JAPANESE
FMS-UI-HANGUL
FMS-UI-JAPANESE
FORMS
FORMS-RT
FORMS-RT-UI-HANGUL
FORMS-RT-UI-HANYU
FORTRAN
GKS
GKS-RT
GKS-RT-UI-JAPANESE
GKS-UI-JAPANESE
GKS3D
GKS3D-RT
LSE
MACRO64
MAILBUS-400-API
MAILBUS-400-MTA
MMOV-DV
MMOV-RT
MMS
NOTES
OPENVMS-ALPHA-USER
OPS5
PASCAL

PCA
PHIGS
PHIGS-RUNTIME
PHIGS-RUNTIME-UI-JAPAN
PHIGS-UI-JAPANESE
RMSJNL
RTR-CL
RTR-SVR
SQL-DEV
SSU
UCX
VAXSET
VMS-UI-JAPANESE
VMSCLUSTER
VOLSHAD
X25
X25-CLIENT
X500-ADMIN-FACILITY
X500-DIRECTORY-SERVER

B

OpenVMS Site Guide

The following is an outline for a site guide, as discussed in chapter 14.

B.1 Site and Hardware Configuration

Equipment inventory

Equipment layout diagrams

Electrical system

UPS, conditioning, emergency shutoff, alarms

Air conditioning—BTU requirements, current usage, alarms

Safety equipment

Halon, fire extinguishers, heat, smoke, water alarms

VMS configuration

Versions in use on each system

Special tailoring

Patches applied

System-parameter settings

Page-/swap-file sizing

System boot procedures

Console subsystem initialization

Configuration of front panel switches

Normal boot procedures

Conversational boot procedures

Stand-alone backup boot procedures

System startup procedures

Flowchart of startup procedures

Special order dependencies

System shutdown procedures

Preshutdown procedures

Configuration of SYSHUTDWN.COM

Normal shutdown

Shutdown with reboot

Installed optional software products

Details on each installed optional product

Date, version, location, startup, and shutdown procedures

Required VMS version, SYSGEN, and UAF requirements

User account management procedures

Username formats

Single ownership of accounts

Preexpiration of new passwords

Organization of UIC groups

Configuration of the DEFAULT account

Password policy

System login procedures

Flowchart of login process

Global symbols defined

Assigning default print queue

Departmental administrative issues

Staff-organization chart

Outline of staff responsibilities

Maintenance agreement strategies

Operation production jobs

Production job schedule

Servicing job requests

Job rerun procedures

Handling job exceptions

Backups

Requirements dictated by business

Backup strategies

Daily backup procedures

Guide to support resources

Internal

HP and third party

Documentation inventory

Books and publications

System-integrity monitoring

Procedures for detecting and handling the following:

- Disk errors
- Low disk space
- Failed job or process
- Runaway jobs
- Network failures

Security procedures

Requirements of business

Security strategy

Security procedures

Default file protection

Specific protection requirements for major areas

Performance management

Tuning and capacity history

Known bottlenecks

Current capacity and estimated future growth

C

Console Summary and Hardware Characteristics

There are two parts to this appendix. The first deals with console commands for the various VAX and Alpha computers. The second, courtesy of Paul Hardy, is a summary listing of all (as of 1998) VAX and Alpha computers, including CPU speed, code names, and so forth.

C.1 Console Summary

Most system-management tasks are similar, whether you manage a MicroVAX or VAX 6000. However, boot procedures can vary dramatically from machine to machine because of the variety of system buses to which a boot device might be attached. Fortunately, systems with the same bus type have similar boot procedures. As a result, boot procedures described in chapter 4 are organized by the various system bus types described in table C.1.

Table C.1 *VMS System Bus Types*

Bus	Systems
QBUS	MicroVAX 2000, VAXstation II/GPX, Microvax 3500/3600, VAXstation 3200/3500, MicroVAX 3800/3900
SCSI	MicroVAX 3100, VAXstation 3100, VAXstation 4000, VAX 4000-100, VAXstation 3520/3540
DSSI	MicroVAX 3300/3400, VAX 4000, VAXft 3000
UNIBUS	VAX 11/730, VAX 11/780, VAX 11/780, VAX 11/785, VAX 8600/8650
BI	VAX 8200/8300, VAX 8250/8350, VAX 8500/8530/8550, VAX 8700/8800, VAX 8810/8820/8830/8840
XMI	VAX 6000, VAX 9000

Table C.1 *VMS System Bus Types (continued)*

Bus	Systems
ALPHA	AXP 3000, AXP 4000, AXP 7000, AXP 10000

C.1.1 QBUS-based Systems

MicroVAX II/VAXstation II

Console CPU	Main CPU	
Console O/S	N/A	
Console modes	Console or program	
Console load device	ROM	
Terminal control	Circle/dot switch	
System restart control	Circle/dot switch	
Console mode switch	<<BREAK>> or <HALT> twice	
Program mode switch	>>> CONT	
Default boot device	N/A	
Default boot control flags	N/A	
Power-on boot	Sniffer Boot	
Manual boot command	>>> B	Same as power-on boot
	>>> B device	Boot from device
	>>> B/xxxxxxxx	Manually specify control flags
Valid devices and sniffer boot order	DUA2, DUA0, DUA1, MUA0, ESA0 (Ethernet)	

Terminal and Restart Control

Terminal Control
Circle/dot Switch

ENABLE

DISABLE

Restart Control
Circle/dot Switch

HALT

BOOT

Sniffer Boot

On these systems you cannot configure a default boot device. Rather, the system attempts to boot from available devices in the order indicated in the following table.

MicroVAX 2000/VAXstation 2000

Console CPU	Main CPU	
Console O/S	N/A	
Console modes	Console or program	
Console load device	ROM	
Terminal control	None	
System restart control	>>> TEST 53	
Console mode switch	Press <HALT> once	
Program mode switch	>>> CONT	
Default boot device	>>> TEST 51	
Default boot control flags	>>> TEST 52	
Power-on boot	Boot from default boot device	
Manual boot command	>>> B	Sniffer boot (note: not same as power-on)
	>>> B device	Boot from device
	>>> B/flags	Manually specify control flags
Valid devices and sniffer boot order	DUA0, ..., DUB0, ..., MUA0, XQA0 (Ethernet)	

Sniffer Boot

On these systems a sniffer boot is initiated when you issue a manual boot (e.g., >>> B), even if you have configured a default boot device. A sniffer boot attempts to boot successively from all available devices in the order indicated in the foregoing above. If you need to perform a manual boot, be sure to specify a device explicitly; otherwise, the system performs a sniffer boot and possibly boots from a device other than the one you intended.

Configuring Default Boot Device

`>>> TEST 51`	Displays current default boot device

`DUA0?>>> device`	Enters new boot device name to change or <<RETURN>> to retain current setting

Configuring Default Boot Control Flags

`>>> TEST 52`	Displays current setting for default boot control flags
`00000000?>>> control flags`	Enter new control flags, or press <<RETURN>> to retain current setting

Configuring System Restart Control

`>>> TEST 53`	Displays current setting for restart control
`2?>>> restart-value`	Enter new restart value (2=BOOT, 3=HALT) or press <<RETURN>> to retain current setting

MicroVAX 3500/3600, VAXstation 3200/3500

Terminal and Restart Control

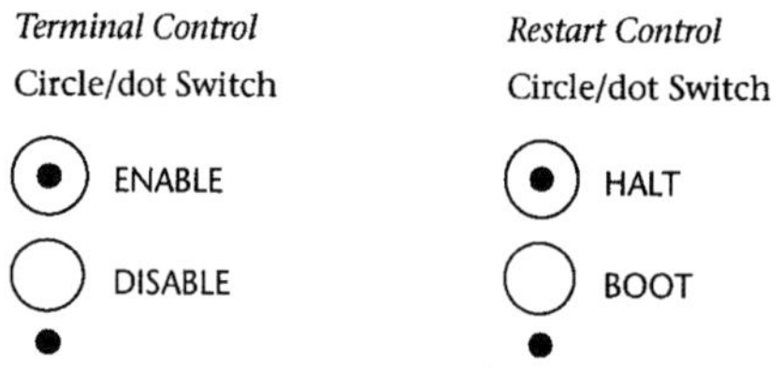

Terminal Control	*Restart Control*
Circle/dot Switch	Circle/dot Switch
(•) ENABLE	(•) HALT
( ) DISABLE	( ) BOOT

Sniffer Boot

On these systems, a sniffer boot is initiated when you issue a manual boot (e.g., >>> B), even if you have configured a default boot device. A sniffer boot attempts to successively boot from all valid devices in the order indicated in the table. If you need to perform a manual boot, be sure to explicitly specify a device, otherwise the system performs a sniffer boot and possibly boots from a device other than the one you intended.

Configuring Default Boot Device

`>>> SHOW BOOT`	Displays current default boot device

Console CPU	Main CPU	
Console O/S	N/A	
Console modes	Console or program	
Console load device	ROM	
Terminal control	Circle/dot switch	
System restart control	Circle/dot switch	
Console mode switch	<BREAK> or <HALT> twice	
Program mode switch	>>> CONT	
Default boot device	>>> SET BOOT device	
Default boot control flags	>>> SET BFLG control-flags	
Power-on boot	Boot from default boot device	
Manual boot command	>>> B	Sniffer boot
	>>> B device	Boot from device
	>>> B/xxxxxxxx flags	Manually specify control
Valid devices and sniffer boot order	Device unit numbers 0 ... 15	

`>>> SHOW DEVICE`	Displays connected devices
`>>> SET BOOT device`	Set default boot device

Configuring Default Boot Control Flags

`>>> SHOW BFLG`	Displays current setting for default boot control flags
`>>> SET BFLG control-flags`	Set default boot control flags

MicroVAX 3800/3900

Console CPU	Main CPU
Console O/S	N/A
console modes	Console or Program
Console load device	ROM
Terminal control	Circle/dot Switch
System restart control	Circle/dot Switch

Console mode switch	<<BREAK>> or <HALT> twice	
Program mode switch	>>> CONT	
Default boot device	>>> SET BOOT device	
Default boot control flags	>>> SET BFLG control-flags	
Power-on boot	Boot from default boot device, if configured; otherwise, boot from query boot	
Manual boot command	>>> B	Same as power-on boot
	>>> B device	Boot from device
	>>> B/xxxxxxxx	Manually specify control flags
Valid devices and sniffer boot order	DJCU, DUCU, MUCU, XQAU (where c = controller and u = unit)	

Terminal and Restart Control

Terminal Control	*Restart Control*
Circle/dot Switch	Circle/dot Switch
ENABLE	HALT
DISABLE	BOOT

Query Boot

When powered on, the system boots from the default boot device. If the device is not configured, the system displays available devices on the console terminal and waits 30 seconds for input. If no input is received within the allowed time, the system attempts to boot from the network device.

Configuring Default Boot Device

`>>> SHOW BOOT`	Displays current default boot device
`>>> SHOW DEVICE`	Displays connected devices
`>>> SET BOOT device`	Set default boot device

Configuring Default Boot Control Flags

`>>> SHOW BFLG`	Displays current setting for default boot control flags
`>>> SET BFLG control-flags`	Set default boot control flags

C.1.2 SCSI-Based Systems

MicroVAX/VAXstation 3100-30,38,48

Console CPU	Main CPU	
Console O/S	N/A	
Console modes	Console or program	
Console load device	ROM	
Terminal control	N/A	
System restart control	>>> SET HALT restart-value	
Console mode switch	<<BREAK>> or <HALT> button	
Program mode switch	>>> CONT	
Default boot device	>>> SET BOOT device	
Default boot control flags	>>> SET BFLG control-flags	
Power-on boot	Boot from default boot device, or if default device is not configured, network device	
Manual boot command	>>> B	Same as power-on boot
	>>> B device	Boot from device
	>>> B/xxxxxxxx	Manually specify control flags
Valid devices	DKAU00, DKBU00, ESA0, MKAU00, MKBU00 (where u = unit)	

Configuring Restart Control

`>>> SHOW HALT`	Displays current setting for restart control
`>>> SET BFLG control-flags`	Set default boot control flags (where 2 = BOOT, and 3 = HALT)

Configuring Default Boot Device

`>>> SHOW BOOT`	Displays current default boot device
`>>> SHOW DEVICE`	Displays connected devices
`>>> SET BOOT device`	Set default boot device

Configuring Default Boot Control Flags

`>>> SHOW BFLG`	Displays current setting for default boot control flags
`>>> SET BFLG control-flags`	Set default boot control flags

MicroVAX/VAXstation 3100-40, 76, 80, 4000-60, 4000-VLC

Console CPU	Main CPU	
Console O/S	N/A	
Console modes	Console or program	
Console load device	ROM	
Terminal control	N/A	
System restart control	>>> SET HALT restart-value	
Console mode switch	<<BREAK>> or HALT button	
Program mode switch	>>> CONT	
Default boot device	>>> SET BOOT device1, device2	
Default boot control flags	>>> SET BFLG control-flags	
Power-on boot	Boot from default boot device or, if default device is not configured, the network device	
Manual boot command	>>> B	Same as power-on boot
	>>> B device	Boot from device
	>>> B/xxxxxxxx	Manually specify control flags
Valid boot devices	DKAu00 or MKAu00 (where u = unit, can boot only from controller A)	

VAXstation 3520/3540

Console CPU	Main CPU
Console O/S	N/A
Console modes	Console or program
Console load device	ROM
Terminal control	N/A
System restart control	CPUxx>>> SET HALT restart-value

Console mode switch	<<BREAK>> or <HALT> button
Program mode switch	CPUxx>>> CONT
Default boot device	CPUxx>>> SET BOOT device1, device2
Default boot control flags	CPUxx>>> SET BFLG control-flags
Power-on boot	Boot from default boot device or, if default device is not configured, query boot
Manual boot command	CPUXX>>> B Not valid (must specify device) CPUXX>>> B device Boot from device CPUXX>>> B/xxxxxxxx Manually specify control flags
Valid boot devices	DKA000, DKA100–DKA700, ESA0, MUA0

C.1.3 DSSI-based Systems

MicroVAX 3300/3400

Console CPU	Main CPU
Console O/S	N/A
Console modes	Console or program
Console load device	ROM
Terminal control	N/A
System restart control	>>> SET HALT restart-value
Console mode switch	<<BREAK>> or <HALT> button
Program mode switch	>>> CONT
Default boot device	>>> SET BOOT device
Default boot control flags	>>> SET BFLG control-flags
Power-on boot	Boot from default boot device or, if default device is not configured, boot from network

Manual boot command	>>> B Not valid (must specify device)
	>>> B device Boot from device
	>>> B/xxxxxxxx Manually specify control flags

Valid boot devices	[NODE$]DIAU, DUCU, DLCU, [NODE$]MIAU, MUCU, ESA0, XQCU

VAX 4000 Model 200,300,400,500,600

Console CPU	Main CPU	
Console O/S	N/A	
Console modes	Console or program	
Console load device	ROM	
Terminal control	N/A	
System restart control	>>> SET HALT restart-value	
Console mode switch	<<BREAK>> or <HALT> button	
Program mode switch	>>> CONT	
Default boot device	>>> SET BOOT device1, device2	
Default boot control flags	>>> SET BFLG control-flags	
Power-on boot	Boot from default boot device, or if default device is not configured, perform query boot	
Manual boot command	>>> B	Not valid (must specify device)
	>>> B device	Boot from device
	>>> B/xxxxxxxx	Manually specify control flags
Valid boot devices	[NODE$]DICU, DUCU, DKAU, MICU, MUCU, EZA0, XQCU	

VAXft 3000-310

Console CPU	Main CPU
Console O/S	N/A
Console modes	Console and program
Console load device	ROM
Terminal control	Local console disable switch
	Pushed in: DISABLED
	Pulled out: ENABLED

System restart control	N/A	
Console mode switch	<<BREAK>> key	
Program mode switch	>>> PIO or SET TERM PROG	
Default boot device	>>> SET BOOT/P DEFAULT device	
Default boot control flags	>>> SET BOOT/P DEFAULT /R5:xxxxxxxx device	
Power-on boot	Boots using boot parameters associated with the DEFAULT boot name	
Manual boot command	>>> B	Same as power-on boot
	>>> B boot-name	Boot using defined boot-name
Valid boot devices	DICU, MICU, EPCU [where c = controller (A,B,F, or G) and u = unit]	

C.1.4 XMI-based Systems

VAX 6000

Console CPU	Main CPU	
Console O/S	N/A	
Console modes	Console or program	
Console load device	ROM or TK tape drive	
Terminal control	Upper front	
	Panel switch	Terminal control
	ENABLE	ENABLED
	SECURE	DISABLED
System restart control	If terminal control DISABLED, then BOOT; otherwise, depends on lower switch settings:	
	Lower front	
	Panel switch	Boot action
	UPDATE	HALT
	HALT	HALT
	AUTO START	BOOT
Console mode switch	<CTRL/P> or <HALT> button	
Program mode switch	>>> CONT	
Default boot device	>>> SET BOOT DEFAULT /... device	

Default boot control flags	>>> SET BOOT DEFAULT /R5:xxxxxxxx/... device	
Power-on boot	Boots using boot parameters associated with the DEFAULT boot name	
Manual boot command	>>> B	Same as power-on boot
	>>> B boot-name	Boot using defined boot-name
Valid boot devices	DUU, ET0, MU0, CSU (where u = unit number)	

Default Boot Device and Control Flags

You can display the currently defined boot names using the following command:

```
>>> SHOW BOOT

DEFAULT       /R5:00000000 /XMI:E /BI:4 /NODE:00000100 DU0
STAB          /R5:E0000000 /XMI:E /BI:4 /NODE:00000100 DU0
CONV          /R5:00000001 /XMI:E /BI:4 /NODE:00000100 DU0
```

By default, the system boots using the parameters and device specified by the DEFAULT boot name. You can modify the default parameters using the following command:

```
>>> SET BOOT DEFAULT/XMI:x/BI:y/NODE:z/R3:a/R5:b DUu
```

where u = disk unit #

x = XMI adapter #

y = BI Bus #

n = HSC[[AU: pls spell out HSC]] node list

a = Value to pass to R3 (for Phase I shadowing)

b = Value to pass to R5 (boot control flags)

Creating Additional Boot Names

The terminal control switch must be set to the Update position before you can modify boot names.

```
>>> SET BOOT CONV/XMI:E/BI:4/NODE:00000100/R5:00000001 DU0
>>> BOOT CONV
```

```
>>> SET BOOT STAB/XMI:E/BI:4/NODE:00000100/R5:E0000000 DU0
>>> BOOT STAB
>>> SET BOOT ALT/XMI:E/BI:4/NODE:00000100/R5:00000000 DU1
>>> BOOT ALT
```

VAX 9000

Console CPU	Modified MicroVAX II	
Console O/S	VAXeln	
Console modes	Console and program	
Console load device	RD54	
Terminal control	Terminal control switch	
System restart control	Front panel switch: BOOT RESTART/BOOT RESTART/HALT HALT	
Console mode switch	<CTRL/P> or <HALT> button	
Program mode switch	>>> CONT or SET TERM/PROG	
Default boot device	Maintained in boot files on console device	
Default boot control flags	Maintained in boot files on console device	
Power-on boot	Executes DEFBOO.CMD boot file located on console device	
Manual boot command	>>> B	Same as Power-on Boot
	>>> B xyz boot	Executes xyzBOO.CMD file
Valid boot devices		

ALPHA and VAX 7000/10000 Systems

Alpha AXP 3000, Alpha AXP 4000

Alpha AXP 7000, 10000 and VAX 7000, 10000

Console CPU	Main CPU
Console O/S	N/A

Console modes	Console or program
Console load device	N/A
Terminal control	N/A
System restart control	N/A
Console mode switch	<CTRL/P> or <HALT> button
Program mode switch	>>> CONT
Default boot device	>>> SET BOOTDEF_DEV device
Default boot control flags	>>> SET BOOT_OSFLAGS control-flags
Power-on boot	Boots from default boot device
Manual boot command	>>> B — Same as power-on boot >>> B -FLAG r,f — Manually specify control flags (where r = system root and f = boot control flags)
Valid boot devices	>>> SHOW device

Default Boot Device and Control Flags

Configure these parameters by establishing values for the environment variables BOOTDEF_DEV and BOOT_OSFLAGS. You can view the current contents of all environmental variables by using the following command:

```
>>> SHOW
```

You can view a list of available devices by entering the following command:

```
>>> SHOW DEVICE
```

Finally, use the SET command to change environment variables, as follows:

```
>>> SET BOOTDEF_DEV DKA100
>>> SET BOOT_OSFLAGS A,1  ! Conversational boot from [SYSA]
```

C.1.5 UNIBUS-Based Systems

VAX 11/780, VAX 11/785

Console CPU	Dedicated PDP-11	
Console O/S	N/A	
Console modes	console and program	
Console load device	RX01 floppy	
Terminal control	**Switch position**	**Terminal control**
	OFF	No power applied to CPU
	LOCAL	ENABLED
	LOCAL DISABLE	DISABLED
	REMOTE	ENABLED
	REMOTE DISABLE	DISABLED
System restart control	ON	Equivalent to RESTART/BOOT
	OFF	Equivalent to RESTART/HALT
Console mode switch	<CTRL/P> or <HALT> button	
Program mode switch	>>> SET TERM PROG	
Default boot device	Configured in boot file: DEFBOO.CMD	
Default boot control flags	Configured in boot file: DEFBOO.CMD	
Power-on boot	Executes boot file: DEFBOO.CMD	
Manual boot command	>>> B	Same as power-on boot
	>>> B xyz	Executes boot file: xyzBOO.CMD
	>>> @file	Executes boot file: file
	>>> B CS1	Boot stand-alone backup from RX01
Template boot files:		
Massbus #1	DB0BOO.CMD	
Massbus #2	DBBBOO.CMD	
Unibus #1	DU0BOO.CMD (for RA-style disks)	
Unibus #2	N/A	
CI	CIBOO.CMD (for HSC-attached disks)	

VAX 8600/8650

Console CPU	Dedicated PDP-11 (T-11)
Console O/S	RT-11
Console modes	Console and program

Console load device	RL02 removable disk	
Terminal control	Switch position	Terminal control
	OFF	N/A
	LOCAL	ENABLED
	LOCAL DISABLE	DISABLED
	REMOTE	ENABLED
	REMOTE/DISABLE	DISABLED
System restart control	Switch position restart control	
	BOOT	BOOT
	RESTART/BOOT	RESTART/BOOT
	RESTART/HALT	RESTART/HALT
	HALT	HALT
Console mode switch	<CTRL/P> or <HALT> button	
Program mode switch	>>> CONT	
Default boot device	Configured in boot file: DEFBOO.CMD	
Default boot control flags	Configured in boot file: DEFBOO.CMD	
Power-on boot	Executes boot file: DEFBOO.CMD	
Manual boot command	>>> B	Same as power-on boot
	>>> B xyz	Executes boot file: xyzBOO.CMD
	>>> @file	Executes boot file: file
	>>> B CS1	Boot stand-alone backup from RX01
Template boot files:		
Massbus #1	DB0BOO.CMD	
Massbus #2	N/A	
Unibus #1	DU0BOO.CMD (for RA-style disks)	
Unibus #2	N/A	
Ci	CIBOO.CMD (for HSC-attached disks)	

C.1.6 BI-based Systems

VAX 8200/8300/8250/8350

Console CPU	Main CPU
Console O/S	N/A
Console modes	Console or program

Console load device	2 RX50 floppy drives	
Terminal control		
System restart control	Lower key: AUTO START—BOOT	
Console mode switch	<CTRL/P> or <HALT> button	
Program mode switch	>>> CONT	
Default boot device	Configured in boot file: DEFBOO.CMD	
Default boot control flags	Configured in boot file: DEFBOO.CMD	
Power-on boot	Executes boot file: DEFBOO.CMD	
Manual boot command	>>> B	Same as power-on boot
	>>> B device	Boot from local device
	>>> B/R5:800 CSA1	Invoke BOOT58
	BOOT58>> @file	Executes specified boot file
	>>> B CSA1	Boot Stand-alone Backups from RX50
Template boot files:		
BI bus	KDBBOO.CMD	
CI bus	CIBOO.CMD	

VAX 8500/8530/8550/8700/8800

Console CPU	Dedicated PDP-11 microcomputer (Pro 380)
Console O/S	P/OS
Console modes	Console and program
Console load device	2 RX50 floppy drives and RD53
Terminal control	ENABLE: >>> ENABLE LOCAL CONSOLE DISABLE: >>> DISABLE LOCAL CONSOLE
System restart control	BOOT: >>> ENABLE AUTO POWERON and >>> ENABLE AUTO BOOT HALT: >>> DISABLE AUTO BOOT
Console mode switch	<CTRL/P>
Program mode switch	>>> SET TERM PROG
Default boot device	Configured in boot file: DEFBOO.COM
Default boot control flags	Configured in boot file: DEFBOO.COM

Power-on boot	Executes boot file: DEFBOO.COM	
Manual boot command	>>> B	Same as Power-on Boot
	>>> B xyz	Executes xyzBOO.COM and passes "u" as drive unit number (R3); xyz can be: BDA, UDA, or BCI
	>>> @file	Executes specified boot file
	>>> @CSBOO.COM	Boot stand-alone backups from RX50
Template boot files:		
BI bus	BDABOO.COM	
Unibus	UDABOO.COM	
CI bus	BCIBOO.COM	

VAX 8810/8820/8830/8840

Console CPU	Dedicated MicroVAX II	
Console O/S	Modified VMS	
Console modes	Console and program	
Console load device	TK50 and RD53	
Terminal control	ENABLE: >>> ENABLE LOCAL CONSOLE DISABLE: >>> DISABLE LOCAL CONSOLE	
System restart control	BOOT: >>> ENABLE AUTO POWERON and >>> ENABLE AUTO BOOT HALT: >>> DISABLE AUTO BOOT	
Console mode switch	<CTRL/P> or <HALT> button	
Program mode switch	PS-CIO-0> CONT	
Default boot device	Configured in boot file: DEFBOO.COM	
Default boot control flags	Configured in boot file: DEFBOO.COM	
Power-on Boot	Executes boot file: DEFBOO.COM	
Manual boot command	PS-CIO-0>> B	Same as power-on boot
	PS-CIO-0>> B xyzu	Executes xyzBOO.COM and passes "u" as drive unit number (R3). xyz can be: BDA, UDA, or BCI
	PS-CIO-0>> @file	Executes specified boot file
	PS-CIO-0>> @CSABOO	Boot stand-alone backup from RD53
Template boot files:		

BI bus	BDABOO.COM
Unibus	UDABOO.COM
CI bus	BCIBOO.COM

C.2 VMS CPU Model Summary (May 12, 1998)

The following table tries to summarizes the whole publicly known Digital VAX and Alpha model range by CPU type, categorized by processor families and then by subtype, giving approximate chronological order. The following information is given:

- The top byte of the SID in hex (containing the CPU type)
- Processor subtype (XCPU or SYSTYPE)
- Processor ID for VAXes
- Clock speed in MHz for AXPs
- Approximate speed, relative to a nominal VAX-11/780:
  - in VUPS for early machines
  - in SPECmark89 (S) for later VAX workstations
  - in SPECint92 and SPECfp92 for most AXPs
  - scaled up SPECint95*38 & SPECfp95*42 for later Alphas
  - scaled up SPECint_rate_base*5.2 & SPECfp_rate_base*5.0 for even later Alphas
- Main I/O bus type (U=UNIBUS, M=MASSBUS, C=CI, Q=QBUS, B=BI, D=DSSI, X=XMI, T=Turbochannel, F=Futurebus+, S=SCSI, E=EISA, P=PCI)
- Model names
- Nickname

Information is from publicly available sources such as DEC brochures and press releases, together with the description of SYS$GETSYI in the VMS documentation, and from $PRDEF, $VAXDEF, and $ALPHADEF in the system macro library. This is supplemented with information from USENET group comp.os.vms. Models thought to be current are marked by a leading '*'.

This list is not an official publication—ask DEC if you want confirmed figures! In the quickly changing world of computer hardware, data probably out of date when written. However, please let me know of any inaccuracies or omissions.

Paul Hardy

Table C.2 *VAX CPUs*

SID	X	Id	VUPs	Bus	Model Name	Nickname
					700 series (1977)	
01	—	780	1.0	U,M,C	VAX-11/780	Star
01	—	780	1.8	U,M,C	VAX-11/782	Atlas
01	—	780	3.5	U,M,C	VAX-11/784	(VAXimus)
01	—	780	1.5	U,M,C	VAX-11/785	Superstar
02	—	750	0.6	U,M,C	VAX-11/750, 751	Comet
03	—	730	0.3	U	VAX-11/730, 725	Nebula, LCN
04	—	790	4.0	U,M,C	VAX 8600,	Venus
04	—	790	7.0	U,M,C	VAX 8650	Morningstar
					8000 series (1986)	
05	—	8SS	0.9–2	B,C	VAX 8200, 8300, 8250, 8350	Scorpio
05	—	8SS	0.9–2	B,C	VAXstation 8000	Lynx
06	—	8NN	3	B,C	VAX 8500	Flounder
06	—	8NN	4/6	B,C	VAX 8530, 8550	Skipjack
06	—	8NN	6/12	B,C	VAX 8700, 8800	Nautilus

Table C.2 *VAX CPUs (continued)*

SID	X	Id	VUPs	Bus	Model Name	Nickname
					MicroVAX I (1984)	**SID = 117440512**
07	—	UV1	0.3	Q	MicroVAX I, VAXstation I	Seahorse
					MicroVAX II series (1985)	**SID = 134217728**
08	1	UV2	0.9	Q	MicroVAX II,VAXstation II	Mayflower
08	1	UV2	0.9	Q	VAXstation II/GPX	Caylith
08	4	410	0.9	none	MicroVAX 2000	TeamMate
08	4	410	0.9	none	VAXstation 2000	VAXstar
08	?	UV2	0.9–28	??	MicroVAX M31	Andromeda
					CVAX chip series (1987)	**SID = 167772160**
0A	1	650	2.8	Q	MicroVAX 3500, 3600	Mayfair
0A	1	65D	2.8	Q	VAXstation 3200, 3500	Mayfair/GPX
0A	1	640	2.4	Q,D	MicroVAX 3300, 3400	Mayfair II
0A	1	655	3.8	Q	MicroVAX 3800, 3900	Mayfair III
0A	2	9CC	2.8	X,B,C	VAX 6000 model 210	Calypso/XCP
0A	2	9CC	3.8	X,B,C	VAX 6000 model 310	Calypso/XCP
0A	3	60	3–10	Q	VAXstation 3520, 3540	Firefox
0A	4	420	2.8	S	VAXstation 3100 models 30, 40	PVAX
0A	4	420	2.4	S	MicroVAX 3100 models 10, 20	Teammate II

Table C.2 *VAX CPUs (continued)*

SID	X	Id	VUPs	Bus	Model Name	Nickname
0A	4	420	3.5	S	MicroVAX 3100 models 10e, 20e	Teammate II
0A	4	420	3.8	S	VAXstation 3100 models 38, 48	PVAX rev#7
*0A	7	510	2.4	D	VAXft model 110	Cirrus
0A	7	520	3.8	D	VAXft model 310	Cirrus
					Rigel chip series (1990)	**SID = 184549376**
0B	1	670	8.0	Q,D	VAX 4000 model 300	Pele
0B	2	9RR	7–36	X,B,C	VAX 6000 model 410-460	Calypso/XRP
0B	4	43	7.6	S	VAXstation 3100 model 76	RigelMAX
0B	4	43?	7?	S	MicroVAX 3100 model 40	??
					Aquarius series (1990)	**SID = 234881024**
0E	—	9AR	40–157	X,B,C	VAX 9000 models 210, 410-440	Aridus
0E	—	9AQ	40–157	X,B	VAX 9000 models 400-800	Aquarius
					Polarstar series (1988)	SID = 285212672
11	—	8PS	6–22	B,C	VAX 8810 to 8840	Polarstar
					Mariah chip series (1991)	SID = 301989888
12	2	1202	13–58	XBCD	VAX 6000 model 510-560	Calypso/XMP
12	4	46	12	T,S	VAXstation 4000 model 60	PMariah
12	4	46	12	S	MicroVAX 3100 model 80	Waverley/M

Table C.2 *VAX CPUs (continued)*

SID	X	Id	VUPs	Bus	Model Name	Nickname
*12	4	46	16	S	MicroVAX 3100 model 85, 88	Waverley/M+
					NVAX chip series (1991)	**SID = 318767104**
13	1	690	16	Q,D	VAX 4000 model 400	Omega
13	1	69D	24	Q,D	VAX 4000 model 500, 500A	Omega/N
13	1	69D	32	Q,D	VAX 4000 model 505A	Omega/N+
13	1	1303	24	Q,D	VAX 4000 model 100, 100A	Cheetah-Q
13	1	1303	32	Q,D	VAX 4000 model 105A	Cheetah-Q+
13	1	1303	???	Q,D	VAX 4000 model 106A	Cheetah-Q++
*13	1	1303	38	Q,D	VAX 4000 model 108	Cheetah-Q++
13	1	700	32	Q,D	VAX 4000 model 600, 600A	Omega/N+
13	1	700	40	Q,D	VAX 4000 model 700A	Legacy
*13	1	700	45	Q,D	VAX 4000 model 705A	Legacy+
13	2	1302	32–150	XBDC	VAX 6000 models 610-660	Neptune
13	4	49	32.8 S	T,S	VAXstation 4000 model 90	Cougar
13	4	49	38.5 S	T,S	VAXstation 4000 model 90A	Cougar+
*13	4	49	46 S?	T,S	VAXstation 4000 model 96	Cougar++
13	4	49	24	S	MicroVAX 3100 model 90	Cheetah

Table C.2 *VAX CPUs (continued)*

SID	X	Id	VUPs	Bus	Model Name	Nickname
13	4	49	32	S	MicroVAX 3100 model 95	Cheetah+
*13	4	49	38	S	MicroVAX 3100 model 96, 98	Cheetah++
*13	7	600	30	D	VAXft model 810	Jetstream
					SOC chip series (1991)	**SID = 335544320**
14	1	660	5.0	Q,D	VAX 4000 model 200	Spitfire
14	4	440	6.2 S	S	VAXstation 4000 VLC (model 30)	PVAX2/VLC
14	4	440	5.0	S	MicroVAX 3100 models 30, 40	Waverley/S
14	7	550	6.0	D	VAXft model 410, 610	Cirrus II
					NVAX+ chip series (1991)	SID = 385875968
17	3	1701	35–120	X,C,D	VAX 7000 models 610-640	Laser/Neon
17	3	1701	35–120	X,C,D	VAX 10000 models 610-640	Blazer
					NVAX5 chip series (1994)	**SID = ?????????**
17	3	1701	50–250	X,C,D	VAX 7000 models 710-760	Laser/Krypton
*17	3	1701	60–300	X,C,D	VAX 7000 models 810-860	Laser/Krypton+

Table C.3 *Alpha CPUs*

SID	S	Clock	SPEC92	Bus	Model Name	Nickname
					EV4 (21064) chip series (1992)	**SID=–2147483648**

Table C.3 *Alpha CPUs (continued)*

SID	S	Clock	SPEC92	Bus	Model Name	Nickname
80	2	160	95/138	F,D,S	DEC 4000 model 610	Cobra
*80	2	190	122/185	F,D,S	DEC 4000 model 710	Fang
80	3	180	103/176	X,C,D	DEC 7000 model 610	Laser/Ruby
80	3	200	133/200	X,C,D	DEC 7000 model 610	Laser/Ruby+
80	3	200	107/200	X,C,D	DEC 10000 model 610	Blazer/Ruby
80	4	150	84/128	T,S	DEC 3000 model 500W or S	Flamingo
80	4	200	130/184	T,S	DEC 3000 model 800W or S	Flamingo II
80	4	133	75/112	T,S	DEC 3000 model 400W or S	Sandpiper
80	4	175	114/162	T,S	DEC 3000 model 600W or S	Sandpiper+
80	4	200	111/164	T,S	DEC 3000 model 500X	Hot Pink
80	4	150	81/110	T,S	DEC 3000 model 300	Pelican
80	4	100	46/63	S	DEC 3000 model 300L	Pelica
80	4	125	68/77	S	DEC 3000 model 300LX	Pelica+
80	4	175	90/102	T,S	DEC 3000 model 300X	Pelican+
80	6	150	81/110	S,E	DEC 2000 model 300 (pc/150)	Jensen
80	9	200	124/160	P,S,E	DEC 2100 model A500MP	Sable
80	9	200	127/161	P,S,E	AlphaServer 2000 4/200	Demi-Sable

Table C.3 *Alpha CPUs (continued)*

SID	S	Clock	SPEC92	Bus	Model Name	Nickname
80	?	200	136/177	P,S,E	AlphaServer 1000 4/200	Mikasa
80	?	166	116/135	P,S,E	AlphaStation 200 4/166	Mustang
80	?	100	75/95	P,S,E	AlphaStation 200 4/100	??
80	?	166	117/140	P,S,E	AlphaServer 400 4/166	Mustang S
					EV45 (21064A) chip series (1994)	**SID=–2147483648**
80	4	225	163/231	T,S	DEC 3000 model 700W	Sandpiper45
80	4	275	189/264	T,S	DEC 3000 model 900W or S	Flamingo 45
80	3	275	201/293	X,C,D	DEC 7000 model 710	Laser/Ruby45
80	?	233	158/184	P,S,E	AlphaStation 200 4/233	Mustang
80	?	233	158/184	P,S,E	AlphaStation 400 4/233	Mikasa
80	9	275	181/260	P,S,E	AlphaServer 2000 4/275	Demi-Sable45
80	9	275	158/184	P,S,E	AlphaServer 2100 4/233	Sable45
80	9	275	200/292	P,S,E	AlphaServer 2100 4/275	Sable45
80	?	233	165/223	P,S,E	AlphaServer 1000 4/233	Mikasa
80	?	266	199/263	P,S,E	AlphaServer 1000 4/266	Mikasa
*80	?	266	199/263	P,S,E	AlphaServer 300 4/266	??
80	?	266	199/263	P,S,E	AlphaStation 250 4/266	??

Table C.3 *Alpha CPUs (continued)*

SID	S	Clock	SPEC92	Bus	Model Name	Nickname
80	?	233	180/230	P,S,E	AlphaStation 255/233	??
80	?	300	215/295	P,S,E	AlphaStation 255/300	??
					EV5 (21164) chip series (1995)	**SID=–2147483648**
80	3	300	336/507	XPFCS E	AlphaServer 8400 5/300	??
80	3	350	432/602	XPFCS E	AlphaServer 8400 5/300	??
80	3	300	336/507	P,S,E	AlphaServer 8200 5/300	??
80	3	250	277/410	P,S,E	AlphaServer 2000 5/250	Demi-Sable5
80	3	250	277/410	P,S,E	AlphaServer 2100 5/250	Sable EV5
*80	?	400	*12/17	P,S,E	AlphaServer 4100 5/400	??
*80	?	466	*14/19	P,S,E	AlphaServer 4100 5/466	??
*80	?	533	*17/22	P,S,E	AlphaServer 4100 5/533	??
*80	?	400	*12/17	P,S,E	AlphaServer 1200 5/400	??
*80	?	533	*17/22	P,S,E	AlphaServer 1200 5/533	??
*80	3	333	*10/13	P,S,E	AlphaServer 800 5/333	??
*80	3	400	*10/13	P,S,E	AlphaServer 800 5/400	??
*80	3	500	*10/13	P,S,E	AlphaServer 800 5/500	??
80	?	266	288/428	P,S,E	AlphaStation 600 5/266	??

Table C.3 *Alpha CPUs (continued)*

SID	S	Clock	SPEC92	Bus	Model Name	Nickname
80	?	333	362/554	P,S,E	AlphaStation 600 5/333	??
80	?	266	280/400	P,S,E	AlphaStation 500/266	??
80	?	333	350/500	P,S,E	AlphaStation 500/333	??
					EV56 (21164A) chip series (1996)	**SID= –2147483648**
80	3	440	*14/17	P,S,E	AlphaServer 8200 5/440	??
80	3	625	*18/21	P,S,E	AlphaServer 8200 5/625	??
80	3	440	*14/17	X,P,F, C,S,E	AlphaServer 8400 5/440	??
80	3	625	*18/21	X,P,F, C,S,E	AlphaServer 8400 5/440	??
80	?	400	420/600	P,S,E	AlphaStation 500/400	Brett
80	?	500	570/840	P,S,E	AlphaStation 500/500	Brett
80	?	433	523/790	P,S,E	Personal WS 433au	??
80	?	500	590/842	P,S,E	Personal WS 500au	??
80	?	600	691/930	P,S,E	Personal WS 600au	??

D

OpenVMS Privileges

OpenVMS privileges are separated into the following six categories:

OPENVMS CATEGORY	Meaning
NORMAL	Grants normal privileges
GROUP	Grants access to users in the same UIC group
DEVOUR	Provides potential to consume system resources
SYSTEM	Potentially affects system processes and resources
FILE	Allows user to bypass file security
ALL	Allows user complete system access

The purpose of the following tables is to give you an idea of the DCL functions enabled by various privileges. These are arranged in ascending order so that, for instance, a user with DEVOUR privilege also has GROUP and NORMAL privileges

Table D.1 *NORMAL Privileges*

Privilege	Allowed Functions	Description
NETMBX	$ SET HOST	Creates an interactive login to a remote system
TMPMBX	$ SPAWN	Creates a subprocess

Table D.2 *GROUP Privileges*

Privilege	Allowed Functions	Description
GROUP	$ SHOW ENTRY $ STOP PROCESS $ SET PROCESS	Affect objects in the same UIC group
GRPPRV	File operations	Access files in the same UIC group via SYSTEM access category

Table D.3 *DEVOUR Privileges*

Privilege	Allowed Functions	Description
ACNT	$ RUN/DETACHED/NOACC	Bypass VMS accounting
ALLSPOOL	$ ALLOCATE device	Allocate a spooled device
BUGCHK	N/A	Create bug-check error log entries
EXQUOTA	$ CREATE	Exceed disk quota
GRPNAM	$ DEFINE/GROUP $ DISMOUNT/GROUP $ MOUNT/GROUP	Define group logical names
PRMCEB	N/A	Create permanent common event flag blocks
PRMGBL	$ INSTALL	Create and map global sections
PRMMBX	N/A	Create permanent mailboxes
SHMEM	N/A	Control multiport memory

Table D.4 *FILE Privileges*

Privilege	Allowed Functions	Description
DIAGNOSE	$ SET HOST/DUP $ SET HOST/HSC	Run online diagnostic programs
VOLPRO	$ DISMOUNT/ABORT $ INITIALIZE	Override volume protection

Table D.5 *SYSTEM privileges*

Privilege	Allowed Functions	Description
ALTPRI	$ SET PROCESS/PRIORITY= $ RUN/DETACHED/PRIORITY= $ SUBMIT/PRIORITY= $ SET ENTRY/PRIORITY	Increase base priority for any process
AUDIT	N/A	Append messages to audit file
OPER	$ DEFINE/CHARACTERISTIC $ DEFINE/FORM $ DELETE/CHARACTERISTIC $ DELETE/ENTRY $ DELETE/FORM $ DELETE/QUEUE $ INITIALIZE/QUEUE $ REPLY $ SET ACCOUNTING $ SET CLUSTER/EXPECTED_VOTE $ SET DAY $ SET LOGINS	Perform queue management and other operation functions
	$ SET PRINTER $ SET TIME $ START/QUEUE $ START/QUEUE/MANAGER $ STOP/QUEUE	
PSWAPM	$RUN/DETACHED/NOSWAPPING	Change process swap mode
SYSLCK	N/A	Lock systemwide resources
WORLD	$ STOP PROCESS $ SET PROCESS	Control any process execution

Table D.6 *ALL privileges*

Privilege	Allowed Functions	Description
BYPASS	Object access functions	Bypass UIC object protection

Table D.6 *ALL privileges (continued)*

Privilege	Allowed Functions	Description
CMEXEC	N/A	Change mode to executive
CMKRNL	$ DELETE/INTRUSION $ SET UIC $ SET PASSWORD/SYSTEM $ SHOW INTRUSION $ START/CPU $ STOP/CPU $ INSTALL $ ANALYZE/SYSTEM	Change mode to kernel
IMPERSON-ATE (DETACH)	$ RUN/DETACH/UIC=	Create a detached process under any UIC
LOG_IO	$ SET PRINTER $ SET TERM/HANGUP $ SET TERM/PERM $ SET TERM/NOSYSPASSWORD $ SET TIME $ SHOW TERM/PERM	Perform logical I/O operations to a device
MOUNT	$ MOUNT	Issue a mount queued I/O (QIO)
PFNMAP	N/A	Map physical memory
PHY_IO	N/A	Perform physical I/O operations to a device
READALL	File operations	Allows READ and CONTROL access all files
SECURITY	$ DELETE/INTRUSION $ SET AUDIT $ SET PASSWORD/SYSTEM $ SHOW AUDIT $ SHOW INTRUSION	Perform security functions
SETPRV	$ SET PROCESS/PRIVILEGE= $ RUN/PRIVILEGES=	Enable any privilege
SHARE	$ OPEN	Access a device allocated by other processes

Table D.6 *ALL privileges (continued)*

Privilege	Allowed Functions	Description
SYSNAM	$ DEFINE/SYSTEM $ CREATE/NAME_TABLE/EXEC $ DISMOUNT/SYSTEM $ START/QUEUE/MANAGER	Define system logical names
SYSPRV	File operations	Access files via SYSTEM [AQ: should be capitalized code?]access category

Sample OpenVMS Command File Tools

E.1 Introduction

Collectively, these sample files are referred to as Tools for Automated System Management (TASM). The procedures for installing TASM are as follows:

1. Create the following directory on the disk of your choice, for instance:

```
$ CREATE/DIR SYS$SYSDEVICE:[TASM]
```

2. Download BALDWIN.ZIP from http://books.elsevier.com/companions/1555582435 to the SYS$SYSDEVICE:[TASM] directory using your favorite browser or FTP client.

   Use UNZIP to expand BALDWIN.ZIP. UNZIP can be downloaded from http://vms.process.com/fileserv-software.html.

3. Edit TASM$STARTUP.COM and configure the TASM$DSK logical to reflect the device you've selected to contain TASM:

```
$ EDIT TASM$STARTUP.COM
$! TASM$STARTUP.COM
$!
$ DEFINE TASM$DSK    SYS$SYSDEVICE:
..
```

   Save the changes and exit to DCL.

4. Execute TASM$STARTUP with the SETUP parameter. This forces the remaining TASM directories and logical names to be created, as follows:

```
$ @TASM$STARTUP SETUP
...
%CREATE-I-EXISTS, TASM$COM already exists
%CREATE-I-CREATED, TASM$ROOT:[BACKUPS] created
%CREATE-I-CREATED, TASM$ROOT:[DOC] created
%CREATE-I-CREATED, TASM$ROOT:[SCRATCH] created
```

5. After you execute TASM$STARTUP, you can refer to all TASM directories by their respective logical names. For example, TASM$COM refers to the [TASM.COM] directory.

6. Edit your system startup files (e.g., STARTUP_PRODUCTS.COM) so that TASM$STARTUP is executed every time the system boots, as follows:

```
$ EDIT SYS$MANAGER:STARTUP_PRODUCTS.COM
...
...
$! Start TASM
$!
$ @device:[TASM.COM]TASM$STARTUP
..
```

   Save the changes and exit to DCL.

7. Execute TASM_SYMBOLS to define TASM symbols, as follows:

```
$ @TASM$COM:TASM_SYMBOLS
Defining TASM symbols. Enter "TASM" for HELP.
```

8. Also add the foregoing command to the login command procedures of users who are to access TASM (see chapter 11). After you define the symbols, issue the TASM command to see the symbols that have been defined, as follows:

```
$ TASM
```

The following TASM symbols are defined:

ACCT	Manage User Accounts
BCK	Perform Backup Functions
MAIL_COMPRESS	Compress VMS Mail Files
SHUT	Display Shutdown Menu
SYSDOC	Access On-line Site Guide
SYSGEN	Run SYSGEN Utility
SYSMAN	Run SYSMAN Utility
TASM	Display this help screen
UAF	Run AUTHORIZE Utility

Once you've installed TASM, refer to the following sections for the procedures on using each TASM component. The files referenced in this appendix are listed in table E.1.

Table E.1 *Common TASM Files*

Procedure Name	Function
TASM$STARTUP.COM	Define TASM logical names
TASM_MENU_ABORT.MSG	Error message file
TASM_MENU_INPERR.MSG	Error message file
TASM_MENUSYM.COM	Define symbols used by command procedures
TASM_SYMBOLS.COM	Define TASM symbols

E.2 Chapter 5

The startup tools referenced in chapter 5 are listed in the table E.2. These files are sample system startup procedures that you can use a guide for designing your startup procedures.

Table E.2 *Chapter 5 Tools*

Procedure Name	Function
STARTUP_APPLICATIONS.COM	Start in-house applications
STARTUP_MOUNT.COM	Mount disks
STARTUP_NETWORK.COM	Start up network components
STARTUP_PRODUCTS.COM	Start vendor products
STARTUP_QUEUES.COM	Set up queues
STARTUP_SDA.COM	Analyze crash dump
STARTUP_SETTERM.COM	Configure terminal devices
STARTUP_SHARE.COM	Install images
SYCONFIG.COM	Configure devices
SYPAGSWPFILES.COM	Install page/swap files
SYSECURITY.COM	Configure security

E.3 Chapter 6

The menu script referenced in chapter 6 is listed in the table E.3.

Table E.3 *Chapter 6 Tools*

Procedure Name	Function
SHUTDOWN_MENU.COM	Shut down system

SHUTDOWN_MENU allows you to execute several commonly used shutdown sequences from a menu. With minor modifications you can customize menu options to reflect the needs of your site. The most important benefit of using this technique is that you can ensure that the procedures you define in the menu are used to shut down the systems. For example, the technique allows you to ensure that certain shutdown options are always selected (e.g., REMOVE_NODE).

The symbol SHUT is defined in TASM_SYMBOLS. It facilitates access to the SHUTDOWN_MENU. For example:

```
$ SHUT
SHUTDOWN MENU
```

```
1--RETURN     Return to previous menu
2--REBOOT     Shutdown now with immediate reboot
3--REBOOT5    Shutdown in 5 minutes, with immediate reboot
4--NORMAL     Shutdown now without reboot
5--NORMAL5    Shutdown in 5 minutes, without reboot
6--POWEROFF   Shutdown, prepare for power shutoff

Enter a number:
```

E.4 Chapter 9

The tools referenced in chapter 9 are listed in the table E.4.

Table E.4 *Chapter 9 Tools*

Procedure Name	Function
ACCT_ADDUSER.COM	Add new user account
ACCT_REMUSER.COM	Remove user account
ACCT_UAFRPT.COM	Produce UAF report
ACCT_MENU.COM	Menu to access ACCT functions

The examples presented in chapter 9 allow you to add and remove user accounts and to produce an account listing. The symbol ACCT is defined in TASM_SYMBOLS, which allows easy access to the ACCT menu. For example:

```
$ ACCT

MANAGE USERS MENU

1--RETURN     Return to previous menu
2--ADDUSER    Add a new user
3--REMUSER    Remove an existing user
4--UAFRPT     Product a report of all existing users

Enter a number:
```

ADDUSER

First, add template accounts using AUTHORIZE and specify all the defaults you want to use for that group of users. For example, to create a template for all executive accounts, issue the following command:

```
$ UAF
UAF> ADD TMPL_EXEC/UIC=[100,1]/ACCOUNT="EXECUTIV"/DEVICE=DSK$EXECUTIVE-
_UAF> /FLAGS=DISUSER/PRIV=(TMPMBX,NETMBX)/DEFPRIV=(TMPMBX,NETMBX)-
_UAF> /PWDLIFETIME="60-0"/OWNER="TEMPLATE ACCOUNT"
```

Next, modify ACCT_ADDUSER.COM to reflect the templates that you've added. You must specify the template name, description, default login device, and UIC group for each template, as follows:

```
$! ACCT_ADDUSER.COM
$! ...
$! Add your template names below (leave first entry blank)
$ tmpl_name = "//TMPL_EXEC/TMPL_BILL/TMPL_HR/TMPL_SHIP/TMPL_SYST/"
$! Define default login device, UIC group, and description
$ tmpl_dev = "//DSK$EXECUTIVE/DSK$BILLING/DSK$HR/DSK$SHIPPING/DSK$SYSTEMS/"
$ tmpl_grp = "//100/200/400/600/700/"
$ tmpl_desc = "//Executive/Billing/Human Resources/Shipping/Systems/"
```

Then invoke ACCT and select ADDUSER from menu. You will then get the following menu listing all the defined templates:

```
ADD USER ACCOUNT

1--RETURN           Return to previous menu
2--TMPL_EXEC        Executive
3--TMPL_BILL        Billing
4--TMPL_HR          Human Resources
5--TMPL_SHIP        Shipping
6--TMPL_SYST        Systems
```

Select a template that you want to use and enter the username, as follows:

```
Enter account template to use: 2
Last name: Simpson
```

```
First name: Homer
Middle initial: A

Owner     Username    UIC     Account     Privs     Pri Directory

TMPL_EXEC [100,1] EXECUTIV Normal 4 Disuser

Chose a UIC Member number, excluding the ones listed above.
```

A list of existing users in the group you selected is displayed. Use this information to locate an available member number and enter it, as follows:

```
Account's UIC Member number: 2
```

The account and its default login directory are then automatically created, as follows:

```
%CREATE-I-CREATED, DSK$EXECUTIVE:[SIMPSONH] created
%UAF-I-COPMSG, user record copied
%UAF-I-RDBADDMSGU, identifier SIMPSONH value: [000100,000002] added
to rights data base

Username: SIMPSONH           Owner: HOMER A. SIMPSON
Account: EXECUTIV            UIC: [100,2] ([EXECUTIV,SIMPSONH])
CLI: DCL                     Tables: DCLTABLES
Default: DSK$EXECUTIVE:[SIMPSONH]
LGICMD: LOGIN
Flags: DisUser
Primary days: Mon Tue Wed Thu Fri
Secondary days: Sat Sun
No access restrictions
Expiration: (none)           Pwdminimum: 6 Login Fails: 0
Pwdlifetime: 60 00:00        Pwdchange: (pre-expired)
Last Login: (none) (interactive), (none) (noninteractive)
Maxjobs: 0             Fillm: 100          Bytlm: 8192
Maxacctjobs: 0         Shrfillm: 0         Pbytlm: 0
Maxdetach: 0           BIOlm: 18           JTquota: 1024
Prclm: 2               DIOlm: 18           WSdef: 150
Prio: 4                ASTlm: 24           WSquo: 256
Queprio: 0             TQElm: 10           WSextent: 512
```

```
CPU: (none)            Enqlm: 100            Pgflquo: 10240
Authorized Privileges:
NETMBX TMPMBX
Default Privileges:
NETMBX TMPMBX

Account added.

Press [return] for main menu
```

REMUSER

The REMUSER option prompts you for the name of an account to delete. It archives the user's default directory (and all subdirectories) to a save-set in the TASM$ARCHIVE directory. The same set is named username.SAV. Then the user's entire directory tree and UAF record are deleted.

To delete a user, select REMUSER from the ACCT menu. When you are prompted for a username, enter the name of the account you want to delete, as follows:

```
Username to delete: SIMPSONH

Are you Sure you want to archive DSK$EXECUTIVE:[SIMPSONH...]*.*;* (Y/N): Y

%BACKUP-S-COPIED, copied DSK$EXECUTIVE:[SIMPSONH]LOGIN.COM;1
%BACKUP-S-COPIED, copied DSK$EXECUTIVE:[SIMPSONH]MAIL.MAI;1

%BACKUP-I-STARTDELETE, starting file deletion pass

Home directory for SIMPSONH has been deleted.

Are you Sure you want to remove the account SIMPSONH (Y/N): Y

%UAF-I-REMMSG, record removed from system authorization file
%UAF-I-RDBREMMSGU, identifier SIMPSONH value: [000100,000002] removed from rights
data base
```

The account, SIMPSONH, has been completely removed.

UAFRPT

The UAFRPT option allows you to generate and optionally print a list of all user accounts. By default, the listing file named SYSUAF.LIS and is located in the TASM$SCRATCH directory. For example:

```
Print Report (Y/N): N

%UAF-I-LSTMSG1, writing listing file
%UAF-I-LSTMSG2, listing file SYSUAF.LIS complete

$ TYPE TASM$SCRATCH:SYSUAF.LIS

Owner            Username      UIC        Account    Privs    Directory

SYSTEM MANAGER   SYSTEM        [1,4]      SYSTEM   All    SYS$SYSROOT:[SYSMGR]
FIELD SERVICE    FIELD         [1,10]     FIELD    All    SYS$SYSROOT:[SYSMAINT]
                 TMPL_EXEC     [100,1]    EXECUTIV Normal Disuser
                 TMPL_BILL     [200,1]    BILLING  Normal Disuser
                 DEFAULT       [200,200]           Normal Disuser
NML$SERVER       NML$SERVER    [376,371]  DECNET   Normal SYS$SPECIFIC:[NML$SERVER]
PHONE$SERVER     PHONE$SERVER  [376,372]  DECNET   Normal SYS$SPECIFIC:[PHONE$SERVER]
MAIL$SERVER      MAIL$SERVER   [376,374]  DECNET   Normal SYS$SPECIFIC:[MAIL$SERVER]
DECNET           DECNET        [376,376]  DECNET   Normal SYS$SPECIFIC:[DECNET]
                 TMPL_HR       [400,1]    HR       Normal Disuser
DSN$NETWORK      DSN$SERVER    [500,1]             Normal SYS$COMMON:[DSN.LOGS]
                 TMPL_SHIP     [600,1]    SHIPPING Normal Disuser
                 TMPL_SYST     [700,1]    SYSTEMS  Normal Disuser

Press [return] for main menu
```

E.5 Chapter 10

The tools referenced in chapter 10 are listed in the table E.5.

Table E.5 *Chapter 10 Tools*

Procedure Name	Function
CUTTER.COM	Archive system log files
CHECK_DISKS.COM	Monitor disk usage

The purpose of CUTTER is to periodically close system log files (e.g., ACCOUNTNG.DAT, OPERATOR.LOG) and archive them to a temporary directory. To make it easier to identify archived files, the files names include a month and date timestamp. By default, files are archived to the directory defined by the TASM$ARCHIVE login name (defined in TASM$STARTUP), as follows:

```
$ @CUTTER

%COPY-S-COPIED, DISK$USER1:[SYSFILES]ACCOUNTNG_BART.DAT;11 copied to
TASM$ROOT:[ARCHIVE]ACC_JUN_2003.DAT;11 (1 block)

%COPY-S-COPIED, SYS$COMMON:[SYSMGR]SECURITY.AUDIT$JOURNAL;5 copied to
TASM$ROOT:[ARCHIVE]SEC_JUN_2003.DAT;5 (1 block)

%COPY-S-COPIED, SYS$SYSROOT:[SYSERR]ERRLOG.SYS;1 copied to
TASM$ROOT:[ARCHIVE]ERR_JUN_2003.DAT;1 (1 block)

%COPY-S-COPIED, DISK$USER1:[SYSFILES]OPERATOR_BART.LOG;75 copied to
TASM$ROOT:[ARCHIVE]OPER_JUN_2003.DAT;75 (2 blocks)
```

The command procedure MONTHLY_PROCESSING (see chapter 12) invokes CUTTER to force this process to occur each month.

E.6 Chapter 11

The tool referenced in chapter 11 is listed in table E.6.

Table E.6 *Chapter 11 Tools*

Procedure Name	Function
DEFINE_SYMB.MAR	Macro code to define DCL symbols
DQ.MAR	Macro code to test disk quota

DEFINE_SYMB.MAR is a VAX macro example that demonstrates how to define DCL symbols from a compiled language. Procedures for using this file are presented in chapter 11.

DQ.MAR is compiled VAX or Alpha macro code that will alert users, at login time, to pending disk-quota problems. Procedures for using this file are presented in chapter 11.

E.7 Chapter 12

The tools referenced in chapter 12 are listed in table E.7.

Table E.7 *Chapter 12 Tools*

Procedure Name	Function
SCHEDULER.COM	Main scheduler
DAILY_PROCESSING.COM	Daily tasks
WEEKLY_PROCESSING.COM	Weekly tasks
MONTHLY_PROCESSING.COM	Monthly tasks

These files comprise a sample automated batch scheduling system. Procedures for using these files are presented in chapter 12.

E.8 Chapter 13

The tools referenced in chapter 13 are listed in table E.8.

Table E.8 *Chapter 13 Tools*

Procedure Name	Function
BCK_CALC_LABEL.COM	Calculate tape label to use
BCK_ERRORS.COM	Backup error codes
BCK_MENU.COM	Main backup menu
BCK_NIGHTLY.COM	Main backup program
BCK_RESTORE_FILE.COM	Perform file restore
BCK_SELECT_FILE.COM	Select file to restore
BCK_SETS.COM	Define backup sets and attributes

Together, these example procedures implement the basic backup, tape labeling, and retention strategies discussed in chapter 13.

To use these procedures you first have to organize your disks into backup sets. Sets are designed to allow you to back up several disks to a single, high-capacity medium (e.g., 4-mm or 8-mm tapes). If you want to perform unattended backups, assign only as many disks per set as will fit on a single tape. For example, consider a system with the following devices:

- DISK$USER1 0.5 GB
- DISK$USER2 0.5 GB
- DISK$SCR1 1.0 GB
- MUA0: 1.0 GB tape drive

Because the capacity of the tape drive is limited to 1 GB, you have to create at least two backup sets, as follows:

```
Set S01:DISK$USER1, DISK$USER2
Set S02:DISK$SCR1
```

Next, edit TASM$COM:BCK_SETS to reflect the backup sets that you've selected. Configure the symbols as indicated in table E.9.

Table E.9 *BCK_SETS Symbol Definitions*

Symbol	Meaning
BCK_NUMSETS	The number of backup sets you have defined
BCK_SETS	List of backup set names separated by slashes; set names must have exactly three characters each
BCK_TAPE	Tape drive to use for this backup set
BCK_OUTQUAL	Any special backup qualifiers you need
BCK_COUNT	Number of devices in the backup set
BCK_DEVICES	List of devices separated by slashes ("/")
BCK_SAVESETS	Names of save-sets to use for each device

The values you establish for the BCK_DAILY, BCK_WEEKLY, BCK_MONTHLY, and BCK_YEARLY symbols determine the backup schedule and the retention period.

The retention period for each backup type is as follows:

DAILY 1 month

WEEKLY	1 month
MONTHLY	1 year
YEARLY	2 years

Configure the symbols in table E.10 to establish the type of backup to perform on each day of the month.

Table E.10 *Symbols To Define Backup Type*

Symbol	Meaning
BCK_DAILY	The days of the week to perform daily backups; select one or more days (Monday–Sunday)
BCK_WEEKLY	Day of the week to perform weekly backup; select one day of week (Monday–Sunday)
BCK_MONTHLY	Week within month to perform monthly backup; select one week number (1–6)
BCK_YEARLY	Month within year to perform yearly backup; select one month of year (1–12)

For example, BCK_SET.COM may be modified to the following:

```
$! BCK_SETS.COM
$! ...
$ bck_numsets == 2
$ bck_sets == "/S01/S02/"
$ bckset = p1
$ goto SET_'bckset'
$! ------------------------------------------
$! Backup Disk Set "S01"
$! ------------------------------------------
$SET_S01:
$ BCK_TAPE == "MUA0:"
$ BCK_OUTQUAL == "/BLOCK=40000/GROUP=10"
$ BCK_COUNT == 2
$ BCK_DEVICES == "/DISK$USER1/DISK$USER2/"
$ BCK_SAVESETS == "/IMAGEU1/IMAGEU2/"
$ BCK_DAILY == "MonTueWedThu"     ! Daily backups on these days
$ BCK_WEEKLY == "Fri"             ! Weekly backup on this day
$ BCK_MONTHLY == "2"              ! Monthly on this week number
```

```
$ BCK_YEARLY == "2"            ! Yearly during 2nd month of year
$ EXIT
$!
$! ----------------------------------------------
$! Backup Disk Set "S02"
$! ----------------------------------------------
$SET_S02:
$ BCK_TAPE == "MUA0:"
$ BCK_OUTQUAL == "/BLOCK=40000/GROUP=10"
$ BCK_COUNT == 1
$ BCK_DEVICES == "/DISK$SCR1/
$ BCK_SAVESETS == "/IMAGES1/"
$ BCK_DAILY == "Mon"           ! Daily backups on these days
$ BCK_WEEKLY == "Tue"          ! Weekly backup on this day
$ BCK_MONTHLY == "2"           ! Monthly on this week number
$ BCK_YEARLY == ""             ! No Yearly backup
$ EXIT
```

If you need more backup sets, add additional entries using the same format.

The resulting backup schedule for backup set S01 is daily backups Monday through Thursday, weekly backups on Fridays, monthly backups on the second week of the month (on Friday), and a yearly backup each February. Once you have specified this information and given a specific date, the backup procedures can always calculate exactly what type of backup should be performed and the tape label that should be used.

This process is automated by the procedure BCK_CALC_LABEL.COM. Before a backup begins, the main backup program (BCK_NIGHTLY) invokes CALC_LABEL to determine if a backup is scheduled for that day and, if so, what label should be used. CALC_LABEL checks the symbols that define the schedule (e.g., BCK_DAILY). If there is no backup scheduled, it does not return a label. If there is a backup scheduled, CALC_LABEL generates one by concatenating the backup set name, the type of backup, and a sequential number.

The first three characters of the label contain the backup set name. The next character is the backup type abbreviated as D, W, M, and Y. The sequential number is set depending on the backup type. For yearly backups, it is set to 1 for odd years and 2 for even years. For monthly backups it is set to the month number (e.g., January = "1," February = "2," etc.) For weekly and daily backups, the sequential number is set to the week or day number, as follows:

```
           S    M    T    W    R    F    S    Week #
           1    2    3    4    5    6    7    1
           8    9   10   11   12   13   14    2
Day #     15   16   17   18   19   20   21    3
          22   23   24   25   26   27   28    4
          29   30   31   32   33   34   35    5
          36   37                             6
```

For example, May 1, 1999, is day number 7, week number 1. May 31 is day number 37, week number 6.

```
May 1999
           S   M   T   W   R   F   S
                                   1
           2   3   4   5   6   7   8
           9  10  11  12  13  14  15
          16  17  28  19  20  21  22
          23  24  25  26  27  28  29
          30  31
```

Given the following dates and the schedule for backup set S01 presented earlier, BCK_CALC_LABEL would generate labels as follows:

- May 1, 1999 No backup
- May 7, 1999 S01M5
- May 14, 1999 S01W3
- May 25, 1999 S01D31
- May 31, 1999 S01D37

Once you have configured BCK_SETS, you should organize all the backup media that you will need, initialize each tape with the required label, and attach a written label to each tape. You can generate a backup schedule to see exactly which tapes will be requested for each day of the month (see the next section).

After you have all your tapes prepared, you're ready to initiate a backup. To start a backup, you have to submit BCK_NIGHTLY as a batch job and pass it through several parameters as indicated in table E.11:

Table E.11 *BCK_NIGHTLY Parameters*

Parameter Name	Meaning
P1	The backup set to process
P2	The scheduled backup date, or "" for the current date
P3	"PRE" if you just want to verify that the proper tape is loaded in the tape drive

To simplify this process you can create a command procedure such as BCK_NIGHTLY_SUB.COM, as follows:

```
$ TYPE BCK_NIGHTLY_SUB.COM
$! BCK_NIGHTLY_SUB.COM
$!
$! P1 - Backup set
$! P2 - Scheduled backup date
$! P3 - If TOMORROW then submit for next day
$!
$ submit/noprint/keep/log=TASM$BACKUPS:BCK_NIGHTLY_PRE.LOG -
  /NAME="BCK_NIGHTLY_PRE"/notify/user=system/param= -
  ("''p1'","''p2'","PRE")/after="''P3'15:30" TASM$COM:BCK_NIGHTLY
$ submit/noprint/keep/log=TASM$BACKUPS:/notify/user=system/param= -
  ("''p1'","''p2'")/after="''P2'23:00" TASM$COM:BCK_NIGHTLY
$ exit
```

Then to submit the backup, issue the following DCL command:

```
$ @BCK_NIGHTLY_SUB S01 ""
```

The foregoing procedure submits BCK_NIGHTLY with the "PRE" option for 3:30 P.M. and without the "PRE" option for 11:00 P.M. When the PRE job runs, it checks the tape drive to see if the proper tape is loaded. If no tape or the wrong tape is loaded, all terminals enabled to receive tape requests (REPLY/ENABLE=TAPES) receive a request message such as the following:

```
%%%%%%%%%%% OPCOM 11-JUN-2003 13:29:44.32 %%%%%%%%%%%
Request 1, from user SYSTEM on BART
BATCH_18, Wrong volume mounted (S01D13), mount S01W2 in MUA0:
and use REPLY/TO.
```

This message alerts you to put the correct tape in before you leave for the day. Once the correct tape is in the drive, issue the following command to respond to the request:

```
$ REPLY/TO = 1

$ 13:31:18.24, request 1 was completed by operator
_BART$OPA0:
```

The PRE job then checks the tape again and sends the following message if the correct tape is loaded:

```
%%%%%%%%%%% OPCOM 11-JUN-2003 13:53:05.76 %%%%%%%%%%%
Message from user SYSTEM on BART

BATCH_25, Tape: S01W2 is loaded and ready for tonight's backup.
Job BCK_NIGHTLY_PRE (queue BART_GENERAL, entry 25) completed
```

Finally, at 11:00 P.M. the backup job begins and performs the backup. During the backup, BCK_NIGHTHLY creates a backup listing file in the TASM$BACKUPS directory that lists every file that is copied to backup media. Additionally, a log file is also written to the TASM$BACKUPS directory.

To force backups to be submitted automatically, you should invoke BCK_NIGHTLY_SUB from an automated scheduling system such as DAILY_PROCESSING.COM (see chapter 12).

The following paragraphs discuss the other components of the backup examples.

BCK_MENU

The symbol BCK is defined by TASM_SYMBOLS to invoke BCK_MENU.COM, which allows you to select a number of backup options from a menu, as follows:

```
$ BCK
@BACKUP/RESTORE MENU
1—<RETURN>          Return to previous menu
2—RESUBMIT          Resubmit BCK_NIGHTLY
3—RESTORE           Restore a file from backups
4—SCHED             Print a backup schedule
Enter a number:
```

RESUBMIT

This invokes BCK_NIGHTLY_SUB to manually resubmit a backup for the current day.

RESTORE

Use the RESTORE option from the backup menu to restore a file from backups. The RESTORE option executes the command procedure BCK_SELECT_FILE. You are then prompted for various information to locate the backup from which you want to restore. BCK_SELECT_FILE then submits BCK_FILE_RESTORE as a batch job, passing it the file name and tape label you selected. The restore procedure copies the restored file to TASM$RESTORE:[*] and notifies you when the restore has completed.

The following is an example restore of [SYS0.SYSCOMMON.SYSEXE]SYSUAF.DAT from DISK$USER1:

```
[Select RESTORE from the Backup Menu]
1--S01
2--S02
Select a backup set (1-2): 1

First choose the backup set that contains DISK$USER1, as
follows:

1-- DISK$USER1- VAXVMSV055 (BART$DUA0:)
2-- DISK$USER2- VAXVMST060 (BART$DUA1:)
Select disk by number (1-2): 1
```

Then select the proper disk. BCK_SELECT_FILE then lists all listing files that exist for that disk.

```
Searching all DISK$USER1 listing files...
```

```
The following is a list of backup listing files that exist. They are
sorted by date of backup (latest backups listed first).

Press "N" for the next page
Press "P" for the previous page
Press <<RETURN>> to return to the previous menu

1--S01W2_IMAGEU1.LIS;1 1999-06-11 13:57:46.4

Enter choice # (1-10), P or <<RETURN>>: 1
```

If there were many from which to choose, you could use N and P to see the next or previous page of listing files. In this case, there is only one choice (S01W2_IMAGEU1).

```
Listfile = TASM$BACKUPS:S01W2_IMAGEU1.LIS;1
```

Enter the filename you wish to restore. Enter the filename in the following format:

```
[directory.subdir.]filename.type
e.g., [USER.SMITH]LOGIN.COM
```

You may leave out any part of the filename, but the less specific you are, the more choices you will have to select from.

```
e.g., LOGIN.COM
Enter filename: SYSUAF.DAT
```

Now, enter the filename you want to restore, in this case SYSUAF.DAT. BCK_SELECT_FILE scans the listing file you selected for all occurrences of that file name. Again, use N or P to scroll from one page to another if there are many entries.

```
1--[SYS0.SYSCOMMON.SYSEXE]SYSUAF.DAT;1 32 17-OCT-1991
2--[SYSFILES]SYSUAF.DAT;1 42 17-OCT-1991 13:36

Enter choice # (1-10), N, P or <<RETURN>>: 1
```

In this case choose selection 1 because it corresponds exactly to the file you want to restore. BCK_SELECT_FILE summarizes the parameters it will use to restore the file and submits BCK_RESTORE_FILE as a batch job, as follows:

```
Tape drive to use [MUA0:]:
label = S01W2
saveset = IMAGE
file = [SYS0.SYSCOMMON.SYSEXE]SYSUAF.DAT;1

Job BCK_RESTORE
_FILE (queue BART_GENERAL, entry 15) started on BART_GENERAL
```

When BCK_RESTORE_FILE is complete, it sends the following broadcast message indicating that the restore was successful.

```
Reply received on BART from user SYSTEM at _BART$OPA0: 11:27:30
File: [SYS0.SYSCOMMON.SYSEXE]SYSUAF.DAT;1 restored to
TASM$RESTORE:[SYS0.SYSCOMMON.SYSEXE]
$ DIR TASM$RESTORE:[SYS0.SYSCOMMON.SYSEXE]/SIZE=ALL/DATE

Directory TASM$RESTORE:[SYS0.SYSCOMMON.SYSEXE]

SYSUAF.DAT;1 32/33 17-OCT-1991 13:36:51.96

Total of 1 file, 32/33 blocks.
```

Once you believe that you have restored the correct file, copy it to its production directory.

SCHED

Use SCHED option to generate a backup schedule for a specific backup set and month. For example:

```
[Select SCHED from backup menu]
Enter a date (DD-MM-YYYY) that is in the month
that you want a backup  schedule
for [CURRENT MONTH]: 01-May-1999
Enter Backup Set [S01]:
Print it (Y/N)? [N]:
```

```
$ TYPE TASM$SCRATCH:BCK_SCHED_S01.RPT

Schedule for MAY 1999
Backup Set: S01

Sat, 1-MAY-1999 :
Sun, 2-MAY-1999 :
Mon, 3-MAY-1999 : S01D9
Tue, 4-MAY-1999 : S01D10
Wed, 5-MAY-1999 : S01D11
Thu, 6-MAY-1999 : S01D12
Fri, 7-MAY-1999 : S01M5
Sat, 8-MAY-1999 :
Sun, 9-MAY-1999 :
Mon, 10-MAY-1999: S01D16
Tue, 11-MAY-1999: S01D17
Wed, 12-MAY-1999: S01D18
Thu, 13-MAY-1999: S01D19
Fri, 14-MAY-1999: S01W3
Sat, 15-MAY-1999:
Sun, 16-MAY-1999:
Mon, 17-MAY-1999: S01D23
Tue, 18-MAY-1999: S01D24
Wed, 19-MAY-1999: S01D25
Thu, 20-MAY-1999: S01D26
Fri, 21-MAY-1999: S01W4
Sat, 22-MAY-1999:
Sun, 23-MAY-1999:
Mon, 24-MAY-1999: S01D30
Tue, 25-MAY-1999: S01D31
Wed, 26-MAY-1999: S01D32
Thu, 27-MAY-1999: S01D33
Fri, 28-MAY-1999: S01W5
Sat, 29-MAY-1999:
Sun, 30-MAY-1999:
Mon, 31-MAY-1999: S01D37
```

You should generate the schedules several months in advance so that you know exactly when you need each tape.

E.9 Chapter 14

The menu script referenced in chapter 14 is listed in the table E.12.

Table E.12 *Chapter 14 Tools*

Procedure Name	Function
SYSDOC.COM	Online site guide

SYSDOC is a tool for creating and accessing online site documentation (e.g., policies, procedures, contact names, configuration information). Before you can use SYSDOC, you must create directories that contain documentation text files. When you invoke SYSDOC, the directory and file names are presented as menu options, allowing you to traverse up and down directories and to view documents.

SYSDOC expects all directories to be created under the directory defined by the logical name TASM$DOC. For example, you might want to store documentation relating to contact names, applications, and emergency procedures. First, create a directory for each of subject, as follows:

```
$ SET DEFAULT TASM$DOC
$ DIR
%DIRECT-W-NOFILES, no files found

$ CREATE [.CONTACTS]/DIR/PROT=(W:RE)
$ CREATE [.APPLICATIONS]/DIR/PROT=(W:RE)
$ CREATE [.EMERGENCY]/DIR/PROT=(W:RE)

$ DIR

Directory TASM$ROOT:[DOC]

APPLICATIONS.DIR;1 CONTACTS.DIR;1 EMERGENCY.DIR;1

Total of 3 files.
```

Then, create as many documents as you want within each directory. When you name a document file, the file name must be DOC, but the file extension can be whatever you want.

```
$ CREATE [.CONTACTS]DOC.DIGITAL
Digital Contacts

Service: (800)-354-9000
Sales: (203)-555-2345 Bill Smith
DECdirect: (800)-344-4825
```

Next, invoke SYSDOC and select CONTACTS, as follows:

```
$ SYSDOC

Online Site Guide

1-- APPLICATIONS
2-- CONTACTS
3-- EMERGENCY

Enter Choice #: 2
```

The documents in the CONTACTS directory are then displayed in a menu. Select the document you want to edit or view.

```
Online Site Guide

1--DIGITAL Digital Contacts

Enter Choice #: 1
E-- Edit
T-- Type
P-- Print
Action: T

Digital Contacts

Service: (800)-354-9000
Sales: (203)-555-2345 Bill Smith
DECdirect: (800)-344-4825
<< Press RETURN to continue >>
```

At any menu just press the <RETURN> key to return to the previous level.

E.10 Chapter 15

The tools referenced in chapter 15 are listed in table E.13.

Table E.13 *Chapter 15 Tools*

Procedure Name	Function
CHECK_DISKS.COM	Monitor disks
CHECK_DISKS.DAT	Define disks to watch
CHECK_PROCESSES.COM	Monitor processes
CHECK_PROCESSES.DAT	Define processes to watch
CHECK_PROCESSES.FDL	Define format to load indexed file from .DAT
CHECK_QUEUES.COM	Monitor queues
DISK.COM	Presents a graphical display of current disk utilization.

You can use the sample procedures in this section to monitor the status of queues, system processes, and disks. All procedures execute as detached processes that send operator request messages in the event a problem is detected. To receive these messages, add the following command to your LOGIN.COM.

```
$ REPLY/ENABLE=CENTRAL
```

The following paragraphs describe each procedure in more detail.

CHECK_QUEUES

CHECK_QUEUES uses the Get Queue Information lexical function (F$GETQUI) to monitor the status of all print and batch queues. By default, every 5 minutes CHECK_QUEUES verifies that all queues are started. If malfunctioning queues are detected, CHECK_QUEUES sends an operator request message to the CENTRAL class.

You can change the polling interval by adjusting the interval symbol defined in CHECK_QUEUES.COM. To start CHECK_QUEUES at system startup time, include the following line in your system startup procedures (e.g., STARTUP_PRODUCTS.COM):

```
$ @TASM$COM:CHECK_QUEUES.COM
```

Add the line after the line that executes TASM$STARTUP so that all required logical names are defined.

CHECK_PROCESSES

CHECK_PROCESSES uses the Get Job Information lexical function (F$GETJPI) to monitor the status of selected system processes. By default, every 30 minutes CHECK_PROCESSES verifies that selected processes exist and are running under the proper usernames. If CHECK_PROCESSES detects the absence of a process or a process executing under the wrong username, it sends an operator request message to the CENTRAL class.

You can change the polling interval by adjusting the interval symbol defined in CHECK_PROCESSES.COM.

Define the processes and usernames that CHECK_PROCESSES monitors by creating TASM$COM:CHECK_PROCESSES.DAT, using the following format:

```
SWAPPER            //00/
ERRFMT             /SYSTEM/00/
OPCOM              /SYSTEM/00/
AUDIT_SERVER       /AUDIT$SERVER/00/
JOB_CONTROL        /SYSTEM/00/
NETACP             /DECNET/00/
EVL                /DECNET/00/
REMACP             /SYSTEM/00/
<Check_Disks>      /SYSTEM/00/
<Check_Queues>     /SYSTEM/00/
```

To start CHECK_PROCESSES at system startup time, include the following line in your system startup procedures (e.g., STARTUP_PRODUCTS.COM):

```
$ @TASM$COM:CHECK_PROCESSES.COM
```

Add this line after the line that executes TASM$STARTUP so that all required logical names are defined.

The first time CHECK_PROCESSES executes, it converts the entries from CHECK_PROCESSES.DAT into an indexed file (CHECK_PROCESSES.IDX) using the included file definition language file (CHECK_PROCESSES.FDL). The indexed file is then used for the life of the detached process. If you make changes to the text data file and you want to make them effective, you must manually stop the detached process and restart it.

CHECK_DISKS

CHECK_DISKS uses the Get Device Information lexical function (F$GET-DVI) to monitor disk space and disk errors. By default, every 15 minutes it verifies that every disk has at least 50,000 free blocks and that error counts have not incremented. When CHECK_DISKS detects disk space below 50,000 blocks or a single disk error (a WARNING state), it sends an operator request message to the CENTRAL class. If disk space drops below 10,000 blocks, or 10 or more disk errors are detected (a CRITICAL state), CHECK_DISKS sends a REPLY message directly to selected usernames.

To adjust thresholds, polling interval, or the destination of messages, modify the following symbols in CHECK_DISKS.COM:

```
$! CHECK_DISKS.COM
$! ...
$ freeblock_warning = 50000 ! Disk space WARNING threshold
$ freeblock_critical = 10000 ! Disk space CRITICAL threshold
$ disk_err_warning = 1 ! Disk error WARNING threshold
$ disk_err_critical = 10 ! Disk error CRITICAL threshold
$ interval = "00:15:00" ! polling interval
$ warning_class = "(central)" ! Opcom class to reply to for warnings
$ critical_list = "(system)" ! Usernames to notify if critical
```

When CHECK_DISKS is started, it determines which disks to monitor by reading the data file CHECK_DISKS.DAT. Before you start CHECK_DISKS, edit this file so that each disk you want to monitor is listed on a separate line, as follows:

```
DISK$USER1
DISK$USER2
```

To start CHECK_DISKS at system startup time, include the following line in your system startup procedures (e.g., STARTUP_PRODUCTS.COM)

```
$ @TASM$COM:CHECK_DISKS.COM
```

Add this line after the line that executes TASM$STARTUP so that all required logical names are defined.

E.11 Chapter 16

The tools referenced in chapter 16 are listed in table E.14.

Table E.14 *Chapter 16 Tools*

Command Procedure	Description
MAIL_COMPRESS.COM	Compresses all MAIL.MAI files contained on a particular disk
MAIL_DEFAULTS.COM	When adding a new user, creates a user [.MAIL] and initializes the user's profile
MAIL_EDIT.COM	Prefixes each line of a mail message with ">" and adds the user's signature

Procedures for using this file are presented in chapter 16.

E.12 Chapter 17

The tools referenced in chapter 17 are listed in table E.15.

Table E.15 *Chapter 17 Tools*

Procedure Name	Function
VMS$PASSWORD_POLICY.COM	Password filter
VMS$PASSWORD_POLICY_LNK.COM	A script to link VMS$PASSWORD_POLICY
CAPTIVE_MENU.COM	Captive login procedure

Procedures for using these files are presented in chapter 17.

E.13 Chapter 18

The tools referenced in chapter 18 are listed in table E.16.

Table E.16 *Chapter 18 Tools*

Procedure Name	Function
BENCH.COM	Gathers resource-usage statistics for an activity
HARD.MAR	Gets hard page-fault count (macro code)

Procedures for using these files are presented in chapter 18.

Digital/Compaq/HP Manuals

The Compaq/HP document titles do not follow any particular standard so the content is sometimes difficult to imagine by reading the title only. Furthermore I find the packing of several manuals under a single title to be occasionally confusing. So I have added some helpful comments to each title to help you recognize their worth. When all else fails, start your search in the *Master Index*. It is very thorough and accurate.

Compaq Availability Manager User's Guide

This product is a GUI for account, disk, and queue management. It can be run from either an OpenVMS terminal or a Windows terminal.

Compaq DECprint Supervisor (DCPS) for OpenVMS

This is not currently available online. This product is licensed with the OpenVMS license.

Compaq OpenVMS Operating System for Alpha and VAX, Version 7.3-1.

This is the OpenVMS SPD (Software Product Description). Also look for versions 7.3-1 and 7.3-2

Compaq TCP/IP Services for OpenVMS Concepts and Planning.

This is the top-level TCP/IP document. It points to the other 10 (or more) that are available.

Compaq TCP/IP Services for OpenVMS Management

This is an invaluable tutorial for OpenVMS TCP/IP. In particular TCP/IP network printers are discussed in Part 6.

Compaq TCP/IP Services for OpenVMS Tuning and Troubleshooting

TCP/IP Services include extensive performance collection capabilities. This manual shows how to monitor and tune TCP/IP effectively and in detail.

DECnet for OpenVMS Networking Manual

This is the bible for DECnet IV.

DECnet-Plus for OpenVMS Introduction and User's Guide.

This references nine additional DECnet-Plus documents.

DECnet-Plus for OpenVMS Network Management

This is the DECnet V management authority. It also discusses migration from DECnet IV to DECnet V.

Guide to OpenVMS File Applications

Describes OpenVMS RMS (Record Management System) files types and their applications.

OpenVMS Alpha System Analysis Tools Manual

Details the Alpha implementation of SDA (System Dump Analyzer).

OpenVMS Command Definition, Librarian, and Message Utilities Manual

This manual is actually a collection of three unrelated utilities.

1. Command Definition manual describes the mechanism which OpenVMS uses to parse command parameters for processing by an application.

2. The Librarian is a utility used throughout OpenVMS for various types of libraries. This manual details for the use of the LIBRARY command.

3. All OpenVMS messages are managed via a database. Compaq/HP recommends that user-written applications also use that database for consistency and this manual describes how to do it.

OpenVMS DCL Dictionary

This is an unlikely title for the manual that describes many of the DCL (Digital Command Language) commands and their options. It includes numerous examples as well. It is a two volume set, A-M and N-Z.

OpenVMS Guide to System Security

This is a philosophy book and well as a detailed 'how to' book. Use this when formulating site security because Digital engineers have solutions for situations that have never crossed your mind.

OpenVMS License Management Utility Manual

This describes software licensing philosophy generally. It also includes a description of the LICENSE command.

OpenVMS Management Station Overview and Release Notes

This is management software that runs on a PC. This document is only a brief description. Full documentation is available, once it is installed on the PC, under HELP feature.

OpenVMS Master Index

This is an invaluable index because it cross-references a given topic to the several documents that discuss it. Furthermore, its subheadings are quite detailed so that often only one probe will lead you to the desired material.

OpenVMS online HELP facility is easy to use and complete. It includes many examples and compliments the *OpenVMS DCL Dictionary* primarily.

OpenVMS Performance Management

This book begins with a philosophical discussion of operating system performance. A manager cannot deal with statements like, "my program takes too long to execute" very well. The manager is encouraged to ask the right questions before attempting to change any of OpenVMS parameters. Then it describes the OpenVMS tuning algorithms in extensive detail. In the process of describing the algorithms, it describes how to use the performance programs available with OpenVMS.

OpenVMS Software Overview

Although a bit dated now is a good introductory document that defines and illustrates many of the OpenVMS capabilities and features.

OpenVMS System Manager's Manual: Volume 1: Essentials

This is the manager's primary reference.

OpenVMS System Manager's Manual: Volume 2: Tuning, Monitoring, and Complex Systems

This is the manager's other primary reference, actually a continuation of Volume 1, a mere packing ploy. If the two were bound together (think hard copy) it would be too awkward to manage.

OpenVMS System Management Utilities Reference Manual

This is another collection of independent manuals required to manage the system divided into two volumes, A-L and M-Z. This manual picks up where the *DCL Dictionary* leaves off. That is, normal users do not have any business poking around in this collection because they are not privileged enough to use them. It includes the various system management utilities needed every day (ACCOUNTING, ANALYZE/AUDIT, AUTHORIZE, BACKUP, DECevent, LANCP,

LATCP and SYSMAN) and describes them completely with many examples.

OpenVMS VAX System Dump Analyzer Utility Manual

Details the VAX implementation of SDA (System Dump Analyzer).

Volume Shadowing for OpenVMS

This manual discusses all aspects of shadowing, including how to backup a shadow set, with many examples.

WWW Resources

I hesitate to add this section because, since the HP acquisition, URLs are bound to change. These addresses are currently valid and I would like to hope Compaq/HP will maintain them in the future.

The primary HP OpenVMS homepage is http://h71000.www7.hp.com/. All official information spins off from there. This is the URL to bookmark.

A fairly extensive collection of current OpenVMS documents can be found at http://h71000.www7.hp.com/doc/os731_index.html. There are links to document sets of several older OpenVMS releases on this page as well.

SPD (Software Product Description) home page is at http://h18000.www1.hp.com/info/spd/.

The best OpenVMS patch site is found at

http://ftp.support.compaq.com.au/pub/ecoinfo/ecoinfo/version.htm. This site is nicely arranged by OpenVMS version number and by patch priority. This site points to OpenVMS and layered product patches at ftp://ftp1.service.digital.com/public/vms. This site includes both VAX and AXP (Alpha) patches for many versions of OpenVMS. Each patch includes a README and installation instructions.

License units required for all VAXes and Alphas can be found online at http://licensing.hp.com/swl/view.slm?page=index in the Reference Material tab. This location contains lots of other information regarding licenses.

I have found the best starting point to reach the user community is http://www.levitte.org/~ava/. This site seems to point to everything else available including DEC/Compaq/HP sites.

Hunter Goatley maintains one of the best OpenVMS software collections at http://vms.process.com/fileserv-software.html

The OpenVMS FAQ is http://h71000.www7.hp.com/wizard/openvms_faq.html. This information is actively updated regularly. However this is not the only FAQ available. See http://www.levitte.org/~ava/vms_faq.htmlx for others.

Ask The Wizard (ATW) is located at http://h71000.www7.hp.com/wizard/. This complements the FAQ.

Hewlett-Packard maintains OpenVMS training for system managers online at http://h71000.www7.hp.com/training.html/.

http://membres.lycos.fr/pmoreau/decw/decw.html is the source of many freeware Motif packages that may interest the system manager.

The home page of Encompass, the HP-sponsored user group, is http://www.encompassus.org/, and in the UK, http://www.hpusers.org.uk/. If you are planning to use OpenVMS as a hobby you will have to join this organization first. You can join for free.

The OpenVMS hobbyist home page is http://www.openvmshobbyist.com/. Once you have your Encompass membership, you can receive free licenses and, for a modest price, media for OpenVMS and several layered products. The user's group was originally called DECUS.

LYNX is a free character-oriented web browser. Many prefer it to the glitzy versions. It can be downloaded from http://lynx.browser.org/

The prime OpenVMS hackers homepage is http://deathrow.vistech.net/. It would be smart to read over that material and assure yourself that you are protected against any of the possible problems described.

Books

Digital Press, CBM Books (which is now part of Digital Press), and others published many VMS (and OpenVMS) titles when DEC hardware and software was in its prime. But many (but not all) of the titles below are out of print today. Clearly Digital Press is still active in the OpenVMS market.

Paul C. Anagnostopoulos and Steve Hoffman, *Writing Real Programs in DCL* 2nd edition, Digital Press, 1999, ISBN 1555581919.

> The is command language bible. It is required reading for system managers.

C. Gordon Bell, J. Craig Mudge and John E. McNamara, *Computer Engineering – A DEC View of Hardware Systems Design*, Digital Press, 1978, IBSN 0932376002.

> Contains the nitty-gritty of the hardware design constraints DEC hardware engineers had to deal with. Gordon Bell was DEC's chief hardware architect. Although technologically dated, Bell's general observations probably still hold in computer design today.

James W. Coburn, *OpenVMS Performance Management*, 2nd Edition, CBM Books, 1994, ISBN 187895640X

> This book addresses specific algorithms used to test and adjust OpenVMS. Also see Sethi.

Roy G. Davis, *VAXCluster Principles*, Digital Press, 1993, ISBN 1555581129

> Clustered VAXes was introduced in 1983 and so the algorithms and data structures presented in this book still hold true. However newer hardware architecture will not be included.

Michael D. Duffy, *Getting Started with OpenVMS*, Digital Press, 2003, ISBN 1555582796

This is a practical introduction to OpenVMS commands and functions from a novice user standpoint.

Ruth E. Goldenberg. Denise E. Dumas and Saro Saravana, *OpenVMS Alpha Internals – Scheduling and Process Control*, Digital Press, 1997, ISBN 1555581560

A detailed description of OpenVMS data structures is found in "the book of Ruth", The earlier titles were either *VAX/VMS Internals and Data Structures* or *OpenVMS Internals and Data Structures* depending on the edition. This book is republished often to keep up with newer versions of OpenVMS. The latest complete VAX/VMS edition is for Version 5.5-2. The latest complete Alpha/VMS edition is for Version 1.5. This newest Alpha edition has been partially updated will continue to be updated.

Patrick Holmay, *The OpenVMS User's Guide*, second edition, Digital Press, 1998, ISBN 1555582036.

The OpenVMS novice is encouraged to read Digital Press' If you've never used OpenVMS before, this is the best introduction available. OpenVMS's basic commands, editors, the file structure, and an introduction to Command Procedures (that is, script writing).

David Donald Miller, *Getting Started with OpenVMS System Management*, Digital Press, 2003, ISBN 1555582818

A short version of Baldwin for those that want an overviews of the key functions of OpenVMS. The book contains references to UNIX commands to make the transition easier.

David Donald Miller, *OpenVMS Operating System Concepts*, second edition, Digital Press, 1997, ISBN 1555581579

Describes several basic operating system concepts (paging, lock management, process communication, and the I/O kernel) and illustrates them using OpenVMS. If you do not know how operating systems work, read this before tackling Goldenberg.

Lesley Rice Ogilvie, David W Bynon and Terry C. Shannon, *Introduction to OpenVMS*_4th edition, CBM Books, 1996, ISBN 1878956612

This is another introductory OpenVMS book directed at the novice. The 5th edition (I have not see it) is sold by Digital Press. This book gives a cursory treatment of OpenVMS (more so than Holmay's *User's Guide*) but covers a broader range of topics, including Motif and some management issues.

Jamie Pearson, editor, *Digital At Work – Snapshots From the First Thirty-Five Years*, Digital Press, 1992, ISBN 1555580920.

This is a composite of recollections by folks who participated in Digital's successes. The book includes some great pictures. This was published in 1992 so no Alpha stories are included.

Joginder Sethi, OpenVMS Performance Management, Digital Press, 1995, ISBN 1555581269.

Oracle, Ingress, Rdb, Motif, ALL-IN-1, and Pathworks tuning are discussed with many examples. Inherent with optimization of disk I/O, CPU, and memory utilization is a discussion of OpenVMS internals.

Glenn Rifkin and George Harrar, *The Ultimate Entrepreneur – The Story of Ken Olsen and Digital Equipment Corporation*, Contemporary Books, 1988, ISBN 0809245590

Ken Olsen's biography, and Digital's too of course, are recorded here. It was published in 1988, during DEC's heyday, so it's not the whole story. The Alpha development is missing completely.

Index